Jefferson Davis's Flight
from Richmond

ALSO BY JOHN STEWART
AND FROM MCFARLAND

The Acrobat: Arthur Barnes and the Victorian Circus (2012)

Antarctica: An Encyclopedia, 2d ed. (2011)

*Byron and the Websters: The Letters and Entangled Lives
of the Poet, Sir James Webster and Lady Frances Webster* (2008)

*Confederate Spies at Large: The Lives of Lincoln Assassination
Conspirator Tom Harbin and Charlie Russell* (2007)

Broadway Musicals, 1943–2004 (2006; paperback 2014)

African States and Rulers, 3d ed. (2006; paperback 2014)

*The British Empire: An Encyclopedia of the Crown's Holdings,
1493 through 1995* (1996)

Italian Film: A Who's Who (1994; paperback 2012)

Moons of the Solar System: An Illustrated Encyclopedia
(1991; paperback 2012)

Jefferson Davis's Flight from Richmond

The Calm Morning, Lee's Telegrams, the Evacuation, the Train, the Passengers, the Trip, the Arrival in Danville and the Historians' Frauds

JOHN STEWART

McFarland & Company, Inc., Publishers
Jefferson, North Carolina

All photographs are from the Library of Congress unless otherwise stated.

LIBRARY OF CONGRESS CATALOGUING-IN-PUBLICATION DATA

Stewart, John, 1952 March 5–
Jefferson Davis's flight from Richmond : the calm morning, Lee's telegrams, the evacuation, the train, the passengers, the trip, the arrival in Danville and the historians' frauds / John Stewart.
 p.   cm.
Includes bibliographical references and index.

ISBN 978-0-7864-7853-8 (softcover : acid free paper) ∞
ISBN 978-1-4766-1640-7 (ebook)

1. Davis, Jefferson, 1808–1889.   2. Richmond (Va.)—History—Siege, 1864–1865.   3. Presidents—Confederate States of America—Biography.   4. Danville (Va.)—History—19th century.   I. Title.
E477.61.S85 2014   973.713092—dc23   2014031850

BRITISH LIBRARY CATALOGUING DATA ARE AVAILABLE

© 2015 John Stewart. All rights reserved

No part of this book may be reproduced or transmitted in any form or by any means, electronic or mechanical, including photocopying or recording, or by any information storage and retrieval system, without permission in writing from the publisher.

On the cover: Jefferson Davis (Library of Congress); Locomotive for the train on which Jefferson Davis fled from Richmond in April 1865 (Southern Methodist University, Central University Libraries, DeGolyer Library)

Printed in the United States of America

McFarland & Company, Inc., Publishers
Box 611, Jefferson, North Carolina 28640
www.mcfarlandpub.com

For Gayle Winston
as always

Table of Contents

Acknowledgments — ix
Introduction — 1

1. Planned Evacuation? — 5
2. April 2 — 25
3. Lee — 28
4. Church — 57
5. The P.M. Dispatches — 89
6. The Mad Rush — 94
7. The Locomotive — 107
8. The President's Car — 119
9. Departure Time — 137
10. Brandy and Morphine — 149
11. The Trip — 154
12. The Confederate Treasure — 192
13. Richmond Left Behind — 199
14. Danville — 206
15. Mallory — 214
16. Stuart — 227

Appendix: The Stuart Article — 241
Bibliography — 270
Index — 295

Acknowledgments

Civil War scholar Jane Singer's input and encouragement have been so tremendous that I think of her almost as a coauthor. (Now there's an idea!)

My dealings with Meghan Glass Hughes, director of collections and interpretation at the Valentine Richmond History Center, constitute one of those stories that researchers dream about—a fabulous custodian who unstintingly goes to bat for you, and, what's more, comes up with the goods.

I am also grateful to all of the following:

Jaclyn Penny, of the American Antiquarian Society, in Worcester, Massachusetts, who supplied the March 17, 1860, issue of *Spirit of the American Press*, and the society itself, that very generously allowed me to use it.

F. Lawrence McFall, Wilford Burson, Christina Williams, and the staff at the Danville Public Library, for their generous and unstinting help.

Albert Lee Atwell, of Danville, for allowing me to pick his brain.

Matthew Turi, manuscripts research librarian at the Wilson Library, at the University of North Carolina in Chapel Hill. Matt supplied the Anna Trenholm "extract" and the original Mallory account. He also patiently guided me through the intricacies of acquiring the Mallory microfilm.

Sean Benjamin, public services librarian, Louisiana Research Collection, Howard Tilton Memorial Library, at Tulane University, who supplied the 1867 Burton Harrison letter to Preston Johnston.

Lynda Crist, famous as the editor of *The Papers of Jefferson Davis*, who, through our mutual friend Jane Singer, took the time and trouble to clear up several questions for me that related to C.E.L. Stuart and to Maggie Howell, and who supplied most of the editions of the *New York Citizen*.

Amber Paranick, of the Library of Congress, who supplied the edition of the *New York Citizen* that I was missing.

Bruce Kirby, manuscript reference librarian at the Library of Congress, who supplied the Beauregard letter and clipping to Alfred Roman.

Henry Fulmer, director, and Graham Duncan, library specialist, Manuscripts Division, both of the South Caroliniana Library, Columbia, SC, who both gave me invaluable analyses of the Anna Trenholm Diary situation.

Nigel Cave and John Buckner, of the Collegio Rosmini, in Stresa, Italy, who explained the Rosminian Order to me, sent me copies of their archival material on Brother MacWalter, spent hours speaking with me, and became good friends.

Acknowledgments

My brother Pete, who unhesitatingly and without charge, acquired British documents for me.

Bob McCloskey, for setting me on the road to seeing the light at the end of the Episcopal Church.

Tom Taber and Dave Holmes, for their advice on old locomotives.

Dave Bright, creator of the fantastic website Confederate Railroads (www.csa-railroads.com). It may well be that Dave knows more about his subject than anyone else, living or dead, and he more than willingly shared with me any and all information and opinions he had on any topic I asked him about.

Introduction

After four years of titanic struggle with the North, the Confederacy was paying the price for its decision to go to war. It was the night of April 2, 1865, and Richmond was doomed. The Union army was at the very gates of the Confederate capital, and would be in the city by morning. Panic reigned. Riots flared in every corner as frightened, famine-stricken mobs ran amok, rampaging and looting. Starving prostitutes were out pounding the streets in one last effort while thousands of terrified citizens fled by horseback, by railroad, by canal boat—any way they could. In a few short hours Richmond would be burning, and the streets would be running with liberated whiskey, and men would be lying on their bellies, slurping it up with the desperation of condemned men. But the fear that overwhelmed all fears—the great Southern nightmare—was that the enemy's negro troops would, out of revenge for two hundred years of slavery, wreak a new hell on the tortured capital. It was during this night, that a little locomotive stood ready at the depot. Each "sshhh" from the smoke-stack was a warning that the sands of time were fast running out.

That there was still any sand at all was only thanks to the bravura performance of the Confederate army. Even as that tattered force braced itself for one last forlorn thrust, even as President Jefferson Davis and his fleeing government lingered at the train station, the hapless Richmonders pinned their hopes on Robert E. Lee to pull the fat out of the fire, as he had always done. No matter how bleak it all looked, no matter how badly their civil leaders had failed them, their great general would triumph in the end.

But the jig was up, and deep down, despite the universal veil of self-deception pulled down tight over the straitened face of Richmond, everyone knew it, except perhaps President Davis and his immediate cronies. The specter of lunacy had long stalked the corridors of power, and now Jefferson Davis, in direct proportion to the speed with which Dixie was dissolving, was beginning his final slide into what at best can be termed a detachment from reality.

It's not that Davis was a coward. Some in his cabinet might have been, but not the president. He just felt it was time to abandon a sinking ship. After all, Richmond was only the capital. It was not the Confederacy, and the Rebels could still carry on a rearguard action from a new seat of government farther south. And there, in a nutshell, lay one of the major reasons why the South had been brought to its knees. Back in 1861, when it all started, they had elected the wrong man. And now came this latest in a long line of costly delusions, and at a time when the odds against Lee in the field were bad and getting worse; when his soldiers were deserting in droves, simply going home; at a time when the dying Confederacy was up against Grant, Sherman, and Sheridan—and the tall man in the stovepipe hat.

Introduction

Given that Davis's harrowing and perilous escape is such a famous event in world history, and because the story contains all the necessary elements of drama and tension, any historian writing on the Civil War has to make at least a mention of it, and yes, in broad, sweeping canvas, the story of the evacuation of Richmond appears to be well told, or, at least, often told. That bright, beautiful Sunday morning, with Davis sitting in his regular pew when he gets the news that he is wanted at the War Department. General Lee's dispatch has just come in, advising the president to leave the city that very night. There would be a mad scramble at the railroad depot, Richmond would be in flames, and a string of trains would carry off archives, treasure, and personnel. After a long and desperately depressing journey, the fleeing Confederate government arrived at the little town of Danville, Virginia, where they attempted to set up the new capital. After a week the news came in of Lee's surrender to Grant at Appomattox Court House, and the Davis party fled again, this time to Greensboro, North Carolina, thence to Charlotte, and from there to a variety of places even deeper south, followers dropping away like flies at every stage, until Davis, almost all alone in the Georgia woods, was caught, some say dressed in women's clothing.

Confederate President Jefferson Davis.

However, only a relatively small number of books and articles have gone beyond a mere mention of the Davis flight. Some of these are histories of the entire Civil War, others narrow down their focus to the last days of the Confederacy itself, while a few deal with just the flight.

In these works you will see not only good, solid, honest history, but also the sort that does not merit those adjectives. But you will not be able to tell the difference between the two unless you take to heart the words of Professor Geoffrey Barraclough: *Anyone who is going to make anything out of history will, sooner or later, have to do most of the work himself.*

Just by being aware, one will see, for example, how writers take from and elaborate upon those who came before, perpetuating errors and making them worse until those errors become part of the accepted canon and the story gets more and more distant from the original. The bigger the historian, the more intimidating his artillery, the more readily he will be believed.

But one cannot just make these accusations. One has to show proof. And, with stacks of books, magazines, and newspapers ranged in front of one, the job of preparing a case for the prosecution is too daunting. The focus has to be narrower than any before. The present work scrutinizes the long two-day period of April 2 and April 3, 1865, the highlight of which was the Jefferson Davis flight from Richmond to Danville.

Forty-eight hours is a manageable time span, which means a handleable body of work from a finite cadre of newsmen and scholars—well known and otherwise, dead and alive—and also from just ordinary folk writing on the subject. So, now able to see the forest and the trees, we are afforded the opportunity of placing this somewhat limited output under the microscope. In the case of the early writers, that is to say the diarists, eyewitnesses, and newspaper reporters—the ones who started this historical ball rolling—we must not fail to avail ourselves of a similar opportunity, that of exposing them to the same degree of minute inspection. Why did they write what they did? In other words, What was their motive? How long after the event did they write it? Is their work original, or was it copied from another source? How reliable were those old newspaper reporters? There were, of course, inevitably—given the supreme historicity of the moment—countless individuals who later claimed to have been on the Davis train, or even in the president's car. We have to be alert to the undeniable fact that some "reputable historians" have used such "eyewitness accounts" without caution. People not only err, they lie. Usually, in the case of "eyewitness accounts," they lie for either money or their fifteen minutes in the sun. "I was there." But were they? As for the famous diaries, purported to have been kept by persons who were on the actual flight, well, we shall see about that.

Only with such a detailed and intense focus are we truly able to get down to the nitty gritty mechanics of how history is made. We can really get to see how it's done, the good and the bad.

As we shall find, a truly astonishing number of historians cannot even copy a date right, or a person's name, cannot reproduce a simple quote without making errors. It's that simple. It's that disturbing, that sad. And there is always the historymaker who, fearing that a fact might be a little bald, let's say, and that his readers might hold him personally accountable for such colorlessness, decides to cross the line of academic rigor by elaboration or even outright invention. Fabrications are then seized upon by other authors, and thus become history. In such cases—and there are many, as shall be seen—what we as readers take in good faith is simply the processed product of the long grind of history making.

Then there is the plagiarizer. There is a saying—if you take from one source, it's called plagiarism, but if you take from several sources, it's called research. There may be something to that. As an exercise in plagiarism-spotting, when you take a sentence, even a whole paragraph, from one writer, and set it right up against that of another writer, and, despite the juxtaposition of certain words, despite the obvious use of a well-thumbed thesaurus, you see it's the same, then that's plagiarism. When there's no attempt at disguise, then that's blatant plagiarism. During the course of this book, we shall find ourselves time after time identifying both forms of plagiarism. But the effort is not just a cheap trick designed to expose plagiarizers. There is a hugely constructive side to all this.

Pick a fact or a concept. Any fact or concept. By tracking it back to its origins, we can see not just what history makers have done with it, but we can also, with a little bit of luck, discover who came up with it in the first place. Only then are we in a position to satisfy ourselves as to the authenticity of that piece of history. If we can manage to witness the birth—or, better still, the conception—we can see who the parent was. The good thing is, this can almost always be done, and often with startling results. In many instances, the parent is not who we thought it was. Illegitimacy runs rampant.

One of the principal and rewarding by-products of this method of investigation is that we can rectify wrongs, so that, in this particular case, we're going to come away with a much more accurate history of the first part of that flight, the train ride from Richmond to Danville.

This book, then, attempts two things. One is to examine what has gone before, how and why the history of this event has been presented so far. The other, by doing the first, is to bring a new understanding to the story of Jefferson Davis's flight from Richmond to Danville and the events that surrounded it, always heeding as respectfully as possible Dallas Irvine's warning: *It is not possible to fix the events of this cataclysmic night in time—either relatively or by hour of the clock—with exactitude or any high degree of reliability, for the recorded recollections of witnesses are generally indefinite and otherwise hopelessly inconsistent with respect to time and sequence.*[1] However, as difficult as it is to fix the events with the definitiveness we would all like, it is possible, after all, to re-create the story in a way that is closer to what Abraham Lincoln had in mind when he said, *History is not history unless it is the truth.*

> The reader will note that in the main text and in the bibliography (but not, for obvious reasons, in the Appendix) quoted passages are in *italics* rather than within "quotation marks." It is thus easier to find such passages but also less confusion is produced with quoted passages containing quoted matter (and sometimes there is a third level of quotation).

---

1. Dallas D. Irvine, "The Fall of Richmond," *Journal of the American Military Institute* (Summer 1939), footnote 24, p. 70.

Chapter 1

PLANNED EVACUATION?

Was the evacuation of Richmond planned? The answer is, yes, of course. The real questions are: When did such plans begin to be discussed and developed? What and who was to be evacuated? How much of those plans had already been put into effect by the time April 2, 1865, arrived? Was Danville planned as the new seat of government?

Rumors of Richmond being evacuated abounded even from the beginning of the war, and Yankee newspapers would occasionally report the evacuation as a fait accompli. All this fed the Northern hopes and the Confederate fears. However, Richmond was Richmond. It had survived against long odds. It was a veritable Gibraltar, an allusion first used by "eyewitness" Dallas Tucker in "The Fall of Richmond," his 1902 article in the *Richmond Dispatch*: *...though several times threatened by raiders, and although we had often heard the cry, "The Yankees are coming," yet, Richmond had come to be regarded, through its long practical siege, as an impregnable Gibraltar, and the army defending it as invincible as a Grecian phalanx.*

Tucker's Gibraltar image has been taken up by surprisingly few historians, notably Ernest B. Furgurson in his book, *Ashes of Glory* (1996): *The Yankees had been turned back so many times, most citizens thought of their capital as an "impregnable Gibraltar,"* and Jay Winik in his famous book, *April 1865* (2001): *Most citizens saw their capital as an "impregnable Gibraltar."* Both of these authors quote and cite Tucker.

But by mid–1864, for realists on both sides of the Mason-Dixon line, the abandonment of the city had become a foregone conclusion. It was just a matter of time before the "impregnable Gibraltar" would be taken.

Frank Leslie's Illustrated Newspaper, in its June 25, 1864, edition, had the following: *There is not the slightest ... doubt as to the result of the present struggle for Richmond. The inevitable issue of the campaign—and it is not far off—will be the occupation of the city by the Union army, and the dissolution, capture, or disappearance of Jeff Davis to parts unknown.*

It is not that *Frank Leslie's* was particularly prescient; this was simply stating the obvious. However, the writer may have been consulting a crystal ball when he expressed his opinion that Grant may be in a position to force a *disastrous evacuation of Richmond, under cover of the night*. The article continued: *The alternative even now presented to Jeff. Davis is, shall Lee's army be sacrificed in the effort to hold Richmond, or shall the city and Virginia be abandoned to save Lee's army?* And this: *Consequently, with the fall of Richmond, which is inevitable ... the Davis Confederacy must collapse, and the war will speedily come to an end.* This neatly summed up the quandary facing the Confederate Government.

The same paper, *Frank Leslie's*, on October 8, 1864, predicted quite correctly that,

When driven to the wall, Lee will abandon Richmond to save his army. Of course, there were always some who simply refused to look at the writing on the wall, let alone try to interpret it. But most were forced to face up to the fact that Richmond would have to be evacuated sooner or later, that the "impregnable Gibraltar" was now a rocky sentiment of the past. However, delusions are a vital part of life, offering hope, as they do. A new, grand, delusion was now beginning to sweep the less realistic elements in Dixie, one that offered compensation for the abandonment of the Confederate capital. If Richmond were evacuated, General Lee would be freed from the necessity of having to defend it, and thus be enabled to roam the countryside for years if necessary, striking at Grant's forces whenever and wherever he chose until the Yankees grew so tired of it all that they offered a settlement advantageous to the Confederacy.

On November 20, 1864, the *Richmond Whig* offered the following on the possible fall of Richmond: *The moral effect of its fall would for a while certainly be great. But there would be countervailing advantages that would more than outweigh it. It would relieve Gen. Lee's army, who then, having no capital to defend, could manoeuvre as it pleased.*[1] This delusion that Lee would save the day continued to prevail in many quarters until the fatal day itself—April 2, 1865. And even beyond.

But what was the Confederate Government doing in those last few months before the fall of Richmond? After all, these men were meant to be not only responsible, but responsible to and for the people of the Confederacy. Back in late 1864 all realistic grounds for hope had gone. Even back then there had been only one sane course of action open to the Confederate Government—surrender. But they did not surrender. As time passed and the day of destiny approached, as the fate of not only Richmond but the whole Confederacy became more and more obvious, surely plans were under way for evacuation.

On February 24, 1865, Secretary of War John C. Breckinridge telegraphed to General Lee, who was then in the field at Petersburg: *Should preparation only be made for evacuation of Richmond? or do you advise the removal at once of public stores, archives, etc?* One must bear in mind that when Breckinridge wrote this, April 2, 1865, was only 36 days away.

Another telegram from Breckinridge to Lee, sent the following day, February 25, 1865, reads: *I have given the necessary orders in regard to commencing the removal of stores, &c., but if pos-*

Confederate Secretary of War John C. Breckinridge.

---

1. *Richmond Whig* (November 20, 1864).

sible would like to know whether we may probably count on a period of ten or twelve days. If the urgency is not very great better order and system can be carried out.[2]

Yet another telegram from Breckinridge to Lee, that same day, February 25, 1865: *I have just heard that General Ewell has an order from you to remove the cotton and tobacco from Richmond and to destroy all that cannot be taken away.*[3] And this: *This morning I called together the heads of bureaus, and directed them to prepare for removal, but I have as yet given no order of execution. I have brought the matter before the President and Cabinet. Nothing has been done.*

By February 27, 1865, there were only 33 days left for Richmond, although no one at the time could possibly have known that number precisely. Evacuation was the dominant theme of every Richmonder's conversations, yet it would seem that the government had not actually made up its mind to evacuate. It was not a done deal. If it had been, then the *Richmond Examiner* of that date was not aware of it, and the *Examiner* was the most important paper in the Confederacy: *The evacuation of Richmond would be the loss of all respect and authority towards the Confederate government, the disintegration of the army, and the abandonment of the scheme of an independent Southern Confederation.* And this: *The hope of establishing a confederacy and securing its recognition among nations would be gone forever.* And, with their own crystal ball functioning perfectly, the paper wrote: *As the army would dwindle in numbers, it would move more and more rapidly westward, and before reaching the banks of the Mississippi would have degenerated into a mere bodyguard for a few officials.*

The *Examiner* was not necessarily promoting the continued defense of Richmond, but it certainly was telling it the way it was—that evacuation of the capital would spell the end of the Confederacy.[4] By March 1, 1865, it was all but decided to evacuate Richmond. But what then? General P.G.T. Beauregard, still showing signs of delusion, or at least of recognizing that the delusion existed, telegraphed to General J.E. Johnston on March 1, 1865: *Present events tending to force the evacuation of Richmond it would seem a necessary part of the strategy of the campaign that the Confederate States Government should be previously removed to some point that would free the army from the necessity of protecting it, and thus at the same time diminish the importance which the enemy attaches to Richmond as the capital of the Confederate States.*

Perhaps Beauregard was not the only general still under the influence of such delusions. According to Jay Winik, in *April 1865* (2001), on March 4 Lee rode into Richmond. *Today he harbored a single daring plan to re-ignite the waning fortunes of the Confederacy. He had come to confer with Davis. Lee's ultimate calculation was as bold as it was simple: abandon Richmond and take his forces south to meet up with General Joe Johnston in North Carolina… From there they could continue the war indefinitely.*

With less than a week to go before the fateful day, the *Richmond Daily Dispatch* of

---

2. On February 28, 1865, Lee would reply to Breckinridge: *I know of no reason to prevent your counting upon the time suggested in your letter.*

3. Richard S. "Fighting Dick" Ewell was Confederate military commander of the Department of Richmond and of the troops remaining on the north side of the James River at the time of the evacuation.

4. John M. Daniel was proprietor and editor-in-chief of the *Examiner*. Initially a supporter of the Davis administration, it was after First Manassas that Daniel and the paper began to lose faith, and from 1862 the editorials against the President became more and more virulent. In late 1863 John Mitchel came over from the *Enquirer* to replace Edward A. Pollard as associate editor. During the last year of the war, Daniel did almost all of the editorial writing for the paper, but died a few days before the fall of Richmond.

March 27, 1865, wrote: *It is said, on the authority of a distinguished Senator in Washington, that General Grant predicts the evacuation of Richmond within ten days.* General Josiah Gorgas, chief of the Ordnance Bureau, kept a diary between 1857 and 1878. His entry for April 16, 1865, reads, in part: *We had been making arrangements to move to Danville on the 3d (Monday).*[5] Frank Bury Woodford wrote the book *Father Abraham's Children* (1961), in which he says: *The move to Danville was part of a prearranged evacuation plan, and the word from Lee putting it into operation was not entirely unexpected.*

Brigadier General William A. Tidwell, in his book *April '65* (1995), wrote: *Judging from the patterns of rainfall and freezing and thawing in the area, the latest feasible date for the planned evacuation would have been the middle of April 1865.* Considering that the evacuation—at least of the government—would be by train, one has to wonder to what degree the Richmond & Danville Railroad would have been affected by these weather conditions.

Perhaps the most telling proof of a planned evacuation of Richmond is that Jefferson Davis sent his wife and children away two full days before he himself got out. Varina says in Volume 2 of her biography of her late husband, published in 1890: *Mr. Burton N. Harrison, the President's private secretary, was to protect and see us safely settled in Charlotte, where we had hired a furnished house.*

Burton Harrison himself wrote, in his 1883 narrative, "The Capture of Jefferson Davis": *We started from Richmond in the evening of the Friday before the city was evacuated.* That was March 31. He goes on to say: *…we got away from Richmond at about ten o'clock.*

There are only three accounts of this Varina flight written by actual participants. Harrison and Varina are two. The third is James Morris Morgan, a young midshipman. In 1917, sixty-two years after the event, and with both Varina's 1890 book and Burton Harrison's 1883 article in front of him, he wrote his own book, *Recollections of a Rebel Reefer*: *It was then the Friday preceding the fall of Richmond.* And then there is this: *It was ten o'clock before our feeble and wheezy locomotive gave a screech and a jerk which started us on our journey.*

Was Varina's train a special one in any way? Harrison says: *It was a special train.* Varina says: *In those days a special train was not contemplated, for the transportation was now very limited.* Morgan seems to back up Varina: *There were no Pullman sleeping-coaches in those days, and it was with great difficulty that an old, creaky passenger car, long a stranger to paint and varnish, had been secured.* And this: *We at once entered the car and seated ourselves on the lumpy seats which were covered with dingy and threadbare brownish red plush, very suggestive of the vermin with which it afterwards proved to be infested. The sleepy little children were laid on the seats and made as comfortable as possible under the circumstances.* Not a special car, then, but an especial train certainly, because, according to Burton Harrison, *the train consisted of only two or three cars. In one of them, the coachman had two carriage horses recently presented to Mrs. Davis by several gentlemen of Richmond.* A regular train—and, as we shall see, there were regular

---

5. Gorgas temporarily ended his diary on March 30, 1865, and resumed on April 16, while at Winnsboro, South Carolina. Hence, his diary of the flight is not a diary at all, rather an account written a few weeks later, and, to boot, relying heavily on newspaper accounts. For this reason alone, it cannot be trusted. This diary did not see the light of day until 1947 when, edited by Frank E. Vandiver, it was published by the University of Alabama Press.

Varina Davis, first lady of the Confederacy.

trains leaving for Danville that evening—would have had a lot more cars than just two or three. So it had to indeed have been an especial train.

As for who constituted the fleeing group, whereas Varina has only this: *Mr. George A. Trenholm's lovely daughters were also to accompany us to remain with friends there,*[6] Burton Harrison is much more detailed: *Our party consisted of Mrs. Davis, Miss Howell (her sister),*[7] *the four children,*[8] *Ellen (the mulatto maid-servant),*[9] *and James Jones (the mulatto coachman). With us were also the daughters of Mr. Trenholm. the Secretary of the Treasury,*[10] *on their way to South Carolina, under the escort of Midshipman James M. Morgan. That young gentleman was then engaged to Miss Trenholm, and afterward married her. There were no other passengers.*

Most modern-day historians who cover Varina's flight also have Jim Limber going with her. Jim was a black child Varina had rescued from the streets, *a free black orphan about six years old,* as Michael B. Ballard describes him in *A Long Shadow* (1986). Jim is not on Burton Harrison's list, nor is he mentioned by James M. Morgan. Varina never mentions Jim leaving with her, nor do her first two biographers, Mrs. Dunbar Rowland and Ishbel Ross. It is not until Hudson Strode compiled his 1966 book, *Jefferson Davis: Private Letters,* that we come across this story, in his relevant footnote: *Mrs. Davis and the children, her sister Margaret, the Negro maid Ellen, the colored coachman James Jones, and Jim Limber, the little adopted black boy, left Richmond by train, escorted by Burton Harrison, the President's private secretary, and a twenty-year-old midshipman named James Morgan.*[11]

So, according to Burton Harrison and James M. Morgan, Mrs. Davis and her party left Richmond about ten in the evening of Friday, March 31. Harrison continues: *It illustrates the then condition of the railways and means of transportation in the Confederate States that, after proceeding twelve or fifteen miles, our locomotive proved unable to take us over a slight up-grade. We came to a dead halt, and remained there all night. The next day was well advanced when Burksville Junction was reached.* He then goes on to say that they stopped at Burkeville, where Harrison sent a telegram to President Davis about what he had heard of the battle between Sheridan and Pickett. *It was Sunday morning before we arrived at Danville.*

All Varina has to say of the trip is: *...as we pulled out from the station and lost sight of Richmond, the worn-out engine broke down, and there we sat all night. There were no arrangements possible for sleeping, and at last, after twelve hours delay, we reached Danville.*

James M. Morgan continues his own account: *We proceeded at a snail's pace for about twelve miles when suddenly we came to a standstill. Our ramshackle locomotive had balked; no amount of persuasion on the part of the engineer could induce it to haul us over a slight*

---

6. George Trenholm (1807–1876), Confederate secretary of the Treasury from July 18, 1864, to April 27, 1865. He and his wife, Anna, would be in the president's car with Jefferson Davis during the flight from Richmond to Danville on April 2–3, 1865. Trenholm, who was rich and handsome, was, some say, the prototype for Rhett Butler in *Gone with the Wind.*
7. Maggie Howell, who will be discussed in Chapter 16.
8. Maggie, aged 9; Jeff, aged 7; Billy, aged 3; and Winnie, aged 9 months.
9. It would seem that Ellen has been identified as Ellen Barnes.
10. There were four Trenholm daughters.
11. It is beyond the mandate of this book to investigate the truth of Jim Limber's participation in Varina's flight.

up-grade, and we remained where we were for the rest of the night. It was the afternoon on the next day when we arrived at Burkesville Junction. He then talks about Harrison telegraphing Davis, and then nothing more about the flight until this: *We did not reach Charlotte until Tuesday; a journey which today requires only six or seven hours, had taken us four days to accomplish!*

That's it. Those three accounts. That's what we have to go on. One has to assume from these three reports that the only delay of any consequence they sustained was at around Coalfield, 12 or 15 miles out of Richmond, because no other individual delay is mentioned.

Of the famous delay, Harrison says that they *remained there all night.* Varina says: *...there we sat all night.* And Morgan writes: *We remained where we were for the rest of the night.* Harrison wrote his account in 1883. Varina's book was published in 1890. Morgan wrote his book in 1917. One suspects, from the wording, that there's a bit of copying going on, which is not to say they're not right. If indeed they were stuck in the area of Coalfield all night, then at what hour would they eventually have started off again and headed toward Danville? None of the three mentions still being at Coalfield during part of the following morning. Harrison says that the day was well advanced when they reached Burkeville, but that could mean anything. Burkeville was 54 miles down the track from Richmond, and about 40 from where they had been stuck all night. It should have taken them about four or five hours, that is if the going was even fair. Morgan says it was afternoon when they arrived at Burkeville. That means, all things being equal, that they left Coalfield around seven or eight o'clock in the morning, and arrived at Burkeville just after noon.

Varina says: *...at last, after twelve hours delay, we reached Danville.* But she does not actually say they were stuck in the area of Coalfield for that length of time. It might well be that what she had in mind was twelve hours total delay before they reached Danville.

However one interprets the wording of any of them, there is only one delay singled out by all three, and, what's more, it was a delay of such enormity that it put them way behind schedule, so much so that they did not arrive in Danville until the morning of Sunday, April 2. If there had been further delays of similar or greater import, then surely these would have been detailed in some way. But there is not even a mention of such delays. Bearing in mind that our knowledge of this event is dependent solely on the narratives of Harrison, Varina, and Morgan, various writers have taken it upon themselves to add a further twenty-four hours of delay to the story. Why would they do this?

Carleton Coffin, in his *Boston Journal* article of April 1865, was the first, in print, to propose Thursday, March 30 as the date of departure, rather than Friday, March 31: *Mrs. Davis and the children left Richmond on Thursday last, but Jeff. remained.* Coffin simply got it wrong, that's all. But his error was perpetuated by certain historians, and even (so we are told by *The Papers of Jefferson Davis*—as shown below) by Varina herself on one occasion. Notwithstanding the fact that March 30 is so obviously wrong, one will still, occasionally, see that date given. For example, Joan Cashin, although she mentions absolutely nothing about the trip itself, writes in *First Lady of the Confederacy* (2006): *They left on the night of March 30,* and James Swanson, in *Bloody Crimes* (2010): *Varina and the children left the White House on Thursday, March 30.*

This confusion of dates is addressed, albeit inconclusively, in *The Papers of Jefferson Davis* (2003): *Varina wrote in June that she departed on Thursday, March 30, and there are documents to support that date (Joseph R. Davis to Davis, March 29, Davis to Breckinridge and Dodamead[12] to Davis, March 30, and Hood[13] to Davis, March 31); two of her traveling companions and the adjutant general said it was late on Friday.* Citing correspondence that took place before an event occurred, even if one is interpreting this correspondence correctly, proves intent, perhaps, but not much more. As for Varina, she can be inaccurate at the best of times, as we have seen, and, as for the date of her departure, she was almost certainly relying on newsman Carleton Coffin or one of his derivatives. Incidentally, in the 2008 volume of *The Papers of Jefferson Davis*, in a footnote on page 77, the editors are not so cautious in their approach to the date: *Varina and the children left Richmond on March 30, a few days before her husband.*

Clint Johnson, in *Pursuit* (2008), says: *On March 30, the day he sent Varina Davis and the children from Richmond, Davis asked Secretary of War John C. Breckinridge by letter if he knew where Stoneman was at that time.*[14] Then he quotes the letter to Breckinridge, part of which says: *My family is about to leave.* About to leave, yes, but when? That day? Or the following day?

If one wishes to get to the bottom of something like this, surely one has to do more than just take a poll of what others have written and swing with the majority. One must work it out for oneself. In a case like this, it does not take much work to achieve clarity.

If March 30 is bad enough, what about March 29? The ubiquitous J.B. Jones, the Rebel War Clerk, who had the advantage of hindsight when writing his diary,[15] places the Varina flight in his entry for Wednesday, March 29: *Mrs. President Davis has left the city, with her children, for the South. I believe it is her purpose to go no farther at present than Charlotte, N.C.* Unfortunately for Jones, hindsight was fast running out on him, and he died on February 4, 1866, just before his famous "diary" was published, and long before anyone other than the occasional newspaper reporter had covered Varina's flight. One such news item was an April 3, 1865, dispatch from Richmond which made all the papers a few days later: *Mr. Jefferson Davis and family left Richmond on Wednesday for Charlotte, North Carolina and it is stated on good authority that they were on their way to Texas.* That's where J.B. Jones got his March 29 date from. For those historians who would usually feel comfortable citing *A Rebel War Clerk's Diary*, this date, the 29th, is rather embarrassing, so they do not mention it.

This from "eyewitness" Phoebe Yates Pember's 1866 article: *The wives and families of Mr. Davis and his Cabinet had fortunately been sent away some weeks previously.* By the time her book, *A Southern Woman's Story*, was published in 1879, she had, perhaps, become a little less Confederate in her tone, but she had learned nothing new about Varina Davis's flight: *The wives and families of Mr. Davis and his cabinet had been sent away some weeks previously.*[16]

Varina's first biographer, Mrs. Dunbar Rowland, writing in 1931 and faced with this confusion, simply decided not even to address the date of departure. Neither did Ishbel

---

12. Thomas Dodamead, recently appointed superintendent of the Richmond & Danville Railroad.
13. General John B. Hood.
14. Stoneman was the raiding Union general.
15. Jones freely admits that he tinkered with his diary after the war.
16. See Pember, in the Bibliography. As she says, in her 1866 article: *From the hill on which my Hospital was built, I had sat all the Sunday of the evacuation, watching the turmoil and bidding friends adieu.* And this: *At eleven o'clock on Monday, the fourth of April.* Given that she is off as to the date, one wonders how much Pember's telescope can be trusted as she looked through it all that day from her hilltop.

1. Planned Evacuation?

Ross, Varina's second biographer, who, in *First Lady of the South* (1958) merely says: *Varina left during the last week of March, 1865.* However she does give us a time of day: *The train puffed out at ten in the evening.* And this: *Late the following day they got to Burkesville Junction. On the Sunday that Richmond was evacuated, they arrived at Danville.* And this: *They finally reached Charlotte ... on Tuesday.* Likewise Hudson Strode, in his relevant footnote in *Jefferson Davis: Private Letters* (1966), in which he merely says *late March, 1865.*

If anything can be proved by sheer overwhelming evidence, it is that Varina left Richmond before her husband. However, there are historians who disagree. In fact, some put forward the theory that she did not leave Richmond at all.

It all began with Edward A. Pollard, who wrote about Jefferson Davis in late 1868, his article coming out in several New York newspapers: *...he nervously prepared at his home his private baggage, assisted by Mrs. Davis.* He goes on to say, *Mr. Davis was accompanied at the first stage of his flight by his family, some of his personal staff, and three members of his cabinet,* and he names them: Breckenridge [sic], Benjamin,[17] and Reagan.[18] Someone pulled him up on his facts, so that by 1869, when his book, *The Life of Jefferson Davis,* was published, Pollard had made some changes, the most notable perhaps being that he now had Mrs. Davis correctly in North Carolina.

In 1903 *Before the Dawn: A Story of the Fall of Richmond*, a novel written by a Kentuckian named Joseph Alexander Altsheler, portrayed Jefferson Davis and his family sitting in the pew at the church that fateful morning when the president receives word from Lee. It's only a novel, but it had influence in quarters where it should not have.

This from Otis Ashmore in his 1918 article, "The Story of the Confederate Treasure": On the presidential train, that night of April 2, 1865, were the *families of Mr. Davis and some of the cabinet members.*[19]

Clement Eaton, writing about the title character in his book *Jefferson Davis*, has this: *...he received the message of doom stoically and immediately gave orders for the removal of the government documents and the scanty supply of specie to Danville, Virginia, where he, his family, and the cabinet followed.* Professor Eaton, perhaps the greatest Civil War scholar of his day—certainly the most patrician—was writing not in 1877, but in 1977.

According to what one reads online, Jean H. Baker, author of *Mary Todd Lincoln*,[20] wrote a review, part of which says: *Charles Lachman has written an absorbing, well-researched account.* The subject of her review was the 2008 book, *The Last Lincolns*. This from the book's blurb: *The Last Lincolns makes the stunning revelation that the notorious skyjacker D.B. Cooper may have worked as a chauffeur for Abraham Lincoln's great-grandson, Robert Todd Lincoln Beckwith.* If this passage does not serve as a warning to the reader, the specific phrase "may have" may. *The Last Lincolns* is not a book about Jefferson Davis, of course, and has only a couple of pages devoted to the evacuation of Richmond, but those pages include this: *To the citizens of Richmond, the first signs of the emergency came on Sunday morning, April 2. President of the Confederacy Jefferson Davis was sitting*

---

17. Judah Philip Benjamin, then Confederate secretary of state.
18. John Henninger Reagan, then Confederate postmaster general.
19. The stated purpose of Ashmore's article *is to present the facts connected with the final disposition of the Confederate and private funds taken away from Richmond at the time of its evacuation by Davis.*
20. Jean H. Baker. *Mary Todd Lincoln: A Biography* (New York: W.W. Norton & Co., 1989). Baker is a professor of history at Goucher College, near Baltimore.

with his wife in the front-row pew at St. Paul's Church when the church sexton came hurrying up the aisle bearing an important message. Lachman goes on to say: *Jefferson Davis boarded a train at 11:00 p.m. leaving his wife and children behind.*

This is how Burton Harrison describes the arrival of the Varina Davis party in Danville on April 2: *It was Sunday morning before we arrived at Danville. While preparations were making there to send on our train toward Charlotte, Morgan and I took a walk through the town and made a visit to the residence of Major Sutherlin, the most conspicuous house in Danville. The train got off again by midday.*

They left Danville on the Piedmont Railroad, bound for Greensboro, passed through that town, and finally arrived at Charlotte on Tuesday, the 4th, by which time Jefferson Davis and the fleeing government were in Danville. In her letter to her husband from Charlotte, written on April 7, 1865, Varina has this to say: *Harrison has been more efficient and attentive than I thought he could be, and very affectionate and kind. I really regret to see him go tomorrow, which is the day he proposes to leave.* In her 1890 biography Varina writes: *Mr. Harrison, after seeing us safely established in Charlotte, fearing he might be separated from Mr. Davis, and hoping to be of use, set out for Richmond to rejoin him.*"[21]

Harrison says that as soon as he could, he made his way back to Danville, *where I arrived late in the evening, and spent the night.* The evening in question was April 9, and the following day Jefferson Davis and his party received news of Lee's surrender at Appomattox Court House: *It was only the next afternoon, however, after my return to Danville, that the President received a communication informing him of the surrender by General Lee of the Army of Northern Virginia, and gave orders for an immediate withdrawal into North Carolina.*

On December 29, 1864, the House of Representatives in the Confederate Congress, alarmed by the constant talk of surrender, passed a resolution providing for the appointment of a joint Senate and House committee to inquire into the Confederacy's present and future means of public defense. The House requested the concurrence of the Senate. On December 30 the Senate proposed some amendments to the resolution, and at the same time appointed Allen T. Caperton, of Virginia; Williamson Simpson Oldham, of Texas; and Benjamin Harvey Hill, of Georgia, as the three senators to sit on this committee. On. December 31 the House agreed to the Senate's amendments, and appointed five congressmen—John B. Baldwin, of Virginia; Willis B. Machen, of Kentucky; James L. Pugh, of Alabama; Charles M. Conrad, of Louisiana; and Arthur S. Colyar, of Tennessee.[22]

Although we have no specific date for the actual physical formation of this committee, it had to have been very early January 1865 when the eight men got together for the first time. Although at the outset the committee had no specific name, it garnered one along the way—the Special Joint Committee on the Means of Public Defense. By January 10 the Virginia Assembly had raised a similar committee and was asking to be able to work in conjunction with its Congressional counterpart, a matter which was deferred until January 12, when Congress, again in secret session, approved the request.

On January 25, 1865, at yet another secret session, the committee's written report was handed in, its job done. The report was never printed, and that was the end of the special committee. However, it was not the end of the written report.

---

21. This should, of course, say Danville, not Richmond. Harrison left Charlotte on April 8.
22. *Journal of the Confederate Congress*, December 29, 30 and 31, 1864.

1. Planned Evacuation?

Someone, almost certainly a Confederate senator or congressman, leaked a copy of it to the enemy. This was almost inevitable, given the number of realists in the Confederate legislature. The leak was quick in springing, and was soon the subject of much gossip. On February 25, 1865, President Davis sent this ominous telegram to Lee: *Rumors assuming to be based on your views have affected the public mind, and it is reported obstructs needful legislation. If you can spare the time I wish you to come here.*

What could this possibly mean? The answer would come precisely a month later. The *New York Daily Tribune* had been a beneficiary of the Confederate leak and, on March 25 published the following, from a Washington correspondent writing two days earlier:

A committee of the rebel senate was engaged early in the present year in an inquiry into the condition of the Confederacy. Among the witnesses summoned before them was Gen. Lee, and the following extracts are from his testimony, on the 24th January, 1865.

Question by Senator Hunter: What is your opinion as to evacuating Richmond, and withdrawing the army to North Carolina?

Answer: In my opinion, it would be a bad movement. The Virginia troops would not go to North Carolina; they would go home.

Question: Do you think we have troops enough for the next campaign?

Answer: I do not. We cannot last till midsummer.

Question: What do you think of the policy of arming 200,000 negroes?

Answer: If we are to carry on the war, that is the least of evils; but in such an event the negroes must have their liberty.

Question: Do you think we could succeed by putting the negroes into the field?

Answer: That would depend on circumstances. We could at least carry on the war for another year.

Question by Senator Hill: What is the sentiment of the army in relation to peace?

Answer: It is almost unanimous for peace. The men will fight longer if necessary, but they believe we cannot continue the war through another campaign.

Question by Senator Graham: What is your individual opinion on the subject of peace?

Answer: I think the best policy is to make peace on the plan proposed by Mr. Stephens. The people and the country ought to be saved further sacrifices.

Question by Senator Walker: If peace be not made before spring, will you consent to take command of all the armies of the Confederacy, with unlimited powers?

Answer: I will take any position to which my country assigns me, and do the best I can, but I do not think I can save the cause now. No

Alexander H. Stephens, vice president of the Confederate States of America.

human power can save it. Had I been assigned such a place one year ago, I think I could have made our condition better than it is now.

Question by Senator Orr: You think, then, General, that the best solution of our difficulties is to make peace on the Stephens plan?

Answer: Yes, that is the best policy now. I think the Army and the people ought to be saved if all else is lost.[23]

Senator Oldham left Richmond on the evening train of Friday, March 31, 1865, and arrived in Danville the following day.[24] Then he caught the train to Greensboro, and made his way to Texas, then on to Mexico, where he wrote his memoirs.[25]

Oldham wrote: *Two or three days after my arrival at the capital, upon the motion of Mr. Caperton, of Virginia, a joint resolution was adopted by the two Houses ordering a joint committee to be raised to inquire into the conditions of the country.* Oldham tells us that the committee consisted of three members of the Senate, *Messrs Caperton, of Virginia, Hill, of Georgia and Oldham, of Texas and of five members of the House; Messrs Baldwin, of Virginia, Pugh, of Alabama, Macklin,*[26] *of Kentucky, and two others, whom I do not remember.* He explains that they immediately entered upon the active discharge of their duties, and availed themselves of every possible source of information, official and unofficial, *including the President, members of the cabinet, and heads of bureaus, military officers, from commanding generals to subalterns, private citizens, as well as official records and documents.* They investigated the strength of the Confederate army, present and absent, and all possible available sources of reinforcement; the resources at their command of arms, ammunition, medical stores, and of all classes of quartermaster and commissary supplies. They also, as far as they were able, inquired into the force and power of the enemy operating against them: *The results were quite satisfactory to the members of the committee.* While they recognized, to the fullest extent, the pressures upon them, and the dangers of the Confederate position, the committee did not believe the cause by any means hopeless; but on the contrary, they came to the conclusion that the Confederacy had a sufficiency of men and military supplies under their control, and subject to their command, to enable them to continue the struggle for an indefinite period of time. The committee wrote: *The result of our investigations and conclusions were drawn up by Mr. Hill, in an able report, and was submitted to the two Houses.* And this: *The report had but little influence on the members of Congress.*

It is of interest to note that Senator Oldham, who one must remember died in 1868, does not make specific reference to General Lee's testimony, does not single it out from the other testimonies. Neither does Ben Hill, in a speech he gave on March 22, 1874, which is reproduced in the book his son compiled in 1893—*Senator Benjamin H. Hill of*

---

23. It is clear from this, and from several other references in the *Journal of the Confederate Congress*, that membership of the committee changed during its month-long life span.

24. This was obviously not the same train Varina Davis took from Richmond that evening.

25. Oldham subsequently went to Canada, was pardoned, and returned to Texas, where he died on May 8, 1868. About two-thirds of his memoirs deal with his career as a Confederate congressman, while the final third describes his harrowing trip from Richmond to Texas. This final third is published in the 1998 book *From Richmond to Texas*, edited and with an introduction by W. Buck Yearns. In October 1869 *Debow's New Orleans Monthly Review* (vol. 6, issue 10) published part of the memoirs under the title "Last Days of the Confederacy." A longer version is in the Oldham Papers at the University of Texas, where his original manuscript and a not particularly faithful typescript of that manuscript are also housed. The original manuscript is called "Memoirs of a Confederate Senator, 1861–1865."

26. He means Machen.

Georgia: His Life, Speeches and Writings. In this speech he says that it was his fortune to be one of a joint committee, recently appointed by the two houses of Congress, and charged with the duty of inquiring into the condition of Confederate resources, present and prospective, for the maintenance of the public defense. After a lengthy examination, the committee had the happiness to conclude and report, unanimously, that their resources were sufficient, and with energy and vigilance, were available for the prosecution of the war until independence was won.

It was not until late June 1881 that Lee's testimony became important enough to Ben Hill for him to talk about it publicly. Just days after Jefferson Davis's book, *Rise and Fall of the Confederate Government*, came out, Hill was interviewed by a reporter from the Philadelphia newspaper, the *Press*. As was the custom in those days, this long interview, titled "Johnston, Lee and Davis. The Three Great Confederate Officials," was picked up in selected portions by several papers throughout the country, including the *Wheeling Register* (West Virginia) of June 29, 1881; the *Daily Arkansas Gazette* of July 2, 1881; and the *Galveston Daily News* of July 3 and 8, 1881.

To the interviewer's question, *Do you know anything about the differences between Lee and Davis as to the surrender of the army?* Ben Hill replied: *Yes, Sir. I have read, with a great deal of amusement, much of the stuff that has been printed about it.* Hill goes on to say that in January 1865 the two houses of the Confederate Congress created a joint committee to inquire into the condition of the army and the means of continuing the war, that he was on the committee upon the part of the Senate, and that the committee held secret sessions and examined almost every prominent man in the Confederacy from Jefferson Davis down. *When Gen. Lee was on the stand I examined him myself and in great detail. When asked about his holding Richmond, he said he could do so until Gen. Grant could get the men and the time to push around upon his flank so as to threaten his communication with the South. He explained that Grant's forces were constantly increasing, and that he had unlimited supplies of men and ammunitions, both of which Gen. Lee lacked. He said that his army was constantly weakened by desertions.*

After General Lee had explained the situation about Richmond, Hill put the question directly to him: *Will the fall of Richmond end the war?*

The old hero raised himself in the chair, and with a great deal of feeling said: "By no means, Sir, by no means. In a military point of view I would be stronger after than before such an event, because it would enable me to make my own plan of campaign and battle. From a moral and political point of view the abandonment or loss of Richmond would be a serious calamity, but when it has fallen I believe I can prolong the war for two years upon Virginia soil. Ever since the conflict began I have been obliged to permit the enemy to make my plans for me, because compelled to defend the capital. When Richmond falls I shall be able to make them for myself." Lee's emphatic statement, said Hill in this 1881 press interview, shaped the report of the committee in favor of continuing the war, *and ought to settle the point conclusively that Lee never thought of surrender until he found that he could not get his army out and was obliged to.*

As one will immediately notice in this 1881 interview, Senator Hill's account of Lee's testimony is totally and diametrically different from that given in the *New York Daily Tribune* of March 25, 1865. It is so at odds with the *Tribune*'s article that there can be no question of interpretation, only one of "one is wrong and the other is right." But how can that be? Senator Hill was part of the committee. It could be that the *Tribune*'s article of 1865 is fiction, and that Hill was simply setting the record straight concerning Lee's responses to the questions asked him by the committee. But if the *Tribune*'s article was lies, why would Ben Hill have waited until 1881 to set the record straight? It may be that Senator Hill, come 1881, was himself lying.

It comes down to the question, Was Lee for the evacuation of Richmond, as Hill says in 1881, or was he against it, as the *Tribune* reported in 1865? If Lee was for it, what was it then that prompted Jefferson Davis's telegram to him on Feb. 25, 1865? In that telegram, Davis said: *Rumors assuming to be based on your views have affected the public mind, and it is reported obstructs needful legislation. If you can spare the time I wish you to come here.*

If one accepts Ben Hill's 1881 version, Lee was as delusional as the president. Yes, Lee did, finally, on April 2, 1865, suggest the evacuation of Richmond, but that was only after adjusting his thoughts as a result of a conversation or conversations with the head of the civil authority—Jefferson Davis. And Lee, being a good officer, was not one to go up against the civil authorities and was not one to force a military takeover of the government, despite what his own personal views might have been on a particular issue.

If Hill was lying, why? What did he have to gain? And would not everyone have known at the time, in 1881, that he was lying? The answer to the second question lies partly in the fact that by 1881 the old *Tribune* article of sixteen years before had been largely forgotten, and one must bear in mind, for what it's worth, that by 1881 Lee had been dead for over ten years, Senator Oldham had died in 1868, and the only other senator on that committee—Allen T. Caperton—had died in 1876.

The first question—What did Hill have to gain by lying?—may perhaps be answered, or at least the answer may be hinted at, by something General Joe Johnston said in an interview he gave in 1881, also in response to the publication of the ex–President's book: *Mr. Davis always kept a class of men about him for witnesses, and Ben Hill was one of the most prominent of them.*

Benjamin Hill was a Davis man all the way. The burning issue in question here in 1881, in the wake of the publication of Jefferson Davis's book, was the surrender of Richmond. Who was responsible for that surrender? Lee or Davis? Naturally, Senator Hill was going to side with Davis.[27]

Thomas Robson Hay wrote a book called *Hood's Tennessee Campaign*, which was published in 1929. In his footnote, on page 225, Hay writes: *Senator B.H. Hill, of Georgia, a close friend and supporter of Davis's, stated, in an interview on July 5, 1881, with a representative of the Philadelphia Press, quoted in the New Orleans Democrat, that Davis was not responsible for the movement into Tennessee.*[28] It must be noted that Hay was concerned not with the joint committee, but with Davis's involvement in Hood's Tennessee campaign. Whatever the nature of Hay's concern, he erred in his date of the Ben Hill interview.

Allan Nevins writes, in *The War for the Union* (1971): *Lee ... in January, in testimony to the Joint Committee on the Condition of the Army,*[29] *is said to have replied to the question,* "Will the fall of Richmond end the war?"; "By no means, Sir, by no means. In a military

---

27. Several of the congressmen who had sat on the 1865 committee were still alive in 1881, some of them still active in politics. Their individual opinions of ex–President Davis would have been one of the several factors which determined whether or not they spoke out against Hill in 1881. Not one of them spoke out.

28. *I see that General Johnston thinks that Mr. Davis was responsible for the Tennessee campaign. That is a most unjust accusation.*

29. This was never the name of the committee.

point of view I should be stronger after than before such an event, because it would enable me to make my plan of campaign and battle. From a moral and political point of view the abandonment or loss of Richmond would be a serious calamity, but when it has fallen I believe I can prolong the war for two years upon Virginia soil. Ever since the conflict began, I have been obliged to permit the enemy to make my plans, because compelled to defend the capital."

For his piece on Senator Hill and the committee, Nevins cites a clipping from the New Orleans *Democrat*, July 5, 1881, an interview with former Confederate Senator Benjamin Hill.[30]

Nevins uses and cites Thomas Robson Hay's book quite extensively, and, in turn, Hay had made much use of Alfred Roman's two-volume book on Beauregard. It was natural, then, for Nevins to go the Alfred Roman Papers.

The Alfred Roman Papers, in the Library of Congress, date from 1861 to 1890 and consist of about 150 items in two folio volumes, all arranged in chronological order. In Volume 1, Nevins found a three-page letter written to Roman from General Beauregard in North Carolina, dated July 6, 1881. Attached to the letter is the newspaper clipping reproduced in part above. There is no date on the clipping itself, no indication of the newspaper it comes from, and no specific reference to it in Beauregard's letter to Roman.

Confederate General Joseph E. Johnston.

For his 1971 book, Nevins copied from the clipping he found in the Alfred Roman Papers, the clipping that Beauregard sent to Roman of Senator Hill's interview. As one can see at a glance, Nevins did not quote accurately from this clipping.

In association with what he found in the Alfred Roman Papers, Nevins uses Hay's footnote to try to settle on a date for the mysterious clipping, and the newspaper it came from. However, Hay's premise that the interview took place on July 5, 1881, is pure guesswork, and hopelessly wrong. Even if it were right, Hay never says that July 5, 1881, was the date the *New Orleans Democrat* carried the article. That date was invented by Nevins.

In a letter from the New Orleans Public Library dated May 18, 2013: *We searched the "New Orleans Democrat" on July 5, 1881, for an interview of Sen. Benjamin H. Hill, but found nothing on that date. Sorry! We searched thoroughly.*

Given the fact that many newspapers of the day carried the Senator Hill interview, or extracts thereof, there would be no reason to suppose that the *New Orleans Democrat* did not either, but it certainly was not in their July 5, 1881, edition, as Nevins claims.

Beringer, et al., in the book *Why the South Lost the Civil War* (1991), tell us that Senator Oldham recalled being a member of a joint House-Senate committee that served in January 1865 *to inquire into our present and future means of public defense. Congress considered the committee report in secret session, and apparently never printed it, so no*

---

30. Alfred Roman Papers. Library of Congress.

official record of its contents exists. But Oldham claimed that after a thorough investigation, which included interviews with Davis, Lee, and various bureau chiefs, the committee "came to the unanimous conclusion and so reported, 'that we were in possession of resources sufficient to enable us to carry on the war for an indefinite period of time.'"

Ernest B. Furgurson, in *Ashes of Glory* (1996), represents the small group of historians who have chosen to write of this committee and yet who seem to be ignorant of the March 25, 1865, *Tribune* article:

For many weeks evacuation had been more than a matter of nervous rumor. As long ago as January, according to Senator Benjamin Hill, Lee had secretly told congressional questioners that leaving Richmond would not necessarily end the war. From a "moral and political" viewpoint, Richmond's fall would be "a serious calamity," Lee reportedly conceded, but once it happened, he could prolong the war for two more years on Virginia soil. Since the war began, he had been forced to let the enemy make strategic plans for him, because he had to defend the capital, but "when Richmond falls, I shall be able to make them for myself."

Jay Winik, in his 2001 book, *April 1865*, writes: *In January, Lee had secretly told congressional questioners that the military evacuation of Richmond would actually make him stronger than before. Richmond's fall, he confided, "from a moral and political viewpoint," might be a "serious calamity," but once it happened, he could prolong the war for a good two more years on Virginia soil. In truth, since the war began, precisely because Lee had been saddled with vigorously defending the nation's capital, he had been forced to let the enemy make strategic plans for him, to dictate far too much of the course of battle, and to determine the place and time of combat. But, he added, striking a more hopeful pose, "when Richmond falls I shall be able to make them for myself."* As Winik says, with appropriate caution, in his notes: *This was according to Confederate Senator Benjamin Hill, quoted in Furgurson.*[31]

In the 2006 book *Rise and Fall of the Confederacy*, edited by Clayton E. Jewett, Oldham's voice is heard on pages 102–103: *I was a member of a joint committee of the two houses of Congress raised in January 1865, to investigate the condition and resources of the country. After most patient and thorough investigation, in which we availed ourselves of the President, Gen. Lee, the Secretary of War, heads of Bureaus and subordinate officers, we came to the unanimous conclusion and so reported, "that we were in possession of resources, sufficient to enable us to carry on the war for an indefinite period of time."*[32]

Was Danville planned as the new capital of the Confederacy? A Confederate War Department confidential circular of February 25, 1865, reads, in part: *...in reference to a possible removal of the Department from Richmond. Whatever may not be deemed [indispensable requisite] will be removed without unnecessary delay to Danville, Va., or points on the railroad beyond Danville.*

This confidential circular very clearly answers three questions regarding the government's position as of February 25, 1865, to wit: They had not yet made up their mind to evacuate; with that uncertainty in mind, they decided to start removing certain material

---

31. Winik also mentions Senator Oldham, and the book by Beringer et al.
32. How much of Oldham can be trusted here? And how much of Jewett? In Appendix 3, "The Confederate Cabinet," Jewett has the secretary of war as Stephen Russell Mallor [sic], and George A. Trenholm as assistant secretary of the Treasury from July 18, 1864, until the end of the war. In his bibliography, Jewett misspells William C. Davis's famous book as *Breckenridge*.

from the capital; and there were no plans at that stage to make Danville the next capital of the Confederacy.

In a secret session of the Confederate Congress, on March 8, 1865, a joint resolution *providing for the removal of the seat of government* was read a first and second time. *That in case of any public emergency which may, in the judgment of the President, render it impolitic for the seat of government to remain at Richmond, or in the case of the evacuation of Richmond, the next session of Congress shall be held at* [this was left blank]. This resolution stipulated that three members of Congress (consisting of two members of the House of Representatives and one member of the Senate) be appointed to make suitable arrangements for the accommodation of Congress and the Executive Departments in case of removal. *Resolved further, that the President is hereby authorized, in the event of removal of the seat of government as provided in the foregoing resolution, to cause the several Executive Departments, with the archives thereof, to be removed to* [left blank]. Mr. Swan moved that all this be replaced with the following words: *That the President be, and he is hereby, authorized, at any time when in his judgment the exigencies of the country require it, to remove the several Executive Departments, with their archives and all other archives, to such point as he may deem the interest of the country and the safety of the archives may require.* The rule went before a select committee of five for consideration, and the bill was passed on March 11. The last session of the Confederate Congress was on March 18, 1865. Never in that session, or any previous session, had there been any mention of Danville as the proposed new capital.

Given the number of leaks of inside information from Richmond to Yankee newspaper correspondents, it is not surprising that Northern papers were almost as up to the minute as those in the Confederacy. Having said that, there was still a lot of guesswork and misinformation, on both sides of Mason and Dixon's Line. Most often, one could not distinguish between the truth and the fabrication. So, the *New York Herald* was able to say, in their March 21, 1865, edition: *...the Rebel President, Cabinet, scrip and archives, will be moved to Danville or Lynchburg.* Roy Z. Chamlee, in *Lincoln's Assassins* (1990), has this: *On the train, Davis discussed the possibility of establishing a new capital at Danville.*[33]

General Josiah Gorgas, chief of the Confederate Ordnance Bureau, was obviously still in the dark on March 29, 1865, and that was just four days before the evacuation. As he says in his diary entry for that date: *We are still discussing as to what place we shall retire to. Danville appears the most feasible, and we are packing up to go there.*

C.E.L. Stuart, who was part of the Jefferson Davis flight, wrote the first ever major account of that adventure, in the July 4, 1865, edition of the *New York Herald*. He tells us that it was not until the fleeing party was approaching Danville that the question, "Whither are we going?" came up for consideration, that to leave Richmond by the safest route, and get clear of Grant, had been the only object in view when starting out from Richmond the night of April 2. *Now that Richmond was abandoned to Grant, and the escaped Government free from immediate danger, its destination was not easily determined. Danville was supposed to be too small for a temporary capital, and the good points of all other eligible cities were discussed generally and warmly. At length Mr. Davis put a stop to the matter by saying that he would not leave Virginia until Lee was whipped out of it.*

---

33. For this passage, Chamlee quotes *Harper's Pictorial History of the Great Rebellion in the United States* (1866), which, in turn, cites Stuart's July 4, 1865, article in the *New York Herald*.

Stuart then reports a dialogue between some of the leading men on the train. *"Then you can make up your mind to a long residence,"* said Mr. Bruce, of Kentucky, confidently.

"A day or two more will decide that," was the wary remark of Mr. Benjamin.

"And if adversely," said the Attorney General, *"Charlotte is our point."* He had been advocating Charlotte from the first, and very naturally, as it was to him a home.

Once it was determined that Danville should bear the burdensome honor of the temporary capital, it became a serious question with most of us how we were to get lodged there.

Confederate Secretary of the Navy Stephen R. Mallory was one of the cabinet members with Jefferson Davis on the flight. He died in 1873, after having written an account of the flight. In this account, he discusses who should or should not be admitted to the train at Richmond as they prepared to flee to Danville: *The order had been given to admit no one whose services were not indispensable to the operations of the government which it was hoped might be re-established "somewhere south."* And this, when Mallory narrates events after they had arrived at Danville: *Beyond a spasmodic effort of Genl. Gorgas to open his irrepressible Ordnance Bureau, there was no attempt to organize departments.*

By April 6, 1865, the fleeing government had been in Danville for three days. They did not know it then, but they had only another four days left there before moving on to Greensboro, North Carolina. The position of Danville as the new capital of the Confederacy cannot be stated more clearly, or by a higher authority, than in a letter Jefferson Davis wrote to his wife from there that day: *We are now fixing an executive office where the current business may be transacted here, and do not propose at this time definitely to fix upon a point for a seat of govt. in the future. I am unwilling to leave Virginia and do not know where within her borders the requisite houses for the Departments and the Congress could be found.*

Michael B. Ballard, in his 1986 book, *A Long Shadow*, tells us that Confederate officials had chosen Danville as their surrogate capital for a number of reasons. *Officials had discussed alternatives to Danville which, with its population of only about six thousand,*

Confederate Secretary of the Navy Stephen R. Mallory.

appeared for some to be too small, even for a provisional capital. Davis had settled the matter by proclaiming "that he would not leave Virginia until Lee was whipped out of it." This last quote is from Stuart.

At the Ballard House, in Richmond, on April 6, 1865, R.D. Francis wrote an article for the *New York Times*, which was published on April 9: *The design of the Confederate Government in leaving Richmond is an attempt to re-establish itself at Columbus, Georgia. They hope to be able to recover that State, making Columbus the capital.*

Danville is called, among other things, "The Last Capital of the Confederacy." This epithet seems to have originated with William D. Coleman, in his article, "Jefferson Davis' Week at Danville," published in the *Times* of Philadelphia on May 28, 1881, in which he refers to Danville as *the last capital of the Confederacy.*[34]

One would have thought that this title, "Last Capital of the Confederacy," would have been too tempting for writers to pass up, but with one notable exception, they did, at least in print, for a full century. The exception was an item that appeared in the *Raleigh Morning Post*, and which was reproduced as the article "Our Last Capital," in the *Southern Historical Society Papers*, Volume 31, 1903. It contained the following: *The last full cabinet meeting which was ever held by the President met with him in one of the sitting rooms of the [William T.] Sutherlin mansion.* The writer was B. Boisseau Bobbitt, an eighteen-year-old North Carolina journalist then living in Danville.[35] The citizens of Danville saw the possibilities, and decided to use the title as a marketing tool. But they did something odd and changed "capital" to "capitol," and applied the new word to the Sutherlin house.

An item, written by the staff of the magazine *Confederate Veteran* in 1916, says: *The City of Danville has acquired the Sutherlin Memorial, better known as the last Capitol of the Confederacy, where President Davis held his last Cabinet meeting.* Today, outside this house, there is a marker that reads: *Last Confederate Capitol. This, the former home of Major W.T. Sutherlin, is regarded as the last capitol of the Confederacy, April 3–10, 1865. Here President Davis stayed and here was held the last full Cabinet meeting, Breckinridge alone being absent.*[36] *The establishment of the Confederate Government in Danville ended when the news of Lee's surrender arrived on April 10.*

Frankie Y. Bailey & Alice P. Green write in the book *Wicked Danville* (2011): *At the end of the war, in April 1865, when Jefferson Davis retreated from Richmond, he stopped in Danville. He stayed at the mansion of William T. Sutherlin, a prominent tobacco factory owner and quartermaster of Danville. During that week (April 3–10) Davis convened his cabinet. Thus, the Danville building gained its place in Civil War history as "The Last Capitol of the Confederacy."*

Finally, someone got around to "The Last Capital." John H. Brubaker III, a Danville historian, explains the thrust of his 1979 book with his very title—*The Last Capital*. But

---

34. William Daniel Coleman (1837–1901) was a Danvillian. After military training at VMI, he became editor of the *Danville Appeal*, and was enlisted for a year by Captain Graves at Danville on April 23, 1861, in Company A of Graves's own regiment, the Danville Blues, the 18th Virginia Infantry, CSA, where, in due time, he made orderly sergeant. He was discharged on September 28 of that year to become the postmaster at Danville. By 1864 Postmaster Coleman was anxious to get back into the army, but only as an officer. After the war, Colonel Coleman was a well-known lawyer in Danville.

35. Benjamin Boisseau Bobbitt would later be editor of the *Long Branch Record*, in New Jersey. He died in Miami in 1967.

36. How could it be a full cabinet meeting if the secretary of war was absent? Actually, Vice President Stephens was also a cabinet member. He was not there either.

as for Danville itself being the last capital, this concept did not really catch on until much later, when it did so with a vengeance. Clara Garrett Fountain, in her book *Danville, Virginia* (2000), says: *Confederate President Jefferson Davis fled Richmond during the last week of the war, bringing his Cabinet to Danville. Arriving on April 3, 1865, he established the last Confederate capital, residing at the home of Major William T. Sutherlin. Davis left the city*[37] *on April 10, 1865, ending Danville's brief reign as "The Last Capital of the Confederacy."* Fountain revisited Danville in 2013, this time with Gary Grant. They write in the book *Danville Revisited: In 1865, Danville was chosen as the last capital of the Confederacy.*[38]

Todd McGregor Yeatts, in *Danville* (2005) has this: *In April 1865, with Federal troops poised to capture Richmond, Confederate President Jefferson Davis and his cabinet boarded a train and headed to Danville. Davis arrived in Danville on April 3, and established the Confederate capital at the home of Maj. William T. Sutherlin.*[39] And this: *For its wartime service as the seat of the Confederacy from April 3 through April 10, 1865, Danville will forever be "The Last Capital of the Confederacy."*

Jeffrey W. McClurken's book, *Take Care of the Living* (2009), says: *...on April 2, 1865, ... the Confederate government had to flee. Jefferson Davis and his cabinet left the Confederate capital on the Richmond and Danville Railroad. Davis arrived in Danville that same evening, hoping to link up with Lee's troops and establish a new Confederate capital in this well-stocked supply depot. On April 10.... What remained of the Confederate government left the "last capital of the Confederacy" by train that same night.*

Larry G. Aaron wrote, in *Pittsylvania County* (2009): *Danville literally became the "Last Capital of the Confederacy." With the arrival of Virginia's governor, William "Extra Billy" Smith from Richmond, the new state capital was also established in Danville.*[40]

Is it true, though, that the last Confederate cabinet meeting took place at Danville? A.J. Hanna, in *Flight into Oblivion* (1938), addresses this question in a footnote to his Chapter 5: *Where was the last meeting of the Confederate Cabinet held? There are those who maintain that the meeting in Richmond on April 2 was the last, whereas some of the inhabitants of Danville declared that the last meeting occurred in that city. Another group claims it for Greensboro and still another for Charlotte. Certain citizens of Fort Mill and Abbeville in South Carolina and of Washington, Ga., assert with surprising fervor that the last meeting was held in their respective cities. Even Shreveport, La., has lodged a claim ... although no member of the Cabinet was ever there.*

The title of Michael C. Hardy's 2012 book, *Civil War Charlotte: Last Capital of the Confederacy*, speaks for Charlotte's claim. *Despite claims by other locales, Charlotte was indeed the last capital of the Confederacy; it was the only place where the entire Confederate cabinet met after the fall of Richmond, Virginia; the papers of various departments were shipped to Charlotte and stored locally; the remnants of the Confederate treasury were deposited in Charlotte's United States Mint building for a time; and official acts, like examining and commissioning officers, took place there.*

---

37. Danville was then a town, not a city.
38. From blurb on the cover. Danville could not have been chosen as the last capital, because no one knew what the future held.
39. Several books and articles on the Civil War misspell the word "capital" as "capitol." Vice versa is comparatively rare. "Capital" means the capital city of a nation or state, and "capitol" means the building within that city that houses the government while in session.
40. William Smith had been given his nickname as the result of his constructive methods of obtaining extra fees while a government mail contractor.

Chapter 2

April 2

The weather in Richmond on Sunday, April 2, 1865, has been described as much as that of any other day in American history. Someone had to be the first to use the word "bright," and it seems to have been C.E.L. Stuart in his *New York Herald* article of July 4, 1865: *The Memorable 2nd of April dawned with glowing promise—a morning such as fitly crowned the glittering hopes of the day before—a morning too bright for melancholy forebodings.*

J.B. Jones wrote in his famous *Rebel War Clerk's Diary* (1866)—which was partly compiled after the war using newspaper articles: *April 2d. Bright and beautiful.* Judith McGuire expanded upon Jones, when she wrote in *Diary of a Southern Refugee* (1867): *The day was bright, beautiful and peaceful.* Sallie Brock, on the other hand, writing in 1867, clearly relies on Stuart: *The morning of the 2d of April, 1865, dawned brightly over the capital of the Southern Confederacy.*[1]

Jones's "bright and beautiful" seemed just the right mix of adjectives for Champlin's 1881 book, *Young Folk's History*: *Sunday morning of April 2d, 1865, was bright and beautiful in Richmond.* And for Church's biography, *Ulysses S. Grant* (1897): *Sunday, April 2d, opened bright and beautiful.* And for the Broun book of 1912: *Sunday, April 2, was a bright, beautiful spring day, and Richmond was assembled at church.*[2] And for Mrs. Amelia Gorgas's so-called diary, published in 1917[3]: *Sunday, April 2, 1865, opened bright and beautiful, false harbinger of the gloom that enveloped the devoted city before the meridian*

---

1. Immediately after the war, Sarah Ann "Sallie" Brock moved to New York, and using the pseudonym "A Richmond Lady," published *Richmond During the War*, in 1867. In 1869 she edited *The Southern Amaranth*, a book of collected poems by various persons, including her own "The Fall of Richmond" (written in 1867 using the pseudonym Virginia Madison) and others. In January 1882, at the age of 54, she married the Reverend Richard F. Putnam. It was only then that she became known as Sallie Putnam.
2. William LeRoy Broun (1827–1902) was a professor of mathematics. In the 1912 book compiled by his son, he is quoted as saying: *After a year's service in the field as artillery officer I was ordered to Richmond and made superintendent of armories, with the rank of major in the regular army, a new office in the Confederate States army.* And this: *Early in 1863 I was appointed commandant of the Richmond arsenal.* He was promoted to lieutenant colonel of ordnance, under General Gorgas, and was in that role when the evacuation of Richmond took place on April 2, 1865. Indeed, the arsenal was blown up at his orders. He continued as a professor after the war. About the arsenal, he says: *Here the greater part of the ordnance and ordnance stores were prepared for the use of the Confederate armies. The arsenal occupied a number of tobacco factories at the foot of Seventh Street near the Tredegar Iron-Works, between Cary Street and James River. It included all the machine shops for working wood and iron, organized into different departments, each under subordinate officers, arranged to manufacture ordnance stores for the use of the Confederate army.*
3. Amelia Gorgas, and her husband, General Josiah Gorgas, were the parents of William Crawford Gorgas who, many years later, would eclipse them in fame as the hero of Panama.

hour. And for David Ryan in his 1993 book, *Four Days in 1865*: *April 2nd dawned bright and beautiful.* And for Catherine Gourley, in *The Horrors of Andersonville* (2010): *Sunday morning, April 2, 1865, dawned bright and beautiful.*

Royal B. Prescott, on the other hand, went in search of something original for his 1900 article, "The Capture of Richmond": *Finally, the morning of Sunday, April 2d, dawned beautifully bright and clear.* So did Richard McGowan Lee, for his book, *General Lee's City* (1987): *Sunday, April 2, dawned beautifully in Richmond.* No less or more original was F. Lawrence McFall, Jr., in his *Danville in the Civil War* (2001): *Sunday, April 2, dawned clear and beautiful in Richmond.* Or William C. Davis, in *The Man and His Hour* (1991), when he described it as a *crisp, beautiful morning*.[4]

On the other hand, true originality is somewhat rare. E.A. Pollard was a professional writer; he had the experience as a creative journalist often under pressure to come up with something new and entertaining for his readers. In his 1869 book, *Life of Jefferson Davis*, he has this: *It was a lovely Sabbath day, and Richmond basked in its beauty and enjoyed more than usual remission from the cares of the week.*

Mallory was, as usual, one of the most descriptive of all the writers: *The 2d of April, in the year of our Lord, 1865, though a clear, beautiful day in Richmond, will ever be remembered as the darkest in her history. The temperature wooed the people abroad; a pleasant air swept the foliage & flowers of the Capitol grounds; the sun beamed upon its bronze group of Conscript Fathers; gossiping idlers lounged upon its shaded seats, & the church bells pealed their invitations as cheerfully as ever to the piously inclined who sought their several places of worship.*

Dallas Tucker writes in his 1902 article, "The Fall of Richmond": *Then too it was Sunday, and this, strange as it may seem, added somewhat to its quiet, sweet brightness. Richmond had had enough during those four years to make it sad, and there were, indeed, many mourners and much sorrow.*

Connie Cary, later Mrs. Burton Harrison, wrote in *Recollections Grave and Gay* (1911): *On the morning of April 2, a perfect Sunday of the Southern spring.*

Finally, there are those historians not driven to come up with something new. They would rather quote. For example, Mike Wright in his book, *City Under Siege* (1995): *The day "dawned brightly over the capital of the Southern Confederacy," Jones recorded.* However, it would have been more effective if Wright had cited the right source. This is not a quote from John B. Jones, as he says, but from Sallie Brock.

It was Stuart, again, who first came up with the word "balmy," in his *New York Herald* account of July 4, 1865, although he was describing April 1, 1865, rather than the following day: *...its balmy delusions.* However, it was too good an adjective to ignore, and so Sallie Brock, in her poem of 1867, applied it to April 2:

> *It was a soft and balmy, cheerful April morn,*
> *The hum of business all was hushed and quiet;*
> *The breezes played like whispers newly born,*
> *With thousand perfumes, wafting odorous riot*

Dallas Tucker, also in "The Fall of Richmond" (1902), writes: *There were no physical portends for superstition to feed on. On the contrary, the day was as perfect a day as Richmond*

---

4. Professor William C. Davis is a major historian of the Civil War and of Jefferson Davis in particular. On Wikipedia he is called "an expert on the American Civil War."

had ever seen: the budding trees, the flowers of spring, the balmy atmosphere, the clear sky, bright sunlight, all combining to make it a spring-day of unsurpassed loveliness. And from Richard McGowan Lee in his book, *General Lee's City* (1987): *The sky was cloudless, the air balmy, and the sun warming for the first time that year.*

Balmy had certainly taken root in the imagination of researchers, as evidenced by Mary Johnston, in *Cease Firing* (1912): *...sunshine and a balmy air.* And William J. Cooper, in *Jefferson Davis, American* (2000): *It was a balmy Sunday morning.* And Rodman L. Underwood in his biography, *Stephen Russell Mallory* (2005): *Sunday, April 2, 1865, was a balmy day.*

A soft haze was what rested over the city of Richmond on the morning of April 2, 1865, at least according to Sallie Brock, writing in 1867: *A soft haze rested over the city, but above that the sun shone with the warm, pleasant radiance of early spring. The sky was cloudless. No sound disturbed the stillness of the Sabbath morn, save the subdued murmur of the river, and the cheerful music of the church bells.*

Today's historian cannot just quote other writers, not if his book is narrative non-fiction. As much as he can, he has to surround a quote with his own prose, lively prose at that, perhaps original here and there, a new phrase, some imaginative words culled from a thesaurus, leave his own individual mark in some way, an imprimatur that, as it always turns out, is more important to himself than to his readers. Michael B. Ballard, for example, in *A Long Shadow* (1986): *Sallie Ann Brock noted "a soft haze rested over the city," but above, the sun glistened brightly in a cloudless sky. It seemed impossible that sounds of war could disturb such a day, when only "the subdued murmur" of the James River and the "cheerful music of the church bells" interrupted the quiet of the morning.*

This is all well and good it you can pull it off, as Ballard does, but Mike Wright in *City Under Siege* (1995), still quoting from J.B. Jones's *Rebel War Clerk's Diary*, has this: *"...a soft haze rested over the city [and] no sound disturbed the stillness of the Sabbath morn."* However, again, it is not from Jones, it is from Sallie Brock.[5] This Mike Wright passage is reproduced in his aptly named 1996 book, *What They Didn't Teach You About the Civil War*: *Confederate diarist John Beauchamp Jones wrote that "a soft haze rested over the city. No sound disturbed the stillness of the Sabbath morn."*

Other people at the time, other than Sallie Brock, seem to have remembered the "soft haze" over the city that morning, at least if we believe David Eicher, in *Dixie Betrayed* (2006): *As Sgt. John Worsham would remember it, the morning of April 2, 1865, had witnessed a soft haze settling over Richmond.* Eicher cites Sgt. Worsham's book, *One of Jackson's Foot Cavalry* (Wilmington, NC: Broadfoot, 1991). However, the original edition of Worsham's book, published in New York in 1912, does not mention the sergeant's memory of the soft haze.

So, Sallie Brock came up with "A soft haze rested over the city." But was there a soft haze that morning? Or was it really "A soft haze rested on the distant landscape" as Harriet Beecher Stowe wrote in *Sunny Memories of Foreign Lands* (1854)?

---

5. Mary Hoehling was co-author of *The Day Richmond Died*. Her review of *City Under Siege* contained the following encomium: *Mike Wright has done a prodigious job of research.*

Chapter 3

LEE

At dawn on Sunday, April 2, 1865, at about half-past four in the morning, the Union forces broke Lee's lines near Petersburg, about 22 miles from Richmond. Aside from Lee's actual surrender at Appomattox Court House a week later, if ever there was a point in time that signaled the end of the Civil War, this was it. Lee and what remained of the Army of Northern Virginia were now on the run. Consequently, Lee sent the famous telegram to the secretary of war, advising the evacuation of the Confederate capital. When that dispatch was received in Richmond, all hell broke loose.

Headquarters, April 2, 1865. General J.C. Breckinridge: I see no prospect of doing more than holding our position here till night. I am not certain that I can do that. If I can I shall withdraw to-night north of the Appomattox, and, if possible it will be better to withdraw the whole line to-night from James River. The brigades on Hatcher's Run are cut off from us; enemy have broken through our lines and intercepted between us and them, and there is no bridge over which they can cross the Appomattox this side of Goode's or Beaver's, which are not very far from the Danville railroad. Our only chance, then, of concentrating our forces, is to do so near Danville railroad, which I shall endeavor to do at once. I advise that all preparation be made for leaving Richmond to-night. I will advise you later, according to circumstances. R.E. Lee.[1]

There is nothing in the records telling us when Lee sent this telegram, but as for when it was received in Richmond those records are clear—10:40 a.m. That is a fixed star, inasmuch as anything can be. Normally a telegram sent from Petersburg would have reached Richmond twenty minutes later, which would imply that Lee sent it off at 10:20.

Douglas Southall Freeman, in *R.E. Lee: A Biography* (1934), can only take a guess at the mechanics of how the 10:40 a.m. telegram was sent: *In a few minutes of relative quiet he dictated to his adjutant general*[2] *a telegram to the Secretary of War, reviewing the facts, outlining his plan, and concluding significantly, "I advise that all preparation be made...." Taylor, in his turn, probably from his rough notes, dictated the fateful message to the telegram operator, who sent it directly to the War Department in Richmond, where it was received at 10:40.* This was the dispatch that was carried to President Davis in Saint Paul's Church.

A. Wilson Greene does not guess. He is certain. In his own book, *Breaking the Back-*

---

1. This is using the words and punctuation as in the *Official Records*.
2. There was only one adjutant general in the Confederacy and that was General Samuel Cooper. There were several assistant adjutants general; one of them was Lee's aide, Lieutenant Colonel Walter Herron Taylor.

bone of the Rebellion (2000), he says this: *About 10 a.m., Lee dictated a fateful message to Secretary of War John C. Breckinridge. Lee's aide, Lieutenant Colonel Walter H. Taylor, then repeated Lee's words to a telegrapher, who relayed them to the capital. Breckinridge read the portentous communication at 10.40 a.m. "I see no prospect...." As Lee's message arrived at the War Department, Postmaster General John H. Reagan, Secretary of State Judah P. Benjamin, and other officials, completed an anxious vigil beside the secretary of war, who had spent a restless night at his office awaiting news from Petersburg.*

It strikes one as odd that Lee would wait so long after his lines had been broken to send his telegram to Richmond. Five or six hours after the catastrophe. There are many ways to explain why he would wait so long, but it still seems strange. What is much more likely, what removes it from the strange to the highly plausible, is that he did not send it off at 10:20 at all, or anywhere close to that time, but hours earlier.

It looks as if there might have been a severe delay in the telegraphic process. John B. Jones, in *A Rebel War Clerk's Diary*, wrote this when discussing that morning at the War Department: *The absence of dispatches there is now interpreted as bad news!* If Jones is to be trusted at all,[3] this sentence may simply mean that no dispatches were coming in from Lee, but it may imply that there had, indeed, been a breakdown in communications between the two cities. But whatever time Lee sent off this dispatch, the record says that it was received in Richmond at 10:40 a.m.

Confederate General Robert E. Lee.

The telegram was addressed to Breckinridge. Where was Breckinridge at the moment the telegram came in? Was he actually physically present at the War Department? Was he on his way to church? After all, most people were. Or was he somewhere else? If he

---

3. Jones himself admits to tinkering with his diary before it was published in 1866.

was at the department, he would have *read the portentous communication at 10.40 a.m.*, as A. Wilson Greene assures us. He would have seen the telegram as it came in, and immediately sent a messenger to President Davis informing him of the cataclysmic contents. To do less would have been a gross dereliction of duty. We know Davis was worshiping at St. Paul's Episcopal Church that morning when he received news of this telegram, and that those services started at 11 o'clock. That means a delay of at least twenty minutes between the time the telegram was received at 10:40 and the time Davis got the news. As the War Department was only a block from the church—only a couple of minutes' brisk walk by messenger—and as everyone knew that if Davis was not already at St. Paul's he would certainly be at the main door just before 11 o'clock, this is not a realistic scenario. No, Breckinridge could not have been at the War Department when the news came in from Lee at 10:40 a.m.

Was he, then, at church? C.E.L. Stuart, in his *New York Herald* article of July 4, 1865, in describing President Davis as he sat in his pew at St. Paul's before the messenger came with news of the 10:40 telegram, writes: *A certain ominous telegram that he received in the early part of the morning was, however, a tormenting demon, manifestly too much for the perfect quiet which would be needed in the house of prayer and praise.* Again, this is before Davis received news of the 10:40 telegram. So, according to Stuart, Davis had received an earlier telegram, the "tormenting demon." Tormenting, yes, but not cataclysmic. However, the cataclysm was only minutes away.

There were a lot of churches in Richmond—Episcopal, Baptist, Methodist, Presbyterian, and so on. They all began their services at 11 a.m. on a Sunday. Stuart, when referring to the various churchgoing activities of the cabinet members at the 11 o'clock services that morning, says: *General Breckinridge went to hear Mr. Duncan lift up his voice… He did not tarry there long. Thoughts of that warning telegram drew him early back to the War Department.*

Or, as Richard McGowan Lee puts it in *General Lee's City* (1987): *On April 2, 1865, President Davis was at St. Paul's when he received word that Richmond would have to be abandoned that night, but his Secretary of War, Major General Breckenridge, was attending Dr. Duncan's service at Broad Street Methodist Church.*

The "warning telegram" haunting the secretary of war was, of course, the very same "tormenting demon" afflicting President Davis at precisely that moment in St. Paul's. If Stuart is to be believed, Breckinridge did not stay long at Broad Street Methodist before he returned to the War Department.

The world over, throughout history, at every church, these are the basic mechanics of attendance: the faithful come from their homes to the church to be ready for the service which begins promptly at, say, 11 o'clock in the morning. They arrive in dribs and drabs anywhere between 10:30 a.m. and 10:55. No later than 10:55, because the service is going to start at precisely 11. They chat a bit with their friends outside the main door, then they go in, gradually and leisurely finding their way to their pews. Stuart never says that Breckinridge was actually inside the church when he decided to leave it. It would make sense that the messenger from the War Department found him before he even went through the doors. The only thing Stuart got wrong was the motive that drove Breckinridge back to the War Department.

So now, at a few minutes before 11 o'clock, Breckinridge, advised of the cataclysm, was about to leave the church steps and return to the War Department as fast as he could. But his first duty must have been to send the messenger on to President Davis at St. Paul's

Episcopal, to tell him that he was wanted urgently at the War Department. And that is exactly what happened. The messenger set off from the church, at the corner of 10th and Broad Streets, and got to Davis about five or ten minutes after the St. Paul's services had begun.

The first indication we have of this "tormenting demon" that Davis and Breckinridge were wrestling with, this telegram that had arrived in the early hours of the morning, is from the *Richmond Whig* of April 6, 1865: *...the Sunday morning preceding the evacuation, when Lee telegraphed to Davis that his lines had been penetrated in a number of places ... and that unless he could regain the lost ground, Richmond must be evacuated the following night.* And this: *A few hours afterward, Lee sent another dispatch to Richmond, to the effect that all efforts to reestablish his lines had proven fruitless, and that Richmond must be given up. On the receipt of this news, the rebel officers hurriedly began their preparation for departure.* However, it is quite clear from the *Whig*'s wording that the two telegrams are one and the same, and that it is the 10:40 telegram. Yet the *Whig*, like Stuart, knew that there had been an earlier telegram. Unlike Stuart, the *Whig* was confused.

Does this mean that Lee sent a telegram earlier that morning? As far as the records are concerned, the first and only dispatch sent by Lee that morning to Richmond is the famous telegram received at 10:40. When Davis got around to replying to that telegram, he said to Lee, *The Secretary of War has shown me your dispatch*. If there had been more than one dispatch then surely Davis would have said "dispatches."

That 10:40 telegram was so shattering, so cataclysmic, that it utterly galvanized the Confederate government from Jefferson Davis down and immediately set in motion the evacuation of Richmond. For those awaiting it, this was the most powerful telegram imaginable, the ultimate in bad news, the end of the Cause and the death knell of their country. If there had been an earlier telegram received, with even anything remotely resembling that message, then it would have had the same effect. But there was no galvanizing before the 10:40 telegram. On the contrary, there was a strange, complacent lack of it.

So, there can be no question at all that there was only one telegram advising evacuation. But, did a telegram come in before 10:40? That's the question, rather than "Did Lee send a telegram earlier that morning?" There's a difference.

Associated Press reporter Carleton Coffin was on the scene just after Richmond was evacuated. Using one of his pseudonyms, "Carleton" wrote a letter to his regular employers, the *Boston Journal*, in April 1865. The paper published it. This letter was copied in the *Boston Liberator* of April 14, 1865, and in other papers. It says, in part: *It was a dispatch from Lee that his lines were broken in three places and that Richmond must be evacuated. It was as if a hand had written once more, "Mene, mene, tekel"—thou art weighed and found wanting; thy kingdom is defeated.*

Nowhere in Lee's 10:40 telegram does he mention that his lines have been broken in three places, so could this be the "tormenting demon?" The answer is no. "Carleton" also says that this telegram contained the news that Richmond must be evacuated. We have already seen that if the Confederate government had received such instructions from Lee before 10:40 a.m., they would have been galvanized then. But they were not. So, what about Lee's lines being broken in three places? In his 10:40 telegram, Lee says of that morning's activities, *enemy have broken through our lines*. The *Whig* of April 6 said *his lines had been broken in a number of places*. "Carleton" mutates this into *his lines were broken in three places.* The telegram Coffin is referring to is the one that came in at 10:40.

Similarly, the *Whig*'s expression "re-establishing lines." Nowhere in Lee's telegram, or any other telegram from Lee to Davis or Breckinridge, is this wording to be found.[4] It originated with the *Whig*. It's not so much that the concept of reestablishing lines is inaccurate. That's not the issue here. The issue is the words themselves.

So, any post-war writer using the words "reestablishing lines" is simply copying from the *Whig*, or from a writer who took from the *Whig*. Likewise, any writer who says that Lee's lines were broken in three places is taking from Carleton Coffin or one of his derivatives. Anyone who uses both expressions together is taking from both the *Whig* and Coffin.

This is especially important to bear in mind, when we come to consider the reliability of Gorgas and Kean as "diarists."[5] When the time came, on April 16, 1865, for General Josiah Gorgas to catch up on his neglected diary, he described two telegrams coming in that morning, just as the *Whig* did. *On the 2d of April news came in, in the morning from General Lee that his lines had been assaulted and broken by the enemy, and in a few hours afterwards a second dispatch that his lines could not be reestablished and that Richmond must be evacuated by eight o'clock that night. This I learned about 1 p.m.*

It is obvious from this that Gorgas, like everyone else, read the *Whig* of April 6. Gorgas was not a fraud, it's just that he wanted to do the right thing in his diary, for posterity. He did not know the facts and had to rely on the newspapers. But, of course, by so doing, he inadvertently wound up doing history a disservice.[6]

Such an easy explanation does not obtain when one considers the case of Garlick Kean and his "diary." Julius Washington Muller, in Volume 6 of his mammoth 1917 work, *Presidential Messages and State Papers*, wrote: *On April 2, 1865, President Jefferson Davis received word from General Lee that his lines were broken in three places and that Richmond must be evacuated.* That Muller was, like most other historians, copying directly or indirectly the inventions of the

Associated Press reporter Carleton Coffin.

---

4. It is, however, to be found in an April 2 telegram Lee sent to General Henry Heth: *Move up to the left with your whole force and endeavor to reestablish lines. Gordon has succeeded in reoccupying most of his.* Perhaps this is where the *Whig* got it from. This telegram is in the R.E. Lee Collection at Leyburn Library, and was reproduced in Clifford Dowdey's 1961 book, *The Wartime Papers of R.E. Lee.*

5. Colonel Robert Garlick Hill Kean, pronounced "Kane." Known as Garlick Kean.

6. It must also be remembered that the Gorgas diary did not see the light of day until 1947.

3. Lee

Whig and Carleton Coffin is a somewhat humdrum revelation, and, besides, is not the real point. What raises this Muller passage to the level of interesting is something that happened forty years after Muller's book came out.

In 1957 Edward Younger edited and had published a book called *Inside the Confederate Government*. This book contains what Professor Younger had just recently authenticated as the diary of Robert Garlick Hill Kean, the head of the Bureau of War at the time of the evacuation of Richmond.[7] In this book we are told that Kean made his last diary entry on March 23, 1865, fled Richmond on the Danville train on April 2, and then, on June 1, 1865, began to fill in the missing diary period from memory: *Since the last entry the Southern Confederacy has been utterly overthrown and destroyed.* He is said to have finished this catching-up chore in December 1865, and on December 30, 1874, to have written an introduction to the manuscript that became known within his family as "The Civil War Diary of Robert Garlick Hill Kean 1861–1866." He died in 1898, and the "diary" was passed down in the family. Finally, 92 years after the event, Colonel Kean's story of the flight emerged into public view.

These purport to be Colonel Kean's words in his June 1, 1865, diary entry (bracketed portion in original): *On the morning of Sunday, April 2, I went to the War Office at 8:00 a.m., as usual; found several persons, Col. F.R. Lubbock [ex–Governor of Texas and a member of Davis's staff], Postmaster General Reagan, etc., etc., sitting there. About 9.30, On April 2, 1865, President Davis received word from General Lee that his lines were broken in three places and he doubted his ability to re-establish them; that preparations should be made to evacuate Richmond at once. Copies sent to President Davis and General Breckinridge at once, and I began to pack the papers and books of the War Office.*

As to the overall content, there can be no doubt, from his wording, that Kean was studying the same *Richmond Whig* of April 6 that Gorgas was studying, as well as the Carleton Coffin article of April 1865, and thus, like Gorgas, he is merely a second-hand witness, repeating a confused *Whig* account.

This from the *Whig*: *...the Sunday morning preceding the evacuation...*

This from Kean: *On the morning of Sunday, April 2...*

This from the *Whig*: *On the receipt of this news, the rebel officers hurriedly began their preparation for departure.*

This from Kean: *...and I began to pack the papers and books of the War Office.*

However, as to the specific wording used by Kean: *On April 2, 1865, President Davis received word from General Lee that his lines were broken in three places and he doubted his ability to re-establish them; that preparations should be made to evacuate Richmond at once*, let's look again at what Julius Washington Muller wrote in 1917, nineteen years after Colonel Kean died and forty years before the Kean "diary" was published by Professor Younger: *On April 2, 1865, President Jefferson Davis received word from General Lee that his lines were broken in three places and that Richmond must be evacuated.*

Colonel Kean's wording is the same as that used by Muller in his 1917 book, even down to "President Davis received word from General Lee" rather than what it should have said—"Secretary Breckinridge received word from General Lee." Muller's wording is Muller's, no one else's. In other words, Muller came up with that precise wording him-

---

7. A diary that takes 100 years to surface must be looked at with great skepticism. One cannot just float a diary out there and insist it's the real thing. It has to have the stamp of approval. It has to be declared authentic. Yet one cannot help remembering the Hitler Diaries.

self; it does not appear anywhere before 1917. Either Muller copied word for word from Colonel Kean's diary or Kean read Muller's 1917 book. As Kean died in 1898, the latter possibility is hard to swallow, but no harder than the first possibility, as Kean's diary did not see the light of day until 1957, and besides, Muller does not cite Kean. Only two other possibilities remain. One is a fantastic coincidence of wording. The other is much more sinister.

Kean opens his narration of this episode with the words, *On the morning of Sunday, April 2.* He then briefly says that he went to the War Office. So, he has given us the date, he has set the scene. Yet, when he begins his very next sentence, he feels obliged to give us the date again—*About 9.30, On April 2, 1865.* Why does he repeat the date only one sentence later? And why a capital "O" for "on," when a small "o" was in order? The answer to both of these questions must be because Julius Washington Muller wrote, *On April 2, 1865.* Muller was beginning a sentence, and so the capital "O" was necessary. Kean was simply copying exactly what he saw in Muller. Yet Muller was writing in 1917, and Kean had died in 1898. So, how can this be? There can only be one answer. Kean did not write his June 1, 1865, "diary" entry. Someone else did. And that someone wrote it after 1917. As we do not know who that was, we shall, for convenience, continue to refer to the writer as Kean.

Kean's diary entry continues: *About 11 a second telegram from General Lee that his efforts to reestablish his lines had failed and that Richmond must be evacuated that night, that he had given the proper orders to General Ewell.*

As we have seen, Kean already has an evacuation telegram coming in from Lee at 9:30, addressed to President Davis. Now he has another one coming in at 11 o'clock, addressee unstated. Where did he get these times from? He did not get them from Muller. And why does he not mention the famous 10:40 telegram addressed to Breckinridge?

The answer is, Kean got this from a combination of two or three sources which he then forged to make his own account. The first source is the *Whig*: *A few hours afterward, Lee sent another dispatch to Richmond, to the effect that all efforts to reestablish his lines had proven fruitless, and that Richmond must be given up. On the receipt of this news, the rebel officers hurriedly began their preparation for departure.*

With this "a few hours afterward" in mind, James Dabney McCabe, in his enormously popular 1866 book on Lee, came up with this: *Having decided to abandon the cities he had so long defended, General Lee at eleven o'clock, on the morning of the 2nd of April, telegraphed to the Government that it was his intention to retire from Richmond and Petersburg that night at eight o'clock, and advised the authorities to have everything in readiness to leave the city that night, unless they heard from him to the contrary in the meantime.*

The third source is Edward A. Pollard's *Life of Jefferson Davis* (1869). Everyone read this book. With Carleton Coffin and McCabe in front of him as he wrote, Pollard has this: *In the morning of the 2d of April, General Lee saw his line broken at three points ... at eleven o'clock in the morning, General Lee wrote a dispatch to President Davis at Richmond, advising him that the army could not hold its position, and that preparations should be made to evacuate the capital that night!* That is how Kean came up with 11 o'clock for the second telegram, and how he computed 9:30 for the first telegram.

As for the 9:30 telegram, Kean has copies being sent at once to Breckinridge and Davis. So, evidently, Breckinridge was not there at that moment. Where was he? Where was President Davis? What did those two gentlemen do when they received their copy?

After all Lee was telling them to evacuate Richmond "at once," a galvanizing message if ever there was one. Kean's supposed 11 o'clock telegram, telling the government to evacuate "that night," is slightly less galvanizing than "at once," yet, when Davis got that one he was, well, galvanized. So, why was Davis not galvanized by the 9:30 telegram which, with its "at once," was even more galvanizing? There's a lot of galvanizing going on here, yet not enough.

Comparing Kean's wording especially to Pollard's, and given that, in both, Davis was the addressee of at least one of these fateful telegrams, and that, like Kean, Pollard gives 11 o'clock, it is more than clear that not only did Colonel Kean have Julius Washington Muller's 1917 book in front of him when he wrote his June 1, 1865, account, but also Pollard's *Life of Jefferson Davis*, which was written in 1869.

Colonel Kean says he arrived at the War Department at 8 o'clock that morning, and that John H. Reagan and Frank Lubbock were already sitting there. Frank Lubbock was Davis's aide, and therefore had a very special responsibility to his chief. If anything of any consequence had happened on Frank Lubbock's watch, Davis would soon have learned of it. If Lubbock was still at the department at 9:30, when, according to Kean, the first telegram came in—and Kean does not mention Lubbock leaving—then surely he, Lubbock, would have been the one to take a copy to the president. Yet Lubbock, in his memoirs, denies any knowledge of an evacuation telegram until he found out about it early that afternoon, after church.[8] So, either Lubbock had left the War Department by 9:30 or he was never there in the first place.

We can see that Kean is just as confused as Gorgas, perhaps even more so. Gorgas was not there, so he had to rely on the newspapers. On the other hand, Kean is meant to have been there. If he had relied solely on memory, as Professor Younger claimed he had, rather than trust to confused and inventive newspaper and book accounts, he would have performed better for history; that is, if he even wrote this so-called diary entry.[9]

But was Kean really there? Was he at the War Department at all that morning? His presence there is not verified by Reagan, Lubbock, John A. Campbell, or anyone else who is said to have been there, so we only have Kean to trust for all this. And it is beyond doubt that Kean is using other sources for pretty much his entire account of this episode. Does Kean bring anything new to the story? Yes, but it is all fiction. Did Kean even write this June 1, 1865, catch-up entry? Highly doubtful. Therefore, at least as far as this issue is concerned, Kean, like Gorgas, must be dismissed from the ever-shrinking roster of reliable witnesses. And, of course, so must any account written by modern day historians who cite Kean or Gorgas as witnesses.

But the *Whig* itself cannot be that easily dismissed. They did not just invent this idea of an earlier telegram. And Stuart did not invent the "tormenting demon." An earlier telegram had, indeed, come in from Lee that morning, and both Stuart and the *Whig* knew it. But the records do not show that Lee sent a dispatch that morning earlier than the famous 10:40 telegram. But, in the days after the flight from Richmond, at that early

---

8. St. Paul's was not Lubbock's church. As Lubbock writes in his book: *I was at church and heard nothing until, stopping at the stable for my horse on my way to dinner, I was informed that a messenger had been there for me ... I repaired immediately to the Executive Office.* Lubbock's account is either accurate or it is not. If inaccurate, then why is he depriving himself of his place in history?

9. This book begins with a long essay by Younger, part of which is a long summary of the "diary," which follows. Younger makes no attempt to explain the several anomalies in Kean's account, at least not in this segment about the telegrams.

stage of the history game, without the benefit of the next 150 years to help them, no one was in a position to interpret this riddle. The *Whig* did the best they could, and, in so doing set the ball rolling toward myth. Yes, there was, indeed, an earlier Lee telegram received in Richmond that morning, and it was the "tormenting demon," but Lee did not send a telegram that morning earlier than the famous one received at the War Department at 10:40. It is a riddle, no question of that, but fortunately we, unlike the *Whig*, have 150 years to help us solve it.

While there is no official record of Lee actually sending a telegram early that morning, he had, in fact, sent one very late the previous night, close to midnight.

The last two April 1 dispatches sent by Lee are reproduced in the 1915 book *Lee's Dispatches*, edited by Douglas Southall Freeman. The penultimate one, numbered 203, is dated *Hd. Qrs April 1, 1865. Rec'd at Richmond 11 o'clock p.m.* It is a very brief telegram to President Davis concerning Governor Watts. The important thing to remember is that it was received in Richmond at 11 o'clock on Saturday night, April 1, 1865. It generally took twenty minutes for a dispatch from Lee's Petersburg headquarters to reach the War Department in Richmond, so this one, #203, was probably sent out at or around 10:40 on the night of April 1.

The last dispatch from Lee that day, also to Davis, is numbered by Freeman as 204, and is dated *Hd Qrs C S Armies, 1st April 1865*. Although not cataclysmic, it is certainly a "tormenting demon." It begins, *The movement of Gen Grant to Dinwiddie C.H. seriously threatens our position, and diminishes our ability to maintain our present lines in front of Richmond and Petersburg.* And this: *...I fear he can readily cut both the south side & the Danville Railroads being far superior to us in cavalry. This in my opinion obliges us to prepare for the necessity of evacuating our position on James River at once, and also to consider the best means of accomplishing it, and our future course. I should like very much to have the views of your Excellency upon this matter as well as counsel, and would repair to Richmond for the purpose, did I not feel that my presence here is necessary. Should I find it practicable I shall do so, but should it be convenient for your Excellency or the Secretary of War to visit Hd Qrs, I should be glad to see you.*

Nowhere is there anything to suggest what time this telegram was sent, and no indication of when it was received in Richmond. But if Dispatch #204 did, indeed, come after #203, as Freeman indicates, then it was almost certainly sent by Lee between 10:40 p.m. and midnight of April 1. If it was sent between, say, 11:40 and midnight, then under ordinary circumstances, it would not have arrived in Richmond until after midnight, thus making it a telegram received in Richmond in the early hours of April 2.

However, at the time this last April 1 telegram was sent, ordinary circumstances might not have obtained. So, it is possible that #204 did not arrive in Richmond until hours after it should have done. Either way, if there was an early morning telegram from Lee, surely this must be it. Surely this must be the "tormenting demon" referred to by Stuart.[10] And if #204 was not received by the War Department until about 9:30 that morning, this would bolster Kean's claim, at least to the time a first telegram came in.[11]

But, as a whole, Colonel Kean's account of this episode itself cannot be bolstered,

---

10. #204 was indeed dire news, but things would get worse. In a few hours, at dawn on April 2, Grant would break the Confederate lines, after which Lee would send the famous cataclysmic 10:40 a.m. telegram of April 2, advising the evacuation of Richmond.

11. The contents of Kean's 9:30 telegram, of course, are not those of #204.

and that is because it is spurious. At best it was copied by Kean from newspapers and books, at worst it was written by someone else after 1917. Either way, when trying to get to grips with the telegram issue of the morning of April 2, 1865, Kean, Gorgas, and the *Richmond Whig* must be ruled out of the equation, especially Kean. To trust anything Kean says is to try to accommodate him, and in so doing historians have landed themselves in the unenviable position of having to try to reconcile the impossible.

Another source who has bedeviled historians since 1901 is Mallory. Writing of Davis sitting in St. Paul's Episcopal Church later that morning—i.e., what we now know to be a few minutes after 11 o'clock—Mallory says: *...yet his heart was agonized, & his brain sorely perplexed by Lee's dispatches of the early hours of the day, telling of Grant's overwhelming charge through his centre, of heavy losses, of his inability to re-establish his lines, and suggesting the abandonment of Richmond.*

Mallory copied extensively from and elaborated upon Stuart's 1865 account (see Chapter 15 and the Appendix). When he was not actually lifting verbatim, he was altering Stuart's sentences, often just for the sake of setting his own imprimatur on the story. These alterations do not necessarily mean corrections. So, now we have more than one Lee dispatch coming in before the famous 10:40 telegram—*Lee's dispatches of the early hours of the day*—and they are all telling Davis that Lee's lines have been broken and to evacuate Richmond. However, as Grant did not break through Lee's lines until dawn on April 2, these telegrams Mallory talks of could not have been the "tormenting demon." Mallory must be talking about telegrams Lee sent after his lines had been broken. But Lee sent only one of those—the 10:40 telegram. Therefore, Mallory's early morning telegrams simply cannot have existed.

However, the wording of these early-morning dispatches from Lee, as given by Mallory, fits that of the famous telegram. As Jefferson Davis himself says of the famous telegram, in his letter to his wife on April 5, 1865: *I was called out of church to receive a telegram announcing that Genl Lee could not hold his position longer than till night, and warning me that we must leave Richmond, as the army would commence retiring that evening.* And, as Davis (or, at least, his ghost writer) says in his 1881 book, *Rise and Fall*: *... General Lee's telegram, announcing his speedy withdrawal from Petersburg, and the consequent necessity for evacuating Richmond, was handed to me.*

The word "announcing" certainly seems to indicate that Lee's suggestion of an immediate evacuation of Richmond was news to Davis. And it is worth noting that Davis never mentions the early-morning telegrams discussed by Mallory and others.

John Taylor Wood remained with Jefferson Davis until the bitter end in the Georgia woods, and then fled to Cuba with Secretary of War Breckinridge.[12] It would seem that on June 14, 1865, while in Havana, he began catching up on his diary entries.[13] The diary

---

12. Taylor Wood was one of Jefferson Davis's aides. In addition to being Zachary Taylor's grandson, Wood was a nephew of Jefferson Davis's first wife, who, of course, was Zachary Taylor's daughter.

13. At noon on June 12, 1865, Wood and Breckinridge arrived in Havana after a series of most desperate adventures, at which point, and only then, did Captain Wood feel he had the luxury of time in which to set down his memories of recent events. He acquired a stout Cuban writing book, and began his chore. On the first page he identifies himself: *J. Taylor Wood. June 18/65 Havanna.* He then scores over the "8" with a "4," makes it too large, and extends the "1" upward to match the size of the "4," thus making it June 14. This is clearly when he began this "diary" of events since Richmond. Or is it? The first entry reads: *2 April 1865 Sunday. While at church with the President, rec'ed a telegram from Genl. Lee announcing that the enemy had broken thro his lines, that he could not reestablish them, and that he must fall back at once. Packed a few things at home, the papers in the office & at the President's house. At 11 p.m. left on* (continued)

itself surfaced in 1941. *While at Church with the President, rec'd a telegram from Genl Lee announcing that the enemy had broken thro his lines, that he could not reestablish them, and that he must fall back at once.*

Like Gorgas and Kean, who were also bringing their journals up to date, Col. Wood was anxious to get it right, and so was studying the *Richmond Whig* for information, the same *Whig* of April 6, 1865, that the other two had before them as they wrote. It is equally clear that Wood did not have Carleton Coffin's account in front of him, otherwise he would have done what Kean did, and write that Lee's lines had been broken in three places.

Richmond must be evacuated by eight o'clock that night. That's what Gorgas wrote in his diary, and he claims to have heard it at about 1:00 p.m. on April 2. But that cannot be true, because the eight o'clock concept itself is not true. Lee could not have given a deadline, except to suggest evening. Anything more specific would have been ridiculous, given that everything was so up in the air, and, of course, in real life, the thought never entered Lee's mind. The idea surely was not invented by Gorgas, so he must have read it somewhere before he wrote, or as he was writing, his own diary entry on April 16. The eight o'clock deadline did not originate in the *Richmond Whig*, but Gorgas got it from somewhere. Where did it come from? Pollard, in his book, *Life of Jefferson Davis* (1869), may well provide the answer when he says: *The reporter of the associated press who was aware that eight o'clock had been designated by General Lee as the hour for evacuation, unless meantime he succeeded in reestablishing his lines, in which event he would telegraph again.*

Pollard must be right. An Associated Press (AP) reporter had to have written that in a newspaper in the week or so after the evacuation, and Gorgas must have seen that item. The only place he could possibly have read it, at such an early date, was in a newspaper. And it had to have been the AP report hinted at by Pollard. Somewhere, not yet found, is a newspaper item, written by an AP reporter, which appeared in the press between April 3 and April 16, 1865.

How did the AP reporter come up with eight o'clock? Newspaper dispatches from as early as April 3 were saying that the Davis party fled Richmond at 8 o'clock in the evening of April 2. Could that be where the confusion comes in?

Or perhaps we get a clue from something Stuart wrote in his July 4, 1865, article in the *New York Herald*? *Orders were issued, about two o'clock, to the principal military and civil officials to have all the government archives not yet removed, and which it was possible to remove, ready by seven o'clock; what could not be easily transported were to be destroyed. Orders were also given to these same personages to meet Mr. Davis at the Danville depot by eight o'clock.*

Or it may be that Lee's intentions for himself and his army were superimposed upon his suggestion for Richmond's immediate future. In his 1866 book on Lee, James Dabney McCabe says: *Having decided to abandon the cities he had so long defended, General Lee at eleven o'clock, on the morning of the 2nd of April, telegraphed to the Government that*

(cont.) *train for Danville with the cabinet & City quiet up to our leaving.* The entry for the next day is: *3. Arrived at Danville at 4 p.m. The citizens took charge of the entire party, questioning all. At Maj. Sutherlin's with the Presidents staff.* Century Magazine (vol. 47, November 1893), features the article "Escape of the Confederate Secretary of War," by John Taylor Wood. Then, in 1941, the Southern Historical Collection at the University of North Carolina, Chapel Hill, acquired the John Taylor Wood Papers from Captain Wood's daughter, Lola M. Wood, of St. Mary's County, Maryland. These papers include the "diary." As Burke Davis wrote, in his 1985 book, *The Long Surrender: The diary of John T. Wood, though helpful, was so sparse as to contribute little drama to the hegira.*

it was his intention to retire from Richmond and Petersburg that night at eight o'clock, and advised the authorities to have everything in readiness to leave the city that night, unless they heard from him to the contrary in the meantime.

But how original is McCabe? Compare his last bit with this from John B. Jones, the Rebel War Clerk, whose "diary" was published earlier the same year, 1866: *Gen. Lee has dispatched the Secretary to have everything in readiness to evacuate the city to-night.* And this: *The Secretary of War intends to leave at 8:00 p.m. this evening. The President and the rest of the functionaries, I suppose, will leave at the same time.*

Bearing in mind that the eight o'clock deadline is a myth, the late Clayton Charles Marlow, in his 1996 book *Matt W. Ransom*, more than hints that the reason Lee gave Davis an eight o'clock deadline was out of revenge. Mid-afternoon of Sunday, April 2, 1865, Davis sent Lee a telegram lamenting the loss of valuables if they were to evacuate Richmond that night (see Chapter 5). Marlow creates the fiction that Davis asked Lee to hold onto his lines at Petersburg for another day, so that he, the president, could take care of those valuables. Whereupon Lee tore up the telegram and, *Refusing President Davis's proposal entirely, General Lee insisted on 8:00 p.m. as the final hour of the government's exit from Richmond.*

So, when it comes to our understanding of the early morning telegrams, we really must eliminate Gorgas, Kean, Mallory, and Taylor Wood as viable sources. Likewise Jefferson Davis and Frank Lubbock, but for a different reason—they make no mention of any such dispatches. However, there are two other participants who left written records of this morning's events, one very important, one much less so—John H. Reagan and John A. Campbell. The big problem is Reagan.

Reagan wrote two accounts of his life or portions thereof. The second was his *Memoirs*, published in 1906 after he was dead, and which is quoted here as "Reagan *Memoirs* 1906." These *Memoirs* were edited—*I edited it no further than was deemed necessary for clearness*—by Walter Flavius MacCaleb. We do not know how far MacCaleb went in his editing, so it is somewhat difficult to work out who is talking at any given time—Reagan or MacCaleb. But we have a clue, probably a good one. We have Reagan's first account.

The first Reagan account was his August 20, 1877, reply, written from Palestine, Texas, to a letter Governor James Davis Porter of Tennessee had addressed to him on July 17. Porter had been disconcerted, as everyone else had been, by Major General James Harrison Wilson's scurrilous attack on the ex–President in the article "The Capture of Jefferson Davis," which had appeared in the July 7, 1877, edition of Alexander Kelly McClure's weekly Philadelphia newspaper, the *Times*, as part of the series "Chapters of Unwritten History."[14] In his letter to Reagan, Porter had included a clipping of the first

---

14. It was Wilson's cavalry who had captured Davis in the Georgia woods. This from Wilson: *On the first Sunday of April, 1865, while seated in St. Paul's church in Richmond, Jefferson Davis received a telegram from Lee, announcing the fall of Petersburg, the partial destruction of his army, and the immediate necessity for flight. Although he could not have been entirely unprepared for this intelligence, it appears that he did not receive it with self-possession or dignity; but with tremulous and nervous haste, like a weak man in the hour of misfortune, he left the house of worship and hurried home, where he and his more resolute wife spent the rest of the day in packing their personal baggage. Those who are acquainted with the character of Mrs. Davis can readily imagine with what energy and determination she must have prepared her family for flight.* And this: *...under cover of darkness, the President of the Confederacy, accompanied by his family and three members of his Cabinet, Breckinridge, Benjamin and Reagan,* (continued)

John H. Reagan, postmaster general (and later secretary of the Treasury) of the Confederacy.

two paragraphs of Wilson's ludicrous article, and had asked Reagan for his comments, and for permission to have those comments published. Reagan sent back a long, detailed account to the governor. This letter from Reagan was, indeed, published, in the September 1, 1877, edition of the offending newspaper, the *Times*, of Philadelphia, as "Flight and Capture of Jefferson Davis," one of the paper's regular "Annals of the War" series. This article was reproduced by McClure and the *Times* in their book *Annals of the War*, published in Philadelphia in January 1879. This reply to Porter is quoted here as "Reagan Letter 1877."[15]

In "Reagan Letter 1877," the former postmaster general says: *I went by the War Department on my way to church.* In "Reagan Memoirs 1906" he has this: *Being anxious about the situation, I was with the Secretary of War until pretty late Saturday night. On the next morning I returned to the War Department at an early hour.*

"Reagan Letter 1877" continues: *When at the department, I was informed of two dispatches, just received from General Lee, stating briefly the circumstances which made it necessary for him to withdraw his army from its position in front of Richmond and Petersburg at seven o'clock that evening, and that it would be necessary for the government archives and public property to be removed at once.*

(cont.) *drove rapidly to the train, which had been prepared to carry them from Richmond. This train, it is said, was the one which had carried provisions to Amelia Courthouse for Lee's hard-pressed and hungry army, and having been ordered to Richmond, had taken those supplies to that place, where they were abandoned for a more ignoble freight.*

15. Not everyone has understood how this Reagan article came about. Heidler and Heidler, for example, in *Encyclopedia of the American Civil War* (2000), have this: *McClure made sure that former Confederates wrote articles for the Annals. These men included ... John H. Reagan.*

"Reagan *Memoirs* 1906" says: *While there the Secretary received two dispatches from General Lee, saying in substance that his whole line would retire from its position at seven o'clock that evening, and making suggestions for the security of the public archives.*

In "Reagan Letter 1877," he says: *On receiving this intelligence, not knowing that Mr. Davis had already received it, I walked towards his residence, which was a few hundred yards off, to confer with him about it, and on the way met him and Governor Lubbock, of his staff.*

And this from "Reagan *Memoirs* 1906": *Immediately on receipt of this information, I started to communicate it to the President, and on the way to the Mansion met him and Governor Frank. R. Lubbock, a member of his staff, on their way to church, and informed him of the dispatches from General Lee to the Secretary of War.*

Those, then, presented side by side, so to speak, are the opening paragraphs of Reagan's two accounts as they relate to the early morning telegrams, the first published in 1877, and the second in 1906. It is quite clear that whoever wrote the 1906 version of these early morning telegrams—whether it was Reagan or his editor, MacCaleb—had the 1877 letter in front of him as he did so. The reasons for the edits are quite easy to determine and to justify. In the 1877 letter, for example, it looks as if Reagan just happened to drop in to the War Department on his way to church. That rather bald fact, although probably true, has a sense of casualness about it. It simply does not convey to the reader a sense of the postmaster general's commitment to the Cause. No, it would be much better to have him burning the candle at both ends, like the faithful and responsible public servant he obviously was.

In both versions Reagan has two telegrams just in from Lee, but it is clear from Reagan's description of them that neither one is the famous 10:40 telegram. If Reagan had seen the 10:40 telegram, how could he have failed to write about the breaking of Lee's lines and, most important, the very keynote of that message—evacuation? It is equally clear that he is describing two telegrams that must have been sent by Lee before his lines were broken at dawn, otherwise Reagan would have mentioned that monumental disaster. These two telegrams Reagan discusses basically revolve around Lee withdrawing at seven o'clock that evening, and Lee's suggestions for the security of the public archives.

Nowhere in the records do we have such a telegram from Lee mentioning seven o'clock, or one mentioning the archives. These two telegrams, at least as described by Reagan, are fiction. Do we find anything, ever written, by anyone, that contains these two concepts within close proximity of each other? How about this, from C.E.L. Stuart's account in the *New York Herald* of July 4, 1865?: *Orders were issued, about two o'clock, to the principal military and civil officials to have all the government archives not yet removed, and which it was possible to remove, ready by seven o'clock; what could not be easily transported were to be destroyed. Orders were also given to these same personages to meet Mr. Davis at the Danville depot by eight o'clock.*

In his 1906 *Memoirs*, Reagan says that Lee's "whole line" would retire. This expression, "whole line" does not appear in his 1877 letter, but it does appear in Lee's famous 10:40 telegram: *If I can I shall withdraw to-night north of the Appomattox, and, if possible it will be better to withdraw the whole line to-night from James River.* We are confronted with the probability that Reagan copied from Lee's 10:40 telegram, or more likely, his editor did.

Could it be that Reagan dropped by the War Department not "early," as he expresses in his 1906 edited *Memoirs*, but just after 10:40? It must be remembered that in his 1877 letter he never mentions "early," just that he was on his way to church. Church began at 11, so that would make sense. But the answer is no. We know that primarily because of what happened next.

Reagan rushes out to find Davis. And he does find him, within a minute or so, no later. In both Reagan versions Davis is walking with his aide, Frank Lubbock, on the street. In "Reagan Letter 1877" Davis and Lubbock are merely walking, out for a stroll, perhaps, or on their way to some office or other. In the 1906 *Memoirs*, Davis and Lubbock are on their way to church.[16] If Davis and Lubbock had truly been on their way to church, then it would have to be the 10:40 telegram Reagan saw. But it was not. Otherwise Davis and Lubbock would have been galvanized. And Davis was not galvanized until later, when he was in church. So, the 1906 Reagan *Memoirs* are wrong. If Reagan ever met Davis and Lubbock on the street, then it was earlier in the morning. The only telegram earlier that morning was the "tormenting demon." Therefore it was that one which Reagan had just seen.

In his 1877 letter, Reagan says: *On receiving this intelligence, not knowing that Mr. Davis had already received it...* This information was omitted in the 1906 *Memoirs*. But it had to be omitted, because the editor had re-worked the scene leading up to it. In his 1877 letter Reagan says: *When at the department, I was informed of two dispatches, just received from General Lee.* In the 1906 *Memoirs* we are told that while Reagan was actually at the War Department, *the Secretary received two dispatches from General Lee.* The two scenarios are very different. The first is probably accurate. The second cannot be.

In his 1877 letter—the one much more to be trusted in this particular case—Reagan says that he was informed of two dispatches just in from Lee. That means he was not there when they actually came in. In the 1906 *Memoirs* he is there when those dispatches come in. If he was there when the dispatches came in, and then rushed out looking for Davis so that he could tell him the contents, and Davis already knew the contents, then, of course, we are reduced to absurdity, and the editor of Reagan's *Memoirs* knew this. So this bit had to be dropped from the *Memoirs*.

If Davis already knew the contents of the telegram or telegrams before Reagan apprised him of them, then he must have been at the War Department before Reagan arrived and seen them. Or perhaps his aide, Frank Lubbock, had rushed out to tell him. And, if Davis already knew the contents, then, as we have seen, they could not have been those of the famous 10:40 telegram, or of a telegram that contained the same information—about Lee's lines being broken and the evacuation of Richmond. Instead, it had to have been the "tormenting demon" sent the night before by Lee.

We know Davis went to the 11 o'clock service at St. Paul's Episcopal, so at about 10:45 he would have been walking to church. With Lubbock? Perhaps. Although Lubbock did not attend St. Paul's that morning, he did attend another church. At the point Reagan found them, they would not have split up yet to go their separate ways. However, if Reagan was conveying news of the 10:40 telegram to Davis on the street, then Lubbock would have heard that news too. And, in his own memoirs, he claims that he never heard such news until early in the afternoon, after church. So, that must rule out the possibility that Reagan was bearing news of the 10:40 telegram.

By 1877 Reagan was confused, as everyone else was. He knew there were two telegrams

---

16. Neither Davis nor Lubbock, in their own writings, ever mention meeting Reagan on the street at any time.

that morning—the "tormenting demon" and the 10:40 one, but he got their timing wrong, as well as the contents. But his confusion was not just over the telegrams. The "tormenting demon" does not mention seven o'clock or the archives and public property any more than the 10:40 telegram does.

On the subject of how Davis and Lubbock took the news given them on the street, Reagan's 1906 *Memoirs* are a total blank. On the other hand, "Reagan Letter 1877" says: *We three then walked on to the Executive Office.* In this same letter, Reagan says that President Davis *then assembled his Cabinet and sent for the Governor of Virginia and the Mayor of Richmond. Directions were then given to prepare the public archives for removal...*

In the first account, the 1877 letter, Reagan's news is of sufficient importance for Davis, Lubbock, and Reagan to forgo church and repair immediately to the Executive Office, where Davis calls the cabinet and so forth. In the second account, the 1906 *Memoirs*, Reagan's news is obviously of insufficient importance for Davis and Lubbock to be deterred from attending church. Perhaps, as some later historians have indicated, Davis was hoping for further messages that were less dire. Which means this one was pretty dire, and should have been acted upon, as it was in Reagan's first account, the one that has Davis not going to church that morning. And if the news was that grim, why did Lubbock not intervene? And why did Lubbock not mention it in his own memoirs?

Reagan concludes this segment of his 1906 *Memoirs* with an attempt to secure a place in history: *In making this statement I am not unmindful of the fact that it has gone into history that President Davis received a dispatch from General Lee that morning while at church, which is assumed to be his first information as to the withdrawal of our army.* He then misquotes Davis from his 1881 book, *Rise and Fall of the Confederate Government*, about the president first hearing the news while in church, and then he continues: *This is true; it is also true that I gave him the first information of that fact. And it is not unnatural, mine being an unofficial communication, that he should state as a historical fact that his first official information reached him while at church.*

From this it is quite clear that what Reagan gave verbally to Davis and Lubbock on the street was the contents of the 10:40 telegram. But that cannot be. If what Reagan says is true, Lubbock would have admitted it in his memoirs. It is impossible to believe that Lubbock would have denied himself such a crucial role in the destiny of the Confederate States of America. What he does deny is any knowledge of such a telegram until he found out about it early in the afternoon.

Historian Douglas Southall Freeman was aware of Reagan's claim, at least as made in the 1906 *Memoirs*, and wrote: *Reagan ... stated that he had informed the President, on his way to church, of the situation at Petersburg. The receipt of the dispatch, therefore, simply confirmed what Reagan had told Mr. Davis.* Given the elusive "seven o'clock" and "public archives and public property," this is merely a justification of Reagan, not a solution to the problem.

There are those who buy Reagan's *Memoirs* completely. A. Wilson Greene, the man who wrote *Breaking the Backbone of the Rebellion*, also wrote *Civil War Petersburg* (2006): *While some accounts state that Davis learned of Lee's message while in church, it is clear that Postmaster General John H. Reagan informed the president of its contents while the chief executive was en route to St. Paul's.* Some historians are not so convinced. Michael B. Ballard, for example, in his 1986 book *A Long Shadow*: *Reagan claims to have gone immediately to inform Davis of the message. He says he met both Davis and Lubbock and told them of the situation at Petersburg.*

By the time John A. Campbell wrote his *Recollections* (1880), he had read "Reagan Letter 1877," as everyone else had. Campbell, knowing full well about the 10:40 telegram, yet reading about the two other telegrams, was thus forced to write, rather uncomfortably: *On Sunday morning, the 2d April 1865, I was as usual at the War Office. During the forenoon three telegrams came from General Lee to the War Office, One reported an engagement and heavy loss the preceding day; the second reported the disaster and loss to have been more serious and heavy than was supposed at first; the third reported the disaster and loss as irreparable, and directed an evacuation of the city.* What is obvious here is that Campbell, by trying to accommodate John H. Reagan, has been rendered impotent as a witness.[17]

Did Reagan truly drop by the War Department that morning? Yes, he probably did. Was he on his way to church? Probably.

Did two telegrams come in from Lee on the morning of April 2, 1865? Yes, the "tormenting demon" of the night before and the famous 10:40 telegram.

Did these two telegrams actually come in while Reagan was at the War Department? Almost certainly not.

When Reagan arrived at the War Department, was he informed, as he says in his 1877 letter, that two telegrams had recently come in from Lee? Almost certainly yes, but not two, only the "tormenting demon," and that only after a mammoth telegraphic delay.

Did Reagan rush out looking for Davis? Yes, he probably did. But only to convey the news of the "tormenting demon."

Did he find Davis and Lubbock walking on the street? He may well have done, but they were not on their way to church.

Did Davis already know of the "tormenting demon?" Quite possibly.

Did Reagan ever carry news of the famous 10:40 telegram to Davis? Certainly not.

In the final analysis then, Gorgas, Kean, Mallory, Taylor Wood, Campbell, and Reagan, cannot be trusted in their accounts of this episode. But, being participants—high officials all—they have weight, and that sheer weight has overwhelmed historians over the years.[18]

How did 19th-century writers cover this telegram business? Mallory, who died in 1873, wrote this: *...Lee's dispatches of the early hours of the day, telling of Grant's overwhelming charge through his centre, of heavy losses, of his inability to re-establish his lines, and suggesting the abandonment of Richmond.*

Mallory, of course, like E.A. Pollard, took from the *Richmond Whig* of April 6, 1865, at least as far as the "re-establishing of lines" is concerned, as did the so-called Amelia Gorgas Diary of 1917 which, when describing the period of time immediately after Jefferson Davis had left the church: *In a moment it was known that Lee's lines in front of*

---

17. In his *Recollections* (written 15 years after the event), Campbell does not mention being in any church that morning, let alone St. Paul's. If he had been in St. Paul's, he would certainly have said so, yet Amelia Gorgas, in her diary (1917) has this to say, of the morning of Sunday, April 2, 1865: *I attended St. Paul's Church, as usual, sitting with Judge John A. Campbell, as our pew was filled with strangers.* This from Campbell's *Recollections* (1880), regarding later on in the day of April 2, 1865: *I remained in the city and was at the War Office till late in the evening. Before midnight the trains had gone and all the public buildings were empty.* The following day Campbell gave himself up to the invading Union forces.

18. Two weighty participants—Jefferson Davis and Frank Lubbock—mention nothing about any early morning telegrams. Neither does the Rebel War Clerk, J.B. Jones, who was at the War Department for at least part of the morning until, as we see in his account, he disappears into the vacuousness of myth.

Petersburg had been assaulted and broken by the enemy and could not be reestablished, and that Richmond must be evacuated by eight o'clock that night. By the time Mrs. Gorgas was writing, she had the advantage of having not only Pollard as a source, but also Mallory, as the secretary of the navy's article had been published by *McClure's* magazine sixteen years before, in December 1900.

As we have seen, the fiction of Lee's line being broken in three places was Carleton Coffin's from his April 1865 newspaper account, so he felt no compunction in using it in his 1866 book, *Four Years of Fighting*, but by now he has gone further; he has invented the actual words for that Lee telegram: *"My line is broken in three places, and Richmond must be evacuated," was Lee's dispatch to Davis. The messenger found him in Rev. Dr. Minnegerode's church.*[19]

The enormously respected Horace Greeley, in his book *An American Conflict* (1866), has Coffin in front of him as he writes: *At 10½ a.m., therefore, he telegraphed to Davis in Richmond a dispatch, containing very nearly these words: "My lines are broken in three places. Richmond must be evacuated this evening." That message found Mr. Davis at 11:00 a.m., in church, where it was handed to him, amid an awful hush; and he immediately went quietly, soberly, out.*

Pollard picks up the false trail in *The Last Year of the War* (1866): *Lee's line broken in three places.* And this: *By daylight, on Sunday, April 2d, these lines were assaulted in three different places by as many different Yankee corps. They were pierced in every place.*

Ben Lossing was perhaps the most popular American historian of his day, so much so that for decades after his death, publishers felt that his name would sell books—and it did.[20] In his *Pictorial History of the United States* (1868), Lossing, who was then still alive, repeated the current myth: *So he telegraphed to Davis at Richmond, in substance, "My lines are broken in three places; we can hold Petersburg no longer; Richmond must be evacuated this evening."*

David MacRae wrote a book called *The Americans at Home*, which, rather oddly, was published in Edinburgh in 1870. Talking about Lee on April 2, 1865, MacRae says: *...his lines were broken in three places.*

Again, another unexpected venue for a lecture was Newcastle, in the north of England. There, on February 8, 1872, American consul Major Evan Rowland Jones, formerly a captain in the 5th Wisconsin Volunteer Infantry, gave a speech on *Personal Recollections of the American War*, in which he said: *Lee's position was now untenable, and he telegraphed Jefferson Davis that his lines were broken in three places, and that Richmond must be evacuated.*[21]

This from the same Jones, this time in his book, *Four Years in the Army of the Potomac* (1881): *Lee's position was no longer tenable; therefore he telegraphed to the President of the tottering Confederacy, saying, "My lines are broken in three places. Richmond must be evacuated." The message was handed to Mr. Davis in church during morning service—it was Sunday. No prophet was here necessary to decipher the handwriting on the wall.*

Ben Lossing again, in *Harper's Cyclopaedia of United States History* (1881): *"My lines are broken in three places. Richmond must be evacuated to-night."*

Philip Sheridan, without doubt a great general, published his *Personal Memoirs* in

---

19. The name Minnigerode is also seen as Minnegerode.
20. Benson John Lossing died in 1891.
21. This lecture was published in the *Newcastle Chronicle* of February 10, 1872.

Union General Philip Sheridan.

1890. For the passage that follows, he relied heavily on Horace Greeley's 1868 book, *The American Conflict*. And so the myth continues. *That morning, Jefferson Davis was in his pew in St. Paul's Church when, before the sermon was ended, an officer walked up the aisle and handed him a telegram from General Lee at Petersburg, dated at half-past ten that morning, in which he read, "My lines are broken in three places; Richmond must be evacuated this evening." He rose and left the church, whereupon the officer handed the telegram to the rector, who, as speedily as possible, brought the services to a close.*

There can be little doubt that Thomas Conolly's diary entry for April 2 and 3, 1865, was written after 1892, and not by him. *A telegram of Disaster at Hatcher's run line broken by masses of the Enemy in 3 places Richmond must be evacuated. Signed R.E. Lee.*[22]

Israel Smith Clare, when writing *The World's History Illuminated* (1897), had before him the late Ben Lossing's *Pictorial History* (1868): *That very Sunday morning Jefferson Davis, while in church, received the following telegram from Lee: "My lines are broken in three places; we can hold Petersburg no longer; Richmond must be evacuated this evening." The Confederate President at once left church without saying a word.*

Should one trust the *Cambridge Modern History* (1903)? The answer is, of course, no—at least not when they rely solely on Horace Greeley; not when they quote telegrams that never existed; not when they fail to do any real research of their own: *The same forenoon,*

---

22. For a brief essay on Conolly, see the Bibliography.

while Jefferson Davis at Richmond sat in his pew at St. Paul's Church listening to the sermon, a telegram from General Lee, dated Petersburg at half-past ten, was handed him, which read, "My lines are broken in three places. Richmond must be evacuated this evening."

Greeley held sway for an awfully long time, as can be seen in the exceedingly anonymous history books that proliferated a half century after the Civil War. This particular Greeley passage refused to die: *He telegraphed to Davis at Richmond, in substance, "My lines are broken in three places. Richmond must be evacuated this evening."*

Burke Davis, without the benefit of "Reagan Letter 1877," and thus relying solely on "Reagan *Memoirs* 1906," wrote, in *To Appomattox* (1959): *John H. Reagan, the old Indian fighter from Texas who was Postmaster General of the Confederacy, had spent most of the night in the War Department. He returned there early this morning.* Burke Davis then goes on to relate that Reagan was at the War Department *when two dispatches came in from General Lee, making it clear that the army must fall back in the evening. Not in so many words was Richmond ordered evacuated but there was a warning to carry off public archives.* It is clear from this that Burke Davis was puzzled by Reagan's failure to mention evacuation. Burke Davis did the best he could to reconcile this, but he took a leap he should not have done when he equated one of the "two dispatches" with the famous 10:40 telegram.

Without the advantage of "Reagan Letter 1877" to give them a bearing, and therefore having to rely solely on the ex-postmaster general's edited and therefore rather suspect 1906 *Memoirs*, historians have, as they were bound to, come up against insuperable problems when considering the moment Reagan finds Davis on the street. In these *Memoirs*, Reagan is carrying news of the 10:40 telegram. If that's the case, and he relays the cataclysmic news to Davis, then why is Davis not galvanized? Burke Davis, for example, in *To Appomattox* (1959), was forced into this: *Reagan found President Davis on the way to church and told him the news from the front, but Davis did not take it as final.* But, of course, if Reagan was bearing any tidings at all, it was of the "tormenting demon" that Lee had sent the night before. Having said that, Burke Davis's conclusion, *... but Davis did not take it as final,* has wreaked havoc on historians who have relied on his deductions, rather than trying to work it out for themselves.

It must be noted that James C. Clark, in his 1984 book *Last Train South*, has the cataclysmic telegram coming in at 8:00 a.m., at which point Reagan dispatched the message to Breckinridge. Then Reagan and the other aides paced the floor in silence for an hour and a half until 9:30, when a new telegram—the one proposed by Kean as the cataclysmic telegram—came in, this time for President Davis. Clark gives in full the contents of this 9:30 telegram, but unfortunately the words he writes are those of the telegram that came in at seven o'clock that night. Clark then has Reagan rushing out to take Davis news of that 9:30 telegram. This alone would be too much for a historian to reconcile, but Clark also had Burke Davis in front of him, and Burke Davis was talking about the 10:40 telegram. Finding Burke Davis's *... but he did not take it as final* to be inadequate, Clark offers the following in his *Last Train South* (1984), not as a suggestion, but as a fact: *Reagan then went looking for Davis to deliver the message personally. Davis was on his way to church. Reagan later wrote that he found Davis and General Frank Lubbock*[23] *on*

---

23. Reagan does not refer to Lubbock as a general, because Lubbock was not a general. He was a colonel. Reagan refers to Lubbock as "Governor."

the street and Davis said he would await another message from Lee before deciding what to do. For this, Clark cites Reagan's *Memoirs* of 1906. As for Clark's *Davis said he would await another message from Lee before deciding what to do*, Reagan never said that.

Having had many comments on his *... but he did not take it as final*, and seeing what difficulties James C. Clark had experienced as a result of that, Burke Davis, when he came to write *The Long Surrender* (1985), had come to the realization that any attempt at a conclusion was hopeless. So he dropped all attempts to do so, which does not do anything but leave the reader thoroughly perplexed and without a resolution: *Reagan was hurrying this news to the presidential mansion when he met Jefferson Davis and Frank Lubbock, who were strolling toward church at a leisurely pace. Reagan reported Lee's dispatch to the President.*

Clark has this: *John H. Reagan, the Confederate postmaster general, spent most of Saturday night in the War Department awaiting further word from Lee.* And this, when talking of Sunday, April 2, 1865: *In the afternoon, the Confederates stiffened, but Lee knew it was only temporary. Lee now sent the first of what would be many messages to Richmond, a telegram to Breckinridge.*

It must be borne in mind that in this last passage Clark is discussing the afternoon of Sunday, April 2, 1865; i.e., church is over, the evacuation of Richmond is underway, and, according to Clark, the Confederates were stiffening. Clark then quotes, in full, and almost accurately, the famous "I see no prospect..." telegram, i.e., the famous telegram which, in actual fact, was received at the War Department at 10:40 a.m.—which, of course, was in the morning, not in the afternoon.

Still with Clark, if possible: *Reagan was waiting when the message arrived at the War Department at eight a.m.* One must admit, as a reader, to being confused on two points at this moment. Here is Clark, in the afternoon of Sunday, April 2, and then suddenly, without warning, it is 8 o'clock in the morning of that same Sunday. Then this 8 o'clock telegram. No such telegram is ever mentioned by Reagan, Kean, Campbell, or anyone else. It seems to originate with Clark. Kean does mention that he arrived at the War Office at 8:00 a.m., but the first telegram he mentions coming in is at 9:30.

Clark continues—and it must be remembered that he is now at 8:00 a.m.: *Reagan dispatched the message to Breckinridge, then waited with other aides.* Although Reagan says that Breckinridge was the one who actually received the early morning dispatches, R.G.H. Kean says that copies of the first telegram were sent to Davis and to Breckinridge. However, Kean is here talking about the 9:30 telegram, by which, as is obvious from his words, he really means the famous 10:40 telegram.

Back to Clark: *They paced the wooden floors without making a sound for nearly ninety minutes.* We are not told why they did this. Nor is it explained why Breckinridge failed to make an appearance at the War Department during those wasted 90 minutes of pacing the floor in silence. After all, Clark says that they had dispatched the message to the secretary of war. And why wasn't President Davis also alerted?

At 9:30 a second telegram arrived, this one for Davis. That is from Clark, who then quotes, in full, and almost accurately, the "I think it is absolutely necessary that we should abandon our position tonight..." telegram. Unfortunately, this telegram is the one that was received at 7 o'clock that evening.

For the telegrams, Clark has relied on the book, *The Wartime Papers of R.E. Lee* (1961), edited by Clifford Downey and Louis H. Manarin. There seems little doubt that, although "Downey" is the spelling used consistently throughout Clark's book, what is meant is actually "Dowdey."

William C. Davis, relying on Reagan's edited *Memoirs* of 1906, and perhaps also on Colonel Kean's account,[24] says, in *The Man and His Hour* (1991): *Reagan had been at the War Department early that morning.* And then that Reagan was *watching the incoming telegrams, and he read Lee's first notice of the disaster as soon as it arrived.* Telegram #204, sent by Lee the night before, as much a "tormenting demon" as it may have been, was not news of the disaster. So, this "first notice of the disaster" that Professor Davis talks about must be another telegram. But there could only have been one such telegram, as we have seen, and that's the 10:40 telegram.

William J. Cooper thinks otherwise. Writing in his 2000 book, *Jefferson Davis, American*, Cooper says: *Grant, on April 2, broke through the Confederate lines. Immediately the news flashed to Richmond. It was a balmy Sunday morning. Postmaster General John Reagan, who had been at the War Department when the telegram arrived...*

General Ulysses S Grant.

The Confederate Lines were broken at dawn, in other words at or around 4:30 a.m. Cooper states that the news flashed immediately to Richmond. Does he mean by telegram? There can be no other reasonable way in which the news could, in those days, have been flashed immediately over that 22-mile distance. If it is a telegram that Cooper means, then it must have been received in Richmond at dawn, or soon thereafter. It certainly cannot refer to the famous 10:40 telegram, which was received six hours after Lee's lines had been broken. Again, we—and that includes Cooper—have no record of such a telegram being either sent or received.

Failing to realize that Kean had copied from the *Richmond Whig* and Carleton Coffin's inventive newspaper reports, and that, therefore, they are not his own memories of the event at all, the Hoehlings tried to solve this telegram problem in their 1981 book, *The Day Richmond Died.* By trying to squeeze Kean into Reagan, so to speak, they made their task impossible: *At 10.40, a third message from Lee arrived at the War Department addressed to General Breckinridge. "I see no prospect of doing more than holding our position here till night. I am not certain that I can do that...." As Kean, Judge Campbell and Postmaster Reagan gravely read on, little doubt was left in their minds that the end was, indeed, at hand ... I advise that all preparation be made for leaving Richmond tonight... R.E. Lee. "Immediately on receipt of this information," Reagan would recall, "I started to communicate it to the President and on the way to the mansion met him and Governor Frank R. Lubbock ... on their way to church and informed him of the dispatches from General Lee to the secretary of war."*

---

24. William C. Davis was aware of "Reagan Letter 1877," but did not understand what it was. He cites it as *account of the evacuation of Richmond, undated clipping in Virginia Clay Scrapbook, Clay Papers, Duke.*

At this point, unable to come to grips with the unsolvable, and unable or unwilling to see that someone was prevaricating, the Hoehlings were reduced to supposition and guesswork. *The Postmaster must have been surprised to learn that the pair planned to attend divine services since Lubbock had been at the department and knew what was coming in from Lee. In turn Lubbock must have told Davis.*

With Burke Davis's 1985 book, *The Long Surrender*, in front of him as he wrestled with the irreconcilable, Don Lowry wrote this, in his own 1995 book, *Towards an Indefinite Shore*: *In Richmond that morning, Postmaster General John H. Reagan was at the War Department at 10:40 a.m. when Lee's telegram to Secretary of War Breckinridge arrived. He hurried toward the Confederate White House and met President Davis, who was on his way to church with Francis R. Lubbock, an aide to the president and a former governor of Texas, Reagan's home state.*

William C. Davis, in *The Man and His Hour* (1991), discusses Reagan's movements: *At once he set out to find Davis himself, and soon encountered Colonel Lubbock, walking with the president, both on their way to church. Reagan told Davis of Lee's news.* It is only in Reagan's *Memoirs* (1906) that the postmaster general says he met Davis and Lubbock on their way to church. In those same *Memoirs* it is the 10:40 news he is conveying to the President, yet, as we shall see, author Davis, in his 2001 book, *An Honorable Defeat*, says that Jefferson Davis did not receive news of this telegram until after church services had begun at 11 o'clock. And again, Frank Lubbock, in his own book, professes ignorance of the entire business until early afternoon.

A. Wilson Greene, in *Breaking the Backbone of the Rebellion* (2000), has this: *Breckinridge accepted Lee's grim analysis with the studied calm of a former field commander, and dispatched Reagan to share the news with President Davis, who at that moment was en route to worship at St. Paul's Church. Reagan explained the contents of Lee's message to the president.*

William J. Cooper, in *Jefferson Davis, American* (2000), says that Reagan *headed to the White House to inform the president. On the way he met Davis en route to church.*

William R. Trotter, writing his book *Silk Flags and Cold Steel* (1988), has this: *The long-dreaded telegram from General Robert E. Lee, announcing that his defensive lines had been ruptured beyond repair, came to Davis's desk at about 10:30 a.m. on April 2.* Although he does not mention the most important element of this dispatch—evacuation—Trotter clearly has in mind here the telegram received at 10:40 a.m. For decades before he wrote this, historians had known that the telegram arrived at 10:40 a.m. The records show it. We do not know why Trotter should be coy on this issue. As for the setting—Davis's desk, etc.—this is entirely Trotter's invention. However, that setting was novel and exciting enough for Clint Johnson to seize and run with in his own 2008 book, *Pursuit*: *By 10:30 that morning, Davis had already spent several hours at his desk in the Executive Mansion poring over maps and reading Robert E. Lee's gloomy Saturday night report describing the recent loss of The Battle of Five Forks on April 1.* It is obvious, from the preceding, that Clint Johnson, unlike William Trotter, knows when the fateful telegram came in. But just to let us know that he knows, he writes this: *Davis had not yet received Lee's telegram detailing the pre-dawn attack on Petersburg itself. Alone with his thoughts now, Davis knew that the end for Richmond could now be measured by hours.* And now for a bit of fiction: *Frustrated that there was no fresh news from Lee, Davis rose from his desk and called to his aide, former Texas governor Frank Lubbock. Davis had promised his wife that he would not neglect going to church no matter how much work piled up on his desk.* But then there is Reagan's 1906 *Memoirs* to contend with: *As Davis walked down the hill toward the church with his head down and his hands clasped behind him, he ignored his surroundings, while Lubbock, a man used to dry, brown, sometimes treeless Texas, reveled in their surroundings.* This sounds as if it is the postmaster general's first day in Richmond, all agog with the wonders of a big Eastern city. *The two were still strolling to morning worship at St. Paul's Episcopal Church when a breathless Postmaster General John Reagan ran up. The portly Reagan, his face flushed with excitement, concern, and over exertion, handed Davis a telegram from Lee addressed to the newly installed secretary of war Breckinridge.*[25] Clint Johnson concludes with: *It was just twenty minutes before church would begin at 11:00 a.m.* One must remember, when reading Johnson's last sentence, that the telegram came in at 10:40 a.m. to the War Department. For his entire account of this, Johnson does not footnote or source.

As will be remembered, "Reagan Letter 1877" says that immediately the postmaster general delivered the news to Davis and Lubbock on the street, *we three then walked on to the Executive Office.* Then Davis called a cabinet meeting. Nothing about St. Paul's or any other church. And "Reagan *Memoirs* 1906" says nothing at all of what happened after the three men met on the street. All it says is that Reagan delivered the news to Davis and Lubbock on the street and got no credit for it in Davis's *Rise and Fall* (1881). Bearing in mind that Reagan is all we have to go on for this episode, and that absolutely no other contemporary mentions it, anything additional to the two Reagan accounts is fiction, unless it is to clarify, or to expand upon an obvious point. Burke Davis, in *To Appomattox* (1959), says that the *president went toward St. Paul's.* This is the sort of additional material that does history no good at all, yet it was good enough for A. Wilson Greene in *Breaking the Backbone of the Rebellion* (2000): *[Davis] ... proceeded to St. Paul's with a deceptively calm demeanor,* and for William J. Cooper, who, in *Jefferson Davis, American* (2000), has Davis on his way to church: *After listening to Reagan, Davis continued on.*

In 1981 the Hoehlings tried to work out what happened after Reagan gave Davis the message, and finally threw up their hands in desperation, resorting to guesswork, fiction, and fanciful quotes: *Although the president appeared to Reagan to be "distracted," he was as well strangely unmoved as if he simply did not believe or possibly even comprehend what his cabinet member was trying to tell him. Davis, as a matter of fact, had always considered the postmaster "unpolished" and "brusque," which may have rendered what the "uncouth" Texan said less credible.*[26]

James C. Clark, in his *Last Train South* (1984), comes up with this: *Davis said he did not recall receiving the message from Reagan.* For this, Clark quotes Reagan's *Memoirs* of 1906. Reagan never said such a thing. On the contrary. And Jefferson Davis never said such a thing either. He never mentions the occasion.

Burke Davis read the Hoehlings' book, and was impressed with what he read. Four years later, when he came to write his own *The Long Surrender,* he felt comfortable saying

---

25. Breckinridge had actually been secretary of war since February 6.
26. One has to wonder about the Hoehlings' use of the three adjectives—"unpolished," "brusque," and "uncouth." They seem to be quotes, but one cannot track down the originals. How did the Hoehlings know that Davis had always considered Reagan thus? If that were true, it would be a little odd when one considers what Joan Cashin says in her book about Varina Davis: *Another of her favorites was John H. Reagan.* Wherever the Hoehlings got this, it did not get many takers in the field—Burke Davis in *The Long Surrender* (1885); Don Lowry in *Towards an Indefinite Shore* (1995), and, in mutilated form, David D. Ryan in his fictional work *Four Days in 1865* (1993).

that Reagan *was taken aback* by the President's reaction. Burke Davis had no idea where the Hoehlings had got their "distracted" from, but he liked it enough to expand on it to make his own quote—*Davis seemed "oddly distracted," as if he did not comprehend the reality of the moment. Nor did Lubbock seem to share Reagan's sense of alarm, despite all he had learned during the night's vigil. Davis walked on toward St. Paul's with his aide, having taken little note of Reagan's message or even his presence, so far as the Texan could observe. Reagan was not one of his close friends, so Davis may have given his report less credence than it deserved. He thought Reagan "uncouth, "unpolished."*

Burke Davis's weight as a famous historian was simply too much for Don Lowry to resist. In his *Towards an Indefinite Shore* (1995), he writes: *Reagan reported the substance of Lee's message, and was surprised that the president, who appeared oddly distracted, did not seem to understand the gravity of the situation. Davis and Reagan were not close. The President considered the Texan unpolished and uncouth, and he may not have paid much attention to his information. War Department messages were not the business of the Postmaster General. Anyway, Davis and Lubbock continued on to St. Paul's Episcopal Church for the 11:00 a.m. services.*

It takes an extraordinary historian to resist peer pressure, unless he is breaking decidedly new ground and can prove it. When all about you are writing one thing, and you're writing another, your readers, overwhelmed by sheer weight of numbers, will think you're wrong. You cannot be seen to be wrong, otherwise you'll lose your credibility, and, of course, you will not sell books. So, something has to give, and, of course, it will be your integrity. When that happens, your writing becomes muddy and indistinct, because it's not yours—it's someone else's. You've betrayed yourself and your readers.

William C. Davis writes in *The Man and His Hour* (1991): *Reagan told Davis of Lee's news, but since the first telegram promised more information later, Davis went on to St. Paul's, where he got a second telegram making it absolutely clear that they must abandon their position that night.*

If that first telegram Professor Davis refers to is the "tormenting demon," then nowhere in that telegram does it say that further information was promised. And even if that first telegram is not the "tormenting demon," there is nothing written by Reagan, Kean, Mallory, or any other early writer to suggest such a promise. On the other hand, the famous telegram of 10:40 a.m. does end with *"I will advise you later, according to circumstances."* That seems to fit the bill; it does sound like the promise of more information later. However, that's not the telegram Professor Davis has in mind because he has President Davis receiving a second telegram while in church, which, it goes without saying, is the famous 10:40 telegram. However, we have a problem. Professor Davis says that this telegram that the president received in church made "it absolutely clear that they must abandon their position that night." Unfortunately, the 10:40 telegram did not contain any such message. That message—*I think it absolutely necessary that we should abandon our position tonight*—would not be received in Richmond until 7 o'clock that night (see Chapter 5).

Referring to the famous telegram of 10:40 a.m., Dr. Nelson Lankford, in his 2002 book, *Richmond Burning*, says: *This was not the first time Davis received bad news from Lee that morning. He had heard an earlier ominous report on his way to church but decided to continue on his walk to St. Paul's in hopes that Lee's next message would be less dire. It was not.*

Dr. Lankford does not source this passage, but it is obviously from William C. Davis. It is equally clear that Dr. Lankford is as uncomfortable as Professor Davis was eleven years before. He has taken the trouble to re-tell this story, which, after all is Reagan's story, so why not mention Reagan? Why does he not give us any details of the "ominous report?" That's what happens when you write something you do not believe in.

A novelist can build fiction upon fiction. When a historian tries that he finds himself in an awful mess. The acme of this process has, of course, not yet been reached, but in the meantime Clint Johnson's *Pursuit* (2008) will serve: *Davis read the telegram with a seemingly unconcerned look on his face. He scribbled a reply to Lee for Reagan to take back to the telegrapher at the War Department. He then continued his leisurely walk toward church.* And this: *Reagan ... was flabbergasted. He had read the telegram. Its meaning was indisputable. Yet, the inscrutable Davis had read it without even changing the expression on his face. Neither had Davis asked Reagan, his own cabinet member, what course he thought the cabinet should take now that Federal forces appeared poised to capture the capital itself. Reagan watched Davis and Lubbock continue their meander down the hill for a few moments while he got his second wind. Reagan rushed back to the War Department to send Davis's reply to Lee.*

So, from nothing—nothing at all—we have a complete and whole scenario built up by a series of historians, each building on the other's fiction.

In order to solve this problem of the early morning telegrams, a new approach was definitely in order. And one was duly presented, in William C. Davis's *An Honorable Defeat* (2001).

It all started with the following passage in that very book: *Then at 10:40 came the word that Lee must abandon his defenses that night, and perhaps even sooner. At once Breckinridge sent a copy of the telegram by clerk to the president. By this time Davis was in church, or at least would be when he received this copy.*

Immediately we have problems. In his earlier work, *The Man and His Hour* (1991), Professor Davis says that the War Department was one block away from the church. We know the telegram was received at the War Department at 10:40 a.m., and Professor Davis confirms that time. So, in *An Honorable Defeat*, we have Breckinridge receiving the telegram at 10:40, and at once sending a copy by clerk to the president. *By this time Davis was in church, or at least would be when he received this copy.* As we have already seen, it could not have taken a messenger more than just two or three minutes to get the news to President Davis, that is if Davis was at church at 10:40, which, of course, he was not—not yet. And if the president was not yet at church, where was he? Was he walking to church with Frank Lubbock? According to Professor Davis, the president did not receive news of this telegram until he was actually in church, so what was the messenger doing between 10:40 and 11 o'clock? Let's think this through. Was he running around town trying to find the president? Why would he do that if he knew that within minutes the president would appear at the steps of St. Paul's Church? Why was it that not until church services had begun did the messenger find Jefferson Davis? None of this works. And, as also seen, Breckinridge could not have been at the War Department when the news came in. He was on his way to Broad Street Methodist Church for the 11 o'clock service there.

Historians writing between 1865 and 2001 had no doubt which service Breckinridge was attending. It was the 11 o'clock. However, in 2001 that would change, in order to accommodate the new approach to the problem.

Garlick Kean, in his "diary," claims that a telegram came in from Lee at about 9:30 that morning, advising the Confederate government to evacuate Richmond "at once." He also says that a copy of this telegram was sent to both Jefferson Davis and John C. Breckinridge. Kean does not say where Breckinridge was at that moment, but one thing is for certain—he was not at the War Department at 9:30, otherwise they would not have had to have a copy sent to him. So, where was the secretary of war at 9:30, when this awful news came in?

Of course, there was no 9:30 telegram concerning the evacuation of Richmond. There was only the "tormenting demon" straggling in from late the previous night. Having been written several hours before Lee's lines were broken, the "tormenting demon" obviously had nothing to do with either Lee's lines being broken or the evacuation of Richmond. The only telegram that morning concerning those two devastating eventualities was the one received at 10:40.

If one believes Kean, or any other "eyewitness"—or, indeed, any source at all, including secondary sources—it means accommodating that account. Sometimes, perhaps even more often than not, the source is impeachable, and thus such an accommodation becomes extremely difficult, if not impossible. In order to avoid this problem, the first thing a historian should do is independently check the source's credentials, something not often done. In short, one cannot just believe a source because it's there on the written page.[27] Similarly, there is a tendency among historians to make deductions from unreliable premises and set them in stone.[28] In both scenarios, one will inevitably paint oneself into a corner.

If you try to make sense of Kean's 9:30 telegram, then a corner is what you're going to find yourself in. In the case of William C. Davis, in his 2001 book, *An Honorable Defeat*, the corner took the form of an early morning service: *Breckinridge went to an early service at the Broad Street Methodist Church the next morning, and while there he received the first in a series of telegrams from Lee intimating that this would likely be the last day he could hold his line...*

When Hattaway and Beringer offer the following passage in *Jefferson Davis, Confederate President* (2002), the most we can do is put it on record as a facsimile of William C. Davis, but with no individual value as far as this particular question goes: *Breckinridge was at an early service at the Broad Street Methodist Church, where he received the first of a series of telegraphs Lee sent.*

Even after consulting the appropriate ecclesiastical authorities in Richmond, we still do not know precisely what time the Broad Street early service began on Sunday, April 2, 1865, but such Methodist services normally began anywhere between 8:30 and 9:00 a.m. After the early service came Sunday School, and finally the main 11:00 a.m. service.

Although there is no Lee telegram on record with precisely the words William C. Davis suggests—*that this would likely be the last day he could hold his line*—this passage would certainly seem to suggest (although Davis does not say this) that the telegram Breckinridge received in church, during that early service, was the last one Lee sent the night before—Stuart's "tormenting demon," telegram #204.

---

27. For just a few examples of this, aside from this current chapter, see W.H. Swallow and E.T. Watehall in the Bibliography; Varina Davis in the first part of Chapter 16, where she throws out the guess that Stuart might have been a clerk in the War Department, and the effect this guess has had on historians; the Northside Depot fiasco in Chapter 14; "Jesus, lover of my soul," in Chapter 4; the locomotive name Charles Seddon, in Chapter 7; the name John C. Hendren, in Chapter 8; and George Trenholm taking morphine in Chapter 10.

28. For just a few examples of this, other than this chapter: In Chapter 16, where we are told why Stuart discontinued his series "Rummaging through Rebeldom"; President Davis having his hand shaken at frequent stops along the route, in Chapter 11; the president's car being crowded, in Chapter 8; the number of passengers in the president's car, also in Chapter 8; and the evacuation of Richmond being a "mixed affair," in Chapter 6.

Professor Davis, continuing the subject of Breckinridge after he has been called out of the early morning service at Broad Street, says: *At once he went to the War Department to await further news...*, while Hattaway and Beringer, in *Jefferson Davis, Confederate President* (2002), have: *The war secretary at once went to his office to await further news.* And this, from David Eicher, in his 2007 book, *Dixie Betrayed*: *Summoned from the Broad Street Methodist Church, Secretary of War John C. Breckinridge scurried to the War Department to await further telegrams.*

Bearing in mind that this was the early service that Breckinridge was attending, he must have left church to return to the War Department some time between 8:30 and 10:00 a.m. That's it. That's the window of opportunity.

The very idea of the early service seems to originate with Professor Davis, in his 2001 book. Although he has made many original contributions over the years to this narrow period of history,[29] in this particular instance he did get it from somewhere. For his information, he cites *Moore's Complete Civil War Guide to Richmond*, a guide book self-published in Richmond by one Samuel T. Moore, Jr., in 1973 and again in 1978 and subsequent years.

Stuart, in 1865, says that Breckinridge was at the 11:00 a.m. service. Professor Davis has an early morning service. So, it comes down to the question, Does one trust a contemporaneous 1865 account written by a journalist in Richmond, or a privately printed 20th-century Richmond guide book that does not cite its source?

Continuing with Professor Davis's new approach to the problem in *An Honorable Defeat*, Breckinridge returns to the War Department between 8:30 and 10 o'clock: *...but when the telegraph wires went silent for some time it seemed an evil portent to all. Benjamin, as well as Kean, Lubbock, and others, joined him at times in the vigil, and Reagan*[30] *and Campbell stopped in on their way to church.*[31]

David Eicher, re-presenting William C. Davis not in style, certainly, but in content, writes, in *Dixie Betrayed* (2007): *The telegraph wires went dead, however, spooking the group of officials left at the building.* And this: *Finally, after a period of silence, the wires reignited, and by 10:40 a.m., word arrived that shocked everyone into silence. Lee sent a message declaring that he would have to abandon his positions that evening or perhaps sooner.*

To sum up: the first telegram from Lee to arrive in Richmond that morning was the "tormenting demon," which had actually been sent the night before. This telegram was subject to a hopeless delay and did not arrive at the War Department until hours later. President Davis was made aware of this telegram very soon after its arrival, possibly by Postmaster General Reagan who found Davis and Lubbock walking on the street. It was depressing news, but not exactly galvanizing. The three men then went to Davis's office

---

29. For example, in Chapter 8 we see that it was Professor Davis who originated the theory that the president's car was crowded; in Chapter 9, we see how he has the Davis party fleeing Richmond on an afternoon train; in Chapter 10 we see that it was he who came up with the idea that it was Anna Trenholm who supplied the brandy; and in Chapter 11 that Milepost #94 on the Davis trip to Danville was named Clover Hill, rather than Clover Station.

30. In his account, C.E.L. Stuart says that on the morning of Sunday, April 2, 1865, Postmaster General Reagan was at Dr. Petre's Baptist Church. Stuart was cited by Ben Lossing in the various pictorial histories of the Civil War which he compiled in the 1870s. *Harper's Encyclopaedia* picks up on Stuart, but chooses to name Petre as Petrie.

31. For this passage, Professor Davis cites, in footnote 32, Reagan's *Memoirs*; John A. Campbell's *Recollections of the Evacuation of Richmond*; Kean; and a clipping he found in the Virginia Clay Scrapbook, a clipping that was actually Reagan's 1877 letter.

to discuss it. Meanwhile, in Petersburg, at dawn, Lee's lines had been broken, and at some stage he sent his first telegram of the morning, advising of the disaster, and that Richmond should be evacuated. That telegram, also almost certainly subject to a delay in transmission, was received at the War Department at 10:40 a.m. This is the only telegram Lee sent to Richmond that morning. It found Breckinridge on his way to Broad Street Methodist Church at about 10:55 a.m., and subsequently President Davis in St. Paul's Episcopal at about 11:05. Davis left the church, hurried to the War Department, and called a cabinet meeting. All parties were galvanized. The evacuation of Richmond had begun.

Chapter 4

CHURCH

Jefferson Davis was called out of church in Richmond, on Sunday morning, April 2, 1865, to go to the War Department, where Lee's telegram had arrived at 10:40, the dispatch that would set in train the evacuation of Richmond. As Mallory tells us: *The members of the cabinet, with the exception of Mr. Benjamin, were similarly called out of church, by special messengers, at their several places of worship.*

Judah Benjamin, not being a subscriber to Christianity, was, of course, not in church that Sunday. C.E.L. Stuart despised the secretary of state for a variety of reasons—Jew, homosexual, unpleasant personality. In the *New York Herald* of July 4, 1865, Stuart describes Benjamin on that fateful morning of April 2: *Mr. Benjamin ... courted his pipe and solitude in the cool verandah of his Main street mansion. His countenance had its never ceasing smile, or glimmer, but his busy, dark eyes and the feverish movements of his hands twirling and tugging his watch-guard, told some of the unpleasant tale so faithfully put in the morning's telegram.* And this: *J.P. Benjamin, who, being no Christian, paid homage to pipe and solitude during the early part of that eventful Sabbath morning.*

Mallory, with Stuart's account in front of him, wrote this: *Mr. Benjamin, having completed his plain & unexceptionable toilette, & scanned the latest foreign papers, pursued his way from his residence on Main Street, beyond Adams, to the State Department, with his usual happy, jaunty air; his pleasant smile, his mild Havannah, & the very twirl of his slender, gold headed cane, contributing to give casual observers, expression to that careless confidence of the last men upon Arrarat who assured Noah of his belief that "it would not be such a h- of a shower after all." But he talked with friends in passing; friends with observing, detective eyes; and they did not fail to see under*

Judah Philip Benjamin, secretary of state of the Confederacy.

St. Paul's Episcopal Church, Richmond, 1865.

that smile, which bore no nearer relations to mirth or contentment than do the dull undulations of the Dead Sea to the sparkling ripples of a mountain stream, no less than in the nervous manipulations of his watch seals, that the astute Secretary was acutely "exercised."

The first Sunday of every month was Holy Communion for those churches, such as the Episcopal, which indulged in this particular ritual. April 2, 1865, happened to be the first Sunday of the month.

Situated at the northwest corner of Capitol Square, St. Paul's Episcopal was the largest church in Virginia when built, and could house 1,000 persons at any one time. As Dallas Tucker writes in his 1902 article, "The Fall of Richmond": *Architecturally this church always seemed to me a rather strange combination of the Greek temple surmounted by a tall, graceful spire. But, nevertheless, it is a tall, dignified, noble building, at the corner of Ninth and Grace streets, near the main gate of the Capitol square, and within almost a stone's throw of the Washington monument.* Or, as Burke Davis wrote in his 1959 book, *To Appomattox: St. Paul's Church stood on the corner of Grace and Ninth Streets, its tower thrusting more than 225 feet into the warm April air.*

The first Sunday service at St. Paul's had been held almost twenty years before, on November 16, 1845, which makes Burke Davis's statement in *To Appomattox—The church was fifteen years old*—somewhat mathematically challenging.

As Congressman Horatio Washington Bruce says in "Some Reminiscences" (1881): *St. Paul's was the church in which President Davis and his family worshipped during the war between the States.*

Church services began every Sunday at 11:00 a.m. Congressman Bruce again: *On Sunday, the 2d day of April, 1865 ... I attended the morning services in St. Paul's Episcopal church ... of which the learned and distinguished Rev. Dr. Minnegerode was then, and is yet, I believe, the beloved pastor.* Or, as A.J. Hanna puts it in his classic 1938 book, *Flight into Oblivion: The popular Dr. Charles F.E. Minnigerode was conducting services in the aristocratic St. Paul's Church.*

Dr. Minnigerode himself wrote in 1890: *The beautiful church of St. Paul, in its chaste simplicity and symmetry, was filled to the utmost, as always during the war.*[1] In 1867 Sallie Brock put it this way: *At St. Paul's Church the usual congregation was in attendance.* Constance Cary would write, in *Recollections Grave and Gay* (1911): *...a large congregation assembled as usual at St. Paul's.*

A general view of that morning in church is given by Mary Johnston, in her 1912 book, *Cease Firing*: *Here and there in the church were members of the Government, here and there an officer of the Richmond defences. Dr. Minnegerode was in the pulpit. The sun came slantingly in at the open windows,—sunshine and a balmy air. It was very quiet—the black-clad women sitting motionless, the soldiers still as on parade.* And by Burke Davis, in *To Appomattox* (1959): *Worshipers thronged up its low, wide stone steps and between the columns, through the facade which had been copied from the Athenian temple known as the Lanthorn of Demosthenes. Inside, settling into quiet, the crowd sat in a spacious room with French gray walls, on pews painted to resemble white oak, capped with rosewood. The seats were none too comfortable, for the fine cushions had been given to the hospitals more than two years earlier.*

Carleton Coffin, in his article in the *Boston Journal* of April 1865, was the first reporter to confirm that Davis *was at church on Sunday morning.* And C.E.L. Stuart, in his July 4, 1865, article in the *New York Herald*, writes in his often cynical way: *Mr. Davis went, as usual, to St. Paul's Episcopal Church, where political and Christian hopes were, once a week, blended for his edification.*

Of course, all the historians have Jefferson Davis at the church that Sunday morning.[2] A sampling over the years. Allen Tate, with his 1929 book, *Jefferson Davis*: *The 2d of April was Sunday, and the President went in the morning to St. Paul's Church.* And William C. Davis, in *The Man and His Hour* (1991): *The following day, Sunday, April 2, Davis turned to God again as he walked out on a crisp beautiful morning to St. Paul's for services.*

The preacher himself, Charles Frederick Ernest Minnigerode (1814–1894) was a German, in the United States since 1839, and in Richmond from 1845 until 1889. As Jay Winik says in his 2001 book, *April 1865*: *Addressed as "Your Eminence," or "Your Excellency," the intensely pious Minnigerode was in his own way a legendary figure in Richmonders' affections.* He might have been all that Winik says, but he seems to have been boring as a preacher, that is if we believe Tom Conolly in his March 26, 1865, diary entry, wherein he says that Minnigerode's sermon "sent me to sleep."

As for the written description of Minnigerode, or, at least, the way it has come down in the history books, we owe it all to Dallas Tucker, who was in St. Paul's that very morning, as a congregant and friend of the minister's. In his 1902 article, "The Fall of Richmond," Tucker has this: *Rev. Charles Minnigerode, a German by birth.... He was a small man, striking in personal appearance, of great learning, earnest religious faith, strongly southern in his patriotism, eloquent in the use of the English language, which, however he spoke with a slight German accent.* And this: *Dr. Minnigerode was delivering one of his stirring and fervid communion addresses (for the communion was to follow) when the sexton of the church was seen to walk up the aisle.*

From Dallas Tucker to Michael B. Ballard's 1986 book, *A Long Shadow: The German-*

---

1. Minnigerode wrote the chapter "My Dead Hero" for the book *Life and Reminiscences of Jefferson Davis* (1890).
2. Not quite all, as we shall see. Landon Knight, in *The Real Jefferson Davis*, has his subject at St. John's.

born Minnigerode, speaking with a slight accent, was delivering, as one worshipper later recalled, "one of his stirring and fervid" Communion Sunday sermons.[3]

Minnigerode was a small man, according to Dallas Tucker, but how small was he exactly? "Diminutive" is Morris Schaff's estimate in his 1912 book, *Sunset of the Confederacy*,[4] and also Clint Johnson's, in *Pursuit* (2008),[5] whereas both Burke Davis, in *To Appomattox* (1959), and Jay Winik, in *April 1865* (2001), describe him as a *tiny German immigrant*.

The slight German accent mentioned by Dallas Tucker would, of course, make sense, given that Minnigerode had come from Germany as an adult. This from Burke Davis in *To Appomattox* (1959): *...whose fervid manner of speech betrayed his native accent after many years in Richmond.* But was Minnigerode's accent "slight," as Dallas Tucker says, or was it as Mike Wright would have us believe?—a *thick thundering German accent.*[6] Or was it, indeed, a new brand of English entirely, as Felicity Allen intimates in her 1999 book, *Unconquerable Heart?*: *On any Sunday, from his high white pulpit centered in the front of the church, where he preached in Germanic English.*

Dallas Tucker's description of the minister's delivery was not quite enough for some historians. His voice had to be filled with something more than just an accent. Why not robust timbre? This from Jay Winik in *April 1865* (2001): *... his accented voice, filled with robust timbre.*

Regarding Minnigerode's facial characteristics, Winik says that *with his thin lips, high forehead, and aquiline nose, he cut a striking figure in the formal regalia.* Clint Johnson gives him a thin face. And Dr. Nelson Lankford, in *Richmond Burning* (2002) has this: *Every Sunday the German-born rector, Charles Minnigerode, looked out from the pulpit through his professorial wire-rimmed glasses on a congregation sprinkled with notables of the Confederate hierarchy, including his frequent dinner guest and confidant President Jefferson Davis.*

It might be of interest to read the description given of Dr. Minnigerode on his June 1866 passport application. Height: 5'7". Nose: straight. Forehead: broad. Eyes: gray. Mouth: large. Chin: prominent. Complexion: pale. Hair: brown, turning gray. Face: oval. It might also be worth bearing in mind that 5'7" was average height for an American male in those days.

Ever since May of 1865, there has been much speculation, not to mention vicious rumor, about the appropriateness of Jefferson Davis's choice of apparel on occasion, especially on the day of his capture in the Georgia woods. James Swanson, in *Bloody Crimes* (2010), clears this up for us once and for all: *On the morning of his capture, Jefferson Davis wore a suit of Confederate gray, and not one of Varina's hoopskirts.* But perhaps some things are best left unsaid.

It may be that the president was wearing such a suit. Others have said so. He was certainly buried in one. Varina, talking of her husband's death in her 1890 book, writes

---

3. Dallas Tucker, whatever failings his account might have, knew his church service better than Ballard did. Minnigerode was, indeed, delivering the opening address, not the sermon, which would have come much later on in the proceedings if they had continued.
4. *Doctor Charles Minnegerode, the rector of St. Paul's, a diminutive, fervid, transplanted German, was delivering his usual tense, extempore address.*
5. *...thin-faced, diminutive Reverend Dr. Charles Minnigerode.*
6. Mike Wright, *City Under Siege: Richmond in the Civil War* (Lanham, MD: Madison Books, 1995).

that *he lay in state, in his suit of Confederate gray.* As was only right, given that he was the president of the Confederate States of America, Jefferson Davis did wear gray habitually. This from Connie Cary (i.e., Mrs. Burton Harrison) in *Recollections Grave and Gay* (1911): *He was always clad in Confederate gray cloth, and wore a soft felt hat with wide brim.*

But was it a suit of Confederate gray that Davis was wearing when he was captured in the woods? Or was it just his vest that was Confederate gray? John W. Headley, talking about Salisbury, North Carolina, some weeks after the Davis party left Richmond and some time before Davis's capture, describes Davis's attire in *Confederate Operations* (1906): *He wore a Prince Albert coat (with a black velvet collar), trousers and vest of Confederate gray cassimere.* Headley got a taker, the august historian A.J. Hanna, no less, and although Hanna was not so taken with the black velvet collar, he was sufficiently impressed with Headley's account to have Davis dressed the same way when he left Richmond. In his *Flight into Oblivion* (1938), he writes: *Upon the arrival of the chief executive of the Confederacy, tall and slim, attired in a Prince Albert coat and trousers and waistcoat of Confederate gray cashmere, the official train creaked out of the station and headed for Danville.* It may well be that President Davis acquired the "black velvet collar" between Richmond and Salisbury.

A.J. Mapp, in *Frock Coats and Epaulets* (1963), when discussing the moment President Davis arrived at the depot in Richmond on April 2, 1865, takes from Hanna and Connie Cary, but Mapp has learned something Hanna never knew—President Davis's breeches were gray too: *Immaculate in Confederate gray waistcoat and breeches and a Prince Albert, a broad brimmed hat on his patrician head.*

In *The Civil War* (1974), Shelby Foote describes the president's sartorial condition immediately prior to leaving for the depot in Richmond. He wishes to elaborate on the Prince Albert coat, and so he does. He wishes to say a thing or two about the President's boots, and so he does. And, finally, he wishes to convey something new about the hat, and so he does. Shelby Foote never cites sources: *...he dressed carefully—trousers and waistcoat of Confederate gray, a dark Prince Albert frock coat, polished Wellingtons, a full-brimmed planter's hat.*

John H. Brubaker III, in *The Last Capital* (1979), when he comes to the moment that President Davis arrives at Danville, also finds himself compelled to elaborate, but this time it is on Davis's breeches: *The man wore a waistcoat of gray cashmere, carefully pressed breeches and a Prince Albert coat.*

But what was Jefferson Davis wearing in church on the morning of April 2, 1865? Burke Davis, in his 1985 book, *The Long Surrender*, talks about the President in church that morning: *Davis wore his familiar "Confederate gray" trousers and vest and a Prince Albert coat.* Mike Wright offers a similar description in *City Under Siege* (1995): *...wearing his now famous gray trousers and vest along with a Prince Albert coat.*

After all this, it comes as a shock to read Jay Winik's description of Davis's clothing in church that morning. This from *April 1865* (2001): *...wearing a natty, dark wool suit, a crisply pressed white shirt, and a traditional black tie.*

Mallory was not in St. Paul's Episcopal Church that morning of April 2, 1865. He was a Catholic, and therefore at St. Peter's Cathedral. So, when the time came for him to write his account of that day, he was creative: *As usual, the President's face was closely scrutinized as he entered St. Paul's alone, & quietly sought his pew.*

The two authors of the book, *The Rebel and the Rose* (2007), unaware that Mallory was simply making this up, elaborated on his fiction: *Those who had arrived ahead of him discretely turned to scrutinize the president, attempting to penetrate the solemn mask for any sign of his state of mind.* Presumably the authors meant "discreetly."

As for Davis's appearance, Stuart, in his July 4, 1865, article in the *New York Herald*, says that he *looked care-worn, yet contrived to tinge his concern with a briskness which warded off suspicion.* Mallory, describing President Davis's face, says: *...but its expression varied not from that cold, stern sadness which four years of harrassing mental labour had stamped upon it.* This wording was basically unchanged by *McClure's* magazine when they published their 1900 article based on Mallory's manuscript, but they did edit it, as will be noticed in their choice of spelling: *...but its expression varied not from that cold, stern sadness which four years of harrassing mental labor had stamped upon it.* Robert McElroy, writing *Jefferson Davis, the Unreal and the Real* in 1937, did not have access to Mallory's original manuscript, and so had to rely on *McClure's*: *According to Mallory, his face was scrutinized as he entered and quietly sought his pew; but its expression varied not from that cold, stern sadness which four years of harrassing mental labor had stamped upon it.*

Hudson Strode was a professor of creative writing, not a history teacher. Yet, because his literary life in the 1950s and 1960s was dominated by his massive and famous three-volume work on Jefferson Davis, does this not entitle him to be called a historian? Of course it does, if for no other reason than for an awfully long time in the public consciousness, the names Jefferson Davis and Hudson Strode were, if not exactly synonymous, automatically linked. Volume 3 of his trilogy, the one we're interested in, is titled *Tragic Hero*, and was published in 1964, twenty years or so after Mallory's original manuscript became openly available for inspection at the University of North Carolina. One would expect Professor Strode to have made such an inspection, but he did not. He chose to use the edited *McClure's* version instead. Even then, he could not get the quote right. In *Tragic Hero* he writes: *In the words of Secretary of the Navy Mallory, his expression in repose "varied not from that cold, stern face which four years of harrassing mental labor stamped upon it."*

The same cannot be said for Allan Nevins, in *War for the Union* (1971): *...but its expression varied not from that cold, stern sadness which four years of harrassing mental labour had stamped upon it.* Not only did Nevins get the quote right, he went to the original Mallory manuscript.

Like Nevins, James C. Clark had access to the Mallory manuscript. Unlike Nevins, he declined to take advantage of it. Clark also failed to understand that Mallory was in another church, and therefore could not have been sitting near the President that morning. This from *Last Train South* (1984): *Navy Secretary Stephen R. Mallory, sitting nearby, said Davis' face, "varied not from that cold, stern sadness which four years of harrassing mental labor had stamped upon it...."*

Equally ignorant of Mallory's whereabouts that morning was Burke Davis, who in *The Long Surrender* (1985) writes: *...as Secretary of the Navy Stephen Mallory observed, Davis wore that "cold, stern" expression that had become so familiar during Richmond's four years of war. The stiffly upright presence not easily forgotten.*

In *Towards an Indefinite Shore* (1995), author Don Lowry, like James C. Clark, has Mallory in St. Paul's: *Secretary of the Navy Stephen Mallory was there, and he noticed that Davis wore his usual cold, stern expression.*

Mike Wright, in *City Under Siege* (1995), with Burke Davis before him as he wrote, has this: *He sat stiffly upright, Secretary of the Navy Mallory noted, and wore a "cold, stern expression."* Mallory never mentions "stiffly upright." That was Burke Davis's invention, based on something he read in E.A. Pollard's 1869 book on Jefferson Davis.[7] And Mallory never says "cold, stern expression."

F. Lawrence McFall, the famous Danville historian, when he came to write his 2001 book, *Danville in the Civil War*, had Burke Davis's *The Long Surrender* in front of him, just as Don Lowry had in 1995. McFall changes Burke Davis's "stiffly upright" to "erect," then, just as Mike Wright had done, in *City Under Siege*, misplaced Burke Davis's quote marks, to come up with this: *Davis sat erect and wore a "cold, stern expression."*

Three other salient features exhibited by the president as he entered St. Paul's that morning were his cold, calm eye, his sunken cheek, and his compressed lip. It is not specified which lip was compressed, nor is it explained what a compressed lip actually is, but everyone agrees that he had one. But then everyone is copying Mallory, who was not even in the church. Yet it was Mallory who started all this, when he wrote: *...the cold, calm eye, the sunken cheek, the compressed lip, were all as impenetrable as an iron mask.*

Allan Nevins reproduces Mallory faithfully in *War for the Union* (1971), but was it only one eye that was cold and calm, or was it both? That Jefferson Davis was blind in one eye probably has no bearing on this question. *McClure's* magazine, when presenting their edited version of Mallory's manuscript in 1900, decided to fall back upon the well-worn device of ocular pluralization: *...the cold, calm eyes, the sunken cheek, the compressed lip, were all as impenetrable as an iron mask.*

Robert McElroy reproduced this passage perfectly in *Jefferson Davis, the Unreal and the Real*, but again, he had no choice. In 1937, the *McClure's* article was all he had to go on. The Mallory manuscript, with its one eye, would not see the light of day until the time of World War II, when, as part of the Mallory Papers, it would become available to the general public. With that in mind, there can be no excuse for James C. Clark, whose *Last Train South* (1984) copies, word for word, either McElroy or the *McClure's* article—it does not matter which.

Harder to account for is the pluralization of "sunken cheek." Both Mallory's handwritten account and its edited version, the 1900 *McClure's* article, have "sunken cheek," yet William J. Cooper, in his book, *Jefferson Davis, American* (2000) prefers "cheeks" to "cheek," and chooses to capitalize "Sunken"[8]: *When Davis entered St. Paul's, one who saw him often noted his appearance: "the cold, calm eye, the Sunken cheeks, the compressed lip, were all as impenetrable as an iron mask."* Needless to say, the "one who saw him often" was Mallory, yet, as we know, Mallory was not a genuine witness to that morning's proceedings at St. Paul's. However, that does not explain "cheeks."

Hattaway and Beringer, in their 2002 effort, *Jefferson Davis, American*, copy directly from, and quote, William J. Cooper, rather than going to Mallory: *Cooper observes that "When Davis entered St. Paul's, one who saw him often noted his appearance: 'the cold calm eye, the Sunken cheeks, the compressed lip, were all as impenetrable as an iron mask.'"*

---

7. *He now sat stiff and alone in the "President's Pew."*
8. In the 19th century, writers would often, and sometimes inconsistently, capitalize words mid-sentence, words that today we render in lower case. But those words were almost invariably nouns, not adjectives.

David J. Eicher, while writing *Dixie Betrayed* (2006), was scanning through Hattaway and Beringer's book when he saw the words "Cooper observes." Hattaway and Beringer were referring to historian William J. Cooper, of course, but Eicher did not grasp that. So he came up with this: *"When Davis entered," wrote Adj. Gen. Samuel Cooper, "one who saw him often noted his appearance: 'the cold calm eye, the sunken cheeks, the compressed lip, were all as impenetrable as an iron mask.'"* Eicher got the wrong Cooper, which therefore makes nonsense of the passage. Incidentally, as both the Rebel War Clerk and Judith McGuire say, Adjutant General Samuel Cooper was at St. James's Episcopal that morning, not St. Paul's.

Despite what seems to be incontrovertible evidence that this description of President Davis originated with Mallory, we find this in Clint Johnson's *Pursuit* (2008): *Constance Cary, the fiancée of Burton Harrison, Davis's private secretary, remembered that the President's "cold calm eye, the sunken cheeks, the compressed lip, were all as impenetrable as an iron mask."* Mallory's account was, of course, written before he died in 1873. Constance Cary's account came out in 1911. One is unable to locate such a remembrance in Connie Cary's "Recollections Grave and Gay." Unfortunately Clint Johnson does not source this passage. However, in the very sentence after this passage, he says: *But another member of the church said, "I plainly saw the sort of gray pallor that came over his face as he read a scrap of paper."* Despite being a misquote, that other member of the church is definitely Connie Cary in "Recollections Grave and Gay."

This error does, however, serve a useful purpose. It leads one to wonder if the compressed lip, the sunken cheek and the eye are truly Mallory's original turn of phrase. It might be worth quoting from the November 1862 edition of *Atlantic Monthly*, in a monograph titled "Conversational Opinions of the Leaders of Secession," in which President Davis is described: *...the thin, compressed, but flexible lips; the almost haggardly sunken cheek; the piercing, not wholly uncovered eye.*

Churchgoers bought pews in those days, and that's where they would faithfully sit, kneel, and stand, Sunday after Sunday. As David Eicher says, in *Dixie Betrayed* (2006), that morning of April 2, 1865, the president sat *in the Davis family pew, sans family*. That is where he was when he received news of Lee's 10:40 a.m. telegram. Ordnance man William L. Broun recounts, as quoted in the 1912 book by his son: *"I was at St. Paul's Church. About four pews in front of me sat President Davis; and in a pew behind me, Gorgas, chief of the ordnance department and my chief."*

Early writers were relatively bald in their mentions of Davis and the pew. For example, Sallie Brock (1867): *President Davis occupied his pew.* Or Pollard (1869): *He now sat stiff and alone in "the President's pew."* Or Mallory: *...& quietly sought his pew.* Dr. Minnigerode has this, from 1890: *Mr. Davis, who never failed to be in his pew unless when sick or absent from the city, was there, devoutly following the services of the church. It was the regular day for the Holy Communion. Nothing had occurred to disturb the congregation, though anxiety was in many a heart.* And Mary Johnston writes, in her 1912 book, *Cease Firing*: *The President sat in his pew at St. Paul's, grave and tall and grey, distinguished and quiet of aspect.* And this: *...the marked man in the President's pew straight, quiet and attentive.* Some latter-day historians followed this practice. Hudson Strode, in *Tragic Hero* (1964), has this: *...the President proceeded with his accustomed dignity and took his seat in his pew just in front of Constance Cary.* And William C. Davis writes, in *The Man and His*

Hour (1991): *He sat alone now, in his regular pew, following the services prior to communion.*[9]

One can sense that some of the 19th-century writers are struggling for freedom of literary expression, a freedom that would duly pervade history-writing over the years, often at the expense of accuracy. A case in point, Congressman H.W. Bruce in "Some Reminiscences" (1881): *President Davis and his family were in their pew that morning.* As President Davis's family had already fled South, one has to wonder where Bruce really was that morning. It was not at St. Paul's, not if he saw Varina and the children.

In 1931, the pew got a number—63. Or it may have been #63 all along. It's just that 1931 is the first time we learn of it. As Elizabeth Wright Weddell wrote that year, in her book, *St. Paul's Church*: ...*pew 63, known as the "Davis pew," middle aisle, it having been the one Jefferson Davis and his family sat in while worshiping in St. Paul's during the war.*

From then on, it was virtually de rigueur to include the number in any mention of the pew. So we have the *Richmond Times Dispatch* of April 30, 1939, writing: *Visitors to St. Paul's will be shown pew No. 63 by the sexton—the seat occupied by Jefferson Davis when he received the news of General Lee's surrender.* James C. Clark in his 1984 book, *Last Train South*: *Davis went directly to his pew, number 63, and sat down.* Mike Wright, with this in *City Under Siege* (1995): *President Davis of the Confederate States of America was in pew number sixty-three at St. Paul's Episcopal Church.* And we have Harry S. Stout writing in his 2006 book, *Upon the Altar of the Nation*: ...*President Davis sat in attendance at his customary pew, No. 63.*

Reagan's 1906 *Memoirs* say that he, Reagan, found President Davis and his aide, Frank Lubbock, on their way to church. Nowhere does Reagan say they were headed for the same church. Before 1959 no historian ever placed Lubbock in St. Paul's with Davis, and that's because Lubbock was not in St. Paul's. One only need read Frank Lubbock's book to see that he was not in St. Paul's that morning, but in a completely different church. This, then, from Burke Davis, in his 1959 book, *To Appomattox*: *It was Communion Sunday, and in the congregation, as usual, were many of the leaders of the Confederacy. President Davis was in his pew, Number 63, with one of his aides, Governor Frank Lubbock of Texas. Behind the President sat General Josiah Gorgas, the chief of ordnance.*

By the time Burke Davis came to write his last book on this subject, *The Long Surrender* (1985)—that's twenty-six years later—he was still maintaining that Lubbock was in St. Paul's: *Today, on the sunlit morning of April 2, Davis and Frank Lubbock went into St. Paul's Church about 11 a.m., and entered the presidential pew, number 63.*

Burke Davis attracted followers, many of them, including the Danvillian historians en bloc—McFall, Carroll, Brubaker, and the reporters for the Danville newspapers. McFall, in his *Danville in the Civil War* (2001), has this: *At 11 A.M. the sun shone brightly as Jefferson Davis and his aide Frank Lubbock entered St. Paul's Episcopal Church. They sat in pew number 63. Another aide, John Taylor Wood ... sat nearby.*

But there are others, not from Danville, who have also been blinded by Burke Davis; for example Millett and White, the authors of *Rebel and the Rose* (2007): *Reaching St. Paul's, Davis climbed the steps with Lubbock and entered the sanctuary through the two large center doors, removed his wide-brimmed hat, and took his place in his family pew.*

---

9. Note, however, that Jefferson Davis is sitting alone. Earlier, William C. Davis has President Davis and his aide, Frank Lubbock, going to church together. Presumably, then, Lubbock sat in another pew. Of course, in reality, we know Lubbock was not in St. Paul's at all that morning.

Shafts of light pierced the windows on the East-facing Ninth-Street side of the church and splashed in patches on the worshipers, brightening the interior. And there is D. Laurence Rogers in *Apostles of Equality* (2011): *It was a gloomy Sunday morning, 2 April 1865. Jefferson Davis ... sat quietly in St. Paul's Episcopal Church.... Davis, gaunt, his face grim with stress and pockmarked by malaria from his younger days, worshiped in pew number 63 in St. Paul's, also joined by his aide, Frank Lubbock, the governor of Texas, and the army's chief of ordnance, Gen. Josiah Gorgas.* By 2001, Pew #63 had become so ingrained in the consciousness of Civil War buffs that Jay Winik was able to say, in his book, *April 1865: And, of course, in pew number sixty three was Confederate President Jefferson Davis.*

Finally, we get good directions to the pew, in Ralph Gary's *The Presidents Were Here* (2008): *His pew, number 63, not quite midway down the center aisle, right side, can still be seen and used. Robert E. Lee and family used number 111, one row in front and to the left of Davis.*

After the congregation, including Jefferson Davis, had made their way to their pews and settled down, the minister opened the ceremonies with the Lord's Prayer, as was the custom. As Burke Davis puts it, in *To Appomattox* (1959): *The service opened with prayers.* Only minutes after the service commenced, with the people still kneeling, and the minister part way through his exhortation, his opening address, the service came to an abrupt end. The time was about 11:05.[10]

As Sallie Brock said in 1867: *It was again the regular monthly return for the celebration of the sacrament of the Lord's Supper. The services were progressing as usual, no agitation or disturbance withdrew the thoughts from holy contemplation.* Mary Johnston says, in *Cease Firing* (1912): *...the white and black form in the pulpit with raised hands, speaking of a supper before Gethsemane—for it was the first Sunday in the month and communion was to follow. The sun came in very golden, very quiet.*

According to Mallory, President Davis *raised his head, after a brief interval, from its devotional position, and turned his furrowed brow to Dr. Minnegerode.* And this: *Not a devotee in all that congregation seemed more gravely attentive to the morning service, or responded to its sublime exhortations more fervently.* As Mallory was not in the church, he must have gotten this from somewhere. Sallie Brock wrote a poem in 1867. It was called "The Fall of Richmond," and was published in *The Southern Amaranth* in 1869. Perhaps this was Mallory's source:

> And one there was, with bowed head, and temples
>   gray with care,
> Who listened meekly to the words that fell like
>   soothing balm,
> And while he listened, fervently sent up a
>   prayer
> That Christ his errors would forgive, and grant
>   him holy calm

---

10. This time is based on the accounts written by persons who claimed to have been in the church that morning, particularly that of the minister himself, the Reverend Charles Minnigerode. From these, one goes to the *Book of Common Prayer*, which gives the required order of service for a Communion Sunday. That, in addition to a logical examination of what must have transpired that morning in regard to the transmission of the 10:40 news, settles the time to within a few minutes.

4. Church

And this:

> *For on his shoulders bent, a nation's load was placed,*
> *And furrows deep, his rounder cheek had plowed;*
> *Across his massive brow broad lines of pain were traced,*
> *And his lithe form from thought, and not with age was bowed*

Wherever Mallory got it from, he did not get any takers.

Again, from Sallie Brock's poem: *"The Lord is in His Holy Temple," said a lowly voice.* "The Lord is in his Holy Temple" is a line used twice in the Old Testament, once in Psalms 11:4 and again in Habakkuk 2:20. Which one Miss Brock had in mind we do not know. Her own words, *said in a lowly voice*, do not help us.

Eventually, of course, we do receive help on this question. William C. Church wrote, in his 1897 book, *Ulysses S. Grant*: *As the worshiping congregation rose in response to the clergyman's invocation, "The Lord is in His Holy Temple, let all the earth keep silence before Him."* But how does he know that this Habakkuk passage is the right one, rather than the Psalm, *The Lord is in his holy temple, the Lord's throne is in heaven*? However, Mike Wright believed him. In his *City Under Siege* (1995), he writes: *Reverend Minnegerode had just intoned, in his thick, thundering German accent, "The Lord is in His Holy temple: let all the earth keep silence before him."* And D. Laurence Rogers believed him. In his 2011 book, *Apostles of Equality*: *A hush enveloped the church as the Rev. Dr. Charles Minnigerode, pastor of St. Paul's, intoned with a German accent, "The Lord is in his holy temple; let all the earth keep silence before him."*

Robert Henrickson, in *The Road to Appomattox* (1998), has this: *The minister had just read Zechariah 2:13—"The Lord is in his holy temple, let all the earth keep silence before him."* If this is true, then the Rev. Dr. Minnigerode's bible must have been a different one to the ones generally in use in the United States at that time. In most Old Testaments, certainly in Richmond, this quote is to be found in Habakkuk 2:20. Zechariah 2:13 is totally irrelevant.

In 1966 something distinctly odd happened. Someone decided that the service at St. Paul's on the morning of April 2, 1865, had been interrupted too soon, that there should be a hymn thrown in. And so they picked one—"Jesus, lover of my soul," the famous song written by Charles Wesley, and first published in 1740. Not a random pick, for it is reputed to have been Jefferson Davis's favorite hymn. The following is to be found in the *Lincoln Herald* (1966): *Jefferson Davis entered St. Paul's Church in Richmond for Sunday worship. The service began. The choir sang "Jesus, lover of my soul...." A message was handed to Davis and he left the church immediately. Richmond, too, must be evacuated.*

This hymn was picked up by William C. Davis, who, in his 1991 book, *The Man and His Hour*, writes: *He listened as the choir sang the hymn, "Jesus, Lover of My Soul," then waited for Minnigerode's sermon.* Or, as David Eicher put it in *Dixie Betrayed* (2006): *In the Davis family pew, sans family, the president listened to the hymn "Jesus Lover of My Soul" as he waited for the Reverend Charles Minnigerode's sermon.*

Most of the historians who have accepted "The Lord is in his Holy Temple" quote that, rather than "The Lord is in his temple," as Jay Winik does in his 2001 book, *April 1865*: *Not a pew was empty. The choir sang "Jesus, Lover of My Soul," and the rector, Dr. Charles*

Minnigerode, his accented voice filled with robust timbre, intoned back: "The Lord is in his temple; let all the earth keep silence before Him."

It would give them a much better understanding of the order of service in an Episcopal Church if historians would only make a quick study of the Book of Common Prayer—the one that was in use in 1865.

While the service was going on, the sexton came up the aisle and alerted President Davis that he was wanted at the War Department. The early newspaper accounts of the sexton, starting with the *New York Daily Tribune* article of April 8, 1865, written by a special correspondent from Richmond on April 6, call the sexton a colored man, and other papers, in the ensuing days, call him a black man. One assumes they're talking about the regular St. Paul's sexton, William Irving, who was, in fact, white.

Dallas Tucker, in his article, "The Fall of Richmond" (1902), claims to have been in St. Paul's that morning: *...the sexton of the church was seen to walk up the aisle. He was a large, pompous, swaggering kind of a fellow, whose Sunday costume at the time was a faded blue suit with brass buttons, and a shirt with waving ruffles at the bosom and wrists. His supreme delight, aside from keeping us boys in order, was seemingly to walk up the aisle with a message for someone. On this occasion, his manner was in perfect keeping with his usual consequential air, only it was more so, for this time he was the bearer of a message to the President of the Southern Confederacy. Gently and respectfully touching Mr. Davis on the shoulder, he handed him something, whereupon the latter immediately arose and left the church.*

Ten years later, this from Morris Schaff in *Sunset of the Confederacy*: *...the sexton, a portly, aging man, with ruffles at his wrists and bosom, and polished brass buttons on a suit of faded blue, advanced up the aisle with soft but stately tread, and after touching the President on the shoulder with solemnity and his one-day-in-the-week lofty importance, handed him a message.*

Ordnance man William L. Broun is meant to have been in St. Paul's that day, but he might not have been, for, like Schaff, he had to rely on Dallas Tucker. This is Broun, quoted in the 1912 book written by his son: *"During service and before the sermon the sexton of the church, a well known individual in the city, stepped lightly forward, and touching Mr. Davis on the shoulder, whispered something to him."*

The year 1912 was a particularly fruitful one for descriptions of the sexton. Mary Johnston, in *Cease Firing*, has this: *He was a large man, with blue clothes and brass buttons and a ruffled shirt. Often and often, in these four years, had he come with a whispered message or a bit of paper to this or that man in authority.* She continues: *Saint Paul's was used to the sexton coming softly up the aisle.*

Yet another who claimed to have been in St. Paul's that very morning was Amelia Gorgas. Her "diary" was published in *Confederate Veteran* in 1917: *I attended St. Paul's Church, as usual, sitting with Judge John A. Campbell, as our pew was filled with strangers. Soon after Mr. Minnegerode began his sermon a messenger swiftly and silently passed up the aisle and whispered to General Cooper and other officers of the War Department news which took them immediately from the church. The sermon proceeded, and all was quiet until the messenger returned and going directly to the President's pew, gave the same whispered message.*

There were other Episcopal churches in Richmond. One was St. James's.[11] Those in

---

11. St. James's, established in 1831, was on the corner of Marshall and 5th, at Shockoe Hill. In 1854 the Reverend Joshua Peterkin became the third rector, and held the position for 37 years. General J.E.B. Stuart's funeral was held here.

attendance at St. James's on Sunday morning, April 2, 1865, included Judith McGuire. In her *Diary of a Southern Refugee* (1867), she says that while the sacraments were being administered, *the sexton came in with a note to General Cooper, which was handed him as he walked from the chancel, and he immediately left the church. It made me anxious, but such things are not uncommon, and caused no excitement in the congregation.*

So, whom do you trust? Mrs. Gorgas or Judith McGuire? There are several items in Amelia Gorgas's account that must be examined. First, the account itself is derivative, and therefore suspect. Second, Amelia Gorgas has herself sitting with Judge Campbell. The judge himself, in his own account, never mentions being in church. If he truly was, then he has deprived himself of a place in the historical sun. Third, why was Mrs. Gorgas's pew filled with strangers, when one stuck to one's own pew Sunday after Sunday? Fourth, Dr. Minnigerode had not gotten to the sermon yet. Nowhere near. Fifth, was Adjutant General Samuel Cooper in St. Paul's, as Amelia Gorgas says, or St. James's, as Judith McGuire would have it? No one else ever mentions General Cooper being in St. Paul's. On the other hand, John B. Jones, the Rebel War Clerk, confirms Judith McGuire when he says that General Cooper was in St. James's that morning. Sixth, in Mrs. Gorgas's account, we have the messenger touching General Cooper on the shoulder, then a certain number of other men, and finally, after all that, the president himself. Why would President Davis be the last to be called out? Seventh, Judith McGuire's account has the ring of truth to it, especially her order of service at St. James's. Generally speaking, the taking of Communion fell about halfway through the service, and Miss McGuire has Cooper just having received the sacrament. The messenger for St. James's would, indeed, have arrived about this time.

Was even General Gorgas himself in the church that morning? William L. Broun thought so, as we have seen. Yet Gorgas's own wife implies quite strongly that he was not. And Gorgas himself indicates that he did not hear of the famous 10:40 telegram until 1:00 p.m. that day, which surely means he could not have been in church.[12] So, if General Gorgas was not in church that morning, then was Colonel Broun really in church? Burke Davis, in *To Appomattox* (1959), wrote: *An officer of the Ordnance Department, Lieutenant Colonel William L. Broun, was in a pew some distance behind the President's.*

Going back to the sexton, Elizabeth Wright Weddell, in *St. Paul's Church* (1931), writes: *Our sexton ... was an Englishman, a Mr. Irving, a very bustling kind of a middle-aged man (who was also the Chief Usher at the old "Marshall Theatre")*. One will also see Irving called a Scotsman. Irving was, in fact, from Pennsylvania. It might be worth noting that Weddell's book is the first to name the sexton.

The 2007 book, *The Rebel and the Rose*, says: *Seventeen year old Emmie Crump, daughter of the assistant secretary of the treasury, Judge William Wood Crump, was in church as well.* Emmie Crump was fifteen, not seventeen. She later became Mrs. Lightfoot, and in 1933 wrote "The Evacuation of Richmond," apparently for her children: *Mr. Irving, our dignified sexton, always well-dressed and self sufficient, came to President Davis, sitting in his pew, and whispered to him. The President left immediately, but the service proceeded to the end, when our beloved pastor, Dr. Minnigerode, dismissed us with the blessing.*

The sexton, in the course of 58 years of history-making, went from large to portly

---

12. As we shall see in Chapter 6, Gorgas was not the only one who did not learn of the telegram until 1 p.m. Attorney General George Davis did not either, and he was, as he says, in another church. Moreover, Frank Lubbock did not hear of the telegram until about that time, so perhaps all three were in the same (unnamed) church.

to stout. Burke Davis writes, in *To Appomattox* (1959): *The stout, aging sexton of the church was William Irving, an Englishman who had served it from the beginning, dressed today in a faded blue suit, with polished brass buttons and ruffles at his wrist and neck.* Dr. Nelson Lankford describes Irving in his 2002 book, *Richmond Burning*: *...a pompous man who glorified in the petty perquisites of his office.*

The authors of *Rebel and the Rose* (2007) have this: *...sexton William Irving, an elderly, somewhat pompous usher and guardian of decorum in the church. Filled with the importance of his mission the sexton stiffly made his way down the aisle to Davis's pew, a curious figure in a faded blue suit with brass buttons and a shirt replete with ruffles.*[13] D. Lawrence Rogers, in *Apostles of Equality,* writes: *The aged sexton of St. Paul's, William Irving.* The sexton, over the course of 100 years of history-making, has ranged from "aging" to "middle-aged" to "elderly" to "aged." He was, in fact, 50.

It is worth observing that Mallory, in his account, writes the following description: *...in his white cravat & irrepressible ruffles, his spotless waistcoat & blue, brass-buttoned coat.* This was reproduced in *McClure's* magazine in December 1900. However, he is not talking about the sexton—he is describing Mayor Mayo on April 2, 1865. Dallas Tucker wrote his article in 1902, in the wake of the *McClure's* article. Tucker, the first to describe the sexton's outfit—blue, ruffles, brass buttons, etc.—has a lot to answer for, but not nearly as much as the historians who have believed him.

Now for the moment the famous telegram was received by Jefferson Davis in church at or around 11:05 a.m. Historians, newspaper reporters, eyewitnesses,[14] and others have, right from the beginning, exerted a tremendous pressure on us to believe that what Davis received in church that morning was the actual telegram, or at least a copy thereof. Despite this overwhelming avalanche of "evidence"—which is not evidence at all, merely derivative reporting from original hearsay—we must bear in mind that what Davis received in church was not the telegram, or a copy thereof, but merely notification that he was wanted at the War Department at once. Davis's April 5, 1865, letter to his wife makes this abundantly clear. *On last Sunday I was called out of church to receive a telegram announcing that Gen'l Lee could not hold his position longer than till night and warning me that we must leave Richmond.*[15] This was written by the president himself, and only three days after that morning in St. Paul's. As fresh as events were in his memory therefore, this letter to Varina, more than any other report, including what appears in Davis's 1881 book—which he probably did not write anyway[16]—has to be given the most credence. If Davis had been handed an actual telegram, or a copy thereof, he would have said so in this letter, rather than what he did say: *I was called out of church to receive a telegram.*

The first newspaper reports were confused as to the time Davis was in church, so why would they not be equally confused about what he received? The *New York Herald's*

---

13. From the door, one stiffly made his way up the aisle, not down the aisle.
14. The difference between a diarist and an eyewitness is that the diarist claims to have written entries in his diary, day by day, so that his memory is, at best, only 24 hours old at the time of writing. Whereas the eyewitness reports what he saw, generally in the form of an article, and usually some time after the event. There is, of course, a third form of witness—the newsman. In the case of April 2–3, 1865, diarists and eyewitnesses have been crawling out of the woodwork ever since.
15. Davis wrote this letter from Danville. Varina was then in Charlotte.
16. See the Bibliography, under Davis, for an explanation of this.

correspondent, writing on April 3, 1865, from Davis's former executive mansion in Richmond, wrote this: *At half past three o'clock yesterday afternoon, Jeff Davis, while in church, received a despatch from General Lee that immediate preparations must be made to evacuate Richmond and its defences at once, as he was wholly unable to make further headway against Grant's further onset on the left.*[17] Similarly, C.A. Dana's dispatch to Stanton,[18] sent at 11:30 a.m., April 5, 1865, from Aiken's Landing[19]: *Gen. Lee telegraphed to Davis at 3 p.m. Sunday, that he was driven back and must evacuate. This was announced in church.*[20] One immediately sees the errors in this small passage. Lee actually telegraphed to Breckinridge, not Davis. And it was certainly not at 3:00 p.m.[21]

Union Secretary of War Edwin M. Stanton.

New York Times and Associated Press reporter Lorenzo L. Crounse was in City Point on April 4 when he wrote: *...an orderly came hurriedly in, handed him a dispatch.* This was published in the *Times* of April 9, 1865. It is the first time the deliverer of the message is identified—an orderly. Carleton Coffin, in his *Boston Journal* article of April 1865, confirms the orderly: *The minister was preaching when an orderly entered and handed a note to the President of the Confederacy. It was a dispatch from Lee that his lines were broken in three places and that Richmond must be evacuated.*

On April 6, 1865, a correspondent wrote an article from the Spotswood House, in Richmond, and it was published by the *New York Daily Tribune* two days later: *At 11½*

---

17. On the evening of April 6, 1865, this report found its way into the papers, and was reproduced in whole or in part in all the dailies of April 7, 1865.
18. Edwin McMasters Stanton (1814–1869) was U.S. secretary of war from January 20, 1862, to May 20, 1868.
19. *Official Records*, series 1, volume 46, part 3, p. 574.
20. Stanton gave this out as a press report later that day, and it was published by various newspapers on April 6, 1865.
21. Charles Anderson Dana, abolitionist, long associated with the *New York Tribune*, became a very good friend of Grant's, and it was partly due to Dana's support that Grant was made supreme commander of the Union Army. Dana was Union assistant secretary of war, 1863–65. On the afternoon of April 4, 1865, he arrived in Richmond with Lincoln's group. On April 5, 1865, he was in Jefferson Davis's house in Richmond. As Wilson says, in his *Life of Charles A. Dana* (1907): *After walking about the town and learning what they could from General Weitzel, who had occupied it on the 3d, Dana began his search for the records and documents of the Confederate government. In this he was but partly successful, for the most valuable papers had been sent off to the South, while the others had been badly disarranged and scattered. Dana gathered up such as could be found, and sent them to Washington, where they became the nucleus of the great collection now in the possession of the government.* And this: *He sent a number of dispatches, which will be found in the Official Records.* Dana arrived back in Washington on April 13, 1865.

o'clock Sunday morning, while seated in his pew at church listening to the lucubrations of the Rev. Dr. Hoge, Jeff Davis was handed a dispatch from Gen. Lee. And this: *The dispatch was to the effect that Richmond must be evacuated during the coming night.*

At least the press had now achieved clarity on which service Davis was attending, but 11:30 is pure guesswork. And it's wrong. Also, Dr. Hoge was not the minister at St. Paul's, of course. It was Dr. Minnigerode. This seems to be the first time this error occurred in reporting. It would not be the last.

The Washington, D.C., newspaper, the *Evening Star*, in its May 10, 1865, edition, has this: *Suddenly the sexton approaching President Davis handed to him a paper, which was perused.* This is probably the first newspaper report in which the sexton is mentioned. Presumably Lorenzo Crounse's orderly gave the message to the sexton, who then delivered it to Davis in his pew.

Those, then, are some of the salient early newspaper accounts. They are confused, and often at variance with one another. One might expect much more unanimity from the eyewitnesses.

General Gorgas was not in St. Paul's at all. So, for his diary entry of April 16, 1865, he had to rely on newspaper accounts, and thus rendered himself unreliable. Talking about Lee, he says: *...and in a few hours afterwards a second despatch that his line could not be reestablished and that Richmond must be evacuated by 8 o'clock at night. This I learned about 1 p.m. We had been making arrangements to move to Danville on the 3d (Monday).* Same with R.G.H. Kean, in his diary entry of June 1, 1865: *About 11 a second telegram from General Lee that his efforts to reestablish his lines had failed and that Richmond must be evacuated that night.* Same with John Taylor Wood in his diary entry of June 14, 1865: *While at Church with the President, rec'd a telegram from Genl Lee announcing that the enemy had broken thro his lines, that he could not reestablish them, and that he must fall back at once.* All three were playing catch-up on their neglected diaries, and all three were copying from the same newspaper, the *Richmond Whig* of April 6, 1865.

C.E.L. Stuart wrote his account in the *New York Herald* on July 4, 1865. Stuart was probably not in any church that morning, but he was in Richmond, and he was a reporter by trade: *Colonel Taylor Wood hastened to the door of St. Paul's and despatched the sexton to Mr. Davis's pew. Only a few words were whispered softly in the ears of the Confederate President—a few words which told him another despatch had come, and that he was immediately wanted. It was enough.*

Here we have Lorenzo Crounse's orderly identified—John Taylor Wood, Jefferson Davis's aide. However, as Taylor Wood himself makes no mention of his having occupied such a role, Stuart's identification may well be inaccurate. But Stuart does bear out Jefferson Davis's letter to Varina of April 5, in which the ex-president makes no mention of receiving a telegram in church—merely a message that he was wanted at the War Department. There is no way Stuart could have seen Davis's April 5, 1865, letter to Varina, and one must remember that at the time Stuart wrote, most reporters were claiming that Davis received the actual telegram while in church. Stuart took the road less traveled by.

Phoebe Yates Pember, in her 1866 article, has this: *On the 2d of April, 1865, while the congregation of Dr. Hoge's church in Richmond were listening to the Sunday sermon, a messenger entered and handed a telegram to Mr. Davis, then President of the Confederate States.* By the time of her 1879 book, *A Southern Woman's Story*, Pember had realized that Dr. Hoge was not, in fact, the pastor of St. Paul's: *On the 2nd of April, 1865, while the congregation of Dr. Minnigerode's church in Richmond were listening to his Sunday sermon, a messenger entered and handed a telegram to Mr. Davis, then president of the Confederate States.*

Pember tells us what this telegram said. First this from her 1866 article: *The telegram that reached Mr. Davis that Sunday morning was to the effect that the enemy had struck, and on the weakest side of the Confederate forces. It told him to be prepared in case a repulse failed; and two hours after came the fatal news that Grant had forced his way through, so that the city must be evacuated that night.* And this from her 1879 book, *A Southern Woman's Story*: *The telegram which reached Mr. Davis that Sunday morning was to the effect that the enemy had struck, and on the weakest point of the Confederate lines. It told him to be prepared in event of the repulse failing. Two hours later came the fatal news that Grant had forced his way through, and that the city must instantly be evacuated.*

The historians began describing this event in books as early as 1866. That year, James Dabney McCabe, relying on newspaper accounts, wrote this in *Life and Campaigns of General Robert E. Lee*: *The first warning of the coming danger was given to the congregation of St. Paul's Church. A messenger from the War Department entered hastily, and approaching the President's pew, handed Mr. Davis a small slip of paper.* And this: *The paper was General Lee's dispatch announcing his purpose to evacuate Richmond.*

Sallie Brock, who claims to have been an eyewitness in the church that day, wrote, in 1867: *...a messenger was observed to make his way up the aisle, and to place in the hands of the President a sealed package.* She also wrote a poem in 1867, part of which reads:

> *Along the Temple's stilly aisle a messenger*
> *   appeared,*
> *With tidings for the man round whom our burdens*
> *   centred.*

Sallie Brock's account seems to be derivative of McCabe, and besides, if Miss Brock was actually an eyewitness, as she claims, then it seems odd that she has the messenger coming up the aisle, rather than the sexton, whose function this would surely have been.

Frank Alfriend, in his *Life of Jefferson Davis* (1868), writes: *President Davis received the intelligence of the disasters while seated in his pew in St. Paul's Church, where he had been a communicant for nearly three years. The momentous intelligence was conveyed to him by a brief note from the War Department. General Lee's dispatch stated that his lines had been broken, and that all efforts to restore them had proven unsuccessful. He advised preparations for the evacuation of the city during the night, unless, in the meantime, he should advise to the contrary.*

Pollard, who had McCabe's 1866 book in front of him, wrote, in his *Life of Jefferson Davis* (1869): *In the midst of the services a man walked noisily into the church, and handed the President a slip of paper,* while Mallory, with a copy of McCabe and a copy of Stuart's July 4, 1865, article in front of him, wrote: *A messenger from the War Department enters the church, steals behind the President, whispers a few words in his ear & withdraws.* Kentucky congressman H.W. Bruce says, in "Some Reminiscences" (1881): *I saw the church sexton go to that pew in the midst of the services and speak to the President.*

It is the grammatically incorrect phrase "in the midst of the services" that shows quite clearly that Bruce had Pollard in front of him when he wrote this. Most people would say, "in the middle of the services." If he had to copy from Pollard, one has to wonder whether Bruce, like most of the supposed eyewitnesses, was actually in St. Paul's that morning.

Bearing in mind that Jefferson Davis's letter to Varina, written on April 5, 1865, just three days after the event, when Davis's memory would not yet be corroded by time or influenced by other writers, includes these words: *I was called out of church to receive a telegram*, his famous book *Rise and Fall of the Confederate Government*, published sixteen years later, has two separate accounts of this episode, one on page 655 and the other on page 667. Why the book should repeat this episode in such a way is probably indicative of how the whole project was handled (see Davis, in the Bibliography). This is the first one: *In the forenoon of Sunday, the 2d, I received, when in church, a telegram announcing that the army would retire from Petersburg at night, and I went to my office to give needful directions for the evacuation of Richmond*. And this is the second: *On Sunday, the 2d of April, while I was in St. Paul's church, General Lee's telegram, announcing his speedy withdrawal from Petersburg, and the consequent necessity for evacuating Richmond, was handed to me.*

Then there is the 1890 book, *A Short History of the Confederate States*, purportedly written by Jefferson Davis, and which has no fewer than three accounts of the episode: *On the forenoon of Sunday, April 2d, I received when in church a telegram announcing that the army would retire from Petersburg at night*. And this: *When, on the morning of April 2d, the main line of the defences of Petersburg was broken, General Lee telegraphed the advice that Richmond should be evacuated that night simultaneously with the withdrawal of his troops*. And this: *On Sunday, April 2d, while I was in St. Paul's church, General Lee's telegram, announcing his speedy withdrawal from Petersburg, and the consequent necessity for evacuating Richmond, was handed to me.*

William Dillon's biography of the great Irish newsman, *Life of John Mitchel* (1888),[22] has this: *It was Sunday, the 3rd of April, and President Davis was at church, when the telegram containing the fatal news was handed to him. General Lee requested that Richmond should be at once evacuated, and that the seat of government should be removed to Danville*. There are too many errors in this short passage for this book to be taken seriously. Just two examples: Sunday was actually the 2nd of April, not the 3rd. And there was no such mention of Danville in Lee's telegram.

Dr. Minnigerode was certainly in church that day. He was, after all, the preacher. He wrote, in 1890: *As the ante-communion service was read and the people were on their knees, I saw the sexton go to Mr. Davis's pew and hand him what proved to be a telegram. I could not but see it*. Does he mean he could not see it, or he could see it? Actually, it does not really matter, because he did not see a telegram. All he saw were other people's accounts in front of him as he wrote.

This from T.C. De Leon, in *Four Years in Rebel Capitals* (1890): *In the midst of a prayer at Dr. Hoge's church, a courier entered softly, and advancing to Mr. Davis, handed him a telegram*. It seems odd that, at this late date, anyone would still be clinging to the notion that it was Dr. Hoge's church.

At least Landon Knight does not have Dr. Hoge in St. Paul's. In fact, he does not have Jefferson Davis in St. Paul's, which is surprising, as he was relying heavily on Pollard's 1869 book for his information. In *The Real Jefferson Davis* (1904) he must have startled his readers: *At last, on Sunday, April 2, 1865, a courier entered old St. John's in the midst*

---

22. Mitchel was one of the editors of the *Richmond Examiner*.

of services and handed the President a telegram. It was General Lee's notice that he could no longer hold his lines. Knight seems to be the only historian who has Jefferson Davis in St. John's church that morning.

Mary Johnston would have seen Mallory's account published in *McClure's* magazine in 1900, in which the messenger from the War Department stole behind the President. She would also have seen De Leon's 1890 book, *Four Years in Rebel Capitals*, in which the courier entered the church softly. So, in her book, *Cease Firing* (1912), she was able to take the leap that the sexton tiptoed up the aisle: *The sexton of St. Paul's walked, on tiptoe, up the aisle ... Mr. Davis read the slip of paper.* And, of course, she also has McCabe and Pollard's "slip of paper."

Morris Schaff, in *Sunset of the Confederacy* (1912) has this: *Doctor Charles Minnegerode, the rector of St. Paul's ... was delivering his usual tense, extempore address, when the sexton ... advanced up the aisle with soft but stately tread, and after touching the President on the shoulder ... handed him a message.* By 1922, when he came to write *Jefferson Davis*, Schaff, who in the intervening decade had been subject to unbearable peer pressure on the subject of the physical telegram, was more specific about what it was Davis received from the messenger. With a reluctance that shows, he wrote this: *Davis was in St. Paul's—it was Communion Sunday—when a messenger brought in the dispatch.*

Hamilton Eckenrode, who, for undoubtedly good reasons is not taken very seriously these days as a historian, was—as one will see when reading his book in its entirety—one of the peers applying the pressure. In his 1923 book, *Jefferson Davis*, he has this: *The President was in church the morning of Sunday, April 2, when the messenger came with Lee's telegram.*

So was Allen Tate, as witness his *Jefferson Davis* (1929): *A messenger came in, and handed Jefferson Davis a piece of paper. It was a telegram from Lee. It said that Grant had broken the Confederate line at Five Forks, that Richmond must be evacuated. The rumor was not unwarranted.* One wonders why Tate should describe the contents of Lee's telegram as rumor. But, rumor or not, the reason it was "not unwarranted" is not because it was not true—nowhere in this telegram does Lee mention Five Forks.

Eisenschiml and Newman, writing *The American Iliad* in 1947, give an essentially accurate picture of what happened. One might accord them more respect as historians if they had been able to transcribe a simple quote correctly[23]: *Jefferson Davis's reaction to the bad news from Petersburg is reported by himself: On Sunday the second of April, while I was in St. Paul's church, a telegram from General Lee was handed to me, announcing his speedy withdrawal from Petersburg and the consequent necessity for evacuating Richmond. I went to my office and assembled the heads of departments and bureaus, as far as they could be found, and gave instructions for our removal that night.*

At the time Ishbel Ross wrote her book about Varina Davis—*First Lady of the South* (1958)—the new era of Civil War historians was being ushered in: *The President was alone in his pew when a courier clattered down the aisle and the congregation watched as he read the message handed him.*[24] And this: *Mrs. Josiah Gorgas thought the courier seemed greatly excited.* When it comes to finding confirmation of the excited courier in the Amelia Gorgas account in the March 1917 *Confederate Veteran*, one must admit to failure.

---

23. Otto Eisenschiml is the same Eisenschiml who wrote *Why Was Lincoln Murdered?* (1937), in which he claims that the mastermind behind the famous assassination was Edwin Stanton.
24. From the door, one clattered up the aisle, not down the aisle.

Burke Davis wrote, in *To Appomattox* (1959): *Near noon a young man in civilian clothes entered the vestibule and approached Irving* [the sexton]. *"I must see President Davis!," he whispered. "I'll call him when the prayer's done." The boy waited impatiently for a moment. "I can't wait longer," he said. He pulled paper and pencil from his pocket and wrote a note: "General Lee telegraphs that he can hold his position no longer. Come to the office immediately. Breckinridge." Irving read the note and took it down the aisle on tiptoes.*[25]

The tiptoes he gets from Mary Johnston's invention of 1912. The rest is Burke Davis's own fiction, and utterly nonsensical fiction at that. "Near noon" is out by practically an hour. And under whose authority would a mere boy sign "Breckinridge" to the bottom of a note he has peremptorily decided to dash off to the President of the Confederate States of America? Would it not have been more effective if the secretary of war himself had dashed off a note and simply handed it to the boy? And, as for the boy, who was he? A boy showing this incredible initiative deserves a name.

James C. Clark, in *Last Train South* (1984), starts off with: *At 10.40, another message came from Lee, this one to Breckinridge.* Then he quotes the entire telegram, but, instead of the famous 10:40 telegram, he quotes the one that came in at 7 o'clock that evening. Then this: *A clerk was dispatched from the War Department to alert Davis. It was nearly noon when the young civilian clerk entered the church and approached church sexton William Irving and whispered "I must see President Davis." Irving replied, "I'll call him when the prayer's done." The youth waited a moment, pacing in the church foyer, then said, "I cannot wait any longer." He scribbled a message for Davis: "General Lee telegraphs that he can hold his position no longer. Come to the office immediately. Breckinridge." Irving read the note and quietly walked to Davis.*

And this from D. Laurence Rogers, in *Apostles of Equality*: *The silence was about to be broken. It was 11 A.M. when the solemnity of the service was invaded by footsteps, whispers, and signs of alarm among the worshipers.* And this: *The aged sexton of St. Paul's, William Irving, stopped the dispatch bearer, an eager young boy, in the vestibule. "I must see President Davis," said the boy, handing him a note. "General Lee telegraphs that he can hold his position no longer. Come to the office immediately. Breckenridge." Irving eased into the sanctuary with the fateful missive from the Confederate secretary of war, Gen. John Breckenridge.*

This Burke Davis dialogue between the sexton and the boy was too much for any historian aside from Clark and Rogers, but F. Lawrence McFall, in *Danville in the Civil War* (2001), did buy into the boy himself: *As the service progressed, a young courier entered the church with a dispatch for the president from General Lee. The message contained the dreaded news that Petersburg could no longer be held. Without the army's protection, Richmond must be evacuated.*

Historians of the 1960s and 1970s tended to be quite unadventurous in their retelling of this episode. For example, Charles Roland wrote a book called *The Confederacy* (1962), in which he says: *The final fateful message reached the President in his pew; the Army faced immediate disaster and the lines could be held for only a few more hours. Richmond was lost.* And Emory Thomas, despite not thinking things through, writes, in *Confederate State of Richmond* (1971): *Lee's dreadful message reached the War Office at 10.40 on that*

---

25. From the door, one took it up the aisle on tiptoes, not down the aisle.

balmy Sunday morning. A courier bore the telegram one block up Ninth Street to St. Paul's Church where Jefferson Davis was on his knees, engrossed in the ante-communion service Dr. Minnegerode was reading. The President took the telegram, read it... While Shelby Foote, in Volume 3 of his masterpiece, *The Civil War: A Narrative* (1974), although he has made no effort to study the order of service in an 1865 Episcopal church, has this: *... a War Department messenger brought to the presidential pew in St. Paul's Church midway through the morning service, Lee's telegram advising that "all preparation be made for leaving Richmond tonight."*

Isolated examples of this trend toward simplicity were still to be found as late as 1990, when Roy Z. Chamlee wrote, in *Lincoln's Assassins* (1990): *During morning worship services, a sexton at St. Paul's Church approached Davis in his pew and whispered that he was wanted immediately.* And even into 2000, when William J. Cooper's book, *Jefferson Davis, American*, was published: *During the service, the sexton brought a dispatch to the presidential pew, Lee's telegram saying that Richmond must be promptly evacuated.* Hattaway and Beringer kept it simple as well, in their 2002 biography, *Jefferson Davis: Confederate President*: *Davis was in his usual place, kneeling for the antecommunion, when the sexton approached him and gave him a telegram reporting that the army would evacuate its lines, including Richmond, that night.* A final example: David Eicher, in *Dixie Betrayed* (2008): *Davis was kneeling during antecommunion when St. Paul's sexton approached the pew and handed him a telegram from General Lee.*

By the 1980s, with the growing pressure being forced upon historians to come up with something called "narrative non-fiction," something akin to Burke Davis's novelistic approach surfaced. Eli Evans, in his biography of the secretary of state, *Judah P. Benjamin* (1988), writes: *At 10.40 A.M. on Sunday, April 2, Secretary of War Seddon received the wire from General Lee advising the evacuation of Richmond. A messenger rushed to St. Paul's Church, where the President was occupying his usual pew, and gave him a sealed envelope.* The secretary of war was, of course, Breckinridge, not Seddon. Seddon had been secretary from November 21, 1862, to February 5, 1865. Breckinridge had taken over on February 6, 1865.[26]

William C. Davis has this, in *The Man and His Hour* (1991): *After a few minutes the sexton walked down the aisle from the front of the church and gently touched Davis on the shoulder to get his attention.*[27] *He handed the president a paper and whispered to him that it came from Breckinridge at the War Department just a block away. When Davis opened it, he saw that it was a copy of a telegram received from Lee less than an hour before. The enemy had broken through his lines, endangering the last remaining avenue of escape. To save his army he had to evacuate immediately. At best he could hold his position only until nightfall.*

Clayton Charles Marlow's book, *Matt W. Ransom*, was published posthumously in 1996. In this passage he comes up with a new theory: that the deliverer of the message

---

26. Catherine Gourley, in *The Horrors of Andersonville* (2010), sets out her mission statement: *The non-fiction writer's challenge is not only to find information but to interpret it in a fair way. I hope I have achieved this.* Then she writes: *James Seddon, the Confederate secretary of war, intended to leave Richmond at six in the evening.* Miss Gourley is relying on J.B. Jones, the Rebel War Clerk, for her information here. This is what Jones actually says: *The Secretary of War intends to leave at 8 P.M. this evening.* Jones does not name the secretary at that point in his narrative, assuming that the reader would know it was Breckinridge.

27. From the door, one walked up the aisle, not down the aisle, and in doing so one walked toward the front of the church, where the altar and the pulpit were.

was a soldier. This theory cannot be substantiated: *St. Paul's Sunday church services were under way with President Davis in attendance when a slight commotion occurred in the rear of the church.*[28] A soldier was insisting he carried an important message. The sexton hurried up the aisle, whispered something to President Davis, and handed him a telegram in which Lee stated his intentions of executing a speedy withdrawal from Petersburg, creating the necessity of evacuating Richmond.

Much of the following passage in Andrew Billingsley's *Mighty Like a River* (1999) is fiction. What remains is based largely on Pollard's 1869 book: *That Sunday, the president of the Confederacy, Jefferson Davis, was worshiping in St. Paul's Church in Richmond. In the midst of the service a messenger brought him a telegram from Gen. Robert E. Lee. The note said simply that Richmond was about to fall. The Confederate forces could hold it no longer. Lee's telegram informed Davis that the last southbound train out of Richmond would be leaving in a matter of hours. The president would be well advised to take that train.*

John Shelby Spong wrote a book called *Here I Stand. My Struggle for a Christianity of Integrity, Love, and Equality* (2000). It is obviously not a history book, nor, apparently, was it subject to the inspired editing one might hope for from a work with this title: *...a messenger from General Lee interrupted the morning worship service to inform President Davis of the surrender at Appomattox.* It must be observed, perhaps unnecessarily—that is, to all except Spong and his publishers—that the surrender at Appomattox Court House took place on April 9, 1865, a full week after the events at St. Paul's church.

This from A. Wilson Greene, in *Breaking the Backbone of the Rebellion* (2000): *April 2 was Communion Sunday and the distinguished congregation knelt to receive the sacrament.* The service was nowhere close to the point yet where the sacrament would have been received. *As Rev. Charles F.E. Minnigerode intoned the service, the church sexton, William Irving, strode down the aisle, tapped Davis on the shoulder, and handed the president a note, apparently Lee's telegram to Breckinridge.*[29] *Davis's eyes scanned the dispatch as the eyes of the parishioners studied the president's facial expression and body language for clues to the contents of the message.*

As we have seen, Lee's telegram included the words, *I advise that all preparation be made for leaving Richmond tonight.* This is a simple quote to transcribe, yet it is the word "preparation" which has defeated some historians. For example, Mike Wright, in *City Under Siege* (1995), says that the Reverend Minnigerode *paused as the church sexton passed a telegram to Davis. It was from General Lee: "I advise that all preparations be made for leaving Richmond tonight."* Another example—Charles Bracelen Flood, author of *Grant and Sherman* (2006): *...on this Sunday morning Lee dictated a telegram to be sent to Confederate Secretary of War John C. Breckinridge in Richmond, reporting the situation, and ending with, "I advise that all preparations be made for leaving Richmond tonight." This message was brought to Jefferson Davis, who was attending a morning service at St. Paul's Church.* James C. Clark, in *Last Train South* (1984) is another victim, but then he has this particular telegram coming into the War Department at 8:00 a.m. Burke

---

28. Marlow is accurate when he says "the rear of the church." People came in the main door and made their way to their pews, which faced the front of the church, where the minister stood. Dr. Nelson Lankford, in *Richmond Burning* (2002) is one of the few other historians who got this right: *Just before communion began, a messenger from the War Department entered the back of the church. He handed a note to the sexton.*

29. From the door, one strode up the aisle, not down the aisle.

Davis does not attempt to quote this telegram in his 1959 book, *To Appomattox*, but in 1985, when he wrote *The Long Surrender*, he does, and uses the word "preparations." Esteemed historian Jean Edward Smith also gets it wrong in his 2001 book on Grant, as, of course, does Lachman in *The Last Lincolns* (2008). But it is not only modern historians who have experienced this difficulty. A.L. Long's 1886 book, *Memoirs of Robert E. Lee* could not copy it right, and the Reverend J.W. Jones, editor of fourteen volumes of the *Southern Historical Society Papers*, fell similarly afoul in his 1906 book about Lee.

The Rebel and the Rose (2007) has this: *A courier was immediately sent to St. Paul's with the telegram. Not wishing to interrupt Minnigerode as he began Communion, the messenger caught the attention of sexton William Irving* [who] *stiffly made his way down the aisle to Davis's pew.... Touching the president lightly on the shoulder, Irving handed Davis the sealed note, an "uneasy whisper" rippling through the congregation as the rector paused momentarily in his Communion sermon.*

To sum up the trend for inaccuracy and/or pure invention, two 2008 books may well be cited. Clint Johnson's *Pursuit* states, *The service had just begun with a hymn and a prayer, when an excited clerk from the War Department yanked open the huge doors and rushed into the vestibule. He started to walk down the aisle when a sexton stopped him with a hand to the chest.*[30] *The prayer was still underway. When Minnigerode finished, the sexton took the folded paper from the messenger's hand and strode down the aisle to Davis's pew. Davis read the note. It was the second telegram from Lee that morning, the one an irritated Lee had written after being admonished by Davis that "many valuables would be lost." "I advise that all preparation be made for leaving Richmond tonight. I will advise you later, according to circumstances," Lee had written.*

The first half of this passage is wrong. As for the second half, Lee's telegram may or may not have been the second one sent by the general that morning, but it certainly was not the one responding to the president's "many valuables would be lost" telegram. As is well known, that one would not be sent from Petersburg until 3:30 p.m.

And finally, Lachman, in *The Last Lincolns*: *Davis was sitting with his wife in the front-row pew at St. Paul's Church when the church sexton came hurrying up the aisle bearing an important message.* Davis's pew, #63, was not in the front row, and his wife had long left Richmond.

Historians say that a gray pallor came over Jefferson Davis's face in church when he read whatever it was the sexton handed him. It was not a gray pallor to start with. It was only with the passing of the years and the liberal application of makeup by "eyewitnesses" and historians that the color evolved into gray. The *New York Times* of April 9, 1865, published the following, written by their reporter Lorenzo L. Crounse on April 4 from City Point: *...his face blanched to a livid whiteness by fear.* However, it may have only looked livid white from a distance. On closer inspection it may not have been quite that bad. As Carleton Coffin reports in his *Boston Journal* article of April 1865: *He turned pale.* But, no, it was definitely white, but not livid white. This from McCabe's book, *Life and Campaigns of General Robert E. Lee* (1866): *The President read it, and it was observed by those near him that his face grew ghastly white.*

---

30. From the door, one walked up the aisle, not down the aisle.

Frank Alfriend passionately objects to any degree of blanching, as that would imply fear. In his 1868 book, *Life of Jefferson Davis*, he rails: *The author has seen an absurd statement, made without any inquiry into the facts, that Mr. Davis was seen to turn "ghastly white" at the moment of receiving the intelligence of the disaster at Petersburg. It is simply one of a thousand other reckless calumnies, with as little foundation as the rest.* Alfriend never reveals how he can be so certain. He's probably right, though.

Mrs. Burton Harrison, the former Connie Cary, wrote her *Recollections Grave and Gay* in 1911. Warned off by Frank Alfriend's indignation, she determined to come up with her own color, and in a fit of inspiration, invented the notorious "gray pallor": *I happened to sit in the rear of the President's pew, so near that I plainly saw the sort of gray pallor that came upon his face as he read a scrap of paper thrust into his hand by a messenger hurrying up the middle aisle.*

But "pale" was one shade that refused to die, at least for a while. Amelia Gorgas's so-called diary (1917) has this: *Pale but composed*, while Hamilton Eckenrode's 1923 book on Jefferson Davis has *Ashy faced but composed*. With Eckenrode, one could sense the shift from a whiter shade of pale to a definite gray. He just didn't have the nerve to follow Mrs. Harrison all the way. Neither did Frank Bury Woodford, in *Father Abraham's Children*, (1961), when he wrote ... *his face strained and gray.*

But Ishbel Ross did, in *First Lady of the South* (1958), albeit only as a quote. Perhaps it was the strain imposed by going all the way to gray that made her unable even to copy a simple quote: *Connie Cary, sitting immediately behind him, saw a "gray sort of pallor" creep over his face.* On the other hand, she is as entitled as any writer of creative non-fiction to change Mrs. Burton Harrison's "came upon his face" to "creep over his face," as long as she does not imply that it is a quote from Harrison. And she does not. So that's all right. But what Professor Hudson Strode did, when writing *Tragic Hero* (1964), was not all right. Instead of consulting Mrs. Burton Harrison's book direct, he had only Ishbel Ross in front of him. Ross had misquoted Harrison's "sort of gray pallor" as "gray sort of pallor," and now Strode does the same thing. But it gets worse. Through his inability to put the end quotes in the right place, Strode misquotes Ross, thus: *Constance Cary, directly behind him, plainly noted a "gray sort of pallor creep over his face."* Professor Strode was one of the leading Davis scholars of his day.

Shelby Foote never cites sources. In the third and last volume of his classic *The Civil War: A Narrative* (1974) he writes: *Nearby worshipers saw "a sort of gray pallor creep over his face" as he read the dispatch, then watched him rise and stride back down the aisle "with stern set lips and his usual quick military tread."* What Foote has done is use Mrs. Harrison, Ishbel Ross, and Hudson Strode to form his own misquote—"a sort of gray pallor creep over his face." And so we reach the greatest distance from the original Connie Cary quote, or rather, we will with Jay Winik's *April 1865* (2001): *Nearby congregants watched "a sort of gray pallor creep over his face."* Winik was so preoccupied with changing Shelby Foote's "worshipers" to "congregants" and "saw" to "watched" that he failed to notice that "a sort of gray pallor creep over his face" was, in fact, Foote's invention.

Mike Wright, in *City Under Siege* (1995), simply copied either Foote or Winik, it does not really matter which: *"...a sort of gray pallor creep over his face."* And Clint Johnson, in *Pursuit* (2008), although he seems to be quoting direct from Mrs. Harrison, comes up with his own misquote: *But another member of the church said, "I plainly saw the sort of gray pallor that came over his face."*

In fact, misquotes are the rule, rather than the exception, so it is startling when an author gets it right. Harry S. Stout, for example, in his 2006 book, *Upon the Altar of the Nation*: *One communicant, sitting behind Davis, was "so near that I plainly saw the sort of gray pallor that came upon his face as he read."*

By 2007, the trend was shifting away from the now hackneyed "gray pallor," and authors were striving for originality again. *The Rebel and the Rose* has this: *...his face perhaps a shade grayer.* And James Swanson's *Bloody Crimes* (2011) ushered in what may well be a trend away from the color gray altogether: *On reading the telegram, Davis did not panic, though the distressing news drained the color from his face.* And, going full circle back to 1865, this from Joseph Wheelan, in *Terrible Swift Sword* (2012): *As Davis read Lee's message, nearby worshippers saw him blanch.*

When President Davis exited St. Paul's Church on receiving the news that morning of April 2, 1865, in what manner did he do it? The Northern newspapers were the first to report this soon to be famous egress. The adverb offered by the *New York Daily Tribune* of April 8, 1865, was "hurriedly": *...he instantly arose and walked hurriedly down the aisle, beneath the questionings of all the eyes in the house.* Carleton Coffin, in his *Boston Journal* article of April 1865, agrees: *...taking his hat, he hurriedly left the church.*

However, the Washington, D.C., newspaper, the *Evening Star*, of May 10, 1865, had diametrically opposing information: *Rising from his seat with singular gravity and deliberation, Mr. Davis left the church.* This version has gained only a few adherents. For example, Ernest B. Furgurson, taking not only from the *Evening Star* but also from Morris Schaff's 1912 book, *Sunset of the Confederacy* (see below), wrote this, in his own 1996 book, *Ashes of Glory*: *Davis rose "with singular gravity and determination," and left quietly, hat in hand. Those watching understood that whatever this meant, it was serious.* And A. Wilson Greene, in *Breaking the Backbone of the Rebellion* (2000): *Convinced of the seriousness of the situation, the ever-dignified chief executive rose "with singular gravity and determination" and quickly left the sanctuary.* It must be noted that while Greene was accurately quoting Furgurson's quote, Furgurson was copying inaccurately from the *Evening Star*.

C.E.L. Stuart, in his *New York Herald* article of July 4, 1865, inclines more toward "hurried," but then he undoubtedly had the April 8 edition of the *New York Daily Tribune* in front of him as he wrote: *The concourse of worshippers within St. Paul's read the whisper by the action of Mr. Davis, who instantly left the church.*

Not many historians have bothered even to look at these early newspapers, which is hardly surprising, given how untrustworthy they are. One historian who did, however, was Doris Kearns Goodwin, for her very famous book, *Team of Rivals* (2005): *"Thereupon"* as an attendant at the service noted, Davis *"instantly arose, and walked hurriedly down the aisle, beneath the questionings of all eyes in the house."* There is a problem here, however. To attribute the quote to an attendant at the service is to take a gamble. All we know is, it was from a Richmond correspondent at the Spotswood House, writing on April 6, a Yankee correspondent at that, and he would not have arrived in Richmond until April 3, 1865. And nowhere does he attribute this to an attendant at the service.

Allen Tate was not completely swayed by the tales of Davis hurrying from the church, but, as he was unable to come up with any convincing alternative for his 1929 biography, *Jefferson Davis*, he was reduced to timidity: *The President quietly and deliberately rose, and with perhaps only a slightly quickened step left the church.* If he had been writing today, Tate would not have used the word "perhaps"; he would have used "likely."

James Dabney McCabe is on safe ground, when he writes about Davis in his influential *Life and Campaigns of General Robert E. Lee* (1866): *Yet, controlling his emotion, he left the church in silence.* Whoever wrote Jefferson Davis's books, *The Rise and Fall of the Confederate Government* (1881) and *A Short History of the Confederate States of America* (1890), obviously liked McCabe's description. Both books say: *I quietly rose and left the church.* Congressman H.W. Bruce of Kentucky, in his 1881 "Recollections," plays it even safer, even though he probably was not even in the church, when he says that he saw *the President retire from the congregation.* Morris Schaff, in his 1922 biography, *Jefferson Davis*, is on the safest ground of all: *He at once withdrew.*

Others who have largely resisted the temptation to invent include Amelia Gorgas, in her so-called diary, published in *Confederate Veteran* in 1917: *Mr. Davis arose, pale but composed, and with great dignity passed out of the church*; Hamilton Eckenrode, in his biography, *Jefferson Davis* (1918): *Ashy faced but composed, the fallen ruler left the church in order to prepare for flight*; William J. Cooper, in *Jefferson Davis, American* (2000): *Upon reading it, Davis rose and quietly walked out*; and Jay Winik, in *April 1865* (2001): *And then Davis rose and quickly walked down the aisle.*

There are always those, of course, who have been keen to leave their imprimatur, in one way or another, upon this event. Phoebe Yates Pember, for example, in her 1866 article, says that Davis *rose immediately, without any visible signs of agitation or surprise, and left the church. No great alarm was exhibited by the congregation.* This is how she tells it in her 1879 book, *A Southern Woman's Story*: *...he rose immediately, and without any visible signs of agitation or surprise, left the church. No alarm was exhibited by the congregation.* T.C. De Leon, has this, in his *Four Years in Rebel Capitals* (1890): *Noiselessly, and with no show of emotion, Mr. Davis left the church, followed by a member of his staff.* And *Landon Knight*, in his 1904 book, *The Real Jefferson Davis*: *Mr. Davis quietly left the church, but all understood, and soon a panic reigned in the quiet old city.* And William L. Broun, as quoted in the 1912 book by his son: *"Mr. Davis immediately arose and walked out of the church, with a calm expression, yet causing some little excitement."* And Mary Johnston, in *Cease Firing* (1912): *Mr. Davis read the slip of paper, rose with a still face, and went softly down the aisle, erect and quiet. Eyes followed him, many eyes.*

The Rebel and the Rose (2007), relying largely on Mary Johnston, has this: *Glancing at the message, the president calmly rose from his seat. Erect and dignified, he quietly exited the church, his face perhaps a shade grayer but still impassive.* The authors then quote the telegram. Unfortunately, it is the wrong telegram; the one quoted is Lee's telegram to Davis himself, received at 7 o'clock that night, not the one to Breckinridge that Davis was called out of church for.

Sallie Brock, writing in 1867, was the first to come up with "unsteadily": *Mr. Davis arose, and was noticed to walk rather unsteadily out of the church.* Michael B. Ballard, almost managing to get the quote right, references this in his 1986 book, *A Long Shadow*: *Sallie Brock similarly recounted that "Davis was noticed to walk rather unsteadily out of the church,"* and "unsteadily" is also favored by Eli Evans, in *Judah P. Benjamin* (1988): *Davis rose and unsteadily made his way up the aisle as uneasy whispers rippled through the congregation.*[31]

This unsteadiness contrasts sharply with the stately step described by Sallie Brock in her poem of 1867:

---

31. Davis would have made his way down the aisle, not up it.

4. Church

No word, or other sign, gave he, of all his
great heart felt—
With eyes as calm and clear—with step as
stately, went he forth

Frank Alfriend it was who invented "measured tread" in his 1868 book, *Life of Jefferson Davis*: *Mr. Davis immediately left the church with his usual calm manner and measured tread. The tranquil demeanor of the President conveyed no indication of the nature of the communication. But the incident was an unusual one, and, by the congregation, most of whom had for days been burdened with the anticipation of disaster, the unspoken intelligence was, to some extent, correctly interpreted.*

Connie Cary (later Mrs. Burton Harrison) liked the "measured tread" offered by Frank Alfriend, enough anyway to rework the wording in her *Recollections Grave and Gay* (1911): *With stern set lips and his usual quick military tread, he left the church.* David Eicher is one of the very few historians to reproduce this. He did so in *Dixie Betrayed* (2008), or at least tried to: *Although Davis had heard the news already, he felt he could remain in the pew no longer, and, "with his usually quick military tread" walked out.* In case one wonders what the first part of Eicher's passage means, it simply reflects a misunderstanding of the contents of Lee's various telegrams to Richmond.

Pollard, in *Life of Jefferson Davis* (1869), did not really agree with Frank Alfriend that Davis was calm when he walked out of church. Or did he? It's hard to tell from Pollard: *Mr. Davis read the paper, rose, and walked out of the church without agitation, but his face and manner evidently constrained.* Mallory, who was not in the church, felt the same way as Pollard, especially after reading Pollard: *All eyes are again fixed upon his face as he follows the messenger the whole length of the aisle; but Lee's later dispatches, telling of new and heavier losses, & urging immediate withdrawal from the capital, are not betrayed by one line of that pale, careworn visage.*

Where Burke Davis, in *To Appomattox* (1959), writes: *Davis glanced at the paper and rose. His face was calm, but many people raised heads to watch him leave, and there were expressions of alarm*, James C. Clark, has this, in *Last Train South* (1984): *[Davis] glanced at it, and left the church.* And D. Laurence Rogers, in *Apostles of Equality* (2011): *Davis and other officials tiptoed out of the service, their grave faces revealing fear that the glorious days of the Confederacy were at last coming to an end.*

Then there is the overcoat. This originates with the Rev. Dr. Minnigerode, writing in 1890: *Mr. Davis took it* [i.e., the telegram] *quietly, not to disturb the congregation, put on his overcoat and walked out.* The overcoat got only a few takers. Emory Thomas, in his *Confederate State of Richmond* (1971), says that Davis *quietly put on his overcoat and left. His departure created no disturbance; affairs of state had interrupted Davis's worship before.* And this led to William C. Davis writing, in *The Man and His Hour* (1991): *Quietly Davis rose, put on his overcoat, and walked out of the church with the sexton.*

So much for the overcoat. Another item of clothing, the hat that Carleton Coffin told us about in his April 1865 article in the *Boston Journal*, might or might not have been picked up by Jefferson Davis as he got up from his pew, but it certainly was not picked up by many later historians, which is somewhat surprising, given that it is a neat detail. Morris Schaff, in his *Sunset of the Confederacy* (1912), says quite a lot about the hat: *Mr. Davis threw his blue-gray eyes rapidly over the fatal dispatch, grasped his soft, creamy-white hat, rose, and withdrew calmly.*

Clint Johnson, in *Pursuit* (2008), writes this: *Without saying a word to Lubbock,*[32] *Davis rose from his seat, turned up the aisle,*[33] *and walked quickly out of church.* And this: *One person recalled that Davis "was noted to walk unsteadily out of the church."* This last passage is almost, but not quite, an exact quote from Michael Ballard's book *A Long Shadow*, wherein Ballard almost, but not quite successfully, quotes Sallie Brock.

There is more from Clint Johnson: *But another watched Davis rise from his seat and "walk softly down the aisle, erect and quiet."* This is almost, but not quite, an exact quote from Ballard, who actually quotes Mary Johnston's 1912 book *Cease Firing*. And from Clint Johnson: *When Davis walked out of the church clutching the telegram in his hand, he glanced to his right toward the Virginia State Capitol lawn. What he saw would have troubled the president of any other nation: clerks building bonfires of paper money and bonds. Much of the remaining wealth of the Confederacy was either burning to ashes or blowing down the street, but no one bothered to rescue any of the $50 bills that featured Davis's idealized portrait showing an unlined, youthful, pleasant, clean-shaven face.* This passage is sheer invention.

The preacher, Dr. Minnigerode, did his best to press on with the service, but he had suddenly taken a distinctly second place to temporal speculation, as more and more dignitaries were called out of the church.

The *New York Daily Tribune* of April 8, 1865, was the first to report what happened in church after Jefferson Davis had made his exit. Misled by false rumors of the sexton's ethnic heritage, they indulged in colorful fiction: *As the preacher closed the services, the colored sexton handed him a note from his ex–Excellency. The face of the preacher waxed, sickly, with despair, while that of the sexton with joy too great for concealment. The chagrin of the one was quite as marked as the grin of the other. The former begged his congregation to tarry and told them in sad utterances that he could not expect to minister to them any more.*

Much more true to events was the report in the Washington, D.C., paper, the *Evening Star*, of May 10, 1865: *...immediately afterwards several prominent citizens were by the same sexton summoned to follow him* [i.e., Davis].

C.E.L. Stuart, in his July 4, 1865, *New York Herald* article, has this: *No telegram ever flashed through the electric wires more swiftly than this unspoken intelligence shot from eye to eye of that dismayed congregation. Had an unseen hand written the coming doom on the wall in letters of fire, the effect could not have been more appalling or more instantaneous.* Or, as Nelson Lankford says, in his 2002 book, *Richmond Burning*: *A navy clerk who was there, searching for a metaphor that could capture the shock of the moment,* [said]: *"Had an unseen hand written the coming doom on the wall in letters of fire, the effect could not have been more appalling or more instantaneous."* Lankford cites "C.E.L. Stuart, in *New York Herald*, July 4, cited in Ballard, *A Long Shadow*, p. 37." This is, indeed, an exact quote from Stuart, but nowhere in his account does Stuart imply that he was in the church (see the appendix); in fact, on the contrary. It's no good just reproducing quotes; one has to have some knowledge of the man who is reputed to have made them.

---

32. The reason he did not say a word to Lubbock is that Lubbock was not there.
33. He would have turned down the aisle, not up it.

James Dabney McCabe, in his *Life and Campaigns of General Robert E. Lee* (1866), wrote: *The agitation of the President caused a vague feeling of alarm throughout the congregation at St. Paul's, and soon the church was emptied.*

Sallie Brock, echoing Stuart, wrote, in 1867: *An uneasy whisper ran through the congregation, and intuitively they seemed possessed of the dreadful secret of the sealed despatch—the unhappy condition of General Lee's army and the necessity for evacuating Richmond.* She also wrote these lines, in her poem of the same year:

> *And quicker than the lightning's flash, then
> through the crowd there ran,
> A whisper, ominous of the woe, that on them was
> to break;
> And friend looked in the face of friend, and
> man on man,
> For light, for help,—that hope might not
> their hopes forsake*

This from Congressman Horatio Washington Bruce, in his 1881 "Recollections": *I was not feeling very well that morning. I felt that something was going wrong with our cause when I saw the President withdraw; and this, in connection with the indisposition referred to, caused me also to retire from the church.* As we shall see when it comes time to get on the train for Danville, Congressman Bruce spent a lot of time sleeping. If it took him until April 2, 1865, to see that something was going wrong with the Confederate cause, then perhaps he slept throughout the entire war.

The moment in time is captured in great detail by the preacher himself, the Reverend Dr. Minnigerode, writing in 1890, twenty-five years after the event. He tells us that on communion occasions he was wont to make a short address from the chancel, and that on this occasion, while so doing, *the sexton came in repeatedly and called out this one and that one, all connected with the government and military service.* Of course the congregation became very restless and he tried to finish his address as soon as he could, without adding to the threatening panic. But when the sexton came to the chancel-railing and spoke to the Reverend Mr. Kepler, who assisted Minnigerode, they began to stir, *and I closed as quickly as possible.* Minnigerode is telling us very plainly that he was giving his address when all this happened. The address came right at the beginning of the service. *Then Mr. Kepler told me the provost-marshal wanted to see me in the vestry room.* So Minnigerode went out and found Major Isaac H. Carrington,[34] who informed the minister that General Lee's lines had been broken before Petersburg, that he was in retreat, and Richmond must be evacuated. *As nothing would occur till the evening, he asked my advice whether the alarm should be rung at once or in the afternoon. We determined to wait till 3 o'clock, and I returned to the chancel.* As Minnigerode entered he found the congregation streaming out of the church, and he sprang forward and called out, "Stop! stop! there is no necessity for your leaving the church"; and most of them (i.e., all who had not left

---

34. Isaac Howell Carrington was born in Richmond on March 7, 1827. Lankford, in *Richmond Burning* (2002), describes him as a *coarse man, rough to the point of brusqueness, he had just the temperament for the job of keeping public order during the evacuation.* Casstevens, in *George W. Alexander and Castle Thunder* (2004), says that Carrington *fled Richmond with Davis, but stayed in the Danville area instead of going farther south. He was arrested and brought back to Richmond, where he was placed in Castle Thunder. It was not known what charges were preferred against him, or by whose order.* He died in Richmond on January 30, 1887. His papers are at the Perkins Library, Duke University, Durham, NC.

before he got back) returned. Then he recalled his appointment for service that night, *told the people that we had met with disaster before Petersburg,* and a meeting of the citizens would be called by the alarm-bell at 3 o'clock in the Capitol square; that there was no occasion for them to leave at once, and he requested the communicants to stay to the celebration. About 250 or 300 remained, and some felt as if they were kneeling there with the halter around their necks. The panic was so great.

Connie Cary had Dr. Minnigerode's account in front of her as she wrote her own *Recollections Grave and Gay* (1911): *...a number of other people rising in their seats and hastening after him* [i.e., President Davis], *those who were left swept by a universal tremor of alarm. The rector, accustomed as he was to these frequent scenes in church, came down to the altar rail and tenderly begged his people to remain and finish the service, which was done. Before dismissing his congregation, the rector announced to them that General Ewell had summoned the local forces to meet for defence of the city at three in the afternoon.*

William C. Davis also relies on Dr. Minnigerode's account for his own book, *The Man and His Hour* (1991): *In the next half hour, the sexton returned again and again, calling other members of the government and military from their pews. Before long, the congregation, who witnessed all this, began spontaneously rising and leaving the church in groups. Even when Minnegerode appealed to them to come back, they continued to wander out to learn what had happened, though most surely suspected well enough. Richmond must be abandoned.*

James Swanson also relies on Connie Cary for his 2010 book, *Bloody Crimes,* but unfortunately he is unable to quote her correctly: "*Before dismissing the congregation,*" Cary remembered, "*the rector announced to them that General Ewell had summoned the local forces to meet for the defence of the city at three in the afternoon.*"

None of these accounts is very specific as to, say, who was the next to be called out by the sexton. Nor are the following, all copying from one source or another: Emory Thomas, in *Confederate State of Richmond*: *Soon, however, the sexton was calling away everyone connected with the government or military.* And Shelby Foote in *The Civil War* (1974): *Some few rose to follow, knowing the summons must be urgent for him to leave before taking Communion this first–Sunday.* And Ernest B. Furguson, in *Ashes of Glory* (1996): *...soon the sexton returned to summon another high official, then another and another. Minnigerode urged his audience to stay and be calm.* And Jay Winik, in *April 1865* (2001): *A few staff members and couriers soon followed the President, but the bulk of the congregation remained in their seats. For these, the well-bred and well-to-do, manners forbade them from making an overt show of concern. So, too, with Minnigerode.*

However, Mary Johnston supplies the answer in her book, *Cease Firing* (1912): *For all it was so hushed in Saint Paul's there came a feeling as of swinging bells.... The sexton, who had gone out before Mr. Davis, returned. He whispered to General Anderson.*[35] The latter rose and went out. She goes on: *Suddenly the sexton was back, summoning this one and that one and the other. "Sit still, my people, sit still, my people"—but the bells were ringing too loudly and the hearts were beating too hard. Men and women rose, hung panting a moment, then, swift or slow, they left Saint Paul's. Going, they heard that the lines at Petersburg had been broken and that General Lee said the Government must leave Richmond—leave at once.*

---

35. Joseph Reid Anderson (1813–1892).

Morris Schaff agrees with Mary Johnston. In his own book, *Sunset of the Confederacy* (1912), he says that hardly had Davis *left the door before the sexton again marched up the aisle, spoke to General Joseph Anderson, who at once took his leave. Then followed two more grand entries.* He continues: *At this fourth presageful march up the aisle, again with a message to a prominent official, anxiety seized the congregation, and like alarmed birds they rose at once and left the church.*

One of the sexton's grand entries referred to by Schaff must have been the one for the benefit of General Gorgas, chief of the Ordnance Department—that is, if we believe William L. Broun as quoted in the 1912 book by his son: "*In a moment, the sexton came back and called out General Gorgas.*[36] *I confess I was made extremely uneasy, and was reflecting on the probable cause when, being touched on the shoulder and looking around, the sexton whispered to me that a messenger from the war department awaited me at the door. I instantly felt that the end had come.*" Broun himself did not merit a grand entry from the sexton, being merely Gorgas's underling. But, more to the point, whereas Mary Johnston and Morris Schaff both have General Anderson being the subject of the sexton's second grand entry, William L. Broun has Gorgas receiving that honor.

Burke Davis certainly went along with Broun. In *To Appomattox* (1959), he writes: *An officer of the Ordnance Department, Lieutenant Colonel William L. Broun, was in a pew some distance behind the President's; while Broun wondered about the departure of Davis, he saw Irving return and tap General Gorgas on the shoulder; Gorgas also left the church. A moment later the sexton called Broun, and then went to the far side of the church and asked General Joseph Anderson, the head of the Tredegar Iron Works,*[37] *to follow him. Minnigerode saw Davis leave, followed by others, and when the prayer was ended, the minister went into the chancel to deliver his usual brief Communion Service talk. Irving called out half-a-dozen other men while he spoke. The congregation, he saw, was restless, and Minnigerode hurried to the end as quickly as he could without giving signs of alarm. At last, when the sexton came into the front of the church, and called Minnigerode's assistant, the Rev. Mr. Kepler, people began leaving the pews. Minnigerode ceased speaking. The rector found the city's Provost Marshal, Major Isaac Carrington, in the vestry room, and was told that Lee's lines were broken, and that Richmond was lost.*

James C. Clark, in *Last Train South* (1984), as usual, uses Burke Davis as his sole template: *As the President walked from the church, Irving went down the aisle, tapping key administration figures on the shoulder. General Josiah Gorgas, head of the Ordnance Department, left quickly and was followed by his aide, Colonel William Groun.*[38] *The minister, Dr. Charles Minnigerode, continued with his sermon, but he was clearly distracted, as more than a dozen men left the church.*

Any writer who maintains that Dr. Moses Hoge was the presiding preacher at St.

---

36. Gorgas claims, in his diary entry of April 16, 1865, that he only learned of the 10:40 a.m. telegram at 1:00 p.m. This seems odd, if he was called out of St. Paul's, as Broun claims. Why would Gorgas deny himself this place in history, unless, of course, he was not in church at all?

37. William L. Broun says: *Cannon were made at the Tredegar Iron-Works, including siege and field guns, napoleons, howitzers, and banded cast iron guns. Steel guns were not made. We had no facilities for making steel, and no time to experiment. The steel guns used by the Confederates were highly valued, and with the exception of a few purchased abroad, were all captured from the Federals.*

38. One assumes this is Broun, rather than Groun. However, William Groun is in Clark's index, but as a general. Following the directions in the index, one goes to page 14 for General William Groun, and finds Colonel William Groun.

Paul's that day does not deserve to be taken seriously. Phoebe Yates Pember, for example, in her 1866 article, says that *several members of the President's Staff followed, till Dr. Hoge brought the service to an abrupt close, and informed his startled flock that Richmond would probably be evacuated very shortly, and they would only exercise a proper degree of prudence by going home immediately and preparing for that event.* Alerted to the fact that she had the wrong minister, this is how the story is told in her 1879 book, *A Southern Woman's Story*: *several members of the president's staff followed him, till Dr. Minnigerode brought the service to an abrupt close, and informed his startled flock that the city would be evacuated shortly, and they would only exercise a proper degree of prudence by going home immediately, and preparing for the event.*

T.C. De Leon is another example. In *Four Years in Rebel Capitals* (1890), he says that another member of Davis's staff *quietly said a few words to the minister; and then the quick apprehensions of the congregation were aroused. Like an electric shock they felt the truth, even before Dr. Hoge stopped the services and informed them that Richmond would be evacuated that night; and counseled that they had best go home and prepare to meet the dreadful tomorrow.*

Clint Johnson sums up the event in his 2008 book, *Pursuit*: *The congregation turned and watched. Unknowing of what the note said and unsure as to how they should react to their president rudely walking out of a church service, they exchanged worried glances and whispers. What could be so important that the president of the nation could not wait an hour before disrupting church? Opinions differed among the congregation as to how Davis reacted when he read the telegram.*

The final word from Jefferson Davis's 1881 book, *The Rise and Fall of the Confederate Government*: *The occurrence probably attracted attention, but the people of Richmond had been too long beleaguered, had known me too often to receive notice of threatened attacks, and the congregation at St. Paul's was too refined to make a scene at anticipated danger. For all these reasons, the reader will be prepared for the announcement that the sensational stories which have been published about the agitation caused by my leaving the church during service were the creations of fertile imaginations. I went to my office and assembled the heads of departments and bureaus, as far as they could be found on a day when all the offices were closed, and gave the needful instructions for our removal that night.*

Mallory says that, in the various churches throughout Richmond that morning, *the faces of all were scanned for information as they withdrew; but though all were fully impressed with the momentous crisis, familiarity with adversity had given to each its inevitable immobility of expression, & they betrayed no evidence of the emotions which filled their hearts.*

Chapter 5

THE P.M. DISPATCHES

This is Jefferson Davis's reply to Lee's famous 10:40 telegram: *Richmond, Va. April 2, 1865. General R.E. Lee, Petersburg, Va.: The Secretary of War has shown me your dispatch. To move to-night will involve the loss of many valuables, both for the want of time to pack and of transportation. Arrangements are progressing and unless you otherwise advise the start will be made. Jeff'n Davis.*

We do not know the time of day Davis sent this telegram from Richmond, but we do know that Lee received it in Petersburg between 3:00 and 3:30 that afternoon.[1] Given the normal twenty-minute time lag between sending and receiving, unless there was a delay in the telegraphic process that afternoon Davis must have sent the telegram from Richmond between, say, 2:40 and 3:10 p.m.

In his 1934 book, *R.E. Lee* (1934), Douglas Southall Freeman says that Davis sent the reply to Lee as he was *going from the church to the War Department*. That would have been between 11:10 and 11:15 a.m. Lee received Davis's reply four hours later; therefore Freeman is of the opinion that a massive delay was afflicting the telegraph on that day. Freeman does not reveal his source for what he wrote.

A. Wilson Greene, in *Breaking the Backbone of the Rebellion* (2000), says that President Davis, upon receiving Lee's 10:40 a.m. telegram at approximately 11:30 a.m., *hastened to his office in the customs house, where he telegraphed Lee, acknowledging receipt of the bad news, and lamenting that "the loss of many valuables,"* etc.

Freeman says, of Davis's reply: *It was a plain request for more time, despite warnings repeatedly given since February 21.* By this Freeman is undoubtedly referring to the telegram Lee sent to Breckinridge on February 21: *In the event of the necessity of abandoning our position on the James River I shall endeavor to unite the corps of the army about Burkeville.* Lee then suggests that Lynchburg or some place west might be a good pace to remove the stores from Richmond, but adds, *This, however, is a most difficult point at this time to decide, and the place may have to be changed by circumstances.*

In Freeman, we learn for the first time in print how Lee reacted when he received Davis's rather petulant telegram about the valuables: *Lee's nerves were beginning to feel the strain of a day in purgatory, and when he read the president's message, he tore it into bits. "I am sure I gave him sufficient notice," he said.* For this anecdote Freeman cites Charles S. Venable to Walter H. Taylor (March 29, 1878, Taylor manuscript).

Shelby Foote renders the episode thus in *The Civil War* (1974): *Lee bristled at the*

---

1. Lee's 3:00 p.m. letter and his 3.30 p.m. telegram—both to Jefferson Davis—bear this out.

implied rebuke—perhaps forgetting that five days ago he had promised Breckinridge a ten- or twelve-day warning—and ripped the telegram to pieces. "I am sure I gave him sufficient notice," he said testily.

It's not Foote's awkward prose that is worrying here. It's the content. Five days before April 2 was March 28, when Lee was in the field at Petersburg. Therefore that day Lee must have sent a telegram or letter to Breckinridge. And he did, too, but it contained nothing about such a warning. But there is an explanation as to how Foote came up with this, and it is not flattering to Foote. As we saw in Chapter 1, Breckinridge had sent a telegram to Lee on February 25, 1865: *I have given the necessary orders in regard to commencing the removal of stores, &c., but if possible would like to know whether we may probably count on a period of ten or twelve days. If the urgency is not very great better order and system can be carried out.* Lee had replied three days later with the words, *I know of no reason to prevent your counting upon the time suggested in your letter.*

Rather than a textbook on elementary arithmetic, it was Foote's book that James C. Clark had in front of him as he wrote his own *Last Train South* (1984). Clark is discussing April 1 when he says, *Three days earlier Breckinridge told Lee that he was preparing to move the government stores, "But if possible, would like to know whether we may probably count on a period of ten or twelve days." Lee replied, "I know of no reason to prevent your counting on the time suggested." Now, Lee was telling Breckinridge that instead of more than a week to complete the job, Breckinridge might have just twenty-four hours.*

Clark then says: *Davis also sent a message to Lee on that Saturday: "The question is often asked, 'will we hold Richmond,' to which my only answer is, if we can; it is purely a question of military power. The distrust is increasing, and embarrasses in many ways."* For this misquoted passage, Clark cites Jefferson Davis's *Rise and Fall* (1881).

Clayton Charles Marlow, in his 1996 book *Matt W. Ransom*, has reduced President Davis's telegram to fiction: *Because he was loath to lose his valuables in a departure too hasty for packing and shipping, Davis requested General Lee to postpone for one day an evacuation of his lines.* And this: *Upon receipt of this request, Lee found it difficult to maintain his usual self-composure; he tore the telegram to pieces, and stomping them into the ground, he muttered, "I am sure I gave him sufficient notice."*

James Swanson, in *Bloody Crimes* (2010), reproduces Davis's telegram more or less faithfully, but, oddly, omits his opening sentence. Then he says: *This was not the answer Lee expected. At this moment his men were fighting and dying to save Richmond, while President Davis was fretting about the loss of valuables. Davis's telegram exasperated Lee. After he read it, he crumpled it into a ball, tossed it to the ground, and complained to his staff: "I am sure I gave him sufficient notice."*

This from Clint Johnson, in *Pursuit* (2008): *While Lee was still riding toward downtown Petersburg, a courier found him with a telegraphed reply from Davis to his earlier message. Aides watched Lee's eyes darken and his face flush and tighten, as he read Davis's reply that Reagan had telegraphed back to Lee. "To move tonight will involve the loss of many valuables, both for the want of time to pack and transportation," Davis had answered.* And this: *With a stub of pencil, Lee wrote out another telegram to Davis briefly describing the military situation.*

Around midday on Sunday, April 2, Lee was forced to evacuate his headquarters of the previous four months, Edge Hill, located about two miles west of downtown Petersburg. They moved to Dupuy House, a mile closer to town.

5. The P.M. Dispatches

The following is a letter written by Lee from Petersburg at 3:00 p.m.,[2] on Sunday, April 2, 1865, to Jefferson Davis, in response to a letter the president had sent him the previous day. It is not a telegram, as claimed by Swanson in *Bloody Crimes* (2010).[3]

It begins: *Hd. Qrs Petersburg. 3 p.m. 2nd. April 1865. Mr. President, Your letter of the 1st is just received.* The part of the letter relevant to this book reads: *I do not see how I can possibly help withdrawing from the city to the north side of the Appomattox to night. There is no bridge over the Appomx. above this point nearer than Goode's & Bevil's over which the troops above could cross to the north side & be made available to us—Otherwise I might hold this position for a day or two longer, but would have to evacuate it eventually & I think it better for us to abandon the whole line on James River tonight if practicable—I have sent preparatory orders to all the officers & will be able to tell by night whether or not we can remain here another day; but I think every hour now adds to our difficulties—I regret to be obliged to write such a hurried letter to Your Excy, but I am in the presence of the enemy, endeavoring to resist his advance—I am most respy & truly yours [signed] R.E. Lee, Genl.*

One will notice that there is no allusion to Davis's telegram to Lee, the one complaining about the loss of valuables; therefore that telegram must surely have been received by Lee after he wrote this 3:00 p.m. letter and before he sent his 3:30 p.m. telegram to Davis.

It is probable that Jefferson Davis never received this Lee letter. In his *Rise and Fall* (1881), there is this: *Had General Lee's letter to me, written on the afternoon of the 2d, been received at Richmond, which I think it was not, the fact that he proposed to march to Amelia Court-House would have been known.* It is also worth noting that in the Lee letter sent at 3:00 p.m. there is no mention of Amelia Court House. Davis must be referring to the 7:00 p.m. telegrams.

Lee's telegram to Davis, sent at 3:30 p.m. in reply to Davis's telegram, says: *Petersburg, April 2d. 3.30 p.m. His Excly Jeffn Davis. Your telegram recd. I think it will be necessary to move*[4] *tonight. I shall Camp the troops here north of the Appomattox the Enemy is so strong that they will cross above us to Close us in between the James & Appomattox Rivers—if we remain.* This telegram would have been received at the War Department at about 3:50 p.m. provided there were no delays.[5]

Of this reply to Davis, Douglas Southall Freeman, in *R.E. Lee* (1934), says that the angry general *replied calmly that it was "absolutely necessary" to abandon the position that night.* Unfortunately Freeman has the wrong telegram. He is citing the one received in Richmond at 7 o'clock that night.

Shelby Foote, relying on Freeman, says, in his *The Civil War* (1974), that Lee *dictated a reply that left no doubt whatever about his intentions*, and then, just like Freeman, he quotes the wrong telegram.

Next was Lee's telegram to Breckinridge, received in Richmond at 4:55 p.m. *Head-*

---

2. The *Official Records* does not include this letter, but *The Papers of Jefferson Davis* does. I have used their wording, spelling and punctuation.

3. Swanson reproduces this letter in *Bloody Crimes* (2010), but his spelling is very different to that in *The Papers of Jefferson Davis*.

4. Some sources have the word "retire" here.

5. This telegram is not in the *Official Records*, but it is in the *Papers of Jefferson Davis*. The manuscript is in the Robert Edward Lee papers, at Duke University.

quarters, April 2, 1865. (Received 4.55 o'clock). General J.C. Breckinridge, Secretary of War, Richmond. I think the Danville road will be safe until to-morrow. R.E. Lee.[6]

H.E. Tremain, in *Last Hours of Sheridan's Cavalry* (1904), says that this telegram was *obviously in response to inquiry*. As Clint Johnson puts it, in *Pursuit* (2008), *Lee knew that Davis and the others would be using the railroad line as an escape route as Breckinridge had asked him in one telegram how much longer the Danville Railroad would be open. "I think the Danville Road will be safe until tomorrow," was Lee's terse if indefinite reply in his only known telegram that seemed to do with the pending evacuation of the cabinet. In reality, Lee had no idea if the Danville Railroad was safe.*

If the telegram was, indeed, in response to an inquiry from Richmond, we do not have that inquiry. As H.E. Tremain said in 1904, it is just a guess that there was such an inquiry. And Clint Johnson's almost accusatory line, *"In reality, Lee had no idea if the Danville railroad was safe,"* is, of course, absolutely in accord with what Lee wrote, *"I think the Danville road will be safe until to-morrow."* One suspects that Lee, if he could, would answer Johnson with *"That's what I said, didn't I?"*

Finally came two telegrams received in Richmond at or around 7:00 p.m. One was to Davis: *Petersburg, April 2, 1865. His Excellency, President Davis, Richmond, Va.: I think it absolutely necessary that we should abandon our position to-night. I have given all the necessary orders on the subject to the troops, and the operation, though difficult, I hope will be performed successfully. I have directed General Stevens to send an officer to Your Excellency to explain the routes to you by which the troops will be moved to Amelia Court-House, and furnish you with a guide and any assistance that you my require for yourself. R.E. Lee.*

The *OR*, whose wording this is, does not give the time of day that this telegram was received. The *Papers of Jefferson Davis*, on the other hand, say it was received at 7:00 p.m., but they have confused this telegram with the similarly worded one from Lee to Breckinridge, which was received at the War Department at 7:00 p.m. However, as the two telegrams are so similar, it seems likely that they were both written and sent at about the same time, and therefore probably both received in Richmond at 7:00 p.m.

Douglas Southall Freeman, in his *R.E. Lee* (1934), analyzes the wording in Lee's telegram to President Davis: *Lee thought at the time that the President would go with the army and he made arrangement to acquaint him with the route and to supply him with a guide.* However, given the 4:55 telegram (see above) about the Danville railroad being open until tomorrow, Freeman's comments are not convincing.

The other telegram was to Breckinridge: *Petersburg, April 2, 1865. General J.C. Breckinridge. It is absolutely necessary that we should abandon our position to-night, or run the risk of being cut off in the morning. I have given all the orders to officers on both sides of the river, and have taken every precaution that I can to make the movement successful. It will be a difficult operation, but I hope not impracticable. Please give all orders that you find necessary in and about Richmond. The troops will all be directed to Amelia Court-House. R.E. Lee.* The *OR* says this was received at 7:00 p.m.

James Swanson, in *Bloody Crimes* (2010), gives a well-reasoned explanation as to why

---

6. This from the *Official Records*.

5. The P.M. Dispatches

Lee sent these two very similar telegrams: *So there could be no doubt of the imminent peril, Lee dispatched a similar telegram to Secretary of War Breckinridge. If Davis could not appreciate the danger, then perhaps Breckinridge, a major general in the Confederate Army, would.*

Swanson quotes both of these telegrams, and then adds this: *At 7:00 p.m. Lee sent a final telegram to Davis and Breckinridge, letting them know he had given the order and was sending the president a rider to inform him of the safest routes west to link up with the Army of Northern Virginia.* It looks as if this passage is from an earlier draft made by Swanson, and should never have been left in.

Chapter 6

THE MAD RUSH

And so his ex–Excellency, the late President of the late Confederacy went forth from the sanctuary where prophesied the favorite high priest of his realm to pack up his "portable property" in hasty preparation for a journey on the Sabbath day. Like a thief in the night he stole away with trepidation and fear, and with an agonizing sense of the shortness of time.[1]

According to John W. Bell, in *Memoirs of Governor William Smith* (1891), Extra Billy was at St. Paul's that morning, and at the conclusion of the services he proceeded to the executive mansion. When he arrived he received a message from the president requesting his personal attendance at the president's house without delay. On his arrival the president handed him the dispatch he had received in church. It was from General Lee, expressing the fear that he would not be able to hold his lines of defense around the city, and that he (the president) should be ready to move at a moment's notice. *About this time, the President had ordered a train to be in readiness to move, and invited the Governor to take a seat in his car. To this information the Governor returned thanks, but said that he was the Governor of Virginia, and must share her fate, and that all his arrangements would have an eye to the protraction of the war, if practicable.* Bell then says that the governor then determined to transfer the Virginia state government to Lynchburg, and ordered all arrangements necessary to that end. The officials and public records, and the officers and students of the Virginia Military Institute were to proceed up the canal (James River and Kanawha), and he and aide Lieutenant Colonel Smith, and servant, were prepared to go through the country, on horseback. The Governor, having seen his boats off, left at the foot of the canal at 1 o'clock that night, taking the towpath for Lynchburg. From Lynchburg, Extra Billy went on to Danville.

After leaving St. Paul's Church, Davis went to the War Department where he read the telegram which had been received there at 10:40 a.m. He then called a summary cabinet meeting. Those seem to be the facts of the matter; it is certainly the way Roy Z. Chamlee interpreted it in his 1990 book, *Lincoln's Assassins: Upon receiving news of Lee's unexpected withdrawal from Petersburg and the subsequent precarious situation around Richmond, he hastily called a cabinet meeting. He informed members that the city would have to be evacuated. Davis ordered the removal of Confederate archives and the destruction of everything that could not be carried.* And this: *Davis told government leaders to meet him at the station at 8:00 p.m.*

---

1. *New York Daily Tribune*, April 8, 1865.

6. The Mad Rush

As Mallory says, and he was one of the cabinet: *In few words, calmly, solemnly, the President expressed to his Cabinet & other high officials gathered around him at his office, his views of the situation & of the measures which it demanded; & each at once entered upon his allotted duty.*

Clayton Charles Marlow, in his 1996 book, *Matt W. Ransom*, which represents itself as being non-fiction, explains how Lee, out of revenge, ordered Davis to be out of Richmond by eight o'clock that night (see Chapter 5). Marlow then comes to the final cabinet meeting in Richmond at about noon that day: *In compliance with these instructions, cabinet members were ordered to join President Davis at the train depot around 10:00 that night.*

One has to assume that Davis, by deliberately being two hours late, was, in turn, exacting his own revenge upon Lee. Fictionalizing the truth can often lead to logistical difficulties.

Not all the cabinet members made that ad hoc noon meeting. In a letter he wrote to Major W.T. Walthall on September 4, 1877,[2] former Attorney General George Davis says: *I was not present at the Cabinet meeting on the first Sunday in April, 1865, when the telegram was received from General Lee announcing that his lines had been broken at Petersburg. I had that day attended service at a church to which I was not in the habit of going, and, in consequence, did not receive the message until about 1 o'clock, p.m. I went immediately to Mr. Davis' office, and found him alone, and calm and composed as usual. He informed me of the orders that had been given and the dispositions made for the evacuation of Richmond. After some conversation I left to make my own preparations for departure.*[3]

It is quite clear from this that the cabinet meeting was over by 1:00 p.m.

Carleton Coffin, in his article for the *Boston Journal* of April 1865, wrote this: *The hour of twelve came. The people as they passed the capitol on their way home from church saw men hurriedly bringing out the State papers and piling them upon the ground and setting them on fire. It was the first intimation they had that the city was to be evacuated.*

However, Coffin's timing is out. At noon that day the cabinet were being assembled for an impromptu meeting. The evacuation had not yet been ordered. It was just before one o'clock in the afternoon when the cabinet meeting broke up. C.E.L. Stuart's account, in the *New York Herald* of July 4, 1865, is much more accurate: *By two o'clock all was known, or what, in result, was all—the evacuation of the rebel capital decided on. Beyond this little was certain. Rumor had her countless tongues at work, and victory was as much*

---

2. The William T. Walthall papers are to be found in the Department of Archives and History, at Jackson, Mississippi.

3. On July 7, 1877, General James Wilson's scurrilous article "The Capture of Jefferson Davis" was published in the *Times*, a Philadelphia weekly issued every Saturday. Major William T. Walthall, former assistant adjutant general of the Confederate Army, immediately set about writing a riposte, "The True Story of the Capture of Jefferson Davis," which would be augmented by letters of testimony solicited by Walthall from various luminaries. He wrote to Preston Johnston on or around July 9 (Johnston replied on July 14, from Lexington, Virginia); to Frank Lubbock on July 28 (Lubbock replied on August 2, from Galveston, Texas); to Admiral Semmes, who replied on August 13, from Mobile, Alabama; and to Attorney General George Davis, on August 14 (the former attorney general replied on September 4, from Wilmington, N.C., after Walthall had finished his article). By mid–August Walthall's article was ready for publication, and he sent it to the Philadelphia newspaper, who agreed to publish it. A few months went by, nothing happened, and a discouraged Walthall took the article back. In March 1878, he sent a copy of the article to General Basil Duke for his comments, and later that month it was finally published in the *Southern Historical Society Papers*, Vol. 5, March 1878.

believed in as defeat. It was only a strategic move, only wise to give Lee full scope and not embarrass him with the defence of such a place, better far that the deed so dreaded when it was more distant, had been consummated two years ago. Nevertheless, for all that flagging hope could urge, the city was quickly an unbroken scene of dismay and confusion.

Alfred Paul was the French consul in Richmond at the time of the evacuation.[4] On April 11, 1865, he wrote a report to French Foreign Minister Drouyn de Lhuys, which first appeared in the *Virginia Magazine of History and Biography*, Volume 73, Number 2, April 1965, as an article titled "A French View of the Fall of Richmond," by Warren F. Spencer.[5] Paul writes that, although long foreseen, the evacuation took place sooner than expected. *Mr. Jefferson Davis was in church when this devastating news was communicated to him. He says that the news spread rapidly throughout the city. Within a few hours the greatest confusion reigned in the streets, within the ministries, and in public establishments.*

Consul Paul says that at about two o'clock in the afternoon, Mr. Benjamin sent for him. So he went to Benjamin's office and found the secretary of state very agitated. Benjamin and the president and his other colleagues were planning to leave town at 5 o'clock that evening, with the exception of Breckinridge, who was going to depart the following morning at 2 o'clock, on horseback. Paul has Benjamin saying, *We are going to Danville. I hope that the railroad will not have been captured at Burkesville Junction and that we will be able to pass through.* Benjamin hoped they would all be able to return in a few weeks. The consul expressed surprise, watching Benjamin *to try to discern if he was motivated by a persisting illusion or by a lack of sincerity, two things which characterize this statesman.* Paul then set about putting his own affairs in order. *The city was in an indescribable state of consternation.*

This from Phoebe Yates Pember, in her 1866 article: *The officers of the different Departments hurried to their offices, speedily packing up everything connected with the Government. The quartermaster's and commissary's stores were thrown open and thousands of the half-clad and half-starved people of Richmond rushed to the scene. Delicate women tottered under the weight of hams, bags of flour and coffee.* And this, from her 1879 book, *A Southern Woman's Story*: *The officials of the various departments hurried to their offices, speedily packing up everything connected with the government. The quartermaster's and commissary's stores were thrown open and thousands of the half-starved and half-clad people of Richmond rushed to the scene. Delicate women tottered under the weight of hams, bags of coffee, flour and sugar.*

Mallory has this: *The disastrous news & warnings of Lee, first whispered to officials only, soon reached the ears of the people, who saw, in the rapid preparations of the several Departments, the immediate withdrawal of the Government from Richmond.* And this:

---

4. During the Civil War there were foreign consuls in several cities in the Confederacy. They came, for example, from the UK, France, Spain, Switzerland, Mexico, Prussia, Russia, Austria, and various principalities. Surprisingly, there were very few in Richmond. For example, Edward William De Voss was consul there from Bremen. He left for Europe in February 1863, and was replaced by Frederick William Haewirickel as acting consul. George Moore was British consul, 1860–63, with Frederick John Cridland his vice consul from May 18, 1861, until November 9, 1862. When Moore was expelled by Judah Benjamin on June 5, 1863, Cridland became acting consul from May to June 1863. Due to the ever increasing anti–British feeling in the Confederacy, there was no further British consul at Richmond. The French had Alfred Paul.

5. Warren F. Spencer, the author of this article, cites the Archives de Ministre des Affaires étrangères, *États-Unis, Correspondence politique des consuls*, Vols. 11–23, and *Correspondence Commerciale*, Vols. 5–7, 14, 15, 21, 22.

6. The Mad Rush

Citizens, gathered here & there in groups, gazed sadly, silently, as if upon the closing scenes of some deplorable drama; &, in the boxes of Government records & papers on their way to the Depot, recognized evidences of the last day of the Confederacy.

C.E.L. Stuart, in his July 4, 1865, *New York Herald* article, writes: *Orders were issued, about two o'clock, to the principal military and civil officials to have all the government archives not yet removed, and which it was possible to remove, ready by seven o'clock; what could not be easily transported were to be destroyed. Orders were also given to these same personages to meet Mr. Davis at the Danville depot by eight o'clock.* And Anna Trenholm, in her account written in or around August 1865, says: *Sunday, 2nd April 1865 we received notice to have every thing ready to leave Richmond that evening.*

General Gorgas, in his diary entry of April 16, 1865, writes: *It was now impracticable to get the family & our effects ready by the time indicated, & Amelia concluded at once to remain & we began moving all our effects up to Marias house.* R.G.H. Kean, in his diary entry of June 1, 1865, has this: *At 6 p.m. got all the records to the Danville depot.* And Taylor Wood, in his diary entry of June 14, 1865, says: *Packed a few things at home, the papers in the office & at the President's House.*

William L. Broun, as quoted in the 1912 book by his son: *I was ordered to report to the war department, where I soon learned that General Lee had telegraphed that his line was broken and could not be repaired, and that the city must be evacuated at twelve o'clock that night. I was ordered to remove the stores of the arsenal as far as could be done to Lynchburg, and was informed that the president and chief officials would proceed to Danville, and the line be reestablished between Danville and Lynchburg. I immediately had the canal boats of the city taken possession of, and began to load them as rapidly as possible with machinery, tools, stores, and so on, to be carried to Lynchburg. As a large supply of prepared ammunition could not be taken, I had a large force employed in destroying it by throwing it into the river."*

After leaving St. Paul's Church, Congressman Bruce repaired to his lodgings on Second Street, not far from the residence of Dr. Morris, on Linden Row, on Franklin Street. *I packed my clothes and some books and papers in my trunk and a traveling-bag. The trunk I had placed in General Breckinridge's baggage wagon, and the traveling-bag I carried in my hand.* And this: *The hours I remained in Richmond on that melancholy Sunday, after leaving St. Paul's, were among the saddest of my life. I felt that our cause was then the Lost Cause.*

There was commotion everywhere, wrote Carleton Coffin in his *Boston Journal* article of April 1865, *among the officials, among the soldiers, among the citizens, and the women; trunks were packed in hot haste, carpet bags were stuffed in a moment.* And this: *Such hurry and confusion never were seen in Richmond before.*

That's definitely the picture Coffin was getting in the day or two after the event. Stuart, in his *New York Herald* article of July 4, 1865, confirms that picture: *From the issuing of these orders to the time of departure, the city assumed the character of a pandemonium. Out of every government building huge cases and boxes tumbled as if a fire were in the rear. These were hurried off in wagons, with jaded mules and horses mercilessly whipped by shouting negroes.* And this: *It was strange and suggestive to observe the hearty will of the "colored officials"—that is to say, the black messengers and servants of the several departments, and the teamsters. They worked with an energy and earnestness which were either the result of sympathy for the predicament of their employers, or an eagerness to be rid of them. Which? Many of them followed the fortunes of the fugitive government to Southern Virginia, as, I presume, the answer for them is easy, but for the others, I am in doubt.*

The wildest disorder, then. That is the image we get from pretty much every so-called first hand account that describes the events of that Sunday afternoon, as well from secondary sources—not that that means much necessarily. Just to cite one example—Jay Winik, in *April 1865: It was generally assumed that the Confederate government had made adequate plans for evacuation. But events that afternoon told a different story.* Winik goes on to say that an official evacuation announcement was finally made, around 4:00 p.m. and it was at that point that any remaining veneer of calm broke.

Mallory, on the other hand, says: *There was no confusion, no noise, no undue excitement; for this contingency had long been anticipated, and, to a large extent, provided for.* And this: *...hundreds were leaving the doomed city by every practicable means, some ... in carriages.* And this: *The African church had, at an early hour, poured its crowded congregation into the streets; & American citizens of African descent were shaking hands & exchanging congratulations upon all sides. Many of them walked the streets with eager faces, parted lips, & hurried strides, gazing anxiously away into the distance, as if to catch the first glimpse of their coming friends.* And this: *Prominent citizens enterchanged views as to the means of protecting the people against the license of the conquering soldiers on the morrow; but so great was the general gloom, arising from the overwhelming conviction that the Confederacy was lost, that all consideration of personal safety or peril failed to arouse attention.*

Mallory's account can only be described as contrary. In Chapter 15 we will get to know the secretary of the navy a little better, find out what drove him to be so contrary, often to the point of sacrificing common sense. With this understanding, it is sometimes necessary to eliminate Mallory from a discussion. There is simply no point in trying to reconcile Mallory's contrariness with the majority of the reports. To try to do so leads one into a trap which it is impossible to get out of, and farce ensues. Hence this from William C. Davis in his 2002 book, *Look Away!: The evacuation itself was a mixed affair, well organized and efficiently executed by Breckinridge and the other department heads ... but to the public it appeared a panicky shambles.* And this: *Looting and confusion were already under way, as rumors of everything, including the death of Lee, spread rapidly.* And this: *For some reason, the panic brought the prostitutes out for a last round of business.* So, the inevitable occurs. We, as the readers, are obliged to gather that the panic in the city described by Professor Davis in this last passage is not the same thing as the panicky shambles of the evacuation, or rather what the public thought was a panicky shambles. Evidently, this is a different panic. One involving prostitutes.

On the afternoon of Sunday, April 2, 1865, during the early stages of the evacuation of Richmond, James Grant dropped by the presidential mansion. Varina Davis, in her 1890 biography of her late husband, says: *Mrs James Grant lived in another fine old house next door to us.*

In his role as editor of *Jefferson Davis: Private Letters* (1966), the renowned Davis historian, Hudson Strode, tends to make cuts and changes to his subject's letters which render many of them incomprehensible. He also writes editorial notes which sometimes

6. The Mad Rush

Railroad yard ruins, Richmond, 1865.

simply do not tally with his sources. For example this, which does not reconcile with what Varina says: *Mr. Grant was a kind neighbor who lived across the street from the Davises*, unless a street intervened between the Davis household and their next door neighbor. But even if that were true, there are conventions in the English language that must be observed.

The episode of the carriage and the cow comes from the letter Jefferson Davis wrote to his wife while in Danville on April 5, 1865. This story has been repeated many times in history books, but only one account is genuine—and that is the original. Not only because Davis himself wrote it, but because it was written only a matter of a few days after the event, and therefore very fresh in his mind. *Mr. Grant was afraid to take the carriage to his house &c. &c. I sent it to the depot to be put on a flat. At the moment of starting it was said they could not take it in that train but would bring it on the next train.*[6] *It has not been heard from since—I sent a message to Mr. Grant that I had neglected to return the cow and wished him to send for her immediately.*

From this, Ishbel Ross, writing *First Lady of the South* in 1958, was able to deduce, perhaps rightly, the daily habits of the cow: *Mrs. James Grant, a close friend and next-door-neighbor, shared a cow with the presidential household, which meant that the Davis children had fresh milk.*

Burke Davis, in *To Appomattox* (1959), not only writes about a second home for James Grant, but has also unearthed the actual words spoken between him and the president:

---

6. This statement suggests that the presidential train was not, or was not expected to be, the last out of Richmond that night.

1201 East Clay Street, Richmond—Jefferson Davis's residence.

James Grant, a wealthy friend, came to help carry off the mansion's treasure to his farm outside the city. "Take Mrs. Davis' carriage with you," the President urged. Grant shook his head. "I don't believe I'd risk that, sir," he said. Davis saw that he feared to have the vehicle on his farm when the enemy arrived. "Well, then," Davis said, "take it to the depot. I'll carry it along." Mr. Grant left with the carriage and a wagonful of household goods. Only after he had gone did Davis notice that the cow had been left. He sent a Negro through the crowded streets with a message for Grant.

And this from James C. Clark's *Last Train South* (1984): *James Grant, a wealthy friend of Davis' stopped by to carry off some items to his farm in the country for safekeeping. "Take Mrs. Davis' carriage with you," Davis urged him, but Grant only shook his head and said, "I don't believe I'd risk that, sir." "Well, then take it to the depot. I'll carry it along," Davis said.* Wisely, Clark refrains from taking on the cow story.

The Hoehlings wrote, in their 1981 book, *The Day Richmond Died*: *He offered his carriage to a country friend, James Grant. When the latter said he was "afraid" for it to be seen on his farm, the President ordered it driven to the depot and "put on a flat."*

When it comes to fixing the location of the Grant house, Burke Davis's book, *The Long Surrender* (1985), trusts to Hudson Strode rather than Varina Davis: *James Grant crossed the street from his house to help carry valuables from the mansion to his farm but declined to take Varina's carriage. "I don't believe I'd risk that, sir," he said. Davis realized that Grant was afraid of retaliation by Federal troops should they discover the carriage on his place. "Well, then," Davis told Grant, "take it to the depot. I'll carry it along with me." As the carriage and the president's light baggage left for the station, Davis remembered the cow and sent a servant after Grant with a message, asking him to send for her.* And, to let us know what happened to the carriage, Burke Davis has this: *The carriage was, indeed, taken to the depot, but there was no room for it on the trains. It was run up against the wall to be burned, but was rescued, albeit in a slightly damaged condition.*

The central character of William J. Cooper's book *Jefferson Davis, American* (2000), *was always accompanied by a cigar. Despite repeated bouts with bronchial troubles, he never gave up cigars. He smoked them constantly and routinely offered them to visitors.*

No one in Richmond, or for that matter in the South, outside of his own family, saw more of President Davis in those days of early 1865 than William W. Davies.[7] He, when about nineteen years of age, had entered the president's service as confidential messenger, and had been with him from the time the Confederate government relocated from Montgomery, Ala. in 1861[8]: *On the Sunday night of the evacuation of Richmond, I was at the President's mansion, assisting in packing up to go South.... When his carriage drove up to the door to carry him to the depot Mr. Davis lighted a cigar, took a seat in the conveyance and was driven to the Danville depot, where he took the train for the South.*[9]

This passage has, of course, been reproduced by historians. Four examples: William C. Davis, in *The Man and His Hour* (1991): *In a few minutes, a carriage arrived to take him to the station. He stepped outside, lit a cigar, and left.* Felicity Allen, citing pages 42–43 of *The Life and Reminiscences of Jefferson Davis*, writes in her own book, *Jefferson Davis: Unconquerable Heart* (1999): *With the president were his courier William Davies [who remembers his lighting up a cigar]...."* William J. Cooper in *Jefferson Davis, American* (2000): *When the carriage arrived to take him to the Richmond and Danville Depot, he lit a cigar and got in.* And Jay Winik, in his 2001 book, *April 1865: Around seven ... Davis climbed into a carriage and headed for the railroad station, a freshly lit cigar clenched between his teeth.*

Various passages from Carleton Coffin's pioneering *Boston Journal* article of April 1865 say that *There was a stampede for the Danville depot,* and that *[C]arriages were driven furiously to the depot.*

Letter from Jeff to Varina, April 5, 1865: *Called off on horseback to the depot, I left the servants to go down with the boxes and they left Tippy—Watson came willingly, Spencer against my will, Robert, Alf, V.B. & Ives got drunk. David Bradford went back from the depot to bring out the spoons and forks which I was told had been left—and to come out with Genl Breckinridge; since then I have not heard from either of them.*

C.E.L. Stuart, in his *New York Herald* article of July 4, 1865, is much more detailed: *Coaches were in waiting at one in every ten houses—coaches which in most cases took their fair fares to the trains to be disappointed, for not one-fifth of those who started to leave*

---

7. William Woodburn Davies was born in 1843, the son of Liverpool-born John Woodburn Davies, a stone mason in Richmond who, ruined by the war, later opened one of the first photographic studios in Richmond. W.W. Davies died in Richmond in December 1903. In the U.K., this name is pronounced "Davis."
8. *Life and Reminiscences of Jefferson Davis* (Baltimore, MD: R.H. Woodward, 1890), p. 41.
9. William W. Davies quoted in *Life and Reminiscences of Jefferson Davis*, p. 42.

were enabled to go. Only a few of the privileged beside the officials were thus favored. And this: *Toward the time of departure, every street poured out its contribution of voluntary exiles—private citizens hurrying to and fro, followed by negroes carrying portmanteaus, boxes, valises, carpet bags and all other sorts of travelling gear.*

This from Phoebe Yates Pember's 1866 article: *All the cars that could be collected were at the Fredericksburg depot, and by three o'clock the trains commenced to move. The scene at the station was one of indescribable confusion.* And this from her 1879 book, *A Southern Woman's Story*: *All the cars that could be collected were at the Fredericksburg depot, and by 3 o'clock p.m. the trains commenced to move. The scene at the station was of indescribable confusion.*

Mallory has this: *The Danville depot was filled by an eager crowd seeking transportation on the train.* And this: *The order had been given to admit no one whose services were not indispensable to the operations of the government which it was hoped might be re-established "somewhere south."* And this: *...generally the heads of bureaus and their chief clerks or assistants.* And this: *The ingenious efforts of many to obtain [passage], & their shifts and devices to circumvent Col. Carrington & Maj. Richardson, who had it in charge, occasioned no little amusement to the insiders.* And this: *...some "Artful Dodgers" contrived to "ring in" upon the ground of their vast importance to some great public interest; claims which, when unsupported by the name of some head of a Department, were never received without opposition & argument highly entertaining to all but the claimants themselves.*

Chamlee, *Lincoln's Assassins*, 1990: *Rebel leaders had trouble pushing through the confused crowds to the train. Near-hysteria gripped the excited multitudes, who were held back by soldiers as Davis and his Cabinet, along with a few select supporters, scrambled aboard.*

This is what Congressman Bruce says about his own berth in his "Reminiscences" of 1881: *About nightfall, I took my seat in a car of the train at the Danville depot preparing to start southward with its sad and disappointed human freight. The President and his Cabinet were on the same train.*

Congressman Bruce was undeniably on the presidential train, and no one should know better his experiences in boarding the train at Richmond than—well—Bruce himself, not even F. Lawrence McFall, the Danville historian, who goes in for bit of harmless (and pointless) invention in his 2001 book, *Danville in the Civil War*: *Congressman Horatio Bruce of Kentucky hurried to take his seat on the presidential train about nightfall. He and his fellow passengers waited in silence for the president to come aboard.* Ten years later, McFall, when he came to write the article, "To Danville," was no less inventive as he reworked his earlier effort: *About nightfall, Horatio Washington Bruce, a Kentucky congressman, rushed to get aboard the presidential car, but then found himself and his fellow passengers sitting in silence for several hours as they endured the delayed departure.*

McFall's 2011 image of Bruce rushing to get aboard the president's car—it is now the president's car, notice, not merely the same train—is very graphic, and quite different from Bruce's own narrative, even though it is obvious, from the opening words, that this time McFall had Bruce in front of him as he wrote. McFall cites three sources for his passage about Bruce: Bruce's own reminiscences; page 148 of Royce Gordon Shingleton's biography of John Taylor Wood (*John Taylor Wood: Sea Ghost of the Confederacy*); and page 14 of James Clark's book *Last Train South*. We have seen what Congressman Bruce has to say. Clark and Shingleton do not mention Bruce in their books.

Continuing with Bruce's narrative: *By this time I had become much exhausted by the*

6. The Mad Rush

fatigues of preparation. And this: *My fellow-passengers, both male and female, in the crowded car.* And this: *I never knew so little conversation indulged by so large a number of acquaintances together, for we were nearly all acquainted with each other. Very few words were interchanged.*

McFall, in an attempt to quote Bruce, writes this in his *Danville in the Civil War* (2001): *Later Bruce recalled: "I never knew so little conversation indulged in by so large a number of acquaintances. Very few words were interchanged."*

Historians must write entertaining creative non-fiction, otherwise they will not find a publisher in the trade-book market. William C. Davis wrote this, in *An Honorable Defeat* (2001): *Congressman Horatio Bruce found himself stuffed into a car with a host of people who looked almost dazed with exhaustion and depression,* and added that *almost all of the fellow government minor officials and employees on the car knew everyone else.*

The last word from Bruce, before he dropped off at the critical moment and rendered himself useless as a witness: *Sleep soon overcame most of us. This, I well remember, was my case, for I dropped to sleep before the train started from Richmond and was not aware of its departure when it left. I slept quite soundly nearly all the night through. I believe we did not leave Richmond until pretty late in the night.*

Robert Lumpkin, a Virginian, a notorious slave dealer in Richmond, was born in 1806. With his brother, Thurston, he had been in the slave-trading business all his life, as slave catcher, slave owner, and slave jailer, and fathered seven children by his slave Mary. Lumpkin died in Richmond in October 1866, and his descendants are alive today.

Carleton Coffin, the famous correspondent, was in on the ground at Richmond from April 3, 1865. Reporting on what he saw and heard, including tales of the previous day and night, he sent article after article to his employers, the *Boston Journal*, in April 1865. In 1866 his book *Four Years of Fighting* was published, and in it we find an account that was not in any of his 1865 newspaper articles, which, for Coffin, is rather odd: *Mr. Lumpkin, who for many years had kept a slave-trader's jail, had a work of necessity on this Lord's day—the temporal salvation of fifty men, women, and children! He made up his coffle in the jail-yard, within pistol-shot of Jeff. Davis's parlor window, and a stone's throw from the Monumental Church. The poor creatures were hurried to the Danville depot. This sad and weeping fifty, in handcuffs and chains, was the last slave coffle that shall tread the soil of America. When the coffle arrived at the depot, the sentinels guarding each entrance told Mr. Lumpkin that his niggers could not be taken. O, what a loss was there! It would have been fifty thousand dollars out of somebody's pocket in 1861, and millions now of Confederate promises to pay, which the hurrying multitude and that chained slave gang were treading underfoot.*

Charles Henry Corey, in *Richmond Theological Seminary* (1895), writes: *Mr. Lumpkin, the keeper of a slave trader's jail, made up a coffle of fifty men, women and children in his jail yard, "within pistol shot of Jeff. Davis's parlor window, and a stone's throw from the Monumental church," and hurried them to the Danville depot. "This sad and weeping fifty, in handcuffs and chains, was the last slave coffle that shall tread the soil of America."*[10] And this: *But there was no room for Mr. Lumpkin and his slaves.*

---

10. He is quoting Carleton Coffin's *Four Years of Fighting*.

This story of Lumpkin at the depot begins with Coffin so, whether he made it up or not, all we know of it comes from Coffin. To deviate from Coffin, unless it is with the intention of safely expanding upon a particular point, is to invent. Thus we find this, in Andrew Billingsley's 1999 book, *Mighty Like a River*: *Lumpkin arrived at the train depot with 50 of his prisoners chained together two by two, valued at $50,000, planning to board this last train and take his property south with him. Alas, there was not room enough on the train for him and his cargo. In a spirit of personal survival, Lumpkin cursed his bad luck and unchained his prisoners, and as they wandered aimlessly about the station, he boarded the train alone.*

We do not know that Lumpkin boarded any train, let alone the last train. This is Billingsley's fiction. Incidentally, Jack Trammell (see below) intimates that Lumpkin himself was refused a berth on the train. However, that refusal might only have applied to "Lumpkin with slaves." The "Lumpkin without slaves" may have boarded the train. But either way, Coffin does not address this issue. It is a modern day fabrication.

Another misinterpretation is the $50,000. Carleton Coffin is quite clear when he says that the value of the fifty slaves was $50,000, but that was Confederate money in 1861, and Confederate money had become so devalued by 1865 that it would have taken millions of such dollars to buy those slaves by that time. Coffin says this. The slaves, in 1865, were not valued at $50,000.

James W. Loewen's book, *Lies Across America* (1999), with the ironic sub-title *What American Historic Sites Get Wrong*, has this: *The Confederate decision to abandon Richmond on April 2, 1865, caught Lumpkin by surprise as he had not yet managed to sell his latest shipment of slaves.*[11] *During that confused evening, Lumpkin marched his coffle—some fifty people, chained together—to the train station, could not get passage on the last train out, marched them back to the jail, and locked them in for the night. It was to be their last night in bondage. The next morning the Union army set them free.* And this: *Robert Lumpkin's occupation—slave dealer—ceased to exist. We do not know how he spent that day, April 3, when his world turned upside down. But soon he realized that he loved Mary Ann, the black woman he had bought a decade earlier who had already borne him two children. Not long after the liberation of Richmond, he married her.* Loewen has Lumpkin dying in 1867.

Beth Brown, in her book, *Wicked Richmond* (2010), talks about the Richmond slave dealers: *...the most notorious of the lot ... was Robert Lumpkin. Lumpkin was described as a "shady businessman," as one would expect from a man who dealt in human slavery.* The author tells us that Lumpkin had failed at several different ventures before moving to the city and building his infamous "Negro jail"; then she describes Lumpkin, his life and family, and his business in considerable detail, and extensively covers Mary's life after the war. However, all she says of Lumpkin attempting to flee Richmond is, *Lumpkin fled Richmond before the city fell, and joined Mary and their daughters in Pennsylvania. Lumpkin fell ill and died not long after the war ended in 1865. In an odd twist of fortune, he left all his property, including that in Richmond, to Mary. Though she had assumed the role of his wife over twenty years earlier, Lumpkin listed her in his will as simply, "a woman with whom I reside."*[12]

Calvin Schermerhorn, in his book about slavery in the antebellum upper South,

---

11. Carleton Coffin, the originator of this story of Lumpkin at the depot, is not cited in either the notes or the bibliography of Loewen's book.
12. Robert Lumpkin's will is to be found in Richmond City Hustings Court Will Book, 24, pp. 410–422.

Money over Mastery (2011), writes: *Just after Richmond fell in April 1865,*[13] *he attempted to evacuate his slave property—some fifty men, women, and children, shackled together and weeping—but before he could reach the railroad depot, he was forced to free them.*[14] Schermerhorn says that Lumpkin died the following year, leaving all his real estate to Mary, that Mary did not stay in Virginia but later ran a restaurant in Louisiana with one of her daughters, and died in New Richmond, Ohio, in 1905, at seventy-two.

D. Laurence Rogers has this, in his 2011 book, *Apostles of Equality*: *Notorious slave dealer Robert Lumpkin was surprised by the Confederate decision to abandon Richmond, as he had not yet managed to sell his latest shipment of slaves.* And this: *Lumpkin had marched his valuable coffle (estimated to be worth $50,000) to the train station the previous night, when they were observed by the author Coffin.*[15] *However, Lumpkin was unable to get passage on the last train out, since it had been reserved for President Davis,*[16] *so he marched the slaves back through the streets of Richmond to the jail and locked them in for the night.* Rogers tells how they were set free the following morning. He then quotes James W. Loewen's 1999 book, *Lies Across America*, which he has actually been taking from all along.

Perhaps the most exhaustive investigation of Lumpkin is to be found in Jack Trammell's 2012 book, *Richmond Slave Trade*. Alphine W. Jefferson, professor of history and director of the Black Studies Program at Randolph-Macon College, in Ashland, Virginia, sets the scene in the foreword to Trammell's book when he says that while awaiting sale, the slaves had to be housed and prepared to garner the highest price and that the most famous of those places was Lumpkin's jail. Virginia's well-established slave mart located near Lumpkin's slave jail and around the Shockoe Slip and Shockoe Creek constituted a contiguous area that was called "the Wall Street of the Confederacy" because of its fast and furious economic trade in human property. *Blacks suffered tremendous brutality, cruelty, humiliation and suffering in Lumpkin's slave jail. Robert Lumpkin was known as "Bully." Some say he was given that nickname because he was cruel. Others say he tended to bully both blacks and whites alike if he were so inclined.* And this: *After the war, Mary Lumpkin, a former slave and legal wife of Robert Lumpkin,*[17] *gave part of her estate to create the educational institution that would become VUU* [Virginia Union University, a private black school in Richmond]. *That a man who was notorious for operating one of the most horrific slave pens in America could love and legally wed Mary, a black slave, is emblematic of the fluid nature...*

This, actually from Jack Trammell, on page 52: *Robert Lumpkin would later illustrate the end of an era as he desperately sought to escape a burning Richmond in 1865 with the last of his chattel property.*[18] *He led them in chains to the Richmond and Danville Railroad Station, where Confederate authorities refused to allow him or his slaves to board one of the last trains out of Richmond.*

---

13. Of course, it was while Richmond was falling, not "just after Richmond fell." Other writers have done this, as we have seen, and shall see again. It's not such a terrible error in itself; it just shows that the writers in question do not have a true command of the concept of the evacuation of Richmond.
14. It was at the depot that Lumpkin was forced to free his slaves, and not before.
15. Coffin, being a Yankee, did not arrive in Richmond until the following day.
16. This is pure invention by Rogers. The last train out did not carry Jefferson Davis. He was on a much earlier one.
17. According to Trammell's book, by 1854 Mary F. Lumpkin, a slave, was living with Lumpkin as his wife, and had five children by him. In 1854 she was 21 or 22.
18. Richmond, of course, was not yet burning.

Trammell rewords this passage on page 107 of his book, perhaps for emphasis, or perhaps because he forgot that he had already covered the subject on page 52[19]: *As for Lumpkin himself, he was desperate to preserve his human capital and save himself. He led a chained group of slaves to the depot for the Richmond and Danville Railroad, where Confederate soldiers refused to let any of them board one of the last trains. According to legend and perhaps in fact Lumpkin's slaves were freed, and were among the African Americans who greeted the Union occupiers and, shortly thereafter, President Abraham Lincoln himself.*

President Abraham Lincoln.

---

19. This book was published by, and presumably edited by, The History Press, of Charleston, S.C.

Chapter 7

THE LOCOMOTIVE

Until 1965 the locomotive that pulled the presidential train from Richmond to Danville a hundred years before was known merely as "the locomotive" or "the engine." For example, Morris Schaff, in his book, *Jefferson Davis* (1922), was only able to write: *The engine, like the Confederacy, had seen its best day, and its speed was slow.* He seems to have known quite a bit about the engine's condition and performance, but he did not know its name, otherwise he would have told us.

That all changed in 1965, when historians discovered that the locomotive had not only a name but a whole history. In short, after a complete century, the engine had finally been identified. Better still, there was a photograph. Lance Phillips's *Yonder Comes the Train*[1] was the first published book to use this black and white photo. The caption beneath the image says: *The little 4-4-0 that pulled President Davis's train out of Richmond on April 2, 1865.*[2] *Built by Rogers Locomotive & Machine Works, her cab panel carried the name Charles Seddon when delivered to the Confederate government in 1864.*[3] *A short time after this trip, the engine was purchased by the Richmond and Danville, and numbered 24 (later changed to No. 14). The picture was made at the roundhouse in Manchester,*[4] *after she had been converted from a wood burner to the use of coal (note pipe from sand dome in front of first pair of drivers, also elaborate scroll work on bellhanger).*

Lance Phillips's find was a major breakthrough in the discipline of Confederate train spotting. Page 6 of Brubaker's *Last Capital* (1979) is fully taken up with an excellent black and white print copy of the locomotive, with the caption: *The engine Charles Seddon pulled the presidential train from Richmond to Danville in April, 1865. After the war, the locomotive was rebuilt as Richmond and Danville Railroad engine number 24, later 14, and converted from wood to coal burner.* The picture and wording were courtesy of the Valentine Museum.

James C. Clark, in his book, *Last Train South* (1984), refers to the locomotive as the *Charles Seddon*, whereas Frank Carroll, in *Confederate Treasure* (1996), uses the spelling favored by Phillips and Brubaker. Clark is the only historian who has adopted the spelling "Sedden."

F. Lawrence McFall, in *Danville in the Civil War* (2001), reproduces the same photo Brubaker used—the only photo in existence, in fact—with the caption: *The engine Charles*

---

1. Quite a magnificent book on railroads, this is not a work about the Civil War.
2. The term "4-4-0" would not be coined for many years yet.
3. This is wrong.
4. This is also incorrect.

Seddon pulled President Davis's train from Richmond to Danville following the evacuation of the Confederate capital in April, 1865.[5] The photo credit is to Valentine Museum, and Danville Museum of Fine Arts and History. McFall simply took his wording from Brubaker's book and added a little from the descriptor provided on the back of the copy of the Valentine print lodged in the Danville Museum. William C. Davis, in *An Honorable Defeat* (2001), when discussing the moment the train arrived in Danville, says: *...the locomotive Charles Seddon brought the cars to a halt.*[6]

In Albert Lee Atwell's unpublished thesis, *Confederate States of America Lost Treasury Gold* (2002), which is used as a source by Danville Library, the photo of the locomotive is reproduced, using Brubaker's caption, and is credited to the Valentine Museum.

And finally, to round out the roster of historians who have named the engine as the "Charles Seddon," the authors of the 2007 book, *The Rebel and the Rose: The Charles Seddon, engine no. 14 on the Richmond and Danville Railroad, was known as an "American," which means it had a 4-4-0 wheel arrangement.* This book, incidentally, is the first to take notice of Lance Phillips's description "4-4-0."

Not all post–1965 historians have accepted the name *Charles Seddon*, yet some, while refraining from naming the locomotive, are still confident enough in their familiarity with it to describe it. For example, Burke Davis, in *The Long Surrender* (1985): *...an ancient engine.* And Clint Johnson, in *Pursuit* (2008): *...a second-rate engine.* Neither of these descriptions is even remotely true.

In 1993, Herman E. Melton wrote and published the book *Picks, Tracks, and Bateaux*, from which a piece called "An Antebellum Tragedy on the old R&D Railroad" was extracted for the *Pittsylvania Packet*. It concerns the explosion on the R&D locomotive *Pittsylvania* in 1859. Melton says that, at that time, the R&D had 19 steam locomotives, six that pulled passenger trains and 13 that hauled freight.[7] Admittedly, that was 1859, not April 1865, but he does say, later in his article, *The records of the most famous of the R & D locomotives, the Seddon, were not available to the writer.* And this: *According to the latter day publications of the Danville Register, it was this locomotive that pulled the train carrying Jefferson Davis to Danville when Richmond fell. It was named in honor of James E. Seddon, who was CSA Secretary of War.*[8]

These latter-day *Danville Registers*. One has to assume Melton is talking about either the April 1965 Centennial splash the paper did on the Civil War, or Brubaker's articles written in the 1970s, or possibly both.[9] As Brubaker explains, in his selected bibliography at the end of his book, *The Last Capital, Not listed here because of their numbers are scores of well-researched articles written by the staff of the Danville Register for that newspaper's day-by-day coverage of historical events during Danville's week-long Centennial celebration in April of 1865* [sic]. *Also ommitted* [sic] *are the author's historical articles, published in the Danville Register from 1970 to 1976, and concluding with an overview of*

---

5. Of course the train left Richmond for Danville during the evacuation, not following it.
6. Professor Davis does not cite a source for his use of the name Charles Seddon, and the name is not indexed in his book.
7. For this information he cites the 1858 Annual Report of the Board of Public Works.
8. The Confederate secretary of war at the time was James A. Seddon.
9. Probably the 1965 centennial articles, one of which—"War News"—reproduces the black and white photo of the locomotive with the name Charles Seddon beneath it. It may be that this article preceded the publication of Lance Phillips's book, *Yonder Comes the Train* (1965), which was the first book ever to reproduce the image of the locomotive.

7. The Locomotive 109

A damaged locomotive, 1865.

Danville's role in the war printed in the July 3, 1976, Bicentennial edition of the newspaper.

Melton does us the service of listing all the locomotives belonging to the R&D, named in order of date, yet, obviously, the *Seddon*, as he is forced to call it, does not appear on this list because, as we know, he could not get access to its records. However, if his story relates only to 1859, then the *Seddon*, which, as we shall soon find out, had not even been built yet, would be irrelevant.

But perhaps an even bigger wonder is why none of the historians who have written about the *Charles Seddon* have ever questioned the name. Surely they must have known that James A. Seddon was the Confederate secretary of war in 1864.

Was there a human being named Charles Seddon? In real life? Curiously, Secretary James A. Seddon had a son Charles, his youngest child, as a matter of fact. He died just after the Civil War, still a young boy. One cannot imagine why a locomotive would be named for him. If he had died during the war, perhaps, but afterwards?—highly unlikely.

Then there is Charles W. Seddon, something of a legend in the railroad boiler-making field. But he was early 20th century. There was no railway superintendent, no politician, with the name. It has so far proved impossible to find a suitable honoree named Charles Seddon. That's because it was not named for anybody called Charles Seddon—it was in fact, as Melton knew but could not prove, named the *James A. Seddon*, after the secretary of war.

In 1859, the Central Southern Railroad, of Tennessee, commissioned Rogers Locomotive & Machine Works, of Paterson, New Jersey, to build them a little five-foot-gauge freight engine. It so happened that the order was diverted, and the Edgefield & Kentucky Railroad took over the commission.

A builder would generally liaise with his client during construction, and, just before completion, would ask for the name of the locomotive. A.G. Green had been one of the founders of the E&K, and so it was his name Rogers affixed to the locomotive's panel as their finishing touch on October 13, 1859. The engine was then delivered to Nashville, to begin its vital but journeyman career pulling freight between the Tennessee capital and western Kentucky.

The most authoritative record we have today of old Rogers locomotives is that published in the fall of 1992 by the Railway & Locomotive Historical Society—Railroad History #167, "Rogers Locomotives: A Brief History and Construction List," compiled by Peter Moshein and Robert R. Rothfus. Rogers would assign a construction number (c.n.) to each of their locomotives, but, chronologically speaking, before c.n. 1245 there are none known to us today; the best we can do is a list of the locomotives, each one being assigned a line in the company record books, each line having a number, i.e., the line number, not the c.n. To put it another way, this line number is not the same as a c.n. To add to this problem, there are about 300 Rogers locomotives that do not even have a line number. They are merely on the list, uncoupled, so to speak. Moshein and Rothfus assigned line numbers they felt were appropriate. Line 883 has been assigned to the *A.G. Green*. However, as educated as that is, it is still a guess. Thomas Townsend Taber III's *Antebellum Railroad Compendium* (2008) attacks the subject of his title state by state, and then road by road. Many of the Rogers locomotives are here, including the *A.G. Green*, belonging to the Edgefield & Kentucky. Taber cites the Moshein & Rothfus line number for the *A.G. Green*, but with a question mark beside it. That was the right thing to do.

The *A.G. Green* was a standard eight-wheeler, a design which, as the authors of *The Rebel and the Rose* (2007) have already told us, would later come to be called "The American," and later still, the 4-4-0. In other words, it ran on four little leading wheels at the front, followed by four big driving wheels behind. Some other locomotive designs, such as the 4-4-2 or the 2-4-2, allowed for trailing wheels behind the drivers, for extra balance, but the American did not. Hence the classification 4-4-0. The drivers for freight engines usually had a diameter of 48" or 54", while passenger locos had 60", 62", 66", or 72". This does not mean to say that under certain circumstances—an emergency, for example—a string of passenger cars could not be hooked up to a 48"; they could, and often were. The *A.G. Green* had 48" diameter driving wheels, and 15" × 24" cylinders.

A new breed of fear had come to Richmond. Not the fear of dying, but the fear of living. By the summer of 1864, as General Grant began the systematic process of squeezing Richmond to death, and reducing the once proud capital of the Confederacy to a beleaguered fortress of starvation and despair, it was just a matter of time before he trapped the city in the bag, sealing it off from the rest of the country.

All eyes strained anxiously South, for both supplies and escape. The depot on Cary Street had become not just the subject of daily attention, but a symbol of hope, for out of this station issued the single-track, five-foot broad-gauge Richmond & Danville Railroad, the tenuous lifeline running the 140 miles southwest through the rolling Virginia countryside to the Dan River hard by the North Carolina line. There, at the little town of Danville, one could, with a bit of luck, pick up the recently built 4 foot 8½ inch standard-gauge Piedmont Railroad, and travel on to Greensboro, and from there to all points deeper South. To freedom.

The Confederate Railroad Bureau, headed by one of the assistant quartermasters general, Colonel Sims, was now working overtime to bring in as many locomotives as it could, by hook or by crook, from all over the Confederacy, to ply one or the other of these two lines. The *A.G. Green* was one of these.[10]

On June 20, 1864, out in Tennessee, the *A.G. Green* and its tender were repaired, at a cost of $5,000 Confederate money, and the following day, for the sum of $100,000 of said Confederate money, Colonel Sims purchased from the Edgefield & Kentucky both the engine and tender for "public service." On August 24, the Bureau paid the repair costs, and on November 14 settled the account for the actual purchase, paying with a voucher, rather, than, say, gold, which Colonel Sims did not have much of. The Confederate government changed the name of the engine to the *James A. Seddon*, after the Confederate secretary of war.[11]

Then nothing. There is absolutely no reference to the *James A. Seddon* after this date. It's as if the locomotive just upped and chugged into Jeff's never never land. But it did not do that, of course.

Huestis Pratt Cook was dying. There was a knock on the door of his Richmond home. Two men stood outside. Lawrence Kocher and Howard Dearstyne were Williamsburg authors, writing a book about old Virginny. They needed good 19th-century illustrations, and had been referred to Cook.

Way back in 1880, famous Civil War photographer (or photographist, as he, like many others of his profession at the time, called himself) George Smith Cook had relocated from Charleston to Richmond, and opened up a major studio. Aside from actual photography, a very important aspect of his business was collecting. Photographists would occasionally go bust, or be obliged to leave town—some in a hurry. Cook made it his business to acquire their collections—photos, negatives under glass, prints—until he had amassed an enviable and renowned super-collection of images. One of the negatives under glass thus collected, from an unknown Richmond photographer (possibly even Cook himself, although not likely), was of a beautiful 4-4-0 Rogers locomotive with 48" drivers, Richmond & Danville engine #14, shown with part of its tender, the shot taken from the foreground on the train's left side front, with a singular-looking building in the right background.

George S. Cook's son, Huestis, got into the business in 1891, and took it over when

---

10. Lieutenant Colonel Frederick William Sims. Black says, in *Railroads of the Confederacy* (1952), that Sims took part in the flight to Danville.
11. National Archives, RRB, 6/21/1864.

the old man died in 1902. Now, in 1951, Huestis P. Cook invited the two book writers into his house, and took them up to his attic. Mouths dropped open as the authors saw what lay spread out before them—10,000 photographic plates. They selected a bunch of these and put together an exhibition for the Virginia Museum of Fine Arts, calling it "Southern Exposures." That was in 1952. Huestis P. Cook was dead.[12]

Kocher and Dearstyne then wrote their book, *Shadows in Silver*, which showed 156 Cook photos. It was published in 1954. They did not use the shot of the old Number 14.

Over the years, visitors to the Valentine Richmond History Center had been dropping coins and things into the donation box as they passed through.[13] By 1954 these offerings had added up to a tidy sum. Long-time Valentine librarian and well-known preservationist Louise Fontaine Catterall, using this fund, successfully negotiated the purchase of the enormous trove of plates from Huestis Cook's widow, Mary Latimer Cook, at a cost of $4,000, and that year the Cook Collection became a major feature of the Valentine Museum. There was a modicum of Richmond press concerning the purchase, and local architectural historian Mary Wingfield Scott agreed to organize and catalogue the collection, at the same time soliciting help from Richmonders to identify as many of the pictures as possible. One of the negatives under glass was of the old No. 14.

Someone, probably Huestis P. Cook, had made a black and white print from this particular negative under glass. The Valentine labeled it *Vintage Print from Cook Studio*. On the back, in Cook's handwriting, it says, *Cook Photo Richmond*. For the sake of convenience, we may call this print "Valentine Image #1." On the back of this print, again in Huestis Cook's handwriting, is the following descriptor, headed *Rich'd & Danville Engine #14*. The text reads: *Carried Davis & party to Danville after evacuation of Rich'd 1865. The engine was built by Rodgers* [sic] *Loco. & Machine Works & delivered to Conf. Gov. 1864 & named Charles Seddon. After the war the engine was bought by R. & D. R.R., numbered 24, later renumbered 14. The picture shows the engine after it was rebuilt & renumbered, changed from wood burner to coal burner.*

You can tell it's a Rogers just by looking at it. But, unfortunately this particular print is somewhat dark, and therefore certain things cannot be made out, even when you blow the image up. For example, there is some wording on the nose of the locomotive, but you just cannot see it well enough. Likewise, there is some sort of plaque on the side of the engine, just behind the nose, and it has wording on it.

Meg Hughes of the Valentine made a special scan, from the original negative under glass, of this particular portion of the train, and the plaque is shown to be a rectangular patent plate with square sides, bolted onto the side of the locomotive. The first two words are illegible, but the rest says *Patent applied for Octr. 26th*,[14] followed by a year that begins with 18 (the pipes get in the way, so we cannot possibly see the actual year). Then comes *Granted Jany 1st*,[15] and then the year again, 18 something, but again the pipes get in the way. That's the patent plate.

There is no builder's plate in evidence on Valentine image #1, but there is a plaque

---

12. This story of Huestis Cook and the two writers is drawn from various sources, perhaps the best being VCU Libraries Digital Collections website article "Through the Lens of Time." http://dig.library.vcu.edu/cdm/landingpage/collection/cook.

13. One of the events luring tourists, in January 1940, had been a month-long exhibition of 100 of Huestis Cook's photos.

14. It's 20-something; cannot be sure it's 26, but it certainly looks like it.

15. It's definitely "Jany," and it looks like "1st"—could be "3rd," however.

on the side of the engineer's cab, and this plaque has wording on it. However, it is indecipherable. Finally, it's obvious that the lamp panel has a number on it, but the resolution will not allow you to get a grip on it.[16] Most important, though, is Huestis Cook's name for this train—the *Charles Seddon*.

By 1882 the Richmond & Danville Railroad was converting its wood burners to coal. The locomotive in the image is a coal burner; therefore the shot has to have been taken after that date.

Our locomotive quite clearly has a sheet-iron smoke-stack. By 1885 the R&D was replacing sheet-iron with the much heavier and—with their curved bases to allow draft—very distinctive cast-iron stacks as quickly as the old ones wore out. Therefore, if our little locomotive ever got the new stack, and there is no reason to suppose it did not, then it would have done so by, say, 1890 at the very latest, probably a lot earlier. Thus, surely we can nail down the date of the photo to between 1882 and 1890.

Tellingly, there is no extension front on the nose of the locomotive. You can immediately tell if a locomotive has an extended front or not, just as you can tell if a man has a long nose or a snub nose. By 1882, fifteen of the freight locomotives on the R&D had extension fronts, but our locomotive, which has a snub nose, obviously was not one of that group.

Then there is this, from the *St Louis Democrat* of mid–June 1884. *The Richmond & Danville Road is having all its engines provided with extension fronts.* The item goes on to inform us that this new improvement is an extension of the boiler front, making it project over the locomotive, that it sifts smoke before it leaves the engine, and that the interior of the extension catches and holds the cinders.

So, by 1884–85, or very closely thereabouts, the locomotives that had not been altered by 1882 now had extended fronts put on. This later group must have included our locomotive, if it was going to see future service. But if this spark-arresting improvement was ever made to this engine, it had not been done by the time this photo was taken. Given all this, then, it seems logical to deduce that the photo was taken between 1882 and 1885. And as the actual negative under glass shows the number 14 on the lamp panel, obviously by then it was already R&D freight engine No. 14.

Another black and white print was made from the negative under glass, "Valentine Image #2," and labeled *Vintage Print from Cook Studio*. The descriptor on the back is in unknown handwriting, but is most likely that of a member of the Valentine Museum staff. The text, again headed *Rich'd & Danville Engine #14*, reads, *Carried Jeff Davis & party to Danville after the evacuation of Richmond—1865. The engine was built by Rogers Loco. & Mach Works and afterwards delivered to the Confed. Gov in 1864 & named Charles Sedden [sic]. After the war this engine was bought by Rich'd & Dan. R.R. & numbered 24 then later renumbered #14. This picture shows the engine after it was rebuilt and renumbered. Presuming it was originally a wood burner engine, but in picture above it is a coal burner.* This print is even darker than the first one, and, again, no writing can be made out. On the other hand, the number 14 is clearly visible on the lamp panel.

Yet another black and white print was made, also probably by Huestis P. Cook, and also labeled *Vintage Print from Cook Studio*. This is "Valentine Image #3." No wording

---

16. The number 14 is quite clearly visible on the original negative under glass, from which several prints have been made. Therefore, if the number 14 is not visible on a particular print, that is the fault of the print, not of the negative under glass.

can be determined, and the number 14 is not visible on the lamp panel. The descriptor on the back is headed *Richmond-Danville Engine #14*. The handwritten text is by two persons, Huestis P. Cook and Louise Catterall. First, Catterall says, *Carried Jeff Davis and party to Danville after the evacuation of Richmond in 1865*. Then Cook writes: *Pulled train over Southern RR. taking Davis south—fall Richmond (Cook)*. Then we have Catterall again: *The engine was built by Rogers Loco. Machine Works and delivered to the Conf. Gov. in 1864 and named Chas Seddon. After the war the engine was bought by R & D RR, numbered 24, later renumbered 14. The picture shows the engine after it was rebuilt and renumbered, changed from wood burner to coal burner*. Then comes a typescript, made by an unknown person, probably a member of the Valentine staff. It seems to be a faithful typescript of the above quoted passage by Louise Catterall, but, in fact, it is not. There's a subtle difference between the two.

This typescript actually reads: *The engine was built by Rogers Locomotive Machine Works and delivered to the Confederate Government in 1864 and named the Charles Seddon. After the war the engine was bought by the R & D RR, numbered 24, later renumbered 14. The picture shows the engine after it was rebuilt and renumbered, changed from woodburner to coalburner*. The typescript ends with, *The Richmond & Danville Engine #14 carried Pres. Jefferson Davis and party to Danville after the evacuation of Richmond*.

Just a comment on Huestis Cook's wording. He writes that the locomotive pulled Jefferson Davis over the Southern Railroad. It did not. The R&D became part of the new Southern only in 1894, but at least we can date Huestis's comment between 1894 and 1951.

Valentine Image #4 is another dark one where no wording can be deciphered, and the number 14 is not visible on the lamp panel. *Print by Valentine Museum made from glass negative*. As may be remembered, the Museum holds the negative under glass, from which all prints have been made. This particular descriptor is headed *Richmond-Danville Engine #14*, and was written by Louise Catterall. *Carried Jeff Davis & party to Danville after the evacuation of Richmond. The engine was built by Rogers Loco. & Mach. Works and afterwards delivered to the Conf. Gov. in 1864 & named Charles Seddon. After the war this engine was bought by Rich'd & Dan. R.R., and numbered 24, then later renumbered #14. The picture shows the engine after it was rebuilt and renumbered. Presuming it was originally a wood burner engine, but the picture shows it to be a coal burner.*

After this comes the number 2535. Then the words "*film neg. Neg. Cabinet file—1971*." Then its says, "*Glass Neg*" followed by something in parentheses which is illegible. Then there is another page, headed 2535, but with no new image on it. It is headed: *Transportation Trains*. The text reads: *Fairly early steam engine No. 14, made by Rogers Locomotive Works, Paterson, N.J*. Then comes *CSP 1960*. Presumably CSP means Cook Studio Photograph, or possibly "print," and "1960" seems to indicate that the print was made in that year. That's a guess. All this wording (i.e., on the second page) is on the envelope storing the glass negative, but it is not known by the Valentine if the wording was transcribed from the original envelope or if it had been developed by Museum staff.

Finally, there is "Valentine Image #5," which is right out of left field. It is labeled *20th century print*, and, although the number 14 is just about visible on the lamp panel, none of the other wording is.

On the back it has *July 12, 1961*, stamped in red. Then, written, *4310*, and a note, *Please credit Valentine Museum, Richmond, Virginia*, stamped in blue. Then comes *6610 345*, which is actually 66.10.345, signifying the 345th item in the 10th donation of 1966.

Finally, a note written by the Valentine, saying *print donated by Richmond Newspapers, Inc.*

The actual text, typed, says, *Chesapeake and Ohio Railway's Locomotive, "Timberlake," built by Rogers Locomotive and Machine Works for the Virginia Central Railroad in August, 1855.* The Valentine added, in a note, ... *assume this was added by newspaper staff Richmond News Leader and Richmond Times-Dispatch.* This last image then, although of the same locomotive, is accompanied by text that says that the name was *Timberlake.*

Rogers, Ketchum and Grosvenor, of Paterson, New Jersey, changed their name in 1856, to Rogers Locomotive and Machine Works. Their emblem changed correspondingly. The *J.H. Timberlake* was built by Rogers, yes, in 1855, but not by Rogers Locomotive & Machine Works, rather by Rogers, Ketchum and Grosvenor. This, just this fact, rules out the name Timberlake. Besides, the *Timberlake* had 66" drivers. Our locomotive has 48" drivers.

Although the name Timberlake is a red herring, it was, nonetheless, on the back of a print received by Richmond Newspapers, Inc. in 1961, and donated by them to the Valentine in 1966. Where Richmond Newspapers, Inc. got that print from is anybody's guess, but that print had to have been made from the original negative under glass before the Cooks got their hands on the negative. Otherwise the name Timberlake would not be associated with it; they would have written Charles Seddon, just as Huestis P. Cook did.

The same goes for two other prints at Southern Methodist University (SMU). These prints were both made from the negative under glass held at the Valentine Museum in Richmond. Like Valentine Image #5, the descriptors on the back of these two prints are radically different from that written by Huestis Cook. Moreover, these two SMU prints are very different one from the other.

The first print, which we may call SMU Image #1, is a very good, untampered with, and reasonably clear digitized image of a 16.6 × 23.9 centimeter gelatin silver straight black and white photographic print taken from the original negative under glass, again the same negative under glass that now resides at the Valentine. In short, it is the same locomotive, with the same building in the background, taken at precisely the same time and from the same angle as all the others. In even shorter terms still, it is a print of the same photo. Where SMU Image #1 differs from any of the other prints is that it shows, in stark relief, the wording on the cab panel—"Richmond & Danville." And, short of the blow-up made by Meg Hughes, it also has the best resolution of the patent plate on the side of the engine. The attached SMU descriptor has this: *Locomotive for train on which Jefferson Davis fled from Richmond in April 1865.* The date given is *ca. 1860–1865.* One supposes that this is an SMU guess at the date the original photo was taken. The SMU descriptor continues: *Print, ca. 1921, from original glass negative. Verso [handwritten] "Jeff Davis engine Rogers."* The final part of the descriptor reads: *Virginia & Tennessee Railroad, Sheldon.*

A check with SMU determined that the original verso is handwritten: *Jeff Davis engine Rogers.* That is the sum total of the real, original descriptor. The rest is SMU's own descriptor. The handwritten verso is correct, in that it is a Rogers locomotive. One will notice that the handwritten verso does not name the locomotive. SMU added their details predicated on their other print.

SMU Image #2 is a digitization of a 24 × 28 centimeter photographic print. It's a photo that has been doctored, airbrushed, and stylized. The building in the background is gone, so that the train can stand alone. The number 14 has been whited-in very prominently on the headlight casing. They could not have got that from SMU Image #1, as the number 14 is not visible on that print, no matter how you try to resolve it. But remember, the number 14 is visible on the actual negative under glass, from which SMU Image #2, as well as all the other prints, have been taken. So, without question, the two photos held at SMU are different prints, very different, but of the same photo, and these two prints probably came from two different sources. Yet they both wound up at Southern Methodist University, which is odd. And they were both made before the Cooks got hold of the original negative under glass, otherwise they would carry Huestis Cook's descriptors.

This is the descriptor for SMU Image #2: *Locomotive for train on which Jefferson Davis fled from Richmond in 1865.* Then, in brackets, it says, *Norfolk & Western, Locomotive No. 14, "Sheldon."* For the date, presumably the estimated date of construction rather than, say, of the actual taking of the photo, SMU states 1858. Then, of the photo itself, it says it was from one of the Rogers Locomotive and Machine Works builders cards. *Copy print from original made ca. 1910.* Then, *Verso [handwritten] "Rogers Loc. & Mach. Co. No. 833, Dec. 1858. As Virginia & Tennessee Tehauntepec* [they mean *Tehuantepec*]*—to Norfolk & Western 14 "Sheldon" pulled the train on which Jefferson Davis fled from Richmond in April 1865.*

Upon studying SMU Image #2, one can see, with no great difficulty at all, the emblem on the nose of the train, where it says, around the rim of the emblem's circle, *Rogers Locomotive & M. Works*, and you can see, inside the circle, in its lower half, *Paterson, N.J.* Above Paterson there is what, at first glance, looks as if it could be some writing, a number perhaps, the builder's number even, and it could be 833. However, what it really is, is three large bolts to hold the emblem to the nose of the locomotive. It's not a number at all.

Again, the descriptor of SMU Image #2 seems so authoritative, this wording about the *Tehuantepec*, and 833, and the builder's card. How could anyone pull the name *Tehuantepec* out of the air, unless they knew what they were talking about? But remember the *Timberlake*. The descriptor says it was Rogers engine 833. It's curious that the line in the Rogers record books assigned by Moshein & Rothfus in the 1990s to the *A.G. Green* is 883, but that's all a red herring.

The *Tehuantepec* was indeed a Rogers locomotive, and it was built pretty much when the verso says it was built, and it did work for the Virginia & Tennessee throughout the war. But we have two immediate and insuperable problems with the *Tehuantepec*. One is that it was a huge 29-ton passenger engine, with 66" drivers, and the other is that its service record militates against its being the locomotive that pulled Jefferson Davis on April 2, 1865.[17]

And the name Sheldon. Where did that come from? One has to admit that the name Sheldon looks like Seddon. Beyond that lies wild conjecture. And Norfolk & Western Locomotive No. 14? That's right out of the blue. Beyond that lies madness.

So, the locomotive in the picture cannot be the *Tehuantepec* or the *Timberlake*. Which leaves the *Charles Seddon* and the *James A. Seddon*. Although we find independent, official, and absolutely confirmed records of the *James A. Seddon*, the name Charles

---

17. Dave Bright's website, *Confederate Railroads*, goes into how many passengers the Virginia & Tennessee locomotives carried in each year of the Civil War—July 1 of one year to June 30 of the next. It is very specific and very detailed. The *Tehuantepec* is one of the locos covered during its term with the Virginia & Tennessee. The figures for 1864–1865, when compared with those of other locos on that line, do not indicate any blip at all in the *Tehuantepec*'s work for that railroad.

7. *The Locomotive*   117

The locomotive, depicted in Valentine Image #1 (Cook collection, Valentine Richmond History Center).

Seddon is never, ever, mentioned, anywhere outside the vicious circle created by Huestis P. Cook.

Lance Phillips, in his book *Yonder Comes the Train*, says of the photograph of the No. 14 (the locomotive reputed to have pulled the train that carried Jefferson Davis from Richmond to Danville on April 2–3, 1865): *The picture was made at the roundhouse in Manchester, after she had been converted from a wood burner to the use of coal.* By Manchester, Phillips means the place he was born and raised in—Manchester, Virginia, now a part of Richmond. A search for the building behind the locomotive in the photograph reveals that it is not in Manchester at all, but in Shockoe Valley, just to the west of Richmond.

In the early hours of the morning of November 11, 1881, a fire destroyed much of the Metropolitan Iron Works, at the corner of Canal and 7th streets, in Richmond. William E. Tanner, the owner, and his partner Alex Delaney decided to rebuild, at a much bigger plant, in Shockoe Valley, on a 12-acre site they had acquired a few years earlier. By 1883 this new and very impressive plant was up and running. By late 1887, Tanner & Delaney had gone bust and had been taken over by the Richmond Locomotive & Machine Works, later called the Richmond Locomotive Works, which in turn was taken over by ALCO (American Locomotive Company) in 1901. There is a very good black and white photograph of the Richmond Locomotive & Machine Works on page 112 of Brian Burns's book, *Lewis Ginter: Richmond's Gilded Age Icon*, and a beautiful color reproduction on Wikipedia (under the entry Richmond Locomotive Works) of the building in 1911, at the time it was owned by ALCO. One can see that this is the building in front of which Jefferson Davis's locomotive was captured in a photograph.

Eighteen sixty-four was the year the R&D gave all their locomotives a number. The *A.G. Green* carried its new name, *James A. Seddon*, only a very short time—a few months at the very most—before it was allotted the number 24. It was as Confederate freight locomotive No. 24 that this grand little engine carried Jefferson Davis from Richmond to Danville. After the war, the R&D purchased the locomotive and renumbered it 14. If it truly was the engine that pulled Davis—and there is no valid reason to doubt that—that would make it one of the famous locomotives of history. Why, then, did it never, ever, get any press until 1965? And what became of the old No. 14 after its photo was taken in or around 1883 at Tanner & Delaney's engine company plant at Shockoe Valley?

Chapter 8

THE PRESIDENT'S CAR

A train consisted of a locomotive, also known as an engine, pulling X number of cars all joined together by couplings. Immediately behind the locomotive was the tender, which contained the wood that the fireman would continually sling into the furnace. This fed the engine. One occasionally sees references to passenger cars immediately behind the tender, but with the choking pine-smoke belching out as the train chugged along, not to mention the sparks, this would have been simply too dangerous and uncomfortable for passengers. It was the freight cars, in fact, that were closest to the engine—express cars, flat cars, boxcars, and horse cars. Finally came the passenger cars, or coaches as they were sometimes called.[1]

An instance, one of many, of the dangers of rail travel was reported in the *Richmond Dispatch* of September 10, 1863: *On Tuesday evening last, as the mail train on the Richmond & Danville Railroad was going up from Richmond when near News Ferry it was discovered that the express car had taken fire on the inside by sparks communicated from the engine. Every attempt to arrest the flames proved ineffectual, and the car, with its entire contents, was consumed.*

The expressive and succinct term "Cabinet Car" seems to have been coined by Confederate Secretary of the Navy Stephen R. Mallory. However, it does not, as is sometimes assumed, refer to the passenger car in which President Davis, most of his cabinet (including, of course, Mallory), and some other eminenti, traveled from Richmond to Danville the night of April 2 and the day of April 3, 1865. To use the term in such a way is wrong, simply because it has been reserved for the "dilapidated, leaky passenger car" in which the staff and cabinet, and other prominent gentlemen, took up their quarters while at Greensboro.[2] Different car, different train, different state. So, to use the term for the car that carried Davis from Richmond to Danville can only confuse. This William C. Davis does, in *An Honorable Defeat* (2001), when talking about the first leg of Davis's journey from Richmond: *More than thirty men crowded the seats in the cabinet car.*

This confusion is tripled in Carolyn Lawton Harrell's 1997 book, *When the Bells Tolled for Lincoln*: *In the cabinet car of his train, Jefferson Davis and the remnants of his fleeing Confederate government continued South from Richmond, through Danville, Greensboro, Lexington, Salisbury, Concord, and Charlotte, North Carolina.* The confusion is tripled because the Davis party started from Richmond, it did not continue on from there; and also because rail travel stopped at Greensboro, at least for the Davis party. From there

---

1. The caboose—the crew's car at the tail end of a train—had been invented by 1865, but was still relatively rare. It is highly unlikely that the Davis train had one.
2. Jefferson Davis was lodged at Taylor Wood's residence.

they were obliged to proceed south by other means. Any travel after Greensboro was not by train.

This is the original quote from Mallory: *The "Cabinet Car" was, however, during those dreary days at Greensboro, a very agreeable resort.* Elisabeth Cutting, in *Jefferson Davis* (1930), makes this rather enigmatic but nevertheless true statement: *This Cabinet Car became a part of all the history of the flight.*

A mere handful of historians simply report it the way it was: Rembert Patrick, in *Jefferson Davis and His Cabinet* (1944): *The other members of the cabinet and officials of the party lived in a railroad coach, the "cabinet car"*; Michael B. Ballard, in *A Long Shadow* (1986): *Occupants of the "cabinet car" remembered the days in Greensboro as uncomfortable.* William C. Davis, in *An Honorable Defeat* (2001), at least when he's discussing the right "Cabinet Car": *In fact, Mallory thought the "Cabinet car" proved to be what he called "a very agreeable resort."* And James Swanson, in *Bloody Crimes* (2010): *Upon their humble quarters, they bestowed the exalted nickname the "Cabinet Car."*

A.J. Hanna, writing *Flight into Oblivion*, in 1938, made the arbitrary decision that Mallory's "passenger car" should be a "boxcar": *...a dilapidated, leaky boxcar. They called it the "Cabinet Car."* Hanna being very influential, several later historians followed his lead, without checking the original Mallory, for example Meade in *Judah P. Benjamin* (1943): *...a leaky, dilapidated boxcar, which they dubbed the "cabinet car,"* and James C. Clark, in *Last Train South* (1984): *Most of their time was spent in a leaky boxcar they nicknamed the Cabinet Car.*

We also have Wright, in *Language of the Civil War* (2001), giving us his explanation of the term "Cabinet Car": *The ironic name given to a dilapidated boxcar used by the cabinet in Greensboro, North Carolina, as they retreated from Richmond at the war's end. They conducted their dwindling business in the leaky boxcar and also slept there, foraging for flour, eggs, and coffee.* And we have Hardy, in his book, *North Carolina in the Civil War* (2006): *Other members of the Cabinet were forced to stay on the train, spending much of their time in a leaky boxcar dubbed the "Cabinet Car."*

It is, of course, disturbing that all this should have happened. But some writers' misunderstandings, especially when perpetuated by other authors, verge on the amusing, if for no other reason than, What can you do but laugh? An example is what happened to Secretary Mallory's "very agreeable resort." In 1988 William Trotter's book, *Silk Flags and Cold Steel*, was published. In it he writes: *Mallory left a vivid and good-humored account of life inside the cabinet's "boxcar," as it was called by its residents.* Trotter wishes to impress upon his readers that he has read Mallory, but he obviously has not, otherwise he would have used the term "Cabinet Car," and he would have described it as a passenger car, as Mallory did, rather than as a box car, as Hanna and his derivatives have done. Moreover, for anyone to fail to grasp the general meaning of the railway term "box car" is simply unbelievable, so one might be forgiven for assuming that something went awry in the editing of Trotter's book.

But one has to wonder, after all, whether that assumption is valid or not. For reasons which are not known, Trotter has rejected the term "Cabinet Car." *Their car, in fact, became known as the "Cabinet Bar," and anyone who dropped in for a chat would have a demijohn opened in his honor.*[3] Doubtless the number of guests increased as the word got

---

3. The demijohn is from Shelby Foote, who invented it, so to speak. But Mr. Foote's demijohn was on the first leg of the flight, between Richmond and Danville—nothing to do with the Cabinet Car in Greensboro, and certainly not enough to warrant that car being called a bar.

around—good whiskey was hard to come by in those days, and the Confederate government still had a supply. And this: Secretary Mallory, whose writing style had a distinctly Dickensian turn now and then, put it this way: *"The 'Cabinet Bar' was, however, during those dreary days at Greensboro, a very agreeable resort."*

Unlike Hanna—who, as we have seen, was able to turn Mallory's passenger car into a boxcar at the stroke of a pen, and by sheer force of reputation to accrue a good number of adherents over the years—Trotter, by being so outrageous, and with no such reputation, has acquired no takers, unless one includes the book, *The Rebel and the Rose* (2007): *The "cabinet car," as Mallory referred to it, became a social center.*[4]

How many people were in the president's car as the train traveled between Richmond and Danville on April 2–3, 1865? In conjunction with this question, another, subtly different, must be asked: How many persons could the president's car accommodate?

Taking the first question first (How many people were in the president's car?), the first answer ever attempted was by Anna Trenholm, in her account of the flight written in or about August 1865: *I was the only Lady, there were about thirty Gentlemen, including the President.* This is the only time an actual number is ventured by a writer until 1991, when William C. Davis wrote, in *The Man and His Hour*: *...nearly thirty men crowded the seats, with only the wife of Treasury Secretary Trenholm to brighten the company.*

If there was a source to inspire "nearly thirty men," it is certainly not Anna Trenholm, who wrote "about thirty Gentlemen." Ten years later, when he came to write *An Honorable Defeat*, Professor Davis wrote this: *More than thirty men crowded the seats in the cabinet car.* If there was a source to inspire this revision, it has not come to light.

F. Lawrence McFall, in *Danville in the Civil War* (2001), shows no uncertainty at all about the figure: *With 31 passengers seated in the presidential car, the official train crept forward from the depot*; nor does Clint Johnson, in *Pursuit* (2008), even though he disagrees with McFall's figure: *...packed train car of twenty-nine men and one woman.*

Regardless of what the actual number was, it's hard to believe that it remained static. There were stops along the route to Danville, and men must have gotten out of one car with some frequency and into another, the president's car included. In fact, we have very strong reason to believe that both C.E.L. Stuart and Congressman Bruce did just that.[5]

When the present author wrote the Danville Historical Society asking if they could provide a list of known names in the president's car during the flight from Richmond to Danville, author F. Lawrence McFall replied on Nov. 18, 2011, *Of the nine trains transporting government workers, baggage, and records, no passenger manifest is known of which I am aware. The ninth train carried the sailors of the James River Squadron.* And this: *The third train to leave Richmond on Sunday, April 2, 1865, contained a passenger coach with 31 known people aboard, including the President.*

Ten days later, a follow-up email from the Genealogical Department of the Danville Public Library arrived: *Attached are copies of a list of people who were on the Davis train. The list is not complete.*

---

4. Having said all that about Mr. Trotter, it is quite possible that I have missed the point of his book.
5. See Clover Station, at Milepost 94, in the discussion of the R&D Route in Chapter 11.

President Jefferson Davis; Colonel John Taylor Wood—Davis's aide; Judah P. Benjamin—Secretary of State and Cabinet member; George A. Trenholm—Secretary of the Treasury and Cabinet member; Mrs. Trenholm—wife of George A. Trenholm and the only female on board; Stephen R. Mallory—Secretary of the Navy and Cabinet member; George Davis—Attorney General and Cabinet member; John H. Reagan—Confederate Postmaster General and Cabinet member; Samuel Cooper—Adjutant General; Francis R. Lubbock—former Texas Governor and now Davis aide; Micajah H. Clark—Chief Clerk of the Executive Office; L.E. Harvic [sic]—President of the railroad; Jules St. Martin; Dr. Garnett—Presidential physician; A.G. Cantley—Post Office Director; Senator Clement Clay—Senator from Alabama; Col. William Preston Johnston; John Hendren—Confederate Treasurer; Dr. Moses Hoge—Prominent Presbyterian minister, outspoken against the Union from the pulpit; Col. Robert G.H.K. [sic] Kean—Chief of the Bureau of War; General Daniel Ruggles—Commanding General of prisors [sic]; General Josiah Gorgas, Chief of the Ordnance Department; Captain Wood; S. Brittain; James Miller; W.R. Bringhurst; General Braxton Bragg—Military Adviser; John Ott; Davis's servant—Spencer; J.B. MacMurdo; Clay Stacker; Two unknowns—one possibly D.F. Kenner, and the other was Viztelly [sic], a war correspondent from England.

The library told me that they had prepared the list using three sources: Mr. McFall himself, the vertical files in Danville Public Library and "Mr. Brubaker's book."[6]

Danville historian J. Frank Carroll's book, *Confederate Treasure*, was published in 1996, a full fifteen years earlier. In it he proposes a list of names of those in the president's car on April 2–3, 1865. *In the Presidential car were thirty men and one woman. Various accounts hint that the following persons shared the same solemn space.* This is Carroll's list:

President Jefferson Davis; Col. John Taylor Wood; Judah P. Benjamin; George A. Trenholm; M.H. Clark; L.E. Harvie; Jules St. Martin; Dr. A.Y.P. Garnett; Senator Clement Clay; A.G. Cantley; James Miller; W.R. Bringhurst; General Braxton Bragg; John Ott; Spencer (Davis's servant); (Unknown Man); Col. Frank. R. Lubbock; Col. William Preston Johnston; Stephen R. Mallory; Anna H. Trenholm (only woman); John Hendren; Rev. Hoge; Samuel Cooper; Robert G. Kean; Captain Wood; S. Brittain; J.B. MacMurdo; Clay Stacker; John H. Reagan; George Davis; (Unknown Man) Possibly D.F. Kenner

How accurate are the lists of Frank Carroll and the Danville Public Library? Of the persons on these two lists, these are the ones who were definitely in the president's car: Jefferson Davis; Judah Benjamin; George A. Trenholm; Stephen R. Mallory; George Davis; John H. Reagan; Clement Clay[7]; Samuel Cooper[8]; Dr. Alexander Yelverton Peyton Garnett[9]; the Rev. Moses Hoge; Colonel Lewis Edwin Harvie[10]; Colonel Preston Johnston[11];

---

6. *The Last Capital*, a book written by former Danville journalist, John H. Brubaker III.

7. Clay was second-in-command of the Confederate Secret Service in Canada, and only hours before had arrived at Richmond. Even in those trouble-torn days, it was not often that you found a rat climbing aboard a sinking ship.

8. Cooper, born in New York in the 18th century, served in the Seminole Wars and the Mexican War, and in 1852 became adjutant general of the U.S. Army. In 1861 he went South, partly because his wife's family was from Virginia, and partly because of his friendship with Jefferson Davis. The highest ranking Confederate general during the Civil War, he was paroled at Charlotte on May 3, 1865, went into farming, and died in 1876.

9. Dr. Garnett (1819–1888) was a surgeon at Robertson Hospital, in Richmond, and was personal physician to General Lee. At President Davis's specific request, Garnett took a seat in the car that was going to carry them all to freedom. Throughout the night, the doctor would keep a close eye on his weary charge, despite the exhaustion he himself was suffering as a result of carrying around a surfeit of names. He was the brother-in-law of John S. Wise, who boarded the president's car at Clover to speak to him.

10. L.E. Harvie, of Amelia, Virginia, former classmate of E.A. Poe, had been president of *(continued)*

Frank Lubbock; John Taylor Wood; Micajah Clark; Jules St. Martin; Anna Trenholm. That's 17 out of 33. As for those who could not pass muster, they will be discussed shortly. First, a word of explanation is in order for some of the ones who did make the cut.

Micajah Henry Clark was 34 years old at the time of the evacuation of Richmond. He was chief and confidential clerk of the Executive Office in Richmond. Normally, President Davis's private secretary was young Burton Harrison, but Harrison was in Danville at that moment, escorting Mrs. Davis to Charlotte as she made her own getaway. Micajah Clark had been nominated to succeed Harrison for the duration. At the end of the Davis flight, in Georgia, Clark served as the last Confederate treasurer, serving under Secretary of the Treasury Reagan,[12] from May 4 to May 10, 1865.

Senator Clement Clay from Alabama.

Clark is the author of an article titled "Last Days of the Confederate Treasury and What Became of its Specie," published in the *Southern Historical Society Papers*, volume 9, November-December 1881, pp. 542–556. This article is headed, *Clarksville, Tenn., January 10th, 1882.*[13] *To the editor of the Courier-Journal: I will state as briefly as possible my connection with the Confederate Treasury, and run hastily over the route from Richmond, Va., to Washington, Ga.* He tells the editor that he left Richmond, Virginia, the night of the evacuation with all the papers of the Executive Office, on the special train containing the president, his staff, his cabinet (excepting the secretary of war, John C. Breckinridge) and many other government officials, being at the time the chief and confidential clerk of the Executive Office. The party reached Danville, Virginia, next day (General Breckinridge arriving a few days afterwards), where the government offices were partially reorganized and opened, remaining there until the 10th of April, when the news of General R.E. Lee's surrender was received. The next move was to Greensboro, North Carolina, the headquarters of General P.G.T. Beauregard's little army. *I had brought out from Richmond the "President's Guard"—disabled soldiers, commanded by three one-armed officers, Captain Coe and Lieutenants Brown and Dickinson.*[14]

There is an article in the *Southern Historical Society Papers* of 1896, titled "Retreat

---

(cont.) the Richmond & Danville Railroad since 1856. Jefferson Davis, in his 1881 book, tells us that Harvie was traveling with him from Richmond to Danville.

11. Johnston was the son of the late General Sidney Johnston.

12. This is not a mistake. Reagan succeeded Trenholm during the flight.

13. How could a letter written by Clark from his home in Clarksville, Tennessee, on January 10, 1882, to the *Louisville Courier-Journal*, and published by them on January 13, 1882, find its way into the *Southern Historical Society Papers* of 1881, especially as the January 10, 1882, date is there for all to see in the Society's article on page 542? Yet, that is what happened, and it is not a unique situation by any means. It has to with post-dating and pre-dating.

14. The President's Guard was also known as Lt. Lawson's Guard, as Capt. Huckstep's Guard, as Lt. Dickinson's Company, President's Guard, and as Capt. Coe's Company, President's Guard. It was formed in February 1864 of disabled soldiers to guard President Davis's mansion in Richmond.

of the Cabinet," taken from the Richmond *Times* of July 2, 1896, which was "Described by President Davis' private secretary." *In response to a request made of him that he would write some personal reminiscences of the late Chief of the Southern Cause ... Mr. Clark has edited, for the perusal of readers of the Times, the following absorbing story.*

It was written by Clark on June 26, 1896, from his home in Clarksville, Tennessee, and published by the *Times* on the date of the laying of the corner-stone of the monument to Jefferson Davis, in Monroe Park, in Richmond. The first part of this article is about Clark, while the second part reproduces portions of his letter. The article says that, under the orders of the Confederate president, Clark packed up all the papers of the office, and left with Davis and his cabinet. At Danville the departments were reopened and a temporary capital was established there. Upon receipt of dispatches, April 10, conveying the news of the surrender of General Lee's army, the president and cabinet retired to Greensboro, North Carolina, where General Beauregard had his headquarters. It goes on that at Charlotte, the president gave Clark a staff appointment with military rank. While in Richmond, Clark was, like all clerks, in the Local Defense Troops. Beginning as a private in the company, he was assigned to duty in the Medical Purveyor's office. And finally, that because Clark was on duty watching papers of the Confederate government until December 1865, he never gave his parole. Then we have this, in Clark's own words: *It was my privilege to be with the President and Cabinet from the evacuation of Richmond until within a few days of the capture of himself and family, a portion of his staff, and the sole Cabinet officer remaining with him.* It was below Sandersville, Georgia, on May 6 or 7, that President Davis ordered Clark on to Florida.

This article was reproduced, in edited form, by the editors of *Confederate Veteran*, vol. 6, July 1898, p. 20, with the new title, "Retreat of the Cabinet from Richmond." The re-working is more or less faithful to the original, but one has to be alert to the cavalier approach to accuracy taken by *Confederate Veteran*.

Colonel Francis Richard Lubbock was governor of Texas, 1861–63. He wrote (or rather, perhaps, did not write) his memoirs, *Six Decades in Texas*, published in 1900. He was definitely in the president's car, as one of Jefferson Davis's aides. C.E.L. Stuart, in his *New York Herald* article of July 4, 1865, describes him thus: *...Colonel Lubbock, ex Governor of Texas.*

Mallory, when copying from Stuart, felt compelled to alter syntax here and there. In this case it was difficult to change Stuart's wording without being awkward, but Mallory succeeded: *Ex Governor Lubbock of Texas, on the President's staff with the rank of Colonel.* Not just awkward but misleading. Davis's aides were all given the rank of colonel, but Frank Lubbock was actually a real-life Confederate colonel.

Frank Lubbock decided that his role in the group would be that of court jester, which, under less stressful circumstances would probably have been well-received casting. However, tonight was not the night for such a performance, what with misery and morbid reflection the dominant mood of his audience. The former Texas governor's tall-tales fell flat, as Stuart says: *Colonel Lubbock, of Texas, was the most loquacious of his party. To him it seemed that the part of an aid-de-camp was not fully performed if he did not say much and bustle more, be doing or seem to be doing a great deal, and he discharged his imagined duty fairly. It was bright and calm, he thought, and all the usual portents denoted good luck.*

Mallory, writing about Lubbock, says that he *evidently regarded himself as, ex officio, bound to "make an effort." An earnest, enthusiastic, big hearted man is Col. Lubbock, who has seen much of life, knows something of men, less of women, but a great deal about horses, with a large stock of pointless Texas anecdotes which he disposed of on the slightest occasion, with infinite enjoyment to himself.*

Jules St. Martin was Judah Benjamin's elegant and well educated brother-in-law, 5 foot 3 inches of Justice Department clerk, no matter what one might read. Benjamin was inordinately fond of Jules, so, although under ordinary circumstances the tiny Creole, given his rather lowly status, would have found himself relegated to a position some way down in the pecking order, the secretary used his considerable weight so he could have the lad in the president's car.

Eli Evans, in his 1989 biography, *Judah P. Benjamin*, says that in June 1861 Benjamin traveled to Richmond with his brother-in-law, Jules St. Martin, now a young man in his late twenties and, though slight in stature, attractive to women, with a shock of black hair and the patrician Creole features of his sister Natalie. *For Benjamin, Jules St. Martin was a link to the roots of his missing family, born to Natalie's parents soon after her marriage to Benjamin,*[15] *and raised almost as their son. Varina said that Benjamin was protective and spoke of his young brother-in-law as if her were a small boy. They lived together at the Davenport house on Main Street throughout the war, and we can assume that Benjamin arranged for Jules's job as a clerk in the War Department.*[16]

George Trenholm was, without question in the presidential car. As C.E.L. Stuart says, in his July 4 article in the *New York Herald: Trenholm was by himself, an invalid, attended by his wife, the only Cabinet-officer who had or needed the gentle care of "sweet woman."* And, as Mallory says: *Mr. Trenholm, Secretary of the Treasury, suffering from a painful attack of neuralgia, was accompanied by a portion of his family.*

The Hoehlings, in their 1981 book, *The Day Richmond Died*, write this: *Secretary Trenholm, suffering from both chronic neuralgia and a stomach ailment, had been taken to the depot in an ambulance.* The depot referred to is the R&D station in Richmond, and here the Hoehlings are discussing the night of April 2, 1865. This is the first mention we have of an ambulance taking Trenholm to the train. Other sources tell us of an ambulance, but that is later on in the flight, not in Richmond. However, the ambulance myth, once promulgated, would not die. Ernest B. Furgurson, in *Ashes of Glory* (1996), has this: *Secretary of the Treasury, George A. Trenholm ... had arrived in an ambulance.* And Trotter, in *Silk Flags* (1988), writes: *On the day Richmond fell, Trenholm was so ill that he had to be taken to the train in an ambulance.*

James C. Clark wrote this in his *Last Train South* (1984): *Mallory wrote that Trenholm had a "never give up the ship sort of air," and "referred to other great national causes which have been redeemed from far gloomier reverses than ours."* This is almost, but not quite, an exact quote from the edited 1900 Mallory article in *McClure's* magazine, but Clark does not cite the *McClure's* article. Instead, he cites Burton Harrison. But the glaring error is that Mallory is not quoting Trenholm, as Clark tells us, but Benjamin.

As for those on the Frank Carroll list and the Danville Library list who were not in the presidential car, one might as well fire the first salvo with *"A little more grape, Captain Bragg."*[17] John Sergeant Wise, in "The End of an Era" (1899), talks about the presidential

---

15. The marriage took place in New Orleans, in February 1833.
16. Jules died in late 1875.
17. General Zachary Taylor is reputed to have made this suggestion, or one very much like it, at the Battle of Buena Vista, in 1847, during the Mexican War.

train stopping at Clover Station while he (Wise) was in command there that morning of April 3, 1865. Wise actually went into the president's car, or so he says. He discusses Davis, then says: *Near him sat General Bragg.* Wise then describes Bragg, for the benefit of anyone not familiar with one of the most well-known faces in Confederate history: *General Bragg, whose shaggy eyebrows and piercing eyes made him look like a much greater man than he ever proved himself to be.* It's not as if Wise could be mistaken; he knew Braxton Bragg personally, and had for years.

Philip Van Doren Stern, in his 1958 book, *An End to Valor*, simply quotes Wise: "*Near him sat General Bragg.*" However, Burke Davis goes further. In his *To Appomattox* (1959), Bragg is no longer merely "near" the president: *Beside Davis sat his military advisor of the last months, General Braxton Bragg, whose striking appearance drew Wise's attention.* Burke Davis then goes on to reproduce Wise's description of Bragg. James C. Clark is even more specific than Burke Davis: *Jefferson Davis sat next to General Braxton Bragg.* And finally this from F. Lawrence McFall, Jr., in his 2001 book, *Danville in the Civil War*: *Seated in silence, like the others, were Generals Braxton Bragg and Samuel Cooper.*

So, in four stages—Wise to Burke Davis to Clark to McFall—we find Bragg sitting "near" the president, then "beside" him, then "next to" him, then "seated in silence."

For the record, on the night of the flight, and on the following day, General Bragg was in Raleigh. He did not catch up with the Davis party until Cokesbury, South Carolina, on May 1.

William Rufus Bringhurst, of Clarksville, Tennessee, was a private in Woodward's Kentucky Cavalry. After the war, he became a hotel operator in Clarksville, and died there on December 4, 1927, aged 83. His obituary had the headline, *Last of Jefferson Davis escort dies.* It continues, *He was the last of the 60 Confederate veterans who volunteered to escort President Davis to the end.* This obituary was reproduced in the book *The Great War of Destruction*, by Russell George LeVan. Curiously, the date ascribed in that book to Bringhurst's death is December 4, 1915, which, of course, is out by 12 years. The 60 referred to in the obit were midshipmen, nothing to do with Bringhurst. There were a few thousand cavalrymen who escorted President Davis, but only from Greensboro onwards. They arrived in Greensboro at midnight on the 14th, from Raleigh, and included Woodward's Kentucky cavalrymen, of whom Bringhurst was one. So, Bringhurst was not in the president's car.

Apparently an officer in the First Auditor's Office, S. Brittain received $50

Confederate General Braxton Bragg.

in gold at Washington, Georgia, on May 4, 1865,[18] but that does not prove he was in the president's car between Richmond and Danville. In fact, he would be much more likely to have been on a separate train altogether, the treasure train that carried the specie from Richmond to Danville, the train that left Richmond about an hour after Davis's train. There would certainly be no reason for him to be in the president's car.

In F. Lawrence McFall's book *Danville in the Civil War, a post office department clerk, A.G. Cantley* is mentioned as being in the president's car. McFall is right in that Audley Gazzam Cantley was a post office clerk, not a director, as the Danville Library list would have it, but, regardless of his status, was he in the car? An interesting background: A dry goods man from Mobile, his father had been shot to death, leaving the family destitute. By his early 30s, now in Palestine, Texas, A.G. became court clerk, and in May 1861 applied to fellow Palestine resident John H. Reagan for a position in the Confederate Postmaster General's Department in Richmond. Cantley might have been in the president's car, but there would have been no obvious reason for it.

The chief of the Ordnance Department was General Josiah Gorgas. Was he in the presidential car? Was he even on the same train? Bearing in mind that the Davis train left Richmond at 11:00 p.m. on Sunday night, this is what Gorgas says in his inimitable prose: *At a little after 1 a.m. Monday morning the train to which the car on which I was belonged moved off but it was 3 o'clock before we left the neighborhood of Manchester. Toward 6 o'clock in the morning as we have since learned the tobacco warehouse on Shockoe Slip was fired, & set that part of the town on fire. About 7 a.m. the three bridges—*[Richmond &]* Danville &* [Richmond &] *Petersburgh R.R.*[s] *were fired & the result was the burning up of a large part of the city, extending from 14th up to 8 and 9 St., and from the Water to Franklin. It was due to our own ill-advised orders. I heard Gen. Breckinridge orders to fire the bridges, & regret I did not interpose, as I had heard Gen.* [Jeremy F.] *Gilmer, Chf Engineer, express* [the] *most decided opinion as to the wanton destruction of R.R. bridges. I had on Saturday addressed a letter to Gen. Ewell deprecating the destruction of tobacco in the warehouses by fire & suggesting that it might be effected as well by breaking barrels of turpentine over the top of it as it lay Stored. The Arsenal was fired from the* [Richmond &] *Petersburgh* [Railroad] *bridge, & the explosion of powder & shells must have terrified the inhabitants of that part of the city, & must have spread the fire. We reached Danville Monday evening & were received by Major Hutter. Here we stayed until the news of the surrender of General Lee made it necessary for the Government to remove still further Southward.*

From easily accessible letters written by Confederate Treasurer Hendren—to Jefferson Davis on April 5, while at Danville, and to General Beauregard, from Greensboro on the 16th—we know he, Hendren, was part of the flight.[19] Was he in the president's car?

This from Mallory, when talking about Secretary of the Treasury Trenholm: "*The coin of his department he had put in charge of Mr. Mallory's Corps of midshipmen placed at his command by the Secretary of the Navy for this purpose, under the immediate orders of Commander W. H. Parker.*" Parker was one of Mallory's officers, so the secretary should have known he was not a commander. In his *Recollections* (1883), Parker says: *I will here remark that neither the Secretary of the Treasury, nor the Treasurer, were with the treasure.*

---

18. Clark, "Confederate Treasury."
19. The Hendren letter of April 16, 1865, is found in the *Official Records*, Chapter 59, pp. 803–804. As for the April 5 letter, *The Papers of Jefferson Davis* cites LNT, LHA Davis Papers, r21, 459–460.

Ruins of the Richmond and Danville Railroad Bridge, Richmond, 1865.

The senior officer of the Treasury present was a cashier.[20] His name was John Newton Hendren. He signed his letters "John N. Hendren." Yet, his name is often seen as John C. Hendren. Why would this be?

On January 10, 1882, from his home in Clarksville, Tennessee, Micajah Clark mailed to the *Louisville Courier Journal* an article he had just written on the Jefferson Davis flight. The paper published it three days later. In the same breath as he discusses Hendren, Clark also talks about John C. Breckinridge, and simply gets the middle initial confused. He should have written John N. Hendren, but wrote John C. Hendren. The Louisville paper did not know to correct it. That is how the initial error came about. One will see this Micajah Clark article quoted by several authors over the years, for example by Otis

---

20. William Harwar Parker (1826–1896) was the Confederate naval officer in command of the midshipmen guarding the treasure train as it left Richmond for Danville on the night of April 2–3, 1865. A U.S. Navy officer, Parker was promoted to lieutenant in 1855. He resigned his commission in April 1861 and went South, being appointed a first lieutenant in the Confederate States Navy. In the summer of 1863, in Richmond, the steamer *Patrick Henry* was fitted up as a school ship, and the Confederate Naval Academy was organized. Lieutenant Parker became its first superintendent and would remain in that position, and that rank, until the end of the war. By the time Parker wrote his *Recollections* he was a captain, but during the Civil War he was a lieutenant. Any author writing of Parker's actions during the Civil War must, therefore, refer to him as Lieutenant Parker.

Ashmore, in his own 1918 article "The Story of the Confederate Treasure" (although Ashmore was under the mistaken impression that the Clark article was an interview the man gave to the paper on January 13, 1882).

Other writers who have fallen into the John C. trap include: Varina Davis, in her 1890 book about her late husband, when she writes... *the Treasurer, Mr. John C. Hendren*; *Harper's Encyclopaedia of United States History* (1905): *...treasurer, John C. Hendren*; Michael B. Ballard, in his 1986 book, *A Long Shadow*: *...Confederate States Treasurer John C. Hendren*; J. Frank Carroll, in *Confederate Treasure* (1996): *John C. Hendren*; and William C. Davis, in *An Honorable Defeat* (2001): *Davis to John C. Hendren, April 15, 1865*.

Then there is the Hendera phenomenon. Somehow, almost certainly through a printing error, the following appeared in Dunbar Rowland's classic 1923 multi-volume book, *Jefferson Davis, Constitutionalist*: *John N. Hendera to Jefferson Davis (From President's Letter Book). Treasury CSA to the President, April 5, 1865.*[21]

Burke Davis, in *To Appomattox* (1959), relying solely on Dunbar Rowland in this instance—rather than going to original sources—has this: *...the Confederate Treasurer John Hendera*. And this: *Hendera went off on his errand*. And this: *Hendera reported that the bank would not cash the huge check*.

The *Danville Register*, in their April 1965 centennial splash, featured an article titled "A Southside Virginia Town Became Home for Thousands During One Week in April," which contains the following: *John Hendera, confederate treasurer*. Another article in that series, "War News," gives a list of persons on various trains that day, including John Hendera. As can clearly be seen by other wording in these centennial articles, they relied too heavily upon Burke Davis, a trait shared by all of the Danvillian historians.

Whatever Burke Davis wrote in *To Appomattox* will probably also appear, often verbatim, in James C. Clark's 1984 book, *Last Train South*. In this case Clark writes: *John Hendera, Confederate Treasurer*. And this: *Hendera returned from the Bank of Richmond with the news that the bank would not honor the check of the President of the Confederacy*. Clark indexes Hendera as Hendra. As William Warren Rogers says, in classic understatement, in his review of *Last Train South*: *There are enough typographical errors to cause concern*.[22]

By 1985—26 years after *To Appomattox*—when he came to write *The Long Surrender*, Burke Davis had not discovered his error, even after all that time. *To John Hendera, the Confederate Treasurer, he gave the check for $28,400*. And this: *About this time John Hendera came....* He is indexed as *Hendera, John*.

This odd use of the name Hendera came under the scrutiny of the authors of *The Rebel and the Rose* (2007): *Some books on the flight of the Confederate government—e.g., Davis, Long Surrender, and Clark, Last Train South—refer to a John Hendera as a treasury clerk. The name also appears in the letter book of President Davis on a note concerning the Bank of Virginia check for $28,244 that the president had wanted cashed.* Actually, the name Hendera appears in Davis's letter book only as a typo in Dunbar Rowland's book, not as Jefferson Davis tells us.

---

21. Volume Eleven of *The Papers of Jefferson Davis*, which was published in 2003, reproduces that letter, but ascribes it to John N. Hendren, because that's how he signed it. The *PJD* tell us that this letter was among the papers taken from Davis's baggage at Fort Monroe on May 24, 1865, just after he had been captured.

22. *Florida Historical Quarterly* 64:2 (October 1985), pp. 206–207.

The authors of *The Rebel and the Rose*, in concluding their research into this anomaly, let us know that they *have not been able to confirm, however, that anyone named Hendera was employed in the Treasury Department. Perhaps Hendera and Hendren were the same person.* In any case, John C. Hendren, apparently, had responsibility as treasurer for the specie when it left Danville.

There are several references in *The Rebel and the Rose* to both "Treasurer John C. Hendren" and "Treasury clerk John C. Hendren." A footnote even cites the April 15, 1865, letter from Jefferson Davis to "John C. Hendren." Despite what appears to have been a rather intensive investigation on the part of the authors into the name Hendren versus Hendera, they obviously failed to spot that his name was John N. Hendren. There is no Hendera, no Hendra, no John C. Hendren. The man's name is John Newton Hendren.

At the very moment the presidential train was moving through the night to Danville, Duncan Farrar Kenner was in England, on a rather bizarre Confederate diplomatic mission. He did not get back until August 23, 1865, on the *Persia*.

According to Micajah Clark in "Last Days of the Confederate Treasury," J.B. MacMurdo received $50 in gold at Washington, Georgia, on May 4, 1865, which, in itself, does not prove that MacMurdo was in the president's car between Richmond and Danville. As James Brown MacMurdo was a Richmond boy, it's possible, but that's as far as one should be prepared to go. By July, J.B. was back in Richmond, as a fully functioning notary public.

James M. Miller was second teller with the Exchange Bank of Richmond. According to Micajah Clark in "Last Days of the Confederate Treasury," *Jas. Miller received $50 in gold at Washington, Ga.* That's true enough, but it does not, in itself, prove that Miller was in the president's car between Richmond and Danville. Indeed, there is something that proves Miller was not in the car, and that's Captain John M. Strother's April 3, 1866, affidavit (see Chapter 12), which says, clear as day, that Miller was on the treasure train, not the presidential train.

John Ott was the 30-year-old chief clerk of the treasurer's office in Richmond. He had started in the Federal Treasury as a young man, and, when war broke out, he went South. It is quite evident, from an affidavit made by Ott a year after the Jefferson Davis flight, that he traveled with the Confederate treasure; therefore he could not have been in the president's car.

The Confederate commissary general of prisons was Daniel Ruggles. He did leave Richmond the night of the evacuation, with his clerks and his newly appointed chief quartermaster, Richard Bayley Winder.[23] Winder had lately been associated with the notorious Andersonville prison camp, which had been under the control of his cousin, General John H. Winder. John H. Brubaker III, in *The Last Capital* (1979), says that General Ruggles and Col. Robert G.H. Kean were traveling on the same train, and they may have been. We do know, from Kean's own account, that he was on the same train as Jefferson Davis, but not in the same car. If Kean had wanted to, he could have said he was in the same car, but he did not. Therefore, we have to believe him. We do know that General Ruggles and Richard Bayley Winder were together on the flight from Richmond to Danville, along with their clerks. That could not have been in the president's car, because Winder is never mentioned—

---

23. 55th Congress, 3rd Session, House of Representatives, Document #314. Reproduced in the *Official Records*, series 2, volume 8, p. 734. Letter from R.B. Winder to Major N. Church, acting assistant adjutant general, written on August 30, 1865, from the U.S. prison at Accomac Court House, in Virginia, Winder's address at the time.

Ruins of the Exchange Bank, Main Street, Richmond, with the façade nearly intact, 1865.

ever, by anyone—as being in the president's car. And all those clerks with Ruggles and Winder? They were not all in the president's car. On the other hand, Kean and Ruggles almost certainly were on the presidential train, although they were definitely not in the president's car.

"Davis's servant—Spencer." This is what the *Papers of Jefferson Davis (PJD)* annotators have to say about this man in volume 11, page 507, footnote 15: *Spencer, a slave not owned by Davis, worked at the White House for about a year. According to Burton Harrison "he had made himself a member of our household, and couldn't be got rid of. Spencer was inefficient, unsightly, and unclean ... he always called Mr. Davis 'Marse Jeff,' and was the only one of the domestics who used that style of address." Spencer traveled to Danville with Harrison and Varina Davis when they left Richmond.*[24] He returned to the capital and

---

24. This is simply not so, as any study of Burton Harrison's writings will show.

accompanied the presidential party as far as Greensboro, where he was charged with the care of John Taylor Wood's family. The *PJD* annotators cite two sources for all this: Fairfax Harrison's *Aris Sonis Focisque*, pages 231–32; and Royce Shingleton's *John Taylor Wood: Sea Ghost of the Confederacy*, page 153.

As one may notice above in Harrison's description of Spencer, as rendered by *The Papers of Jefferson Davis*, there is an ellipsis after *inefficient, unsightly, and unclean*, indicating missing words. Those words, written by Harrison, are indeed unfit for print, but for the sake of completeness, they are, with of course the appropriate trepidation and reluctance, included in this footnote.[25]

Harrison tells anecdotes about Spencer's unacceptability that in all conscience, cannot be reproduced here, even as a footnote, and then continues: *This Spencer had accompanied the* [Jefferson Davis] *party from Richmond to Danville, but had made the journey in a box-car, with a drunken officer, who beat him. The African was overwhelmed with disgust at such treatment, and announced in Danville that he should go no further if* [blank] *was to be of the party.*

Upon finding that the drunken officer was to remain in Danville, Spencer changed his mind, wanted to go on with the flight. Harrison placed him in a box-car with General Raines' fuses, until someone told the Negro that they would explode.[26] A panicked Spencer then demanded alternative accommodations, whereupon Harrison informed him that *he couldn't travel in any other car*. Spencer then declared he was going back to Richmond, and, as he did, according to Harrison, he uttered the words, *Den Marse Jeff'll have to take keer of hisself.* That Spencer left Danville there can be little doubt, but one has to wonder how he got back to Richmond.

This bit about Spencer being in Greensboro looking after the Wood family does not come from Burton Harrison, but it does come from Royce Gordon Shingleton's *Sea Ghost of the Confederacy*, page 153, with no source cited. So, where did Shingleton get it? It was not from Taylor Wood, or from Burton Harrison. It appears that, using Shingleton's unsourced and uncorroborable statement as their only guide, *The Papers of Jefferson Davis* have set this Greensboro business in stone.

Henry Clay Stacker. Known as Clay. Stacker was a Virginia Military Institute (VMI) cadet, just turned 18, a guard for the president. *He was one of the escorts to accompany President Davis on his departure from Richmond, after Lee's surrender, accompanying him as far as Washington, Ga.*[27] What this means, of course, is that Stacker accompanied the president only after Lee's surrender, which took place on the 9th.

In February 1865 Clay Stacker dropped from the VMI rolls to become a private in the 2nd Kentucky Cavalry; Stacker and the 2nd Kentucky Cavalry were in Southwest Virginia when Jefferson Davis made the train ride to Danville; when news of Lee's surrender reached the 2nd Kentucky, they were ordered to Charlotte to rendezvous with the fleeing president. And Charlotte was where they met up with Davis, on April 18, 1865.[28] Interestingly, J. Frank Carroll's *Confederate Treasure* came out a decade before *The Corps Forward*, so one does not know how he came up with Stacker's name.

There are published sources which hint that Frank Vizetelly, the famous illustrator,

---

25. *...a black Caliban,—and had the manners of a corn-field darky.*
26. Gabriel Raines was head of the infamous Torpedo Bureau.
27. William Couper, ed. *The Corps Forward* (Buena Vista, VA: Mariner, 2005).
28. There are many sources that verify this date, one being *Basil Wilson Duke, CSA*, by Gary Robert Matthews. Duke commanded the 2nd Kentucky.

8. The President's Car

Illustrator Frank Vizetelly is rumored to have been on the Davis train, although he was not.

was on the presidential train from Richmond to Danville, but those sources are vague, at best. For example, Joshua Brown, in his *Pictorial Reporting: Everyday Life, and the Crisis of Gilded Age America* (2002), which, after describing how Union Secretary of War Stanton had refused Vizetelly permission to travel with the army, says that Vizetelly *went South to depict the Confederacy at war from the Battle of Fredericksburg in 1862 to Jefferson Davis's ignominious departure from Richmond in 1865.*

However, Vizetelly was not on the train from Richmond to Danville. Michael B. Ballard, in *A Long Shadow* (1986), says that by the evening of the 17th of April the Davis party had almost reached Salisbury, North Carolina. *Frank Vizetelly, an artist-correspondent for the* Illustrated London News, *had joined the fugitives in Greensboro. He had left Virginia just before Lee's surrender to report on the Johnston-Sherman campaign.* And, as Douglas Bostick says in his book about Vizetelly—*The Confederacy's Secret Weapon* (2009): *Vizetelly boarded a train at Durham's Station and traveled to Greensboro hoping to intercept President Davis fleeing south after the fall of Richmond.* And this: *Vizetelly did find Davis and his entourage in North Carolina as his train pulled into Greensboro on April 15.*

Clint Johnson, in *Pursuit* (2008), also has Vizetelly joining the Davis party for the first time at Greensboro. And Hudson Strode, in *Tragic Hero* (1964), confirms Greensboro. Moreover, even though we do have well-known Vizetelly illustrations drawn later on in the Davis flight, none are from the Richmond to Danville period, and there's no way Frank was going to miss those.

Both the Frank Carroll list and the Danville Library list feature Colonel John Taylor Wood, whom they correctly annotate as President Davis's aide. They also feature a Captain Wood, unannotated, a mystery man. Neither Carroll nor the Library has a clue who this man is, yet somehow he made both lists. So, who was he, that he should gain a berth in the presidential car? The answer is, We do not know. But we can hazard a guess. President Davis made all his aides Colonel,[29] so this explains Taylor Wood's title: Colonel. However,

---

29. In 1865 the common spelling of "aide" was "aid."

in real life, when he was not Davis's aide, Wood was a famous naval captain, Captain Wood, the Confederate Sea Ghost.

Those who were in the car, but not on the Frank Carroll list or the Danville Library list, include: Dr. Duncan, Ives, Macfarland the banker, and, for part of the way, Congressman Horatio Washington Bruce. All these names were given to us by Stuart, in 1865, and they all make absolute sense.[30] There may well have been others, Stuart himself, for example, especially as the train stopped at several stations, and people migrated from car to car for parts of the trip.

Joseph Christmas Ives was *among Davis' entourage on the retreat from Richmond*, says *The Papers of Jefferson Davis*. The *Papers* continue: *Staying on in Danville when the president left, he was relieved as Davis' aide on April 12, and ordered to report to Engineer Chief Jeremy F. Gilmer, who traveled with Breckinridge from Richmond, and was paroled at Washington, Georgia, on May 9.* For this, the *PJD* cites Stuart's July 4, 1865, *Herald* article. Therefore, for what it's worth, *The Papers of Jefferson Davis* believe Stuart and thus validate him, at least in regard to Ives being in the president's car. It is worth bearing in mind that not only was Stuart the first to report Ives' presence in the President's car, he's the only one. And, as the three other aides were in the car—Lubbock, Wood, and Johnston—then so, surely, must Ives have been.

The Reverend James Armstrong Duncan, Methodist minister at Broad Street Church, was editor of the *Christian Advocate*. The *PJD*, vol. 11, p. 504, footnote 1, reports that *A prominent Richmond minister, James A. Duncan, recalled seeing Davis in Capitol Square after church* [that is, on Sunday, April 2], and then that *although Duncan said he wished to remain in this city, Davis insisted that he leave "for his preaching to the lines had brought him such prominence, that he would be captured."*

Was the President's car crowded? As William C. Davis says in *The Man and His Hour* (1991): *Not until 11 p.m. did Breckinridge finally escort Davis to his seat in the crowded presidential car.* And Clint Johnson, in his 2008 book, *Pursuit*, has this: *Most everyone in the packed train car of twenty-nine men and one woman....*

Where did these two historians get the idea that the car was crowded? It certainly was not from any of the participants' accounts. It might have been from something Burton Harrison wrote in his article in *Century* magazine, 1883: *There we all were in our seats—crowded together—waiting to be off.* However, this passage refers to the train as it left Danville bound for Greensboro. Different train, different railroad line, different state.

A boxcar was one inch short of eight feet wide. A passenger car was about a foot wider. In 1865 the interior of a common wooden coach was fully open; i.e., it had no compartments. Everyone sat in the same large space. A central aisle, no more than a foot or so wide, ran from one end of the car to the other, with pairs of reversible, hard-backed, and rather austere benches on each side of the aisle. Therefore, if a passenger car was nine feet wide, with a central aisle of about a foot, then the benches are going to be four feet long, with seating on each bench for two persons. This is somewhat confirmed by the occasional illustrations one sees in newspapers of the time. It is further confirmed by none other than Secretary Mallory, who says that the seats (he means "benches") were

---

30. Stuart writes a lot about Macfarland on the flight. See the Appendix.

four feet long on the Piedmont Railroad running from Danville to Greensboro. Four feet was standard by then, in passenger cars all over the country, regardless of gauge.

Long distance cars, and that's probably the one we're talking about here, had better appointments (at least in theory), more comfortable seats, and longer pitch (i.e., leg room) than their short-distance counterparts. The president's car would have had a wood stove for heating, two greasy, smoky oil lamps for light, and a barrel for drinking. There was a small bathroom across from the water barrel, the two fixtures differing sufficiently in aspect so that passengers would not confuse one with the other, unless pressed.

Of course, the question remains, how many passengers could a car normally take? To put it another way, how many pairs of reversible seats were there in a passenger car?

Albert A. Nofi's *A Civil War Treasury* reveals that a passenger car could take 56 persons, 80 at a pinch, maybe even 100. Then we have Arthur Lyon Fremantle, a British visitor in Texas, traveling by train in 1863,[31] who states that a passenger car had a central aisle, with 12 "seats" (he means "benches") on either side, each seat taking two persons. That makes 48. That was Texas, but most of the cars used on the Southern railroads were pre-war cars, built by manufacturers in the North. In brief, one does not find too many references to how many passengers a Confederate car could hold, but all indicate between roughly fifty and sixty.

F. Lawrence McFall, in "To Danville" (2011), says that Breckinridge was not on the train, but that all *other members of the President's cabinet found seats in the same coach, as it accommodated thirty-one people.* This mathematics implies eight rows of benches on one side of the aisle and seven on the other, with one individual seat set apart, presumably for the president. That makes 31.

J. Frank Carroll confirms Albert Nofi when he says that passenger cars normally had a seating capacity of 55 to 58 persons, but in this case the president's car was not a common car—it was an executive car, and had seating capacity for 32 persons.

Directly contradicting Carroll, James Swanson, in *Bloody Crimes* (2010), assures us that Jefferson Davis took his place in a common coach packed with the heads of the cabinet departments, key staff members, and other selected officials. He does not mention anything about a doctored car. On the contrary, he says that this was not a private, luxurious sleeping car constructed for a head of state. He does, however, subscribe to the theory that the car was packed.

One finds no mention anywhere that Jefferson Davis ever had what might be called his own executive car. There seems to have been no need for one. He apparently never went anywhere that would require one. He had never even been to Danville, for example.[32] The other reason is that this train had to have been cobbled together on the spur of the moment, using whatever cars could be impressed for this particular service. To believe anything else is unreasonable. Davis had to take what there was available in Richmond that Sunday. No time to create a special car. Even the locomotive pulling the train was not a passenger engine, but, rather, a little freight lad. If Davis had had a special train waiting in the wings, then it would have had a full-size passenger locomotive to pull it. The very necessary ad hoc atmosphere of April 2 is borne out by James W. Raab,[33] who

---

31. Fremantle, *Three Months in the Southern States, April–June 1863.*
32. At least, according to Mr. Johnson, in *Pursuit.*
33. James W. Raab, *J. Patton Anderson, Confederate General.*

says that President Davis ordered several ten-car trains to be brought up for removing the government to Danville. Raab does not cite his source for this unique contribution to history, but his point is well taken.

If, then, there were seats for fifty to sixty persons, and yet only thirty or so people occupied the presidential car, it can only mean that impedimenta crowded the rest of the benches. There was very little floor space, and it is most unlikely that these dignitaries would trust their belongings to a boxcar.

Chapter 9

Departure Time

I have already heard from six credible witnesses as many different stories of the time when, and the way in which, Jefferson Davis left Richmond. I expect to hear at least as many more before I get to the truth.

That is an excerpt from a reader's letter, published in the *Milwaukee Daily Sentinel* of April 11, 1865, only eight days after the flight to Danville. It could have been written today.

There was great turmoil in Richmond as the train was leaving, and this was compounded over the course of the next few days with Union troops entering and occupying the city. Moreover, there are no official Confederate records that enable us to nail down Jefferson Davis's departure time. "Let's get the hell out of here!" is not a state of mind conducive to the leaving of a paper trail. Nevertheless, one is continually surprised that such an important event as the Confederate government deserting its people should not have been faithfully recorded—by someone. Yet, perhaps it was. Perhaps among the welter of conflicting reports, one is true. If that is the case, we cannot recognize it when we see it.

General Shepley has information that several millions of dollars in gold left by railroad Saturday and Sunday for Danville. This is probably the gold from New Orleans banks and the mint.[1]

An early news dispatch from Richmond, dated April 3, 1865, shows what rumors were flying around at the time. *Mr. Jefferson Davis and family left Richmond on Wednesday [March 29] for Charlotte, North Carolina and it is stated on good authority that they were on their way to Texas. Mr. Davis returned to Richmond and was in church yesterday, when a despatch was handed to him from General Lee, stating the position of affairs was desperate. He left Richmond at once.* This dispatch went via Washington on April 5, 1865, reached New York on April 6, was shipped from New York to the UK on that date, and arrived in London by the 20th, when the *Times* printed it.[2]

A *Richmond Whig* article of April 4, 1865, was based on much more solid ground: *The evacuation of Richmond commenced in earnest Sunday night, closed at daylight on Monday morning with a terrific conflagration.* The article describes primarily the effect of the conflagration upon Richmond. It does not mention the president's flight.

---

1. General Weitzel to Ulysses S. Grant, April 3, 1865. *OR*, p. 535.
2. The *Times* had started publishing accounts of the fall of Richmond as early as April 15, 1865, but it was not until April 20, 1865, that the British public were able to read a version of the Davis flight.

A Richmond correspondent wrote on Tuesday evening, April 4, 1865, a dispatch that was sent via Washington on the 6th, and published in the papers on the 7th: *It appears that General Lee sent Davis a despatch Sunday p.m., saying he could not hold out, and the city must be evacuated immediately. Davis, and most of his cabinet, left within three hours, and the soldiers and citizens began to leave about dark.*

At 11:30 a.m., on April 5, 1865, C.A. Dana sent a dispatch to United States Secretary of War Stanton from Aiken's Landing: *All the leading men got away that evening.*[3] Stanton sent this out as a press report later that day. At the very end of this busy day, at 11 o'clock, Stanton issued another official bulletin, the verbatim copy of a telegraph that had come in from Grant at Nottoway Court House: *Davis left Richmond by the Danville railroad Sunday evening, with all the members of Congress.*[4]

Carleton Coffin was one of the journalists who arrived in Richmond on April 3. His article for the *Boston Journal* reflected the confusion—some parts true, some false—that reporters were experiencing in trying to piece together the facts of the Davis flight: *Jeff. Davis went in the first train, leaving his housekeeper in charge of his house, important papers in his private room upon the table.*

This sense of confusion has been perpetuated over the years by some of the participants themselves—if not all of them—until it has become more of a vagueness, as if the memory has been clouded.

In his affidavit made on March 12, 1866, Adair Pleasants, the corresponding clerk of the Confederate States Treasury Department, wrote that, at the time of the evacuation of Richmond, *on the night of the 2d of April 1865*, he *left the city on the train with Mr. Davis and his cabinet.*

Jefferson Davis probably did not write a lot of his famous 1881 book, *The Rise and Fall of the Confederate Government*, but it does not really matter when we are considering this statement: *In the night of the 2d ... I left Richmond.* Because it's true. Bald, but true.

William Harwar Parker, in his 1883 *Recollections*, says that the presidential train left *"sometime in the evening."* Parker is clear that his own treasure train left at close to midnight, and that fact is confirmed by others. There can be little doubt that the treasure train left after the presidential train. Ergo, Jefferson Davis left before midnight.

Taylor Wood, in his 1893 published article, "Escape of the Secretary of War," says: *I left Richmond with him and his cabinet on April 2, 1865, the night of evacuation.* Again, bald but true.

Some historians have remained noncommittal about the specific time of night that the presidential train left the Richmond depot, which, perhaps, is just the right attitude to take, given that we simply do not know the time. This, for example, from Lance Phillips, in his book, *Yonder Comes the Train* (1965): *President Davis and his official party had left the turmoil on the first train, early Sunday night; and following close behind, wheezing but game little woodburners pulled other trains loaded with archives, gold and silver bullion, and personnel of governmental departments, plus evacuees who managed to get aboard.* It would seem that he got this from a line in Carleton Coffin's 1865 *Boston Journal* article, *Jeff. Davis went in the first train.* However, as we have seen, Coffin was writing at a moment of extraordinary confusion, a brief period of time when myths were made.

John H. Brubaker III, in *The Last Capital* (1979), says, in prose that seems to detach

---

3. *OR*, ser. 1, vol. 46, part 3, p. 574.
4. These two bulletins were published in the newspapers the following day, April 6, 1865.

the principal passenger from his vehicle, that Davis *finally took his seat in a car behind the Charles Seddon and watched his train move off into the darkness before midnight*, while Joan Cashin, in *First Lady of the Confederacy* (2006), merely has this: *On April 2, Jefferson Davis received a telegram ... and that night he left the city with his staff for Danville, Virginia.*

On the other hand, right from the beginning, certain writers, agitated beyond endurance by the vagueness of the departure time, have determined to remedy this, even it if means being creative. Some have chosen afternoon, rather than night. For example, the *Vermont Watchman* of April 14, 1865, quoting the New York *Herald*'s correspondent: *Jeff. Davis left at 1:00 p.m. for Danville.* Or Pollard, in his 1866 book, *The Lost Cause*: *In the afternoon a special train carried from Richmond President Davis and some of his cabinet.* Or McCabe in *Life and Campaigns of General Robert E. Lee* (1866): *In the afternoon, President Davis and his family, accompanied by several of his cabinet, left the city on a special train.*

Afternoon quickly died a death, and rightly so. The weight of historical opinion against it was simply too strong. So, it is not surprising that after 1866 no one ever mentions afternoon. That is, until 2001, when this appears in William C. Davis's book, *Look Away!*: *Davis and most of the Cabinet went out on a late afternoon train.* Professor Davis does not cite his source.

It may be apropos here to mention that nobody except Walter Coffey, in his 2011 book, *The Civil War Months*, has President Davis leaving Richmond before he even received the telegram from Lee: *By 11 a.m. on April 2, Davis boarded a special train ... with other top Confederate officials, and about $500,000 in gold. Each government department was assigned a freight car.*

Other history makers have preferred the hour or two before and after nightfall. For the record, nightfall is when night falls, i.e., when it becomes dark. First comes sunset, when the sun disappears over the horizon, then comes the period of dusk, and finally comes nightfall. That evening, April 2, 1865, in Richmond, sunset was at 6:15 p.m. The following day it was a minute later (the days were getting longer).[5]

While Congressman Bruce, in "Some Reminiscences" (1881), can be no more specific than that he took his seat on the Davis train about nightfall, an item about Davis appeared in several British newspapers of April 22, 1865, saying that he *remained in the city until near nightfall, when he left in the 5.30 train*, whereas the *New York Daily Tribune* of April 8, 1865, has him taking *the train at half past 6 in the evening*.

At 1:00 p.m. on April 5, 1865, C.A. Dana sent a dispatch to Union Secretary of War Edwin M. Stanton from Jefferson Davis's house in Richmond. Stanton received it at 8:25 p.m.,[6] and gave it out as a press report, and so late editions of that day were able to let the public know that Jefferson Davis *left at 7 p.m. by the Danville railroad*, and that all *the members of Congress escaped*. The *Richmond Whig* of April 6, 1865, also says: *Davis left at 7 o'clock*.

The *New York Herald*'s correspondent, writing on April 3, 1865, from Davis's former executive mansion in Richmond, had this to say: *Davis left this city last night at eight o'clock by rail for Danville.* This item found its way into some of the evening newspapers

---

5. Robert K. Krick's book, *Civil War Weather in Virginia*, gives a chart of sunrise, sunset, and temperatures in Richmond for April 2 and 3, 1865.
6. *OR*, ser. 1, vol. 46, part 3, p. 574.

of April 6, 1865, and was reproduced in whole or in part in all the morning papers of April 7.

A dispatch by the London *Times* special Southern correspondent, written in New York on April 11, and published in the *Times* on April 26, 1865, had this: *About eight in the evening, President Davis, accompanied by all the members of his Cabinet, except General Breckenridge, started by an express train for Danville.*

John B. Jones's *A Rebel War Clerk's Diary* was published in 1866. By his own admission, he compiled his April 2, 1865, entry after the war, using newspapers as his guide, as he did with other entries. By so doing, he destroyed the credibility of his diary: *The Secretary of War intends to leave at 8:00 p.m. this evening. The President and the rest of the functionaries, I suppose, will leave at the same time.* And this: *It was after 2 o'clock p.m. before the purpose to evacuate the city was announced; and the government had gone at 8:00 p.m. Short notice! and small railroad facilities to get away.*

W.H. Swallow, an eyewitness who was not really an eyewitness at all,[7] likewise copied from the newspapers for his "Retreat of the Confederate Government" (1886): *It was fully eight o'clock when the train departed.*

C.E.L. Stuart is the only reporter known to have been on the presidential train that night who actually wrote anything of the flight (*New York Herald*, July 4, 1865). He is very definite as to the departure time. He was a reporter by trade and by instinct. He wrote, *And then and there began the flight—there, at ten o'clock on the night of April 2, 1865.*

Daily Saratogian (New York), April 1, 1890: *At 10 o'clock that Sunday night, a closely packed train left the station for Danville. It contained Jefferson Davis, his cabinet, the archives of the Southern Confederacy, a guard of picked men, and the contents of the Treasury.* John W. Bell, in his *Memoirs of Governor William Smith* (1891), writes: *The President left by 10 o'clock p.m., on his train.*

There have been no further takers, which is a pity, because, although Stuart was the only person on that train who comes up with 10 o'clock, he was a trained journalist, with a keen nose for detail.

The first time the world ever became aware of 11 o'clock as a possible departure time was in December 1900, when Mallory's account was published in *McClure's* magazine. *By the arrangements of the Secretary of War, the Danville train of cars assigned to the President and those to accompany him, was to leave Richmond at half past eight P.M.; and before this hour the heads of Departments and their chief assistants were ready at the depot. There were good reasons for delay, however, and the cars did not move until eleven P.M.* And this: *At 11 o.c. P.M., the President ... took his seat in the cars, and the train moved in gloomy silence over the James River.*

This article was based on Mallory's original manuscript, which in turn was based on Stuart's July 4, 1865, *New York Herald* article. We are used to Mallory changing Stuart's wording when it suits him. Did he do that here? Did he come up with 11 o'clock just in order to be different from Stuart?

The relevant entry in Robert Garlick Hill Kean's diary purports to have been written on June 1, 1865. However, as there are items in it which can only be explained by a rather serious post hoc situation, and as the diary in its entirety did not see the light of day until 1957, this entry must be regarded with extreme caution. *The train (on which the President*

---

7. See Swallow in the Bibliography for an explanation of this.

and Cabinet also went) did not start until 11 p.m. If, indeed, the Kean entry was written after 1917, which seems to be the case, then whoever wrote it would have read the 1900 Mallory account in *McClure's* magazine.

Even though John Taylor Wood's "diary" was not made available to the public until 1941, it cannot be subject to exactly the same caveat. His April 2, 1865, entry seems, on the surface, at least, to have been written on June 14, 1865, while Wood was in Havana. *At 11:00 p.m. left on train for Danville with the Cabinet.*

All things point to Anna Trenholm writing her diary in or around August 1865. However, it did not emerge until around 1914, when it was donated to the South Caroliniana Library by her daughter. *We left the depot at eleven o'clock in an especial car.*

It's very unlikely that Mallory would have seen any of these three accounts—Kean, Wood, or Mrs. Trenholm—and so, as he also has 11 o'clock, it may be then that, despite Stuart, the train did leave at 11:00.

Mallory did not catch on immediately with history makers, not really until after World War II, but when he did, he did so with a vengeance, and it is now extremely rare to find an author who offers any time other than 11:00 p.m.

James Ford Rhodes, in his *History of the Civil War* (1917), seems to have been the first to accept Mallory's account: *Davis, with all the members of his cabinet except Breckinridge, a number of his staff and other officials, got away at eleven o'clock in the evening on a train of the Richmond and Danville Railroad.*

Robert Douthat Meade thought about 11 o'clock, decided it was just a little too vague, and, in his 1943 biography of the secretary of state, *Judah P. Benjamin*, with absolutely nothing to go on, offered: *...soon after eleven o'clock.*

Shelby Foote, in his book, *The Civil War* (1974), merely writes: *...at 11 o'clock ... the train creaked out of the station.* But he does give 11 o'clock, and this is worth remembering when we come to Chapter 11, and Milepost #94—Clover Station.

By the 1970s, then, eleven o'clock had long been the standard, so to speak. Some examples: Don A. Grigg in his untitled article in the *Danville Register & Bee*, July 4, 1976: *Only hours before Union troops set torch to the city, a train carrying Confederate gold bullion, government records, arms, rations, the President's Cabinet, and Jefferson Davis himself, left at 11 p.m.* Felicity Allen, in *Unconquerable Heart* (1999): *...by eleven that night* [they were] *on the way to Danville.* William J. Cooper, in *Jefferson Davis, American* (2000), says that Davis *climbed aboard, and at 11 p.m. the locomotive chugged out of the city.* Jay Winik, in his famous 2001 book, *April 1865*: *...it was not until eleven that Davis at last bade farewell to Richmond, as the train pulled away.* Jane Singer, in *Confederate Dirty War* (2005): *Finally, at 11 P.M. Davis boarded the train for Danville.*

But even after Mallory's article came out in *McClure's* in 1900, there were others who stuck by their own versions. John H. Reagan, the Confederate postmaster general, was dead when his *Memoirs* came out in 1906. They were edited by Walter Flavius Mac-Caleb, and so we really do not know who wrote the following, but these *Memoirs* were the first to mention the concept of just before midnight. *It was near midnight when the President and his cabinet left the heroic city.*

The Reagan *Memoirs* gained adherents. Morris Schaff, for example, writing in *Jefferson Davis* (1922): *...that night, toward midnight,* [Davis] *boarded a train for Danville.* And, rather surprisingly for such late writers, Katharine M. Jones, in her 1962 book, *Ladies of Richmond*: *At midnight, the train on the Danville Railroad bore off the officers of the government.* And Simon Neiman, in his biography, *Judah Benjamin* (1963): *They* *fled at midnight.* And, even more surprising, Roy Z. Chamlee, in *Lincoln's Assassins* (1990): *Mounted horsemen guarded the train as it pulled out about midnight.* Not so surprising is Hans Kuenzi, in his article, "Search for the Lost Confederate Gold" (2008): *The two trains left Richmond at midnight,* but this last cited does show that Reagan's midnight is still alive and well.

Beginning with Wise, in 1899, April 3 became a fad for a while, rather than April 2. As Wise puts it, in his "End of an Era": *After midnight.* The great William E. Dodd, writing in his 1907 book, *Jefferson Davis,* says this: *The next day, April 3d, a long train of cars laden with the archives of the Confederacy, and crowded with civil officials, from the President himself down to the anxious citizen who had forced his way into it, drew slowly across the James River.*

William L. Broun, as quoted in the 1912 book by his son: *By midnight the boats laden with stores were placed under charge of officers and started for their destination, which they never reached. What became of them I never knew. About two o'clock in the morning General Gorgas came to the arsenal to tell me that he was about to leave with the President for Danville, and to report to him there. I never reported to him til [sic] fifteen years later, when I met him at Sewanee, Tenn.*

When considering spurious eyewitnesses, little more need be said about E.T. Watehall than that his name was really Walthall (see the Bibliography), and that his 1909 article appeared in the magazine *Confederate Veteran*. It is a truly historical fact, beyond impeachment, that Richmond was evacuated during the night of Sunday, April 2, 1865, and the early morning of Monday, April 3, and that at or around 8:15 on Monday morning the Union forces entered the city. So, really, one can say, with more than a small degree of truth, that the fall of Richmond took place on April 3, 1865. With this in mind, the title of the Watehall article, "Fall of Richmond, April 3, 1865," seems innocent enough. However, it is more than clear, from the content of the article itself, that Watehall thinks April 3 was Sunday. And so does *Confederate Veteran*.

Jefferson Davis, of course, received Lee's dispatch on Sunday, April 2, 1865. One of Professor Dodd's major disciples, Armistead Gordon, wrote *Jefferson Davis* in 1918: *On the day after receiving Lee's despatch, he left Richmond with the members of the cabinet and many civil officers, who took with them the archives of the government.* Professor Dodd was still a legend in 1923, when Dunbar Rowland published his mammoth work, *Jefferson Davis, Constitutionalist,* in 1923: *April 3. Leaves Richmond, Va., with the Confederate Cabinet, for Danville.*

But that was it for April 3. The concept was so obviously out of synch with other accounts that after 1923 only an extraordinarily daring individualist could possibly have resurrected it. Alfred H. Bill was such a man. In his 1946 book, *Beleaguered City,* he writes: *Faithful Benjamin met President Davis and other cabinet members at the Danville station about midnight, where a special train awaited them.*

In the morning of Monday, April 3, 1865, just before daybreak, four riders guided their horses out of the apocalypse that was Richmond, and headed toward the southern roads. For Secretary of War Breckinridge, Quartermaster General Lawton,[8] Commissary

---

8. Alexander Robert Lawton (1818–1896), graduate of West Point, 1839, and subsequently a Harvard lawyer. A general in the war, he was severely wounded, and Jefferson Davis appointed him quartermaster general. He was paroled at Charlotte on May 12, 1865.

9. Departure Time

General St. John,[9] and chief of the Engineer Corps, Jeremy F. Gilmer,[10] it would be a rough ride, but the four horsemen would eventually catch up with Jeff Davis.

As Breckinridge wrote in a telegram to Davis on April 8, 1865, as he was riding through Virginia: *Evacuation of Richmond completed in order on morning of third.* And this: *Genls. Gilmer, Lawton and St. John are with me.*

The *Richmond Whig* of April 6, 1865, was the first to report the basic elements of this individual adventure: *Breckinridge, who seems to have been the pluckiest of the lot, waited until the following morning, when, at an early hour, he started out on horseback, intending to follow the fortunes of the army.*

The *New York Daily Tribune* of April 8, 1865, expanded upon the *Whig*'s information: *John C. Breckinridge, who had remained behind to superintend the work of destruction, was among the last to leave. His assistants in this work were General Ewell and Maj. Dick Turner, of Libby Prison notoriety.*

Burke Davis, in his 1985 book, *The Long Surrender*, has this to say: *The companion adventure of John Breckinridge in escaping was first told in a letter to his son Owen, written from the British steamer Shannon and mailed in London in July 1865. The account, presented as a diary, appeared in the Register of the Kentucky State Historical Society, Oct. 1939, edited by A.J. Hanna.*[11]

In 1866, Moses Purnell Handy wrote a seven-part series of articles for the short-lived New York newspaper, *The Watchman*.[12] The paper called it "A Courier's Experience During the Great Retreat," and it takes the form of daily diary entries from the year 1865, beginning at April 1. Each installment included a subtitle, "From his Journal." For some reason the series ended abruptly at April 9. In *The Watchman* of March 10, 1866, we are with Handy in the morning of Monday, April 3, 1865. The sun has already risen, and sunrise that morning was at 5:49, and Handy is on the Manchester side of the about-to-be-burned Mayo Bridge. *I recognized the well-known form of General J.C. Breckinridge crossing the bridge. He too halted and reviewed for a few moments the passing troops. He wore a suit of plain black, with a short cape or talma thrown over his shoulders. None present would have presumed that the confederate Secretary of War was before them, although he was attended by several officers in dress uniform. But notwithstanding his unassuming garb, many soldiers recognized the familiar face of "Old Breck," and acknowledged his presence*

---

9. Isaac Munroe St. John (1827–1880), a Yale graduate, newspaper editor, civil engineer, and railroad man, joined the Confederate Army as a private, rapidly being promoted to captain. In 1862 he became chief of the Mining and Nitre Bureau, and on February 16, 1865, replaced Lucius Northrop as Commissary General of the Confederate States Army, with the rank of brigadier general. He retired his position on May 4, 1865, while on the run, and surrendered to the Union forces on May 23, at Thomasville, Georgia.

10. Jeremy Francis Gilmer (1818–1883), graduate of West Point, 1839, and a veteran of the Mexican War.

11. Breckinridge left Havana on July 7, 1865, aboard the *Shannon*, and spent a part of the transatlantic trip writing this letter to his son, John Witherspoon Breckinridge, known as "Owen." The steamer arrived in Southampton on July 28. The Hanna article Burke Davis refers to is "John Cabell Breckinridge, as revealed by his diary," and appears in *The Register of the Kentucky State Historical Society*, 1939, vol. 37, p. 323, et seq. In 1939 the letter to Owen was in the possession of Mrs. Lee Breckinridge Thomas, of Berkeley, California, the granddaughter of General Breckinridge, and Owen's daughter. A.J. Hanna tells us that part of the account had been printed in an undetermined edition of the *Frankfort Yeoman* (a Kentucky newspaper whose actual name was the *Kentucky Yeoman*). Unfortunately the letter to Owen begins with the events of May 16, 1865.

12. *The Watchman*, founded, published and edited by Charles Force Deems, ran for 52 issues from January 10, 1866.

by hearty cheers, which the secretary returned by touching his cap. Handy goes on to say that while they were all gazing at the Breckinridge party the Confederate fleet blew up. This, then, places the Breckinridge episode at or around 4:35 a.m. Handy then says that the cause of the explosions was confirmed about half an hour later when Admiral Semmes's boys *steamed up to Manchester in their wooden gunboats.*

Mallory writes this: *The Secretary of War, with the chief of the Engineer Corps, General Gilmer, Quartermaster-General Lawton, Commissary-General St. John, with a handful of men, had left Richmond on horseback about three hours after the President, expecting to join him at Danville.*

F. Lawrence McFall, in *Danville in the Civil War* (2001), relies here on Mallory: *Accompanying him were Chief Engineer Jeremy F. Gilmer, Quartermaster General Alexander R. Lawton, and Commissary General Isaac Munroe St. John, along with "a handful of men."*

Speaking only of I.M. St. John, the Jefferson Davis book, *Rise and Fall* (1881), has this to say: *On the morning of the 3rd, the Commissary-General left Richmond and joined General R.E. Lee at Amelia Springs.* William Harwar Parker, writing of Breckinridge, says, in "Gold and Silver" (1893): *The General went out of the city on horseback.*

A.J. Hanna, in his classic 1938 book, *Flight into Oblivion*, says: *Early Monday morning, April 3, 1865, Breckinridge, accompanied by a group of high army officials, rode out of this city of Roman-like hills and proceeded toward General Lee's headquarters.*

If we believe Purnell Handy, and are prepared to dismiss as faulty memory his assertion that sun had already risen, then the Breckinridge party was in Manchester at 4:35 that morning of the 3rd. So, from this, and from all the other evidence, there seems to be no question that Breckinridge, Lawton, St. John, and Gilmer all left Richmond on the morning of the third, by horseback, to join General Lee and from there pressed on to rendezvous with Jefferson Davis. However, there is a dissenting voice. C.E.L. Stuart in his *New York Herald* article of July 4, 1865, has Breckinridge, Lawton, and St. John on the presidential train as it left Richmond. *On we whisked briskly but cautiously—on until we were close to the last battle field of the last campaign, about twenty three miles from the city, and abreast of Petersburg. There we stopped. There General Breckinridge and Quartermaster General Lawton and Commissioner [sic] General St. John left us to find their way to Lee's headquarters, and there gather consolation or offer it.*

Why would Stuart offer this? It seems to be an outrageous fabrication, and it may well be.

Upon orders from Secretary of the Navy Mallory, Admiral Raphael Semmes and his James River Squadron stayed behind in Richmond to scuttle the Confederate fleet in the early hours of the morning of Monday, April 3, 1865. A very basic summary of the event can be found in Spencer C. Tucker's *The Civil War Naval Encyclopedia* (2011): *On the orders of squadron commander Rear Admiral Raphael Semmes, the* Richmond *and other ships of the James River Squadron were destroyed on April 3, 1865, to prevent their capture by Union forces, just prior to the fall of Richmond.*

Semmes himself, in his 1869 book, *Memoirs of Service Afloat*, recounts what led up to the event: *As I was sitting down to dinner, about four o'clock, on the afternoon ... on board my flagship, the* Virginia,[13] *one of the small steamers of my fleet came down from Richmond, having on board a special messenger from the Navy Department. Upon being introduced into my cabin, the messenger presented me with a sealed package.*

---

13. The actual name of Semmes' flagship was the *Virginia II*. He referred to it as simply the *Virginia*.

This is what Semmes read: *General Lee advises the government to withdraw from this city, and the officers will leave this evening, accordingly. I presume that General Lee has advised you of this, and of his movements, and made suggestions as to the disposition to be made of your squadron. He withdraws upon his lines toward Danville, this night, and unless otherwise directed by General Lee, upon you is devolved the duty of destroying your ships this night, and with all the forces under your command joining General Lee. Confer with him, if practicable, before destroying them. Let your people be rationed, as far as possible, for the march, and armed and equipped for duty in the field. Very respectfully, your obedient servant, S.R. Mallory, Secretary of the Navy.*

Admiral Semmes must surely be the most trustworthy of all the people who have ever written of this event. After all, it was his event. It is his story, as told by him. When he says he was sitting down to dinner, then we must believe he was sitting down to dinner. However, Burke Davis, in his 1959 book, *To Appomattox*, was not happy with dinner[14]: *Admiral Raphael Semmes was waggling his spectacular waxed mustaches over late luncheon in the wardroom of his flagship,* Virginia, *at four in the afternoon when a messenger handed him a sealed dispatch. It was from Secretary Mallory.*

Semmes picks up the tale: *This was rather short notice. Richmond was to be evacuated during the night, during which I was to burn my ships, accoutre and provision my men, and join General Lee!* With his captains he then planned the night's work. The job would have to wait until after dark, otherwise they would arouse the suspicions of the enemy, whose lines were only four or five miles away. When night came, Semmes got all his ships together, and ran them up to Drewry's Bluff, where he planned to blow up the ironclads.

It was between two and three o'clock in the morning of April 3 when the crews of the iron-clads were all safely aboard the gunboats, and the iron-clads were well on fire. My little squadron of wooden boats now moved off up the river, by the glare of the burning irons-clads. They had not proceeded far, before *an explosion, like the shock of an earthquake, took place, and the air was filled with missiles. It was the blowing up of the Virginia, my late flag-ship.* As he says, *the pyrotechnic effect was very fine, and the explosion shook the houses in Richmond.*

As they came in sight of the lower part of Richmond, they could see the school ship *Patrick Henry* burning. *The rear guard of our army had just crossed, as I landed my fleet at Manchester, and the bridges were burning in their rear. The Tredegar Iron Works were on fire.* Semmes says that he had 500 sailors, all on foot, as they walked up to the Manchester depot and found that the

Confederate Navy Captain Raphael Semmes.

---

14. In the South, the meal at midday or conveniently thereafter, was called "dinner," as it still often is today. Burke Davis, being from North Carolina, should have been aware of that.

A crippled locomotive in Richmond, 1865.

last train to Danville had left at daylight. They found a small engine lying on the track, but without fuel. There were several cars just sitting around, full of people. Semmes turned the people out, lined the cars up behind the engine, and put his men in the cars. For fuel he cut down a picket fence in front of a residence, and then an engineer and fireman were detailed for the locomotive. *In a very few minutes we had the steam hissing from its boilers.* But then it was found that the engine did not have the power to make even the slightest upgrade. They were still in full view of Richmond across the river, and they could clearly see the enemy pouring into the capital. Then a better engine was found, and they were soon on their way. *My railroad cruise ended the next day—April 4th—about midnight, when we reached the city of Danville.*

The *Richmond Daily Whig*, of April 4, 1865, was the first organ to report this incident: *About daylight on Monday morning, the city was shaken to its foundations by the explosions proceeding from the blowing up of the Confederate ironclads in the river. The Patrick Henry was in flames at Rocketts, and the Navy Yard and all the public buildings therein situated were in process of destruction. Several of the smaller vessels were burned at the city wharves.*

It was not long before other newspapers were writing about the destruction. For example, Carleton Coffin says, in his April 1865 *Boston Journal* article: *At four o'clock the iron-clads, one after another, were blown up.* And this from the *New York Daily Tribune* of April 8, 1865: *About half past 6 o'clock the last train of the retreating Rebels crossed the Danville Railroad bridge.*

Then the "eyewitnesses." This from Phoebe Yates Pember's 1866 article: *...near midnight, and then the schoolship, the Patrick Henry ... was fired at the wharf in "Rocketts," the extreme east end of the city. Her magazine blowing up seemed a signal for the work of destruction to commence. Explosions followed from all points.... The warehouses of tobacco were fired next and communicated the flames to the adjacent houses and shops, which were soon in a flame along Main Street.* And this from her 1879 book, *A Southern Woman's*

9. Departure Time

Story: ...near midnight, when the Patrick Henry ... was fired at the wharf at Rocketts (the extreme eastern end of the city). The blowing up of her magazine seemed the signal for the work of destruction to commence. Explosions followed from all points. The warehouses and tobacco manufactories were fired, communicating the flames to the adjacent houses and shops, and soon Main Street was in a blaze.

William L. Broun, as quoted in the 1912 book by his son, says that every *possible effort was made to prevent the destruction of the arsenal. I, as commanding officer, visited every building between three and four o'clock in the morning of the third of April,* and that he had the gas extinguished and the guards instructed to shoot any man who attempted to fire the buildings. He then says that one hour afterward, while he was four miles from the city, the rapid and terrible explosion of shells heard in the distance proved that part of the city occupied by the arsenal was being made desolate by the torch applied by the frantic mob. *Shortly after the president left the city the gunboats were blown up. After witnessing the explosion from the steps of the arsenal I sent for the keeper of the magazine, and satisfying myself that life would not be endangered by its destruction, wrote an order for him to explode the magazine at five in the morning, the last order of the ordnance department, and among the last orders of the Confederate government given in the city of Richmond. As I rode out of the city in the early dawn, I saw a dense cloud of smoke suddenly ascend, with a deafening report, that shook the city to its center. Thus ended the surrender of the city of Richmond. The mob immediately took possession, looted the stores, and fired the city. A large part of beautiful Richmond was burned to the ground. The Federal troops marched into the burning city in splendid order, took possession, dispersed the mob, and saved by their energy and discipline the city from total destruction.*

Dr. Nelson Lankford's book *Richmond Burning* (2002), quoting from the *Official Records*, is more specific as to the time of the explosion: *At 4:35 a heavy explosion in W.N.W. direction.*

So, ever since the scuttling of the fleet, newsmen and historians have known pretty much the exact time in the morning of April 2–3 that it took place. They've certainly known which morning it was. Which makes Clint Johnson's account of the event, in his 2008 book, *Pursuit*, all the more surprising. Johnson is discussing Secretary Mallory's thought processes as the Davis train waited at the depot on the night of April 2, several hours before the explosions took place: *Mallory sat in the rocking car pondering his future even before the train got out of sight of the station. Just the night before he had heard the Confederate-instigated explosions that splintered the last of the James River Squadron ships he once commanded.* This puts the scuttling a full twenty-four hours before the generally accepted time, thus making it the night of April 1, or at best before sunrise on April 2.

As Semmes himself says that he arrived at Danville at midnight on the 4th, there has been little disagreement, if any, from historians. In other words, Semmes arrived at the tail end of Tuesday, April 4. But can "midnight on the 4th" be interpreted as the midnight that brings you into the 4th, rather than the midnight that takes you out of it—into the 5th? Is that what Semmes had in mind? Did he actually arrive at the end of Monday, April 3, only seven hours or so after Jefferson Davis?

We know he left Richmond on the morning of Monday, April 3, and that, from Manchester, he was watching the Yankees entering Richmond. The Union troops started entering the conquered city at 8:15 that morning, so if Semmes left Manchester at, say, 9:00 a.m. and arrived at Danville at midnight that same day, then it would have taken his train 15 hours to make the trip. Very possible.

The Rebel and the Rose (2007) is equally unclear on this point: *The last train to escape Richmond arrived in Danville around midnight on April 4. On it were Adm. Raphael Semmes and four hundred to five hundred crewmen from the small fleet he had commanded.* However, William H. Parker, in his 1893 article "The Gold and Silver in the Confederate States Treasury," is very clear: *On Monday night, Admiral Semmes arrived with the James River squadron. His was the last train out of Richmond.*

McFall, in *Danville in the Civil War* (2001) is also without doubt. While discussing Tuesday, April 4, he says: *The previous night Admiral Raphael Semmes and his 400 sailors of the James River Squadron arrived in Danville.*

Chapter 10

Brandy and Morphine

C.E.L. Stuart, in his *New York Herald* article of July 4, 1865, is the first to mention alcohol on the presidential train: *Attorney General Davis took an occasional pull at a brandy bottle which was kept by Harrison and others to arrest the progress of discomfort if not of drowsiness.* One knows, from Stuart's account of the party's arrival at Danville, that he is referring here to Burton Harrison, yet Burton Harrison was not on the train. This is Stuart's error, and thus, at the outset, the entire brandy episode must be regarded with suspicion.

While Anna Trenholm, writing her post-war account in or around August 1865, does say that her husband used brandy and cologne in order to revive himself, she was referring to Danville on April 10. Despite the fact that she must have read Stuart's account of the flight, she does not mention alcohol during the trip from Richmond to Danville. She was the only woman in the car for a lot of hours, so it simply would not have been appropriate for her to allude to anything that might have stimulated the imagination of whatever readership she had in mind—even if there is any truth to Stuart's article.

Mallory wrote this about Secretary of the Treasury George Trenholm: *...as usual with men of his practical sense and mature knowledge of the fitness of things, he was provided with abundant supplies for the inner man, which his companions shared. As the morning advanced, our fugitives rescued their spirits; a process which was doubtless aided somewhat by Mr. Trenholm, the astute Secretary of the Treasury, whose well filled hampers and stock of "old Peach" seemed inexhaustible; & by the time the train reached Danville at 5:00 p.m. all shadows seemed to have departed.*

On the surface, it would appear that Mallory is confirming Stuart's brandy story, at least in its basic ingredients. Mallory knew full well that Burton Harrison was not on the train, so he had no choice but to change the purveyor to Trenholm, and decided, at the same time, to add a bit of flavor to Stuart's bare brandy. And it may have been Trenholm's brandy, and it may have been peach. However, Mallory knew a good story when he saw one, and was as well practiced in elaboration as Stuart. Neither man can be trusted, certainly, but, as far as this brandy story goes, they are all we have. Finally, it is important to note that, whereas Stuart has only one brandy bottle being swigged from relatively early on in the trip, Mallory has masses of the stuff, but partaken of only as the morning advanced. One bottle seems much more reasonable, all things considered.

A.J. Hanna, in *Flight into Oblivion* (1938), is the first 20th-century historian to address the subject of alcohol aboard the president's car: "*As the morning advanced,*" said Secretary Mallory, "*our fugitives recovered their spirits, a process which was doubtless aided somewhat by Mr. Trenholm, the astute Secretary of the Treasury, whose well filled hampers of 'old peach' seemed inexhaustible."*

Hanna's book was published in 1938, and he is quoting from the 1900 edited version of Mallory's account, the one that appeared in *McClure's* magazine. It would be another few years before Mallory's original manuscript would become available to the general public, so *McClure's* was all Hanna had to go on, hence his use of the word "recovered" instead of Mallory's own word, "rescued." However, by omitting the words "and stock"—which are in both the Mallory Papers and the *McClure's* article—Hanna altered the meaning of Mallory's narrative. In Mallory, the well-filled hampers and the stock of "old Peach" are quite clearly two separate and distinct items, and they both seemed inexhaustible. The hampers, without question, contained food, not alcohol. The process of how a story is handed down—in this case, from Stuart's "brandy bottle" to Mallory's "stock of 'old Peach'" to Hanna's "well-filled hampers of 'old peach'"—illustrates the way in which history can be re-written. Hanna was very influential, and those writers who have studied him at the expense of Mallory have perpetuated this error.

Alfred H. Bill, in *The Beleaguered City* (1946), says that Trenholm *brought along a large quantity of old peach, which proved a godsend to the party, and seems to have been about the only luxury they had for their journey.* And Roy Nichols says, in *The Stakes of Power* (1961): *Secretary Trenholm's generous store of peach brandy.* The Hoehlings, influenced by Roy Nichols' vocabulary, wrote this in their 1981 book, *The Day Richmond Died*: *...a generous amount of "old peach" brandy.* *The Rebel and the Rose* (2007), has this: *No doubt Trenholm's peach brandy had helped as well.*

All four of these passages are quite acceptable, if one accepts Mallory. What is not acceptable is what Philip Van Doren Stern did to the story, in his 1958 book, *An End to Valor*: *As soon as the city was left behind, the members of the Confederate cabinet turned for solace to the plentiful supplies of old peach brandy, which George Trenholm, the wealthy Secretary of the Treasury, had been thoughtful enough to provide.* Again, history is being changed here. Secretary Trenholm was in extremis as he boarded the train at Richmond. Thoughtfulness—in the form of supplying liquor for his friends on the trip—would have been one of the last things on his mind. And, again, nowhere does Mallory indicate that drinking took place until well into the following morning. This is all invention on the part of Stern.

Judging from what follows, and from the 1958 date, it would appear that Hamilton Cochran wrote his book *Blockade Runners of the Confederacy* in tandem with Stern: *Mrs. Trenholm went along with her husband, who had thoughtfully brought with him a quantity of old peach brandy, which helped.*

In his 1964 book, *Tragic Hero*, Hudson Strode introduced an element to the story which had interesting but not serious consequences. He ascribes ownership of the brandy not only to George Trenholm, but also to his wife: *In the morning the party was refreshed by good things from the hampers of food the well-to-do Trenholms had brought along, including inexhaustible supplies of 'Old Peach.'*

Professor Strode's invention led to another, by William C. Davis. In his 2001 book, *An Honorable Defeat*, he decided that it was not George Trenholm at all who supplied the brandy, but rather his wife who did: *...some of the peach brandy that Anna thought to bring along.* He does not source this passage. Professor Davis's sheer prestige clearly overwhelmed Margaret Middleton Rivers Eastman when she came to write her 2011 book, *Old Charleston Originals*. Talking about Anna Trenholm, she says: *Her seemingly inexhaustible* supply of peach brandy cheered the thirty Confederate officials as they continued on to Danville. She seems to be Professor Davis's only taker.

Outright, unashamed fiction was bound to happen, and it did, in the unsurprising form of Burke Davis, who in 1959 wrote in *To Appomattox*: *There was a secret source of merriment and comfort in the Presidential car. Secretary George Trenholm had managed to bring aboard two well-filled hampers of old peach brandy, and the invalid became the most popular member of the cabinet.* Burke Davis decided that the hampers of old peach brandy deserved a number—two. *Mallory of the Navy, at least, was won, and proclaimed, "Our fugitives recovered their spirits."* Actually Mallory did not proclaim that. What he actually wrote was, "Our fugitives rescued their spirits." As we have already seen, the word "recovered" was only in the edited *McClure's* magazine version. By 1959 the Mallory papers had been available for years.

Because Burke Davis had two hampers, we have this from James C. Clark, in *Last Train South* (1984): *To help Trenholm cope with his illness, two hampers of peach brandy had been brought aboard, but Benjamin quickly found nonmedical uses for it. Navy Secretary Mallory sampled the brandy, and wrote, "Our fugitives recovered their spirits."*

John D. Wright, in his unique 2001 book, *The Language of the Civil War*, says that "old peach" was a nickname for peach brandy. He should have stopped there, instead of quoting A.J. Hanna and/or Burke Davis: *When the Confederate cabinet escaped south by train from Richmond at the war's end, the secretary of the treasury, George A. Trenholm somewhat revived their sadness with his inexhaustible "well filled hampers of old peach."*

Burke Davis changed the mood on the train from somber to cheery, when he describes the brandy as being a "secret source of merriment." James Swanson, in *Bloody Crimes* (2010), prefers this to the original: *Trenholm contributed an essential ingredient to the cheery mood aboard the train: a seemingly inexhaustible supply of "old Peach" brandy.* And this, quoting Mallory: *"As the morning advanced, our fugitives recovered their spirit [sic], and by the time the train reached Danville ... all shadows seemed to have departed."* Swanson is using *McClure's* magazine, rather than the Mallory Papers, as is evident from his use of the word "recovered" rather than "rescued." However, the misquote of "spirit" for "spirits" not only spoils the secretary's rather clever double entendre, but, unfortunately, alters the entire meaning of the passage.

Shelby Foote often created his own history in his classic three-volume *The Civil War: A Narrative*. In Volume 3 (1974), he writes: *Trenholm, down with neuralgia and attended by his wife, the only woman in the party, had brought along a demijohn of peach brandy, presumably for medicinal purposes, though it helped to ease the tension all around, especially for Benjamin, who smiled in his curly beard.* The "demijohn," invented by Foote, has been copied by, for example, Ken Bivin in his May 1995 article "The Fall of Richmond." When all is said and done, though, even if the inexhaustible supply of peach had truly been limited to the one mere vessel proposed by Foote, it is somewhat disappointing to observe that he and all other writers copying from him have deprived themselves of the chance to make a play on the word that is synonymous with "demijohn"—carboy.

Burke Davis originated the two-hamper theory. Ernest B. Furgurson came up with the one hamper. In his *Ashes of Glory* (1996), he says that Trenholm *also brought a hamper of "supplies for the inner man."* This one-hamper theory gained at least one notable adherent, the eminent Nelson Lankford, in his book, *Richmond Burning* (2002). Dr. Lankford says that Trenholm *boarded the carriage well provisioned for the trip with a hamper of peach brandy—"supplies for the inner man" in the words of a colleague. It did him little good, as self-medication with alcohol and morphine made Trenholm a very sick man indeed.* The morphine story comes from the Anna Trenholm diary (1865). However, Mrs. Trenholm's reference to morphine is when the party arrived at Danville, not as it was leaving Richmond, and then certainly not in connection with alcohol.

Rodman L. Underwood wrote the latest biography of Secretary of the Navy Mallory, in 2005. When it comes to discussing the brandy episode, Underwood is apparently not satisfied with either the one-hamper theory, or the two-hamper theory, so he makes it more than two: *Of Secretary of the Treasury Trenholm, he* [i.e., Mallory] *wrote that Trenholm "was provided with abundance of supplies for the inner man, including some 'inexhaustible' hampers of 'Old Peach,' all of which he shared generously with his companions."*

Another fiction that was bound to happen sooner or later was a new flavor for the brandy, or rather that there were two flavors. This, from Clint Johnson's *Pursuit* (2008): *Bored and unable to sleep as readily as his traveling companions who had liberally partaken of the apple brandy Secretary of the Treasury George Trenholm was passing around, Mallory started glancing around the train car.* Then this: *Trenholm, a man of great wealth accumulated by owning blockade-running ships,[1] did not seem as ill as he usually did, but then again, he was passing around what seemed like an inexhaustible supply of "Old Peach." Most everyone in the packed train car of twenty-nine men and one woman, Mrs. Trenholm, seemed to welcome the chance to drink some liquor to smooth the transition from government official to war refugee.*

As for the morphine, Anna Trenholm wrote her account of the flight in or around August 1865. Discussing the moment they arrived at Danville, she says: *Mr. Trenholm was quite sick from the effects of Morphine, as well as the pain in his head.*

The Hoehlings paraphrased this, in their book, *The Day Richmond Died* (1981: *Mr. Trenholm was quite sick from the effects of the morphine as well as the pain in his head.* A historian who reworked the passage in his own words was Ernest B. Furgurson, in *Ashes of Glory* (1996): *Ailing with neuralgia, using morphine for his pains, he also brought a hamper of "supplies for the inner man."*

Burke Davis brings us a bit of fiction in *The Long Surrender* (1985): *The Secretary of the Treasury had been sedated by a doctor before departure, treatment for neuralgia and a stomach ailment, and he was now "quite sick from the effects of the morphine as well as the pain in his head."* It must be noted that he is quoting from the Hoehlings, rather than from Anna Trenholm.

Perhaps not fiction, but certainly creative nonfiction, was William C. Davis's account of this in *An Honorable Defeat* (2001): *Poor George Trenholm had to lie down across a seat much of the time, suffering from neuralgia and some internal complaint for which the morphine that he took only made him sicker.*

Edward Lee Spence, in *Treasures of the Confederate Coast* (1995) says that *there is some evidence that, like many of the very wealthy men of his time, Trenholm was addicted to morphine.* And that may be. However, the evidence for such an addiction is not to be found in any of the accounts of the Davis flight. But then, Spence never says that. An addict, however, would surely know not to mix drugs with alcohol, especially when in such desperate straits, which makes Nelson Lankford's concoction in *Richmond Burning* (2002) hard to swallow when he discusses the moment Trenholm boards the train at

---

1. Actually, Trenholm was one of the richest men in the United States before the Civil War even started.

Richmond, at the very beginning of the trip: *...self-medication with alcohol and morphine made Trenholm a very sick man indeed.*

Lankford got a taker—not for the mixing of the two substances, but for Trenholm's being medicated before leaving Richmond. *The Rebel and the Rose* (2007), relying not only on Lankford but also on Burke Davis, has this about the unfortunate Secretary of the Treasury Trenholm, as he boarded the train at Richmond: *Trenholm was suffering not only from neuralgia but also the effects of the morphine given to him by his physician before leaving Richmond.* This is not footnoted.

History has indeed come a long way from the time Anna Trenholm wrote her account. It has come even farther since Stuart wrote his.

Chapter 11

THE TRIP

Whatever the distance is between the two cities as the crow flies, the Richmond & Danville Railroad main line between the two termini comprised 140.6 miles of track running, as A.J. Hanna put it in *Flight into Oblivion* (1938): *southwest ... through the sloping Piedmont section,* or as John H. Brubaker III re-phrased it forty years later in his book *The Last Capital* (1979): *southwest through the sloping Piedmont countryside.*

Notwithstanding the fact that 140.6 miles is absolutely correct,[1] there are those historians who have expressed variance. For example, William J. Cooper, in *Jefferson Davis, American* (2000), writes: *Danville, some 145 miles southwest of Richmond,* while Flood, in his book *Grant and Sherman* (2005), has this: *Davis and most of his cabinet left Richmond on a special train, heading 120 miles southwest to Danville, Virginia.*

The Richmond & Danville Railroad ran the 140.6 miles from the Confederate capital to the small Virginia town on the Dan River hard by the North Carolina line.[2] Here, at Danville, on, say, April 2–3, 1865, one could pick up the recently constructed Piedmont Railroad[3] for the 48-mile stretch through North Carolina to Greensboro.[4] In theory, one could proceed from Greensboro to all points south. However, in practice, the Piedmont, like all other roads, was subject to broken tracks.

J. Frank Carroll, in *Confederate Treasure* (1996), writes: *Because the narrow gauge lines were in poor condition and individual cars needed attention along the way, the 140-mile journey to Danville required sixteen worrisome and tedious hours.*

The R&D, running between Richmond and Danville, was a single-track road, which means that up trains and down trains could not pass; one of them would have to back up and pull into a siding. When the Richmond & Petersburg line was cut in 1864, the R&D remained the only rail route out of Richmond open to the south.[5] It became the lifeline,

---

1. *Annual Report of the Railroad Companies of the State of Virginia,* for the year ending September 30, 1859, p. 580; Henry Varnum Poor, *Poor's Manual of the Railroads of the United States* (New York: H.V. & H.W. Poor, 1868), p. 152.
2. The efficiency of the Confederate rail system was severely hampered by the fact that there was no standardized gauge in the South. There were three types of railroad gauge in the Confederacy—broad, standard, and narrow. Broad was 5 feet, standard was 4 feet 8½ inches, and narrow was anything smaller than standard. The Richmond & Danville was broad gauge, whereas the Piedmont was standard.
3. Opened May 19, 1864.
4. Because of the difference in gauges, shipment by rail from Richmond to Greensboro, or vice versa, meant offloading and reloading at Danville. See John E. Clark, Jr., *Railroads in the Civil War.*
5. The Richmond and Petersburg Railroad came out of Richmond, crossed the James River into Manchester, where it then crossed the Richmond & Danville Railroad, and then headed due south to the left of Manchester Cemetery, and, running parallel with the Richmond and Petersburg Old *(continued)*

and, as such, was kept in better shape than it had ever been. However, having said that, in the months immediately preceding April 1865, with the extraordinarily heavy flow of men and subsistence for the armies in front of Richmond and Petersburg, the road was taxed beyond its capacity. In those dying days of the war, with the Confederate States in desperate trouble, neither labor nor material in sufficient quantities could be produced for the proper repairs of the railroad and machinery.

Lee surrendered at Appomattox Court House on April 9, 1865. Up trains continued to run on the R&D from Danville to Keysville until April 12, when the bridge over the Staunton River was burned.[6] Subsequently they ran only as far as Clover, that is until April 24, when the advance of the Union's Sixth Corps made that impossible.

The next few segments of this chapter rely to a considerable extent upon railroad company ads and schedules published in newspapers, but also upon an analysis of the following sources, which, although individually not always completely trustworthy, do present, as an overall compendium, something closely resembling a good picture of the lay of the R&D land at the time:

1856—*Smith's Hand-Book for Travellers Throughout the United States.*
1857—*Mitchell's New Travellers' Guide Through the United States.*
1858—*Virginia Gazetteer.*
1859—*Smith's Hand-book for Travellers Throughout the United States.*
1859—*W. Alvin Lloyd's Southern Steamboat and Railroad Guide.*
1862—"Map of the Country Surrounding Richmond, Virginia, Showing the railroads, principal roads, water-courses, etc.," which was shown in *Harper's Weekly*, August 23, 1862. On this map we see the following R&D depots marked: Richmond, Manchester, Coal Mines, Tomahawk, Powhatan, Mattox [sic], Chula, and Amelia Court House.
1862—*Hill & Swayze's Confederate States Rail-road & Steam-boat Guide* of 1862.
1863—Gilmer map.
1863—*W. Alvin Lloyd's Southern Railroad Guide.*
1864—Nordendorf Map of Danville.
1864—*W. Alvin Lloyd's Southern Railroad Guide.*
1865—*Appleton's Illustrated Railway and Steam Navigation Guide.*
1865—Nordendorf Map of Danville.
1867—"Thirty-five miles around Richmond, Va.," a map produced by Jedediah Hotchkiss.
1881—*Official Railway Guide.*
1888—Map of Chesterfield County, compiled by J.E. La Prade, County Surveyor.

According to Shelby Foote, in *The Civil War: A Narrative* (1974), in 1865 a train would normally have covered the 140 miles from Richmond to Danville in four hours. *The normal four-hour run had taken just four times that long.* That's an average of 35

(cont.) Turnpike, it passed through Temple Station, Phillips Crossing, Drewry's Bluff Station, Centralia, Chester, and Port Walthall, going all the way to Petersburg.

6. In this part of Virginia, the Roanoke River is called the Staunton River.

mph. One must repeat, Foote is implying an average here, which means taking into account stops at stations along the way and other delays. At times, then, the train would have been hitting speeds of 50 or 60 mph, in order to maintain the average. Foote is not alone in his optimistic assessment. Far from it.

Hudson Strode, in *Tragic Hero* (1964), assures us that *the journey should have been completed by dawn*. Dawn that morning was 4:30 a.m. Given that the presidential train left Richmond the previous night at about 11 o'clock, that would mean a traveling time of between five and six hours. That's an average of about 26 mph. Strode found a taker in Danville historian, John H. Brubaker III, who says, in his slim but very influential 1979 book, *The Last Capital*: *The government trains should have reached Danville by a little after dawn on the morning of April 3, but a combination of events conspired to turn the trip into a 15-hour nightmare.* So, Strode invented "dawn," and Brubaker elaborated on that, making it "a little after dawn." This is all pure fiction based on sloppy research, or rather, no research at all.

James C. Clark has this in his 1984 work, *Last Train South*: *...the 140-mile trip to Danville should have taken four hours, but the train crawled along at barely nine miles an hour*, while Clint Johnson, in *Pursuit* (2008), comes up with this: *A 140-mile train trip between Richmond and Danville should have taken no more than four to five hours.*

In 1857 it took a train nine hours to get from Richmond to Danville, under ordinary, normal circumstances. That was the schedule, including a stop at Burkeville Junction.[7] In 1861, the scheduled time for the mail train was 7 hours and 58 minutes, and 20 minutes faster on the return trip. Mind you, that was 1861. A year of war had its effects on the R&D schedule. This from *Hill & Swayze's Confederate States Rail-road & Steam-boat Guide* (1862):

Richmond—4:00 p.m.
Manchester
Powhite—8 miles, 4:40 p.m.
Coalfield—13 miles, 5:10 p.m.
Tomahawk—18 miles
Powhatan—22 miles, 6:03 p.m.
Mattoax—27 miles, 6:30 p.m.
Chula—30 miles, 6:48 p.m.
Amelia Court House—36 miles, 7:33 p.m.
Jetersville—43 miles, 8:16 p.m.
Jennings Ordinary—50 miles
Burkeville Junction—53 miles, 9:00 p.m.

And this:

Richmond—7:30 a.m.
Manchester
Powhite—8 miles
Coalfield—13 miles, 8:37 a.m.
Tomahawk—18 miles
Powhatan—22 miles, 9:27 a.m.
Mattoax—27 miles, 9:52 a.m.
Chula—30 miles, 10:09 a.m.
Amelia Court House—36 miles, 10:52 a.m.
Jetersville—43 miles, 11:24 a.m.
Jennings Ordinary—50 miles
Burkeville Junction—53 miles, 12:02 p.m.
Price's—61 miles
Meherrin—65 miles, 1:03 p.m.
Keysville—73 miles. 1:46 p.m.
Drake's Branch—81 miles, 2:23 p.m.
Mossingford—84 miles, 2:39 p.m.
Roanoke—90 miles, 3:10 p.m.
Clover—94 miles, 3:51 p.m.
Scottsburg—100 miles, 4:14 p.m.
Wolf Trap—104 miles
Boston—109 miles, 4:47 p.m.
News Ferry—117 miles, 5:18 p.m.

---

7. *Richmond Daily Whig*, March 17, 1857. Advertisement for Richmond & Danville Railroad.

11. The Trip

Barksdale—127 miles, 5:53 p.m.
Ringgold—135 miles, 6:25 p.m.
North Side—140 miles
Danville—141 miles, 6:45 p.m.

The up train left Danville at 6:30 a.m. and arrived at Richmond at 5:25 p.m. That's eleven hours. The up train from Burkeville Junction left at 12:30 p.m. and arrived in Richmond at 6:00 p.m. That's 5 hours and 30 minutes—and that's just the 54 miles from Burkeville to Richmond.

The *Richmond Sentinel* of July 27, 1863, carried a change of schedule notice issued on July 23 by James H. Lester, General Ticket Agent at the office of the superintendent of the Richmond & Danville Railroad: *On and after Tuesday, July 28th, the passenger trains on this road will run as follows: Way Train leaves Richmond, daily, (except Sunday) at 7.30 A.M. and arrives in Danville at 6 P.M. Leaves Danville at 6 A.M. and arrives at Richmond at 5 P.M.* This was repeated in the *Sentinel* of August 12, 1863. That's the summer of 1863, and the trip, either way, between Richmond and Danville was taking eleven hours.

This from the *Augusta Constitutionalist* of August 11, 1864, quoting the *Danville Register*: *...passenger trains now pass over the entire line of the Richmond & Danville Railroad. The track is much better than it was before, the flat iron having been replaced by the heavy T.*

By December 1865, and on into 1866—in other words, several months after the war, after the track had been somewhat normalized—the trip was taking nine and a half hours, including the stopover at Burkeville. The return trip took 15 minutes longer.[8] In 1882, after 17 years of peace and major strides forward in railroad technology, this was the schedule for passenger trains[9]:

12:07 p.m.—left Richmond
2:32 p.m.—arrived at Burkeville Junction
6:43 p.m.—arrived at Danville
Total: 6 hours and 37 minutes

In 1888 it took 5 hours and 35 minutes to make the trip.
By 1891 they'd gotten the time down a bit:

3:00 p.m.—left Richmond
5:11 p.m.—arrived at Burkeville Junction
5:54 p.m.—arrived at Keysville
8:22 p m.—arrived at Danville
Total: 5 hours and 22 minutes

It was not until almost World War I that a train was able to equal Shelby Foote's four hours.

It may be instructive to see at a glance how historians have described the motion of the train as it made the trip to Danville:

1906. Reagan—*rolled along*
1907. Dodd—*dragged along*

---

8. *Daily Richmond Examiner*, February 6, 1866. Advertisement for the Richmond & Danville Railroad.
9. *Richmond Daily Whig*, February 15, 1882. Advertisement for the Richmond & Danville Railroad.

1920. Walmsley—*crept along*
1923. Eckenrode—*humped its way southward*
1958. Cass Canfield—*crawled*
1974. Shelby Foote—*rolled creakily*
1984. Clark—*crawled along*
1985. Burke Davis—*laboring westward*
1986. Ballard—*rattled forward*
1993. Ryan—*inched forward*
2000. William J. Cooper—*chugged, clanked slowly*
2001. Winik—*jerking and clacking*
2001. William C. Davis—*by fits and starts, crawled*
2007. *The Rebel and the Rose*—*lurched and belched*
2008. Johnson—*herked and jerked and wheezed, clattering along*
2011. Swanson—*creep at a slow speed, groaned, rolled*

Obviously the speed of the presidential train varied as it ran between Richmond and Danville on April 2–3, 1865, as it would on a trip of 140 miles on an uncertain road. Uncertain, yes—the poor, unmaintained track, the threat of Sheridan's cavalry—but it is important to bear in mind L.E. Harvie's words in a letter to General I.M. St. John on January 1, 1876: *Neither the road nor the telegraph was cut or disturbed until the day after the evacuation of the city.*

C.E.L. Stuart writes, in his July 4, 1865, *New York Herald* article: *On we whisked, briskly yet cautiously.* However, Mallory says: *The progress of the train was slow & its interruptions frequent; & it was not until the bright beams of the morning sun shone cheerily into the cars, as they "drew their slow length along" at the rate of about ten miles an hour, that any relief from the general gloom was felt.*

This is the first time that 10 mph is ever mentioned, and only after the sun had come up on the morning of Monday, April 3. But Mallory's manuscript was not made public until *McClure's* magazine published it, in edited form, in 1900. Between the time Mallory wrote his manuscript and 1900 no mention is ever made by anyone of the speed of the train. So, effectively, the first time we read of a speed is in 1900.

William E. Dodd, the greatest historian of his age, and later U.S. Ambassador to Nazi Germany, wrote, in his 1907 classic, *Jefferson Davis*: *The Davis train dragged along the Danville Railroad at the rate of ten miles an hour, taking all day and the following night to traverse the distance which is now but a matter of three or four hours.* And this: *Sheridan's cavalry were on the lookout for the escaping president and his cabinet. Every member of the anxious and disconsolate company expected at any time to be halted by a detachment from the army of Grant, and forced to surrender at discretion. However, they reached Danville in safety."*

It is quite clear from "all day and the following night" that Professor Dodd had very little, if any, understanding of the event. And he has completely misjudged the context in which Mallory was discussing "ten miles an hour."

Dodd was so influential that he was bound to acquire disciples. Walmsley, for example, in his 1920 article, "Break-up of the Confederate Cabinet": *...the party arrived at Danville at 3 P.M. on Monday, April 3, having crept along at less than ten miles an hour, expecting capture every moment.* And Meade, in his biography of the Confederate secretary of state, *Judah P. Benjamin* (1943): *The engine could go only about ten miles an hour* *over the war-worn Confederate railroad and the Davis party passed a gloomy night, only partly relieved by the sunshine the next morning.* And Cass Canfield, in *The Iron Will of Jefferson Davis* (1958): *...as the Davis train crawled along the Danville railroad at ten miles an hour, Sheridan's cavalry was scouring the countryside, looking for the President and his Cabinet.*

Of course, Canfield took the speed from Dodd, as he did the piece about Sheridan. But was Sheridan truly on the lookout for the fleeing party? He was certainly on the loose in the general area, but was he even aware that Jefferson Davis had departed Richmond? How could he have known of it, at that early stage? There were no telephones then. There was telegraph, yes, but who in the Confederate capital would have telegraphed this Union general to tip him off that Davis had fled? And even if someone had wished to do this, how would he have known where to telegraph to, with Sheridan roaming around the countryside as he was?

Yearns and Barrett, in their *North Carolina Civil War Documentary* (1980), commenting on Southern railroad speeds, have this to say: *By 1864 the average speed of passenger trains had fallen to ten miles an hour, and some rails and roadbeds were in such poor shape that five miles an hour was considered dangerous.* James C. Clark, in *Last Train South* (1984), was somehow able to refine the mathematics for us: *...the train crawled along at barely nine miles an hour.* Rather speciously, William C. Davis, has this, in his 1991 effort, *The Man and His Hour*: *The train moved slowly over the poor roadbed, doing barely more than ten miles an hour at times, and there were frequent stops at which people gathered to gawk at the president and shake his hand.*

It must be borne in mind, especially by those who have ever traveled by train, that during any trip of some considerable length, at any time in railroad history, anywhere in the world, a locomotive will do "barely more than ten miles an hour at times."

Even after a hundred years, Professor Dodd was still exerting the pressure of his enormous reputation. William C. Davis, in *An Honorable Defeat* (2001), felt compelled to write: *By fits and starts, at ten miles an hour, the presidential train crawled through the night toward the west.* This was as the train was heading west toward Powhatan, before it made the turn to the south. We have no idea how fast or slow the train was moving at this early stage of the journey, except Stuart's "briskly" and Mallory's "slow."

F. Lawrence McFall, in his book *Danville in the Civil War* (2001) writes: *Frequent interruptions slowed the average speed of the train to less than ten miles per hour. With the arrival of dawn, the sun began shining through the dingy windows of the railroad car.*

Although Clint Johnson in *Pursuit* (2008) toes the Dodd line, we learn a good deal more: *The engine herked and jerked and wheezed down the rails toward Danville at a measly ten miles per hour, barely four times the pace a soldier could march, and at half the pace a regiment of cavalry could have maintained.*

James Swanson, in *Bloody Crimes* (2010), describes the departure of the presidential train from Richmond that night, through the eyes of 1st Lt. William Harwar Parker. Like most other historians, Swanson has elevated Parker in rank: *Captain Parker watched the train gather steam and creep out of the station at a slow speed, no more than ten miles per hour.* It is better for all concerned if a train creeps out of a station, rather than rushing out at tremendous speed. Regardless of that, this is the actual quote, from Parker's *Recollections* (1883): *After a short delay in Manchester, we steamed away at the rate of some ten miles an hour.* The problem is, Parker was talking about the treasure train, not the presidential train, as can be confirmed by what he says next: *We went along at a slow rate of speed, stopping at Amelia Court House and other places, and arrived at Danville on the afternoon of April 3d. We found the Cabinet here.*

Again from Swanson: *It had taken 18 hours to travel just 140 miles. The train had averaged less than ten miles per hour, and at some points, especially on uphill grades, it could barely move at all. Sometimes the train stopped completely. This sorry performance demonstrated the lamentable state of the Confederate railroad system.* Working with Swanson's math, the train averaged just over 7 mph.

Now for a reference section, the R&D route from Richmond to Danville:

Richmond

On the night of April 2, 1865, the train upon which so many hopes now rested, and on which so much humanity was crammed, jolted slowly west out of the R&D depot on Cary Street, and headed toward the James River.

Rocketts

The train passed the entrance of the branch to Rocketts, a branch completed in 1851.

James River

They left Henrico County and inched over the stone bridge that crossed the James River into Chesterfield County, and more specifically into the city of Manchester.[10] As Stuart wrote, in his July 4, 1865, *New York Herald* article: *The night was supremely clear and calm—the dome of heaven spread out its radiance, glittering as I have rarely seen it— "silent as if watched the sleeping earth."* Or, as Mallory put it: *...and the train moved in gloomy silence over the James River.*

Stuart talks more about the night: *Yet it seldom shed its peaceful effulgence on more desperate deeds—seldom flung its glittering mantle over more dismal and degrading scenes—seldom threw its myriad rays of "perfect quiet" into horrors more demoniac. What was transpiring in the city we were fleeing from we had not the least conception of—knew nothing of the fearful acts with which the half starved mob so [illegible] the doomed city while we were jolting along the Danville road, wondering why we were going, or whither our course tended. No, none of the fiendish feats which marked Richmond as a prey for that night, under that serene, seductive canopy of a beaming spring day—none of these had for a moment occurred to any of us as possible. We were all thinking not of the horrors in the city but of the carnage in the vicinity of which we were passing. It was in what seemed likely to confront us in the front, not in what was raging in the rear, that all our speculations centered.*

This from Mallory: *A commanding view of the river front of the city was thus afforded, and as the fugitives receded from its flickering lights, many and sad were the commentaries they made upon the Confederate Cause.*

---

10. Richmond's first bridge across the James had been built in 1788 by John Mayo, Jr., but it had proved insubstantial and was destroyed by river ice in the first winter. Mayo rebuilt it several times over the following years. Owning it, as he did, he collected tolls, and the structure became known as Mayo's Bridge.

11. The Trip

Top: Ruins on Cary Street, Richmond, 1865. *Bottom:* A view of Rocketts and the James River.

Milepost 0.7
Manchester

After crossing the James, one immediately found oneself both in Chesterfield County, Virginia, and the city of Manchester. Every train stopped at the great junction there. Passing through town, and crossing over the Richmond & Petersburg Railroad tracks, the long, long Davis train was an object of wonder to the folks by the side of the road. The contorted silhouette of the demon fireman, already blackened by the belching pine-smoke and flying sparks, slinging wood from tender to furnace with the vigorous abandon of a lost soul, appeared to be the very ferryman of the Styx, as the train picked up speed and headed out into C.E.L. Stuart's "supremely clear and calm night," hugging the west bank of the river. The sands of time had run out for the Lost Cause.

The 2007 book, *The Rebel and the Rose*, has this to commence its Chapter 2: *The train carrying the fugitive Confederate government lurched and belched its way through the suburb of Manchester on the south side of the James River; the locomotive's whistle screeched into the night.*

Manchester is a part of Richmond today, but back then it was not a suburb of Richmond, or of any other city, but an independent entity. Between 1870 and 1876 it would be the county seat of Chesterfield County and from 1874 to 1910 one of Virginia's "independent cities." Only at that latter date did it merge with Richmond.

Milepost 2.0
Belle Isle Spur

The train, running along the main R&D line, passed the entrance to a short spur line that went out to the right, to Belle Isle, in the middle of the James River.[11] The train carried on, passing Granite Quarry on its left,[12] and Hickory Island to its right.[13] With Hickory Island in view, the train swung west in the direction of Granite Station, while a longish spur continued up the south coast of the river crossing Gilbert's Creek to the Westham Granite Quarries off Barrett Island.

Milepost 2.6
Rockfield

This was where the track crossed Reedy Creek. In a Richmond newspaper of December 23, 1851, Rockfield appears in an R&D ad as a station for passengers only, but is not mentioned in the 1858 *Virginia Gazetteer*. Rockfield is shown on Hotchkiss's map of 1867, but not on La Prade's 1888 map.

Milepost 4.0
Fourth Mile Post/Hutcheon and Donald Siding

There was a siding here, a short spur line leading over Powhite Creek to the Old Dominion Quarries, which, in reality, formed part of the community of Granite. If it was

---

11. The spur line to Belle Isle was opened in 1851. Much later it came to be known as Smithsyde.
12. Granite Quarry was just a quarry, not an inhabited place, as such.
13. Like Belle Isle, Hickory Island was in the middle of the James River. Unlike Belle Isle, there was no spur line running to it.

11. The Trip

Belle Isle Railroad Bridge and Old Dominion Iron and Nail Works, Richmond.

called anything at that time, it was Fourth Mile Post. By 1915 it was known as Hutcheon & Donald Siding.

Milepost 4.5
Granite

Granite is not shown in the 1858 *Virginia Gazetteer*, nor on Jed Hotchkiss's 1867 map, but oddly, and almost certainly erroneously, the latter has "Powhite St." at this exact location [*see* Powhite, next stop]. Granite is listed at Milepost #5 in the 1881 *Official Railway Guide*, and on La Prade's 1888 map it is a definite community, rather spread out, with Granite Station located where, at that period of time, the tracks crossed the River Road, and also at the point where Powhite Creek intersected.[14] As for newspaper mentions of "Granite Station," they begin only in 1904.

After leaving Granite, the R&D tracks continued west, with the River Road running parallel to the north.

Milepost 7.9
Powhite/Bonair

According to the R&D advertisements in the Richmond papers from December 23,

---

14. Today, this is where Forrest Hill Avenue and the Powhite Expressway cross the railroad tracks.

1851, to April 1853, the train stopped at Powhite,[15] in Chesterfield County. This was obviously a depot of some sort, and there had to have been a water tank here as well.[16] After April 1853 Powhite is not mentioned in the ads, nor is it mentioned in the 1858 *Virginia Gazetteer*. However, *Hill & Swayze's Confederate States Rail-road & Steam-boat Guide* of 1862, which gives the stations along the Richmond & Danville Railroad, shows Powhite at Milepost #8, as does *Appleton's Guide* of 1865. On the map *Thirty-Five Miles Around Richmond, Virginia*, compiled by Jed. Hotchkiss in 1867, the R&D tracks are clearly shown, and "Powhite St." is shown where Granite Station should be, at Milepost 4.5.[17] Immediately to the south of Milepost #8, on Hotchkiss's 1867 map, we see the name Brown rather dominating the landscape (the original name of this site, before the railroad came, was Brown's Summit), but we also see the name Bon Air. This was the Bonair Company, who ran a coalfield here.

There never was a town, village, or any other form of community here with the name Powhite. However, from Granite Station at Milepost #4.5, as one can see on various maps, Powhite Creek runs to the south of the railroad, and very roughly parallel with it, until, just south of Milepost #8, it swings up sharply in a northward bow, flowing just to the west of the milepost, so close, in fact, that one can see why the name Powhite Station was given to some sort of depot here.

In 1879 a village was built on the R&D line, seven and a half miles from Richmond, and named Bon Air. The Bon Air Hotel was built in 1880, as were the new Bon Air depot and water tank. The hotel annex went up the following year. In 1880, according to ads in the Richmond papers, the passenger train left Richmond at 7:00 p.m. arriving at Bon Air at 7:20, and at Coalfield at 7:30. In the *Official Railway Guide* of 1881, and also on an 1892 railroad timetable, Bonair is at Milepost #8, and it is marked thus on the 1888 map, right on the border of Midlothian Magisterial District and Manchester Magisterial District; a fair sized village, arranged in a grid, four streets by four streets.

Leaving Bonair, the main track continued west.

Milepost 8.7
Tompkins Mill

On the 1863 and 1867 maps this mill lies immediately to the south of the main R&D track. It is not a depot, and, because it is not a community it is not mentioned in the 1858 *Virginia Gazetteer*.

Milepost 10.0
Lee Park

This name does not appear on the 1863 or 1888 maps. Newspaper mentions begin only in 1906. Jefferson Davis would not have known this name.

---

15. Pronounced Pow-hite, or Po-White.
16. This may sound rather vague, but even after much consultation with local historians, it is the best we can come up with.
17. This is undoubtedly an error, perhaps brought about by the fact that, by at least 1859, the Powhite Quarries, named for Powhite Creek, were located five miles above Richmond on the R&D. The Powhite Granite Works were still in operation there as late as, if not later than, 1871.

Milepost 10.5
Robiou's

Still in Chesterfield County, this depot was named for the Robiou family, who owned land here. On December 23, 1851, it was listed by the Richmond & Danville Railroad Company in an ad in a Richmond newspaper as one of their passenger-only stations. In the 1858 *Virginia Gazetteer*, it is listed as Robio's, a station on the R&D, 10 miles southwest of Richmond. On the 1863 map it is where the R&D track crosses the Lynchburg or River road, and is shown as "Robiot St." *Appleton's Guide* of 1865 does not list it on their timetable; however it is shown on Jed Hotchkiss's 1867 map and on La Prade's 1888 map as "Robious Sta."

On the 1888 map, after Robious and before Coalfield was another short right hand spur, leading to the Blackheath Mines. Back on the main tracks, after they crossed Falling Creek, there was another, longer, spur, about half a mile before Coalfield Station, leading left and south down to the highly populated Midlothian Coal Mines and terminating at Grove Shaft (see Midlothian, below). The main track then went on into Coalfield.

Milepost 13.0
Coalfield

By 1850 the R&D had completed track from Richmond to Falling Creek. The Falling Creek Coal Pits were located about 250 yards from the track, and thus the R&D had access to the mines theretofore served by the Chesterfield Railroad Company. On January 1, 1851, the R&D commenced regular passenger service from Richmond to these pits. From there Boyd & Edmonds Stage Company took passengers on to Powhatan and other places west. On December 23, 1851, a Richmond newspaper ran an ad for the R&D, in which their passenger-only stations were listed. Coal Field was one of them. Coalfield is not in the 1858 *Virginia Gazetteer*, but Hill & Swayze (1862) shows Coalfield at Milepost #13. The place is on the 1863 map as "Coalfield St.," and *Appleton's Guide* of 1865 lists Coalfield at Milepost #13. It figures on the 1888 map as "Coalfield Sta." On that particular map, the Falling Creek Old Turnpike had been running parallel to the main R&D tracks to the south for some time, and soon after leaving Coalfield, the tracks cross Michaux Creek and then cross this turnpike road, proceeding in a now southwesterly direction. An 1892 timetable shows Midlothian at Milepost #13.

Coalfield Station was destroyed by the enemy on May 13, 1864—the depot, water tank, wood shed, and five loaded boxcars. By 1865 a new depot had been built.

John W. Headley, writing in the first person in his 1906 book, *Confederate Operations in Canada and New York*, was coming from Lynchburg. The date was April 2, 1865[18]: *... we left Lynchburg and arrived at Burkesville Junction in the afternoon, where we waited some time for the train from Danville going to Richmond. At last we got this train and were on the way to Richmond, but, at Coalfield station, nine miles from Richmond, we were halted again about 9 o'clock p.m.* Coalfield, it must be remembered, was 13 miles from Richmond. *After waiting here for hours, the passengers, nearly all soldiers, began to get hungry, but at this small station there was nothing to eat. All got out and walked about to*

---

18. Headley made a mistake with the date. He writes April 1, but he means Sunday, April 2. In fact, within a few paragraphs his chronology has righted itself.

take exercise, thinking every moment we would make another start, but the hours dragged on, and were still side-tracked at midnight. About one o'clock in the morning, a train was heard coming from the direction of Richmond. It soon whistled and slowed up at the station. It was a long passenger train, and we soon learned that President Davis, his Cabinet and the other civil officers of the Confederate Government were on board, and that General Lee, having evacuated Petersburg and Richmond, was now retreating.

Headley's companion, Martin, went into the car containing the cabinet and found Judah Benjamin, secretary of state. *He said General John C. Breckinridge, who was now Secretary of War, was in North Carolina with General Joseph E. Johnston.* The truth is, at that moment, Breckinridge was still in Richmond, something Benjamin knew. The secretary of war would get out of Richmond on horseback later that morning and make his way to Lee's headquarters. Either Benjamin lied to Martin for security reasons, or Headley is making this up.

Secretary Benjamin told Martin that he and Headley *could report at Danville. Everything was now in confusion, and it was an hour of consternation. Still, no one seemed to lose courage or hope.* What Headley means here is that Richmond, having been evacuated and now in flames, was no longer a valid destination for the up train from Burkeville, and that the train was now going to turn around at Coalfield, and follow the Davis train to Danville.

After the Government train had passed, ours was made ready, and left at 2:30 for Burkesville. It arrived there before day, but was detained for some time. As it happens, Headley and his companion never made it to Danville, having become side-tracked back to Lynchburg.

But Headley and Martin do not exeunt our story quite yet. After some adventures in and around Lynchburg, they stole a handcar and railroaded themselves to North Carolina, where they ran into President Davis and Secretary Benjamin at Saulsbury.[19] They would remain with Davis until the bitter end.

This Headley account has to be compared with the chapter "Fellow Fugitives," in Stuart's July 4, 1865, account in the *New York Herald*: *We passed a train of cars between Burkesville and Richmond—a train filled with fugitives—chiefly ladies—from Petersburg, expecting to find shelter in Richmond. Imagine their dismay on discovering that our train contained the emblem of the protection they sought, and bore away from the sanctuary they were flying to, all that made it, in their eyes, sacred and substantial. At first they were loath to credit what was told them; but when the assurance was put so that it was no longer reasonable to doubt, some cried, while most held their heads down in utter consternation.*

"All is up," shrieked a young soldier in that train, on his way to rejoin his command under Lee; "all is up," and he could not utter another word.

"No, Sir," cried Colonel Wood, "all is down, unless absentees like you hasten to the front!"

The young soldier jumped from the cars, and with a heart teeming with blended sorrow and rage, dashed to the window from which he was thus reproached, shrieking,

"Damn you, had all the bombproofs like you been as often to the front as myself, you wouldn't be on the back track now."

What might have ensued no one can tell, for the soldier was in for fighting his friends

---

19. This spelling of Salisbury was often used in the 19th century.

since he could not immediately get at his foes; but the cars rolled off, and left him to his mutterings and the colonel to a mild rebuke from headquarters-in-the-cars.

Milepost 14.0
Midlothian

The Midlothian Coal Mining Company was incorporated in 1835. They owned and dug the Midlothian Coal Pits in Chesterfield County. Midlothian may be the name of the town today, but it is not in the 1858 *Virginia Gazetteer*, and the name in 1888 still applied only to the coalfields (and, to the magisterial district). There was no actual town called Midlothian then, but there is a newspaper reference to Midlothian Station which ran in a land ad from December 1855 for a couple of months. The Midlothian Coal Pits and the community of people working those mines, perhaps as many as a thousand of them, were served by Coalfield Station. By that time the Midlothian Pits were being referred to as Old Coalfield. By 1863, at least, the community had an English Church and an African Church.

Milepost 15.5
Dodamead

On the 1863 map, about 2 miles past Coalfield, the R&D track crosses the Buckingham Road. In this immediate vicinity, on the 1867 Hotchkiss map, appears Mark's Turnout. This must be the Mark's Siding that one will see once or twice erroneously being located at Milepost #14. As for a depot, or anything like it, nothing appears on the 1863, 1867, or 1888 maps, and it does not seem to be until 1915, in the *Virginia Annual Report*, that the name Dodamead appears here as a freight station. As a point on the R&D, Dodamead is not a name Jefferson Davis would have known, and this is not surprising, given that Thomas Dodamead did not become the R&D superintendent until early 1865.

Milepost 17.0
Dry Bridge/Watkins

Neither name appears in the 1858 *Virginia Gazetteer*, or on the 1863 or 1888 maps. They are much later names (1915).

Milepost 17.5
Tomahawk/Hallsboro/West

The train had now crossed over into Powhatan County. This depot (and the post office within the same building) was originally named Tomahawk, for Tomahawk Creek, and served the community of Hallsboro, which was located about one mile south of the tracks. On December 23, 1851, the R&D ran an ad in a Richmond newspaper, listing Tomahawk as a passenger-only station. In the 1858 *Virginia Gazetteer*, Tomahawk appears as a station on the R&D, 17 miles west by south of Richmond. There is no Tomahawk here on the 1863 map, the only name like it being Tomahawk Church, which appears way to the southeast of Milepost #17.5. *Appleton's Guide* of 1865 lists Tomahawk at Milepost #18. However, Tomahawk does appear where it should on the 1867 map, at Milepost #17.5.

It was still called Tomahawk Station in 1875, but by the time of the 1888 map, that name had been discarded in favor of Hallsboro Station. Both names, Hallsboro and West, appear as freight stations in the 1915 *Virginia Annual Report*.

Milepost 20.0
Turpin

This name does not appear in the 1858 *Virginia Gazetteer* because it was neither a community nor a depot, and on Jed Hotchkiss's 1867 map the tracks cross Swift Creek at this point. But that's all. On the 1888 map, the name Turpin indicates a family homestead just south of the main tracks. Dr. William T. Turpin lived at Hallsboro during the Civil War. In 1915 Turpin appears at Milepost #19, as a freight station.

Milepost 22.2
Powhatan/Moseley

On the Chesterfield-Powhatan county line. Powhatan Station, or Powhatan Depot, was listed by the R&D in an ad they took out in a Richmond newspaper on December 23, 1851, as one of their passenger-only stations. It was there in 1856. The Snipsville Road passed the railroad at this station. The community of Powhatan is there in the 1858 *Virginia Gazetteer*, but a depot is not mentioned, yet that is simply an omission because Powhatan Station was there in 1860. Powhatan Station—depot, freight house, water tank and 12 cars loaded with forage—was burned by the enemy on May 13, 1864. It was rebuilt.

Toward midnight, and well on schedule, the fleeing Davis party reached Powhatan, where the track ceased its westward course and swung sharp south. Here they stopped for a while. Once the train got rolling again out of Powhatan, they discussed their fears for the immediate future. Had the road ahead of them been taken by Union troops? Was Sheridan waiting for them? Of course there was no way, at that early stage of the game, for Sheridan to know anything of the evacuation of Richmond, but was he just sitting there on his great horse Winchester, listening for a train—any train—coming down the line? Of course, they could not know the answers to these questions, but they had to sleep. They resolved unanimously and arbitrarily that the road ahead was uninvested.

Appleton's Guide of 1865 has Powhatan at Milepost #22, and Powhatan Station is shown on the 1867 Jed Hotchkiss map. By the time of the 1891 railway timetables, Powhatan Station had been supplanted by the new Moseley, at Milepost #21. Moseley is actually at Milepost #22.2.

Milepost 23.0
Dorset

On 1891 timetables, and, apparently not before that date, Dorset is at Milepost #23.

Milepost 24.0
Clayville/Petersburg Road

Neither name appears in the 1858 *Virginia Gazetteer*. As a depot, Clayville is never mentioned in the newspapers, but in 1915 it appears as a freight station at Milepost #24. The name has occasionally been seen as Petersburg Road.

Milepost 26.0
Payne/Pilkington

Neither name is mentioned in the 1858 *Virginia Gazetteer*. In 1915 Pilkington appears as a freight station at Milepost #26. The name has occasionally been seen as Payne.

Milepost 26.8
Mattoax/Appomattox River

Mattoax is a town on the Appomattox River, a watercourse which serves as the line between Powhatan and Amelia counties. In an ad run by the R&D in a Richmond newspaper on December 23, 1851, the depot appears as a passenger-only station, not, however, with the name Mattoax, but Appomattox River. Mattoax Depot was mentioned as a station on the R&D in newspapers of 1852 and 1857, and it is in the 1858 *Virginia Gazetteer*. *Appleton's Guide* of 1865 has it at Milepost #27. There was also a post office there.

Milepost 30.4
Chula

A community in Amelia County, the depot was mentioned in *Smith's Hand-Book*, 1856, and in *Mitchell's Guide*, 1857, located at Milepost #30. Although Chula is not in the 1858 *Virginia Gazetteer*, *Appleton's Guide* of 1865 has the depot at Milepost #30. Chula Station was destroyed by the enemy on March 13, 1864, but rebuilt.

Milepost 33.0
Scott's Shop

One of the stopping places for passengers only on the R&D as early as 1851, it appears as such in an R&D ad in a Richmond newspaper of December 23, 1851. In the 1858 *Virginia Gazetteer* it is listed as a station on the R&D, 33 miles southwest of Richmond, in Amelia County.

Milepost 34.0
Winterham

In the 1850s it was a post office in Amelia County, but does not appear in the 1858 *Virginia Gazetteer*. There was certainly no depot here in 1865. In 1915 it appears as a freight station at Milepost #34.

Milepost 35.9
Amelia Court House

David S. and Jeanne T. Heidler, in their *Encyclopedia of the American Civil War* (2000), identify Amelia Court House as *a rail station thirty-nine miles southwest of Richmond.*

The R&D tracks reached Milepost 35.9 in 1851, and a depot was built. In an ad run by the R&D in a Richmond newspaper of December 23, 1851, it is listed as a station for passengers only. In the 1858 *Virginia Gazetteer* it is described as the community of Amelia, on the R&D, but no depot is mentioned. However, *Appleton's Guide* of 1865 has the depot at Milepost #36.

On April 2, 1865, General Robert E. Lee, his lines broken by the enemy, informed Secretary of War Breckinridge and President Davis by two individual telegrams that he was going to retreat to Amelia Court House.[20] These two telegrams were received at the War Department in Richmond at 7:00 p.m., the very moment that most of the Confederate higher-ups were rushing for the train, so it is doubtful that Davis ever received this notification from Lee. However, someone, probably Breckinridge, did receive these two telegrams. Later that night, just before 11 o'clock, and just before the presidential train left for Danville, Breckinridge and Davis were ensconced in intense private conference in L.E. Harvie's office at the railroad depot. It is distinctly possible—probable, in fact—that the secretary of war did, at that meeting, transmit to the president the news of Lee's intended movement to Amelia Court House. But so what? If Davis was indeed told, then all he would have learned was that Lee was heading toward Amelia Court House. That's all. Or was it?

There were huge Confederate dumps at Richmond, Danville, Lynchburg, and other points on the railroads, from which Lee's army was supplied daily. It was a system well in place by April 2. The Commissary General was used to sending Lee supplies, to wherever he was fighting on any given day. So, when Lee telegraphed saying he was heading toward Amelia Court House, he might well have felt no need to spell out a request for supplies to be sent there. Just assumed they would be. That's what his aide, Colonel Walter Taylor, claimed, in 1906. And it may be true. It seems a little careless, though, on Lee's part. Anyway, there were no supplies of the right type waiting for Lee at Amelia Court House when he and his army arrived there on the morning of Tuesday, April 4.

The Reverend J.W. Jones—not to be confused with the late J.B. Jones, the Rebel War Clerk—published his reminiscences in 1874. In this book Jones claims to present for the first time a letter Lee wrote to Davis on April 12, 1865, from near Appomattox Court House, outlining the events surrounding the famous surrender. The letter includes this: *...upon arrival At Amelia Court House on the 4th ... and not finding the supplies ordered to be placed there, nearly twenty-four hours were lost in endeavoring to collect in the country subsistence for men and horses. This delay was fatal and could not be retrieved.*

On the same day that Lee is supposed to have written this letter to Davis, April 12, 1865, Jerome B. Stillson, of the *New York World*, wrote a report from Grant's headquarters that did the rounds of the newspapers in the ensuing weeks: *Several railroad trains, loaded with supplies, for which Lee had telegraphed to Danville, were taken on the road.* What Stillson meant was "captured on the railroad tracks by Sheridan's cavalry."

So, had Lee actually sent his telegram to Danville, rather than Richmond? Is this why we do not have a record of it? Not so, apparently. It does, indeed, seem to have been Richmond, at least originally. Douglas Southall Freeman has investigated this question of Amelia Court House in more depth than any other historian. In his *R.E. Lee: A Biography* (1934), he indicates that the supplies had originally been ordered from Richmond. Now, on discovering that there were no supplies at Amelia Court House, Lee sent his chief commissary, Colonel R.G. Cole, to Jetersville (the line had been cut between there and Amelia Court House) to send off a telegram to Danville for the supplies of 200,000 rations

---

20. This information was written in the two telegrams, not in the 3 p.m. letter to Davis (see Chapter 5).

to be sent to Burkeville. Cole was to send another similar telegram to Lynchburg. That, then, was on the 4th. Anyway, the dispatch was not sent for one reason or another, and Sheridan found the written message when he arrived at Jetersville later that day. He sent it off by rider to Burkeville, and from there had it transmitted to Danville, in the hope that Danville would duly send on the supplies and he could capture them. The commissary at Danville discovered the condition of the road, and made no shipment.

As early as November 1865 a long newspaper article was going the rounds. Written by London *Times* reporter Frank Lawley, the Amelia episode is covered. Lawley expresses the opinion that there can be little doubt that Lee's design was to recruit his army with rations that he hoped to find at Amelia Court House, and to fall in detail upon the Federals. *Two days rations at Amelia Court House for 40,000 men would possibly have made a great difference in the immediate, though, as I believe, not in the ultimate history of the Continent of North America.* He feels that it is hardly necessary to state that at Amelia Court House Lee found not a ration. *I shall not pause now to blame, or to investigate, who was at fault. All that I have to state is that the fault was not Lee's, whose orders on this subject for a fortnight past had been urgent and precise.* He then says that it became necessary for Lee to break nearly half his army up into foraging parties to get food.

There are no records indicating Lee's "urgent and precise orders" on this subject of sending rations to Amelia Court House. Or, if there are, perhaps they are as cunningly disguised as those purporting to be in his telegrams of April 2. But more telling is that, two weeks before April 2, how could Lee have known he was going to have to retreat on Amelia Court House?

By 1881, when Davis's book, *The Rise and Fall of the Confederate Government*, was published, he had been under attack for some time in memoirs and newspaper articles. Confederate apologists, keen to explain Lee's collapse, or rather to shift the blame from Lee to someone else, had come up with the idea that Davis and his government had refused to act upon Lee's request. That, of course, is absurd, given Davis's fanatical and delusional determination to carry on the fight, a determination that was infinitely greater than Lee's.

The attack that really caused a stir was General James Harrison Wilson's inflammatory article in 1877. When he comes to the train that carried Davis and the fleeing government to Danville, Wilson says: *This train, it is said, was the one which had carried provisions to Amelia Court House for Lee's hard-pressed and hungry army, and having been ordered to Richmond had taken those supplies to that place where they were abandoned for a more ignoble freight. As a matter of course the starving Rebel soldiers suffered, but Davis succeeded in reaching Danville in safety.* It was this article, more than anything, which prompted Davis to riposte with: *Neither the president of the railroad, who was traveling with me, nor I, knew that there was anything which required attention at Amelia Court House or any other station on the route. Had General Lee's letter to me, written on the afternoon of the 2d, been received at Richmond, which I think it was not, the fact that he proposed to march to Amelia Court House would have been known; it would have been unjust to the officers of the commissary department, however, to doubt that any requisition made or to be made for supplies had received or would receive the most prompt and efficient attention.*

William Swinton wrote *Campaigns of the Army of the Potomac* (1882). In it he says that when Lee determined to abandon Petersburg and Richmond, he dispatched orders that large supplies of commissary and quartermaster's stores should be sent forward from Danville to Amelia Court House, there to await the arrival of his columns. When, however, on Sunday afternoon, the loaded train of cars reached Amelia Court House, the officer in charge was met by an order from the Richmond authorities to bring on the train to Richmond, it being the design to use the cars in the transportation of the personnel and property of the Confederate government. Interpreting this order in the sense that the train and its contents should be taken to Richmond, the officer, without unloading the stores at Amelia Court House, carried on cars, freight and all; *and the rations upon which Lee had depended for the subsistence of his army were consumed in the general conflagration of Richmond!*

However, Swinton's book has an appendix, one of the items being titled "The Question of Lee's Supplies at Amelia Courthouse." Swinton has just read Jefferson Davis's 1881 book, *Rise and Fall*, and has decided to be less certain in his history-making. He recognizes Davis's obvious honesty on this issue, and he also realizes that he, Swinton, has been more than a little naive in accepting without question General Wilson's vicious account. In his appendix, therefore, Swinton attempts to make amends, when talking about Lee and the large supplies of stores *it is alleged he had ordered to be forwarded to Amelia Courthouse.* He then cites Davis's book, which in turn cites Commissary General I.M. St. John, who denies any such request by Lee, or anyone else, official or unofficial, for supplies to be sent to Amelia Court House. Breckinridge also did not recall such a request. On or around April 6, at Lee's headquarters, Breckinridge and St. John were both with Lee when the Commissary General mentioned to Lee that he had about 80,000 rations stored away at a convenient point on the railroad, and what would Lee like being done with them. Lee did not know.

Swinton has, by the time of this appendix, come to believe that if any such order was sent by Lee, it was not received. And that makes sense. As can clearly be seen from Lee's dispatches of April 2, the concept of Amelia Court House did not occur to him until late that afternoon or in the evening. Even then, his 7:00 p.m. telegrams mention Amelia Court House as a destination, but supplies are not even hinted at. Seven o'clock was just about the last time a telegram could have been received at the War Department before it closed its doors for the last time. From then on everyone was on the run. So, if Lee had, indeed, sent such a request, it would not have been received. And why would he have sent any telegram after that hour? He was the one who had suggested evacuation, and surely he would not have expected the government to be there still. It makes no sense for him to have sent such a telegram.

Fitzhugh Lee, writing in 1894, said: *...if Lee's supplies had been there as ordered.*[21] But then Fitz was the general's nephew.

Many sources, following Wilson's 1877 article, say that, yes, the supplies were sent up from Danville, and yes, they did reach Amelia Court House, but then a misunderstanding took place, and the train took the supplies on to Richmond. But that implies that the government did receive Lee's telegrammed request late in the night of April 2, and that can hardly be possible. Even if it had been, Richmond would have had to get on to Danville in the middle of the night, arrange for the supplies to be gathered together at Danville, loaded on to a train, which in turn would have had to be made up, and then run up to Amelia Court House, 104 miles up an uncertain track. That would have taken the best part of 12 hours to achieve, on that Monday morning, April 3.

---

21. Fitzhugh Lee, *General Lee*, edited by James Grant Wilson (New York: Appleton, 1894).

Other sources have the order being received but the supplies coming down from Richmond. Again, it is not possible that such a Lee request was made before 7:00 p.m. so who was it who received the order? Breckinridge. perhaps? But, if he did, could he have put the order into effect? Given all that was going on in Richmond that night, there is no way that this order could have been complied with. And even if someone had tried, a train was necessary to run it the 36 miles down to Amelia Court House.

Emory Thomas says, in his biography of Lee, *It is now impossible to know what happened to Lee's directive to deliver food to Amelia Court House, if in fact a written order ever existed.* And that may be.

At Amelia Court House, in the morning of April 3, 1865, the presidential train veered southwest, and from that time on would essentially maintain that bearing all the way to Danville.

Did Jefferson Davis make a stop at Amelia Court House? William Harwar Parker has the treasure train stopping there, but, as for the presidential train, Jefferson Davis himself says that it did not stop here: *If, however, I had known that General Lee wanted supplies placed at Amelia Court House, I would certainly have inquired as to the time of reaching that station, and have asked to have the train stopped so as to enable me to learn whether or not the supplies were in depot. The unfounded calumny, after perhaps having been given more consideration than it was worth, is now dismissed.*

Milepost 37.0
Otterburn

In Amelia County. This place is not in the 1858 *Virginia Gazetteer*. In 1865 Phillip Stephen Hunter lived here. There was a station here, but only much later than 1865.

Milepost 40.0
Maplewood

Not in the 1858 *Virginia Gazetteer*. In 1915 it appears as a freight station at Milepost #40. There was no depot here in 1865.

Milepost 41.0
Raen

In 1915 it appears as a freight station at Milepost #41. There was no depot here in 1865.

Milepost 43.0
Wyanoke

The R&D tracks reached Milepost #43 in late 1851, and the company built a depot here, calling it Wyanoke Station. It is to be found in newspaper schedules of June 1852. It is listed in *Smith's Hand-Book*, 1856, and in *Mitchell's Guide*, 1857, both times at Milepost #42, and in the 1858 *Virginia Gazetteer* it is listed as a station on the R&D. Then it disappears, to be fully superseded by Jetersville.

Milepost 43.3
Jetersville

The R&D opened regular passenger service between Richmond and Jetersville on December 23, 1851. The train stopped for passengers only at Manchester, Rockfield, Powhite, Robiou's, Coal Field, Tomahawk, Powhatan, Appomattox River, Scott's Shop, Amelia Court House, and now Jetersville. The train took less than three hours to get from Richmond to Jetersville. From Jetersville one could catch Flagg & Company's stages to Burkeville, and on to Danville. In the 1858 *Virginia Gazetteer*, Jetersville is 41 miles west-southwest of Richmond as the crow flies. *Appleton's Guide* of 1865 has it at Milepost #43.

As the fleeing Davis party pulled into the tiny depot at the comfortable and respectable little village of Jetersville, with its couple of stores, blacksmith shop, post office, and its dozen homely dwellings, rumors were abroad that Sheridan's cavalry were on a raid in the vicinity, and the dozers in the President's car were all awakened to learn of this new threat. For a while they talked big, adjusted their spurs, fingered their revolvers, and postured about getting their horses out of the boxcar and making a break for it across country, although Benjamin, not physically adapted to violent action, thought more than once about following such a course.[22] In the end, though, after more solid inquiry, it was found that there were not actually any boys in blue in the area at all, and so, with a deep sigh of relief, the train proceeded along its way.

Milepost 46.0
Fowden

Only much later did Fowden become a station. In 1915 it appears as a freight station at Milepost #46. There was no depot here in 1865.

Milepost 49.7
Jennings Ordinary

Nottoway County. On February 19, 1852, regular passenger service on the R&D began from Richmond to Jennings Ordinary. This was now the R&D railhead, and the company built a depot. Flagg & Company moved their offices here from Jetersville, and continued to provide passengers with ongoing stagecoach services. In *Mitchell's Guide*, 1857, it is listed at Milepost #50, and in the 1858 *Virginia Gazetteer* it is listed as a post office on the R&D line, but with no depot mentioned. *Appleton's Guide* of 1865 has it at Milepost #50. It seems, from Stuart's account, that the presidential party pulled into Jennings Ordinary at, or very close to, 4:25 a.m., stopped there for perhaps fifteen or twenty minutes while they contemplated the possibility of taking to the horses to avoid a rumored Union cavalry patrol, decided to stay on the train, and left at about 4:45 a.m., heading south the three or so miles to Burkeville Junction.

---

22. Newspaper accounts hitting the streets as early as April 6, 1865, say that a box car contained horses for President Davis, his cabinet, and staff, in case anything went wrong on the track and the refugees had to take to alternative means of transportation.

Milepost 52.0
Haytokah

The train stopped here in 1853, 1854, and 1855. In *Smith's Hand-Book*, 1856, it is at Milepost #53. In *Mitchell's Guide*, 1857, it is at Milepost #54. In the 1856 and 1859 editions of *Smith's* it is listed at 52 miles on the R&D. It is not in the 1858 *Virginia Gazetteer*, having been superseded by Burkeville Junction.

Milepost 53.4
Burkeville Junction

In February 1829, the name of the post office here was changed from Miller's Tavern to Burkeville, and as Burkesville it features as a post office in the 1835 Virginia gazetteer. The R&D opened regular passenger services from Richmond to Burkeville on May 17, 1852. Given that it was such an important R&D station—their most important station between Richmond and Danville, in fact—it is odd that it is not listed on timetables until the war. *Appleton's Guide* of 1865 has Burkeville Junction at Milepost #53.

In July 1861 it took precisely three hours for the Sunday mail train to run from Burkeville to Richmond. By November of that year it was taking 15 minutes longer. In 1862 it took an R&D train four hours to make the trip from Richmond to Burkeville Junction. In 1882, 17 years after war's end, it would take 2 hours 25 minutes, and by 1891 the time would be down to 2 hours 11 minutes.

The morning of April 3, 1865, the presidential train pulled into Burkeville Junction at about 5:00 a.m., to take on wood and water, a halt which afforded the passengers the luxury of being able to get out and stretch their legs. If it had not been for the stops along the way, the #24 would have had them at the junction an hour or two earlier.

Dawn that morning was at 4:30 (Richmond time), and sunrise was at 5:49. Sunrise is not dawn. It is a very different thing. Dawn is the time that marks the beginning of that period of morning twilight before sunrise. With dawn comes a weak sunlight, but the sun is still about six degrees below the horizon when dawn breaks. The sun has not yet made its physical appearance. Sunset is when the leading edge of the sun itself appears above the horizon. So, there is a distinct period between the onset of dawn and sunrise, during which things become ever more visible to the naked eye. That period is known as morning twilight. As for the term daybreak, that can mean anything from dawn to sunrise. It depends on the speaker, but usually implies dawn.

Robert K. Krick's book, *Civil War Weather in Virginia*, gives a chart of sunrise, sunset, and temperatures in Richmond for April 2 and 3, 1865. In Richmond, on April 2, 1865, sunrise was at 5:45 a.m. The following day, it was at 5:44 a.m. Those were the days before Daylight Savings Time.

That was Richmond. Every nine miles you go west of Richmond, sunrise occurs a minute later, so, at Burkeville Junction, for example, sunrise occurred at 5:49 that morning of April 3. At Roanoke (i.e., the Roanoke on the Staunton River, at Milepost #90) and at Clover Station (Milepost #94), it was at 5:52 a.m. What makes it more confusing is that people set their clocks by the time the sun came up, and in those days there were no set time zones. So Clover time was different to Richmond time, albeit by only eight minutes. However, to all intents and purposes sunset in this part of Virginia, on April 3, 1865, occurred about ten to fifteen minutes before six a.m.

Stuart says, *Toward day we reached the next station north of the Burkesville Junction.* It is hard to say precisely which station Stuart has in mind here. Strictly speaking, Jennings Ordinary was the next station up the line, 3.7 miles north of Burkeville Junction, and it is probably that one he means, rather than, say, Jetersville, which is ten miles up the track from Burkeville. Jetersville was very well known to anyone who had ever traveled this line, and so it would be a name easily called to mind, whereas Jennings Ordinary is a name that could just as easily have slipped Stuart's memory. Although only guesswork, one has to settle on Jennings Ordinary.

However, it is not difficult to work out exactly what Stuart had in mind when he said "toward day." It is his next sentence which gives us the clue: *A cavalry raid was expected to interfere with our progress, and all the drones were unceremoniously awaked.* That almost certainly means it was dark as they pulled into Jennings Ordinary, but because Stuart says "toward day" it must have been getting very close to dawn. If it had already dawned, at least some of the drones would have been awakened by the encroaching gray light. The party evidently stopped for about ten or twenty minutes at Jennings Ordinary, to try to decide what to do about the threatened Union patrol, settled on doing nothing, stayed on the train, and, as Stuart says, *On rolled the train into the gray clear of morning.* That means dawn had broken as they left Jennings Ordinary, with Jefferson Davis and his fellow passengers now fully awake. *No hostile cavalry was in sight*, says Stuart, which means they could see, which means it was daylight.

The distance between Jennings Ordinary and Burkeville Junction being only three miles, it would have taken the train only ten to fifteen minutes to cover that distance, and, as Stuart says in his next passage, they arrived at Burkeville Junction *shortly after daybreak*. This really must mean in the area of 5:00 a.m.

Stuart is consistent: *Burkesville, which we reached shortly after daybreak, was the first place at which any of our distinguished men got off the train—it was also the first place we had a clear-eyed view of since the night before. I am particular in mentioning this, for there was something ominous in that first place and first view. It was a wreck—a woeful ruin—one of the saddest havoc sights Mr. Davis had yet seen. Raiders had torn it to pieces, and the pleasant, bustling little junction of other days was only visible in its vestiges. Mr. Davis got out and walked a few minutes on the platform. Owing to his unsightly spectacles, he was not at once recognized by the people who were even that early at the station.* And this: *As soon as the few stragglers at the station knew that the train contained their President, they sought him, crowded around him, kindly and respectfully spoke in smothered tones, and looked most sorrowful.*

On April 4, 1865, General Grant at Wilson's Station sent a dispatch to General Philip Sheridan: *An engineer from the S.S. Railroad is just in from Burkesville.*[23] *He reports that Davis and his Cabinet passed there about 3:00 a.m. yesterday going South."*[24]

That day, April 4, Sheridan established his Cavalry Headquarters at Jetersville. That day he wrote to General Meade: *The enemy are moving from Amelia Courthouse, via Jetersville and Burke's Station, to Danville, Jeff. Davis passed over this railroad yesterday to Danville.* To some extent, Sheridan may have been reflecting the dispatch he had received from Grant, but one must remember that Sheridan was actually right there, in

---

23. The South Side Railroad ran east from Lynchburg, through Appomattox Station, Farmville, and Burkeville Junction, to Petersburg, intersecting the R&D at The Junction.

24. *OR*, ser. 1, vol. 46, part 3, p. 557.

Jetersville, on the 4th, ten miles north of Burkeville, and without question would have obtained plenty of first-hand local confirmation of the engineer's tale.

According to Stuart, then, the train arrived at Burkeville at about 5 o'clock that morning. But that is nowhere near the 3:00 a.m. time given by the engineer. However, as we see in the Grant telegram, the engineer's time is approximate. Stuart, on the other hand, is very definite. But one thing is certain—the presidential train pulled into Burkeville between 3 and 5 that morning.

Congressman Bruce, writing in 1881, says that *when dawn broke in on us the morning of April 3d we were somewhere in the neighborhood of Burkeville Junction, probably between that place and Roanoke.*[25] Bruce is horribly imprecise, for that is a distance of 37 miles, too wide a geographical field to shed any light on the problem. On the other hand, he is not altogether wrong. When dawn broke, the train was, indeed, somewhere in the neighborhood of Burkeville Junction—it's just that it was to the north of the Junction, not the south. Clint Johnson, obviously perplexed by this, as we all are, made the decision, in his 2008 book, *Pursuit*, to be as definitive as Bruce was vague: *Congressman Bruce awoke the next morning, April 3, as the train pulled into Burkeville Station*. If the congressman did, indeed, awake as dawn broke—and he never says that—then surely he would have known he was pulling into such a major junction as Burkeville.

The train almost certainly stayed at Burkeville Junction for at least half an hour, so it would have been about 5:30 when it pulled out, heading south for Keysville, twenty miles down the track.

The engineer's tale and Stuart's account, when read in conjunction, are important not only for fixing the arrival time at Burkeville, but particularly so in ascertaining the time the train pulled into Clover Station, a further 40 miles down the track. We will duly arrive at Clover—Milepost #94.

Milepost 59.0
Liberty Church

The Richmond & Danville had certainly built their track as far as Liberty Church by August 1852, because in newspaper ads for the line we see that trains stopped at the depot here, as they did in April 1853 and throughout 1854 and 1855. In *Mitchell's Guide* of 1857, Liberty Church is listed at Milepost #59, but the place is not in the 1858 *Virginia Gazetteer*. By the time Jefferson Davis came through here, Liberty Church depot had probably gone, supplanted by Green Bay, two miles down the track.

Milepost 60.9
Green Bay

In *Smith's Hand-Book* of 1856, Green Bay is listed at Milepost #60, but it is not in the 1858 *Virginia Gazetteer*. On June 23, 1864, a large column of Yankee cavalry, under General Wilson, destroyed the depot here, but it was rebuilt. It is at Milepost #62 in the *Official Railway Guide* of 1881.

---

25. This is not the Roanoke we know today. See below, at Milepost 90.

Milepost 61.0
Price's

Appleton's Guide of 1865 lists it at Milepost #61. It is probably the old Green Bay.

Milepost 64.9
Moore's Ordinary/Meherrin

Prince Edward County. In 1748 George Moore received a license to keep an ordinary at his house.[26] It became known as Moore's Ordinary. Regular R&D passenger service was opened between Richmond and Moore's Ordinary on August 16, 1852, and a depot, containing a post office, was opened there. At that date, trains left Richmond at 7:00 a.m., and arrived at Moore's Ordinary at 1:50 p.m. That's 6 hours, 50 minutes. Although in the 1858 *Virginia Gazetteer* Moore's Ordinary is described as a post office 61 miles west-southwest of Richmond, and there is a community there, no depot is mentioned. That is because the depot, at least, had become known as Meherrin, at least as early as 1855, and that is how it is listed in *Smith's Hand-Book* of 1856, and in *Mitchell's Guide* of 1857, both times at Milepost #65. However, Meherrin is not in the 1858 *Virginia Gazetteer*. On June 23, 1864, Gen. Wilson's Yankee cavalry destroyed the depot, but it was rebuilt, and *Appleton's Guide* of 1865 has Meherrin at Milepost #65. It was probably approaching 7:00 a.m., when the presidential train pulled into Meherrin.

Milepost 67.0
Virso/Clark's

Neither name is mentioned in the 1858 gazetteer, and it was not until much later that these names were applied. In 1915 Virso appears as a freight station at Milepost #67.

Milepost 73.4
Keysville

Keysville became the railhead of the R&D on November 8, 1852, and a depot was built. In *Smith's Hand-Book* of 1856, Keysville is listed at Milepost #73, as it is in *Mitchell's Guide* of 1857, but in the latter erroneously as Kingsville. In the 1858 *Virginia Gazetteer* Keysville is described as 66 miles southwest by west of Richmond, which, of course, is as the crow flies. No depot is mentioned. In the 1856 and 1859 Smith Guides it is listed at 71 miles out of Richmond on the R&D. On June 23, 1864, the depot was destroyed by General Wilson's Yankee cavalry, but it was rebuilt. *Appleton's Guide* of 1865 has it at Milepost #73.

There is nothing in any of the participants' accounts to indicate anything untoward happening between Burkeville Junction and Keysville, so, if we assume the train averaged 10 mph, and allowing for the inevitable stops along the way, either at stations or just the occasional halt on the track, the fleeing Davis party would have arrived at Keysville between about 8 and 8:30 a.m., on Monday, April 3, 1865.

---

26. An ordinary was a tavern or inn providing a meal at a fixed price.

Milepost 81.0
Drake's Branch

Trains were stopping here from at least 1853, and the depot is listed at this milepost in *Smith's Hand-Book* of 1856, and in *Mitchell's Guide* of 1857. On June 23, 1864, the depot here was destroyed by Yankee cavalry under General Wilson, but rebuilt soon afterwards. *Appleton's Railroad Guide* of 1865 has it at Milepost #81. It is hard to imagine the Davis train arriving at Drake's Branch any sooner than 9:00 a.m.

Milepost 83.8
Mossingford/Overby's

The R&D line reached here in December 1853, and the company built a depot. In *Smith's Hand-Book* of 1856 it is listed as Mossingford, and in *Mitchell's Guide* of 1857, as Mossing Ford, at Milepost #84. Not under any name is it mentioned in the 1858 *Virginia Gazetteer*. On June 23, 1864, General Wilson's Union cavalry destroyed the depot, but it was rebuilt, and *Appleton's Guide* of 1865 has it at Milepost #84.

Milepost 87.0
Saxe

This name is not in the 1858 *Virginia Gazetteer*. It only came into being a lot later. In 1915 it appears as a freight station at Milepost #87.

Milepost 89.0
Vey

This name is not in the 1858 *Virginia Gazetteer*. It only came into being a lot later. In 1915 it appears as a freight station at Milepost #89.

Milepost 89.7
Roanoke/Staunton River

This Roanoke is not the Roanoke we know today. That's a different place entirely, several miles to the west. The one we're talking about here is the old estate of John Randolph, and is right on the Staunton River. The Roanoke of today was called Big Lick back then, for obvious reasons.

Roanoke, as a depot on the R&D, was in operation from 1854, and is listed in *Smith's Hand-Book* of 1856, and also in *Mitchell's Guide* of 1857, both times at Milepost #90. Not being a community as such, it is not in the 1858 *Virginia Gazetteer*. On June 23, 1864, General James Wilson's Union cavalry destroyed the depot here, but it was rebuilt, and figures in *Appleton's Guide* of 1865, as at Milepost #90, and in the *Official Railway Guide* of 1881, at Milepost #91. Also in the 1881 guide, Staunton River is listed at Milepost #90.5. By 1915 there would be a freight station named Randolph, at Milepost #90.

Probably about 10 o'clock on the morning of April 3, 1865, the presidential train crossed the 613-foot-long bridge over the Staunton River at Milepost 90, into Halifax County, Virginia. The bridge would be destroyed by Confederate forces on April 12, 1865.

Milepost 94.9
Clover

By September 1854, the R&D had completed the laying of their track as far as Clover, and a depot was built there.

The presidential train crossed the Staunton River into Halifax County about 10 o'clock in the morning of Monday, April 3, 1865. It could not really have been much earlier than that. Another four or five miles brought them to Clover Station, where they pulled in for wood and water, probably at or approaching 10:30 a.m.

How far was it from Richmond to Clover? The three most common ways of measuring the distance between two towns are by road, by rail, and as the crow flies. For anyone telling the story of Jefferson Davis's flight along the Richmond & Danville Railroad, only the rail distance is meaningful. We are discussing one thing only, the distance covered by a train—not a horse or a crow. As the fugitives' train pulled into Clover, they were 94.9 miles from Richmond by rail.

It may be eighty miles or so as the crow flies, but that imparts nothing in real terms to the readers of Burke Davis's *To Appomattox* (1959), in the passage where he describes Clover: *...a cluster of houses on the Richmond and Danville Railroad, some eighty miles southwest of Richmond in Halifax County*, or to the readers of James C. Clark, who wrote in his 1984 book, *Last Train South*, *Clover Station, some eighty miles from Richmond*, or to those of Don Lowry's book, *Towards an Indefinite Shore* (1995): *...the little town of Clover Station, Virginia, some eighty miles southwest of Richmond.*

For any historian who cares to look up the distance by rail from Richmond to Clover, the information is freely and quickly available. 94.9 miles. So, with such detail at his fingertips, it is odd that Philip Van Doren Stern felt himself under the obligation to be approximate, when he wrote in *An End to Valor* (1958): *Clover Station about one hundred miles south of Richmond.*

One can always look at this question from another angle—how far was Clover from Danville? In other words, how many more miles did the fleeing Davis party have yet to go before they reached their destination? James Swanson chooses this approach in his *Bloody Crimes* (2010), when he states that Clover was *about sixty miles northeast of* Danville. One has to agree that Clover is northeast of Danville, but by rail it was 46 miles between the two towns. As the crow flies it was 30, and remains so to this day.

Lieutenant John Sergeant Wise of General Walker's command was on duty at Clover Station the morning of April 3, 1865. We do not actually know how long Wise had been on duty at the depot. One must bear in mind that our sole source for this Clover Station episode is Wise's 1899 account, "End of an Era,"[27] and all he says is, *I was for the time at Clover Station.* However, Burke Davis wrote this, in his 1959 book, *To Appomattox*: *John Wise was the eighteen-year-old son of General Henry Wise, the aging ex–Governor of Virginia.*[28] *For some weeks he had been on duty at Clover Station.*

Using Burke Davis's description of Wise, Hudson Strode wrote this, in *Tragic Hero* (1964): *At Clover Station, Lt. John S. Wise, eighteen-year-old son of the ex–Governor, General Henry Wise.* We learn more of young Wise and his father in Clint Johnson's *Pursuit* (2008): *Lieutenant John S. Wise, a son of former governor Henry Wise whom Davis had*

---

27. Republished in 1901, in book form, with the same title.
28. Governor Wise was then 58.

appointed a general early in the war. Johnson then says that *Wise, just 19 years old,*[29] had first seen combat just a year earlier at the battle of Newmarket, Virginia, *under the command of then General Breckinridge.* We are given even more biographical data in James C. Clark's *Last Train South* (1984), which describes Lt. John S. Wise as *the son of one of Lee's aides.* And finally this, from James Swanson, in *Bloody Crimes* (2010): *A young Army lieutenant, eighteen years old John S. Wise.*

It must be stressed that everything we know about the events at Clover that morning comes from Wise, and therefore we have absolutely no corroborating evidence to prove that it ever happened. Having said that, it might be worth noting that soon after the Clover episode, Wise ran messages between Davis and Lee, an astonishing adventure well-proved by others. In June 1886, the *New York Mail* and *Express* published Wise's account of this segment of his life. Nowhere does he mention the train passing through Clover. It was not until 1899, when his "End of an Era" was published, that he came up with that story. Consequently, we should not be too eager to believe it. As Clint Johnson says, in *Pursuit: While some historians question Wise's account, others credit him with having a keen sense of what he was observing.*

Whether Wise is wrong, right, or both, whether he is lying or telling the truth, "The End of an Era" is all we have, and any subsequent historian's deviation from that account, no matter how small a deviation, is a fictional elaboration, unless, of course, the intention is to correct an obvious error in Wise or to expand on a point when it can be done safely.

As Wise says: *Train after train, all loaded to their capacity with whatever could be transported from the doomed capital, came puffing past Clover station on the way southward.* He says that these trains bore many men who, in the excitement, were unwilling to admit that all was lost. They frankly deplored the necessity of giving up the Confederate capital, but insisted that the army was not beaten or demoralized, and was retreating in good order. They argued that Lee, relieved of the burden of defending his long lines from Richmond to Petersburg, and of the hard task of maintaining his communications, would draw Grant away from his base of supplies, and might now, with that generalship of which everyone knew him to be master, be free to administer a stunning if not a crushing blow to Grant in the open, where strategy might overcome force.

Philip Van Doren Stern sums it up in *An End to Valor* (1958): *John S. Wise, who was at the station, recorded the train's passing.* But then the fiction writers began to take over. This from Burke Davis, in *To Appomattox* (1959): *Last night, the first of the trains came through, and by midnight they had become a procession. Most of them stopped for wood or water, and Wise listened eagerly to the Confederate officials who came out to reassure the little crowd.* James C. Clark says, in *Last Train South* (1984): *Lt. John S. Wise ... said the first evacuation trains began to pass him about midnight, stopping for water and wood.*

For a start, we do not know the size of the crowd. It probably was little, but Wise never mentions it.[30] And why wouldn't all of the trains stop for wood and water, rather than just most of them? Wise does not mention wood or water. And, if the first of the trains came through Clover last night, that means, given the twelve hours or so that it took to cover that 95 miles, they would have had to have left Richmond no later than 11:30 in the morning of Sunday, April 2. Finally, if by midnight the trains had become a procession through Clover, Jefferson Davis, having taken one of the first trains, would

---

29. John S. Wise was, actually, 18, as all the other historians say.
30. James C. Clark does, though, in his 1984 book, *Last Train South.*

have been at Clover by that hour, and would therefore have had to have left Richmond no later than midday on April 2. Yet we know that is nowhere close to the time he actually fled the capital. None of this comes from Wise. It is all from Burke Davis.

Professor Hudson Strode, in *Tragic Hero* (1964), writes about Wise that he *had watched refugee train after train go past loaded to capacity with men clinging to the cars. He had seen the treasure train go by.* This passage firmly places Strode in the camp that believes that the treasure train preceded the presidential train, a camp inhabited also by Shelby Foote, who wrote in the third volume of his classic, *The Civil War* (1974): *A young lieutenant posted there watched the treasure train go through at daybreak, loaded with bullion and cadets.* Foote never cited sources. He never mentions Lieutenant Wise by name. And one must bear in mind that this is the treasure train Foote is talking about. Finally, one must remember that it was much later than daybreak when the treasure train went through Clover.

Clint Johnson, in *Pursuit* (2008), writes, rather enigmatically, that Wise *happened to be watching at one station when the train passed. He too focused on Davis. Wise was still appreciative of the president.* James Swanson, in *Bloody Crimes* (2010), merely says that Wise *saw the train pull into the station.*

There is nothing in Wise's account that gives a time of day for the presidential train arriving at Clover, except that he does say it was the morning. *Monday morning, April 3, a train passed Clover bearing the President, his cabinet and chief advisers, to Danville. They had left Richmond after the midnight of that last Sunday when Mr. Davis was notified, while attending St. Paul's Church, that the immediate evacuation of the city was unavoidable.* Everything he writes seems to indicate it was in daylight, rather than in the dark, and daylight came to Clover at 4:30 that morning.

So, we just have "morning," that's all, nothing more specific. Hudson Strode was on safe ground in his 1964 book, *Tragic Hero*, when he wrote: *And now came the presidential train*, as was Shelby Foote, in *The Civil War* (1974): *...and now came the one with the Chief executive and his ministers aboard, all obviously feeling the strain of a jerky, sleepless night.* Burke Davis was certainly right in *The Long Surrender* (1985), when he said: *Long after midnight, the President's train slowed to a stop at Clover Station.*

But history makers soon found the vagueness intolerable, and were compelled to supply a time of morning. Hence Stern in *An End to Valor* (1958): *Early on Monday morning, April 3, the train carrying Jefferson Davis and his cabinet passed Clover Station.* Stern cannot possibly know, from Wise's account, that it was early morning. Wise just says "Monday morning." But Stern did get takers. William J. Cooper, for example, in *Jefferson Davis, American* (2000): *As the cars passed a rural station early on the morning of the third....*[31]

Burke Davis it was who came up with the exact time, in his 1959 book, *To Appomattox*: *At 3 A.M., however, the train bearing Jefferson Davis and the Cabinet drew into the torchlit station, and, with a glimpse of the President, Wise felt despair.* Again, all we have to go on for the Clover episode is Wise's account, and Wise only says "Monday morning." Three o'clock originates with Burke Davis in 1959. The presidential train left Richmond at either 10 or 11 o'clock the previous night—of that there can be little doubt—and Burke Davis's suggested arrival time at Clover, 95 miles from Richmond, would require the train

---

31. Cooper does not give the name of the station.

to have traveled at an average speed of between 19 and 23 miles per hour, which, of course, is simply not feasible for April 2, 1865. Unfortunately, many historians have relied upon Burke Davis. This from James C. Clark, in *Last Train South* (1984): *The Davis train came through about 3:00 a.m.* And Don Lowry, in *Towards an Indefinite Shore* (1995): *At 3 a.m., Jefferson Davis's train stopped briefly at* [Clover]. And James Swanson in *Bloody Crimes* (2010): *At about 3 a.m., while en route to Danville, Davis's train stopped at Clover Station.*

There was a dissenter, Shelby Foote. He has the presidential train pulling into Clover *about 7 o'clock* on the morning of April 3. But then he goes completely off the rails: *... already some eight hours behind schedule, with other delays to follow—the presidential special crossed the Roanoke and rolled creakily into Clover station, two thirds of the way to Danville.* Foote has already had the presidential train leaving Richmond at 11 o'clock the previous night: *Finally, at 11 o'clock ... the train creaked out of the station.* That means, according to Foote, that eight hours elapsed between the time the train left Richmond and the time it arrived at Clover. Yet, again according to Foote, the train was "already some eight hours behind schedule" when it arrived at Clover. The only way for Foote's statement to make any sense at all is to admit the possibility of instantaneous travel, and that had not been invented yet.

We know, by using both the engineer's tale at Burkeville and Stuart's account, and by making deductions from Mallory's account and that of Congressman Bruce, that the presidential train arrived at Burkeville Junction about 5 o'clock that morning, and that it left there around 5:30. It is another 40 miles from Burkeville to Clover, so it is most likely that the train, after a stop at Keysville, pulled into Clover at about 10:30 a.m.

Then there is President Davis sitting at a car window, smiling and being cheered by the crowd. This from Wise, in 1899: *Mr. Davis sat at a car window. The crowd at the station cheered. He smiled, and acknowledged their compliment.* Clint Johnson, in *Pursuit* (2008), simply replicates this wording, as does Professor Strode, in *Tragic Hero* (1964)—well, almost: *Mr. Davis sat at a car window. The crowd at the station cheered. He acknowledged their compliment.* Shelby Foote, in *Civil War* (1974), actually quotes Wise: "*Mr. Davis sat at a car window. The crowd at the station cheered. He smiled and acknowledged their compliment.*"

Historians feel driven to rework other writers' wording, of course, their motive being to leave their own imprimatur on whatever they can, otherwise they feel they're not being creative, that they're simply copyists. Only one in a million readers will ever detect this change, or even care that it has been effected, so, unless the new version is a distinct improvement upon the original, or a tremendously wild variation thereof, it will have been done solely for the benefit of the writer. Michael B. Ballard, in *A Long Shadow* (1986) has this: *At one stop, during the morning hours of 3 April a waiting crowd saw Davis sitting next to a window of his car. Cheers rang out. "He smiled and acknowledged their compliment."* And William J. Cooper, in *Jefferson Davis, American* (2000), writes: *...a crowd cheered the president, who sat by a window. Acknowledging the notice, he "smiled."*

Burke Davis came up with the waving hand in *To Appomattox* (1959): *Davis sat at a window of the train ... waving a hand and smiling to acknowledge the cheers of the crowd.* The president might have smiled, as Wise writes, but his other manifestation of acknowledgment, if there was one, may just have been a nod. There is nothing in Wise's account to hint at waving. This from William C. Davis's *An Honorable Defeat* (2001): *He just smiled and waved to them from his window.* And from James Swanson's *Bloody Crimes*: *Through one of the train's windows he* [i.e., Wise] *spotted Davis, waving to the people gathered at the depot.* James C. Clark, on the other hand, steers clear of the waving hand. In his *Last Train South*, he merely writes: *Sitting beside the window, Davis smiled to the cheers of the small crowd.*

F. Lawrence McFall, in *Danville in the Civil War* (2001), has taken the specific and rendered it as the general: *President Davis sat at the car window and smiled to the crowds who gathered and cheered at each stop.*

However, a smile was not the only thing that showed on Jefferson Davis's face. As Wise says, in "End of an Era," 1899: *...his expression showed physical and mental exhaustion.* Wise is generally quoted accurately on this point—Burke Davis in *To Appomattox*, Professor Strode, Shelby Foote, James C. Clark, Michael B. Ballard, and Clint Johnson. However, William J. Cooper in *Jefferson Davis, American* (2000) has this: *...an eyewitness thought "his expression showed mental and physical exhaustion."* Cooper does not mention his eyewitness by name. It is certainly not Wise.

In his 2001 book, *Danville in the Civil War*, McFall discusses the interchange between Wise and Dr. Garnett in the presidential car as it stopped at Clover: *During their conversation even Wise noted that Davis's face "showed physical and mental exhaustion."* And this: *Davis's outward demeanor disguised his physical and mental exhaustion. An occasional facial expression betrayed his false composure.*[32]

As F. Lawrence McFall has already mentioned, Lieutenant Wise entered the president's car to chat with Dr. Garnett. Unfortunately, except to mention the president and General Bragg, Wise does not go into any more details about the occupants of the car, which is somewhat surprising, given that he was so palpably aware of the historic event he was part of: *In this car was my brother-in-law, Dr. Garnett, family physician to Mr. Davis. I entered, and sat with him a few minutes, to learn what I could about the home folk. His own family had been left at his Richmond residence, to the mercy of the conqueror.*

Burke Davis shows restraint in his version of this incident, when writing in *To Appomattox*: *Wise saw his brother-in-law in the car, a Dr. Garnett, who was physician to the President.* So does James C. Clark: *...nearby was the president's physician, Dr. Garnett.*

It is most likely that the presidential train remained at Clover for perhaps half an hour. Whatever time it was that the train left—and it must have been about 11:00 a.m.—it was a bright, sunny day, and well advanced into the morning. They should be in Danville by four o'clock in the afternoon—if things went well. But, of course, there was always the unexpected delay to take into account.

Wise does not mention the departure of the train at all. Once again, it must be stressed that Wise is the sole source for this episode, and therefore any actual description by historians of the train's departure from Clover—whenever it departs from Wise—is pure fiction.

Thus, in *To Appomattox*, we have Burke Davis letting us know it was still dark when the train left Clover: *The train soon pulled away, and Wise watched its lantern dwindle away in the direction of Danville.* And, as he writes twenty-six years later, in *The Long Surrender*: *The train was soon on its way laboring westward with a dwindling of its lanterns and a subdued soughing of its ancient engine.*

Shelby Foote, keenly aware that it could not possibly have been night time, merely

---

32. It would be interesting to know how this facial expression manifested itself.

says this: *Finally the engine chuffed on down the track and over Difficult Creek, drawing its brief string of coaches and boxcars.*

Other trains soon arrived at Clover Station. As Wise says: *The Presidential train was followed by many others. One bore the archives and employees of the Treasury Department, another those of the Post Office Department, another those of the War Department. I knew many in all these departments, and they told me the startling incidents of their sudden flight.* James Swanson sums up in his 2010 book, *Bloody Crimes*: Later Wise witnessed the train carrying the Confederate treasury pass, and others too.

The next passage by Wise is a classic, and has been copied verbatim by almost every historian. *I saw a government on wheels. It was the marvelous and incongruous debris of the wreck of the Confederate capital. There were very few women on these trains, but among the last in the long procession were trains bearing indiscriminate cargoes of men and things. In one car was a cage with an African parrot, and a box of tame squirrels and a hunchback! Everybody, not excepting the parrot, was wrought up to a pitch of intense excitement.*

Wise continues: *The last arrivals brought the sad news that Richmond was in flames. Our departing troops had set fire to the tobacco warehouses. The heat, as it reached the hogsheads, caused the tobacco leaves to expand and burst their fastenings, and the wind, catching up the burning tobacco, spread it in a shower of fire upon the doomed city. It was after dark on Monday*[33] *when the last train from Richmond passed Clover Station bound southward.*[34] *We were now the Northern outpost of the Confederacy. Nothing was between us and the enemy except Lee's army, which was retreating toward us—if indeed it were coming in this direction.*

Some historians—not many—have confused Clover Station in Halifax County with Clover Hill in Chesterfield County, just outside Richmond. For example, William C. Davis in *An Honorable Defeat* (2001): *…but when one crowd at Clover Hill cheered him from the platform that morning, Davis did not rise and come out. He just smiled and waved to them from his window, while out in the crowd some could see the exhaustion and anguish on his face.* And Hattaway & Beringer in *Jefferson Davis* (2002): *A soldier on the platform at Clover Hill, Lieutenant John S. Wise.*

Milepost 98.0
Ockward/Logdale

It is highly doubtful if either Ockward or Logdale existed in 1865. Neither one features in the 1858 *Virginia Gazetteer*. In 1915 both names appear as freight stations at Milepost 98.

Milepost 100.6
Scottsburg

Halifax County. In *Smith's Hand-Book* of 1856, and in *Mitchell's Guide* of 1857, Scottsburg is listed at Milepost #100. In the 1858 *Virginia Gazetteer*, it is a small village on the line of the R&D, 87 miles southwest of Richmond as the crow flies, with about 50 or 60 inhabitants. No depot is mentioned. *Appleton's Guide* of 1865 has it at Milepost #100.

---

33. He means that Monday night, the 3rd.
34. Admiral Raphael Semmes (1809–1877) commanded the last train out of Richmond.

The Davis train went through Scottsburg probably at about 11:30 that morning. Scottsburg is still there.

Milepost 101.0
Banister

There was a stop here on the R&D in 1855, but the place is not listed in the 1858 gazetteer. In *Smith's Hand-Book* of 1856 and 1859, it is listed as 101 miles out of Richmond on the R&D.

Milepost 104.5
Wolf Trap

There was no depot here in 1855, and Wolf Trap is not in the 1858 *Virginia Gazetteer*. However, it is at Milepost #103 in the 1881 *Official Railway Guide*. Wolf Trap is still there.

Milepost 108.0
Berry Hill

Halifax County. Berry Hill was the palatial home of the Bruce family, built in the 1840s. One of the great Virginia plantations, it took in most of what is today Boston, Virginia. The R&D line reached here in January 1855, at "109 miles." That month, trains left Richmond at 7:00 a.m., stopped at Robiou's, Coal Field, Tomahawk, Powhatan, Mattoax, Chula, Amelia Court House, Wyanoke, Jennings Ordinary, Haytokah, Liberty Church, Meherrin, Keysville, Drake's Branch, Mossingford, Roanoke, Clover, Banister, and arrived at Berry Hill at 12:45 p.m. That is 5 hours, 45 minutes. The return trip left Berry Hill at 10:30 a.m. and arrived at Richmond at 4:45 p.m. which is 6 hours, 15 minutes. By later in January 1855 the track had reached South Boston, and Berry Hill was discontinued as a station; hence it is not in the 1858 *Virginia Gazetteer*.

Milepost 108.9
Boston

Still in Halifax County, the R&D line reached South Boston in January 1855, and there the company built a depot. This depot superseded Berry Hill. In *Smith's Hand-Book* of 1856 and 1859, Boston is listed at 108 miles out of Richmond on the R&D, and in *Mitchell's Guide* of 1857 it is listed at Milepost #109. Neither Boston nor South Boston is in the 1858 *Virginia Gazetteer*. *Appleton's Guide* of 1865 has Boston at Milepost #109.

It was probably close to 12:30 p.m. when the presidential train passed Boston. Stuart, in his *New York Herald* article of July 4, 1865, says: *About forty miles*[35] *beyond the junction*[36] *we came up with two trains which had stopped.* Stuart says that both contained minor officials and convalescent soldiers, and both had gone off the track. The foremost train had one of its cars broken, five lives being the cost of the accident. *Everything appeared burdened with a portent of evil, thus far. The five victims of this accident were laid out*

---

35. It was actually 54 miles.
36. I.e., Burkeville Junction.

11. The Trip

Remains of a wrecked train on the track, perhaps similar to the scene near South Boston.

near a grove as we came up. They were wounded soldiers from Alabama—gallant men who had dragged their lives most gloriously from the battle field, to have them most ingloriously sacrificed by incompetent or reckless railway officials. There they lay, all their aspirations for the home to which they hoped themselves bound, sunk forever within the confines of one common, coffinless grave preparing for them. There was no need to give sadder zest to the sadness we all felt; but this calamity, upon which we so unexpectedly trod, left us "stunned by death's twice mortal mace." Mr Davis got out to inquire into the circumstances of the disaster; all the others got out too; but no one except myself went over to where the "nameless heroes lay," in a most melancholy row—a neighboring farmer keeping the flies from their ghastly faces, and two negroes digging a long hole in which what was left of the luckless soldiers was to be deposited.

"Taking this interruption as an omen, I don't relish it," said Benjamin, when his companions were once more seated.

"Yet it is preferable to the kind we expected," remarked a Major Wheeler immediately behind him, who had a holy terror of Sheridan.

"Not preferable," cried Lubbock, sharply; "some may distrust their personal safety, but we are enough to whip a whole brigade of raiders. Give me an interruption from living Yankees, whom I can slay, but no interruption like this."

"It was to be," whined one of the preachers, emphatically.

Mr. Davis said not a word, sighed, and leaned back to peer vacantly at dim distance. In about twenty minutes we were again moving on slowly and drearily.

Mallory does not mention this significant incident at all.

In the article "War News" published in the *Danville Register* in April 1965, it is stated that: *Because of the war-torn condition of the railroad, the journey itself was painfully slow, and a further delay came during the morning at South Boston when a mishap to an Army troop train in front of the President's claimed the lives of several soldiers and took some time to clear the tracks.*

In that same issue of the *Danville Register*, the article "Wreck at South Boston Delayed President" says that: *Captain R. Walton Sydnor of Danville, on April 3, 1865, was commander of the 1st Regiment, Virginia Reserves, stationed at Staunton River Bridge on the railroad, about 50 miles east of Danville, when he was ordered to return to Danville with his command.* "We boarded a freight train—old box cars—which had on it a number of sick and wounded soldiers from the hospital in Richmond on their way home to Georgia. Soon after leaving Staunton River our train was wrecked. In some way, the trucks of one of the cars turned and got out of place and the bottom of the car fell through, and the soldiers who were in this box car were caught right under the wheels and were terribly mangled; five or six were killed outright. As this train was just preceding the one which carried President Davis and staff, we had to act promptly. I had charge of a detail of men to bury the dead soldiers. We took up their bodies on the old car doors, carried them up the slope some fifty or one hundred yards, and buried all in one grave, protecting them as best we could with boards from the old car." *It was not until nearly 60 years later that the details of this tragedy were recounted by Capt. Sydnor. He wrote his account for the "Confederate Veteran" magazine in Aug. 1924, after seeing an appeal in the same magazine from Halifax United Daughters of the Confederacy chapter for information about the all-but-forgotten wreck. The UDC chapter later erected a marker at the burial spot, about two miles east of South Boston.*[37]

John H. Brubaker tells of this incident in his slim 1979 book, *Last Capital*: *At South Boston, about 30 miles east of Danville, the convoy was halted when the bottom fell out of one of the cars in a train just ahead of the president's. Five or six soldiers were killed outright beneath the moving wheels; others were badly mangled. The dead were buried and the tracks cleared as quickly as possible so the government could move on to Danville.*

J. Frank Carroll reports the incident in his *Confederate Treasure* (1996): *The ramshackle and rotted floor of one overloaded car collapsed, and some of the passengers fell to their deaths underneath the wheels of the train, necessitating a quick, but sad, burial near the tracks. [The dead were all soldiers from Georgia].* Carroll is definitely implying that this incident happened to one of the cars on the presidential train. That's not what Brubaker says. He says it was the train immediately preceding the president's train.

McFall agrees with Brubaker. In *Danville in the Civil War* (2001), he talks about the presidential train, and says that it *stopped once more, this time two miles east of South Boston. The train in advance of the president's derailed following the collapse of the floor in a boxcar. Five Georgia soldiers fell beneath the train to their deaths. Captain R. Walton Sydnor, on board the fatal train, helped to bury the victims within 100 yards of the tracks.* McFall, in his 2011 article, "To Danville," says that the presidential train was delayed by the derailment of an earlier train just east of South Boston. For this, he cites Ballard.

William C. Davis, in *An Honorable Defeat* (2001), writes: *On one occasion, as they slowly started off again after being stopped by a train that had derailed, Davis looked out his window and saw wounded soldiers lying beside the track where they had been thrown by the wreck of their train, and some of them horribly mangled. It was not a sight to cheer him or his companions.*[38]

---

37. Robert Walton Sydnor (1847–1931) was commander of the Nottoway Company at the age of 17. In August 1924 he told his story of the South Boston train wreck in the magazine *Confederate Veteran*.

38. For this passage Professor Davis cites the Beverley Randolph Wellford Diary of April 2, 1865. Wellford, of Fredericksburg and Richmond, Virginia, was a judge, and chief clerk of the Confederate War Department. The White, Wellford, Taliaferro, and Marshall Family Papers, consisting of letters, diaries, writings, and other papers of Wellford and Taliaferro, and including Wellford's 1865 diary of the flight of *(continued)*

11. The Trip

If Stuart's account is to be trusted, and one feels it should be, then the presidential train left the scene of the accident no later than about 12:45 p.m. From there to Danville the going would be easier. Today, the Dan, among other things, separates the city of Danville from its northern suburb, North Danville, which in 1865 was called Northside. As all travelers did heading south on the Richmond and Danville Railroad, the fleeing Davis party first encountered the Dan long before Danville—in fact, at South Boston— then stayed with it for a while on its northern bank, before heading out across the countryside. They would next encounter it at Danville, where they would cross via the railroad bridge into downtown Danville.

Milepost 117.0
Gianal

In 1915 it appears as a freight station. Certainly Jefferson Davis would never have known this name.

Milepost 117.4
New's Ferry

The line reached here in August 1855, and a depot was built. In *Smith's Hand-Book* of 1856, it is listed at Milepost #117. It is not listed in the 1858 *Virginia Gazetteer*, but *Appleton's Guide* of 1865 has it at Milepost #117.

Milepost 118.0
Noding

It is not in the 1858 *Virginia Gazetteer*, and is not a name Jefferson Davis would have known. In 1915 both New Ferry and Noding appear as freight stations at Milepost 118.

Milepost 122.0
Pace/Marseilles

Marseilles was a community here, on the north bank of the Dan River, from at least the early 1800s. Occasionally one will see it on a railroad schedule, but not as early as 1865. One also sees the name Pace, otherwise Pace's, or Paces. None of these variants is listed in the 1858 *Virginia Gazetteer*, but in the 1893 *Official Railway Guide* Pace's is listed at Milepost #122. At that milepost, in 1915 Pace appears as a freight station. Paces is still there.

Milepost 126.9
Barksdale's

Still in Halifax County, the R&D line was completed to this point in September 1855, and a depot was built. In *Smith's Hand-Book* of 1856 it is listed as Barksdales, at Milepost

---

(cont.) the Confederate cabinet, are stored in the Southern Historical Collection at the Wilson Library, University of North Carolina at Chapel Hill, and are available on microfilm #01300 (318 items). One cannot help feeling, though, that the diary entry quoted—April 2—should be April 3.

#127. In the 1858 *Virginia Gazetteer* it is listed as Barksdale, a post office, 98 miles southwest of Richmond, on a corner of the Roanoke River. *Appleton's Guide* of 1865 has it at Milepost 127.

Milepost 129.9
Sutherlin's Mill

There was no depot here in 1865. In the 1881 *Official Railway Guide* Sutherlin's is listed as a depot at Milepost #130. Sutherlin is still there, on the Halifax–Pittsylvania County Line.

Milepost 135.2
Ringgold

Pittsylvania County. The line was completed to this point in February 1856. In the 1858 *Virginia Gazetteer* it is described as a post office, 120 miles west-southwest of Richmond. No depot mentioned. *Appleton's Guide* of 1865 has it at Milepost #135.

Milepost 140.0
North Danville/Dundee

The line was completed to this point in March 1856 (Dan River), and a depot was built. *Appleton's Guide* of 1865 has Northside at Milepost #140

Milepost 140.6
Danville

On May 16, 1856, the R&D line was completed all the way to Danville.[39] In *Smith's Hand-Book* of 1856, Danville is listed as the terminus, at Milepost #141. In the 1858 *Virginia Gazetteer*, it is described as 123 miles southwest by west of Richmond as the crow flies. *Appleton's* 1865 guide has it at Milepost #140.

Finally, how many trains left Richmond for Danville on April 2–3, 1865? The 2007 book, *The Rebel and the Rose*, gives us the background to how the trains were gathered and made ready for the flight: *Secretary of War Breckinridge was given the responsibility of ensuring that enough engines and cars were standing by at the station. One train would be for Davis and his cabinet while a second train would contain the remainder of the treasury.*[40] And this: *Rounding up train crews would be as much a challenge as locating adequate rolling stock and engines that could hold a head of steam. The problem was quickly assigned to Capt. Peter Helms Mayo, a quartermaster with Lt. Gen. A.P. Hill's Third Corps.* Mayo

---

39. We know it as Danville today, and we knew it as Danville in the 19th century. However, back then, unlike today, there was an alternate spelling used by many people—Dansville. A.C. Bancroft sometimes spells it Danville in his 1889 book *The Life and Death of Jefferson Davis*, but the spelling he prefers is Dansville.

40. The authors of *The Rebel and the Rose* have subscribed to the theory that the treasure went out on two trains (see Chapter 12).

11. The Trip

had previously been in charge of the movement of soldiers on trains running between Richmond and Petersburg. He was no longer needed for that purpose.[41] And this: *Quartermaster Peter Helms Mayo had done his job well. Summoning the train crews to the depot with blasts from a shift-engine steam whistle, he had somehow found the cars and engines to make up the trains he needed, and the fireboxes of the cabinet and treasury trains were glowing with hot coals.*[42]

There were not just two Danville trains, but several; perhaps as many as nine. J.B. Jones wrote the famous *Rebel War Clerk's Diary*. After the war, using sources that had been unavailable to him during the evacuation of Richmond, he reworked his diary, especially the most celebrated entry, April 2, 1865. The book was published in 1866, by which time Jones was dead. Nevertheless, he seems to have been the first person to come up with an actual number of trains: *Eight trains are provided for the transportation of the archives, etc. No provision for civil employees and their families.*

Alfred H. Bill, with J.B. Jones's book on his desk, wrote the book, *Beleaguered City*, in 1946: *Eight trains had been reserved for the archives.*[43] *One pulled out with the last of the armory machinery and many of the armory mechanics. But no provisions had been made for the transportation of the department clerks and their families.*

No one really disagrees with eight. Burke Davis in *To Appomattox* (1959): *Jones ... grew more concerned as he found that eight trains would leave for Danville during the night.* Richard E. Prince in *Steam Locomotives and Boats* (1965): *Eight trains were made available.* James C. Clark in *Last Train South* (1984): *There would be eight trains leaving for Danville.* Michael B. Ballard in *A Long Shadow* (1986): *Eight trains had been reserved for an emergency evacuation.* F. Lawrence McFall in *Danville in the Civil War* (2001): *Eight trains were made ready in Richmond for the evacuation of the Confederate government.* *The Rebel and the Rose* (2007): *A total of eight trains would be made up, a task especially difficult on a Sunday.* And Larry Aaron in *Pittsylvania County* (2009): *That afternoon, eight trains were readied to take Confederate officials and important documents to Danville.*

And a grand total of six thousand refugees riding in, on, or underneath passenger cars, boxcars and flat cars. As for the presidential train itself—the one Jefferson Davis was on—there were close to eight hundred souls, 99 percent of them unknown to posterity.

---

41. In May 1861, Peter Helms Mayo (1836–1920) and his two brothers enlisted as privates in the Governor's Mounted Guard, 4th Virginia Cavalry, Confederate States Army. Peter was made captain and quartermaster in charge of railroad transportation of supplies and troops to and from Richmond. He surrendered with Lee at Appomattox Court House, and returned to Richmond under parole. "Episodes of a Busy Life," typescript in the Peter Helms Mayo Recollections, at the Southern Historical Collection, UNC.

42. The trains were wood-burners, not coal-burners (see Chapter 7).

43. If this seems like a lot of trains just for the archives, it is. What the Rebel War Clerk had actually said was: "*Eight trains had been reserved for the archives, etc.*"

Chapter 12

THE CONFEDERATE TREASURE

Legend has it that Jefferson Davis took the Confederate treasure out of Richmond when he fled, and that it subsequently "disappeared." People are still digging.

This is how the whole affair started. William Harwar Parker says, in his *Recollections* (1883): *I received a dispatch from the Secretary of the Navy which read as follows, "Have the corps of midshipmen, with the proper officers, at the Danville depot today at 6:00 p.m."* That means, of course, the Richmond & Danville Depot, in Richmond.

One of those young midshipmen was Robert H. Fleming, who purportedly kept a diary of events as they unraveled. "The Confederate Naval Cadets and the Confederate Treasure. The Diary of Midshipman Robert H. Fleming" appeared in 1966 (see the Bibliography, under Herndon, G. Melvin). In his entry for Sunday, April 2, Fleming says that the midshipmen were marched at quick time to get ready to leave. *Left quarters about 4 armed. Arrived at Danville Depot at 5. It was announced today that we were picked out by the Sec. to guard a very valuable train loaded with specie.*

John W. Harris, who did not actually get to go on the train,[1] says that the midshipmen marched to the depot, where they were informed by John H. Reagan that they had been selected "for a service of peculiar danger and delicacy." *To their guardianship was to be committed a valuable train, containing the Archives of the government, with its money.* Harris continues: *They then marched into the station, where the train was receiving its freight.* Guards were placed, and the building cleared of all except those in charge. Two midshipmen, with loaded revolvers, were placed in each car with the government boxes, one to sleep while the other watched.

But what exactly was this treasure? According to Harris, the treasure consisted of small, square boxes, supposed to contain gold and bullion; and kegs, resembling beer kegs, which were believed to be filled with silver.

Otis Ashmore, in his 1918 article, "Story of the Confederate Treasure," explains in more detail: *...there were two separate and distinct funds which were brought away from Richmond under the same guard and on the same train. One was the public fund of the Confederate Government, and the other the private property of certain Virginia banks*

---

1. John W. Harris (1848–1890) was appointed midshipman in the Confederate States Navy in January 1865. He was the author of two articles, "Confederate Naval Cadets" and "The Gold of the Confederate Treasury" (see the Bibliography). Burke Davis says in his 1959 book, *To Appomattox: Naval cadet John W. Harris, son of a Charlottesville physician, lay abed in the Belleview Hospital, a victim of dysentery. He was not quite seventeen, but was a veteran who had fought with the raider John Mosby before entering the Navy. For all his discomfort, he was a lighthearted warrior.*

12. The Confederate Treasure

whose officers decided to seek safety and protection for their funds under the same military escort provided for the Confederate funds. Both of these funds were transported southward by rail ... to Danville.

To put it another way, there were two separate and distinct "treasures" in play here—the Confederate Treasury treasure and the Confederate War Department treasure. These two treasures were never intermingled and they remained separate throughout the entire flight.

Captain John M. Strother was in charge of the War Department money, and commandeered one of the train cars carrying the treasure from Richmond to Danville. In an affidavit he made on April 3, 1866,[2] Strother explains exactly what the War Department treasure was—$300,000 which had been raised from loans by the Bank of Virginia, the Farmer's Bank of Virginia, the Exchange Bank of Virginia, as well as a few other Richmond banks and a bank in Petersburg. Courageous representatives from these banks crowded into Strother's car in order to keep a watchful eye on their own contributions.[3] As J. Frank Carroll puts it, in his 1996 book, *Confederate Treasure*: *The Virginia bank funds were supervised by Judge W.W. Crump who was assisted by junior clerks from six banks. The bank funds were placed in the second forty-four-foot long freight car earmarked with the stamp of each bank. These boxes were not opened during the journey south.*

So, Strother was the military overseer of the War Department funds and Crump was the civilian in charge of those funds.

Frances H. Casstevens, in *Edward A. Wild and the African Brigade* (2005), writes this: *On April 3, 1863, the "midnight train" from Richmond, Virginia, carried two separate treasures—the Confederate treasure and the private bank funds. The Virginia bank funds were supervised by Judge W.W. Crump and junior clerks from six banks. Each container was stamped with the name of the bank from which it came. These were not opened on the journey south.* Aside from the fact that the author places the event in the wrong year, the rest of this passage seems to be accurate. Casstevens does, in fact, cite J. Frank Carroll.

A separate car was allocated to the Treasury treasure, which was *placed under the care of Walter Phillbrook [sic], Chief Teller of the Confederate Treasury. It was packed in boxes, bags, chests and kegs, which were labeled with the seal of the Confederacy and located in the first freight car. Clerks from the Confederate Treasury judicially insured the integrity of their charge on its way south.*[4]

It is clear from everything so far that both treasures went out on the same train—the treasure train, also known as the specie train—which left Richmond about midnight for Danville. Parker's sixty midshipmen guarded both treasures. But there is another school of thought.

F. Lawrence McFall proposes that the Treasury treasure went on the presidential train. This from his *Danville in the Civil War* (2001): *Two cars of the presidential train carried the records, personnel and specie of the Treasury Department.* And this from his 2011 article, "To Danville": *Two cars of the Presidential train transported the personnel,*

---

2. Captain Strother's affidavit of April 3, 1866, was made before John S. Loomis, assistant special agent, Treasury Department, Richmond District, Virginia. 45th Congress, 2nd Session, House of Representatives, Document #5, "Petition of William B. Isaacs & Co, of Richmond, Virginia, representatives of certain banks in Richmond, praying for the restoration of certain coin belonging to them now in the Treasury of the United States."
3. The representative for the Exchange Bank was second teller James M. Miller.
4. J. Frank Carroll, *Confederate Treasure in Danville* (Danville, VA: URE Press, 1996).

records, and specie of the Treasury Department to Danville. One implication is reasonably clear here—the War Department treasure went out on a different train, obviously the treasure train. Another implication is that the sixty midshipmen were split up between two trains. This flies in the face of all we have learned so far—one treasure train for both sets of treasure, and that train leaving at midnight, with all sixty midshipmen aboard it. So where did McFall get this?

J. Adair Pleasants, in an affidavit he made on March 12, 1866, in Washington, D.C., wrote: *At the time of the evacuation of Richmond, on the night of the 2d of April 1865, I was corresponding clerk of the Confederate States treasury department, and left the city on the train with Mr. Davis and his cabinet.* By this, does he mean he was traveling in the presidential car? Probably not. Why would a corresponding clerk be traveling with the big wigs? No, he must mean he was simply traveling on the same train as the president.

Adair Pleasants continues: *At Danville, the specie belonging to the Confederate Government was in the custody of, and under the control of, the treasurer (Mr. Hendren), and that of the Richmond banks was in a different train, and in charge of officers of the banks. The same was the case at Greensborough, N.C.*

One must remember that at Danville everybody and everything, including both sets of treasure, was unloaded from the R&D trains to await replacement on their new Piedmont Railroad trains that would take them on to Greensboro. Pleasants is very specific about what happened to both sets of treasure while at Danville and Greensboro, but he does not mention how either one was conveyed from Richmond to Danville. All he says is that he, Pleasants, was on the presidential train during that first leg of the flight. We cannot infer from this that the Treasury treasure, or even the War Department treasure, was as well. In short, nowhere does Pleasants say, or even imply, that the two sets of treasure did not go from Richmond to Danville on a separate and distinct treasure train.

And neither does John Ott, chief clerk of the Treasurer's office, and one of Adair Pleasants's immediate colleagues. One year to the day after the train arrived at Danville, Ott swore his own affidavit in Richmond: *All the specie belonging to the Treasury Department was sent off on a train about six o'clock Sunday evening, April 2, 1865. The specie belonging to the War Department I knew nothing about, as it did not come under my cognizance. Walter Philbrook, the first teller of the Treasurer's office, went in charge of the Treasury specie.*

It is absolutely clear from this report that the Treasury treasure left Richmond on a separate and distinct treasure train. Six o'clock is six hours too early, however. We simply have too much evidence in favor of midnight. Just a mistake on Ott's part, perhaps.

Ott goes on to say that, upon the arrival at Danville, $50,000 in gold and an equal amount in silver, was taken out of the Treasury funds by order of George Trenholm, the secretary of the Treasury, and placed in the Bank of Danville. The balance, of $200,000, was left in the railroad cars for a week under the care of Philbrook, along with all the other effects of the treasurer's office, and then, still under Philbrook, *went on South on Sunday, the day of Lee's surrender.*[5]

Of the $100,000 in the Bank of Danville, they sold $9,000 of the silver at 70 to 1, which left $91,000. On Monday, April 10, the Davis party fled Danville, heading for Greensboro on the Piedmont Railroad, taking that $91,000 with them.

---

5. From *The Papers of Jefferson Davis*, p. 547: *The treasure had left Danville about April 6 and traveled to Greensboro.*

Two other works repeated McFall's story. The first was Douglas W. Bostick's book about Frank Vizetelly, the Civil War illustrator—*The Confederacy's Secret Weapon* (2009). When discussing the presidential train, Bostick has this to say: *Also on the train was a group of sixty handpicked midshipmen from the Confederate Naval Academy led by Captain William H. Parker. Parker and his sailors were escorting $500,000 in gold nuggets, coins and silver bars, the last of the Confederate treasury.* The problem with this is that Bostick has placed all the midshipmen on the presidential train, the implication being, therefore, that the treasure train never existed. So, Bostick's argument here must be dismissed.

McFall's version of events also appears in a note in *The Papers of Jefferson Davis: Under guard of mostly navy and marine personnel, the Confederate treasury was carried in the train that left Richmond on the 2d with Davis.* However, second thoughts creep in with the very next sentence: *In addition to the deposits of the Confederate Treasury Department and those of several Richmond banks, the 'specie train' also included government records.*[6]

There are also two theories about which train left Richmond first out of the two—the presidential train or the treasure train. Lt. Parker was in command of the treasure. He should know something about its movements that night. In his 1893 article, "The Gold and Silver in the Confederate States Treasury," he says: *Sometime in the evening the President, his Cabinet, and other officials left the depot for Danville. The train was well packed. General Breckinridge, Secretary of War, however, did not start with the President. He remained with me at the depot until I got off, which was not until somewhere near midnight.* We know that Parker left with the treasure, so his statement, which is unequivocal—at least as far as he is concerned—says that the treasure left subsequent to the presidential train.

Otis Ashmore, in "Story of the Confederate Treasure" (1918), concurs: *It is well known that a large amount of gold, silver, bonds, etc., followed Mr. Davis on his journey southward.* However, Ashmore perhaps disqualified himself as a source when he wrote this: *The train bearing this treasure ... together with the funds of the Virginia banks, the families of Mr. Davis and some of the Cabinet members, and the armed escort under Capt. Parker, left Richmond on the night of April 2nd, and arrived at Danville, Va., on the afternoon of April 3rd.* The only cabinet family on the entire flight was Mrs. George Trenholm, and she was in the same car as her husband and Jefferson Davis, and that was, of course, on the presidential train, not the treasure train.

Dallas Irvine, in his 1939 article, "The Fall of Richmond," says: *...the passenger train bearing the higher officials pulled out, to be followed at intervals by trains of freight cars carrying the impedimenta and minor personnel. The last of these trains, which got off shortly before dawn, carried the government's treasure under guard of the midshipmen.* Dawn that morning in Richmond was at 4:30. That does not tally with Parker's "somewhere near midnight." And how does Irvine know the treasure train was the last train out? Regardless of how he knows, Frances H. Casstevens, in *Edward A. Wild and the African Brigade* (2005), certainly believed him: *The treasure train was the last train to leave Richmond before it was evacuated by Confederate troops.* She cites Medora Fields Perkerson's book *White Columns in Georgia*.

Midshipman Fleming agrees with Parker. When talking of a separate treasure train,

---

6. *The Papers of Jefferson Davis*, vol. 11, p. 509, footnote 29.

Fleming says in his diary: *The train left the Depot about 12 midnight*. Midshipman Harris also has a separate treasure train, and also gives midnight for its departure from Richmond.

The separate treasure train theory is certainly subscribed to by Hudson Strode, who, in his 1964 book, *Tragic Hero*, says: *The treasure train was ordered to proceed to Danville as soon as it was ready, independent of the movement of the presidential train.*

Eli Evans is very clear in his biography, *Judah P. Benjamin* (1989): *The two trains, one with the gold and the other bearing the President and the Cabinet, pulled out at midnight. Diaries described hearing the train blow its whistle with a mournful sound of sorrow that some would remember the rest of their lives.* As is J. Frank Carroll, who wrote *Confederate Treasure* (1996): *Two separate treasures, the Virginia bank funds and the Confederate treasure, departed Richmond on the same midnight train.*

James Lee Conrad is also of the opinion that there were two separate trains. In *Rebel Reefers* (2003), he says: *...both the President's train and the Treasure train were packed—not only inside, but on top, in the platforms, on the engine, everywhere, in fact, where standing room could be found.* And this: *The treasure train's departure was delayed for several hours. Secretary Breckinridge and Superintendent Parker spent some very apprehensive hours waiting in the depot for the train to depart.*

James Swanson, in *Bloody Crimes* (2010), has this: *The presidential train was not the last to leave Richmond that night.* And this: *A second one carried another precious cargo from the city—the financial assets of the Confederacy, in the form of paper currency, and gold and silver coins, plus deposits from the Richmond banks.*

However, Shelby Foote, in *Civil War* (1974), is at pains to say that the treasure train left before the presidential train: *All got aboard the waiting coach, but there was another long delay while the treasure train, preceding them with its cargo of precious metals and its sixty nattily-uniformed midshipmen, cleared the southbound track, and the bridge across the James.* Later, when the trains get to Clover Station, en route to Danville, Foote will strongly reiterate their order. Foote does not source his information, but he may have got it from John Ott: *All the specie belonging to the Treasury Department was sent off on a train about six o'clock Sunday evening, April 2, 1865.* And Foote knew that the presidential train left at eleven o'clock that night. Or Foote might have got it from something Hubbard Taylor Minor, Jr., said in his diary: *At 6 p.m. all the midshipmen left Richmond for Danville, as did many other persons, & it was rumored that Richmond was being evacuated.*[7] There is a real problem with Minor at least. His time of 6:00 p.m. is six hours before midnight, and midnight is when Parker, Fleming, and Harris all say the midshipmen left Richmond. However, as we have seen, Lt. Parker, who was in command of the middies, had his orders to have his men assembled at the depot in Richmond by 6:00 p.m.

Weighing up the evidence, though, both from eyewitness accounts and secondary sources, there can be little doubt that the treasure train and the presidential train were two separate and distinct entities, and that the treasure train left Richmond about midnight, an hour or two after the presidential train, and that the treasure train was carrying both sets of treasure.

---

7. Minor (1845–1874) wrote three diaries, only the third—December 1864–April 1865—being of relevance to this book. These diaries are archived at the US Army Military History Institute, at Carlisle, Pennsylvania.

12. The Confederate Treasure

There is not much recorded about the actual trip of the treasure train, but what there is waves a red flag of suspicion. Lieutenant William Harwar Parker was in command of the midshipmen on the treasure train. According to Otis Ashmore, in his 1918 article, "The Story of the Confederate Treasure," Parker was *with the treasure train during the entire period of its movements from Richmond.* If we have to trust anyone, it might as well be Parker. In his 1893 article, "Gold and Silver," he writes: *Our train being heavily loaded, and crowded with passengers—even the roofs and platform-steps occupied—went very slowly. How we got by Amelia Courthouse without falling in with Sheridan's men has been a mystery to me ever since. We were unconscious of our danger, however, and took matters philosophically.*

Midshipman Fleming's supposed diary has this entry for April 3, 1865, and, bearing in mind Fleming's diary did not see the light of day until 1966, it sounds here eerily reminiscent of Parker: *Morning. We find ourselves switched off from our train and left on our track just across the river. The smoke of the burning city is rising up in dense columns. I hear the glad sound, another train is coming. We will yet get off, but no, it will not stop. But here comes another. Away we scramble on top, can scarcely get a place to sit down. Away we go, leaving the burning city behind.* And this: *We travel very slowly.*

James Lee Conrad's book, *Rebel Reefers* (2003), merely reworks the Fleming prose: *Finally the train pulled out, only to stop across the river at Manchester. From here the midshipmen could see the smoke of the burning city rising up in dense columns. After a short delay, the train slowly steamed on, leaving the blazing city behind.*

We hear from Midshipman Fleming again later that day, April 3, this time at Burkeville, about 54 miles down the track: "*Evening. Burkeville Junction. Yankees reported 4 miles off.*" As we have seen earlier, Fleming has the treasure train leaving Richmond at midnight on the 2–3 April, which tallies with most of the other reports. Bearing in mind that the presidential train left Richmond an hour or so before the treasure train, and arrived at Burkeville about 5 o'clock in the morning, Fleming is asking us to believe that it took the treasure train about 12 hours longer to get to Burkeville. At that rate it would never have gotten to Danville. Yet it did, apparently at about 4:30 the next morning, Tuesday the 4th. This from Fleming: *Danville, April 4th. Arrived here at daylight.*

Of the treasure train's arrival at Danville, William Harwar Parker writes this, in "Gold and Silver" (1893): *Monday, April 3d, in the afternoon, we arrived at Danville, where we found the President and his Cabinet, save General Breckinridge, who came in on Wednesday.* And this: *We did not unpack the treasure from the cars at Danville.*

Of the same event, this is J. Frank Carroll, in *Confederate Treasure* (1996), with a wealth of new detail: *No fanfare heralded the appearance of the treasure train that haltingly inched its way across the trestle* [i.e., of the bridge over the Dan River] *one hour after the Confederate officials arrived and made a right turn onto siding number two.* And this: *This particular siding had been chosen for several laudable reasons. The end of siding number two was in an elevated position at Linn Street. Due to incessant rainy conditions during the winter and early spring, the ground had become a quagmire. The treasure train was extremely heavy because the immense amount of hard money ("specie") exceeded eleven tons. The other three sidings, situated on lower ground, would not support the weighty burden of such excessive proportions over an indeterminate period.* Linn Street is downtown, on the south side of the river. *Gray overcast skies and an early dusk helped to mask the coming of the treasure train that quietly lumbered through the fine mist to Linn Street. The distance between Linn Street to Craighead Street on siding number two was limited. The nose of the engine rolled quietly to a stop, followed in sequence by the two freight cars holding the Confederate treasure and the Virginia bank funds as well as three passenger cars.*

Otis Ashmore wrote this, in "Story of the Confederate Treasure" (1918): *The treasure was not unpacked from the cars at Danville, except to make some payments for the use of the government. The treasure train remained in Danville till about April 6, when it proceeded to Greensboro, N.C.*

Chapter 13

RICHMOND LEFT BEHIND

Phoebe Yates Pember wrote, in her 1866 article: *The scream and whistle of the cars never ceased all that weary night.* And this from her 1879 book, *A Southern Woman's Story*: *The scream and rumble of the cars never ceased all that weary night.*

On the night of April 2, 1865, and into the early hours of the following morning, as the evacuation of Richmond was taking place, the city was ravaged not only by screaming train whistles, but by fire, explosions, and looting mobs. Antoni's Confections, a candy store in the St. Nicholas Saloon, next to the Exchange Bank, on Main Street, was one such victim of the looters. The name of the store was actually "Antoni's Confections, Richmond," not "Antoni's Confectionery," as is sometimes seen. Andrew Antoni and Benny Catogni were Corsican confectionery cousins.

The *Richmond Whig* of April 5, 1865, was the first to report that this particular confectionery had been ill-used: *The following are some of the stores thus robbed: …Antoni's confectionery store.*

For the talented young writer, Moses Purnell Handy, that *Whig* news item was the only prompting he required for a good story, and that story duly appeared in the February 3, 1866, edition of *The Watchman*. In it he says that at about 2 o'clock in the morning of Monday, April 3, he was walking the streets of Richmond: *As I passed the old Market-House, I met a tall fellow with both arms full of candy, dropping part of his sweet burden at every step. "Stranger," said he, "Have you got a sweet tooth?" I told him that I did not object to candy upon all occasions, expecting that he was about to make me a present. "Then go up to Antoni's and get your belly full—and all for nothing." With this unrefined remark he left me, and I directed my steps toward the store of the principal Richmond confectioner, on Main Street, near the American Hotel. I rather doubted the fellow's statement, being at a loss to imagine why such articles should be distributed to the soldiers free of charge.* Handy says that when he reached the store, the stock had been disposed of, and upon inquiry he learned the true state of the case. That true state, according to Handy, was that a squad of soldiers, led by unruly citizens, had demanded admittance into the establishment, and being refused by the proprietor, had broken down the door and crowded in, pell-mell, *eager to taste the sweetmeats, tropical fruits, and other dainties so temptingly displayed upon the shelves and tables.* On discovering that he was to lose his wares in any event, the confectioner compromised, by offering to give his stock to the crowd, provided his store were abandoned and no more furniture abused. As soon as this promise was made, the reserves made their appearance, and prevailed upon the mob to evacuate the premises; but they still demanded candy, and the merchant adhered to his promise, and dealt out all the sweets, *even to the last stick of peppermint.* From the

The ruins of Richmond, 1865.

proprietor's broken remarks, Handy received this version of the affair. *When I reached the scene of the riot, he stood upon the counter, surveying, with gloomy countenance, the ruins of his stock.* Broken glassware, candy, oranges, cakes and jellies; fancy goods and children's toys had been trampled underfoot in confusion, and if any of the half-starved children who crowded the streets of Richmond had been about at that unseasonable hour, they would doubtless have been given some of the candy by the mob. Handy wrote: *A bystander kindly gave me about a pound of cream-candy, which I crammed into my coat-pockets, and walked off well-satisfied, expecting to sell it for a good sum in the country.*[1]

The following passage from Carleton Coffin's book, *Four Years of Fighting* (1866), is taken from Handy, whose account had been printed in *The Watchman* earlier that year: "As I passed the old Market House," writes a Rebel soldier, "I met a tall fellow with both arms full of sticks of candy, dropping part of his sweet burden at every step." "Stranger," said he, "Have you got a sweet tooth?" "I told him that I did not object to candy." "Then go up to Antoni's and get your belly full, and all for nothing."

E.T. Walthall, who, through no fault of his own, has gone down in history as E.T. Watehall, wrote in his 1909 *Confederate Veteran* article "The Fall of Richmond": *I saw some men wearing Confederate uniforms break into Antoni's confectionery. The woman inside asked them not to break the jars, but to take all the candy they wanted.*

Burke Davis, in *To Appomattox* (1959), says that Watehall *watched men in Confederate uniforms smash the door of Antoni's Confectionery, the city's famed candy shop. Women in the store begged them not to break the jars on shelves. "Take all you want,"* they said, *"but don't ruin us."* And this, from James C. Clark, in his 1984 book *Last Train South* (1984): *...stopping by Antoni's Confectionery, and found men in Confederate uniforms*

---

1. This narrative was reproduced, with commentary, as the article "The Fall of Richmond in 1865," in *The American Magazine and Historical Chronicle*, Autumn/Winter, 1985.

smashing the door in. One of the employees screamed, "Take all you want, but don't ruin us."

This is from Dr. Nelson Lankford's *Richmond Burning* (2002): *At Antoni's confectionery store, the proprietor offered to give the mob all of his wares if they would not wreck the shop. Guards arrived just as he gave away the last stick of peppermint. Broken glassware, candles, jellies, cakes, and children's toys were trampled underfoot. Handy stuffed a pound of cream candy into his pockets, a present from a looter.*

When one reads Handy's account in its entirety—not just his astonishingly detailed stories of the night of depredation—one gets a really good picture of how unreliable he is as a witness. Nevertheless, this Antoni's adventure caught on—because it is colorful.

This from the *Richmond Whig* of April 5, 1865: *Drunk with vile liquor, the soldiers ... roamed from store to store ... followed by a reckless crowd.... With the butts of their muskets, they dashed in the plate glass of the store doors, and entering, made a wreck of everything.... The following are some of the stores thus robbed: Jennet's Jewelry Store, Mitchel and Tyler's jewelry store.*

Again taken from the *Whig*, this from Moses Purnell Handy's account in the *Watchman* of 1866: *I passed by a jeweler's. His shelves were empty, and the broken glass and mashed woodwork of the windows told me that the removal of the goods had been accomplished by violence.* And this, from Carleton Coffin's 1866 book, *Four Years of Fighting*: *First attacking the clothing, boot, and hat stores, then the jewellers' shops and the saloons, and lastly the dry-goods establishments. Costly panes of glass were shivered by the butts of their muskets, and the reckless crowd poured in to seize whatever for the moment pleased their fancy, to be thrown aside the next instant for something more attractive.* An ingenuous footnote says, "A Rebel Courier's Experience." This means Handy's account in *The Watchman*, but, of course, Coffin was taking just as liberally from the *Whig*.

E.T. Watehall, who somehow managed to find himself in every corner of Richmond in which something of historical interest was going to happen, writes in his 1909 article, "The Fall of Richmond": *I also saw a jewelry store and one or two others broken open, but this was not by the soldiers.* Perhaps Watehall was in company with Purnell Handy that night.

Burke Davis, in *To Appomattox*, 1959, relying on Watehall, wrote: *A nearby jewelry store window was broken and rifled by civilians*, while James C. Clark, in *Last Train South* (1984), merely reworks Burke Davis's prose: *A nearby jewelry store window was broken and the counters had been rifled by the crowd.*

The *Richmond Whig* of April 4, 1865, had this: *When it was made known on Sunday morning that the evacuation of Richmond was a foregone conclusion, the City Council held a meeting, and, in secret session passed an order for the destruction of all the liquor in the city. Accordingly, about the hour of midnight the work commenced, under the direction of committees of citizens of all the wards. Hundreds of barrels of liquor were rolled into the street, and the heads knocked in. The gutters ran with a liquor freshet, and the fumes filled and impregnated the air. Fine cases of bottled liquors were tossed into the street from third-story windows, and wrecked into a thousand pieces. As the work progressed, some straggling confederate soldiers, retreating through the city, managed to get hold of a quantity of liquor. From that moment law and order ceased to exist, chaos came, and a Pandemonium reigned.*

The *New York Daily Tribune* was quick to pick up on the *Whig* account. In their April 8, 1865, edition, they say this: *Fortunately the city authorities, and a Committee of citizens, on Sunday evening, anticipating the probability of ... violent scenes had visited the liquor establishments and poured their contents into the gutters.*

And now we come to Purnell Handy's dramatized and fictional account in *The Watchman* (1866), an account that comes, as it were, courtesy of the *Richmond Whig* of April 4, 1865: *And now I turned into Thirteenth street, and from thence into Cary, when a strong odor of whisky greeted my nasal organs. The cause was soon revealed. Just before me a voice cried: "Look out below!" And a moment after a barrel of whisky was hurled from the third-story window of a warehouse,*[2] *used as a commissary store, and dashed to pieces against the pavement, the liquor running in streams down the gutter.*[3] *A crowd was gathered around the door of the medical purveyor's office, where stood a guard with fixed bayonets. From this building barrels of liquor were rolled into the street and knocked to pieces.*[4] *The streets literally ran with whisky. A lieutenant standing at the door informed me that it was to prevent "the Yankees from getting tight when they should enter the city." Unfortunately, the confederate officers were allowed full liberty to fill their canteens, or the offense was at least winked at.* And this: *As I was watching this scene, the Capitol bell struck three. Turning my steps again toward headquarters, I perceived that day was just dawning.*[5]

J.B. Jones, the Rebel War Clerk, has in his diary entry for Monday, April 3, 1865: *At 7 A.M. Committees appointed by the city government visited the liquor shops and had the spirits (such as they could find) destroyed. The streets ran with liquor; and women and boys, black and white, were seen filling pitchers and buckets from the gutters.*

Historians have been only too glad to seize upon Jones's graphic image of the humans in the gutters, and to expand upon it with abandon, but they have chosen to disbelieve his assertion that it all took place after 7 o'clock in the morning. As for the former, it must be borne in mind that this is Jones's post-war invention, created to titillate the readers of his book, with questionable concern for the truth. For historians to use his report even on a basic level is to perpetuate a myth. For them to elaborate upon it is simply to show their worth, which, of course, they do. As for historians choosing to disregard "7:00 p.m.," when all around them are proclaiming midnight, they may have good reason. After all, Union troops would be entering the city at 8:15, so it does not leave much time to slurp booze out of the gutters.

That same year, 1866, Pollard's book, *Southern History of the War*, was published. For the account of the whiskey, he relies heavily on the *Whig*: *The City Council had met in the evening and had resolved to destroy all the liquor in the city, to avoid the disorder consequent on the temptation to drink at such a time. About the hour of midnight, the work commenced, under the direction of committees of citizens in all the wards. Hundreds of barrels of liquor were rolled into the street, and the heads knocked in. The gutters ran with a liquor freshet, and the fumes filled and impregnated the air. Fine cases of bottled liquors were tossed into the street from third-story windows, and wrecked into a thousand pieces. As the work progressed, some straggling soldiers, retreating through the city, managed to get hold of the liquor. From that moment law and order ceased to exist.*

James Dabney McCabe also relies on the *Whig*, and on the Rebel War Clerk, for his account in his *Life and Campaigns of General Robert E. Lee* (1866), but he cannot believe that Richmonders would actually lower themselves into the gutters like animals: *At nightfall a scene of the wildest confusion set in. There was a large quantity of liquor in the city,*

---

2. Compare with the *Whig* article above.
3. Ibid.
4. Ibid.
5. Not in Richmond—dawn that morning was at or around 4.30 a.m.

and the Municipal Authorities, as a measure of safety, ordered this to be destroyed. The heads of the casks were knocked in, and the liquor poured into the gutters. The worst classes of the inhabitants, white and black, turned out en masse, and a rush was made for the business quarter in the lower part of the city. The commissary stores were appropriated in an amazingly short time—stores of considerable value, which had been denied to the hungry troops in the field. The shops of the merchants were broken open, and entered at pleasure. The contents—jewelry, dry-goods, provisions, property of all kinds—were seized and carried off by the rioters, the owners making no effort to save them, everyone being convinced that the city would be sacked by the enemy the next day. Hundreds of drunken men and boys roamed through the streets, adding to the confusion by their cries and yells. To these noises were joined the shrieks and screams of terrified women and children.

Sallie Brock, of a sensitivity similar to that of McCabe, writing in 1867, relies on both Handy and Pollard for her account: *The city council met and ordered the destruction of all spirituous liquors, fearing lest, in the excitement, there would be temptation to drink, and thus render our situation even more terrible. In the gutters ran a stream of whiskey, and its fumes filled and impregnated the air. After night-fall Richmond was ruled by the mob.*

Whereas the Rebel War Clerk stopped short at the people filling pitchers and buckets from the gutters, his prose inspired Clement Sulivane to sink further into the amber stream of degradation. Sulivane wrote an article called "The Fall of Richmond," which forms a chapter in Volume 4 of *Battles and Leaders of the Civil War* (1888): *The gutters ran whisky, and it was lapped as it flowed down the streets.* Similarly inspired by the War Clerk, but considerably more delicate than Sulivane, was Amelia Gorgas, in her so-called diary, published in *Confederate Veteran* in 1917: *Then began wild scenes of confusion on the streets. Liquor from the medical stores emptied in the gutters offered temptation to those who wanted to forget their fate.*

From then on the story started by the *Richmond Whig* of April 4, 1865, became the property of 20th-century historians, some of whom reported it pretty straight. E. Merton Coulter, for example, in his 1950 book, *The Confederate States of America*: *The gutters ran with whisky from the staved barrels.* And D. Laurence Rogers in his *Apostles of Equality* (2011): *Whisky gushed in the gutters from smashed barrels.* But *Life* magazine of March 3, 1961, is too influenced by J.B. Jones: *Vast stores of whisky had been emptied in the streets, and plundering mobs drank from the streaming gutters.*

Most historians have been only too eager to leave their own individual literary imprint on such a graphic story, and some even more keen to invent those colorful little details that are so delightful, and so wrong. Mary Newton Stanard, in *Richmond: Its People and Its Story* (1923), obviously took this from Jones: *In one of the warehouses they [i.e., the mob] found a quantity of whisky stored, and as the barrels were rolled into the street they were met by those outside, promptly burst open with clubs, the contents literally filling the gutters as from a shower of rain. Numbers of them grabbed up tubs and buckets, dipped to the brim the fiery liquid, which the more generous of them freely dispensed to our men with the tin cans, cups, etc., lying around.*

Nelson Lankford, the generally acknowledged leader in the field of *Richmond Burning* (2002), has this: *The first sign of chaos sprang from the city council's efforts to prevent it. About midnight ... the ward committeemen designated to destroy the city's liquor began their work. They easily identified the major legal supplies and soon had whiskey barrels by the dozen rolling out of warehouses and into the streets. A sharp stroke with the blunt*

A lithograph of the fall of Richmond by Currier and Ives.

end of an ax was enough to send the contents cascading into the gutter. They threw bottles of brandy and wine out of the windows to smash on the cobblestones below. Following orders, they handed out receipts pledging the city would make good on the loss at a later date. Government commissaries undertook the same task at the Confederate storage building at Cary and Pearl streets, a former wholesale grocery store where they kept huge quantities of medicinal whiskey and brandy. And this: ...ominous sounds of thumping axes and shattering glass attracted attention, and enough unbroken whiskey casks remained to cause mischief. As if by magic, the actions of the committeemen conjured up a crowd intent on plunder, lured by the alcoholic scent that presaged the collapse of law and order. Soon, intoxicated men, women, and, it was later said, even children[6] *crouched down on their knees to scoop up the liquid from the gutters in their hats and hands. The city council had inadvertently encouraged the very thing it had hoped to avoid.*[7]

Bill O'Reilly, with Martin Dugard, wrote in *Killing Lincoln* (2011): *Their* [i.e., the Confederate leaders'] *first reaction was to destroy the one thing that could make the Yankees lose control and vent their rage on the populace: whiskey.* We are told that Union troops had gone on a drunken rampage after taking Columbia, South Carolina, two months earlier, and had then burned the city to the ground. As for Richmond on the night of April 2–3: *Out came the axes. Teams of men roamed through the city, hacking open barrel after*

---

6. It was J.B. Jones in 1866, who came up with "children."
7. For this, Dr. Lankford cites Pollard, *Lost Cause*, p. 695.

barrel of fine sour mash. Thousands of gallons of spirits were poured into the gutters. But the citizens of Richmond were not about to see all that whiskey go to waste. Some got down on their hands and knees and lapped it from the gutter. Others filled their hats and boots. And this: *Perfectly respectable men and women, in a moment of amazing distress, found a salve for their woes by falling to their knees and quenching their thirst with alcohol flowing in the gutter.*

Chapter 14

DANVILLE

Northside[1] was the name given in those days to the area of land on the north shore of the Dan River, across that river from the town of Danville. Today it is called North Danville, and is part of what is now the city of Danville. In May 1862, just before the battles around Richmond, it was deemed prudent by the Richmond & Danville Railroad to abandon the machine, carpenter and smith shops in Manchester—just outside Richmond—and to remove to a place of safety the items indispensable to the working of the road, and which might, in case of a reverse, be lost to the Confederacy without the means to replace them. The Manchester shops were given up as a hospital for the wounded. The relevant machinery and materials were duly removed to Northside, and placed in temporary buildings where for several months all the machine work of the railroad was carried out.

After the threat to Richmond had subsided, and before October 1, 1862, some of the machinery was moved back, and the Manchester shops were again in use. However, the shops at Northside were retained, and, to house them, the railroad erected a brick building in which it was intended to place the machinery permanently. By the end of 1864 the buildings had been much improved, but the problem was one of personnel. Due to the inability or reluctance of the railroad to house the families of the employees, machinists were leaving Danville.

Beginning in late 1863 earthworks, redoubts, rifle pits and similar defenses were built around Danville by military commander Colonel Robert Withers, with the help of an Austrian engineer cum music teacher named Nordendorf. These efforts did not amount to much, but they served in some measure to assuage the fears of the local citizenry. In 1864 Nordendorf made a very detailed topographical map of these defenses, including those north of the river. On this map one can see railroad lines marked "Richmond & Danville RR" coming in from the north, across a bridge into downtown Danville. One can see the bridge. The tracks come in right to the depot on Craghead Street. Issuing south from that same depot are railroad tracks saying "Piedmont RR to Greensboro, N.C."[2] To the left of the railroad bridge, as one looks north from the depot, is a separate bridge, the Main Street Bridge.[3]

---

1. Also spelled North-side and North Side.
2. That was 1863–64. At that point of time, even though the Piedmont Railroad had not yet been completed, it was under construction.
3. Robert D. Ricketts, "Stratford College, Danville Virginia," http://stratforddanville.blogspot.com, 2010.

As for the way Northside is depicted on the map, about 250 yards north of the river, immediately to the right of the tracks as one heads north toward Richmond, we see two buildings, both quite small and very close together. Immediately to the south of them are what look like five or six sheds. Immediately to the east of these sheds is a casemated battery. This is all in the area known today as Dundee, but which was then known as Tippit's Crossing. In addition to all this, there was the Cleburn farm just north of the Main Street Bridge over the Dan, and the Gordon farm some way to the west. Those are the only named settlements north of the river, but on the South Boston Road there are clearly a few more, unnamed, and scattered around are what look like more sheds.

That is how Northside looked in 1864. There was not much there. However at least three modern-day historians have proposed that, in April 1865, the Danville terminus of the Richmond & Danville Railroad line was situated at Northside. In other words, whereas the town of Danville was south of the river, the R&D's terminus was north of the river. If the R&D terminus had truly been in Northside, there would have been no railroad bridge over the Dan into downtown Danville. If there had been such a bridge, trains would have crossed it. Of course, there was a bridge, as we have seen on the Nordendorf map of 1864. Northside Depot is a myth, at least as the terminus of the R&D.

Danville historian John H. Brubaker III, it seems, was the first to promulgate this myth, in his 1979 booklet, *The Last Capital*: *After 3:00 p.m. a train of cars pulled by the engine Charles Seddon reached the Richmond and Danville Railroad Depot at Northside, immediately across the water from the town. Other trains soon followed, bearing a government in flight and all the personnel and baggage which that government could in haste assemble.*

Brubaker got two takers. William C. Davis in his *An Honorable Defeat* (2001): *Finally between 4:00 and 5:00 p.m. the government train pulled into the Richmond and Danville railroad depot just across the Dan River from its namesake town of six thousand. A considerable number of those people stood around the station as the locomotive Charles Seddon brought the cars to a halt.* And Rodman L. Underwood, in his 2005 biography, *Stephen Russell Mallory*, takes from Davis: *The presidential train ... arrived at around 5:00 p.m. the following afternoon, April 3, at the railroad depot across the Dan River from Danville, Va. The presidential party remained there for five days.*[4]

There was no such terminus as Northside, not in 1865 anyway. The train crossed the bridge all the way to downtown Danville. The confusion arises partly from the fact that Northside appears on various rail timetables for the period at Milepost #140. And there was a depot there, built when the tracklayers reached this point in March 1856. Northside then became the railhead, but only until May of that year, when they completed the half mile or so of line across the river from Northside into downtown Danville. At that point, downtown Danville became not only the railhead, but the southern terminus of the R&D. The Northside depot remained, but only for passengers wanting to get on or off there.

As for the main reasons for the confusion, F. Lawrence McFall stated the case in his 2001 book, *Danville in the Civil War*, 2001: *A misconception has existed for more than fifty years*[5]

---

4. One assumes, when Underwood says that the party "remained there for five days," that he is talking about Danville itself, rather than Northside. The Davis party was actually in Danville from April 3 until April 10.
5. McFall is referring to the article "Tunstall's Folly Grew into Southern Railway; Great Celebration Here," which appeared in the October 29, 1956, edition of the *Danville Register*. The author of that news item, confused by something he had read in a June 1956 edition of the *Richmond Enquirer*, *(continued)*

that the Richmond and Danville Railroad Depot was located on the north side of the river. And this: *The R&D RR purchased the land in 1850 to erect the depot. It paid Nathaniel Wilson $1,000 for four acres on the south bank of the Dan River.* And this: *An Oct. 28, 1859 deed map of 240 acres of the John Noble estate on the north side of the Dan River, which adjoined the railroad's right-of-way, depicts the railroad bridge.* And this: *Town Council minutes, Feb. 16, 1863, state that the R&D RR wished to pave Craghead Street from its depot to the Corporation limit (located at Loyal Street). Much of the confusion on the location of the Richmond and Danville Depot was brought about in 1873 when the newly formed Virginia Midland built its own depot on the north side of the river.*[6]

There has been much confusion, and even debate, about when the Davis train arrived at Danville. It was on April 3, 1865, yes, but what time of day?

F. Lawrence McFall, in *Danville in the Civil War* (2001), says: *The time of the train's arrival in Danville is cited in various accounts from 11 a.m. to 5 p.m. on April 3, with Davis in Rise and Fall being the earliest and Mallory in Reminiscences being the latest.*

John H. Averill,[7] the R&D's trainmaster in Danville, writing in 1897, says: *Daylight brought the first train*[8]—*the President of the Confederacy, his Cabinet, their families,*[9] *and many members of Congress.* Averill continues: *Other trains soon followed. There were women and children in box-cars, many without baggage, few with anything to eat. It was a sad scene, but the doors of the Danville houses were wide open, and they were soon housed as comfortably as possible.*

So daylight is the earliest time given, not Davis's 11:00 a.m. As for McFall's "11 a.m.," this is what was actually written in Jefferson Davis's *Rise and Fall*: ...*reached Danville on*

(cont.) had proceeded to write a very confusing piece in the *Danville Register*, which implies that the terminus was at Northside. He says that some 5,000 people turned up here.

6. As for what happened to the Virginia & Midland Depot, McFall writes: *The building's site is today bisected by River Street, just northeast of the northern end of Main Street Bridge. About 1935 railroad workers demolished the depot. In 1950 road workers unearthed and destroyed it's* [sic] *foundation during the widening of River Street in front of Dan River Mills' Riverside Division's Mill No. 6. In 1995, Dan River, Inc. demolished its Mill No. 6.* As for the railroad bridge across the Dan, this from McFall: *This bridge spanned the Dan River until replaced in 1898 by a four-span, iron-truss structure of approximately 900 feet in length. Built by the A.P. Roberts Company, for the Pengoyd Iron Works of Pengoyd, Pa., the bridge rests on the original 1856 piers of Chesterfield County, Virginia quarried stone. In 1999 the City of Danville removed the rails from the bridge and planked its floor to make it part of a walking trail.*

7. Averill (1843–1907) was the author of "Richmond, Virginia: The Evacuation of the City and the Days Preceeding It." This article tells how the news of Jefferson Davis's flight was received in Danville. *Some of the closing scenes of the Confederacy are vividly recalled* [32 years later]. Colonel Averill says that it was a quiet Danville Sabbath noon, and with no inkling in the sleepy town of what was happening in the capital, when the telegraphic news reached him of the evacuation. *Hold all trains in Danville. Send nothing out.* At that very moment, the regular northbound passenger train was scheduled to leave Danville for Richmond, and people were waiting. Eventually another message came through the keys from Richmond: *Come to Richmond with all engines and empty passenger and box cars you can pick up. Bring no freight or passengers.* Averill then got together the four engines he had in the yard, together with what cars they could scrape together, and reported for running orders. He was told to await further instructions, which duly arrived: *Too late. Richmond is being evacuated. We will all leave this p.m. Arrange for all track room possible in Danville.* Colonel Averill then goes on to tell of the dismal effect this had on the waiting passengers, and how Danville received the news, and how the town got ready to receive the refugees.

8. Daylight that morning was about 4:30 a.m.

9. The only wife was Mrs. Trenholm. There were no children.

the next morning. But that must be discounted too, because there is no way the train could have completed the trip by morning.[10]

A decade later, McFall wrote the article "To Danville" as a chapter in the book *Virginia at War, 1865*: *The train's time of arrival in Danville varies widely in post war accounts, from 11 a.m. to 5 p.m. with Davis citing the earliest and Mallory the latest.*

In his 2001 book, McFall writes: *Since Mallory's work was the only contemporary account by a major participant in the Confederate government's retreat to Danville, it is accepted by the author over others. Mallory kept his diary in late–1865, while imprisoned in Fort Lafayette, N.Y.*[11]

While one might not necessarily disagree with McFall's conclusion that 5:00 p.m. was the time, one must certainly be a little worried about how he reached that conclusion. To use only one source on which to build a conclusion is always dangerous, especially when that source is Mallory.

Anna Trenholm wrote her account in or around August 1865. It has been available to the public since 1914. McFall was writing in 2001. If he had made use of Mrs. Trenholm's diary, his case would have been considerably strengthened, for Mrs. Trenholm confirms Mallory: *Arrived in Danville at five o'clock the next day where there was an immense crowd to welcome the President. We were hospitably entertained at Mr Sutherlin's. Mr Trenholm was quite sick from the effects of the Morphine as well as the pain in his head.*

But it is obvious that McFall was not even aware of the Anna Trenholm diary. If he had been, he would not have called Mallory the only major participant. There are also, for what it's worth, the accounts of Robert G.H. Kean (written on June 1, 1865) and Taylor Wood (written on June 14, 1865), just to mention two much more supposedly contemporary accounts by major participants.

The fact that both Anna Trenholm and Mallory give 5 p.m. and that neither one of these major participants could have seen the other's account, might lead one to the conclusion that they are right, and that it had to be 5 o'clock. However, there is a problem with this argument.

Both Kean and Wood give 4:00 p.m. and, at least on the surface—the same murky surface upon which float Mallory and, to some extent, Anna Trenholm—they are no less potent as witnesses than the other two. As Kean writes, in his diary entry of June 1, 1865: *Reached Danville at 4 p.m. on April 3. Citizens hospitably took us in.* And as Taylor Wood says, in his diary entry of June 14, 1865: *Arrived at Danville at 4 p.m. The citizens took charge of the entire party, quartering all. At Maj. Sutherlin's with the President & Staff.*

Just as in the Mallory–Anna Trenholm situation, neither account was influenced by the other. So, whom do you trust? Is it 5 p.m. or 4 p.m.?

Again, in the article, "To Danville" (2011), Lawrence McFall maintains exactly the same position he had held way back in 2001. He has not moved forward: *Since Mallory's work was the only contemporary account by a major participant, 5:00 is preferred by the author.*

That the Davis party arrived in Danville on Monday, the 3rd, we have known since

---

10. It must be stressed that Jefferson Davis probably did not actually write this—his ghost writer almost certainly did (see the Bibliography, under Davis).
11. Even a cursory glance at the Mallory Papers or at their finding aid at the University of North Carolina will show that the 1865 diary in question has no relevance to the Jefferson Davis flight. See Chapter 15.

the following day's newspaper reports, published on the 5th. The *Raleigh Confederate*, for example: *The Evacuation of Richmond. Danville, April 4. The evacuation of Richmond commenced Sunday afternoon. President Davis and Cabinet arrived here Monday. Very few persons were able to leave the city,*[12] *except Government officials, in consequence of the suddenness of the movement.* The report continues: *...the Banks in the city, and the specie belonging to the Government were removed."* Finally, *The President will probably remain here for the present.*

Or the *Columbia Phoenix* (South Carolina), which issued their April 5 extra edition at 2 o'clock in the afternoon. *Danville, April 4. The evacuation of Richmond was commenced on Saturday* [sic] *afternoon. President Davis and Cabinet arrived here on Monday. Very few persons were able to leave the city, except Government officers, in consequence of the suddenness of the movement.* The report continues, *The valuables of the banks in Richmond were brought away and the specie belonging to the Government."* Finally, *The President will probably remain here for the present.*

It was definitely the 3rd. And it was, without question, in the afternoon. The Washington, D.C., paper, the *Daily National Republican*, ran this in their April 10, 1865, edition: *Parties have arrived from Danville within our lines, who report that the fugitive insurgent, Jef. Davis, arrived at Danville on Monday afternoon last, covered with dust and perspiration. His only baggage consisted of three dilapidated trunks, which looked hardly fit for a journey to Mexico. Jef. was accompanied by two or three members of his cabinet, and the whole party seemed to be in an extremely demoralized condition. Breckinridge, the Rebel secretary of war, had not turned up, and was not heard from, although diligent inquiries were being made for him.*

And, as C.E.L. Stuart says, in his July 4, 1865, article in the *New York Herald*: *We who had arrived in the afternoon.*

Mallory and Anna Trenholm give 5 p.m. Kean and Taylor Wood give 4 p.m. Sooner or later someone was going to come up with something different. William D. Coleman, in his 1881 article, "Jefferson Davis' Week at Danville," writes this: *About 3 p.m. five trains of cars reached Danville, bringing President Davis, several members of his cabinet and other government officials, some members of the Virginia legislature, and a few private citizens of distinction.* It is unlikely that five trains arrived at the same time.

All three arrival times—5 p.m., 4 p.m. and 3 p.m.—have gained their adherents.

William C. Davis, in *An Honorable Defeat* (2001), says of J. Frank Carroll's 1996 book, *Confederate Treasure*, that it *is so careless with sources and so confuses and jumbles events, that it is unwise to accept much on its authority alone without corroboration from other sources."*[13]

As we know, the railway station in Richmond from which President Davis departed for Danville was known as the Richmond & Danville depot, or the Danville Depot for short. That's because the line that connected the two places was called the Richmond & Danville Railroad. So, one cannot help but be confused when one reads J. Frank Carroll: *The engine of the Presidential Train and the ten cars that followed it had departed*

---

12. The city here referred to is Richmond. At that time, Danville was a town.
13. A criticism well-founded, of course, but Professor Davis perhaps should not cast the first stone.

from the Danville and Midland Depot in Richmond precisely at 11:00 p.m. on Sunday, April 2.[14]

Inseparable from this, Carroll goes into the story of Given Campbell, using Micajah Clark's 1882 article, "Last Days of the Confederate Treasury":

Clark: *Captain Given Campbell (an active, efficient officer).*

Carroll: *"...an active and efficient officer."*

This from Micajah Clark, when talking about Captain Campbell at Greensboro, some considerable way into the Davis flight: *...his company from the Ninth Kentucky Cavalry were detailed for special service with the President, his men being used as scouts, guides and couriers, the cavalry force not traveling as a rule upon the same road as the party.* And this, from Frank Carroll: *They had been detailed for special service with the President, acting as scouts, guides and couriers for the 140-mile journey from Richmond to Danville.*

Not until May 4, 1865, was Captain Campbell selected by President Davis to lead his last escort, and he was captured along with Davis on May 10. Given Campbell is not exactly obscure. He wrote a journal, "Memorandum of a Journal Kept Daily During the Last March of Jefferson Davis," 1865. It is dated April 15–May 10, 1865, and is 9 pages long. The typescript is owned by the Library of Congress. Frank Carroll does not list this source in his bibliography.

Carroll says that the first of the Richmond evacuees to arrive in Danville was Captain Campbell. It was 1:00 p.m. on Monday, April 3. Campbell *frowned against the sting of the chilly mist that awaited him on the north side of Danville's Free Bridge where he planned to rendezvous with his troops.*[15] *He rested there, occasionally chatting with fifty-year-old Charles Slaughter, Danville's only bridgekeeper.*[16] Continues Carroll: *Within minutes his company of twelve from the Ninth Kentucky Cavalry joined him.* And this: *The horsemen had traveled by a circuitous route. Acting Treasurer, M.H. Clark explained that "the cavalry force did not travel as a rule upon the same road as the party" (i.e., President Davis's party). Although fatigued by a sleepless night, Captain Campbell arranged the group into a formation of six rows of two to make an orderly entrance into town.* And this: *The impressive parade crossed over the tributary barely one hour ahead of the train bearing the officials of the Confederate government.*

There is also this, from Carroll, when he describes Captain Given Campbell riding into Danville, *past the tall Exchange Hotel on the right and turned left onto Craighead Street where was situated the Danville and Midland depot.*

The "Danville and Midland Depot" here mentioned by Carroll is in Danville. It is not to be confused with the one he has earlier in Richmond (*see* above). It is not a typographical error, for when he comes to the scene where the Danville citizens are awaiting the arrival of the trains from Richmond: *Further down the street, on the left at the Danville & Midland Railroad Depot, a crowd...*

As distinct from Brubaker and William C. Davis, who have the Richmond & Danville Railroad's terminus north of the Dan River, at Northside, Carroll has the crowd waiting at the Danville & Midland depot on Craghead Street (which he spells Craighead), in downtown Danville. To prove what he says, he includes a black and white illustration with the

---

14. The Danville & Midland is discussed below.
15. The bridge did not become a free bridge until 1873.
16. Charles Darwin Slaughter was born on January 17, 1814, so he was 51.

caption *Danville and Midland Depot*, and the sub-caption *(From* Sketchbook of Danville, 1885, *by Edward Pollock).*[17]

On page 77 of Pollock's Sketch Book is the very picture Frank Carroll used in his book, the shot of the Danville & Midland Depot. However, the caption says, *Depot of the Danville and New River Railroad.* This is the same photo, but with different captions. Pollock includes a very detailed history of the Danville and New River Railroad, and its 3-foot gauge track running to Martinsville, Virginia. He got this history from the former president of the road, Major W.T. Sutherlin. The company was chartered in 1873, and the road finished in 1881. In 1884 it was extended to Stuart, Virginia, and in 1887 went bust.

The only railroad depot in downtown Danville in 1865 was on Craghead Street. This depot served both the Richmond & Danville Railroad coming in from the north, and the Piedmont Railroad coming in from the south. There never was a Danville & Midland Railroad, just as there never was an R&D Railroad terminus at Northside.

The hospitality of the Danvillians on April 3, 1865, as the thousands of evacuees from Richmond poured into town, is legendary.

On April 10, 1865, Jefferson Davis wrote to Mayor Walker of Danville, thanking him and the council of Danville for their hospitality. C.E.L. Stuart, a reporter by trade, was there. In his *New York Herald* article of July 4, 1865, he wrote: *There was hospitality for you—genial, genuine, grand. Nothing like the Virginian hospitality of Danville has come within my observation in any other American state. It was pure and catholic and unstinted.*

Anna Trenholm wrote her account in or around August 1865. She must have seen the Stuart article. She writes: *...there was an immense crowd to welcome the President. We were hospitably entertained...*

Mallory certainly saw Stuart's article. Indeed, he had it in front of him as he wrote his own account: *...with that spirit of hospitality, as universal & cheering in Virginia as the dews of Heaven.* On the other hand, if F. Lawrence McFall had had Mallory before him as he wrote his 2001 book, *Danville in the Civil War,* then surely the following would not have appeared: *Mallory observed that the President received a cordial greeting "with that spirit of hospitality as universal in Virginia as the dews of Heaven."*

Jefferson Davis's book, *The Rise and Fall of the Confederate Government,* was published in 1881, although it is doubtful if he wrote all of it, or even most of it. Whoever did write it had to rely largely on writers who had gone before: *Nothing could have exceeded the kindness and hospitality of the patriotic citizens. They gave us an "Old Virginia welcome," and with one heart contributed in every practicable manner to cheer and aid us in the work in which we were engaged.* Exactly the same wording is to be found in the 1890 book, *A Short History of the Confederate States,* which also purports to have been written by Jefferson Davis. As Clint Johnson sums it up in *Pursuit* (2008): *Davis himself felt very welcome in the town he had never before visited. He remembered years later that "nothing could have exceeded the kindness and hospitality of the patriotic citizens."*

William Daniel Coleman, in his 1881 article, "Jefferson Davis' Week at Danville," writes: *...throwing open the houses in the town for the hospitable reception and entertainment*

---

17. Pollock's book was actually titled *Sketch Book*, not *Sketchbook*.

of President Davis and the other government officials and the private citizens accompanying him.

William C. Davis, in *The Man and His Hour* (1991), quotes Jefferson Davis's aide, Preston Johnston: *"We had a good time at Danville,"* and then says: *Sharing the Sutherlins' hospitality proved to be very comfortable.* James Swanson has this, in his 2010 book, *Bloody Crimes*: *With fine Virginia hospitality, leading citizens opened their homes to the president and other dignitaries.*

But Danville may not have been as hospitable as the canon insists. Herndon's 1966 article, "Confederate Naval Cadets," which includes what purports to be Midshipman Fleming's Diary, offers this in the diary entry for April 4, 1865: *Danville is a small place of about 2000 inhabitants—people are very inhospitable, and we are tired of the place.*

German-born Christopher Gustavus Memminger was Confederate secretary of the Treasury before Trenholm. As McFall writes, in his 2001 book, *Danville in the Civil War*: *Several sources erroneously state that Christopher G. Memminger was in Danville. Memminger resigned as Confederate Secretary of the Treasury on June 15, 1864, and retired to his country home in Flat Rock, N.C.* Pollock's *Sketchbook*, 52, is the earliest work noted citing this error.

The 1903 article, "Our Last Capital," by B. Boisseau Bobbitt, cited in Chapter 1, describes the cabinet meeting held in Major W.T. Sutherlin's house in Danville: *There were present Judah P. Benjamin ... Trenholm, Secretary of Treasury, S.R. Mallory ... Davis, the Attorney-General, J.H. Reagan ... and Mr. Memminger, formerly Secretary of the Treasury; also Mr. Harrison, the President's private secretary.* And this: *Mr. Memminger, who had been confined to his bed for several days with a severe attack of neuralgia.*[18]

Jane Hagan, in an effort to copy from the Bobbitt article, writes in her little 1950 book, *Story of Danville*: *President Davis was entertained by Major W.T. Sutherlin at his recently completed home on the outskirts of the village, with Hon. A.R. Mallory, Secretary of the Navy, and Hon. C.G. Memminger, Secretary of the Treasury.*

---

18. A problem that also afflicted Mr. Trenholm.

Chapter 15

MALLORY

Because Stephen Russell Mallory was the only secretary of Navy the Confederacy ever had, and because he fled Richmond with Jefferson Davis in April and May 1865, much has been written about him. But although he figures in the appropriate reference books, and is mentioned quite a lot in history books of the period, there have been only five biographies of the man.

1936. Miss Occie Clubbs. "Stephen Russell Mallory, The Elder." Master's thesis written at the University of Florida.

1944. Philip Melvin. "Stephen Russell Mallory: Naval Statesman." *The Journal of Southern History*, volume 10, no. 2, May 1944, pp. 137–160.

1947. Miss Occie Clubbs. "Stephen Russell Mallory: United States Senator from Florida and Confederate Secretary of the Navy." *Florida Historical Quarterly*, January, April, and July 1947. This was her 1936 thesis expanded into a three-part article.

1954. Father Joseph T. Durkin. *Stephen R. Mallory: Confederate Navy Chief.* Chapel Hill: University of North Carolina Press. This book was republished by the University of South Carolina Press, in 1987 as *Confederate Navy Chief: Stephen R. Mallory*, and edited by William N. Still.

2005. Rodman L. Underwood. *Stephen Russell Mallory: A Biography of the Confederate Navy Secretary and United States Senator.* Jefferson, NC: McFarland.

Everyone agrees that Mallory was born in Trinidad, but not everyone is in accord about his father's name. Miss Occie Clubbs, his first biographer, calls the father Charles, while Father Joseph T. Durkin, who wrote the first book on Mallory, calls him John.

As for Mallory's date of birth, both Underwood and Clubbs say that Mallory's headstone, in the family burial plot at St. Michael Cemetery in Pensacola, Florida, shows 1812, but that Mallory's own daughter thought the secretary was born in 1813. And Ruby did think that.[1]

This from Underwood: *Several reference sources give birth dates ranging from 1811 to 1814. The consensus is that he was born around 1813*. Philip Melvin simply says that Mallory was born around 1813 on the island of Trinidad. He does not name the parents. For his sources, he cites, among others, Miss Clubbs's 1936 thesis. This from Father Durkin, in 1954: *There is some doubt as to the year of Stephen Mallory's birth. It was certainly 1810 or 1811. The latter date, it would seem, is the more probable.*

---

1. She says 1813 in the introduction to the *McClure's* article in 1900, and that was just before she died.

Going from secondary sources to easily accessible primary sources, one finds that on March 17, 1846, at Key West, Mallory's mother, *Ellen Mallory, of Key West, widow of Charles Mallory deceased, of Reading, in the state of Connecticut,* deposed before notary public Fernando J. Moreno, in support of her son's passport application. She swears that she, the said deponent, is the *widow of Charles Mallory, who died at Key West in the year One thousand eight hundred and twenty four.* She further swears that her late husband, the said Charles Mallory, was born in Connecticut in 1777, raised in and about the town of Bridgeport, and that he first left the United States, for a temporary absence, in or about the year 1812, when he was thirty-five years of age. *That during this temporary absence, at the Island of Trinidad, in October 1814, Stephen R. Mallory (at present Collector at Key West) the only living child of the said Charles Mallory and this deponent, his lawful wife, was born.—That soon afterwards, to wit in the Year One thousand eight hundred and fifteen, the said Charles Mallory and this deponent returned to the United States of America, to wit: to the State of Connecticut and the town of Bridgeport aforesaid, bringing with them their child, the said Stephen R. Mallory, then but a few months old.* She then goes on to say that she and her son Stephen have resided in the United States ever since.[2]

By 1900 there had been a massive resurgence of interest in the Civil War, and people were in need of a new light to be shone on the flight of Jefferson Davis. Mrs. Ruby Mallory Kennedy filled that need. She dug out an old handwritten manuscript that had been written by her father, and submitted it to the prestigious *McClure's* magazine, who edited it and published it in their December 1900 and January 1901 editions, as a two-part article, "The Last Days of the Confederate Government."

It was a long and very detailed account, and, of course, written by one of the principal players in the drama that had been Jefferson Davis's flight. It was the definitive first-hand account, and revolutionized the way historians look at the government's escape from Richmond. Indeed, it became far and away the major source for the event, the sine qua non, and remains that way. If one had to put a figure on it, perhaps eighty percent of what we know today of the Davis flight comes from Mallory's account in *McClure's*.

Then, in March 1940, Mallory's grandson, Thomas Seilles Kennedy, donated two unbound manuscript volumes (what became known as the Mallory Papers) to the Southern Historical Collection at the University of North Carolina at Chapel Hill, papers which included the handwritten manuscript that Ruby Kennedy had submitted to *McClure's* all those years before. As was agreed, UNC furnished Mr. Kennedy with six typed and bound copies in August 1941, and they got to keep the items that he had given them. Since then, the university has owned the two manuscript volumes, and their bound, typed copy of the same coming to 250 pages.

The first volume of handwritten manuscript consists of scattered diary entries written by Mallory from May 30, 1861, to September 19, 1862; i.e., his first diary. This is the only diary he wrote during the Civil War. At the beginning and end of this diary are several pages of financial accounts from the years 1862 and 1865. Volume 2, the one we're interested in, consists of Mallory's Second Diary, Letterbook, and Recollections. This second

---

2. National Archives and Record Administration (NARA), Passport Applications, 1795–1805; Collection Number: ARC Identifier, 566612/MLR Number A1 508; NARA Series: M1372; Roll #: 18, April 1, 1846–September 30, 1846.

diary of Mallory's, which, one should stress, has nothing to do with the flight, covers the periods June 3 to July 17, 1865, September 10 to December 31, 1865, and January 18 to March 8, 1866. For all three of those periods he was a political prisoner in Fort Lafayette, in New York Harbor. It is a prison diary, a journal of his life behind bars. The Letterbook consists of three categories of letters written by Mallory: (1) Ones he wrote while in prison (Mallory, like many other people in those days, made handwritten copies of his letters), from June 21, 1865, to April 1866, and which pertain chiefly to his application for parole (these particular letter copies were placed by Mallory under the appropriate dates of his diary, and thus form an integral part of that diary); (2) letters written by Mallory from Bridgeport, after his release from prison; and (3) letters and notes written from Pensacola, dated between July 1866 and September 1867. Then comes a series of recollections and miscellany, much of it written for his son, Buddy. All of this Mallory material has been committed to a reasonably faithful typescript. Pages 360–326 of the manuscript (working in reverse; he was writing with the blank-book upside down) are those that deal with the Davis flight, and these pages are represented by pages 43 to 80 on the typescript. It must be stressed that this account of the flight was not written while Mallory was in prison.[3]

When one reads either the typescript or (much better) the original handwritten manuscript account of the flight, one is immediately struck by the fact that, for 90 percent of its length, it is written in the third person. Rather than "I" or "me," it is "Mr. Mallory" or "the Secretary of the Navy" almost all the way through the text.

Mallory's daughter, Ruby Kennedy, wrote that her father drew up this account purely for his children. So, why would he wish to present himself to his children as "Mr. Mallory," rather than, say, "I," or "your dear papa?" It's only in the last few pages that it turns to the first person, and then it does so with abundance, if not abandon.

This is so odd, that right away, one knows that all is not what it appears to be. One automatically suspects that Mallory did not write this account; that Ruby did, and that it's a fake. However, one would be forced to think again. A quick study of the other items on the UNC microfilm is all one needs to prove it is all the same handwriting. That means one of two things. The first is that this very strange style of writing in the third person was employed by Mallory for his own unfathomable reasons, perhaps to give the impression that he is a somewhat detached author. But that cannot be, for as we have seen, for a few pages at the end, the account is, indeed, in the first person. The second possibility is that someone else, namely Ruby, copied everything, not just the account, but everything on the microfilm, including Mallory's signatures on the letters. But that cannot be either, for a rapid analysis of Mallory letters extraneous to the microfilm shows the same hand. No, there can be no question. This account on the microfilm was written by the secretary himself, mostly, and deliberately, in the third person. But why?

---

3. This original manuscript is on microfilm #2229 in the Southern Historical Collection, in the Wilson Library, at UNC. Before I ordered it in 2012, only a handful of orders had been placed for it before mine; the latest being in 2011, in 2009, and 2008, respectively, and all through university libraries. Getting this microfilm is the hard part. By that it should not be inferred that the actual process of ordering it is necessarily difficult in any way, it's just that one has to know that the microfilm exists, which not many historians do. When one makes a request for the Mallory Papers, the typescript is what one is told about, not the original manuscript on microfilm. Naturally, one is led to believe that the typescript is the pot o' gold, so to speak, and in a way it is, but there's an even more definitive pot o' gold—the original handwritten manuscript—and one really has to push to find out that there even is such a thing. Acquiring the typescript from Chapel Hill is so much easier; one can get it by e-mail.

The editors of *McClure's*, back in 1900, evidently had their doubts about the authenticity of what Ruby was showing them; their edited version is something of a masterpiece in the field of sleight of hand.[4] They generally did away with those references to "Mr. Mallory" and "the Secretary of the Navy," especially in their December 1900 edition, thus making it look much more as if Mallory wrote it, which, of course, he did.

As previously mentioned, the account of the flight occupies pages 43 to 80 of the typescript. These are some of the oddities which arrest the reader of either the original handwritten version or the typescript; it doesn't matter which:

On pages 46 and 47 Mallory jeers at the folks trying desperately to get on the train at Richmond. It's hard to believe that Mallory's daughter would allow him to be portrayed for eternity as a heartless fool. Yet, she does. It's even harder to believe that the secretary would wish himself to be remembered that way by his children, bearing in mind that it was for them that he wrote this account. But that's what happened. One cannot explain why this was left in. Not yet, anyway. But the answer will come.

On page 48 it is clearly revealed that this Mallory narrative is being written in hindsight, as opposed to, say, on the train. *The Secretary of the Navy's occupation was therefore, gone. But there sat Mr. Mallory, probably reflecting upon the..., etc. ... looking like a man who had done his best and been whipped, but who still had a "heart for every fate."* Because it looks so much as if Mallory is not writing this, *McClure's* took out this whole passage.

On page 49 the account talks about Secretary Trenholm being accompanied by *a portion of his family*, an odd phrase indeed when one considers that the only "portion" of Trenholm's family to accompany him was his wife, Anna. Then, still on Trenholm, Mallory says, *The coin of his department he had put in charge of Mr. Mallory's Corps of midshipmen placed at his command by the Secretary of the Navy for this purpose, under the immediate orders of Commander W. H. Parker.* This is about the only time in history that Parker is referred to as Commander Parker. Most of the time he is called Captain Parker. He was, in fact, 1st Lieutenant Parker, something Mr. Mallory, as secretary of the Navy, really should have known.

On page 50 Mallory goes on about the history of the treasure until way after the end of the war, when it was returned to Judge Crump in Richmond. This definitely rules out any diary written by Mallory on the train, or, indeed, during the flight at all. Indeed, it confirms what Ruby says, that her father wrote the account while he was in jail, or rather that he wrote it during a period of his life that could only have begun when he was in jail.

On page 61, referring to the cabinet in the car, the typescript says, "*its distinguished hosts.*" Why would Mallory glorify himself that way?

There is reference on page 65 to an event that happened on June 12, 1865. By that time Mallory was in prison in New York Harbor. And we must remember that he did not write this account while he was in prison.

Page 68 introduces the mysterious unnamed cabinet member (it's obviously Mallory), an old personal friend of General Joe Johnston's. The page is basically taken up with old Joe's conversation with this cabinet member, in which the cabinet member suggests that Johnston tell his defeatist views to Davis. This mysterious member of the cabinet is

---

4. *Civil War Times Illustrated* reproduced this *McClure's* article many years later, and other magazines and books have done likewise. Some historians have preferred to rely solely on these latter-day reproductions.

re-introduced on page 72, where he immediately seats himself at the writing table, takes up a pen, and offers to act as old Joe's amanuensis.

On page 73 Mallory writes: *In leaving Greensboro Mr. Reagan, Mr. Breckenridge & Mr. Mallory rode with Mr. Davis.* For the first half of the page it is all "they" and "their," and then suddenly, without warning, it switches to *Mr. Davis was very moody and unhappy, and this was the first day on which I had noticed in him a thorough surrender & abandonment of the cause of Southern independence.* Dramatically, for the first time since the beginning of the account, we are in the first person.

Page 74 starts off in the third person, and then, and only for the second time in the whole manuscript, we go into the first person, but only for the rest of the page. By the next page, it's back to the third person, and remains that way until the second half of page 78. From there on in, until the end of the manuscript on page 80, it remains in the first person.

Obviously, there is a problem which must be solved. We need to travel back in time to 1867, to observe a moment in literary history that has been completely forgotten, that moment when Frank Alfriend was compiling his book, *The Life of Jefferson Davis.*[5] That summer, Alfriend contacted various persons who had been on the Davis flight in April and May 1865, to see if they would contribute their reminiscences. *Mr. Alfriend has had the cooperation and assistance of the leading Confederate officials in the preparation of this work, as will be apparent to all on examination.*[6] One of the people thus contacted was Mallory. The former Confederate secretary of the Navy, by now living in Pensacola, agreed to write an account for Alfriend, but was worried about compromising himself, it being so soon after he had been granted parole by the former enemy. Those immediate post-war years were dangerous days for ex–Rebels. So, he wrote it in the third person, and concealed his identity as well as he could. That was Mallory's first account of the flight.

Perhaps it should be called the Stuart account. When Mallory sat down at his desk in Pensacola to write this piece, he realized that he could not remember much at all about the flight, not enough in detail, anyway, to come across as historically authoritative. So he copied largely from C.E.L. Stuart's July 4, 1865, *New York Herald* article. In the end, though, he need not have worried about being exposed. By the time Alfriend's book came out in 1868, the political climate had changed so drastically that secrecy no longer mattered. Nevertheless, even though Alfriend openly and at all times credits Mallory as the author of his long segment, the account remains in the third person, just as Mallory had written it.

At some point between the summer of 1867 and 1873, when he died, Mallory rewrote the account he had supplied to Frank Alfriend. This second account of the flight was for his private use only, and has never seen the light of day. Even his family did not know of it. It was still in the third person. So, if no one ever saw this second account, how do we know it ever existed?

When one examines the handwritten account at UNC, the one Mallory's daughter Ruby submitted to *McClure's*, two things are very evident. One is that it's a work in progress,

---

5. Frank Heath Alfriend, born January 10, 1841, was editor of the *Southern Literary Messenger*. He had just been appointed assistant librarian of the Senate when he died of rheumatism of the heart, in Washington, D.C., on May 3, 1887.
6. This quote is from the book's blurb.

unfinished, and that, therefore, he was working on it when he died—otherwise he would have finished it. It is also very clear that Mallory was reworking, not creating, and that for this reworking he had something in front of him other than the 1867 Alfriend account. One can tell that by the wording. Therefore, it has to be a second account, one that he wrote between 1867 and 1873, one that no one ever saw except Mallory. If Ruby, his daughter, for example, had ever known about this second account, she would have used it, to make sense of the account she did submit to *McClure's*. Because this reworking—the one he was compiling when he died—differs from the second account, it is therefore Mallory's third account.

For this revision, this third account, he employed two methods at the same time—the desultory and the systematic. The first is evidenced by the sporadic points where the text differs from the Alfriend account. One sees these differences throughout the text from the beginning to the end of the manuscript. As for his systematic approach, this takes two forms. The first was literally cutting and pasting. On the original 1873 manuscript one can actually see this handiwork—a different brand of paper inserted at strategic places in the text, different writing modes, different ink. And then we come to the changing of the third person to the first person. Working from the end of the text to the beginning, as many people do—as Mallory is known to have done—rather than from the beginning to the end, he began changing all instances of "Mallory" to "I," again in a rather sporadic fashion, and then he died, part way through his chore, thus leaving the bulk of the text unchanged. This is why some portions of this third account make no sense, at least on first inspection.

This third account, in manuscript form, remained within the Mallory family until 1940.

One may ask, with considerable justification, how come this revelation is new? Why don't all the relevant historians know about Alfriend, for example? The answer is in the proof. They don't know, otherwise they would have said something. Only a few modern historians have even heard of Frank Alfriend, let alone seen the Mallory account in his book. And no one has ever tried to work out what happened.

By 1900, when the *McClure's* article came out, Frank Alfriend's biography of Jefferson Davis, although quite easily obtainable as a rare book—as it is today—had all but disappeared into abject obscurity, and Stuart's account from 1865 had well and truly vanished into the mist that sooner or later envelops all ephemera. To all intents and purposes, then, the *McClure's* article was the first Mallory account seen by the world, at a time, moreover, when interest in the Civil War was at a peak.

It must be said about the *McClure's* article, edited as it is, that it has one distinct advantage over the chapter in Alfriend's book. Alfriend picks up Mallory's account not from the time the train left Richmond on April 2, but from much later in the flight. So, for the first portion of the flight, we do not have Mallory's voice in Alfriend. In *McClure's* we do. And for that, we have Ruby Kennedy to thank.

One can see, by placing the Alfriend account next to either Mallory's third account or the *McClure's* account, that large passages are identical, but one can also see the substantial differences between the two accounts. They are actually two different stories, not in the overall concept, perhaps, but in detail. And as the second depends on the first, and the first depended on Stuart, both, then, are derivative of Stuart.

The versions most used by researchers are, in order: the *McClure's* account (i.e., the fourth account), the typescript at Chapel Hill (i.e., the fifth account), and the handwritten account at Chapel Hill (i.e., the third account). No one except Mallory ever actually saw the second account, and the first account, readily available in Frank Alfriend's book, has rarely, if ever, been used by researchers.

As Professor William C. Davis warns us, when he writes about the Mallory account in *An Honorable Defeat* (2001): *Except where otherwise cited, this account of the train ride to Danville, and the comments on the cabinet members aboard, are taken from Mallory Recollections, Mallory Papers, Southern Historical Collection. An edited version of this account appeared in* McClure's *Magazine, XVI (December 1900, January 1901) as "The Last Days of the Confederate Government," but in most instances the original document has been used since it contains material omitted from the published version.*

One must expand upon Davis's warning. As intimated above, the typescript is almost, but not quite, faithful to the original handwritten manuscript. Spellings and punctuation occasionally differ, but, most important, on the original one sees how Mallory cut and pasted, one can ascertain how and why he drew up this third account. The typescript, of course, cannot show this. So one really has to look at that handwritten manuscript if one is to have an absolutely true idea of what one is talking about. Go to the original. Always go to the original. Joseph T. Durkin, the Jesuit priest who wrote the first book-length biography of Mallory, was never a man slow to toot his own off-key horn[7]: *The Library of Congress has an authenticated typescript copy of the diary. The present author has used this copy and checked all references against the original.* What does he mean by "authenticated?" And when he says he has used the typescript copy in the Library of Congress, but has checked all references against the original, this surely implies he has studied the original as well. Was it the one at Chapel Hill? So why did he not just use the original? Why did he bother to cite the Library of Congress? Again, when he talks about the original, does he mean the original typescript or the original handwritten manuscript? His words are ambiguous, but one suspects he means the original typescript. But the original typescript of what? Mallory's account of the Davis flight from Richmond, or Mallory's diary? The diary has nothing to do with the flight. From his statement, it would seem that it's the diary that Durkin is talking about. Either way, he mentions nothing about the original handwritten manuscript.

The original manuscript and the typescript both use Mallory's spellings, which tend to be somewhat British, or even just plain wrong. For example, Mallory uses "harrassing mental labour" when talking about Jefferson Davis in church. *McClure's* magazine Americanized this to "harassing mental labor." Some authors, such as Allan Nevins, quote the original Mallory, as opposed to *McClure's*. Durkin quotes the *McClure's* spelling. This in itself suggests that Durkin never actually saw the original or the typescript at UNC or anywhere else. If he had, the temptation to use Mallory's spellings would have been too great to resist.

There is also the myth of Mallory busily scribbling in his notebook as he fled from Richmond. Mrs. Ruby Kennedy, when she submitted her father's 1873 handwritten account

---

7. For example, in the preface of his book, Father Durkin avers that *he is confident that he has at least found all the important Mallory sources that are or will be in the future available.* In addressing this most astonishing claim, Rodman Underwood, in 2005, shows remarkable restraint: *It should be noted that considerable scholarship, about Mallory and the Confederate Navy, that was unavailable to Durkin, has been made available in the past half-century.*

of the flight to *McClure's*, wrote an introduction to that article, in which she says, quite openly: *The manuscript of the accompanying article was written by my father in 1865 while he was a prisoner of war in Fort Lafayette, in New York Harbor, and while the events which it chronicles were still fresh in his mind.*

Mrs. Kennedy is wrong. Mallory did not write the manuscript while in prison in 1865. He wrote it in 1873. She is wrong too when she says that the events were still fresh in his mind. They were never fresh in his mind. Even when he wrote the 1867 account for Frank Alfriend, he had to rely largely on Stuart's July 4, 1865, article in the *New York Herald*. Nevertheless, Mrs. Kennedy is quite certain that her father did not write his account on the train. Notwithstanding, two, and perhaps more, historians, have the secretary of the Navy scribbling in the president's car as he fled Richmond on April 2–3, 1865.

Mallory's latest biographer, Rodman L. Underwood, writing in 2005, says: *During the flight of the cabinet toward Danville, Stephen Mallory wrote brief portraits of other cabinet members.*

Millett & White's 2007 book, *The Rebel and the Rose*, has this rather ambiguously worded passage: *Stephen R. Mallory wrote an account of Jefferson Davis and his administration during the flight south from Richmond to Danville.*

And Clint Johnson, in his 2008 book, *Pursuit*, writes: *Without any ships to command, Mallory had time to write down his thoughts. Bored and unable to sleep as readily as his traveling companions who had liberally partaken of the apple brandy Secretary of the Treasury George Trenholm was passing around, Mallory started glancing around the train car. He realized that he and the other members of the cabinet were making history this night. He started writing down impressions in his diary of the things that were happening and of the people who would be with him until they escaped or they were captured. After four years of writing dry cabinet reports to a president who wanted and expected just that, Mallory must have welcomed the chance to spread his literary wings by inserting some visual imagery into his own diary.*

In this passage, Johnson claims that Mallory was writing in his diary. Mallory did compile a diary—two, as a matter of fact—but not during the flight. And nowhere in those diaries does he write anything pertaining to the Davis flight.

Finally, for the student of Mallory, a small reference section on comparative analysis. When we talk about *McClure's*, we're talking about the editions of December 1900 (pages 97–107) and January 1901 (pages 239–248), in which was published the two-part edited version of Confederate Secretary of the Navy Stephen R. Mallory's account of the Jefferson Davis flight of April and May 1865.

For the most part, *McClure's* presented the original quite faithfully, but there are differences. Below are a number of what might be termed couplets, the first line being the 1873 Mallory (as seen in the Mallory Papers), and the second being the edited *McClure's* version. They are arranged in the order in which they appear in the Mallory text.

When a historian quotes from Mallory, that quote usually contains something from these couplets, so one can almost unfailingly determine which source is being used—the 1873 manuscript at Chapel Hill or *McClure's*—despite what it may say in footnotes or a bibliography.

Those who have used the original are few, and include Allan Nevins. On the other hand, those who have relied solely on *McClure's*, or even the one or two periodicals and books which have reproduced the *McClure's* article, include Michael B. Ballard, James C. Clark, Joseph T. Durkin, Shelby Foote, Ernest B. Furgurson, A.J. Hanna, the Hoehlings,

Clint Johnson, Robert Douthat Meade, James Swanson, and Rodman L. Underwood. Some historians, such as Burke Davis and William C. Davis, have used both.

Here are the differences between Mallory's original account and the *McClure's* version.

> Original: The 2d of April in the Year of Our Lord, 1865
> *McClure's*: The 2d of April, 1865
> Original: Rumours spoke of a flight
> *McClure's*: Rumors spoke of a fight
> Original: four years of harrassing mental labour
> *McClure's*: four years of harassing mental labor
> Original: the cold, calm eye, the sunken cheek
> *McClure's*: the cold, calm eyes, the sunken cheek
> Original: seemed more attentive to the morning service
> *McClure's*: seemed more attentive than he to the morning service
> Original: Lee's dispatches
> *McClure's*: Lee's despatches
> Original: Grant's overwhelming charge through his centre
> *McClure's*: Grant's overwhelming charge through his center
> Original: "peace on Earth and goodwill to men"
> *McClure's*: peace on earth and goodwill to men
> Original: All eyes are again fixed upon his face
> *McClure's*: All eyes are again fixed upon Mr. Davis' face
> Original: Lee's later dispatches
> *McClure's*: Lee's later despatches
> Original: careworn visage
> *McClure's*: care-worn visage
> Original: emotions which filled their hearts
> *McClure's*: emotions which filled their breasts
> Original: plain & unexceptionable toilette
> *McClure's*: plain and unexceptionable toilet
> Original: beyond Adams
> *McClure's*: beyond Adams Street
> Original: his mild Havannah
> *McClure's*: his mild Havana
> Original: the last men on Arrarat
> *McClure's*: the last man outside the Ark
> Original: which bore no nearer relations to mirth or contentment[8]
> *McClure's*: which bore no resemblance to mirth or contentment
> Original: than do the dull undulations of the Dead Sea to the sparkling ripples of a mountain stream, no less than in the nervous manipulations of his watch seals
> [Deleted from *McClure's*]
> Original: Heaven bless them
> *McClure's*: Heaven bless them!
> Original: husbands, brothers, sons, lovers

---

8. Compare this with *approaching to mirth or contentment* from Charles Dickens, *Pickwick Papers*.

15. Mallory

McClure's: husbands, brothers, sons and lovers
Original: Prominent citizens enterchanged views
McClure's: Prominent citizens interchanged views
Original: that all consideration of personal safety
McClure's: that considerations of personal safety
Original: his spotless waistcoat & blue, brass-buttoned coat
McClure's: his spotless waistcoat and his blue, brass-buttoned coat
Original: gazing anxiously away into the distance
McClure's: gazing anxiously into the distance
Original: and those to accompany him
McClure's: and those who were to accompany him
Original: to leave Richmond at half past eight p.m.
McClure's: to leave Richmond at half-past eight o'clock p.m.
Original: the cars did not move until eleven p.m.
McClure's: the cars did not leave until eleven p.m.
Original: carriages, carts & waggons
McClure's: carriages, carts, and wagons
Original: Col. Carrington
McClure's: Colonel Carrington
Original: who had it in charge
McClure's: who had charge of the train
Original: occasioned no little amusement to the insiders
McClure's: occasioned no little amusement to those already aboard
Original: generally the heads of bureaus and their chief clerks or assistants
[Deleted from *McClure's*]
Original: "Artful Dodgers"[9]
McClure's: artful dodgers
Original: opposition & argument highly entertaining
McClure's: opposition and argument, highly entertaining
Original: crinoline at the South
McClure's: crinoline in the South
Original: mans arbitrary rules
McClure's: man's arbitrary rules
Original: of wealth or professional distinction
McClure's: of wealth and professional distinction
Original: and yet they performed their duties as assiduously and strictly under what they felt was the last order
McClure's: and yet they performed their duties as assiduously and strictly, under the last order they would ever receive
Original: At 11 o.c., P.M.
McClure's: At eleven o'clock P.M.
Original: During the preceeding hour
McClure's: During the preceding hour
Original: Railroad President

---

9. From Dickens, *Oliver Twist*.

McClure's: railroad president
Original: better news from Lee's ["army" is crossed out]
McClure's: better news from Lee
Original: as the fugitives receeded
McClure's: as the fugitives receded
Original: the Adjutant General Cooper
McClure's: Adjutant-General Cooper
Original: the material and personel of his office
McClure's: the material and personnel of his office
Original: and a half a dozen log cabins
McClure's: and a half-dozen log cabins
Original: tents, or even waggons
McClure's: tents, and even wagons
Original: James river squadron
McClure's: James River squadron
Original: iron clads
McClure's: iron-clads
Original: lain like chained and sulky bull dogs to prevent the ascent of the enemy's ships, under the command of Rear Admiral Raphael Semmes
McClure's: lain like chained and sulky bulldogs under the command of Rear Admiral Raphael Semmes to prevent the ascent of the enemy's ships
Original: The Secretary of the Navy's occupation was therefore gone. But there sat Mr. Mallory, probably reflecting upon the construction of some new "iron gophers," as Gov. Wise called his iron clads, in one of the way rivers or creeks hidden from the enemy's fire-brands looking like a man who had done his best and been whipped, but who still had "a heart for every fate."
[deleted from *McClure's*]
Original: he had long kept up mail communications
McClure's: he had kept up mail communications
Original: A glance at Judge Reagan
McClure's: A glance at Judge Reagan, Postmaster-General
Original: Silent & sombre
McClure's: Silent and somber
Original: now scraping abstractedly the palms of his hands with his knife
[deleted from *McClure's*]
Original: the judge sat
McClure's: he sat
Original: a truer, "bigger hearted" man
McClure's: a truer, bigger-hearted man
Original: keeping up his mails
McClure's: keeping up the mails
Original: was evidently "bothering" him
McClure's: was evidently bothering him
Original: mature knowledge of the fitness of things[10]

---

10. Yet another Dickens quote ("the fitness of things"), this one from *A Tale of Two Cities*.

McClure's: knowledge of the fitness of things
Original: Mr. Mallory's Corps of midshipmen
McClure's: the corps of midshipmen
Original: & these young aspirants for nautical fame
McClure's: These young aspirants for nautical fame
Original: three hundred thousand dollars
McClure's: $300,000
Original: Washington, Geo.
McClure's: Washington, Georgia
Original: somewhat in favor of the latter "gobble"
McClure's: somewhat in favor of the "gobble"
Original: apart from considerations of personal peril, which were generally disregarded
McClure's: apart from the consideration of personal peril, which was generally disregarded
Original: grim spectors of anarchy, tyrany & terrorism
McClure's: grim specters of anarchy, tyranny, and terrorism
Original: which rose up behind this utter annihilation
McClure's: which rose behind this utter annihilation
Original: bright beams of the morning sun shone cheerily into the cars
McClure's: bright beams of the morning sun shone into the cars
Original: Mr. Benjamin's deep brunette complexion
McClure's: Mr. Benjamin's deep olive complexion
Original: Had he been a Hildebrand, a Loyolo, a Tell or a Kosiosko, a stern enthusiast with sword or scrip, & "Words that burn," he might, perhaps, have aroused his hearers & inspired hope; but as he sat there, in form and feature, and in expression, so jolly, the very picture of contentment, smiling sweetly, & talking "so like a waiting gentlewoman," dividing his attention between his listeners & his luncheon, he convinced some—of course the ill natured grumblers, not of his sincerity, not that he had any idea of fighting, bleeding & dying for the cause,—but that he was "outward bound...."
[deleted from *McClure's*]
Original: "badge of all the tribe"
McClure's: "badge of all their tribe"
Original: than with humiliation
McClure's: than humiliation
Original: rank of Col.
McClure's: rank of colonel
Original: is Col. Lubbock, who has seen much of life, knows something of men
McClure's: was Colonel Lubbock, who had seen much of life, knew something of men
Original: pointless Texas anecdotes which he disposed of upon the slightest occasion, with infinite enjoyment to himself, & in a style earnest & demonstrative as garulous. The merits of his nag Blue Tail, which he had with him, were frequently the staple of his irrepressible talk
McClure's: Texas anecdotes, which he disposed of in a style earnest and demonstrative
Original: Colonels Taylor Wood and Preston Johnston
McClure's: Colonels John Taylor Wood and William Preston Johnston (son of the lamented Albert Sidney Johnston)

Original: our fugitives rescued their spirits
McClure's: our fugitives recovered their spirits
Original: "Old peach"
McClure's: "old Peach"
Original: reached Danville, at 5:00 p.m.
McClure's: reached Danville at five o'clock p.m.
Original: There was none of the old, wild, Southern enthusiasm, however [deleted from *McClure's*]
Original: , & there was that in the cheers which told almost as much of sorrow as of joy
McClure's: but there was that in the cheers which told as much of sorrow as of joy
Original: as universal & cheering
McClure's: as universal
Original: they opened their houses & provided
McClure's: the people of Danville opened their houses
Original: Secretaries of the Treasury & Navy
McClure's: Secretaries of the Treasury and the Navy
Original: Col. Southerlin
McClure's: Colonel Sutherlin
Original: the Atty. General
McClure's: the Attorney-General

Chapter 16

STUART

There must have been several journalists who took part in the flight of the Confederate government from Richmond in 1865, but we know of only two. George Bagby wrote nothing about the event.[1] On the other hand, C.E.L. Stuart not only wrote about the flight, his long, meaningful account in the *New York Herald* of July 4, 1865, was the first such ever published. Most of what we know today about the flight comes from Secretary of the Navy Mallory, and as Mallory ruthlessly mined Stuart's *Herald* article, it all goes back therefore, ultimately, to Stuart. Hence the importance of Stuart.[2] He has rarely been biographized, and only then in brief outline.

The hugely respected *Papers of Jefferson Davis* has this potted biography: *Charles E.L. Stuart (c1823–), born in Ireland, was a clerk and journalist in New York before the war and a clerk in the Confederate Post Office and War Departments (1861–64).*[3] *Saying he had "boast[ed] for the South while at the North"—as editor of the short-lived New York Volunteer—and was "personally and politically devoted to" Davis, he frequently applied for a commission; in 1864 he served in a local Richmond defense unit. Stuart returned to Brooklyn and in 1870 worked as a wholesale grocer.*[4] *In "Rummaging Through Rebeldom," a series of articles published in 1867, he claimed an insider's knowledge of Confederate officials.*[5]

In three books, William C. Davis has written bits and pieces about Stuart which amount to a brief sketch of the man's life. Below are relevant biographical extracts from Professor Davis's works.

From *Government of Our Own* (1994): *Once editor of a pro-secession paper in New York called the* Volunteer,[6] *he brought a host of eccentricities with him. He claimed descent*

---

1. George William Bagby (1828–1883) had been editor of the *Southern Literary Messenger*, and associate editor of the *Richmond Whig*. He was on the presidential train as it traveled between Richmond and Danville, but within two weeks returned to Richmond.
2. See the Appendix.
3. Stuart was never in the War Department.
4. There was a Charles Stuart in Brooklyn, in both the 1860 and 1870 censuses, an Irishman born about 1823. In the earlier census he is a clerk (he was actually a clerk in a grocery store, although it does not actually say that in the census), and in the latter a wholesale grocer. But this is not C.E.L. Stuart. Stuart was not a clerk, of any sort, before the war. In 1860 he and his family missed the census by virtue of being in Richmond when the New York census was taken, and being back in New York when the Richmond census was taken. In 1870 C.E.L. Stuart and his family were not living in Brooklyn. Nowhere near it. In short, the *Papers of Jefferson Davis* has the wrong man.
5. *The Papers of Jefferson Davis*, vol. 12, 2003, p. 57, footnote 14.
6. The *Volunteer* was the campaign organ for the Breckinridge–Lane ticket of 1860; i.e., "John C. Breckinridge for President."

The front page of the *Spirit of the American Press* on March 17, 1860, featured woodcut likenesses of famous New York newspaper editors of that year (courtesy American Antiquarian Society, with thanks to Jaclyn Penny). Stuart is fifth from right.

from the royal Stuarts of England,[7] *was born in Poland,*[8] *and raised a Catholic.* And this: [He] *boasted a smattering of military training and experience in Europe, and occasionally maintained that he was a rightful heir to the throne of England.* And this: *Stuart fancied that he looked a bit like Shakespeare with his long hair, beard, and loose-flowing garb... He wanted Davis to make him a general.*

From *An Honorable Defeat* (2001): *Though born in Poland, he declared that he was descended directly from the Royal House of Stuart, and was in fact rightful heir to the English crown.*[9]

From *Leaders of the Lost Cause* (2004): *Charles E.L. Stuart of the War and later Postmaster's departments.*[10]

C.E.L. Stuart appears out of nowhere in March 1860, with startling suddenness, and for a solid year his name was constantly in the newspapers, as an important figure in both journalism and politics.

From the *Spirit of the American Press*, March 17, 1860: *Dr. Charles Edward Louis Stuart, editor-in-chief of the New York Daily News, was born at Naples, Italy, on the 12th of February, 1830. In the church of St. Domenico Maggiore ... the baptismal record ... reads: "Charles Edward Louis Cassimer John Walter Stuart, Feb. 18, AD 1830."*[11] The article then goes on to say that Stuart was chiefly educated by his mother while a boy, and that he was entered in the Neapolitan Army in his fourteenth year, as an honorary member, *"by the grace" of the late King Ferdinand commonly called Bomba*. In his fifteenth year, *he "smelt powder" at the Alps, and received some bullet wounds.* According to the article, his life for the next three years seems to have been a romantic wandering with his brother and other members of his family. He journeyed through all Europe and the East, but was back in time to share in the Italian troubles of 1848. *He then took sides against what we in this country deem the popular cause.* We are then told that he was in Ireland in the latter part of the same year, 1848, that in 1851 he graduated at Trinity College, Dublin, and in 1854 took an ad eundem degree at Cambridge. Then he came to the United States, where he began as a journalist *and is now the chief of a daily organ, which represents the greatest national party in this great country. Dr. Stuart has written several works in history, fiction, and travel, most of them under the cognomen of "Oliphant." So he wrote, and still writes, for Blackwood's and other magazines.* In this piece it is claimed that Stuart is a fellow of the Royal Literary Society of London, and holds an LL.D. from the University of Edinburgh, and that he *also conducts, privately, several weeklies of our city, in addition to the News, all of which enjoy success and popularity from the attractiveness of his productions in their columns. Joined with a manly bearing, Dr. Stuart has a refinement of taste and feeling, and, at the same time, has such a versatility in literary genius, that in style (as he is considered in looks) he may be termed the Shakspere of the New York Press.*

This edition of *Spirit of the American Press* also sports a woodcut reproduction of

---

7. If one is to name a political entity of which the Stuarts were monarchs, then Britain or Great Britain would be the only appropriate one, at least after a particular date. If one were to select a subdivision of Great Britain, then Scotland would be the logical choice, rather than England.
8. Stuart was not born in Poland.
9. There is no English crown. It is a British crown.
10. Again, Stuart was never with the War Department.
11. His date of birth seems to be right. The place is very definitely not. The baptismal details are humbug, as is most of the biographical material in this article.

that year's crop of famous New York newspaper editors, including C.E.L. Stuart of the New York *Daily News.*

The article on Stuart was reproduced in the Richmond *Sentinel*, January 8, 1864, as part of a letter from "Amicus."[12] By way of introducing the article, "Amicus" has this to say: *Dr. Charles Edward Stuart ... who is this bright light that has burst forth so suddenly in our midst?* He then says that the doctor started the *Volunteer*, the only Breckinridge paper at the North, with the aid only of General Gustavus Smith.[13] *It did not succeed like his other editorial undertakings. He lost much by it.* "Amicus" then says that Stuart was president of the New York Breckinridge and Lane Club, and chairman of the first public meeting to confirm their nomination, that he never took the oath of allegiance to the United States, but so soon as Secession began to break forth, moved South, and took the oath of allegiance to the Southern Confederacy. *He and his family now reside in Richmond. His lady belongs to a noble and distinguished English family. His face resembles that of Charles I more than that of Shakespeare.*

Long after the war, the *New York World* had occasion to write this about Stuart in their January 11, 1870, edition: *Though he has led an eventful life, both as soldier and journalist—having served as an officer both in the Royal Army of Naples during the time of King Bomba, and more recently in the Confederate army....*[14]

That, then, sums up the available biographic material on Stuart—with the exception of certain correspondence between Jefferson Davis and his wife. In her November 7, 1865, letter to her husband (then a prisoner at Fort Monroe), Varina Davis explains that she has been trying to send him photographs of the children, but that they have *been intercepted by an adventurer, a Dr. Stuart in New York who was once somehow connected with the Confed. Treasury, or perhaps War Office*[15]—*he foisted himself upon Ma, by offers of service, and thus obtained permission to go with her to Canada—as escort—You know the old lady has not much judgement of character—if people speak fair—he then came back to New York, and as my agent, accepted aid for me and for the children, as far as I can learn ... to the amount of seven or eight hundred dollars, which he put to the use of paying William Waller and his Wife's bill at the New York Hotel,*[16] *and after settling them, and being generous with the money in other ways, he had left as he said $75—which he gave to W.W.* And this: *In short, he is a finished scoundrel with a good education.*

In a reply to Varina, Mr. Davis wrote, on November 21, 1865: *The adventurer you mention always was a trifling fellow and was formerly suspected of being unfaithful. He was said to be well connected and exhibited letters purporting to be written to him by distinguished persons abroad. His impudence has however passed supposible* [sic] *bounds.* He then says that Stuart deserves *to be put into the penitentiary for getting money under false pretences. It is intolerable to have one's name used by such sharpers in a manner so humiliating.*

---

12. "Amicus" was Stuart. Since 1861, he had been using that byline in various Richmond newspapers, from whom, while prosecuting his main employment as a Confederate departmental clerk, he supplemented his income as a writer of obituaries and miscellaneous articles.

13. Gustavus Woodson Smith (1821–1896). As cofounder of The *Volunteer*, he used the pen name James Monroe. On September 19, 1861, he was commissioned a major general in the Confederate army.

14. At the time the *World* published this, Stuart was no longer in New York.

15. It was this vague guess of Varina's that led both Professor Davis and the editors of *The Papers of Jefferson Davis* to believe Stuart was in the War Department. She was wrong.

16. W.W. is William Griffin Waller, who was married to Varina's sister, Jennie Howell. Is one imagining it or could Varina not even bring herself to mention her sister's name? There will be more on this in a little while.

Varina Davis's sister, Maggie Howell, was made the subject of a rather bizarre scandal created by Joan Cashin in her book, *First Lady of the Confederacy* (2006), in which she says that, after the war, *Varina's mother and six siblings, who gathered in Montreal, consumed much of her energy. In fact, they got into more trouble than ever.* And this: *A charlatan named Mr. Stuart insinuated himself with the Howells and bilked them out of some money.*[17] And this: *After Margaret Howell left her watchful older sister* [i.e., Varina], *she became pregnant, and would give birth to a son, Philip, in June 1866. Margaret was engaged to yet another man in 1865 before the match was broken off,*[18] *but she did not name the baby's father, who could have been one of several men: Stuart, her ex-fiancée, or one of the ex–Confederates who visited Montreal.*

Professor Cashin continues: *Varina learned of the pregnancy by the start of 1866, when she said "the new addition to the family circle" made her and "all parties" unhappy.* This is almost, but not quite, an exact quote from the letter Varina wrote on January 11, 1866, from Augusta, Georgia, to her friend and confidant, William Preston "Dobbin" Johnston.[19]

In this letter, Varina goes on: *The expense of her return is a serious matter to me*, but she does not identify "her." It is almost as if she cannot even say the name. However, Joan Cashin can. *She* [Varina] *knew that an out-of-wedlock pregnancy could make a respectable marriage impossible for her sister, and she was determined to salvage Margaret's prospects. The Davis children may have been told that the boy was their brother, the son of Varina and Jefferson, and the family maintained its silence forever after on Philip's paternity. Varina's unbreakable love for her siblings had survived the war.*

By dint of sheer circumstance, Maggie was not the only member of the Howell family pregnant at precisely that time; Jennie Waller was too. Two sisters, both almost identically close to term. Referring to Jane Howell Waller and her husband William G. Waller, who lived in New York City immediately after the war, *The Papers of Jefferson Davis* has this: *By April Jennie was in Montreal and there gave birth to a second daughter Margaret Howell Waller.*[20]

Professor Cashin does not mention Jennie Waller's pregnancy.

This from Jefferson Davis's letter to Varina, March 13, 1866. *Margaret looks 'ill at ease.'* She would be ill at ease if she was, as Cashin asserts, eight months pregnant. As for Maggie's sister, Jennie, in the same letter Davis asks, *What has become of W.W.? He has not been mentioned when you have spoken of J., at least since he was noticed as being in N.Y.* It is obvious that something has gone awry with the Waller marriage.

According to the April 14, 1866, letter from Varina to her husband, Maggie is in Montreal, but not in good shape. The doctor said it was *a nervous shock which had upset her.*

Cashin says that Maggie's illegitimate son, Philip, was born in June 1866, in Montreal. However, there is no birth or baptism record. Jennie Waller's daughter was born in the same city on July 9, 1866, legitimate and duly documented. Why should Jennie's child be duly recorded, and Maggie's not? A birth is a birth, a baptism is a baptism, regardless of

---

17. Cashin does not give Stuart a first name, and he is not indexed in her book.
18. Cashin does not name this man.
19. *I have felt it all along—feared the new addition to the family-circle which has always rendered me and all parties unhappy.*
20. *The Papers of Jefferson Davis*, vol. 12, p. 134, footnote 39, which cites the following: Jefferson Davis to Varina, August 21, 1865, and December 25, 1869; Varina to Jefferson Davis, November 7, 1865, April 14–16, 1866, and December 16, 1866.

the legal status of the child. Anyway, all of a sudden the Howell household was blessed with two single-mother situations. One would have been bad enough, given their uncertain finances, but the shame of Philip must have been overpowering.

In 1868 Jefferson Davis and his family relocated to England. Professor Cashin writes that later, *Margaret Howell arrived from Canada, apparently without her son.*

The following year, at the Liverpool home of the Campbell family, Maggie met the small, mustachioed Bavarian consul to Liverpool, a businessman with the unlikely name of Le Chevalier Charles William Peter de Wechmar Stoess. The Chevalier was then 47, a widower, with a grown-up son. He was not Bavarian at all. He was not Serbian either, even though he was also Serbian consul to Liverpool. Son of physician Charles de Wechmar Stoess, he was, in fact, born in Strasburg to a good Alsatian family.

In the ensuing months, Herr Stoess was seen dancing with Maggie at the occasional ball for distressed foreigners. At 11 o'clock in the morning of April 23, 1870, at St. Peter's Church, Belsize Park, London, the rector, the Reverend Francis W. Tremlett, joined them in holy matrimony.

The Stoesses had two children, both in Liverpool. Christy was born in January 1872 and Philip on June 27, 1873.[21] Maggie now had two sons named Philip—one illegitimate, born in 1866 in Montreal, perhaps the son of C.E.L. Stuart, and the other legitimate, born in 1873 in Liverpool, definitely the son of Herr Stoess. And both Philips were born in the month of June, which is a curious coincidence.

Professor Cashin found that the illegitimate Philip died in Seattle in 1942. She writes that she got a "certified copy" of his death certificate, dated February 3, 1942, in which it states that Philip was 75 years 7 months and 8 days old. This certificate was obtained from the Washington State Department of Vital Statistics, King County, Seattle, and is therefore official and, presumably, unimpeachable. Cashin subtracted 75 years 7 months and 8 days from February 3, 1942, and, of course, came up with the correct mathematical answer—June 1866. For Cashin, the most telling fact on this certificate is: "Parents: unknown." That, then, is the illegitimate Philip, although we know nothing of his life between the time he was born and the time he died. Nothing at all.

The legitimate Philip, on the other hand, the one born in 1873—Herr Stoess's son—is very well documented. For example, in 1880 Maggie and her two legitimate children sailed for the United States, to visit the Davises at Beauvoir, in Mississippi. The ship's manifest lists one of the passengers as Master P. de Stoess, aged 6. The illegitimate Philip did not make the trip. In the 1891 Liverpool census we find the legitimate Philip aged 17, living with his widowed mother and his sister. No illegitimate Philip, in this or any other British, Canadian, or American census—ever. Later in 1891 we find the legitimate Philip coming to the Americas, aged 18, a clerk bound for British Columbia. As an adult, we find him in the 1900 U.S. census, in Shoshone, Idaho, a single man, an assayer, born in England in June 1873. His 1924 passport application has him being born on June 27, 1873, in England. Other references to his age and place of birth are numerous, and consistent. They never vary.

In one of those odd twists of fate, the legitimate Philip also died in Seattle on February 3, 1942, in the same hospital. Same day, same hospital as the illegitimate Philip. The *Seattle Daily Times* obituary of February 4, 1942, gives his age as 69, and his birth place as Liverpool. It says that less than a month before his death, Philip had been bruised and

---

21. This from the English birth, marriage and death records.

shaken in an auto accident in downtown Seattle. It was while in a very confused state that he gave the hospital the particulars that hospitals so crave. Whether those particulars are right or wrong does not matter, as long as they fill out the paperwork. And those particulars were the ones that appeared on the death certificate.[22]

An older Jefferson Davis.

In 1867, two years after the Civil War, the *New York Citizen* was being published weekly by Charles Halpine from their office at 32 Beekman Street. On April 6 they began a series of historical articles called "Rummaging Through Rebeldom." There were 25 rummages, week after week, until September 21, all written by "Col. C.S. Armee," and giving the reader an inside look into the Confederate government of 1861, from its birth in Montgomery, Alabama, until the transfer to Richmond.

Jerrold Northrop Moore advises us that this "Col. C.S. Armee" has been identified by William C. Davis as Charles E.L. Stuart.[23] The truth is, Stuart had been outed as the author before William C. Davis "identified" him—in fact, 127 years before. As soon as the rummages appeared, back in 1867, everyone was talking about it.

Burton Harrison wrote a letter to William Preston Johnston, the style of which must not be taken too seriously. Dated New York, June 29, 1867, it opens with, *Dear Johnston, or rather Hated Johnston, my enemy, who abuses me.* Harrison is sending Johnston two numbers of the *New York Citizen*, in which are to be found copies of communications styled *Rummaging in Rebeldom, or some such alliteration. Folk here say that they were written by that vile Bohemian Stuart.* Harrison goes on to describe Stuart as a free lancer of a fellow who was a clerk in the Post Office Department in Richmond, and who employed a large part of his time in writing to the chief applications for appointment to be a colonel or brigadier, in swearing that he was a descendant in the right line from the royal Stuarts, that he had been an officer in the Neapolitan service at the early age of 14, and that he ought now to be King of England, Ireland & France, and defender of the faith. *You may remember that he filled the newspapers with lies about the circumstances of the chief's capture, &c &c., asserting that he was a member of the Staff & knew all about it &c.*

---

22. Miss Cashin's book was published by Belknap. The paperback version of this book was put out by Harvard University Press. According to Miss Cashin, in her acknowledgments, the "thoughtful and careful" editor of this work was Joyce Seltzer. Joyce Seltzer had been senior executive editor of Harvard University Press since coming over from the Free Press in 1994.

23. Moore, *Confederate Commissary General: Lucius Bellinger Northrop and the Subsistence Bureau of the Southern Army*, 1996, p. 50 and p. 226.

Harrison then goes on to say that folk in New York are affirming that Stuart wrote the aforesaid Rummagings, *but I can't believe it. I once saved his afflicted wife, his wretched progeny, & his miserable self from starvation by inducing his official superiors to double his pay*. Harrison says that his young faith in human justice forbids him to think that even the ungrateful could be so ungrateful as to assail a benefactor, a gentle, kind & good benefactor with the opprobrious epithets thrown at him in one of these articles. *No, I had no difficulty in divining the real author. I know your style, Johnston*.[24]

So, as everyone has always known that Colonel C.S. Armee was C.E.L. Stuart, "reidentified by William C. Davis for his readers" might be more accurate.

The *Citizen* touted the rummages as being the work variously of "A Late Private Secretary of Jeff Davis," "A Late Colonel in the Confederate Service," and "Col. St. Armee," implying, respectively (one supposes) Burton Harrison, William Preston Johnston, and C.E.L. Stuart. Although the byline "Col. C.S. Armee"—indeed, any byline at all—was discontinued after the 12th Rummage (June 22, 1867), there can be no doubt that all 25 rummages were written by the same man, and that man was Stuart.

"Rummaging through Rebeldom" simply came to an abrupt end when the author had scarcely taken his readers through the summer of 1861, and Stuart would not finish it in any other venue. According to William C. Davis, *He or Halpine apparently just lost interest*.[25]

But that is not why the series came to an end. Not at all. It's because Stuart had a plan. It involved Brazil.

First of all, Stuart faked a letter of introduction from Jefferson Davis.[26] Then he forged some letters of credit on the names of some of the most prominent men in New York. Stuart was nothing if not bold, for his victims in this case included Horace Greeley, of the *Tribune*; Henry J. Raymond, of the *Times*; James Gordon Bennett, Sr., of the *Herald*; as well as industrialists A.T. Stewart and August Belmont. The forged letters of credit, to the tune of 250,000 American dollars, were dated November 17, 1867. How he hoped to get away with all this is almost beyond comprehension.

With all these documents, and a glowing letter of introduction from his old friend, John McGill, Bishop of Richmond,[27] Stuart set sail from New York on November 23, 1867, traveling steerage to Rio de Janeiro.[28] Four days before Christmas the *South America*

---

24. Letter in, and courtesy of, the Mason Barrett Collection, at Tulane University.
25. William C. Davis, ed. *Secret History of Confederate Diplomacy Abroad*, p. xviii.
26. *To whom it may concern. This is to certify that C.E.L. Stuart was an officer in the service of the Confederate States from the opening to the close of the war. He was always, during that time, in the most intimate official relation with the undersigned, and he gave the utmost satisfaction as an officer and a gentleman. Whether in the field or at the seat of Government in Richmond (where most of his duties were) Col. Stuart proved himself to be eminently worthy of the high confidence reposed in him by the Government. I am glad to be able to testify that a more faithful friend or qualified officer than he was not in the service. (signed) Jefferson Davis, Montreal, Canada, October 7, 1867.* It was quite a clever fake, in that, on that particular date, October 7, 1867, ex–President Davis was, indeed, in Montreal.
27. This letter is in the University of Notre Dame Archives, in South Bend, Indiana, ref. 1867/1211.
28. Aside from newspapers—Brazilian and American—it is a rare source indeed that mentions Stuart in Brazil. One is Gerald Horne's book *The Deepest South*. While discussing U.S. speculators in Rio after the war, the author says, *There was, for example, Charles Edward Lewis Stuart*, "calling himself General of the late Confederate Army," who had "forged," and was also "swindling by false representation." That's all there is, however, and Horne got it from one source only—the *Richmond Whig* of October 20, 1868, and the *Whig* got it from the April 7 issue of the *Anglo-Brazilian Times*.

docked in Rio,[29] and on January 3, 1868, Stuart cashed his letters of credit with the famous discount house of Messrs. Wright & Co.

The amiable, learned and immensely rich Dr. Stuart (Colonel Stuart of the Virginia Cavalry), noted writer and journalist, former member of Jeff Davis's staff, descendant of the royal line, and now special correspondent for the *New York Tribune* and advance man for that trio of newspaper giants—himself, Greeley, and Raymond—finally revealed his scheme to an astonished and, one must say, skeptical Rio. His was a grand mission, of course, to set up a gigantic daily newspaper in the English language, a *New York Herald* and London *Times* all in one. The paper, to be called the *Herald*, was to open in May.[30]

Stuart tripped insouciantly, but with great fanfare, around the central business district, making grand offers on several of the city's most magnificent buildings, such as the San Pedro Theatre, and even approaching William Scully with a fabulous deal for his paper, the *Anglo-Brazilian Times*. None

John McGill.

of these propositions was workable, though, and everyone knew it, Stuart included. He even urged upon the Brazilian government, "for the safety of the public treasury and the banks," the establishment of a corps of North American policemen to guard his future downtown real estate. For a sane man, this would all be an utter waste of valuable time, but Stuart's overwhelming drive to be perceived as a magnifico outweighed any sanity he might still have had left. And, given that anyone with half an eye could see that he was heading inexorably toward a very nasty destiny, that sanity was the insanity of a suicide

---

29. For Stuart's stay in Rio de Janeiro, I have relied principally on Brazilian newspapers of the day. They are listed in the bibliography. Most of them are in old Brazilian-Portuguese, and refer to Stuart as Carlos Eduardo Luiz Casimiro João Walter Stuart, or some variation thereof.

30. Letter of May 18, 1868, written by Jefferson Davis Howell in Montreal to Jefferson Davis. *Among the few who were doing well* [in Brazil] *was Dr. Chas Stuart, who was representing to people that he was a member of your staff. I did not cowhide him for fear of going to jail, but took every opportunity to expose him as a thief & a scoundrel & a liar; he claims to have letters from Davis on the strength of which he had introduced himself into some very influential society.*

bomber. The short-lived bubble was about to burst, and the dazzling pyrotechnic that was Stuart was on the point of fizzling out into a squib.

The telegram sent from Messrs. Wright's head office in New York caused a panic in their Rio branch when it arrived there on March 18. *Letters of credit on New York editors, taken out by Stuart, are false.* The police came for Carlos Eduardo Luiz Stuart on March 26, 1868. The charge was forgery and swindling.[31]

News of Stuart's arrest and trial made the U.S. newspapers. Dr. George Bagby wrote in the *Richmond Whig* of October 20, 1868, that Stuart had been a clerk in the Post Office Department of the Confederate States, had written for the *Whig* and *Southern Literary Messenger*, had followed Davis to Georgia, had written an account of his capture for the *New York Herald*, and had collected money for Davis's benefit. That he had started South as a correspondent for the *Herald*, got into a row in Richmond; *and that is the last we heard of him*. The *Whig* itself editorialized: *We remember him very well—a plausible, pushing, presuming fellow*. Like other sources, the paper says that Stuart would claim to be of the royal Stuart line, and that he held an LL.D. from the University of Edinburgh. Apparently they had done some digging into his Neapolitan background, coming to the conclusion that if he had been born in Naples, it was by a process of which the church preserved no record. The *Whig* actually calls him an impostor. *When we last saw him, some three years ago, he represented himself to be the "commissioner of the New York Herald for the Southern States and South America." The Herald published several of his letters from the South.*

On November 6, 1868, the Rio jury acquitted Stuart of the charge of forgery, but convicted him of fraud, and sentenced him to six years imprisonment with labor, and a fine of 20 percent of the damage and costs.[32]

Finally, after a round of unsuccessful appeals, Stuart began his prison sentence in June 1871. At that point, he enlisted the rather reluctant aid of George H. Preston, British consular chaplain in Rio. On December 20, 1871, Preston wrote to Jefferson Davis, asking if he had ever known anyone by the name of C.E.L. Stuart, *who is and has been for several years past in trouble, but he only made application to me for help in July last, but until I can ascertain the truth of his statements, I do not feel justified in acting as he wishes. He states then that in the fall of 1865 he was enabled to take your family to Canada, and that he left them at the Clifton Hotel, Niagara—he also states that your children were photographed with himself in the same picture.* The chaplain wished to know if there was any truth to all this, and, if Stuart was, indeed, known to the ex–President, was he worthy of credit? *I am anxious to receive an answer as soon as possible, in case I may have to petition the Emperor*[33] *in his favour on his return to Brazil.*[34]

Jefferson Davis wrote back to Chaplain Preston on February 10, 1872. This letter has

---

31. Jefferson Davis Howell wrote to Jefferson Davis on June 28, 1868: *You were quite right in regard to Dr. C.E.S., as since my departure from Rio I understand he undertook a forgery and was caught & now is paying the penalty in jail.*

32. At his trial, Stuart claimed to be variously 37 and 39, the son of Charles Edward Louis Stuart and his wife Amalia Julia, that he was born in Naples, was a bachelor, and a British citizen. As for his profession, he claimed both journalist and "man of letters." He also claimed to have been on Jefferson Davis's staff during the war.

33. The emperor, Pedro II, returned to Brazil from his European trip on March 31, 1872. Whether Preston interceded with the emperor on Stuart's behalf is not known, but it is unlikely.

34. This letter is in the Davis Collection, Museum of the Confederacy, Richmond, Virginia.

not been found, but Preston replied to it on April 17, 1872: *...your handwriting in the note you wrote to me is very unlike what purports to be your handwriting in a paper affixed to the written account of C.E.L. Stuart's trial, a copy of which I inclose. Will you kindly state whether you ever furnished him with such a testimonial? He has passed himself off as general Stuart,*[35] *and there seems to be so much mystery about him, that I begin to think he is not the injured person he represents himself to be.*

On May 23, 1872, Jefferson Davis wrote to the Reverend Geo. H. Preston, Chaplain, Rio de Janeiro. *The circular letter, of which you enclosed a copy, and which purports to have been written by me at Montreal, Canada, Oct. 7th, 1867, is a forgery. It's* [sic] *statements are destitute of the truth. The C.E.L. Stuart who was in Richmond during the War was a clerk of the Navy Dept. He never had any official relations with me individually, and the extent of confidence exhibited by me, in him, was that in one instance when his fidelity was impugned, I accepted his defence as conclusive against the charge. His conduct in New York, subsequent to the war, caused me to fear that I had in that instance been more credulous than just; and the evidence you furnish of the crime of forgery is in keeping with the reports which have reached me of the false pretences on which he procured money from my friends while I was a prisoner at Fortress Monroe. It is always a disagreeable duty to condemn; but the attempt to make me the instrument of deception, has left me no option.*

On July 7, 1877, the *Times*, a Philadelphia newspaper, published an article called "The Capture of Jefferson Davis." It was part of the paper's famous "Annals of the War. Chapters of Unwritten History" series. This particular article was written by Major General James H. Wilson, and in it Wilson ascribes certain statements to an anonymous written source, a source who sounds very much like Jefferson Davis's former secretary, Burton Harrison. In September, Harrison, in a bit of a panic, wrote a memo to his old chief disclaiming having never, himself, published anything on the subject. *As a conjecture, merely, as to the person who is, possibly, the one intended to be quoted by Genl Wilson, I would remind you that there was a person (who had served in Richmond, as a Clerk in the Navy Department, I think), calling himself Stuart, and said to claim descent from the Royal Stuarts, who is in this connection quoted by Horace Greely* [sic] *in a footnote in his "History" as authority for some of Greely's statements about the incidents of Mr. Davis' capture. Stuart seems to have met Mrs. Davis, or Mrs. or Miss Howell, at Savannah or Augusta, Georgia, after Mrs. Davis was taken back there when her husband was imprisoned at Fortress Monroe. Stuart appears to have made himself useful to one or more of those ladies, and perhaps acted as escort to Mrs. and Miss Howell on their journey to Canada. At any rate, he seems to have passed himself off in New York, "shortly after" our capture, as having been a Staff Officer of Mr. Davis, and he is said to have addressed to a New York Newspaper a letter describing the circumstances of the capture. Mr Greely, if I recollect aright, cites the letter entire in a footnote, in his "History."*[36]

By this time, however, unknown to Burton Harrison or anyone else in the United States, things had been happening on the Stuart front in Brazil. The June 24, 1877, edition of the newspaper *Diario de São Paolo* says that Stuart had been set free.

---

35. The word "general" is underlined.
36. One senses Harrison is prevaricating here. He knew exactly who Stuart was—had very good and painful reason to know, as we have seen from his 1867 letter to Preston Johnston.

From 1860 to 1877 C.E.L. Stuart was frequently in the press in both North America and Brazil. In June 1877, from the moment he stepped through the prison gates back into the free world, this extraordinary character disappears, forever, never to be seen again. In the seventeen years he had graced the world's stage, he had talked much about his past, and so had other people, but none of it was true. Never had he revealed anything to indicate his real origins. He had lived behind a perfect smokescreen. He had let nothing slip—nothing, that is, except two things.

The first thing was that Bonnie Prince Charlie's name had been Charles Edward Louis John Casimir Philip Sylvester Severino Maria Stuart. At least those are some of the multitude of forenames one sees credited to the Young Chevalier. But, without question, those names he did have were Charles Edward Louis Casimir John, the last two not necessarily in that order. C.E.L. Stuart, by his own admission, was Charles Edward Louis Casimir John Walter. The Bonnie Prince never had Walter in his name. Why, then, did our man? The name Walter must have been of exceeding importance to him. But why he attached such importance to the name Walter could not possibly become evident until after we had found the second and most important thing that gave Stuart away—*Tales of Ireland and the Irish*. It was during an unguarded moment, when his bragging got the best of him. It was in 1863, in Richmond, and he had just written a novel called *Casimir*.[37]

This from the *Richmond Examiner* of March 7, 1863: *Casimir, an original novel in three books by C.E.L. Stuart, LL.D., formerly chief editor of the New York Daily News..., of the "Volunteer" ... and also of the New York Illustrated News. Author of Tririvin,*[38] *Katie Stewart, Athlings,*[39] *Tales of Ireland, and the Irish, etc etc. J.W. Randolph, publisher.*

It was that mention of *Tales of Ireland and the Irish*, and that alone, which pierced the hitherto impenetrable veil covering up the past—and the future—of C.E.L. Stuart.

John George MacWalter was born on February 12, 1830,[40] in the village of Knockaney, in county Limerick, the son of James MacWalter, of the British Army, and his wife Julia O'Dwyer. Superbly educated at St. Jarlath's College, the famous school in Tuam, Galway, he graduated with dazzling honors in the summer of 1848.[41] He could have gone to any of the great universities, but chose journalism as a career. Raised a Catholic, he had suffered a conversion on the road to Dublin,[42] and went to work for the rabid Protestant organs, the *Dublin Warder* and the *Dublin Evening Herald*.

On January 12, 1850, he married Wilhelmina Phillips, the very young daughter of

---

37. *Casimir* was never published.
38. It turned out to be *Frirwin*, a novel by Octavia Oliphant, published in London in 1856.
39. It turned out to be *The Athelings*. That and *Katie Stewart* were both written anonymously, but, in fact, were by the famous British novelist, Mrs. Oliphant.
40. Even this innocent truth he kept from his second wife. She knew he was born somewhere in Ireland, but thought the date was March 18, 1830. What he told people in the Americas, while he was posing as C.E.L. Stuart, was that he was born in Naples on February 12, 1830, and baptized on February 18. Later in life he would give his birth date as February 8, 1831, and baptism date as February 12. Taking all things into consideration, and given that February 12 seems to be something of a constant, he was born probably on February 12, 1830.
41. *Freeman's Journal* (Dublin), July 8, 1848.
42. London *Morning Post*, October 1, 1852; *London Daily News*, October 29, 1852.

Dublin solicitor, William Phillips. Two years later their only child, John George Patrick, was born,[43] but in the intervening time MacWalter had become somewhat famous as the author of the book, *Reformation of the Irish Church*. His follow-up works, *Table Tapping*, *The Scarlet Mystery*, and *Tales of Ireland and the Irish*, would cement not only his fame all over the United Kingdom, but also his pocket.

They tried hard to find MacWalter, but, now with a nice nest egg and tired of the domestic life, he had simply disappeared. Wilhelmina and the child went to live with the widowed Mr. Phillips, and they did the best they could. It was all very sad, but not for J.G. MacWalter, who reappeared in Dorset, as John Going Gort Mac Walter, editor of the *Dorset Chronicle* and of the *Southern Times*, man-about-town, and well-respected figure of Dorchester society. On July 16, 1855, forgetting to tell anyone that he already had a wife and child in Dublin, he married twenty-year-old Emily Newton,[44] niece of the local prison governor. A year later, he and Emily had their first child, Henrietta.[45]

By day he was Mac Walter in provincial Dorset, by night he was Sir Oscar Oliphant, Knight, writer and kilted society lion in London.[46] He cut quite a figure, as presumably did Octavia Oliphant,[47] who was actually never seen in public, at least not at the same time as Sir Oscar.

MacWalter allowed himself to be nominated as member of Parliament for Weymouth, and thus began making the papers again in a big way. It was the year of the national elections, and, as was inevitable, someone in Dublin saw his name. With the Irish authorities hot on his trail, the candidate fled to London with his Dorset family, but they found him, and then it was up to Liverpool, where one August day he, Emily and Henrietta boarded the *Harvest Queen* bound for New York. The name MacWalter definitely had to go, for good, and on September 5, 1857, Charles Edward Stuart stepped off the ship in New York.

Sir Oscar Oliphant, from the frontispiece of his 1856 book, *Collected Poems.*

---

43. Born March 15, 1853, at 16 Lower Gardiner Street (*Freeman's Journal*, March 17, 1853). Moved to the United States, married twice, and died in 1934, no children.
44. Parish records of Moreton, Dorset, a village just outside Dorchester.
45. Henrietta Maria Gort McWalter. Dorchester parish records, July 4, 1856. The father is listed as J. Going Gort McWalter, Esq., barrister-at-law.
46. In 1857 Sir Oscar wrote a book about China and also had published a book of poems.
47. The mysterious Octavia Oliphant wrote the novel *Frirwin*, published in London in 1856. She is not to be confused with the famous British writer, Mrs. Oliphant (Margaret Oliphant).

They moved to Kingston, in upstate New York, where he got a job as a reporter on the *Ulster Democrat*. The following year, he and the family moved to New York City, rented a home in Staten Island, and Stuart became a reporter with the *Daily News*. By March 1860 he was the editor, a role he quit in July of that year to found the Breckinridge & Lane campaign newspaper, *The Volunteer*. His man lost the election, of course, to one A. Lincoln, and Stuart then became editor of the *New York Illustrated News*. In March 1861 he quit and went South.

In Rio, then, in June 1877, C.E.L. Stuart walked through the prison gates and emerged into the bright sunlight of freedom as John Gabriel Stuart MacWalter. He had a plan. It involved the Catholic Church.

He immediately took passage to England and became Brother MacWalter in the Rosminian Order of Charity, spinning the yarn that he had survived a shipwreck which had taken the life of his wife. It sounded tragic, and would have been, but for the fact that, unknown to Stuart, after he had gone to Brazil in 1867, Emily had left the United States and returned to England, with her two surviving daughters. She became a lady's companion in Devon, and the girls were put into a convent in Plymouth. And, it must be remembered that Stuart's first wife, Wilhelmina, now Mrs. Stedman and quite well off, was living happily in London, while Stuart's son, by that first marriage, was living in Dublin.[48] It was all very cozy, as long as all the parties remained in a certain state of mutual ignorance.

In 1879 Brother MacWalter was assigned to the Rosminians' chapel in London, St. Etheldreda's, to assist the famous Father William Lockhart in literary matters. And then he began to write a book on Rosmini, the founder of the order, even going to Italy to gather material. In 1882, as "a member of the institute," his translation of Rosmini's *Discourses on Moral and Religious Subjects* was published, and, in 1883, came Volume 1 of his *Life of Antonio Rosmini Serbati*, written by Gabriel Stuart MacWalter.[49] By now, Emily was living in Camberwell with Lily. The elder daughter, Henrietta, was still at the convent in Plymouth, as a teacher. She would shortly become a nun and spend most of her working life in Liverpool.[50]

Brother MacWalter's book was reviewed extensively in the British press. Someone, sooner or later, was going to see the name Gabriel Stuart MacWalter and put two and two together, and that's exactly what happened. Emily and Lily appeared at St. Etheldreda's with an interesting tale to tell to Father Lockhart. The next thing was that a very surprised Brother MacWalter was out on his ear.[51]

After two years of degradation and increasing depression, Brother MacWalter was fished out of the Thames on December 3, 1885.

---

48. Emily died in 1915, in Hertfordshire. Wilhelmina died in January 1927.
49. There was a volume 2, but it was written by Father Lockhart after Brother MacWalter's death.
50. Henrietta died in London in December 1926, still a nun. If her half-brother, John George Patrick MacWalter, had known of her existence, which he did not, he might have gone to the funeral. Curiously, he was visiting London from the USA at that very time. Lily, who never married, died in Brighton in 1922. Three children having died young, and John George Patrick having no children, Brother MacWalter had no more descendants.
51. Through the clouds, the sun was shining on Lago Maggiore. A shaft of its bright light forked through a nimbus, bringing clarity into the little town of Stresa. With his thumb, the Rosminian archivist flipped up the rusting metal clasp, unlocking the leather-bound volume. With appropriate respect and care he began to turn the ancient pages of the Institute's register, finally coming to the letter M. Then he found what he was seeking. Written in Italian, long ago, in a spidery hand, were the records for "Mac Walter, Gabriello." I duly received an e-mail.

APPENDIX: THE STUART ARTICLE

C.E.L. Stuart's account of the flight was published in the *New York Herald* on July 4, 1865. For two main reasons it is presented here in its entirety. The first is that it has not been seen as such since 1865, and, because it was the first ever full-length account of the adventure, and by a man who traveled on Jefferson Davis's train—and a highly skilled reporter, to boot—this 150-year omission must be rectified.

The second, and much more important reason, is to set the record straight. Most of what we know about the flight comes from Mallory's account. A good deal of what Mallory wrote he took from Stuart's article. The Stuart article presented below has a certain number of footnotes appended, which show just how Mallory cribbed.

THE APRIL FOOL DAY OF THE REBEL CONFEDERACY

The 1st of April, 1865,[1] was, to the citizens of Richmond, a veritable "All Fools Day." It became this in a most positive and comprehensive sense. Spring was bursting out in its earliest rural charms, and the despondency which had long clutched the rebel capital in a wintry grip was loosened. The whole population was buoyed up with hopes such as the most sanguine had not indulged since Grant's army encompassed the city. The touchstone of these delusive hopes was to be found in the price of gold—forty for one was about the lowest price paid for the precious metal at any time within six months prior to the evacuation, and it was more than once, under certain phases of public depression, as high as eighty-five for one; yet, on the 1st of April, it was sold, in many instances, as low as forty for one; sold by sage brokers—by absolute Solomons! Within twenty-four hours you could not purchase it at five hundred for one.

But the 1st of April and its balmy delusions, and its variety of Fools Paradises, passed away, and Richmond, if not all the confederacy, lulled itself to sleep in a confidence so complete that its fallacies cannot rob it of a sublimity which need not be denied it. The infatuation just then was as invincible as the necessity crowding on it was inexorable.

---

1. Mallory says: ...*in the year of our Lord, 1865.*

The Memorable 2nd of April[2]

dawned with glowing promise[3]—a morning such as fitly crowned the glittering hopes of the day before—a morning too bright for melancholy forebodings[4]—A Sunday morning with nought but faith, in its widest, deepest sense, illuminating every countenance. Every? No; there were notable exceptions, and these pertained to certain notabilities. It was the conglomeration known as the "general public" which reflected the beaming[5] brightness of the day, and basked in brilliant hope. Behind the "general public," whose spirits naturally bounded up with the glow of spring,[6] there were the "particular few" who did not deem it expedient to fling dim clouds over so much complacent confidence. These "particular few" were aware of preparations which threatened to test the resistive power of Lee—they were aware of the strength about to be hurled at their own comparative weakness—they were aware of movements which should quickly and inevitably touch the very vitals of their "grand experiment."[7] They were, therefore, reverentially grave, in spite of efforts to assume an air of ease and satisfaction somewhat in harmony with the feeling of confidence they wished to inspire and gladly saw existing—existing spontaneously—existing so soon after a universal gloom, and so close to destruction—existing, as does the painless interval which precedes the death of a much suffering patient. They were all at their respective churches[8]—all of this "particular few"—all except J.P. Benjamin,[9] who, being no Christian, paid homage to pipe and solitude during the early part of that eventful Sabbath morning.[10]

Jeff Davis Praying Amidst Impending Ruin

Mr. Davis went, as usual,[11] to St. Paul's Episcopal Church,[12] where political and Christian hopes were, once a week, blended for his edification. He looked care-worn,[13] yet contrived to tinge his concern with a briskness which warded off suspicion.[14] A certain ominous telegram that he received in the early part of the morning[15] was, however, a tormenting demon, manifestly too much for the perfect quiet which would be needed in the house of prayer and praise.[16]

Benjamin Smoking While Richmond Burned

Mr. Benjamin, as I have said, courted his pipe[17] and solitude in the cool verandah of his Main

---

2. Mallory says: ...*ever be remembered 2d of April.*
3. Mallory says: ...*a clear beautiful day in Richmond.*
4. Mallory says: ...*the darkest in her history,* meaning Richmond's history.
5. Mallory says: ...*the sun beamed.*
6. Mallory says: ...*the temperature wooed the people abroad.*
7. Mallory says: ...*yet, at that very moment, the hours of the Confederacy ... were being numbered by the dread arbitrament of blood.*
8. Mallory says: ...*the members of the Cabinet, with the exception of Mr Benjamin, were similarly called out of church by special messengers, at their several places of worship.*
9. Mallory says: ...*with the exception of Benjamin.*
10. Mallory sets the scene the same way, also in a long paragraph
11. Mallory says: ...*as usual.*
12. Mallory says: ...*entered St. Paul's alone.* Even though Mallory was not there, he is quite categoric that Davis entered the church alone. In other words, Frank Lubbock, his aide, did not go to church with him.
13. Mallory says: ...*pale careworn visage.*
14. Mallory says: ...*its expression varied not,* meaning, of course, Jefferson Davis's face.
15. Mallory says: ...*Lee's dispatches in the early hours of the day.*
16. Mallory says: *The dull, booming sounds of distant guns were mingled with the impressive words of the service, forming strange and startling responses to its invocations for peace on earth and good will to men.*
17. Mallory says: ...*his mild Havana.*

street mansion.[18] His countenance had its never ceasing smile,[19] or glimmer, but his busy, dark eyes and the feverish movements of his hands twirling[20] and tugging his watch-guard,[21] told some of the unpleasant tale so faithfully put in the morning's telegram.[22]

Breckinridge Nervous Over the Approaching Catastrophe

General Breckinridge went to hear Mr. Duncan lift up his voice for the lifting up of the now responsive popular heart, as he had often before done with effect. He did not tarry there long. Thoughts of that warning telegram drew him early back to the War Department. In him, however, you could trace nothing of apprehension, nothing of alarm.

Trenholm Sick at the Prospect Before Him

Mr. Trenholm was indisposed,[23] and therefore the indications noticed in him were readily ascribed to his feeble health, rather than to a fear-provoking telegram, of which the "general public" as yet knew nothing, or next to nothing.

Mallory at Mass

Mr. Mallory was at mass, in St. Peter's Cathedral, betraying no marked symptoms of what must have distracted his devotions.

Reagan and the Attorney-General Looking Sombre

Mr. Reagan was at Dr. Petre's Baptist church, as morose looking as man could seem; and Attorney General Davis as sombre as a judge digesting a death charge.[24]

This of the Cabinet. The "particular few," as exposed to the "general public," included more than these; but they were of the staff, or comparatively irresponsible gentlemen, who did not feel the burden, or realize the danger in its full force. They were, however, mysteriously reticent, and foolishly "important"; felt their position, if not the occasion.

The Handwriting on the Wall

At length, while heaven was being assailed for favor and protection in every church of Richmond, Colonel Taylor Wood hastened to the door of St. Paul's and despatched the sexton to Mr. Davis's pew.[25] Only a few words were whispered softly in the ears of the Confederate President[26]—a few words which told him another despatch[27] had come, and that he was immediately wanted. It was enough. The concourse of worshippers within St. Paul's read the whisper by the action of Mr. Davis, who instantly left the church.[28] No telegram ever flashed through the electric wires more swiftly than this unspoken intelligence shot from eye to eye of that dismayed congregation. Had an unseen hand written the coming doom on the wall in letters of fire, the effect could not have been more appalling or more instantaneous. In other churches a kindred scene ensued,[29] and thus, from pulpit and sanctuary, although the people were expressly gath-

---

18. Mallory says: ...*his residence on Main street.*
19. Mallory says: ...*usual happy, jaunty air; his pleasant smile.*
20. Mallory says: ...*the very twirl of his slender, gold-headed cane.*
21. Mallory says: ...*nervous manipulations of his watch seals.*
22. Mallory says: ...*Benjamin mask which fooled no one.*
23. Mallory says: ...*suffering from a painful attack of neuralgia.*
24. Later, Mallory uses "silent" and "somber" to describe Judge Reagan.
25. Mallory says: *A messenger from the War Department enters the church.*
26. Mallory says: ...*whispers a few words in his ear.*
27. Mallory says: ...*Lee's later dispatches.*
28. Mallory says: ...*follows the messenger the whole length of the aisle.*
29. Mallory says: ...*the members of the Cabinet ... were similarly called out of church by special messengers, at their several places of worship.*

ered together for such a purpose, the dismal tidings spread that the day of doom had dawned for Richmond,[30] prayed they ever so fervently to the contrary.

The Dismay of the People

By two o'clock all was known,[31] or what, in result, was all—the evacuation of the rebel capital decided on.[32] Beyond this little was certain. Rumor had her countless tongues at work, and victory was as much believed in as defeat. It was only a strategic move, only wise to give Lee full scope and not embarrass him with the defence of such a place, better far that the deed so dreaded when it was more distant, had been consummated two years ago. Nevertheless, for all that flagging hope could urge, the city was quickly an unbroken scene of dismay and confusion.[33]

The Evacuation

Orders were issued, about two o'clock, to the principal military and civil officials to have all the government archives[34] not yet removed, and which it was possible to remove, ready by seven o'clock; what could not be easily transported were to be destroyed. Orders were also given to these same personages to meet Mr. Davis at the Danville depot by eight o'clock.

Pandemonium

From the issuing of these orders to the time of departure, the city assumed the character of a pandemonium. Out of every government building huge cases and boxes tumbled as if a fire were in the rear. These were hurried off in wagons, with jaded mules and horses mercilessly whipped by shouting negroes.

It was strange and suggestive to observe the hearty will of the "colored officials"—that is to say, the black messengers and servants of the several departments, and the teamsters. They worked with an energy and earnestness which were either the result of sympathy for the predicament of their employers, or an eagerness to be rid of them. Which? Many of them followed the fortunes of the fugitive government to Southern Virginia, as, I presume, the answer for them is easy, but for the others, I am in doubt. Toward the time of departure, every street poured out its contribution of voluntary exiles—private citizens hurrying to and fro, followed by negroes carrying portmanteaus, boxes, valises, carpet bags and all other sorts of travelling gear. Coaches were in waiting at one in every ten houses[35]—coaches which in most cases took their fair fares to the trains to be disappointed,[36] for not one-fifth of those who started to leave were enabled to go. Only a few of the privileged beside the officials were thus favored.[37]

How the Negroes Appreciated the Situation

As I was myself on the way to join Mr. Davis' party one scene struck me with singular force. It is a scene of which the *Tribune* may, perhaps, make much; although I saw it in a far different light from any which Mr. Greeley may view it, as I shall take occasion to tell you at another time.

---

30. Mallory says: ...*the last day of the Confederacy.*
31. Mallory says: ...*the disastrous news ... soon reached the ears of the people.*
32. Mallory says: ...*the immediate withdrawal of the government from Richmond.*
33. Mallory says: ...*there was no confusion, no noise, no undue excitement.*
34. Mallory says: ...*boxes of government records & papers.*
35. Mallory says: ...*hundreds were leaving the doomed city by every practicable means, some ... in carriages.*
36. Mallory says: ...*the Danville depot was filled by an eager crowd seeking transportation on the train.*
37. Mallory says: ...*the order had been given to admit no one whose services were not indispensable.*

I am now narrating, not commenting. It is this: Coming down the upper part of Franklin street, above Fourth street—all around being utter disorder and consternation—rushing hither and thither of excited men equipped as refugees and followed by, or following, such worldly goods as it was possible for them to transport or get transported—coming down amid all this wild bustle of white men, whiter than usual, I crossed a stream of placid negroes and negresses, just emerged from the Second African church.[38] They either did not comprehend the excitement or were indifferent to it. They were dressed in that gorgeous excess that I have only noticed among negroes in the South, and looked on, in quiet wonderment, at what was taking place before them. Their sang froid was enviable.[39] Said the eager gentleman in that shoving throng to a sable [illegible] "Jack, come and help me with this trunk to the Danville cars."

"I've to see Jane home, Sir, or I would," and Jack coolly walked on in his slow gait, in no way disturbed, as Jane whisked her satin dress, as though to say, "What impudence!," not in Jack, but in his white acquaintance.[40]

Another Strange Phase

amid the tumult was this:—At all the private houses I passed—houses of regular Richmond families—the balconies were filled with ladies,[41] evidently resolved to brave the dangers consequent on being left alone.[42] They were mute. They looked terror stricken, and in many cases powerless and irresolute. The crisis had come with fearful suddenness upon them, although for years it impended. "Wolf" was cried so often that, when at last it came, they could not credit the fact, or, crediting it, they were palsied. It was not resignation; it was nearer akin to desperation. The chances of getting away were few; the ability to make the effort was of the faintest description. They beheld fate and saw nothing for it but such a reluctant embrace as necessity enforced.[43] It was woeful to witness their sturdy, stolid sadness.[44]

The Escape

All the way to the rendezvous assigned for the flying "Presidential party" was blocked by panting fugitives, or by groups of wonder-gapers. At last the Danville depot is reached through a crush of eager men scrambling for admission to the platform.[45] Two militia regiments had parties on duty.[46] None were admitted to the "Presidential train" except a specified few.[47] Other trains had gone, others were to go. The crowd must push aside. Provost-Marshal Carrington, with a select guard, saw that no one entered unless duly authorized.[48] He called for each cabinet officer to designate his special few.[49] It was done amidst fierce confusion.

After all descriptions of annoyances from throning citizens and soldiers,[50] the "Presidential train" was made up, the platform incontinently cleared—many a respectable and venerable citizen having been sent off under guard because his anxiety overlooked official routine

---

38. Mallory says: *...the African Church had, at an early hour, poured its crowded congregation into the crowded streets.*
39. Mallory says: *...many of them walked the streets with eager faces, parted lips & hurried strides.*
40. Mallory says: *American citizens of African descent were shaking hands & exchanging congratulations on all sides.*
41. Just like Stuart, Mallory devotes a paragraph to the women of Richmond.
42. Mallory says: *...noble women.*
43. Mallory says: *...ready to surrender life itself.*
44. Mallory says: *...wept in the streets.*
45. Mallory says: *The Danville depot was filled by an eager crowd seeking transportation on the train.*
46. Mallory says: *Members of the Home Guard ... were on duty in charge of the depot and train.*
47. Mallory says: *The order had been given to admit no one whose services were not indispensable.*
48. Mallory says: *Colonel Carrington & Major Richardson, who had it in charge.*
49. Mallory says: *...generally the heads of bureaus and their chief clerks.*
50. Mallory picks up on this, and elaborates with a few instances.

in such a scuffle for opportunity to fly[51]—and all was ready. Mr. Davis took his seat in a close car,[52] attended by his Cabinet[53]—General Breckinridge alone being for a while absent, seeing to some military matters at the other side of the city, and waiting for a fresh and, perhaps, more encouraging despatch from Lee.[54] The other portion of the "Presidential party" included General Cooper, the ranking general of the army and Adjutant General,[55] General Terry and General Stuart,[56] Colonel Preston Johnston,[57] Colonel Burton Harrison, Colonel Ives, Colonel Taylor Wood,[58] and Colonel Lubbock, ex Governor of Texas.[59] In an adjoining car were the various heads of bureaus and other chiefs.[60]

By eight o'clock all intended for this train were seated and ready to go.[61] Several other trains were in course of preparation. But it was ten o'clock before the Davis train moved.[62] The delay begat a variety of surmises.[63] Some held that Lee had won a great victory, and that the necessity for going had passed away. Others imagined that the Southern army was unable to defend the road, and that the necessity for staying was imperative. Meanwhile, the militia, who were doing guard duty, began gradually to "go home"; and, before we left, not half the number were at their posts; meanwhile, also, pillage and riot had begun in the city, of which we were blissfully ignorant[64]; meanwhile, too, a guard of two hundred picked men entered a car ready for them between the engine and the Davis carriage; finally, General Breckinridge arrived with news for the Davis party that Lee could not save the city, but that the road was clear, and likely to remain so until this precious freight was out of immediate danger.

THE FLIGHT BEGUN

Then Mr. Davis and his party tightened their spurs to their heels (horses were in a car for the Cabinet and staff), saw to their small arms, leaned back on their seats,[65] and the signal puff was given. And then and there began the flight—there, at ten o'clock on the night of April 2, 1865—there, amid a turmoil seldom equaled, and thence through scenes and incidents as varied and harassing as any in history.[66]

---

51. Mallory says: ...*some "Artful Dodgers" contrived to "ring in" upon the ground of their vast importance to some great public interest.*
52. Mallory says: ...*took his seat in the cars.*
53. Mallory says: ...*with the Secretary of War and other members of the government.*
54. Mallory says: ...*in anxious expectation of better news from Lee.*
55. Mallory says: *Adjutant General Cooper.*
56. General Stuart is, of course, C.E.L. Stuart, who, of course, was never a general. As for General Terry, there were eight Confederate officers named Terry during the Civil War, but only one general with that name—William Richard Terry (1827–97). On May 31, 1864, he was promoted to brigadier general, and on March 31, 1865, suffered his seventh war wound while fighting at Dinwiddie Court House. He remained with the Army until its surrender at Appomattox Court House on April 9. So, this General Terry cannot be the man Stuart has in mind.
57. Mallory says: *Preston Johnston.*
58. Mallory says: *Taylor Wood.*
59. Mallory says: ...*ex-Governor Lubbock of Texas, on the President's staff with the rank of Col.*
60. Mallory says: ...*heads of bureaus and their chief clerks.*
61. Mallory says: ...*the Danville train ... was to leave Richmond at half-past eight P.M., and before this hour the heads of Departments and their chief assistants were ready at the depot.*
62. Mallory says: ...*the cars did not move till eleven P.M.*
63. Mallory says: *There were good reasons for the delay however.*
64. Mallory says: ...*the rabble who stood ready to plunder during the night.*
65. Mallory says: ...*took his seat in the cars.*
66. Mallory says: ...*the cars did not move until 11 P.M.*

The Thoughts of the Flying Parties

The night was supremely clear and calm—the dome of heaven spread out its radiance, glittering as I have rarely seen it—"silent as if watched the sleeping earth."[67]

Yet it seldom shed its peaceful effulgence on more desperate deeds—seldom flung its glittering mantle over more dismal and degrading scenes—seldom threw its myriad rays of "perfect quiet" into horrors more demoniac. What was transpiring in the city we were fleeing from we had not the least conception of—knew nothing of the fearful acts with which the half starved mob so [illegible] the doomed city while we were jolting along the Danville road, wondering why we were going, or whither our course tended. No, none of the fiendish feats which marked Richmond as a prey for that night, under that serene, seductive canopy of a beaming spring day—none of these had for a moment occurred to any of us as possible. We were all thinking not of the horrors in the city but of the carnage in the vicinity of which we were passing. It was in what seemed likely to confront us in the front, not in what was raging in the rear, that all our speculations centered.[68]

At Petersburg

On we whisked[69] briskly but cautiously[70]—on until we were close to the last battle field of the last campaign, about twenty three miles from the city, and abreast of Petersburg. There we stopped. There General Breckinridge and Quartermaster General Lawton and Commissioner General St. John left us to find their way to Lee's headquarters, and there gather consolation or offer it.

It was close on midnight, and to the dense darkness of the "nether earth" stood out the bold brightness of the "upper air." Cooped up in that train, with the dim lights of a gasless station flitting here and there on the platform, one could not avoid feeling the touch of doom[71] sending its direful spasms to his heart. The wind grew bolder and bolder, and each gust had a dolesome melody. "Spirits of the uncoffined slain/Sudden blasts of triumph swelling/Came that night in misty train/Rushing round our narrow dwelling."

"Sleep No More"

Sleep was as yet attempted by no one, and no one appeared to be less susceptible of its influence than Mr. Davis. He was anxious, not nervous; doubtful, not daunted; irritated, not irresolute. As he wore travelling spectacles, which completely encased his eyes, it was, of course, not possible to detect how far the "indexes of the soul" betrayed what was passing within him. He spoke little and only by way of question. Colonel Lubbock, of Texas, was the most loquacious[72] of his party. To him it seemed that the part of an aid-de-camp was not fully performed if he did not say much and bustle more,[73] be doing or seem to be doing a great deal,[74] and he discharged he imagined duty fairly. It was bright and calm, he thought, and all the usual portents denoted good luck. To which a wag too pertinently replied, from Coleridge's ballad of "Sir Patrick Spens":—"Late, late yestreen, I saw the new moon/With the old moon in her arm/And I fear, I fear, my master dear/We shall have a deadly storm."

---

67. Misquote from Coleridge: *Silent as though they watched the sleeping Earth!*
68. Mallory says: *As the fugitives receded ... many and sad were the commentaries they made upon the Confederate Cause.*
69. Mallory says: *...at the rate of about ten miles an hour.*
70. Mallory says: *...the progress of the train was slow and its interruptions frequent.*
71. Mallory says: *...general gloom.*
72. Mallory says: *...garrulous.*
73. Mallory says: *With a large stock of pointless Texas anecdotes which he disposed of upon the slightest occasion.*
74. Mallory says: *...bound to make an effort.*

On we went from this halting place abreast of Petersburg—on without exactly knowing how affairs stood as to the battle.⁷⁵ That the Southside road—long a disputed prize—that the avenue of escape was uninvested, we felt pretty certain, and in the security of this knowledge many gradually yielded to sleep, and asked the god of dreams to bless them with sweeter visions than reality. Indeed there were several who suspected that the whole thing was a dream, and made comical efforts to arouse from it; comical yet serious efforts. Few could comprehend the calamity which occasioned this flight; few could grasp it in its details or its effects. Among these few was Mr. Macfarland, the Richmond Bank President, a gentleman once pronounced by the Richmond *Examiner* as "the most exquisite soul in Virginia."⁷⁶ He bore the horrors of the flight with fashionable bravery, as became the venerable exquisite he indubitably was. He was among the last to pay tribute to Somnus, and Mr. Benjamin among the first. Had Mr. Macfarland the faintest idea of the sacking and scrimmaging, the distractions and destructions, at that very time going on in the city of his love, he, who had so much personally at stake there, would have been the most miserable of all in that misery-filled train.

How the Conspirators Looked

Among the earliest to evince somnolence, and to give audible evidence of its force, were two distinguished preachers, who saw fit to quit the flocks they had so often aroused. These were Messrs Duncan and Burrows⁷⁷; both eminent each in his way. It was amusing and yet it was melancholy—a passing, practical paradox—to note the efforts of the famous men who held the central portion of the "Presidential car" to avert or ward off sleep. All were long since drowsy, yet few cared to be caught napping. Benjamin whiffed his cigar till midnight, and was soon after midnight whiffed off by Morpheus. Mallory dozed with a good humored smile playing on his features, a smile made pleasanter by the flickering light which fell indirectly on him. Trenholm was by himself, an invalid, attended by his wife,⁷⁸ the only Cabinet-officer who had or needed the gentle care of "sweet woman." Attorney General Davis took an occasional pull at a brandy bottle which was kept by Harrison and others to arrest the progress of discomfort if not of drowsiness.⁷⁹ Reagan chewed his tobacco and ruminated in a lonely way.⁸⁰ The only one of all the throng who seemed, as compared to the rest, a very king in dignity, even to the resistance of sleep, was Jefferson Davis, yet was he a sad and sobered looking one. "My God!

---

75. This chapter is very difficult to interpret. Remember, Stuart has the Davis train leaving Richmond at 10 o'clock. By *the last battle field of the last campaign*. Stuart must mean Appomattox. *Abreast of Petersburg*. What does this mean? Wherever they were, they stopped, and it was close on midnight. If the train had left Richmond at 10:00, as Stuart claims, then, yes, 23 miles would have taken them about two hours to accomplish, but that's 23 miles of track—not 23 miles the way the crow flies. And Powhatan was 22 miles along the track. That could be the place Stuart has in mind when he said they stopped. Yet Powhatan is abreast of Richmond, not Petersburg.

76. Macfarland, Judge Halyburton, Judge W.H. Lyons, Judge John A. Meredith, and Loftin N. Ellett were all elected on April 2 as a Committee of Citizens who, led by Mayor Mayo, would welcome the Union forces into Richmond on the morrow.

77. John Lansing Burrows (1814–1893). In 1854 he became pastor of the First Baptist Church, in Richmond, a position he would hold for twenty years. On December 20, 1883, Burrows gave a lecture in Augusta, Ga., on the Fall of Richmond. In it he said that President Davis was in his pew at St. Paul's Church when a soldier walked down the aisle and handed him a note. That note was from General Lee, stating that the line had been broken through and the city must be evacuated. Burrows described the pouring of the whisky into the gutters, to keep it out of the hands of the Union troops [*Augusta Chronicle*, December 21, 1883].

78. Mallory says: ...*accompanied by a portion of his family*.

79. Mallory switches the ownership of the brandy to Trenholm, at the very same point in his account.

80. Mallory says: ...*sat chewing and ruminating in evident perplexity*.

It was a melancholy thing/For such a man, who would full fain preserve/His soul in calmness, but perforce must feel/For all his fighting brethren. Oh my God!/It weighs upon the heart, that he must think/What uproar and what strife may now be chasing/This way or that thro' the silent night."

"Silent night." Verily, it was silent in all outside our train except the city we had fled from.[81] Grant and Lee were resting on their arms, with bated breath, ready to resume the fierce and bloody and noisome struggle at dawn, and we were hastening as far as prudent and practicable from the vicinity of the conflict. But Richmond, far behind us, was not silent. Alas! the tumult there was of the most furious quality, and a "silent night" can only be thought of in connection with it if we deem it a silent night or the regions of Pluto. Of that, however, I presume you have already heard quite enough. For the rest, I have only to say that our car at last slept as it slipped along. I certainly slept, maugre the snoring sounds around me.[82]

Preparing for an Expected Raid

Toward day we reached the next station north of the Burkesville Junction.[83] A cavalry raid was expected to interfere with our progress, and all the drones were unceremoniously awaked. It was a scene for the pen of a Thackeray or the pencil of a Doyle—no, of a Hogarth; none other could do it complete justice. Some of the Cabinet officers were very ponderous gentlemen. Benjamin, one of these, though of low stature, had aldermanic bulk. He did not propose to ride—perhaps he could not—in case of an attack[84]; all the others were ready to mount at a moment's notice. "Ye won't surely leave me," he cried, as he shivered from the first effect of rousing. The appeal uttered by him, in a Frenchy tone and somewhat piteously, had a ludicrous effect, and yet so full of concern and mortification were all upon whom the effect told, that no one ventured to laugh, though more than one felt so disposed. On rolled the train into the gray clear of morning, Mr. Davis and all around him shaking themselves with a tremor or a yawn, or a nervous stretch. No hostile cavalry was in sight; no trace of it could be found on inquiry. Then again repose resumed such sway as was possible under the jolting circumstances of the case.

Fellow Fugitives

We passed a train of cars between Burkesville and Richmond—a train filled with fugitives—chiefly ladies—from Petersburg, expecting to find shelter in Richmond. Imagine their dismay on discovering that our train contained the emblem of the protection they sought, and bore away from the sanctuary they were flying to, all that made it, in their eyes, sacred and substantial. At first they were loath to credit what was told them; but when the assurance was put so that it was no longer reasonable to doubt, some cried, while most held their heads down in utter consternation.

"All is up," shrieked a young soldier in that train, on his way to rejoin his command under Lee; "all is up," and he could not utter another word.

"No, Sir," cried Colonel Wood, "all is down, unless absentees like you hasten to the front!"

The young soldier jumped from the cars, and with a heart teeming with blended sorrow and rage, dashed to the window from which he was thus reproached, shrieking,

"Damn you, had all the bombproofs like you been as often to the front as myself, you wouldn't be on the back track now."

What might have ensued no one can tell, for the soldier was in for fighting his friends

---

81. Mallory says: *Silence reigned over the fugitives*.
82. Mallory studiously avoids any reference to sleeping.
83. Stuart must mean Jetersville, which is abreast of Petersburg.
84. Mallory says: ... *not that he had any idea of fighting*.

Burkesville

which we reached shortly after daybreak, was the first place at which any of our distinguished men got off the train—it was also the first place we had a clear-eyed view of since the night before.[85] I am particular in mentioning this, for there was something ominous in that first place and first view. It was a wreck—a woeful ruin—one of the saddest havoc sights Mr. Davis had yet seen. Raiders had torn it to pieces, and the pleasant, bustling little junction of other days was only visible in its vestiges. Mr. Davis got out and walked a few minutes on the platform. Owing to his unsightly spectacles, he was not at once recognized by the people who were even that early at the station. Judge Reagan was also out, and, even that early, busy at whittling a stick[86] and chewing his quid. As soon as the few stragglers at the station knew that the train contained their President, they sought him, crowded around him, kindly and respectfully spoke in smothered tones, and looked most sorrowful.

Passing from the junction and its traces of destruction—burned buildings, charred remains of railroad stock, and distorted iron, twisted into most fantastic forms by the action of raiding fire, passing through miles and miles of war devastation, our party felt the claims of hunger, and as dainty provisions were in abundance,[87] we fared sumptuously enough for coerced travellers.

The morning was very fine, and as the level sunshine[88] glimmered with green light over the landscape[89] all looked fruitful, though neglected. The corn, wheat and oat crops seemed most promising, but sic vos non vobis was the sad commentary of the fugitives.[90]

A Break Down

About forty miles beyond the junction we came up with two trains which had stopped. Both contained minor officials and convalescent soldiers, and both had gone off the track. The foremost train had one of its cars broken, five lives being the cost of the accident. Everything appeared burdened with a portent of evil, thus far. The five victims of this accident were laid out near a grove as we came up. They were wounded soldiers from Alabama—gallant men who had dragged their lives most gloriously from the battle field, to have them most ingloriously sacrificed by incompetent or reckless railway officials. There they lay, all their aspirations for the home to which they hoped themselves bound, sunk forever within the confines of one common, coffinless grave preparing for them. There was no need to give sadder zest to the sadness we all felt; but this calamity, upon which we so unexpectedly trod, left us "stunned by death's twice mortal mace."[91]

Mr. Davis got out to inquire into the circumstances of the disaster; all the others got out too; but no one except myself went over to where the "nameless heroes lay," in a most melancholy

---

85. When Stuart says that Burkesville was the first place that any of the passengers got out, what he means is get out and stretch legs. He is not referring to Breckinridge, Lawton, and St. John, who had got out earlier—permanently.
86. Mallory says: *...now whittling a stick down to the little end of nothing without ever reaching a satisfactory point.*
87. Mallory says: *...well filled hampers.*
88. Mallory says: *...bright beams of the morning sun.*
89. Mallory says: *...shone cheerily into the cars.*
90. Mallory says: *...the general gloom was felt.*
91. From Coleridge's *Ode to the Departing Year.*

row—a neighboring farmer keeping the flies from their ghastly faces, and two negroes digging a long hole in which what was left of the luckless soldiers was to be deposited.

Evil Omens and Predestination

"Taking this interruption as an omen, I don't relish it," said Benjamin, when his companions were once more seated.

"Yet it is preferable to the kind we expected," remarked a Major Wheeler immediately behind him, who had a holy terror of Sheridan.

"Not preferable," cried Lubbock, sharply; "some may distrust their personal safety, but we are enough to whip a whole brigade of raiders. Give me an interruption from living Yankees, whom I can slay, but no interruption like this."

"It was to be," whined one of the preachers, emphatically.

Lee Responsible for the Burning of the Bridges at Richmond

Mr. Davis said not a word, sighed, and leaned back to peer vacantly at dim distance. In about twenty minutes we were again moving on slowly and drearily.[92] At the next station, as indeed at all on the road, anxious inquiries were made for news—a message from Lee, or Breckinridge, or anyone. At the next station we had a message, but only in allusion to the burning of the bridges over the James, at Richmond. This gave rise to a tart despatch as to the necessity or policy as such an act as thus to cut Richmond off completely from the South. Mr. Macfarland would have been strong in his denunciation of it had not the responsibility been shown to belong to Lee. That was sufficient for any Virginian, if not for any Southerner.

No Hope or Consolation for Others

Although the trains on this road, as on all the Southern roads, had of late been most irregular, our train was the occasion of much wonder—so long, so thronged, so much better looking than the customary cars, and so unusually early. Tidings of the evacuation had floated down the road, but so vaguely that it was only the presence of the evacuators which really brought the news along. Every face was solemn, doom glanced out of every throng which pressed to exhibit the sympathy for their flying President. He could tell them nothing of all they were eager to know beyond the fact his journey itself told. In vain were crowds clamorous to discover how Lee was whipping Grant; for in spite of evacuation, that was the theory—in vain were eager sisters and mothers piteously asking if this or that brigade was in the fight yet. Words of hope were spoken—glittering consolation freely given; but though the Southern government, body and soul, was in this train, it had no information with which even to feed its own hopes, or gild its own consolation. Nothing to animate it, except a proud, defiant confidence that all would yet be well. I did not hear one word of doubt at any side as to the final issue; ultimate triumph in the teeth of staggering disaster was the creed of all, or nearly all. For himself the flying President said little, and what he did say bore rather the sign of determination to see the struggle through to exhaustion than a braggart confidence in its own success.

Playing the Braggart with Their Tongues

Approaching Danville, the question, "Whither are we going? came up for consideration. To leave Richmond by the safest route, and get clear of Grant, was the only object in view at starting. Now that Richmond was abandoned to Grant, and the escaped Government free from immediate danger, its destination was not easily determined. Danville was supposed to be

---

92. Mallory does not mention this South Boston incident at all.

too small for a temporary capital, and the good points of all other eligible cities were discussed generally and warmly. At length Mr. Davis put a stop to the matter by saying that he would not leave Virginia until Lee was whipped out of it.

"Then you can make up your mind to a long residence," said Mr. Bruce, of Kentucky, confidently.[93]

"A day or two more will decide that," was the wary remark of Mr. Benjamin.

"And if adversely," said the Attorney General, "Charlotte is our point." He had been advocating Charlotte from the first, and very naturally, as it was to him a home.[94]

Once it was determined that Danville should bear the burdensome honor of the temporary capital, it became a serious question with most of us how we were to get lodged there. The fortunes of war—the fate of Lee's army, or of Grant's—were things which grew little for the few minutes that this selfish subject occupied our thoughts. Hastening to a town of very scant dimensions, with the prospect of having its population alarmingly increased by a sudden influx of officials and refugees,[95] it was not easy to feel assured that one in ten of all could obtain even ordinary shelter. Those who had friends and acquaintances and those in high places were pretty certain of homes; but those who had none of these were naturally afraid of Danville. While we were contemplating the subject in no hopeful humor, an assurance was brought that the city was alive to the occasion, and provision would be made for the whole "Presidential party" at least. This was a vast relief to most of us. Nearly five hundred persons, almost all more or less distinguished, and some two or three hundred soldiers were on our train. Behind us, on the road, were trains bringing about five or six thousand more fugitives—all for Danville. Here there was a ready made population for a goodly sized town to come in a few hours into what was only a goodly sized town. But our party was made sure of shelter, and gave itself little concern for the rest. Am I ashamed, for myself and the others, to confess this? Why should I "Strive to expel strong nature? 'Tis in vain—/With double force she will return again."

Taking Care of Number One

While in doubt as to what might become of ourselves we only thought of ourselves. Once pretty certain of being provided for, we could afford to think of others,[96] and we gave at least our pity to those not likely to be so fortunate as telegraphic promise induced us to imagine ourselves. Sympathy, compassion and all that sort of thing are exceedingly cheap. We had a superabundance of the article the instant our condition was favorably fixed. We had even more. We had practical suggestions. Why not camp all others out? Provisions—commissary provisions were abundant—let all others be fed on soldiers' fare. We, we—emphatically we—would fare as sumptuously as Danville's hospitality allowed. Then again, let half the expected officials go on to Charlotte, N.C., or some other city. There was no reason why these unimportant entities should cumber us. And, verily, it was so decided before we reached Danville. The minor officials of the Treasury and Post Office Departments—the most numerous—were not to remain in Danville. A representation of each would answer every purpose—say, the head of the department and his principal subordinates. The War and Navy Departments were

---

93. Stuart has Bruce in the president's car here. And he may well have been. If he was, then he probably changed cars at Clover.

94. At first sight it would seem that Stuart is wrong about Charlotte. Attorney General Davis was from Wilmington. But his wife was dead, his Wilmington home had been seized by the Federals, and his children were staying with friends in Charlotte. Charlotte may not have been his home, but as Stuart says, it was "a home." After Danville, after Greensboro, when the fleeing government arrived at Charlotte, this is where the attorney general, in fact, stayed.

95. Mallory says: *Danville had received from Richmond a large addition to her population.*

96. Mallory says: *But apart from considerations of personal peril, which were generally disregarded.*

to remain intact at Danville. As the State Department had nobody but Mr. Benjamin, and his assistant, Mr. Washington, there was no trouble about that. As the Navy Department had only Mr. Mallory and three others, there was no trouble about that. As the Department of Justice had only Mr. George Davis himself, there was no trouble about that. The War Department had General Cooper and a host of clerks; that was the only trouble left. By sending all the Quartermaster's and Commissary General's clerks on to Charlotte, the difficulty was brought to a practicable bearing. This settled, the new condition of the Government was fixed, and Danville was, for the time being, to be its focus.

Looking to the Rear Again

Then again, we began to ponder on what was taking place in our rear. Whether Lee was winning or losing. Whether Richmond was sacked or yet surrendered. Whether the Confederacy was dying in spasms or recovering in glory. And thus speculating, we drew in sight of Danville, or rather of the covered bridge leading to the town. We had already seen the Dan at the very point where Nat Green made his successful passage when pursued by Lord Rawdon in the last year of the Revolution—near the spot where the Virginia militia made a most triumphant resistance to an assault upon them about a year ago. The river looks as yellow as the Savannah, and nothing more tawny than that is to be found out of China.

The destroying hand of the raider was to be found everywhere up to the bridge. There, fortunately for us, its work of destruction ceased, and we cautiously steamed over the Dan into Danville. The first thing which attracted my attention was the evidence of mechanical taste and industry apparent in the railroad shops. A superb new carriage, designed for the Piedmont Railroad, was standing out in bold relief from a vast quantity of rubbish. The buildings around were most creditable, and everything seemed to denote the power of the South to be its own manufacturer as well as factor.

At Danville

At the depot in Danville, a crowd, but not a great one, awaited us.[97] All was silence and sadness.[98] Mr. Davis divested himself of spurs, spectacles, and other similar appurtenances. So did all those who with him had prepared themselves for an attack and a different sort of flight across the country. He walked out to the platform, accompanied by Colonels Johnston, Lubbock and Ives. After him went his Cabinet, followed by Generals Cooper, Terry and Stuart. Colonel Harrison, Mr. Davis's private secretary, remained to see to the presidential baggage. On the platform were gentlemen representing the city of Danville, to offer its hospitalities[99] to the capitalless President and his fleeing followers. Major Sunderland, one of the most eminent citizens of Danville, was present to invite Mr. Davis and Mr. Mallory to the most palatial residence in the place.[100] The Mayor (Walker) was indefatigable in his attentions to all others.[101] He was chief of a committee having charge of the hospitalities, and his committee did all that men could do to uphold old Virginia's claim to genial generosity.[102] Every private house in the

---

97. Mallory says: *A large number of the people of Danville were assembled at the depot as the train entered it.*

98. Mallory says: *There was none of the old, wild, Southern enthusiasm, & there was that in the cheers which told almost as much of sorrow as of joy.*

99. Mallory says: *...with that spirit of hospitality.*

100. Mallory says: *The President, with the Secretaries of the Treasury & Navy found quarters prepared for them at the house of Col. Southerlin.*

101. Mallory says: *Secretary Benjamin, the Atty. General, Postmaster General, Adjutant General and others, were in like manner cared for.*

102. Mallory says: *...hospitality, as universal & cheering in Virginia as the dews of Heaven.*

city was thrown open to all in our train[103]; not a being along with us was unprovided with a home ten minutes after the arrival of the train.[104] The Mayor himself took three distinguished gentlemen who, to use their own words, 'fared as they never did since the war began.' I myself was invited to the home of a veritable Southern Yankee—a Massachusetts Virginian, who was lavish of kindness, he and his.

Touching that, let me tell you this Virginiaized Yankee was de tout mien coeur for the South; and in truth, so I found them all; heartily, absolutely rebels. That they were so at all, in the face of a bitter local hatred to the very idea of their nativity was a puzzle to me, a foreigner de toto; yet, I but give my experience when I assure you I found them in all, or nearly all cases, more Southern than the Southerners.

Virginia Hospitality

The better to comprehend the quality and the spirit of the good old Virginia hospitality[105] extended to the Richmond fugitives in Danville, I shall just relate an incident or two immediately following our arrival. While standing with General Terry opposite the Tunstal [sic] Hotel—the Astor House of Danville—three gentlemen approached us, knowing us to be strangers.

"Are you provided with homes?," asked one of them, in a most courteous manner.

I replied that we were, but that some gentlemen who had arrived since we came, and who were near at hand, needed the kindness proffered to ourselves. Instantly, they met these gentlemen and assigned them homes at most respectable families, where they, or such as they, were expected.[106]

Another Instance

Walking quietly along a by-street, we passed a noble looking house. Two ladies and a gentleman—all advanced in years—were standing on the balcony. Seeing us sauntering down that unfrequented way, and being impressed with the peculiarity of the occasion, they accosted us thus:

"Do you require a home, gentlemen?" We made our obeisance, and answering, thanked them.

"Then," said the elder of the ladies, "be good enough to send us two or three. No one has come here yet, and we are ready to make at least three comfortable."

There was hospitality for you—genial, genuine, grand. Nothing like the Virginian hospitality of Danville has come within my observation in any other American state. It was pure and catholic and unstinted.

No Word from Lee

But, aside from this, what a sad plight we were in! Not a word of encouragement from Lee—not a word, at all, in fact. Rumors there were in great abundance—rumors that Lee had far the best of it[107]—now that he was relieved of the Richmond embarrassment—rumors that Grant had sacrificed so many lives that he could not continue the contest without yielding up

---

103. Mallory says: ...*they opened their houses.*
104. Mallory says: ...*& provided as far as practicable for the accommodation of the members of the Government.*
105. Mallory says: ...*with that spirit of hospitality, as universal & cheering in Virginia as the dews of Heaven.*
106. Mallory says: ...*they opened their houses & provided as far as practicable for the accommodation of the members of the Government.*
107. Mallory says: ...*not one of which, however, involved Lee's defeat.*

his prestige.[108] These, however, were only rumors. Not a direct word was yet had from Lee, and it was only the unswerving confidence which all fixed on the success of the cause that could possibly sustain them in this suspense. Every fresh train from Richmond—and trains continued to come all night filled with fugitives and archives—was besieged by crowds of citizens and sojourners. The news, the least particle of news, was asked for with the intensest eagerness. We who had arrived in the afternoon passed the neighborhood where the news was making or to be made, while its manufacture was suspended. Those who came later were supposed to have had opportunities greater than ours—the latest, the exact. Every fresh-come batch of "reliable gentlemen"[109] felt the importance of the position to which impatient news-cravers elevated them.

And they had news—more in most cases than could be well digested. Lee was giving Grant a fearful castigation[110]; so enfeebled were the Yankees that, although Richmond was open to them, they did not enter it—Richmond was in ashes—Richmond was filled with Nigger soldiers—Richmond was not disturbed—Richmond has ceased to be—Grant was gathering his army up to fly away[111]—it was not possible for him to hold out against Lee's braves another day. To each item of this character which your "reliable gentlemen" delivered to gaping listeners, they invariably added an averment which clinched its truth. And all that was so far known of the actual condition of things—known even to Mr. Davis—consisted of wild and contradictory stories like those I have summed up. It was on that sort of stuff we slept our first night at Danville.

Getting Brave Again in Words

Next morning, the street and depot news was slightly more definite. Mr. Davis was up very early, and out on the portico of his Danville residence, anxiously awaiting the arrival of a despatch or a courier.[112] None, however, came, and both Lee and Breckinridge were pronounced remiss. He issued a proclamation to reassure the public and to persuade them that it was for the special accommodation of Lee's new tactics—field tactics as opposed to entrenched positions—that Richmond was abandoned. The proclamation was very spirited, and breathed defiance to the last.

The News Gatherers

In the absence of authentic news the government dignitaries had to content themselves with such gossip as was brought by the latest arrivals. This was fragmentary as such as scared fugitives were likely to process—in all cases distorted and exaggerated, but in no case unfavorable.[113] Danville was one moving mass of news tellers and news seekers—citizens and strangers huddled together[114] at every porch or shady nook—discussing probabilities and possibilities with feverish earnestness. Occasionally a self-constituted courier would create a sensation by some story of a "despatch to the President," which he had just delivered. Its contents would be mysteriously hinted at, and gradually a consistent piece of information—consistent at least in form—would result. Then Mr. Davis would be beset for "further particulars," and the imposition exposed.

---

108. Mallory says: ...*strange & startling rumors of military events.*
109. Mallory says: ...*very reliable gentlemen just in.*
110. Mallory says: *Lee had gained a glorious victory, held his army well in hand, and was steadily pursuing Grant.*
111. Mallory says: *Lee ... was steadily pursuing Grant.*
112. Mallory says: *All confidently looked for news from, or of, Lee.*
113. Mallory says: ...*fugitives were constantly arriving with strange & startling rumours of military events, not one of which, however, involved Lee's defeat.*
114. Mallory says: ...*herding together.*

Establishing a Capital

Having nothing else to do, and confident that "no news was good news,"[115] Mr. Davis resolved on establishing his capital.[116] An executive office was rented, and the President's aids set to work opening and referring letters. General Cooper started a War Department, and Mr. Mallory an office for the Navy. Judge Reagan seized the Masonic Hall for a post-office department, and had chiefs of bureaus to go on with public business. Captain Lee—the General's brother, went through the usual red tapeism of an order and detail office for the navy, and found himself soon as busy as ever he was in Richmond. Attorney-General Davis and Mr. Benjamin rested—law and foreign affairs were in abeyance.[117]

The New Rebel Treasury Operations

Mr. Trenholm opened the Treasury at one of the banks and delighted all Danville, resident and fugitive, by offering Mexican silver for Confederate notes—seventy dollars for one! That struck me as a significant commentary—the government in the market to depreciate its own currency! About $40,000 in silver was thus disposed of in the course of two days. This course of the Treasury Secretary, though most acceptable as accommodation, had the effect of neutralizing the good impressions produced by the President's proclamation.

Morning, noon and evening of the 4th of April, no news, and every sign of building, or arranging, rather, a new capital. Eligible structures were impressed for some sort of circumlocution office. Admiral Semmes put all his navy—officers and men—into one grand brigade for the defence of the new Richmond. He was dubbed a brigadier general as well as admiral, and assigned to the batteries. Much fuss and no little fustian was the immediate consequence. Guns were mounted, sighted and tested on all the knolls around the city. Stoneman was expected. Two of his men, escorted by five mounted Confederates were passed in triumph through the city. Semmes would be ready in a day to give Stoneman a stunning reception. Every fugitive was to be put in service if he was capable of carrying a gun. At least ten thousand muskets and a goodly artillery force were thus to hold the new capital against all comers. Things looked brisk and bright, only not a word yet from Lee or Breckinridge.

John Mitchel Arrives

The evening of the 4th of April grew stormy, and the latest arrivals came in drenched with rain. Among them was John Mitchel.[118] I was very glad to buttonhole Mitchel. If any latest arrival was to have news, surely he was the man, yet he knew very little beyond the fact that a fierce and sanguinary contest was raging—that General Hill was killed and Lee was changing his base, and that an immense conflagration had ravaged Richmond. One incident in his journey is worth repeating as an illustration of the frightful uncertainty surrounding all. When at a wayside station, almost forty miles from Danville, he got out of the train—it was the last that left Richmond—and was instantly accosted by a young lady who knew him.

"Oh, Mr. Mitchel, how did you leave them at home?"

---

115. Mallory says: ..."*no news is good news*," and uses quotation marks.
116. Mallory says: ...*thus were passed five days*.
117. Mallory says: *Beyond a spasmodic effort of Genl. Gorgas to open his irrepressible Ordnance Bureau, there was no attempt to organize Departments.*
118. Mitchel had been an editor of the *Richmond Examiner*. As William Dillon says, in his *Life of John Mitchel* (1888): *Mitchel determined to go to Danville with the government. He wished to "keep within the Confederate lines so long as they had any lines at all."* Early in May, Mitchel returned to Richmond, and later that month headed for New York, where he would become editor of C.E.L. Stuart's old newspaper, the New York *Daily News*. It was not long before his inflammatory articles had him arrested and thrown into Fort Monroe. He died in 1875.

Mitchel is very near sighted, and for a moment did not know his questioner, with whom and whose family he was intimate. The instant he recognized her he recoiled. She noticed the movement, and, taking it as a boding of evil, clung to him with questions. The lady was Miss Pegram, sister of the young general who was killed only a few weeks before, and a few days after his marriage. She had left Richmond prior to the evacuation, and was staying in the neighborhood where she then met John Mitchel.

"Do tell me what is the matter with them!," she implored.

"Nothing. I left them all well at home—vey well, indeed."

"And Willie. What of him? His command, they tell me, has been hotly engaged."

"I fear he is badly wounded, Miss Pegram."

"Badly wounded! Tell me all, Mr. Mitchel; oh, tell me all, your look is fearful."

Mitchel hesitated. He had seen her poor brother's corpse a few hours before—the third victim which that one family had offered on the altar of the struggle. But how could he tell her that the young and gallant colonel—the brave brother in whom all her sister's love was centred—tell her, as a climax to her many sufferings, that he indeed was slain. Yet he told it; for his looks spoke more than words, and the afflicted girl read the awful truth in his hesitation. She fainted, and was borne away just as he had to reenter the train.

MACFARLAND DETERMINES TO GO BACK TO RICHMOND

The 5th of April came, and yet no news. Rumors crept out with wonderful fecundity, and all rather of the pleasant order—all except what related to Richmond. No rumorist put the horrors of the riot and fire in Richmond in other than the most appalling colors. The effect was that all the natives of Richmond who were with us, or others whose families were there, felt the keenest alarm. Even divesting rumor of its grossness, of its most outlandish phases, sufficient horror remained to terrify the least timid. Poor Mr. Macfarland, the exquisite old banker, was in perpetual agony. Sitting by one of the notched pillars of the Tunstall House, watching the rain and pondering on probabilities, he looked the most forlorn specimen of human greatness I have yet observed. He may not like my pity, but he had it to the fullest extent, and it followed him when he fled back to Richmond next day, unable longer to endure the suspense, and ready to risk his chance with Grant.[119]

OMINOUS SILENCE

The 6th, 7th and 8th of April came and went,[120] yet not a word from Lee.[121] Most ominous silence! In vain rumorists got up pleasing fictions; to no purpose were sweeping theories devised; apprehension laid hold of every one, and some misfortune was expected. Mr. Davis evinced uneasiness, but no alarm. He was exemplary in his patience. It was that sort of patience which may be called carnage in repose. Scipio and Tell were noble fellows, but Regulus and Arnold Van Wincklebried[122] were of a grander mould. The placid endurance of the latter, their

---

119. Another refugee was James D. Halyburton (1803–1879), who, despite being one of the Committee of Citizens elected to welcome the conquering Union forces into Richmond the following morning, had decided to take the train to Danville, where he and Congressman Bruce boarded at the house of Wicher Kean. Like Macfarland, Halyburton left Danville to return to Richmond, but five days later, following the news of Lee's surrender. Judge Halyburton had sworn Jefferson Davis in at the President's second inauguration in 1862.

120. Mallory says: *...thus were passed five days.*

121. Mallory says: *...the fourth, and the succeeding four days passed without bringing a word from Lee or Breckinridge.*

122. Stuart means Winkelried, the 14th-century Swiss hero.

self control, their martyrdom of mind, surpassed, in very majesty, the dash and enthusiasm of the others.[123]

An Encouraging Story

Late on Saturday evening, the 8th, a handsome story crept out and bloomed all over the city. A despatch was said to be received—indeed, Captain Lee, the General's brother, told me it was received—and it read thus: "We have squarely beaten the Yanks in two days' fight. Lee is all right, and his army well in hand. Breckinridge."

This sent a thrill through the city, and when Sunday came, with fine, clear weather, the capital looked happy, halcyon. As such a delightful fiction had a Sunday to bask in—a day on which only persons connected with him troubled Mr. Davis—it flourished without exposure. It was a warm, genial Sunday, and for the first time since my arrival, I thought of viewing the city as a city.

Danville

is what may be termed a very pretty town, and if the war had not baulked its efforts would by this time have been a very thriving one.[124] The opportunities for mills of all descriptions and machinery which can be worked by water are as great as in Richmond. Some cloth and other factories stood on the river's edge, finished and unfinished in spectral silence. Decay had set in before the place was ripe. The city is hilly and neatly laid out, many of its mansions being of a most imposing character.[125] Taking it all in all, I would style it a ragged and abridged edition of Richmond, with villa advantages peculiar to itself.

Danville Gladdened at Its Brightening Prospects

Mr. Davis was, of course, at the Episcopal Church on that first Sunday in his new capital, and heard a most encouraging discourse. Benjamin had no synagogue, and Mallory no Catholic chapel, so they alone, of all the Cabinet, could not pray according to public formula. Governor Smith and other State notabilities arrived during the day, and enjoyed the seductive rumor of the previous evening. Arrangements were advanced for completing the official accommodation, and that night Danville had made up its mind to be the capital. Lee was falling back at his leisure to have his lines on the Staunton, and the condition of the Confederacy was serene and steady. There was only one regret—the specie had been sent off to Charlotte in the charge of the midshipmen, who were armed as soldiers. Danville was desirous of being burdened with it, and could see no reason, in the light of things as they now looked, for despatching it to any other place. Stoneman was much more likely to get it where it was going than in the security of confident Danville. But it would be brought back, and Danville was very sanguine of its own safety and its own claims.

Storm Gathering

Everything looked prosperous on Monday morning, the 10th—everything but the weather, and that was lowering. About the usual breakfast time, however, people's faces wore a sombre

---

123. Here, Mallory's plagiarism is outrageous. While describing Benjamin, he insinuates William Tell into his account. Not only that, Tell is one of a group of four heroes mentioned, just as in Stuart, although Mallory has had the decency to choose three new names to fill out the quartet. He even uses the word "enthusiast" in the context.

124. Mallory will rework this later, when he says that Greensboro had been a flourishing town.

125. Mallory, when describing Greensboro, says that there were many commodious and well-furnished residences.

appearance. The brilliant news bubble which gaily floated all day before was burst, and no news was still the answer to all inquiries about Lee. The effect was worse than if the fiction had not been invented. Toward mid-day the anxious crowds in the vicinity of the hotel, or loitering around the improvised department offices, or lounging at the railroad depot, began to be more than lugubrious. The railroad track at Burkesville was at last known to be torn up; the telegraph wires in that locality were known to be cut; the federal army was known to be between us and Lee. Alas for the hopes of Danville, and the defensive efforts of Brigadier-General and Admiral Semmes! Information of all this was too positive and too perplexing. Early in the afternoon[126] it took a shape which scattered to the winds the fond speculations of Sunday. On every countenance you read panic. News, aye, positive, distinct, and direct news had at last arrived from Lee.

The Storm Bursts

But, heavens! what news it was. The consternation in Richmond at the evacuation was as nothing when compared with the dismay depicted on every face in Danville as soon as that news leaked out. Lee had been whipped. Well, he can recover from the blow.[127] But Lee had surrendered. Impossible! What, Lee Surrender![128] Robert E. Lee do any such thing! The very thought seemed absurd.[129] Yet the fact was so; and slowly and reluctantly it had to be credited. Gloom the densest was abroad, and in harmony with its horrors the sky poured out its torrents,[130] making Danville the most miserable and muddy place I ever tried to drag my feet through.[131]

Evacuating Danville

Orders were given for the evacuation of Danville at five o'clock[132] on the evening of Sunday, the 10th of April.[133] The place was filled with naval and other stores, and these had been mostly niggardly husbanded. Now they were to be destroyed or wasted. Mr. Davis was at the depot by half-past five o'clock. Mr. Trenholm, who was very ill, was carried there in an ambulance. Mr. Mallory rode about the city, issuing orders, and doing hard work, to secure the transportation of all that was most valuable belonging to the navy. At the depot, amid a crush little inferior to that in Richmond eight days before, Judge Reagan sat moodily on a trunk. Near him was Mr. Benjamin, couched on some soft baggage, and the Attorney-General seated on a valise.[134] Confusion was supreme,[135] and it was half an hour before there was order enough to enable the President's train to receive its evacuating freight. At length, the turmoil was over, and Mr. Davis, accompanied by the same party as when leaving Richmond (with the exception of Colonel Ives, who remained in Danville), started off[136] for Greensboro, in North Carolina.[137]

---

126. Mallory says: *...in the afternoon of the 9 of April.* He is a day early.
127. Mallory says: *The President received the unexpected blow.*
128. Mallory says: *Lee's surrender.*
129. Mallory says: *It fell upon the ears of all like a fire bell in the night.*
130. Mallory says: *...much rain had fallen.*
131. Mallory says: *...mud knee-deep.*
132. Mallory says: *...eight o'clock.*
133. This error on Stuart's part (Sunday was the 9th of April, not the 10th) led to Mallory's error two segments earlier.
134. Mallory says: *At ten o'clock Cabinet officers & other chiefs of the Government, each seated upon, or jealously guarding his baggage.*
135. Mallory says: *...a confusion such as it was never before the fortune of old Danville to witness.*
136. Mallory says: *...moved off.*
137. Mallory says: *Greensboro, N.C.*

The news, which was long looked for and so unwelcome when it came stunned all. Its effect on most of the old citizens of Richmond was to deter them from going further, and thus the second stage of the evacuation had fewer to follow the fortunes of Davis than had the first. The silence in the immediate vicinity of Mr. Davis was dolesome. No one seemed to have an opinion of heart to give it utterance.[138] From Richmond to Danville all were more or less loquacious, but from Danville to Greensboro the "dismals" ruled so despotically that the very men whose natures appeared to "talk" were dumb.[139]

A Narrow Escape

A short distance on the road an accident occurred to our engine, and we had to wait for a fresh one. Had the delay been much longer, our train would have run a close chance of capture.[140] Scarcely had we passed a point of the road within a few miles of Greensboro when a raiding party tore up the track and assailed a train which we only met ten minutes before.[141] But we got to Greensboro in safety.

Our progress was the progress of ill news speeding apace.[142] As tidings of the evacuation of Richmond had not preceded but accompanied us, so intelligence of Lee's surrender was born along by our presence. No one in Greensboro even suspected it. We arrived early in the day. Both Johnston and Beauregard—the latter first, he being in command there—were soon with Mr. Davis. This interview was short and evidently only a preparatory one.[143]

The Inhospitality of Greensboro

In Greensboro, as in Danville, the naval store was well stocked.[144] Fortunately it was, for in Greensboro, as not in Danville, its people were inhospitable. The home of the flying President was a railroad car. Not a soul offered the slightest courtesy.[145] Mr. Trenholm, alone, being very ill, was tendered the shelter of a house, and he was taken to Governor Morehead's.[146] All the others, Cabinet and staff, roomed and mealed in the cars.[147]

It rained furiously in Greensboro, and a more pitiable sight you cannot well imagine as that presented by our distinguished party[148] resisting the drainage of leaky cars.[149] Most fortunately for me, I found a friend "uptown," and got a room of a most luxurious quality. Willingly would I have surrendered it to Mr. Davis if there had been propriety in the doing so, or to any of his Cabinet, who were all unaccustomed to "rough it," but they had resolved to let Greensboro's hospitality as severely alone as it threatened to leave them. In the case of Mr. Davis, he was persuaded to adopt a compromise—to sleep at a little house in which the wife and family

---

138. Mallory says: *For some moments, a silence, more eloquent of great disaster than words could have been, prevailed.*
139. Mallory says: *...a little silent group by themselves.*
140. Mallory says: *...it was a lucky escape.*
141. Mallory says: *...upon reaching Greensboro it was found that a body of Federal Cavalry had cut the road at a point which the train had passed but five minutes before.*
142. Mallory says: *...our progress was consequently very slow.*
143. Mallory says: *On the 11 of April, Generals Johnston & Beauregard reached Greensboro for a conference upon the military situation.*
144. Mallory says: *...the Navy store supplied bread & bacon.*
145. Mallory says: *...their doors were closed ... against the members of a retreating government.*
146. Mallory says: *Mr Trenholm, who was very ill, and who found quarters at the large and elegant mansion of Gov. Morehead, was the only exception.*
147. Mallory says: *...here they ate, slept and lived during their stay.*
148. Mallory says: *...distinguished hosts.*
149. Mallory says: *...dilapidated, leaky passenger car.*

of Colonel Taylor Wood had for some weeks been staying,[150] and to spend the rest of his time with his companions in the cars.

THE CONFEDERACY COOPED UP IN A CAR

It would have been ludicrous if it had been less provocative of painful reflections, to think of the whole rebel government cooped in these miserable cars. And there and thus for five days, Jefferson Davis and his Cabinet and staff, with other high officials,[151] lived.[152] Colonel Lubbock acted as sort of foraging officer,[153] and General Stuart as caterer, and fare rather better than camp fare was the result of their efforts. It was not so unpleasant,[154] this feasting in the cars—eating at no set hours, but just as we felt hungry. There was something novel about it, and for one, I think Mr. Benjamin[155] enjoyed it greatly.[156] The further he got South, the more buoyant became his spirits. Attorney General Davis[157] thought it fine,[158] but Judge Reagan, the most robust of all, relished it least.[159] He impressed me with a conviction that the crisis was weighing more heavily on his spirits than on any of his peers.

GENERAL BRECKINRIDGE

joined us at Greensboro, and brought all the details of Lee's surrender. Soon after he arrived, he and Mr. Davis and Generals Johnston and Beauregard had a prolonged consultation.

AN HISTORIC SPOT

It was held on the slope of a little hill, just off the railway track. The little hill was itself historic. It was there that Nat Greene, of Revolutionary fame, held his council of war the night before the battle of Guildford [sic] Court House. It was there that on the day after Greene's death, Lord Rawdon had his headquarters. It was near to there that the churlish Quaker refused Greene the hospitality of his house, saying, "Get thee hence, wicked man; I have nought to do with such as thee." It was there that Greensboro first laid its claim to the cold unconcern which marked its conduct toward the tottering fortunes of the Confederate chiefs. It was there these chiefs were now grouped—Davis, Breckinridge, Beauregard and Johnston forming one picture; Benjamin, Mallory, Reagan and Geo. Davis another. Here and there, in clusters of fives and sixes, were other generals and other high functionaries. Altogether that little hill presented a series of gatherings which an artist would have had much difficulty in arranging better for purposes of scientific effect.

JOHNSTON REFUSES TO OBEY DAVIS' ORDERS TO FIGHT

Neither Johnston nor Beauregard betrayed a trace of despondency. It was obvious, however, that they regarded the struggle as over.[160] Mr. Davis felt much concern, and rather showed

---

150. Mallory says: *Col. Wood ... provided him with a bed at the limited & temporary quarters of his family.*
151. Mallory says: *...the staff and Cabinet, with other prominent gentlemen.*
152. Mallory says: *...the times were sadly out of joint, just then, and so was the Confederate Government.*
153. Mallory says: *...active foraging of Paymaster Semple & others of the party.*
154. Mallory says: *...a very agreeable resort.*
155. Mallory says: *...there was the clever Secretary of State.*
156. Mallory says: *...busily dividing his attention between a bucket of stewed dried apples, & a haversack of hard boiled eggs.*
157. Mallory says: *...here was the astute Minister of Justice.*
158. Mallory says: *...his face bearing unmistakable evidence of the condition of the bacon.*
159. Mallory says: *...here was a Postmaster General, sternly & energetically running his Bowie knife through a ham, as if it were the chief business of life.*
160. Mallory says: *...it was evident, notwithstanding their effort to present a military front, that they regarded the cause as irretrievably lost.*

it. He distrusted Johnston, but relied on Breckinridge to foil him in an untimely move. Johnston was instructed to fight. He did not approve the order, and disputed not only the wisdom, but its power over his action. He left the hill at last, undetermined as to his course, reserving to himself a right of decision in accordance with the development of events. Mr. Davis saw him no more. He had gone to his army headquarters near Hillsboro. Beauregard, whose headquarters were a railway car, not far from our train, we often saw afterward.

The Confederacy Despaired Of

Although the collapse of the Confederacy was evident to every one since the surrender of Lee's army, the completeness of that sudden and outstanding collapse was not thoroughly manifest until after this interview on the little hill beside the railroad at Greensboro. The indecision and vacillation of the "constitutional advisers" of Jefferson Davis were distressing. Neither he nor they seemed to know what next should be attempted, or what they should do even with themselves. They were utterly powerless, and evinced an absolute incapacity to deal with the dangers which encircled them as individuals.

The first startling evidence of the reported demoralization of the Southern army which I witnessed was during this dreary stay at Greensboro.[161] The cars—homes for thousands of fugitives—were systematically pillaged by soldiers. Cavalrymen broke into public and private stores,[162] and the military authorities were unable to give redress or protection.[163] It was anarchy all around us. The commissary warehouses were demolished and all descriptions of goods hauled openly through the streets, paraded as plunder. One day, a spasmodic attempt was made to arrest this, and three or four of Wheelers' rather notorious cavalry were shot by an infantry guard sent to curb their depredations.[164] After that there was more order and fewer outrages.

Evacuating Greensboro

I, for one, was rejoiced, for a more lawless place than that pretty Quakerish town was then I never visited. Among the more civilized incidents of our sojourn, I should mention a speech by Governor Smith of Virginia. He had a large audience in front of the Court House near the Brittan Hotel, but, spoke he ever so fervently and ever so hopefully, not a spark of enthusiasm could be evoked. The masses—citizens and soldiers—were indifferent.

"A Poor, Weak and Dispirited Old Man"

As the railroad was cut at Jamestown, twelve miles from Greensboro, the very morning of our arrival at the latter place, it was decided that the "Presidential party" must take to horses and wagons.[165] Accordingly, a train was provided and the hour and order of departure agreed on, Major Maynard having charge of arrangements. The horses and wagons were to have been

---

161. Mallory says: *Those scenes of wild disorder which marked the return of disbanded Confederate soldiers ... commenced at Danville on the night the Presidential party left there, and next appeared at Greensboro, during his stay there.*

162. Mallory, talking of Capt. Cheesman, the quartermaster, says that his stores were *charged, taken possession of & the raides* [sic] *helped themselves.*

163. Mallory says: *...the futility of all further effort in behalf of the Confederacy.*

164. Mallory says: *...attempt made by some sixty of Cavalry on the morning of the 12 of June* [sic]*, upon a Commissary's store, a faithful guard was found which fired upon the raides* [sic] *who fled, leaving three of their number wounded.*

165. This is an absolutely key piece of information, without which we would be left wondering why the party took to the byways on horseback rather than continuing on by train. Mallory does not tell us this in his account. If his account had been an honest one—i.e., if he had written it himself rather than plagiarizing Stuart—he would have.

at the cars by three o'clock on the morning of Easter Saturday. The hour arrived. It was pouring rain. No horses—no wagons. Four, five, six, aye ten o'clock, and yet none. There was, of course, some mistake—a common thing in the last days of the fallen Confederacy, a mistake. The mistake was discovered, rather an amusing one, if those to whom it is told had no share in the annoyances it entailed. The horses and wagons started punctually at the hour they were ordered, and in the direction of their instructions but they neglected the somewhat important duty of calling for their passengers. There we were then, the whole Confederate government and its followers, left most miserably in the lurch. Colonel Preston Johnston was despatched after the horses and wagons, and succeed in overtaking them near Jamestown, where he brought them to a halt. Now the condition of the weather was such as rendered the roads almost impassable. To have this wagon train retrace its course was out of the question. It became a case in which Mahomet must go to the mountain, since the mountain would not come to him. But how? Easily, of course, inasmuch as Greensboro was alive with mules and chock full of ambulances. Not so easily after all, for the whole authority of his Presidential character was insufficient after four hours' effort, to procure Jefferson Davis, for himself and party, more than three ambulances. Tell it not in Gath. I am ashamed to tell it anywhere, and do not yet comprehend the mystery which underlaid that fact. Some threw the blame on Johnston, to whose army all these mules, horses and wagons belonged; but, be the blame where it may, it was as much as could be done by the head of the Confederate government to procure means of transporting the few—very few—who were now of his party. I say very few, for, as at Danville, the fugitives grew less, so at Greensboro they grew also less, and the thousands were reduced to half a dozen.

Thanks to the indefatigable efforts of Mr. Mallory, the three ambulances I mentioned were obtained. General Cooper, seeing the cramped accommodation, grew vehemently angry, and declared he would not go farther. Mr. Mallory, who was on horseback, soon succeeded in soothing the enraged soldier, and he found himself at last seated by Mr. Benjamin in a wretched ambulance. Reagan, Mallory and Breckinridge, with the members of his staff, etc., accompanied Mr. Davis on horseback.[166]

The Agreement with Sherman

I said it was raining, pouring.[167] A bleaker evening's ride, under circumstances, too, sadly in keeping with the drenching character of the weather and the miry quality of the roads, no equestrian party ever took. We camped in a wood near Jamestown, and had a soaking soldier's night of it. Next morning, for potent reasons, Breckinridge, accompanied by Reagan, returned to Greensboro.[168] What Johnston might choose to agree on in his convention with Sherman was a matter which needed looking into. The terms first submitted were Breckinridge's. These were rejected. They were the only terms Johnston was authorized to make, so far as Mr. Davis could give him authority. The compromise terms afterwards allowed by Breckinridge were not approved[169] at Washington, and, after waiting two days[170] in the neighborhood of the negotiations, Breckinridge consented to permit General Johnston to do the best he could. As I was

---

166. Mallory says: *...in leaving Greensboro, Mr. Reagan, Mr. Breckenridge and Mr. Mallory rode with Mr Davis & his three aides on horseback, and Mr Trenholm, Mr. Geo. Davis, and Mr. Benjamin, comprising the six members of the Cabinet, were in ambulances, with Genl Cooper & other officers.*
167. Mallory says: *...the roads were bad from recent rains.*
168. Mallory says: *Breckenridge (who had, with Mr. Reagan, returned to Greensboro, to Johnston's camp).* Mallory was so hard pressed to plagiarize Stuart at this point, that this miserable construction was the best he could do.
169. Mallory says: *...were disapproved.*
170. Mallory says: *...three days.*

with General Breckinridge during this time, and until he rejoined Mr. Davis at Charlotte, I cannot tell you what occurred in the "Presidential trip" to Charlotte from Greensboro.

THE PAROLED SOLDIERS TAKE POSSESSION OF DAVIS' TRAIN

Breckinridge, Reagan and myself reached the break on the railroad at Jamestown on the night of the 19th of April. We there heard the "end" of the negotiations—Johnson's [sic] surrender. Breckinridge was most eager to get on, and a train from Salisbury was waiting to take us on. But soldiers returning from Lee's army had got into it and on top of it and crammed themselves into every groove in it where it was possible for a man to be. Breckinridge spoke to them, showed them the danger of running the train with such a load, and implored them to suffer himself and his friends to go off, as it was vitally important to avoid delay. To all his entreaties and remonstrations they paid not the least attention. We had therefore to abandon the notion of leaving till next day. Roughing it for the night, and taking stock of the demoralization we were now in constant contact with, we dragged through till morning. Another appeal to the paroled soldiers hived like bees all over the cars, was productive of no good. They would go— were much obliged for his interest in their safety, and not much concerned in his hurry or its importance. We had therefore to get into the tender and ride with the engineer. Breckinridge sat on the ward; Reagan on a tool chest; and I on a pump. Thus we dashed off for Salisbury. Passing through Lexington, we gave the first news of Lincoln's assassination.

THE COMMENTS ON PRESIDENT LINCOLN'S ASSASSINATION

Here, by the way, I should mention that when General Breckinridge heard of the deplorable affair through Sherman's headquarters, he did not credit it.[171] When convinced that it was so he was greatly shocked, and said not a word. Most of those who heard it were horrified, and I only found a few ready to rejoice—not so much that Mr. Lincoln was murdered as at what might ensue from the outrage. It was taken to inaugurate a new and frightful, but it was supposed a saving, phase in the contest, which they did not know to be already over.

AN ACCIDENT

Within three miles of Salisbury, General Breckinridge's predictions of danger for the jam of soldiers had well nigh a fatal fulfillment. We were passing over a portion of the track with which Stoneman's cavalry had been playing terrible pranks. It was "jobbed" into running order and unstable. Off went one of the centre cars, then another and another; off fell the soldiers on top and out rolled those inside. There was a panic, but, luckily, most escaped with a scare. No one was killed, and only a few badly hurt.

AT SALISBURY

A carriage from Salisbury carried me into that town—a town yet smoking with the ravages of cruel war.[172] We were to have gone directly away, and went down to the unburned portion of the track at the other side of the city where a train was expected—a special train—from Charlotte. No train. Soldiers had seized it, and forced the engineer to go back and spare them the fatigue of a march. There was nothing for it but to wait until morning.

We did, and then, after much difficulty succeeded in rescuing another "special train," or rather, obtaining room in it.

---

171. Mallory decides that it was not Breckinridge who was unbelieving, but rather himself: *I expressed my utter disbelief at the assassination.*

172. Mallory says: *...much of the town, including the valuable depot & rail road buildings, had been destroyed.*

Mr. Davis, who was anxiously awaiting our arrival in Charlotte, amazed at this repeated interruption, sent a third special train with a determined guard of men from General Duke's command. This we met near Concord, and getting into it left the refractory soldiers to their chances of further transportation.

ATTENTION TO DAVIS AT CHARLOTTE

Charlotte, unlike Greensboro, had yet some consideration for the dying Confederacy. The hospitality of Danville was approached.[173] But Charlotte, like Danville, and unlike Greensboro, had hopes of being honored as the capital. As was the case of all the Southern towns, trade was nearly altogether suspended, and a very promising city bore every symptom of premature decay. It was only in and around government depots that one traced plenty, especially in the naval stores, which were there, as everywhere else, teeming with substantial things that were now luxuries—brandies, coffee, tea and sugar, cloths, candles, mats and sundries enough to honor a most extensive miscellaneous grocer's establishment.

To think, however, of what would become of all this was painful. The stores kept in Richmond with miserly care had at last to be lavished—no, destroyed. Those in Danville and Greensboro fared no better, and here in Charlotte the penny wise and pound foolish policy was, perhaps, to reproduce itself with extravagant variations.

On the one hand hungry soldiers and famishing families—and on the other squandering what, rightly applied, would have at the right moment relieved one and both. I sickened of what I saw in that way all through the country.

I am led to these remarks on entering Charlotte because the stores and their surroundings were the first things to attract my attention there. The next thing was the military bustle in Main street, which we soon mixed in. All, or nearly all, moving about, were soldiers.

Passing the first noteworthy mansion on our route "uptown," there was Mr. Benjamin in the porch, hatless, smoking, sleek and smiling.

"Ah! General. We feared you were run off with. Glad, most glad it isn't so."

"Our travelling trucks were slightly out of order, nothing more, Secretary."

"And is it really true that Lincoln is killed?"

"No doubt of it, I'm sorry to say."

"Indeed," and Benjamin's smile vanished, and we passed on.

I should mention that General Breckinridge telegraphed, among other things, to Charlotte, the mere fact that President Lincoln was killed.[174] The circumstances were not known until our arrival. Except some thoughtless enthusiast, no one heard the particulars and was unshocked. Mr. Davis said nothing in my hearing in the least like the remarks that have been ascribed to him.[175] He made an inquiry similar to that of Benjamin, and looked rather than spoke his horror, when the facts were put before him. "It is awful," was all I heard him say.

About the plainest looking house in Main street was the temporary residence of the Confederate President. You would have looked for him in any other house before thinking of an inquiry there. It was a Yankee's house too—Mr. Bates, the express agent at the place. I was myself nobly lodged within shade of the very trees beneath which Lord Cornwallis had his headquarters during his Carolina campaign. And my hostess, a genial North Carolina lady, whose husband was killed in battle, felt piqued that a Northerner should entertain Jefferson Davis. The choice was his own, and led to no few remarks, all of a jealous hue. Very likely, his treatment in Greensboro had stung Mr. Davis to indifference on that point. It was the only

---

173. Mallory says: *...received and treated with the utmost kindness & courtesy.*
174. Mallory says: *...a dispatch was read from Mr. Breckenridge.*
175. Mallory says: *I was not with Mr. Davis when he read it.*

How Davis Took the News of Johnston's Surrender

Mr. Davis was little pleased with the information brought by General Breckinridge, but he resolved to let events guide him. If Johnston had to surrender his army—for, mind you, Johnston had no right, expressed or implied, to surrender a department, inasmuch as he commanded no department—if he surrendered his Army, Mr. Davis resolved to gather the fragments of armies around him and find or force his way to the Trans-Mississippi. A truce was now in force, and pending that, he would not move.

Wade Hampton came for instructions before the truce expired, and he left Charlotte with the determination not to surrender himself or a man in his command. He was chief of the Confederate cavalry, and the most uncompromising cavalier in all the South. Intense, indeed, must have been his mortification when, on repairing to his command at Hillsboro, he found himself and force already surrendered. It was idle for him to telegraph for instructions, to deny Johnson's [sic] authority, to impugn the deed that was done. His troopers were satisfied, and so had he to be, murmur ever so much his brave, undaunted spirit.

The first positive information received in Charlotte as to Johnston's surrender came in the form of a telegram to his wife, then staying there. It advised her to remain in Charlotte, and he, paroled, would soon join her.

Evacuating Charlotte

Next day,[176] accompanied by a cavalry escort of about two thousand men,[177] Jefferson Davis, Cabinet and staff evacuated Charlotte,[178] somewhat undetermined as to a future course. There had been some semblance of a capital, some show of governmental routine, some pretence of the power he was elected to wield, up to this; but now all that was vanished, and thenceforth the Confederate President was a fugitive, with hardly the shadow of authority. He looked sad, and indeed hopeless. Never a word escaped him which betrayed the faintest yielding. The principle he had contended for was still as dear to him as ever, only the opportunity to give it honor or stability, or to reflect its features himself, was irrevocably gone. He felt himself unseated but not unthroned—*c'est une autre chose*.

Davis' Treasure

Much has been said, and more supposed, in regard to the treasure he was carrying off in his train. The Confederate treasure was never with him or his train. It was the Richmond bank specie that was fastened to his train at any time—its custodians deeming that course the safest. The Confederate specie was usually far away from him. It left Charlotte in charge of the midshipmen before he arrived there. What became of it finally I know not, although I know that a portion of it was used to pay off certain troops and others at various points from Charlotte to Washington, in Georgia.

The Flight from Charlotte

As Davis practically ceased to be a President from the day he evacuated Charlotte, and his course after that was an incessant flight, I can quickly tell all I have to add. From Charlotte, the Presidential party, attended by a more imposing escort than yet honored its progress, went

---

176. Mallory says: ...*after about a week's stay at Charlotte.*
177. Mallory says: ...*with an escort of some two or three hundred cavalry.*
178. Mallory says: ...*they started south.*

to the Catawba river. It was like the sun setting—this array—the expiring glories of a four years gallantly maintained power. George Davis had resigned the Attorney Generalship in Charlotte. Mr. Trenholm resigned the Treasury Secretaryship on the banks of the Catawba. Not only had the "Presidential party" grown "small by degrees and beautifully less," but the high officials had begun to dwindle away, and the whole party, official and not, was at length reduced to scanty numbers[179] though its escort was at length large. Judge Reagan was appointed acting secretary of the Treasury at the Catawba—about the last executive deed of the flying President.

Delays were now not thought of, and on toward Abbeville, via Yorkville, the party struck, taking full soldiers allowance of turmoil, and camping all the journey. Only intent on pushing to certain points on the Florida coast, onward it went. Rumors of Stoneman, rumors of Wilson, rumors even of the ubiquitous Sheridan, occasionally sharpened the excitement.[180] The escort for the sake of expedition was shorn of its bulky proportions, and by the time we reached Washington, in Georgia, there were only enough to make a fair fight with a respectable raiding party.

Scrambling for Gold

At Washington there was a scramble for specie. It was determined to give the cavalry some few dollars each; they were impatient and helped themselves as soon as they discovered where to get it. The result was an inequitable distribution—many got much, many got nothing, and "dust hunters" picked up a good deal the following day—a good deal that was trampled underfoot during the contemptible scramble.

It was manifest at Washington that the disintegration which had been apparent more or less from the outset among the Presidential followers had culminated. It was equally clear that Mr. Davis had little to expect from the cowed and trembling people. Except at Charlotte, and there only qualifiedly, he experienced little like cordiality since leaving Virginia. North Carolina was positively cold or lukewarm. South Carolina displayed no marked indications of sympathy, and now, in Georgia, and near to the house of Alexander H. Stephens, what could he expect?

His companions all saw how it was, if not how it was so soon going to be. The personal safety of each became a question, and each was urged to secure it as best he could. Mr. Mallory quietly left his horses in charge of a friend and boldly ventured himself in a railroad train to Barnett Station, and thence on to Atlanta, where the federals were in force. That far he was accompanied by Louis Wigfall,[181] the quondam General and Texas Senator. From Atlanta the Confederate Navy Secretary took the West Point train and successfully reached Lagrange,[182] where his family were,[183] and where he was lately captured.[184]

Benjamin Mysteriously Disappears

Mr. Benjamin disappeared before Washington, no one knows how or where. Thus, the Confederate President had left him only one Cabinet Officer, and that one the Postmaster General. It is true he was recently made Secretary of the Treasury as well, and felt the importance of the dual responsibility. Now he was the whole Cabinet—Trenholm and Geo. Davis resigned,

---

179. Mallory says: ...*reduced to a handful of men.*
180. Mallory says: ...*we heard crude statements of cavalry parties of Federals upon all sides.*
181. Mallory says: ...*joining Genl Wigfall & wife.*
182. Mallory says: ...*took the cars for Atlanta & La Grange.*
183. Mallory says: ...*where my wife & children were.*
184. Mallory says: ...*where some days later I was taken prisoner.* It is quite clear from this entire segment that, without Stuart to guide him, Mallory would hardly have known his own name.

Benjamin and Mallory flown away. Breckinridge near but "rowing his own boat," there was no one but John H. Reagan to answer the Cabinet roll call of the Confederate States. The whole party at this time consisted of Reagan, Lubbock, Harrison, Stuart, Wood, and two or three volunteers by the way. An adjoining party there was—one taking the same track, headed by Breckinridge. But for reasons best known to the ex–Vice President, its movements were only confided to a few.

No Longer Escorted

No longer leaning on the least particle of his Presidential dignity—no longer trusting to the hopes of any political Micawber—Jefferson Davis started from Washington, bent on finding a loophole for himself on the Florida coast. Thence "the Lord direct him." He was completely subdued, yet lost not an iota of his manliness, no portion of faith in the rectitude of his cause. We know nothing as yet of the reward which was, at that very time, flaunted all over the South—a reward for him as the accomplice of assassins. It was reserved for his capture—for the concentration of sorrows on his head—the announcement of this reward. He was, however, happily ignorant of it. I grant you that neither the death of Mr. Lincoln nor the doom of his murderers so greatly grieved him as the demise of the Confederate States. He thought much more of Johnston's unauthorized surrender of a department. More of the faintheartedness which had overcome the people; more of what was sacred to him as country and cause, than of all else beside. Thoughts of this sort fretted him fearfully, and day by day betokened the progress of depressing spirits. Added to all this came frequent intelligence of lawless acts by soldiers once in the Confederate service. No narration of these outrages failed to affect him keenly.

Davis Rushes to His Wife's Rescue

At last[185] he got information[186] that his own wife and family[187] were in danger from the assaults of military marauders. Mrs. Davis, with her three children, and accompanied by her sister, Miss Howell, had a wagon train of her own, about twenty or thirty miles from her husband's party.[188] She was very anxious to go her own way and be no embarrassment to him. She felt equal to the task of protecting herself from reckless Confederates, and felt sure of avoiding federals. But, no sooner did he ascertain that she was in danger, that two gangs had concocted a scheme to seize all her trunks under the impression that she carried the rebel gold, than he resolved, at all hazards, to go to her rescue. It was a fond husband's, a fond father's infatuation. No remonstrance prevailed. He set out[189] and rode eighteen miles to meet the object of his love and solicitude. He met them, and the first to rebuke him for his excess of fondness was the anxious wife and mother. A tent or two was already pitched, and he, weary to exhaustion, went to sleep, intending to retrace his steps before morning. Had he not gone to assure himself of his wife's safety, and had he not been excessively fatigued while there, Colonel Pritchard would be without the honor of capturing him, for nothing was easier than his escape, as Breckinridge and Wood and the writer of this know, and by meeting no interruption themselves have proved. Their immunity might have been his.

---

185. Mallory says: ...*at about this time.*
186. Mallory says: ...*he found.*
187. Mallory says: *Mrs. Davis & family.*
188. Mallory says: ...*were some twenty miles off.*
189. Mallory includes this, but says he learned it later from Judge Reagan. However, he only mentions Reagan in his revised account, not in the original Alfriend account.

The Capture

But Davis ran his risks and took his chances, fully conscious of imminent danger, yet powerless, from physical weariness, to do all he designed doing against the danger. When the musketry firing was heard in the morning, at "dim, gray dawn," it was supposed to be between the rebel marauders and Mrs. Davis' few camp defenders. Under this impression he hurriedly put on his boots and prepared to go out for the purpose of interposing, saying: "They will at least as yet respect me."

As he got to the tent door thus hastily equipped, and with this good intention of preventing an effusion of blood by an appeal in the name of a fading but not wholly faded authority, he saw a few cavalry ride up the road and deploy in front.

"Ha, Federals!" was his exclamation.

"Then you are captured," cried Mrs. Davis with emotion.

In a moment she caught an idea—a woman's idea, and as quickly as women in an emergency execute their designs. It was done. He slept in a wrapper—a loose one. It was yet around him. This she fastened ere he was aware of it, and then, bidding him adieu, urged him to go to the spring, a short distance off, where his horses and arms were. Strange as it may seem there was not even a pistol in the tent. Davis felt that his only course was to reach his horse and arms, and complied. As he was leaving the door, followed by a servant with a water bucket, Miss Howell flung a shawl over his head. There was no time to remove it without exposure and embarrassment, and as he had not far to go he ran the chance exactly as it was devised for him. In these two articles consisted the woman's attire of which so much nonsense has been spoken and written, and under these circumstances, and in this way, was Jefferson Davis going forth to effect his escape. No bonnet, no gown, no petticoats, no crinoline, no, nothing of all these. And what there was happened to be excusable under ordinary circumstances, and perfectly natural as things were.

But it was too late for any effort to reach his horses, and the Confederate President was at last a prisoner in the hands of the United States.

What attended his capture you have heard in all forms,[190] and what followed it too; but many things remain to be told and corrected touching that and other events germane to it. These, with your permission, I shall take another opportunity of relating.

---

190. Mallory says: *...his capture has been published & commented upon very fully.*

BIBLIOGRAPHY

Aaron, Larry G. *Pittsylvania County, Virginia: A Brief History*. Charleston, SC: History Press, 2009.
Aberdeen Journal (Scotland) May 9, 1856.
Addey, Henry Markinfield. *Life and Imprisonment of Jefferson Davis, Together with the Life and Military Career of Stonewall Jackson*. New York: Michael Doolady, 1866.
_____. *Life of Jefferson Davis Together with the Life of "Stonewall Jackson."* Philadelphia: Keystone, 1890.
Alfriend, Frank Heath. *The Life of Jefferson Davis*. Bedford, MA: Applewood Books, 1868.
Allen, Felicity. *Jefferson Davis: Unconquerable Heart*. Columbia: University of Missouri Press, 1999.
Allibone, Samuel A. *Critical Dictionary of English Literature, and British and American Authors*. 1854, 1871, 1891 (the last edited by John Foster Kirk).
Altsheler, Joseph Alexander. *Before the Dawn: A Story of the Fall of Richmond*. New York: Doubleday, 1903.
Amicus (C.E.L. Stuart). Items in the *Richmond Daily Dispatch*: April 2, 1861; June 18, 1861; September 20, 1861; December 18, 1861; June 11, 1862; September 1, 1862; February 6, 1863; May 9, 1864.
Anglo-Brazilian Times (Brazil) April 7, 1868; November 22, 1869.
Annual Report of the Railroad Companies of the State of Virginia, for the Year Ending Sept. 30, 1859. 1859.
O Apostolo (Brazil).
Armee, C.S. (C.E.L. Stuart). "Rummagings Through Rebeldom." *New York Citizen*. 1867.
Ashmore, Otis. "The Story of the Confederate Treasure." *The Georgia Historical Quarterly* 2:3. (September 1918).
Athenaeum. 1854.
Atwell, Albert Lee. *Confederate States of America Lost Treasury Gold*. Danville, VA: Unpublished. A copy of this manuscript reposes in Danville Public Library, and is cited by them as an authority.
Auburn Daily American (NY). May 2, 1859.
Auburn Daily Union (NY). April 26, 1860.
Avary, Myrta Lockett, ed. *A Virginia Girl in the Civil War, 1861–1865: Being a record of the actual experiences of the wife of a Confederate officer*. New York: D. Appleton & Company, 1903. The editor has suppressed the name of her interlocutor, and, as the Hoehlings say, in *The Day Richmond Died* (1981), *Concerning Myrta Lockett Avary ... history will never know if* [her character] *was one or a composite of two or three people, or in greater part the creation of Myrta's fertile brain.* Myrta Harper Lockett (1857–1946) married James Corbin Avary in 1884.
Averill, John H. "Richmond, Virginia: The Evacuation of the City and the Days Preceeding It." *Richmond Dispatch*, July 4, 1897 (reprinted from the *Nashville Banner*). Reproduced in *Southern Historical Papers* 25 (1897), pp. 267–273.
Bailey, Frankie Y., and Alice P. Green. *Wicked Danville*. Charleston, SC: History Press, 2011.
Ballard, Michael B. *A Long Shadow: Jefferson Davis and the Final Days of the Confederacy*. Jackson: University of Mississippi Press, 1986. In his preface, Ballard writes that most historians of the Civil War South have ignored the final days of the Confederate States of America, including the government's April–May retreat from Richmond. *The only previous scholarly account* [i.e., the only one prior to Ballard's scholarly account], *Alfred Jackson Hanna's* Flight into Oblivion, *was published in Richmond in 1938.*

Bancroft, A.C. *The Life and Death of Jefferson Davis, Ex-President of the Southern Confederacy.* New York: J.S. Ogilvie, 1889. On April 2, while sitting in his church pew at Richmond, Mr. Davis received a telegram announcing Lee's speedy withdrawal from Petersburg, and the consequent necessity for the evacuation of Richmond. On the opening of that day Mr. Davis started, with his personal staff, for Dansville, where, on the 5th, he issued another of his reassuring proclamations. Dansville was abandoned within a week, and Mr. Davis made his way to Charlotte, N.C., via Greensboro, N.C. There he heard of the assassination of Lincoln. He overtook his wife near Irwinsville, Ga., and there, on May 10, he and his whole party were captured. That's it, as far as the flight goes.

Belfast News-Letter (Ireland). April 4, 1854; April 14, 1854; May 8, 1854; May 10, 1854.

Bell, John. *Confederate Seadog: John Taylor Wood in War and Exile.* Jefferson, NC: McFarland, 2002.

Bell, John W, ed. *Memoirs of Governor William Smith of Virginia: His Political, Military and Personal History.* New York: Moss Engraving, 1891. Bell was a private in the Culpeper Minute-Men and the 13th Virginia Regiment, and later quartermaster of the 49th Virginia and of the 4th Brigade (Smith's) of Early's Division.

Benjamin and Phelps. "That School Swindler Again!" *American Educational Monthly* (March 1864).

Benton, Scott. *Last Train from Richmond. The Plot to Assassinate Jefferson Davis, CSA.* Lincoln, NE: Universe, 2006. A novel.

Beringer, Richard E., Herman Hattaway, Archer Jones, and William N. Still, Jr. *Why the South Lost the Civil War.* Athens: University of Georgia Press, 1986.

Bill, Alfred Hoyt. *The Beleaguered City: Richmond, 1861–1865.* New York: Knopf, 1946. H.J. Eckenrode's review of this book, in *The Journal of Southern History* 12:3 (1946), begins with: *It is human, but perhaps unfortunate, that authors usually strain facts to justify theses. This sometimes leads to a confused idea of history, a modeling of history in a shape often discordant with the truth.* Eckenrode concludes with *While he has written a good book, it could have been made much better, and could have made a genuine contribution to history.* Bell Wiley reviewed it in *The American Historical Review* 52:2. January 1947, *For pleasant reading,* The Beleaguered City *is superb; as history it leaves much to be desired.*

Billingsley, Andrew. *Mighty Like a River: The Black Church and Social Reform.* New York: Oxford University Press, 1999.

Bivin, Ken. "The Fall of Richmond." *America's Civil War,* May 1995.

Black, Robert C., III. *The Railroads of the Confederacy.* Chapel Hill: University of North Carolina Press, 1952.

Blackburn Standard (England). April 26, 1854; May 10, 1854; June 21, 1854.

Blackford, W.W. *War Years with Jeb Stuart.* Introduction by Douglas Southall Freeman. New York: Charles Scribner's, 1945. There is nothing in this book which furthers our knowledge of April 2.

Blackwood's Magazine. July 1852.

Bleser, Carol K., and Lesley J. Gordon. *Intimate Strategies of the Civil War: Military Commanders and Their Wives.* New York: Oxford University Press, 2001.

Bolles, John A. "Porter-Humphreys-Hardin, a Chapter from the Romance of Rascality." *Old and New.* February 1871.

Bostick, Douglas W. *The Confederacy's Secret Weapon: The Civil War Illustrations of Frank Vizetelly.* Charleston, SC: History Press, 2009.

Boston Evening Transcript. April 23, 1860.

Bradford Observer (England). May 11, 1854.

Bradley, Mark L. *This Astounding Close: The Road to Bennett Place.* Chapel Hill: University of North Carolina Press, 2000. The Bennett Close referred to is a farmhouse in North Carolina where the armistice was signed between Confederate general J.E. Johnston and his Union counterpart, William T. Sherman.

Bright, David L. *Confederate Railroads.* http://www.csa-railroads.com.

Bristol Mercury (England). May 27, 1854.

Brock, Sallie. *Richmond During the War: Four Years of Personal Observation.* New York: G.W. Carleton, 1867. This review from *Scott's Monthly Magazine* 5 (1868): *It is in the main a dull, prosy book.*

_____, ed. *The Southern Amaranth.* New York: Wilcox & Rockwell, 1869. A book of collected poems by various persons celebrating the Lost Cause, including Brock's own "The Fall of Richmond" (written using the pseudonym Virginia Madison) and others. See Madison, Virginia.

Brooklyn Daily Eagle. April 17, 1860.

Broun, Thomas L., comp. *Dr. William LeRoy Broun.* New York: Neale, 1912.

Brown, Beth. *Wicked Richmond*. Charleston, SC: History Press, 2010.
Brown, Joshua. *Pictorial Reporting: Everyday Life and the Crisis of Gilded Age America*. Berkeley: University of California Press, 2002.
Brubaker, John H. III. *The Last Capital: Danville, Virginia, and the Final Days of the Confederacy*. Danville: Danville Museum of Fine Arts and History, 1979. Brubaker once edited the *Danville Register and Bee*.
Bruce, Horatio Washington. "Some Reminiscences of the Second of April, 1865." *Southern Historical Society Papers* 9 (May 1881), p. 208 et seq. This was a paper originally read by Bruce before the Louisville branch of the Southern Historical Society in 1881.
Burger, Nash Kerr, and John Knox Bettersworth. *South of Appomattox*. New York: Harcourt, Brace, 1959.
Bulwark. 1852.
Burns, Brian. *Lewis Ginter: Richmond's Gilded Age Icon*. Charleston, SC: History Press, 2011.
Butler, Pierce. *Judah P. Benjamin*. Philadelphia: George W. Jacobs, 1907.
Callahan, James Morton. *The Diplomatic History of the Southern Confederacy*. Baltimore: Johns Hopkins Press, 1901. Callahan was the first to write a book that mentions the *McClure's* article, when he says that Mallory *wrote an interesting account of the removal from Richmond, which has just been published by his daughter, under the caption "The Last Days of the Confederacy" [McClure's Mag., Dec., 1900, and January, 1901]*. The *McClure's* article is actually called "The Last Days of the Confederate Government."
Campbell, Given. "Memorandum of a Journal Kept Daily During the Last March of Jefferson Davis," 1865. The typescript of this diary is owned by the Library of Congress.
Campbell, John A. *Recollections of the Evacuation of Richmond, April 2d, 1865*. Baltimore, John Murphy, 1880.
Campbell, R. Thomas, ed. *see* Minor, Hubbard T.
____, ed. *Voices of the Confederate Navy: Articles, Letters, Reports, and Reminiscences*. Jefferson, NC: McFarland, 2008.
Canfield, Cass. *The Iron Will of Jefferson Davis*, New York: Harcourt Brace Jovanovich, 1958. Canfield was senior editor at Harper & Row.
Carroll, J. Frank. *Confederate Treasure in Danville*. Danville, VA: Ure Press, 1996.
Cary, Connie. See Harrison, Constance.
Casdorph, Paul D. *General R.S. Ewell: Robert E. Lee's Hesitant Commander*. Lexington: University Press of Kentucky, 2004.
Cashin, Joan E. *First Lady of the Confederacy: Varina Davis's Civil War*. Cambridge, MA: Belknap, 2006. "*On April 2, Jefferson Davis received a telegram from General Lee stating that Richmond would have to be evacuated, and that night he left the city with his staff for Danville, Virginia.*" This is the only passage concerning the flight to Danville.
Casstevens, Frances Harding. *Edward A. Wild and the African Brigade in the Civil War*. Jefferson, NC: McFarland, 2003.
____. *George W. Alexander and Castle Thunder: A Confederate Prison and Its Commandant*. Jefferson, NC: McFarland, 2004.
Chamlee, Roy Z. *Lincoln's Assassins: A Complete Account of the Capture, Trial, and Punishment*. Jefferson, NC: McFarland, 1990.
Champlin, John D., Jr. *Young Folk's History of the War for the Union*. New York: Henry Holt, 1881. The term "Young Folk's" is somewhat misleading, as both the content and layout are consistent with an adult book, at least by today's standards.
Christian, William Asbury. *Richmond: Her Past and Present*. Richmond, VA: L.H. Jenkins, 1912.
Church, William Conant. *Ulysses S. Grant and the Period of National Preservation and Reconstruction*. New York: G.P. Putnam's, 1897.
"Civil War, Day by Day, 50 Years Ago." *Washington Herald*, April 4, 1915.
Civil War Papers, Read Before the Commandery of the State of Massachusetts, Military Order of the Loyal Legion of the United States. Boston: Commandery, 1900. See Prescott, Royal B.
Clark, James C. *Last Train South: The Flight of the Confederate Government from Richmond*. Jefferson, NC: McFarland, 1984. William Warren Rogers, in his review in the October 1985 edition of the *Florida Historical Quarterly*, p. 206: *Clark is obviously not aiming at profundity*
Clark, John E., Jr. *Railroads in the Civil War*. Baton Rouge: Louisiana State University Press, 2011.
Clark, Micajah Henry. "Last Days of the Confederate Treasury and What Became of Its Specie." *Southern Historical Society Papers* 9 (November–December 1881), pp. 542–556.
Cleveland Plain Dealer. February 21, 1860.

Clubbs, Occie. "Stephen Russell Mallory: United States Senator from Florida, and Confederate Secretary of the Navy." *Florida Historical Quarterly*, January, April, and July 1947. This was Clubbs's 1936 thesis expanded into a three-part article. Clubbs writes that, through the kindness of the surviving members of Mallory's family, she was privileged to have in her keeping during the writing of this study, two diaries of the Secretary's. It is worth noting that she does not mention the Davis flight, or Mallory's account thereof. In fact, she skips over it entirely, as if it did not happen. These 1947 articles had long been in print when Father Durkin's book biography came out on Mallory. He does not mention them, nor does he mention Philip Melvin's biography of Mallory.

_____. "Stephen Russell Mallory, the Elder." MA thesis, University of Florida, 1936. This is the first biography of Confederate Secretary of the Navy Mallory, written while the author was principal of the Agnes McReynolds Grammar School.

Cochran, Hamilton. *Blockade Runners of the Confederacy*. New York: Bobbs-Merrill, 1958.

Coffey, Walter. *The Civil War Months: A Month-by-Month Compendium of the War Between the States*. Bloomington, IN: AuthorHouse, 2012.

Coffin, Charles Carleton. *Four Years of Fighting: A Volume of Personal Observation with the Army and Navy*. Boston: Ticknor & Fields, 1866.

Coleman, William D. "Jefferson Davis' Week at Danville." *Times* (Philadelphia), May 28, 1881.

Collins, Donald E. *The Death and Resurrection of Jefferson Davis*. Lanham, MD: Rowman & Littlefield, 2005.

Confederate Veteran. A 32-page magazine published monthly at Nashville, Tenn., between January 1, 1893, and 1932. It was originally intended as an organ of communication between Confederate soldiers and those who were interested in them and their affairs. S.A. Cunningham was the first editor and manager. He edited the first issue from his sickbed. The first issues were 5 cents, or 50 cents for a year's subscription. It was revived in 1984, by the Sons of Confederate Veterans.

Connelly, Thomas Lawrence. *The Marble Man: Robert E. Lee and His Image in American Society*. New York: Alfred A. Knopf, 1977.

Conolly, Thomas. *An Irishman in Dixie: Thomas Conolly's Diary of the Evacuation of Richmond*. Edited by Nelson D. Lankford. Columbia: University of South Carolina Press, 1988.

Thomas Conolly

On February 23, 1865, the blockade runner *Owl* left Nassau, and three days later deposited Member of Parliament Tom Conolly on the shores of North Carolina. A Southern sympathizer, Conolly seems to have come over from Ireland purely for the adventure. He certainly had his adventure, and then left New York on May 17, 1865. As Nelson Lankford writes, in *An Irishman in Dixie* (1988), Conolly *met Jefferson Davis, dined with Robert E. Lee, saw Richmond fall, fled northward, and returned home to tell his tale*. And this: *When Thomas Conolly returned home to Castletown House in 1865, he carried with him a diary containing his day-by-day observations of America at the close of the Civil War. What he did with this account is not known.* That 1865 diary, which begins the day he left Nassau, on February 23, ends on May 26, when he arrived back in Ireland.

Between 1967 and 1983 three relevant events of significance occurred in connection with this diary. First, in 1979 Conolly's old house in county Kildare was acquired by the Castletown Foundation, one of the trustees of this group being *Desmond Fitz-Gerald, the twenty-ninth Knight of Glin, of Glin Castle in County Limerick and an authority on Irish art, architecture, and furniture.* Second, Dublin antique dealer Ronnie McDonnell brought something to the attention of The Knight of Glin, who immediately recognized Conolly's diary. *The diary is now one of the prized manuscripts on the Conollys owned by the Castletown Foundation*. The quoted passages are from Lankford's *An Irishman in Dixie*. The third event of significance happened in 1983. The Knight of Glin was at a party on an obscure Yugoslav island, where he happened to meet *FitzGerald Bemiss, a trustee of the Virginia Historical Society*. Of course, one thing led to another, and *a photocopy of the Civil War diary of Thomas Conolly was soon made available to the Virginia Historical Society by the Castletown Foundation*. The quoted passages are from Nelson Lankford's *An Irishman in Dixie*.

In early 1986 the senior librarian of the Virginia Historical Society brought the diary to the attention of Civil War historian Nelson Lankford. The *Virginia Magazine of History and Biography*, in their January 1987 edition, published a portion of this diary, the portion covering the period March 8 to April 2, 1865, Conolly's stay in Richmond, including the details of the fall of the capital. The Castletown Foundation simply could not keep up with the expenses of maintenance and renovation, and Conolly's old house was purchased by the Irish government in 1994. It is of interest that in the "Further reading" section of Castletown's website, Lankford's book was conspicuously absent when I visited.

As can be seen by his comments, Lankford is well aware of the possibilities of forgery, but it is difficult to determine his level of skepticism from a passage such as: *Tom Conolly had had his share of close calls. Reaching the North Carolina coast—without incident, on the last blockade-runner, after the closing of the last port—required extraordinary luck. Giving hardly a thought to this good fortune, he then managed to avoid the northern army that had just taken Wilmington, walk inland through miles of pine barrens and swamps, and leave Fayetteville only days before it too passed from southern hands.* As for Conolly's subsequent adventures—his time in Raleigh and Richmond; being under fire with Lee in the field; the fall of Richmond; his departure from the burning capital; and his dramatic escape to the North—Lankford says, *Conolly surely put the luck of the Irish to a stern test.* As for Conolly's death, Lankford writes: *The* London Times *was strangely silent on Conolly's demise, with only two lines appearing in the death notices (12 August 1876).* For the record, this death notice read: *On the 10th Aug., 1876, at Castletown, Celbridge, Thomas Conolly, Esq., M.P., aged 53.* However, despite what Lankford says, that was not all the *Times* had on Conolly's demise. This from August 11, 1876: *Death of Mr Conolly. Our Dublin Correspondent telegraphed last night:—"Thomas Conolly, M.P., died to-day at his residence, Castletown, Celbridge. He succeeded his father in the representation of the county of Donegal, for which he sat since 1849. Although a Conservative, he was very popular, and was able to retain his seat, in spite of the legislation of the last few years which destroyed the dominant power of the landlords, and secured to the electors comparative freedom in the exercise of the franchise. There will be a determined struggle for the vacant seat, which has long been kept in view by the Home Rule party."* There is also a brief discussion in the *Times* of August 14, about what would happen now in Donegal after Conolly's death. And the M.P.'s death is also mentioned briefly in the *Times* of August 15. This from Lankford: *Thomas Conolly recorded his American diary in a large ledger, bound with a leather spine and marbled paper covers, on the title page of which he wrote, "Log of 1st. Expedition to America beginning 23rd. day of February 1865 being two days before my birth day Thomas Conolly."*

Lankford goes on to say that the transcription of the diary in his book, *An Irishman in Dixie*, was made from the Richmond photocopy, and that the original diary is owned by the Castletown Foundation. Questionable passages in the photocopy were checked against the original when Lankford made his trip there in 1987. The entry for April 1, 1865, ends with: *...little did we know what a day would bring forth.* Lankford, referring to the entire diary entry for that date, which he calls "the passage," says, in a footnote, *Conolly wrote this passage at least several days later.* Then he says, *The following entry, for Sunday, 2 April, was written on pages that were inserted and not part of the original diary. Conolly left in the bound ledger space only for the title of the passage he intended to insert later on the events of 2 April, "Crisis of Richmond Fate."* The only entry in Conolly's diary of relevance here is this April 2 one, the one that was inserted later as a loose sheet. Not all of it is of interest to us, or to anyone, frankly. These are the two segments that are: *Go to Church with Miss T. one of the most beautiful mornings I ever saw in my life... But what is the matter the sexton having stealthily whispered to Jeff. Davis he rises & leaves the Ch then the same operation to one & a second member of the Govt both follow suit, people begin to whisper, when as if curiosity long suppressed had ignited they rose (the whole congregation) in tens & 20 & left the Church, outside the secret was soon abroad a telegram of Disaster at Hatcher's run line broken by masses of the Enemy in 3 places Richmond must be evacuated signed R.E. Lee. Then painful rumours follow thick on one another A.P. Hill killed Fitzhugh Lee, great carnage, Petersburg in the hands of the Yanks &c &c, and as the day goes on the confirmation of all! The Govt. officials all leave for Danville by train. Streets filled with departures, a regular stampede has begun.* And this: *...at last at 4 o'clock a.m. Then the awful shock the magazine exploded There is the death knell of Richmond & then another & another and sure it was so—I went out and what a sight at that hour the streets filled with all the ragamuffins cheifly* [sic] *niggers running & hurrying about & then another crash another explosion & all the windows of the Spottswood are rent asunder as also of all the stores in Main Street & now the plundering begins men & women grabbing more than they can carry & bustling on under their burthens now the mills are on fire & the crowd rush to get the flour & begin rolling out barrels thro' the street & carrying bags & sacks of flour the white meal & the black ashes making the nigger face most damnably ludicrous, hurry & bustle &*

noise everywhere..." It looks very much as if Conolly did not even write this entry. He died in 1876.

In Carleton Coffin's book *The Life of Lincoln* (1892) he devotes a few paragraphs to the fall of Richmond, substantially different from any of the accounts he had previously written, either in articles or books, and heavily influenced, as he always was, by the 1866 *Watchman* account of Moses Purnell Handy. That the Conolly entry for April 2 is taken directly from these few paragraphs in Coffin's 1892 book there can be little doubt. Below is a series of what might be termed couplets:

COFFIN: *...sacks of flour, meal...*
CONOLLY: *...sacks of flour the white meal*
COFFIN: *...men and women...*
CONOLLY: *...men & women...*
COFFIN: *...their backs bending low beneath the heavy sacks...*
CONOLLY: *grabbing more than they can carry & bustling on under their burthens*
COFFIN: *...plunder...*
CONOLLY: *...plundering...*
COFFIN: *...rolling barrels...*
CONOLLY: *...rolling out barrels*
COFFIN: *Haxall's Mills were burning*
CONOLLY: *...and now the mills are on fire*
COFFIN: *...were breaking open stores and shops*
CONOLLY: *...are rent asunder as also of all the stores*
COFFIN: *A little past four o'clock in the morning...*
CONOLLY: *...at last at 4 o'clock a.m....*
COFFIN: *...the tocsin sounded...*
CONOLLY: *...the death knell...*
COFFIN: *...Main Street...*
CONOLLY: *...Main Street...*
COFFIN: He was staying at the Spotswood Hotel, which he spells *Spottswood*.
CONOLLY: *...all the windows of the Spottswood are rent asunder...*

Coffin's book is not the only source used by whoever wrote Conolly's April 2 entry. Coffin's famous April 1865 article in the *Boston Journal* has the word "stampede" to describe the events of the afternoon of April 2, 1865. Conolly uses the word too. In the same *Boston Journal* article, Coffin invents the concept of Lee's lines being broken in three places, and he also comes up with the immediately subsequent expression, "Richmond must be evacuated." Conolly does the same thing, but by 1892 many writers had copied Coffin in this respect. Conolly's sexton whispering to Jefferson Davis in church was created by Stuart in his July 4, 1865, article in the *New York Herald*, and subsequently copied many times. One must say, therefore, that whoever wrote the page inserted into the Conolly diary did so after 1892. Rather interestingly, Ella Lonn, in her book *Foreigners in the Confederacy*, calls him Peter Connolly. *The Honorable Peter Connolly, an Irish member from Donegal, was present to see the death throes of the Confederacy. At the request of General Lee he was allowed a room in the cottage of a Mrs. Pryor near Petersburg and messed with the general on his scanty fare. He ran the blockade on the Owl.*

Conrad, James Lee. *Rebel Reefers: The Organization and Midshipmen of the Confederate States Naval Academy*. Cambridge, MA: Perseus Press, 2003.
Cooper, William J., Jr. *Jefferson Davis: American*. New York: Knopf, 2000.
____. *Jefferson Davis and the Civil War Era*. Baton Rouge: Louisiana State University Press, 2013. A series of essays, this book is not relevant to the Davis flight.
____, ed. *see* Davis, Jefferson.
Corey, Charles Henry. *A History of the Richmond Theological Seminary, with Reminiscences of Thirty Years' Work Among the Colored People of the South*. Richmond, VA: J.W. Randolph & Co., 1895.
Cork Examiner (Ireland). June 11, 1864.
Correio da Victoria. (Brazil).
Correio Mercantil, e Instructivo, Politico, Universal (Brazil). March 31, 1868.
Coulter, Ellis Merton. *The Confederate States of America, 1861–1865*. Baton Rouge: Louisiana State University Press, 1950.
Couper, William, ed. *The Corps Forward: Biographical Sketches of the VMI Cadets Who Fought in the Battle of Newmarket*. Buena Vista, VA: Mariner, 2005.

Cozzens, Peter, ed. *Battles and Leaders of the Civil War*. Vols. 5–6. Urbana: University of Illinois Press, 2004. Part Eleven of Volume 5 has a section titled "The Last Days of the Confederate Government," by Stephen R. Mallory. This is the *McClure's* article. See Johnson, Robert Underwood.
_____, and Girardi, Robert I., eds. *The New Annals of the Civil War*. Mechanicsburg, PA: Stackpole Books, 2004.
Crist, Lynda Lasswell, ed. *see* Davis, Jefferson.
Crump, Emmie *see* Lightfoot, Emmie Crump.
Culpepper, Marilyn Mayer. *All Things Altered: Women in the Wake of Civil War and Reconstruction*. Jefferson, NC: McFarland, 2002.
Cutting, Elisabeth Brown. *Jefferson Davis, Political Soldier*. New York: Dodd, Mead, 1930.
Daily National Intelligencer (Washington, D.C.). July 6, 1854; July 12, 1854.
Daily News (London). October 29, 1852; April 1, 1854; April 3, 1854; April 5, 1854; April 6, 1854; April 29, 1854; June 3, 1854; June 5, 1854; June 6, 1854; June 7, 1854; June 8, 1854; June 9, 1854.
Daniel, John M. *The Richmond Examiner During the War, or the Writings of John M. Daniel*. "With a memoir of his life by his brother, Frederick S. Daniel." New York: printed for the author, 1868. This book was republished in 1970 by Arno Press. John M. Daniel had died only a few days before the fall of Richmond.
Danville Register (Virginia). This newspaper ran four anonymous articles in its April 1965 bonanza on the Civil War. "War News," "A Message from Lee Touched Off Exodus," "There Were but Five Trains and Everyone Wanted Ride," and "A Southside Virginia Town Became Home for Thousands During One Week in April."
Davis, Burke. *The Long Surrender*. New York: Random House, 1985. Herman Hattaway reviewed this book in *Military Affairs* 50:1 (January 1986), pp. 57–58. *It is hard to imagine this book enjoying a wide readership.* And this: *Certainly the volume is interesting and fun to read; if one likes the "tell me about what happened to everyone after the war was over" type of history.* The reviewer points out that Burke Davis's research is admirable, but flawed [!]; that he has used a good variety of secondary sources, and some printed primary ones, but has been spotty by omitting certain newer works; that there is an embarrassing number of errors in the text, but while reviewer Hattaway *found no major misstatements, there are so many small ones, and even egregious ones, that it engenders uneasy doubt about any given passage.*
_____. *To Appomattox: Nine April Days, 1865*. New York: Rinehart, 1959. The book deals with the period Saturday, April 1, 1865, through Sunday, April 9, 1865, and focuses on the adventures of both Robert E. Lee and Jefferson Davis during the period in question.
Davis, George. Letter to W.T. Walthall, September 4, 1877.
Davis, Jefferson. *Jefferson Davis: Private Letters*. Edited by Hudson Strode. New York: Harcourt, Brace, 1966.
_____. *Jefferson Davis: The Essential Writings*. Edited by William J. Cooper, Jr. New York: Knopf, 2000.
_____. *Jefferson Davis, Constitutionalist: His Letters, Papers and Speeches*. Edited by Dunbar Rowland. Jackson: Mississippi Dept. of Archives and History, 1923.
_____. Letter to Gen. Gustavus W. Smith, November 22, 1861 (G.W. Smith papers, University of Georgia, Athens, GA).
_____. Letter to George H. Preston, May 23, 1872.
_____. *The Papers of Jefferson Davis*. Vols. 11–12. Edited by Lynda Lasswell Crist. Baton Rouge: Louisiana State University Press, 2003, 2008. *The Papers of Jefferson Davis* (*PJD*) is a mammoth, ongoing effort based at Rice University and published by Louisiana State University Press. Each volume is heavily annotated, and, being huge and so guaranteed by celebrity historians, has the unofficial reputation of infallibility. This work is usually known as "The Jefferson Davis Papers," but one of the hallmarks of a book's greatness is to have its name abused. The Book of Revelations springs to mind. The first volume was published in 1971, and the latest, Volume 13, in 2012. Fifteen volumes are planned altogether. There have been various editors of the *PJD* over the years, but since 1983 the effort has been led by Lynda Lasswell Crist. There is an introduction written for each volume by an eminent historian: Bruce Catton, Richard E. Beringer, Frank E. Vandiver, James I. Robertson, Jr., William J. Cooper, Jr., to name but a few. The volumes that interest us the most are 11 and 12, published in 2003 and 2008, respectively, covering the periods September 1864 to May 1865 and June 1865 to December 1870.
_____. *The Rise and Fall of the Confederate Government*. 2 vols. New York: Appleton, 1881. The history of the writing of this book is presented by William C. Davis in *The Man and His Hour* (1991). Much of Volume 1 was written by former Assistant Adjutant General Major W.T. Walthall, and pretty much all of Volume 2 by W.T. Tenney. Author Davis says, *It would be difficult to tell with*

certainty just which portions came from the pen or mouth of Jefferson Davis himself and which from Walthall and Tenney. Jefferson Davis had very little idea of what was actually in the book. The working title was *Personal Memoirs of Public Events.* By June 3, 1881, the two volumes were printed *and on their way to the nation's bookstores.*

_____. *A Short History of the Confederate States of America.* New York: Belford, 1890.

Davis, Varina. *Jefferson Davis, Ex-President of the Confederate States of America: A Memoir.* New York: Belford, 1890.

Davis, William C. *Breckinridge: Statesman, Soldier, Symbol.* Baton Rouge: Louisiana State University Press, 1974.

_____. *"A Government of Our Own": The Making of the Confederacy.* New York: Free Press, 1994.

_____. *An Honorable Defeat: The Last Days of the Confederate Government.* New York: Harcourt, 2001.

_____. *Jefferson Davis: The Man and His Hour.* New York: HarperCollins, 1991. Despite David Herbert Donald's words in his *New York Times* review of this book, *The fullest and best biography yet written,* this is not a biography as such, not a study of a life—only a portion thereof, the only part of Jefferson Davis's life that truly interests people, hence the carefully chosen title, "The Man and His Hour." Nevertheless, Professor Davis predicted, *Some will perceive what seems to be an imbalance of coverage.* And he was right. Michael B. Ballard says, in *The American Civil War* (1996), *The biography is not definitive because it suffers from the same problem, albeit to a lesser extent, as Eaton's, in that Davis' significant postwar years are not examined in depth.* Reviewer Gary Marotta, of the University of Southwestern Louisiana, warns that *the reader seeking to discern an overall shape in Jefferson Davis's biography is in for drudgery* (*Louisiana History: The Journal of the Louisiana Historical Association* 35:1 (Winter 1994)). However, reviews contained more good than bad.

_____. *Look Away! A History of the Confederate States of America.* New York: Free Press, 2002.

_____, ed. *see* DeLeon, Edwin.

DeLeon, Edwin. *Secret History of Confederate Diplomacy Abroad.* Edited by William C. Davis. Lawrence: University Press of Kansas, 2005.

De Leon, T.C. *Belles, Beaux and Brains of the '60s.* New York: G.W. Dillingham, 1909. Notable for its many wonderful portraits, including Lee, Mosby, Jefferson Davis, De Leon himself, Beauregard, the White House, Varina Davis, Maggie Howell and her husband Mr. Stoess, Mallory and his daughter Ruby, Alec Stephens, Joseph Ives, Beverley Tucker, John S. Wise, Breckinridge, Semmes, Jefferson Davis Howell.

_____. *Four Years in Rebel Capitals: An Inside View of Life in the Southern Confederacy from Birth to Death.* Mobile, AL: Gossip, 1890. From original notes collated in the years 1861 to 1865 by T.C. De Leon.

Derby Mercury (England). May 10, 1854; June 21, 1854.

Dew, Charles B. *Ironmaker to the Confederacy: Joseph R. Anderson and the Tredegar Iron Works.* New Haven, CT: Yale University Press, 1966.

Diario de São Paolo (Brazil). June 24, 1877.

Diario do Rio de Janeiro (Brazil). March 28, 1868.

Dillon, William. *Life of John Mitchel.* 2 vols. London: Kegan Paul, Trench, 1888.

Dodd, William Edward. *Jefferson Davis.* Philadelphia: George W. Jacobs, 1907. From the American Crisis Biographies Series edited by Ellis Paxson Oberholtzer. *Of the biographies of Jefferson Davis the one published seventy years ago by Professor William E. Dodd is the most scholarly but is not deeply researched and is dated* (Clement Eaton, in *Jefferson Davis,* 1977).

Dorchester Directory (England). 1855.

Dowdey, Clifford. *Experiment in Rebellion.* New York: Doubleday, 1946. There are many books which misspell Dowdey's name as "Dowdy," but only two of those are referenced in this book: Michael Ballard's *A Long Shadow* and Mike Wright's *What They Didn't Teach You About the Civil War.* Everyone else spelled the name right, except James C. Clark, who throughout *Last Train South* spells it "Downey."

_____, ed. *see* Lee, R.E.

Dublin City Directory. Dublin Ireland, 1852.

Dublin Review (Ireland). January 10, 1852.

Dublin University Magazine (Ireland). February 1836.

Dublin University Magazine Advertiser (Ireland). October 1846.

Duke, Basil Wilson. *The Civil War Reminiscences of Basil Duke, C.S.A.* New York: Doubleday, 1909.

Dunaway, Philip, and Melvin Evans. *A Treasury of the World's Great Diaries.* New York: Doubleday, 1957.

Dunbar, Rowland, ed. *see* Davis, Jefferson.

Dundee Courier (Scotland). May 10, 1854.

Durkin, Joseph T. *Stephen R. Mallory, Confederate Navy Chief.* Chapel Hill: University of North Carolina Press, 1954. The first book written on Mallory's life. The book was republished in Columbia, by the University of South Carolina Press, in 1987 as *Confederate Navy Chief: Stephen R. Mallory*, and edited by William N. Still, Jr.

Eastman, Margaret Middleton Rivers. *Old Charleston Originals: From Celebrities to Scoundrels.* Charleston: History Press, 2011. One of the chapters is "Rhett Butler and the Blockade Runners," about George Trenholm.

Eaton, Clement. *Jefferson Davis.* New York: Free Press, 1977.

CLEMENT EATON

It is noted on the dust jacket of Eaton's biography of Jefferson Davis that it was the first Davis biography in 25 years. It is further stated that *Clement Eaton has given us the most complete picture available of Davis the politician and Davis the man.* That is, a complete picture, in 334 pages. However, the publishers seem to have overlooked Hudson Strode's three-volume work on Jefferson Davis published between 1955 and 1964. Still on the dust jacket, Thomas L. Connelly (author of *The Marble Man: Robert E. Lee and His Image in American Society*) calls Eaton "The Elder Statesman of Southern Historians." Connelly says: *No one understands Jefferson Davis as well as Clement Eaton does.* Also from the dust jacket: *Clement Eaton has written a brilliant book* [Bruce Catton]; *...the best yet of the Davis biographies* [Bell Wiley]. Eaton himself says: *My biography of Jefferson Davis is based on manuscript sources to a much greater degree than any previous biography. The particular value of using manuscript sources is that they give a more intimate view of the subject—relatively free of self-consciousness—than do the formal printed sources.*

F.N. Boney, of the University of Georgia, reviewed Eaton's book in the *Virginia Magazine of History and Biography* (July 1978): *Not always totally convincing.* And this: *Unfortunately, the book is rather roughly and unevenly written, a few sections are much in need of another proofreading, and some of the Civil War chapters allow Davis to fade too far into the background.* And finally, this: *Interesting and informative, it is well worth reading, but a definitive study of the leader of the Confederacy has yet to be written.*

The September 1978 edition of the *Indiana Magazine of History* carried Norman D. Brown's review of Eaton's book, and included the following about Jefferson Davis's postwar years: *... deserves fuller treatment than the six pages Eaton gives to them.* Brown wraps up his review with: *Eaton's book, based on a lifetime of research on the Old South and the Confederacy, is superior to any of its predecessors, but it is still not the definitive biography of this puzzling figure who presided over the South's experiment in rebellion.*

The book is a disappointment, writes Ludwell H. Johnson of the College of William and Mary, in his review of Eaton's book in *The Journal of Southern History*, August 1978. He describes Eaton's handling of the war years as *often superficial and digressive*, and then goes on to mention the mistakes and copy-editing errors. *And perhaps the biggest mistake of all is not a matter of fact, but is the author's decision to allot only four pages to the last twenty-four years of Davis's life. No biography can hope to provide a full understanding of the man without an account of these years of struggle and defeat.* He wraps up with: *There is no pleasure in writing an unfavorable review of this book, whose author I have long admired and whose accomplishments I could never hope to equal; and it is a little intimidating to express opinions so utterly at variance with those expressed by the five famous historians quoted on the dust jacket. To do otherwise, however, would be to play fast and loose with the high standards of scholarly achievement that Professor Eaton has done so much to uphold during his long and distinguished career.*

Richard M. McMurry, of Valdosta State College, wrote a review of Eaton's book in the July 1978 edition of the *Florida Historical Quarterly*. In it he talks about the dearth of books on the Rebel president, and then says, *Professor Eaton's Jefferson Davis does not fill the void.* McMurry then goes on to say, *This book is not really a biography. It is, instead, a history of the nineteenth-century South and the Civil War strung together around a factual sketch of the events in Davis's life.* He notes how far, and for what great stretches of the book, Jefferson Davis is lost in the welter of unrelated and somewhat irrelevant material, including William Gilmore Simms' hemorrhoids and enlarged testicle. *Jefferson Davis still awaits a good biography.*

As Michael B. Ballard says, in *The American Civil War* (1996), *Clement Eaton's 1977* Jefferson Davis *is a solid, scholarly effort, but he devotes only a few pages to Davis's postwar years.*

Eckenrode, Hamilton James. *Jefferson Davis: President of the South.* New York: Macmillan, 1923.
Eicher, David J. *Dixie Betrayed: How the South Really Lost the Civil War.* Boston: Little, Brown, 2007.
Eisenschiml, Otto, and Ralph Geoffrey Newman. *The American Iliad: The Epic Story of the Civil War as Narrated by Eyewitnesses and Contemporaries.* Indianapolis, IN: Bobbs-Merrill, 1947.
Era. May 14, 1854.
Evans, Eli N. *Judah P. Benjamin: The Jewish Confederate.* New York: Free Press, 1989.
Evening Star (Washington, D.C.). November 5, 1859; May 10, 1865.
Ewell, General Richard S. *The Letters of General Richard S. Ewell, Stonewall's Successor.* Edited by Donald C. Pfanz. Knoxville: University of Tennessee Press, 2012.
Examiner (London). December 27, 1856.
Exeter Flying Post (England). April 27, 1854; May 11, 1854.
Fleming, Midshipman Robert H. *see* Herndon, G. Melvin, ed.
Flood, Charles Bracelen. *Grant and Sherman. The Friendship That Won the Civil War.* New York: Farrar, Straus and Giroux, 2005. Republished by HarperPerennial, New York, 2006.
Foote, Shelby. *The Civil War: A Narrative. Vol. 3: Red River to Appomattox.* New York: Random House, 1974.
Fountain, Clara Garrett. *Danville, Virginia.* Charleston, SC: Arcadia, 2000. One of the Postcard History series.
_____, and Gary Grant. *Danville Revisited.* Charleston, SC: Arcadia, 2013.
Frank Leslie's Illustrated Newspaper. April 28, 1860; June 25, 1864; October 8, 1864.
Freeman, Douglas Southall. *A Calendar of Confederate Papers.* Richmond, VA: Confederate Museum, 1908.
_____. *R.E. Lee: A Biography.* New York: Charles Scribner's, 1934.
_____, ed. *see* Lee, Robert E.
Freeman's Journal (Dublin). July 8, 1848; January 11, 1850; May 24, 1851; April 24, 1852; January 10, 1853; March 17, 1853; April 23, 1853.
Fremantle, Arthur Lyon. *Three Months in the Southern States, April–June 1863.* New York: John Bradburn, 1864.
Furgurson, Ernest B. *Ashes of Glory: Richmond at War.* New York: Knopf, 1996.
Gallagher, Gary W., and Joseph T. Glatthaar, eds. *Leaders of the Lost Cause: New Perspectives on the Confederate High Command.* Mechanicsburg, PA: Stackpole, 2004.
Gary, Ralph. *The Presidents Were Here: A State by State Historical Guide.* Jefferson, NC: McFarland, 2008.
Goodwin, Doris Kearns. *Team of Rivals: The Political Genius of Abraham Lincoln.* New York: Simon and Schuster, 2005.
Gordon, Armistead Churchill. *Jefferson Davis.* New York: Charles Scribner's, 1918.
Gorgas, Mrs. Amelia. "The Evacuation of Richmond: Personal Recollections of Mrs. Amelia Gorgas, as Recorded in Her Diary." *Confederate Veteran* 25:3 (March 1917), 110–11.
Gorgas, Josiah. *The Civil War Diary of General Josiah Gorgas.* Edited by Frank Everson Vandiver. Tuscaloosa: University of Alabama Press, 1947.
_____. *The Journals of Josiah Gorgas, 1857–1878.* Edited by Sarah Woolfolk Wiggins. Tuscaloosa: University of Alabama Press, 1995. This book supersedes the 1947 work edited by Frank Vandiver.
Gourley, Catherine. *The Horrors of Andersonville: Life and Death Inside a Civil War Prison.* Minneapolis: Twenty-First Century Books, 2010. This is a children's book.
Greeley, Horace. *The American Conflict: A History of the Great Rebellion in the United States of America, 1860–65.* Hartford, CT: O.D. Case, 1866. Chapter 35, titled "Southward Flight of Jefferson Davis," is in Volume 2, p. 756.
Greene, A. Wilson. *Breaking the Backbone of the Rebellion: The Final Battles of the Petersburg Campaign.* Mason City, IA: Savas, 2000. This book was republished by the University of Tennessee Press in 2012, as *The Final Battles of the Petersburg Campaign: Breaking the Backbone of the Rebellion.*
_____. *Civil War Petersburg; Confederate City in the Crucible of War.* Charlottesville: University of Virginia Press, 2006.
Grigg, Don A. Untitled article. *Danville Register & Bee* (July 4, 1976).
Hagan, Jane. *The Story of Danville.* Danville, VA: Stratford House, 1950.
Hairston, Lora Beatrice Wade. *A Brief History of Danville, 1728–1954.* Danville, VA: Dietz Press, 1955.

Hampshire Advertiser (England). April 8, 1854; May 6, 1854; June 10, 1854.

Handy, Moses Purnell. "The Fall of Richmond in 1865." *The American Magazine and Historical Chronicle* (Autumn-Winter 1985). An edited version of the seven-part Handy series that first appeared in the New York newspaper, *The Watchman*, in 1866.

Moses Purnell Handy

Born April 14, 1847, in Warsaw, Missouri, Moses Purnell Handy was referred to as Purnell Handy in 1865, but later as Moses Handy. His name has also been seen as M.P. Handy and M. Purnell Handy. The Civil War began while Handy was at the Virginia Collegiate and Military Institute, in Portsmouth, and he joined the fight, was assigned to the staff of General Walter H. Stevens, Lee's chief of Engineers, and purportedly served with gallantry in the closing months of the war. As *The American Magazine and Historical Chronicle* says, Handy's narrative *apparently exists in but one file at Duke University, and in clippings in Handy's papers, which*, about 1985, *were placed at the Clements Library* [University of Michigan] *by his descendants.* The Handy Papers do include an 1863 pocket diary in which the year has been crossed out, and "1865" substituted, with entries in pencil and pen for April 1 through April 30 and slightly variant entries for April 1 through April 20 repeated in the book under the heading, "Copy of Diary." The notes are sketchy, not having the wealth of detail or literary qualities of the printed version, but they agree in factual matter. Presumably this is the original diary upon which he constructed his narrative, filling in the details from memory of the events less than a year in the past. The published installments are a vivid, nearly contemporary account which, because of their obscure place of publication, have escaped the richly deserved attention of historians. Of the seven parts which were printed in The Watchman, the first and most of the second are reprinted here, tracing his movements from the evening of April 1 until the morning of the 3rd. The other five printed installments, not re-published here, trace Handy's march toward Appomattox. It must be mentioned that in Handy's article, there is not a single mention of the Jefferson Davis flight. Shortly after the war, Handy became a reporter with the *Richmond Dispatch*, in the 1870s went to the *New York Tribune*, and later joined the *Philadelphia Press*, as a reporter. From 1880 to 1885 he was editor of the *Press* (at the time the paper interviewed Ben Hill [see Chapter 1]). He was later editor-in-chief of the *Chicago Times Herald* and died on January 8, 1898, at the Hotel Bon Air, Augusta, Georgia.

Hanna, Alfred Jackson. *Flight into Oblivion*. Richmond: Johnson, 1938. A seminal work. *Hanna focused on the fortunes of President Jefferson Davis's cabinet during the retreat* [from Michael Ballard's book, *A Long Shadow*]. And this, from a review by W.W. Davis in the *Florida Historical Quarterly* 17:3 (January 1939): *Professor Hanna's book ... is a unique as well as a notable contribution to the history of the closing weeks of the Civil War. The inclusion of fifty-seven illustrations by John Rea lend the right atmosphere to the volume and add to its charm.*

Hardy, Michael C. *Civil War Charlotte: Last Capital of the Confederacy*. Charleston, SC: History Press, 2012.

_____. *North Carolina in the Civil War*. Charleston, SC: History Press, 2011.

Harrell, Carolyn L. *When the Bells Tolled for Lincoln: Southern Reaction to the Assassination*. Macon, GA: Mercer University Press, 1997.

Harris, John W. "Confederate Naval Cadets." *Confederate Veteran* (April 1904), p. 170.

_____. "The Gold of the Confederate Treasury" *Southern Historical Society Papers* (1904), pp. 259–60.

Harrison, Burton N. "The Capture of Jefferson Davis." *Century Magazine* (November 1883), pp. 130–144. This article was reproduced in the 1910 book *Aris Sonis Focisque* (see Harrison, Fairfax).

_____. Letter to Jefferson Davis, September 1877.

Harrison, Constance. "Recollections Grave and Gay." *Scribner's Magazine* 49 (January–June 1911). In 1911 Scribner's published this as a book using the same title. Constance Harrison was, before her marriage to Burton Harrison, Connie Cary, and as such is often quoted (and misquoted). She did not go with Harrison and Varina. *After an intolerably slow journey by interrupted trains, Mr. Harrison succeeded in establishing Mrs. Davis and her party at Charlotte, where, on Wednesday, the 4th of April, he received a telegram from President Davis at Danville, merely announcing that he was there.* This was their first news of the evacuation of Richmond on April 2. Wednesday was actually April 5. This is what her husband had written in his 1883 *Century Magazine* article, "The Capture of Jefferson Davis": *Mrs. Davis received a telegram on Wednesday, from the President at Danville, merely announcing that he was there.*

Harrison, Fairfax, ed. *Aris Sonis Focisque. Being a Memoir of an American Family, The Harrisons of Skimino, and particularly of Jesse Burton Harrison and Burton Norvell Harrison*. Privately printed, 1910. Edited by Fairfax Harrison from material collected by Francis Burton Harrison, and privately printed by both men in 1910, this book's version, as opposed to the magazine article, has notes by Jefferson Davis, never before printed. In 1883 Harrison had sent the proof sheets to Jefferson Davis, inviting his comments. Those comments were now inserted on the proofs by "J.D." It must be said that Harrison did not adopt all of J.D.'s suggestions.

Harwell, Richard Barksdale, and Marjorie Crandall. *More Confederate Imprints*. Issue 4. Richmond: Virginia State Library, 1957.

Hattaway, Herman, and Richard E. Beringer. *Jefferson Davis: Confederate President*. Lawrence: University Press of Kansas, 2002.

Haw, Joseph Richardson. "The Last of the C.S. Ordnance Department," in *Confederate Veteran* 34 (December 1926), p. 440. Cited in Burke Davis's *To Appomattox* (1959), in Ballard's *A Long Shadow* (1986), and in McFall's *Danville in the Civil War* (2001).

JOSEPH RICHARDSON HAW

Born on December 14, 1845, in Hanover County, Virginia, Joseph Richardson Haw was the brother of John Hugh Haw and George Pitman Haw. He served as a private in Company A of the 1st Virginia Infantry Battalion He was mustered out on May 10, 1865, at Washington, Georgia. In addition to the article above, Haw had other articles published in *Confederate Veteran*—"The Burning of Hampton," in October 1924, "The Battle of Haw's Shop Community, Virginia," in 1925, "The Haw Boys in the War Between the States," in 1925, and "Corse's Brigade," in 1926.

Burke Davis said of Haw in *To Appomattox*, 1959: *Joseph Haw was a young clerk in the Ordnance Department. He went to a Presbyterian church on this Sunday morning and heard the Rev. Moses Hoge announcing the breaking of Confederate lines at Petersburg. When he went outside and passed the capitol, Haw saw a man building a bonfire of new, unsigned Confederate money in the street.* And this: *The Ordnance Department clerk, Joseph Haw, was one of the fortunates ordered to the Danville depot to join the retreat by rail. When they pushed through the mob and passed the ring of midshipmen with bayonets, the Ordnance men found they were few indeed, no more than twenty, Haw estimated. Even so, they could find no place on the train then in the station. They waited for hours.* And this: *When they returned to the depot there were more hours of waiting, but at last the Ordnance men got into a freight car, clambered over piles of pig lead and bullet molds, and were jammed in a jumble of mattresses and household furniture, the property of some fleeing officer. Joe Haw saw men atop the car, and soon realized that wounded from hospitals in the city covered the train. At last, very late, the wheels groaned into motion and they were off.*

James C. Clark, *Last Train South*, 1984: *Haw and his Ordnance men returned to the depot hours later and were able to jam into a freight car, sitting on top of pig lead and bullet molds. The car also contained mattresses and household furniture belonging to fleeing Confederate officials. As the train moved, Haw heard sounds from the top of the train and wondered who was on top. He soon realized that wounded soldiers had been placed on top of the cars.* For this, Clark cites Burke Davis rather than Haw.

F. Lawrence McFall, Jr., *Danville in the Civil War*, 2001: *Joseph R. Haw, and his brother-in-law, C.P. Cross, plus eighteen other employees of the Richmond Arsenal, arrived in Danville well after dark. Reporting to Major Hutter the next morning, they found much of the material and machinery that had been sent down from Richmond and Lynchburg on April 1, lying scattered about the ground, with no protection.*

After the war, Haw lived for years in Richmond as a machinist, around the turn of the century moving to Newport News. He died in Hampton in 1929, and his wife, Mary Cumming, died in 1934. "A Christian gentleman, a loyal soldier of the cross and of the C.S.A."

Hay, Thomas Robson. *Hood's Tennessee Campaign*. New York: Walter Neale, 1929.
Headley, John W. *Confederate Operations in Canada and New York*. New York: Neale, 1906.
Heck, Frank H. *Proud Kentuckian: John C. Breckinridge, 1821–1875*. Lexington: University Press of Kentucky, 1976.
Heidler, Davis S., and Jeanne T. Heidler, eds. *Encyclopedia of the American Civil War: A Political, Social, and Military History*. New York: W.W. Norton, 2000.
Herndon, G. Melvin, ed. "The Confederate Naval Cadets and the Confederate Treasure. The Diary of Midshipman Robert H. Fleming." *The Georgia Historical Quarterly* 50:2 (June 1966), p. 209.

The editor of the journal wrote in a note that he was indebted to Mary R. Fleming, Robert Fleming's daughter, for the use of the diary and additional papers in her collection. Herndon was a member of the faculty of the Department of History at the University of Georgia.

Hoehling, Adolphus A., and Mary Duprey Hoehling. *The Day Richmond Died*. San Diego: A.S. Barnes, 1981. Republished by Fairfax Press, New York, in 1986, as *The Last Days of the Confederacy*, and reprinted with the new title by Random House's Value Publishing in 1987. In 1991 Madison Books of Lanham, Maryland, offered to reissue the book with the original title, *The Day Richmond Died*. Both Fairfax Press and Madison Books list 1981 as the publication date, but omit mention of a republication date. This, combined with the fact that there have been two titles, has led to much confusion in citations. Some authors have even listed both titles in their bibliographies, as if they were two books.

Hoge, Peyton Harrison. *Moses Drury Hoge: Life and Letters*. Richmond: Presbyterian Committee of Publication, 1899.

Hoke, Jacob. *The Great Invasion of 1863, or General Lee in Pennsylvania*. Dayton, OH: W.J. Shuey, 1887.

Horne, Gerald. *The Deepest South: The United States, Brazil, and the African Slave Trade*. New York: New York University Press, 2007.

Howell, Jefferson Davis. Letters to Jefferson Davis. May 18, 1868; June 28, 1868.

Huddersfield Chronicle (England). June 17, 1854.

Hull Packet (England). May 19, 1854; May 26, 1854.

Illustrated London News. July 8, 1854.

Inter Ocean Curiosity Shop. Vol. 3. Chicago: Inter Ocean, 1881.

Ipswich Journal (England). May 6, 1854.

Irvine, Dallas D. "The Fall of Richmond." *The Journal of the American Military Institute* (Summer, 1939).

Jackson's Oxford Journal (England). May 6, 1854; May 13, 1854.

Jewett, Clayton E., ed. *see* Oldham, Williamson S.

John Bull (England). May 20, 1854.

John Bull and Britannia (England). February 7, 1857.

Johnson, Clint. *Pursuit: The Chase, Capture, Persecution, and Surprising Release of Confederate President Jefferson Davis*. New York: Citadel Press, 2008.

Johnson, Robert Underwood, and Clarence Clough Buel, eds. *Battles and Leaders of the Civil War*. New York: Century. Four volumes were published in 1887, 1888, 1888, and 1889, and collectively titled *Battles and Leaders of the Civil War*. In 2004, military historian Peter Cozzens edited Volumes 5 and 6 (see Cozzens, Peter).

Johnston, Mary. *Cease Firing*. Boston: Houghton Mifflin, 1912.

Johnston, Mary Tabb, and Elizabeth Johnston Lipscomb. *Amelia Gorgas: A Biography*. Tuscaloosa: University of Alabama Press, 1978.

Jones, Evan Rowland. *Four Years in the Army of the Potomac: A Soldier's Recollections*. London: Tyne, 1881.

Jones, J.W. *Life and Letters of Robert Edward Lee, Soldier and Man*. New York: Neale, 1906.

Jones, John Beauchamp. *A Rebel War Clerk's Diary at the Confederate States Capital*. Philadelphia: Lippincott, 1866.

John Beauchamp Jones

In March 1866, at Onancock, Accomac County, Virginia, a short preface was written for a meaningful book. *A Rebel War Clerk's Diary at the Confederate States Capital* was meaningful because of its author, John Beauchamp Jones (also known as J.B. Jones and John B. Jones), and would become very famous. It's a fun read, as diaries go, and much scoured and sourced by writers on the Civil War. The diary entries begin on April 8, 1861, and end on April 19, 1865.

Jones had died, aged 55, on February 4, 1866, a month before the preface bearing his name was written. A Southern novelist of some note, he sought and obtained a position in the Confederate War Department at Richmond when hostilities broke out, with the frank intention of making literary capital out of the war through the books he hoped to write. To serve his purpose, he kept a day-to-day diary in which he entered information to which he had official access, supplementing it by personal observations (*A Treasury of the World's Great Diaries*, by Philip Dunaway and Melvin Evans. New York: Doubleday, 1957).

Surely *A Rebel War Clerk's Diary* contains an absolutely contemporary record of the flight to

Danville. Or does it? Surely it's as close as we're going to get to what we do not have—official Confederate records of the flight. Or is it? Nursing, as one must, a healthy distrust of the authenticity of "diaries," especially 19th-century efforts, one approaches Jones as a (good) district attorney might.

Jones, in his April 10, 1865, entry, warns himself and us that he is nearing the end of the diary, and intimates that his daily habit will be hard to break. He adds, *I may find sufficient employment in revising, correcting, etc., what I have written.* In fact, he did just that, then traveled to Philadelphia, where he secured Lippincott to publish the book in April 1866.

Jones, Katharine Macbeth. *The Ladies of Richmond, Confederate Capital.* New York: Bobbs-Merrill, 1962.
Jornal da Tarde (Brazil).
Kean, Robert Garlick Hill. *Inside the Confederate Government: The Diary of Robert Garlick Hill Kean, the Head of the Bureau of War.* Edited by Edward E. Younger. New York: Oxford University Press, 1957. This is a book presenting what purports to be Kean's diary. The June 1, 1865, entry reads (in part): *At 6 p.m. got all the records to the Danville depot. The train (on which the President and Cabinet also went) did not start until 11 p.m. Reached Danville at 4 p.m. on April 3. Citizens hospitably took us in.* This from the book's introduction by Prof. Younger: *By six o'clock Kean had his records packed and at the Danville depot. With them he boarded the same train which at eleven carried away the President and his Cabinet. The next afternoon they arrived at Danville.*
Jornal das Familias (Brazil).
Knight, Landon. *The Real Jefferson Davis.* Battle Creek, MI: The Pilgrim Magazine Company, 1904.
Kocher, Alfred Lawrence, and Howard Dearstyne. *Shadows in Silver: A Record of Virginia, 1850– 1900, in Contemporary Photographs Taken by George and Huestis Cook, with Additions from the Cook Collection.* New York: Scribner, 1954.
Krick, Robert K. *Civil War Weather in Virginia.* Tuscaloosa: University of Alabama Press, 2007.
Kuenzi, Hans. "The Search for Lost Confederate Gold." *The Charger* 29:7 (March 2008).
Lachman, Charles. *The Last Lincolns: The Rise and Fall of a Great American Family.* New York: Sterling, 2008.
Lady's Newspaper (England). May 26, 1854.
Langhein, Eric. *Jefferson Davis, Patriot: A Biography.* New York: Vantage, 1962.
Lankford, Nelson D. *Richmond Burning: The Last Days of the Confederate Capital.* New York: Viking, 2002. William C. Davis reviewed the book in *The Journal of American History* 90:2 (September 2003). *Surely no one knows this story better.* And this: *Outstanding scholarship, sound judgment and enviable writing.* Emory Thomas reviewed this book in *The Journal of Southern History* 69:4 (November 2003), pp. 927–928. *Nelson Lankford has written the best book about the fall of Richmond.* Richmond Burning *is the definitive study of this fascinating and significant series of events.* And this: *Nelson Lankford's research is exhaustive.* And this: *...he knows more about his subject than anyone else ever has.*

_____, ed. see Conolly, Thomas.
Law Times (England). July 12, 1856.
Lee, Fitzhugh. *General Lee.* New York: Appleton, 1894. Foreword by James Grant Wilson.
Lee, Richard McGowan. *General Lee's City: An Illustrated Guide to the Historic Sites of Confederate Richmond.* McLean, VA: EPM Publications, 2007.
Lee, Robert E. *Lee's Dispatches. Unpublished Letters of General Robert E. Lee, CSA, to Jefferson Davis and the War Department of the Confederate States of America, 1862–65.* Edited by Douglas Southall Freeman. New York: G.P. Putnam's, 1915. From the private collection of Wymberley Jones de Renne, of Wormsloe, Georgia. With an introduction by Freeman.

_____. Various telegrams and letters in the *OR*, and in *The Papers of Jefferson Davis*.
_____. *The Wartime Papers of R.E. Lee.* Edited by Clifford Dowdey and Louis H. Manarin. Boston: Little, Brown, 1961.
LeVan, Russell George. *The Great War of Destruction.* Raleigh, NC: Pentland, 2000.
Leyburn, John McDowell. "The Fall of Richmond." *Harper's New Monthly Magazine* 33 (June 1866), pp. 92–96. Leyburn (1814–1893) was minister at Tabb Street Presbyterian Church in Richmond. Despite being much cited as a source in books concerning the Davis flight, Leyburn's five-page article does not aid us in our inquiry.
Life. March 3, 1961.
Life and Reminiscences of Jefferson Davis. Baltimore: R.H. Woodward, 1890.
Lightfoot, Emmie Crump. "The Evacuation of Richmond." *Virginia Magazine of History and Biography* 41 (July 1933), p. 219.

Limerick Chronicle (Ireland). September 9, 1829; December 2, 1829; November 17, 1830; April 30, 1831; June 4, 1831; June 30, 1831; January 9, 1850.

Lincoln Herald. Vols. 67–68, page 9. Harrogate, TN: Lincoln Memorial University Press, 1966. A quarterly magazine devoted to historical research in the field of Lincolniana and the Civil War.

Literary Gazette (England). February 7, 1857.

Lloyd's History of the Great Rebellion. New York: H.H. Lloyd, 1866.

Lockhart, William, ed. *Life of Antonio Rosmini Serbati*. Vol. 2. London: Kegan Paul, Trench, 1886.

_____. *An Outline of the Life of the Very Rev. Antonio Rosmini*. London: Richardson, 1856.

Loewen, James W. *Lies Across America: What American Historic Sites Get Wrong*. New York: New Press, 1999.

Long, A.L. *Memoirs of Robert E. Lee: His Military and Personal History*. London: Sampson & Low, 1886.

Lossing, Benson John, ed. *Harper's Encyclopaedia of United States History*. New York: Harper, 1905. Foreword by Woodrow Wilson. Lossing, long associated with *Harper's Magazine*, had died in 1891. This book is based upon his plan.

_____, ed. *Pictorial Field Guide of the Civil War*. Three volumes in one were published in 1874.

_____, ed. *Pictorial History of the Civil War in the United States of America*. Vols. 1-2. Philadelphia: G.W. Childs, 1866, 1868.

Lowry, Don. *Towards an Indefinite Shore: The Final Months of the Civil War, December 1864–May 1865*. New York: Hippocrene Books, 1995.

Lubbock, Francis Richard. *Six Decades in Texas, or Memoirs of Francis Richard Lubbock, Governor of Texas in Wartime, 1861–1863: A Personal Experience in Business, War and Politics*. Edited by C.W. Raines. Austin, TX: Ben C. Jones, 1900. Lubbock finished his manuscript in the spring of 1897, when he was 82 (32 years after the event). In his short preface, Lubbock admits that these memoirs are from his memory. The editor warns that this is a book about Texas history, and that Lubbock's involvement with the final days of the Confederacy is but subsidiary to this idea. All we have from Lubbock, then, about the actual flight is: *I met him [Davis] at the hour appointed, and accompanied him, with the other members of his staff, to the train. This was the saddest trip I had ever made, for I could but feel grieved—sorely distressed; a sorrow that was ominous of the future. Arriving safely at Danville, we went into quarters.*

MacCaleb, Walter Flavius, ed. *see* Reagan, John H.

MacWalter, J.G., trans. (anonymous). *Discourses on Moral and Religious Subjects* by Antonio Rosmini Serbati. Dublin: James Duffy, 1882.

_____. "Hugh O'Hegan's History" (short story). *Ainsworth's Magazine* (August 1854).

_____. *The Irish Reformation Movement*. Dublin: George Herbert, 1852. This book is also known as *The History of the Irish Church*.

_____. *The Life of Antonio Rosmini Serbati*. London: Kegan Paul, Trench, 1883.

_____. *The Modern Mystery, or Table-Tapping*. London: J.F. Shaw, 1854.

_____. *The Scarlet Mystery*. London: James Nisbet, 1854.

_____. *Tales of Ireland and the Irish*. London: J.F. Shaw, 1854.

Madison, Virginia. "The Fall of Richmond." In *The Southern Amaranth*. New York: Wilcox & Rockwell, 1869. A long poem, written on March 18, 1867. Virginia Madison is really Sallie Brock. (See Brock, Sallie Ann.)

Mallory, Stephen Russell. "The Flight from Richmond." *Civil War Times Illustrated* 11: 1 (April 1972). This is a reprinting of the *McClure's* magazine 1900 edited version of Mallory's account retitled.

_____. "Last Days of the Confederate Government." *McClure's* magazine (December 1900, January 1901).

_____. Letter to James A. Seddon, November 4, 1864 (National Archives).

_____. Mallory Papers. Wilson Library, University of North Carolina at Chapel Hill.

Manchester Times (England). May 10, 1854; May 17, 1854.

Manning, H.G. *Unwavering Duty: Jefferson Davis*. Bloomington, IN: Xlibris, 2011. A novel.

Mapp, Alf Johnson. *Frock Coats and Epaulets: Psychological Portraits of Confederate Military and Political Leaders*. New York: T. Yoseloff, 1963. Reissued in 1982 with the subtitle "The Men Who Led the Confederacy." With its original subtitle it was republished by Jameson Books, of Ottawa, Illinois, in 1985.

Margotti, Giacomo. *Roma e Londra*. Torino: Tipografia Fory e Dalmazzo, 1858.

Marlow, Clayton Charles. *Matt W. Ransom: Confederate General from North Carolina*. Jefferson, NC: McFarland, 1996. Marlow died on July 24, 1996, just before his book was published.

Matthews, Gary Robert. *Basil Wilson Duke, CSA: The Right Man in the Right Place*. Lexington: University Press of Kentucky, 2005.

McCabe, James Dabney, Jr. *Life and Campaigns of General Robert E. Lee*. New York: National, 1866.
McClure, Alexander Kelly. *Annals of the War Written by Leading Participants North and South*. Philadelphia: *Times*, 1879.
McClure's. December 1900, January 1901.
McClurken, Jeffrey W. *Take Care of the Living: Reconstructing Confederate Veteran Families in Virginia*. Charlottesville: University of Virginia Press, 2009.
McElroy, Robert. *Jefferson Davis, the Unreal and the Real*. 2 vols. New York: Harper, 1937. The *long-felt need of an adequate biography of Jefferson Davis has not been met by this superficial study* [*The Mississippi Valley Historical Review* 25:3, (December 1938)]. *Professor Robert McElroy, a history professor at Princeton University, published* Jefferson Davis, the Real and the Unreal, *in 1937, but it is superficial and undistinguished* [Clement Eaton, in his own book, *Jefferson Davis*, 1978]. As Michael B. Ballard writes, in *The American Civil War* (1996), *Robert McElroy's two-volume* Jefferson Davis: The Unreal and the Real *(1937) is at times superficial but was probably the most thorough account of Davis's life up to that time.* As Charles F. Strong said in his well-balanced review in *Annals of the American Academy of Political and Social Science* 198 (July 1938), *The exhaustive critical bibliography does not adequately compensate for the omission of footnotes*. Most reviews were bad, and all criticized this lack of footnotes, a lack that was made worse by McElroy saying, on page 699, that *the full text, with footnotes attached, has been deposited in the New York Public Library.*
McFall, F. Lawrence, Jr. *Danville in the Civil War*. Lynchburg, VA: H.E. Howard, 2001.
_____. "To Danville." A chapter in *Virginia at War, 1865*. Edited by William C. Davis and James I. Robertson, Jr. Lexington: University Press of Kentucky, 2012. As McFall stated to reporter Susan Elzey in an interview for *GoDanRiver.com*, December 21, 2011, "*I detail the events of April 2 through April 10, 1865.*"
McGovern, Bryan P. *John Mitchel: Irish Nationalist, Southern Secessionist*. Knoxville: University of Tennessee Press, 2009.
McGuire, Judith W. *Diary of a Southern Refugee During the War*. "By a lady of Virginia." New York: E.J. Hale & Son, 1867.
Meade, Robert Douthat. *Judah P. Benjamin: Confederate Statesman*. New York: Oxford University Press, 1943.
Melton, Herman E. "An Antebellum Tragedy on the Old R & D Railroad." *Pittsylvania Packet* (Winter 1993). An article taken from the author's book.
_____. *Picks, Tracks and Bateaux: Industry in Pittsylvania County, 1750–1950*. Privately printed, 1993.
Melvin, Philip. "Stephen Russell Mallory: Naval Statesman." *The Journal of Southern History* 10:2 (May 1944).
"A Message from Lee Touched Off Exodus." *Danville Register* (April 1965).
Miller, Fannie Walker. "The Fall of Richmond." *Confederate Veteran* (1905). She mentions that she had been appointed as a copying clerk in the Bureau of War by the Hon. A.J. Seddon, which, of course, should be J.A. Seddon. *I was spending the day with my mother and sister, who were matrons at Howard Grove Hospital, consequently was not in my accustomed seat at dear old St. Paul, of precious memory*. There is nothing in this article about the Davis flight.
Millett, Wesley, and Gerald White. *The Rebel and the Rose: James A. Semple, Julia Gardiner Tyler and the Lost Confederate Gold*. Nashville: Cumberland House, 2007.
Minnigerode, Charles. "My Dead Hero." A chapter of the book *Life and Reminiscences of Jefferson Davis*. Baltimore, MD: R.H. Woodward, 1890.
Minor, Hubbard T. *Confederate Naval Cadet: The Diary and Letters of Midshipman Hubbard T. Minor, with a History of the Confederate Naval Academy*. Edited by R. Thomas Campbell. Jefferson, NC: McFarland, 2007.
Moore, Jerrold Northrop. *Confederate Commissary General: Lucius Bellinger Northrop and the Subsistence Bureau of the Southern Army*. Shippensburg, PA: White Mane, 1996.
Morgan, James Morris. *Recollections of a Rebel Reefer*. Boston: Houghton Mifflin, 1917.
Morning Chronicle (London). July 20, 1855; July 11, 1856; March 24, 1857; June 2, 1857.
Morning Post (London). October 1, 1852; April 1, 1854; April 3, 1854; April 4, 1854; April 19, 1854; June 3, 1854; June 5, 1854; June 6, 1854; July 29, 1854; August 8, 1854; July 20, 1855; January 10, 1857; March 24, 1857; March 27, 1857; May 2, 1857.
Moshein, Peter, and Robert R. Rothfus. "Rogers Locomotives: A Brief History and Construction List." Railroad History #167, Railway & Locomotive Historical Society, 1992.
Mott, Frank Luther. *A History of American Magazines, 1860–1865*. Cambridge, MA: Harvard University Press, 1938.

A Nação (Brazil) April 17, 1873.
Nation (Dublin). December 18, 1852.
Neiman, Simon I. *Judah Benjamin*. New York: Bobbs-Merrill, 1963.
Nevins, Allan. *War for the Union: The Organized War to Victory, 1864–1865*. New York: Scribner, 1971.
New York Citizen.
New York City Directory. 1860, 1861.
New York Daily News. May 14, 1856; September 22, 1859.
New York Daily Tribune. September 10, 1857; April 17, 1860; June 13, 1860; July 18, 1860; July 19, 1860; March 25, 1865; April 8, 1865. The *Tribune* was founded by Horace Greeley in 1841. In 1922 it merged with the *New York Herald* to form the *New York Herald-Tribune*.
New York Evening Express. March 10, 1863.
New York Herald. April 17, 1860; June 10, 1861; March 21, 1865; April 6, 1865; April 8, 1865; July 4, 1865; December 21, 1869; June 20, 1872. The *Herald* was started by Gordon Bennett in 1835. In 1922 it merged with the *New York Daily Tribune* to form the *New York Herald-Tribune*.
New York Times. June 27, 1857; April 9, 1865.
New York Volunteer.
New York World. January 11, 1870.
Nichols, Roy Franklin. *The Stakes of Power, 1845–1877*. New York: Hill & Wang, 1961.
Nofi, Albert A. *A Civil War Treasury*. Conshohocken, PA: Combined Books, 1992.
North Wales Chronicle. July 8, 1854.
Nottinghamshire Guardian. April 20, 1854; May 11, 1854; June 8, 1854; June 29, 1854.
Oldham, Williamson S. *From Richmond to Texas: The 1865 Journey Home of Confederate Senator Williamson S. Oldham*. Edited by W. Buck Yearns. Dayton, OH: Morningside Press, 1998.
_____. *Rise and Fall of the Confederacy: The Memoir of Senator Williamson S. Oldham*. Edited and with an introduction by Clayton E. Jewett. Columbia: University of Missouri Press, 2006.
Oliphant, Octavia. *Frirwin*. London: J. Hope & Co., 1856. 2 vols. *The author inscribes these volumes to Mrs. MacWalter as slight token of deep affection and high admiration*. Allibone has this novel as *Firwin*, and being written by Oscar Oliphant. The *Dublin Review* has it as *Kirwin*. Both are wrong. However, Octavia Oliphant is Sir Oscar Oliphant.
Oliphant, Sir Oscar. *China—A Popular History*. London: J. Hope, 1857.
_____. *Collected Poems*. London: J. Hope, 1856. Sir Oscar Oliphant is a pseudonym used by J.G. MacWalter.
Opinião Liberal (Brazil).
O'Reilly, Bill, and Martin Dugard. *Killing Lincoln: The Shocking Assassination that Changed America Forever*. New York, Henry Holt, 2011. A special illustrated edition of this book came out the following year, titled *Lincoln's Last Days*. Dugard does not appear as co-author. Dwight Jon Zimmerman does.
Parker, William H. "The Gold and Silver in the Confederate States Treasury." *The Southern Historical Society Papers*. Vol. 21, 1893, pp. 304–308. This article is reproduced in the book *Voices of the Confederate Navy* (see under Campbell, R. Thomas, in this bibliography).
_____. *Recollections of a Naval Officer, 1841–1865*. New York: Charles Scribner's, 1883.
Patrick, Rembert Wallace. *The Fall of Richmond*. Baton Rouge: Louisiana State University Press, 1960. This book commits to print, in expanded form, the Walter Lynwood Fleming Lectures delivered by Patrick at Louisiana State University. Illustrative materials are drawn in the main from the Confederate and Valentine museums.
_____. *Jefferson Davis and His Cabinet*. Baton Rouge: Louisiana State University Press, 1944.
Paul, Alfred. Report to Drouyn de Lhuys, April 11, 1865.
Pearce, Haywood Jefferson, Jr. *Benjamin J. Hill: Secession and Reconstruction*. Chicago: Chicago University Press, 1928.
Pedro II (Brazilian newspaper).
Pember, Phoebe Yates. "Reminiscences of a Southern Hospital. By Its Matron." Serialized in four consecutive editions of *The Cosmopolite* (published by De Leon and Co. of Baltimore): 1:1 (January 1866), pp. 70–89; 1:2 (February 1866), pp. 203–215; 1:2 (March 1866), pp. 297–309; 1:4 (April 1866), pp. 350–369. The first page of this memoir has it copyrighted 1865 by T.C. De Leon in Maryland. It is the fourth part that is relevant to this book. Phoebe Yates Levy Pember (1823–1913) was the matron at Chimborazo Hospital in Richmond during the Civil War. See Wiley, Bell I.
_____. *A Southern Woman's Story: Life in Confederate Richmond*. Edited by Bell I. Wiley. Jackson, TN: McCowat-Mercer, 1957.

Perkerson, Medora Fields. *White Columns in Georgia*. New York: Rinehart, 1952. The book has a chapter titled "Lost Gold of the Confederacy," in which Perkerson gives an account of the movements of the treasure under Parker and the midshipmen.

Pfanz, Donald C., ed. *see* Ewell, General Richard S.

_____. *Richard S. Ewell: A Soldier's Life*. Chapel Hill: University of North Carolina Press, 1998.

Phillips, Lance. *Yonder Comes the Train: The Story of the Iron Horse and Some of the Roads It Traveled*. South Brunswick, NJ: A.S. Barnes, 1965.

Pollard, Edward Alfred. *Last Year of the War*. New York: C.B. Richardson, 1866. This book was one of a series of books called "The Southern History of the War."

_____. *The Life of Jefferson Davis: With a Secret History of the Southern Confederacy*. Philadelphia: National, 1869. This book was reprinted the same year by Applewood Books, of Bedford, Massachusetts.

_____. *The Lost Cause: A New Southern History of the War of the Confederates*. New York: E.B. Treat, 1866. As Frank E. Vandiver says of Pollard in his article "Jefferson Davis—Leader without Legend," *In 1862 his* First Year of the War *appeared, followed by annual volumes, each more anti–Davis than the last. In 1866 Pollard culled his multi-volume diatribe into one,* The Lost Cause.

Pollock, Edward. *Illustrated Sketch Book of Danville, Virginia: Its Manufactures and Commerce*. Danville: 1885. This book is usually mis-cited as *Sketchbook*. Pollock (1842–1887) was an English journalist and publisher, son of William Pollock, Archdeacon of Chester. He moved to Canada in 1871, and in 1880 came with his family to Richmond, Virginia, later living in Portsmouth, Virginia, where he died. Known as the "sketch book man," what he did for Danville, he also did for Petersburg, Suffolk, Portsmouth, Norfolk, Lynchburg, and other cities, his money coming from advertising in the books.

Poor, Henry Varnum. *Poor's Manual of the Railroads of the United States*. New York: H.V. & H.W. Poor, 1968.

Prescott, Royal B. "The Capture of Richmond." A chapter in *Civil War Papers* (1900). See The Commandery.

Preston, George H. Letters to Jefferson Davis: December 20, 1871; April 17, 1872.

"Pretenders." *All the Year Round*. November 27, 1869. Author possibly Charles Mackay.

Procter, Ben Hamill. *Not Without Honor: The Life of John H. Reagan*. Austin: University of Texas Press, 1962.

Pryor, Mrs. Roger Atkinson. *Reminiscences of Peace and War*. New York: Macmillan, 1904. Chapter 23 is titled "Richmond Surrenders," and reproduces an eyewitness account of one "Agnes," written from Richmond on April 5, 1865, in which "Agnes" says: *I am sure you will have heard the grewsome story of Richmond's evacuation. I was at St. Paul's Sunday, April 1, when a note was handed to President Davis. He rose instantly, and walked down the aisle—his face set, so we could read nothing*. The value of this work may be judged from this passage.

Quinn, James. *John Mitchel*. Dublin: Historical Association of Ireland, 2008.

Raab, James W. *J. Patton Anderson, Confederate General: A Biography*. Jefferson, NC: McFarland, 2004.

Radley, Kenneth. *Rebel Watchdog. The Confederate States Army Provost Guard*. Baton Rouge: Louisiana State University Press, 1989.

Raines, C.W., ed. *see* Lubbock, Francis Richard.

Reagan, John H. Letter to Governor Porter, August 20, 1877, reproduced in the *Times* (Philadelphia), September 1, 1877.

_____. *Memoirs: With Special Reference to Secession and the Civil War*. Edited by Walter Flavius MacCaleb. New York: Neale, 1906.

"Retreat of the Cabinet from Richmond." *Confederate Veteran* 6 (July 1898). An article about Micajah H. Clark.

Rhodes, James Ford. *History of the Civil War, 1861–1865*. New York: Macmillan, 1917.

Richmond Daily Dispatch. January 2, 1863; January 3, 1863; September 10, 1863; March 27, 1865.

Richmond Daily Whig. December 8, 1863; November 20, 1864; April 4, 1865; April 5, 1865; April 6, 1865; October 20, 1868; February 15, 1882.

Richmond Examiner. March 7, 1863; February 27, 1865; February 6, 1866.

Rogers, D. Laurence. *Apostles of Equality: The Birneys, the Republicans, and the Civil War*. East Lansing: Michigan State University Press, 2011.

Roland, Charles P. *The Confederacy*, Chicago: University of Chicago Press, 1960.

Rosmini Serbati, Antonio *see* MacWalter, J.G.

Rosminian records. Collegio Rosmini, Stresa, Italy.

Ross, Ishbel. *First Lady of the South: The Life of Mrs. Jefferson Davis.* New York: Harper, 1958.

Rowland, Dunbar, ed. *see* Davis, Jefferson.

Rowland, Eron. *Varina Howell: Wife of Jefferson Davis.* New York: Macmillan, 1927. Eron Rowland was the wife of Dunbar Rowland.

Royal Literary Fund Records. British Library, Western Manuscripts Division Area, Loan 96, RLF 1/2310. The RLF was a fund set up to provide relief for writers down on their luck. Widows and orphans might also be provided for by the terms of its charter, and in May 1889, Emily Mac Walter applied, from 8 Hetherington Road, Clapham. 30 pages of application; letters written by Emily MacWalter and her daughter Elizabeth Mary Beatrice "Lily" MacWalter, forms they filled out, testimonials, masses of stuff on MacWalter. This was the find that proved beyond doubt that J.G. MacWalter was Stuart.

Rubin, Anne Sarah. *A Shattered Nation: The Rise and Fall of the Confederacy, 1861–1868.* Chapel Hill: University of North Carolina Press, 2007.

Ryan, David D. *Four Days in 1865: The Fall of Richmond.* Richmond: Cadmus, 1993. This work is generally presented as nonfiction, although not by the author, who actually says that his book is fiction. It even has an index, something unusual in a novel. The danger is, it appears cited, sourced, or in the bibliographies in some historical books about the Davis flight, for example: *The Rebel and the Rose*, Swanson's *Bloody Crimes*, and *The Papers of Jefferson Davis*. *The president climbed into the creaky passenger car and seated himself on one of the benches. He began to pen a letter to Varina*, and then Ryan cites a portion of the letter, the famous April 5 letter which, of course, was not written until two days after Davis had reached Danville.

Schaff, Morris. *Jefferson Davis: His Life and Personality.* Boston: John W. Luce, 1922. Unannotated and unsourced.

_____. *Sunset of the Confederacy.* Boston: John W. Luce, 1912. *So, then, with Davis's train speeding on, and he, from his seat beside a window, looking out into the black night, ends Sunday at Richmond.*

Schermerhorn, Calvin. *Money Over Mastery, Family Over Freedom: Slavery in the Antebellum Upper South.* Baltimore, MD: Johns Hopkins University Press, 2011.

Sentinel. January 8, 1864.

Sheffield and Rotherham Independent. April 22, 1854.

Shingleton, Royce Gordon. *John Taylor Wood: Sea Ghost of the Confederacy.* Athens: University of Georgia Press, 1979.

Singer, Jane. *The Confederate Dirty War: Arson, Bombings, Assassination and Plots for Chemical and Germ Attacks on the Union.* Jefferson, NC: McFarland, 2005.

Smith, Jean Edward. *Grant.* New York: Simon and Schuster, 2001.

"A Southside Virginia Town Became Home for Thousands During One Week in April." *Danville Register* (April 1965).

Spence, Edward Lee. *Treasures of the Confederate Coast: The "Real Rhett Butler," and Other Revelations.* Charleston, SC: Narwhal Press, 1995.

Spirit of the American Press. March 17, 1860.

Spong, John Shelby. *Here I Stand. My Struggle for a Christianity of Integrity, Love, and Equality.* New York: HarperCollins, 2000.

Standard (London). April 30, 1831; October 15, 1852; October 19, 1852; November 20, 1852; April 19, 1854; May 31, 1854; June 1, 1854; June 26, 1854; September 7, 1857.

Stern, Philip Van Doren. *An End to Valor: The Last Days of the Civil War.* Boston: Houghton, Mifflin, 1958.

Stoddard, Nikki Schofield. *Alas Richmond: A Civil War Romance.* Bloomington, IN: AuthorHouse, 2011. A novel.

Stout, Harry S. *Upon the Altar of the Nation: A Moral History of the Civil War.* New York: Viking Penguin, 2006.

Strode, Hudson. *Jefferson Davis: American Patriot.* New York: Harcourt, Brace, 1955.

_____. *Jefferson Davis: Confederate President.* New York: Harcourt, Brace, 1959.

_____. *Jefferson Davis, Tragic Hero, the Last Twenty-Five Years, 1864–1889.* New York: Harcourt, Brace, 1964.

_____, ed. *see* Davis, Jefferson.

Hudson Strode

Upon the publication of Strode's third volume, J.B. Joyner, of Miami University in Ohio, wrote a review of the entire Strode phenomenon, in *The Journal of the Illinois State Historical Society* 58:2 (Summer 1965), pp. 217–219: *In 1951 Professor Strode began what he hoped would be the definitive biography of Jefferson Davis. His purpose was to reveal the truth about "the most misunderstood man in history." This was to be done by combining biography and history in an acceptable synthesis, using care not to let the man become lost in the setting in which he had lived. At that stage, the author thought the story could be told in two volumes. The first would carry the narrative to 1861. The final volume would deal with the War Between the States and Davis's later life. But, as the work progressed, Prof. Strode found the information on Davis so vast, and the source material that had never been used before by other biographers so great, that a third volume would be necessary.* Of all three volumes, he says: *...the author has painted a sensitive and glowing portrait of a great man... He writes with balance and good judgement.* On the other hand, Clement Eaton, in his 1978 book, *Jefferson Davis*, wrote: *Hudson Strode, a professor of English at the University of Alabama, wrote three volumes of a Davis biography, beginning in 1950, which are pleasant and interesting, but they are all-admiring and written in a political vacuum.* Norman D. Brown [in *The Indiana Magazine of History* 74:3 (September 1978), pp. 282–284], while reviewing Clement Eaton's 1978 book *Jefferson Davis*, could find little good to say, so, instead, he offered this: *To date, there has been no satisfactory life of Davis. The best of a rather poor lot is Hudson Strode's laudatory three-volume work,* Jefferson Davis, *completed in 1964.* Or, as Michael B. Ballard says, in *The American Civil War* (1996), *Beautifully written, Strode's volumes are nevertheless marred by a blind partisanship that attempts to transform Davis into an inerrant icon.*

Strother, John M. Affidavit, April 3, 1866.
Stuart, C.E.L. "Anglo Saxon Mania." *Southern Literary Messenger*, vol. 35, November and December 1863. Written as Dr. Stuart.
_____. "History of the Last Days and Final Fall of the Rebellion." The name given by certain U.S. newspapers when reprinting Stuart's July 4, 1865, *New York Herald* article. The title was not used by the *Herald*. The reprints continued to use the *Herald*'s anonymous by-line, "a Rebel staff officer." Although the identity of the author was common enough knowledge, at least among the in-crowd, it was not until Horace Greeley's 1866 book, *The American Conflict*, that the world learned that this staff officer was "Lt. C.E.L. Stuart."
_____. Letter to Confederate Secretary of War Leroy P. Walker, September 10, 1861.
_____. Letters to Jefferson Davis. October 10, 1861 (National Archives); December 19, 1861 (Library of Congress); February 10, 1862 (National Archives).
Stucker, Augustin. *Lincoln & Davis: A Dual Biography of America's Civil War Presidents*. Bloomington, IN: AuthorHouse, 2011.
Sulivane, Clement. "The Fall of Richmond. Part 1. The Evacuation." In *Battles and Leaders of the Civil War* 4 (1889), pp. 725–726.
Swallow, W.H. "Retreat of the Confederate Government from Richmond to the Gulf." *Magazine of American History* (1886), pp. 596–608.

W.H. SWALLOW

Colonel Swallow was serving with the troops in defense of Richmond during the evacuation. Twenty-one years after the event, he wrote his short but often-sourced account. He comes with impressive credentials. A Marylander in the Confederate army, an engineer in Jubal Early's division at Gettysburg, he wrote definitive, although not entirely accurate, first-person articles about Gettysburg, in *Southern Bivouac* in 1885 and 1886. Ever since Jacob Hoke's classic book, *The Great Invasion of 1863*, was published in 1887, the reader interested in Gettysburg is going to come across Swallow. As for the evacuation of Richmond on the night of April 2, 1865, Swallow writes, *It was fully eight o'clock when the train departed. Many failed to obtain seats in the cars and were greatly disappointed, for there was little, if any, prospect of another train leaving before the "Yankees" should arrive in the town.* He only mentions that one train, and his information comes primarily from J.B. Jones's *A Rebel War Clerk's Diary*.

Some researchers have tried to locate Colonel W.H. Swallow in the Army records, but have been unsuccessful. The general conclusion is that W.H. Swallow is an alias, or pseudonym. But that's where it stands.

An examination of old newspapers and other records reveals the following: Isaiah J. Porter was born in Little York, Pennsylvania, in 1834. Young Porter, all fired up by the prospect of making a living, chose the rather unusual occupation of arsonist. Of course, he was put away in a place where he could not harm himself or, especially, anyone else. Emerging from incarceration, he proceeded over the next seven years, under literally a hundred aliases, to bilk, forge, bigamize, and generally make a nuisance of himself in practically every state of the Union. He was an epidemic. He did time, got off, did time, broke out, until finally, in 1862, he was thrown into the lunatic asylum at Sing Sing, which is where he was languishing when the Battle of Gettysburg occurred. Inexplicably, and to the great chagrin of many interested parties, Porter was pardoned by the governor on New Years Day 1864, and after the war continued along his course of crime, but with double the vigor. He was a ubiquitous disease, a boil on the buttocks of American society, turning up here as Colonel Alex H. Nelson of the 59th Fusiliers, there as Governor Porter of Arkansas; here as former rebel Major General Edward Humphreys, there as the Rev. Dr. Barnes. The man was the most indefatigable crime figure of the 19th century. Finally, in 1882 he was bagged again, and began submitting, from prison, first-person Confederate history articles to reputable magazines under the pen name of W.H. Swallow, a pointed jab at a despised parson from his past.

Jacob Hoke, who lived in Chambersburg, Pennsylvania, was a frequent correspondent of Convict Swallow's, and relied heavily on the incarcerated man for information for his great work on Gettysburg. Some historians who have written on Jefferson Davis's flight from Richmond have cited Swallow including:

- Michael B. Ballard. *A Long Shadow*, 1986.
- Mark L. Bradley. *This Astounding Close*, 2000.
- Nash K. Burger and John K. Bettersworth. *South of Appomattox*, 1959.
- James C. Clark. *Last Train South*, 1984.
- Alfred Hanna. *Flight into Oblivion*, 1938.
- Herman Hattaway and Richard E. Beringer. *Jefferson Davis*, 2002.
- Dallas D. Irvine. "The Fall of Richmond," 1939.
- Nelson D. Lankford. *Richmond Burning*, 2002.
- *The Papers of Jefferson Davis*, September 1864–May 1865 (p. 552, notes).
- T. Harry Williams, ed. *Military Analysis of the Civil War*, 1977.

Noah Andre Trudeau wrote the book *Gettysburg*. Like most other writers on the subject of Gettysburg, M. Trudeau cites Swallow. However, he does not mention Swallow in *Out of the Storm*, his book that covers the Jefferson Davis flight.

Experts contributed chapters to the 2004 book *Leaders of the Lost Cause* (see Gallagher). The chapter on Confederate Adjutant General Samuel Cooper was written by William C. Davis. As the editors say in the preface about Davis, he *mines a wide array of sources to present the first modern day portrait of the seemingly invisible adjutant and inspector general of the Confederacy.* One of the sources mined by Davis was W.H. Swallow.

In his book *An Honorable Defeat* (2001), William C. Davis gives Swallow the title "government clerk," something Hattaway and Beringer picked up on the following year. W.H. Swallow is not only a cited source in Davis's book; he is a central character in the story. Events are built around Swallow, as they have been in books about Gettysburg. To some extent—albeit a relatively small one—William C. Davis's shape of the Civil War, and that of those writers who have used Davis as a secondary source, has been determined by a bilker.

It is not difficult to get information on Swallow. The interested reader may care to go to, among many other newspaper articles, the *Baltimore Sun* of August 19, 1886; the *New York Times* of August 20, 1886; the *Kansas City Times* of August 24, 1886; the *Atlanta Constitution* of September 2, 1886; the *Baltimore Sun* of September 9, 1886; and the *Wheeling Register* (West Virginia) of November 13, 1891. For a good early history of Swallow, one may wish to read the letter sent by Benjamin and Phelps, principals of Mt. Pleasant Military Academy, to the *American Educational Monthly* (New York: Schermerhorn, Bancroft), and published by them on pp. 86–87 of their March 1864 issue, under the title "That School Swindler Again!" A post–Civil War biography of some length can be enjoyed in "Porter-Humphreys-Hardin, A Chapter from the Romance of Rascality," by John A. Bolles, in the magazine *Old and New*, edited by Edward Everett Hale, February 1871, vol. 3.

Swanson, James L. *Bloody Crimes: The Chase for Jefferson Davis and the Death Pageant for Lincoln's Corpse*. New York: William Morrow, 2010.

_____. *Bloody Times. The Funeral of Abraham Lincoln and the Manhunt for Jefferson Davis*. New York: Collins, 2011. This is a children's version of *Bloody Crimes*.

Syracuse Courier Union. July 31, 1861.

Syracuse Daily Courier. June 8, 1859.

Taber, Thomas Townsend, III. *Antebellum Railroad Compendium*. http://rlhs.org/Reference/antebellum.shtml. 2014.
Tate, Allen. *Jefferson Davis: His Rise and Fall, A Biographical Narrative*. New York: Minton, Balch, 1929.
"There Were but Five Trains and Everyone Wanted Ride." *Danville Register* (April 1965).
Thomas, Emory M. *The Confederate State of Richmond: A Biography of the Capital*. Austin: University of Texas Press, 1971.
_____. Review of Nelson Lankford's book *Richmond Burning*. The Journal of Southern History 69:4 (November 2003), pp. 927–928.
Thorne, Robert, ed. *Fugitive Facts*. New York: A.L. Burt, 1890.
Tidwell, William A. *April '65: Covert Action in the American Civil War*. Kent, OH: Kent State University Press, 1995.
Times (London). June 1, 1854; June 12, 1854; June 15, 1854; June 21, 1854; June 26, 1854; July 4, 1854; July 6, 1854; April 20, 1865; April 26, 1865; August 11, 1876; August 12, 1876).
Times (Philadelphia). July 7, 1877; September 1, 1877.
Toalson, Jeff, ed. *No Soap, No Pay, Diarrhea, Dysentery & Desertion: A Composite Diary of the Last 16 Months of the Confederacy from 1864 to 1865*. Lincoln, NE: Universe, 2006.
Trammell, Jack. *The Richmond Slave Trade: The Economic Backbone of the Old Dominion*. Charleston, SC: History Press, 2012.
Tremain, Henry Edwin. *Last Hours of Sheridan's Cavalry*. New York: Bonnell, Silver and Bowers, 1904.
Trenholm, Anna. Anna Holmes Trenholm Diary, 1865. Southern Historical Collection, Wilson Library, University of North Carolina at Chapel Hill.

Anna Trenholm

The Anna Trenholm diary, written by the wife of Confederate Secretary of the Treasury, George A. Trenholm, is not, in fact, a diary, rather an account, written in one session soon after July 9, 1865, probably inspired by the publication of C.E.L. Stuart's anonymous article in the *New York Herald* of July 4, and relating in somewhat terse form the flight of Jefferson Davis from Richmond in April and May of 1865, at least as that flight relates to the Trenholms. There are three known versions of this account. The original manuscript of "the Mrs. George A. Trenholm Diary" is in the South Caroliniana Library at the University of South Carolina, donated in or around 1914 by the Trenholms' daughter, Mrs. Eliza Macbeth (1847–1926), as part of the George A. Trenholm Papers. It consists of 10 small (4.3 inches by 6.7 inches), unbound, handwritten pages that span the period 2 April 1865, to 9 July 1865. These pages have obviously been detached from the binding. Just before donating the papers, Macbeth made a handwritten copy of her mother's account, one she could—and did—hand down to her own daughter Kate (1883–1956), who had recently become Mrs. Edward Padelton Taft, of Greenville, South Carolina. Macbeth calls this copy an "extract," but it is in fact the entire account.

Extract from Diary of Anna (Holmes) Trenholm wife of George Trenholm, Secretary of the Treasury (Eliza's great grandmother). The Eliza in the parentheses is Mrs. Taft's daughter, Eliza Williams Taft (1913–2005), later Mrs. John Bentley. Macbeth made her copy of the Anna Trenholm Diary before the Tafts had their second child, Edward P. Taft, Jr., in 1915, and their third, Josephine, in 1917. That is why Macbeth does not mention them. Thus we can date the copy at 1914 and the subsequent donation to the University of South Carolina at about that time.

At the bottom of the "extract" are the words, *An account of my father's flight with President Davis & the Cabinet from Richmond, Va., written by my Mother & copied from her diary by her daughter Eliza Trenholm Macbeth*.

At the same time Macbeth was copying her mother's account, she was compiling historical and genealogical notes on the Trenholm family.

What follows is a quick comparison of the two accounts—Anna Trenholm's and Eliza Macbeth's. This is how the original opens:

1865.

Sunday 2d April we received notice to have every thing ready to leave Richmond, that evening we left the Depot at eleven oclock, in an especial Car. I was the only Lady, there were about thirty Gentlemen, including the President and Suite.

And this is how the Macbeth copy opens, complete with opening quote mark: *"Tuesday 2nd*

April 1865 we received notice to have every thing ready to leave Richmond that evening. We left the depot at eleven o'clock in an especial car. I was the only Lady, there were about thirty Gentlemen, including the President (Davis) & Suite.

Of course, Macbeth somehow misread Sunday as Tuesday. Aside from that, one sees immediately how the alteration of punctuation has changed the meaning of the original.

The original continues: *Arrived in Danville at five oclock the next day, where there was an immense crowd to welcome the President. We were hospitably entertained at Mr Sutherlin's. Mr Trenholm was quite sick from the effects of Morphine, as well as the pain in his head.*

The Macbeth extract continues: *Arrived in Danville at five o'clock the next day where there was an immense crowd to welcome the President. We were hospitably entertained at Mr Sutherlin's.— Mr Trenholm was quite sick from the effects of the Morphine, as well as the pain in his head.*

In November 1947, Eliza Taft briefly loaned her "extract" and the genealogical notes her mother had compiled to the Southern Historical Collection (University of North Carolina at Chapel Hill), who made a typescript and promptly returned the original. Knowing full well that Anna Trenholm's original had been at the South Caroliniana Library for several decades, Taft made this gesture more for the sake of the historical and genealogical notes than for the account itself. Unlike their deal with the Mallory Papers, Chapel Hill did not get to keep the handwritten copy made by Macbeth. The typescript is all they have. However, Macbeth's handwritten pages remain in the possession of her descendants.

Trotter, William R. *Silk Flags and Cold Steel. The Civil War in North Carolina: The Piedmont*. Winston-Salem, NC: John F. Blair, 1988.

Trow's City Directory for New York. 1856.

Trudeau, Noah Andre. *Out of the Storm: The End of the Civil War, April–June 1865*. Boston: Little, Brown, 1994. This is the third volume of a trilogy, the previous two being *Bloody Roads South* and *The Last Citadel*. It relies on first-hand accounts to tell the story of the Confederacy's death throes.

Tucker, Dallas. "The Fall of Richmond." *Richmond Dispatch*, February 3, 1902. This was reproduced as an 11-page article in the *Southern Historical Society Papers*, vol. 29, 1901. The flight of Jefferson Davis is never mentioned. At the time of the evacuation of Richmond, Tucker's father was connected to the medical department of Libby Prison. In 1902, when he wrote his article, the Rev. Tucker, now of Bedford, Virginia, was describing the events of 46 years earlier. He claims they are *as fresh in my mind as though they were of yesterday*, yet he is convinced that the fateful Sunday in Richmond fell on April 3. *...as late as Sunday morning, April 3, 1865—the fatal day— there was hardly a thought among the people that such a thing as the evacuation of the city was either near of probable.* And this: *Among these churches to which, perhaps, an unusually large crowd might have been seen going on Sunday, April 3, 1865, none was more popular and has become so historically interesting as St. Paul's.*

Tucker, Spencer C., ed. *The Civil War Naval Encyclopedia*. Santa Barbara, CA: ABC-CLIO, 2011.

U.K. Census. London: 1841, 1851, 1861, 1871, 1881, 1891, 1901, 1911.

Underwood, Rodman L. *Stephen Russell Mallory: A Biography of the Confederate Navy Secretary and United States Senator*. Jefferson, NC: McFarland. 2005.

U.S. Census. Washington, D.C.: 1850, 1860, 1870.

U.S. War Department. *War of the Rebellion: A Compilation of the Official Records of the Union and Confederate Armies*. 128 volumes. Washington, D.C.: Government Printing Office, 1881–1901. Known popularly (and in references in this book), as the *OR*. The references relevant to the Jefferson Davis flight are to be found in Series 1, Volume 46, Part 3 (Appomattox Campaign), Chapter 58.

Vandiver, Frank Everson. *Jefferson Davis and the Confederate State*. Oxford: Clarendon Press, 1964.

_____. "Jefferson Davis—Leader without Legend." *Journal of Southern History* 43:1 (February 1977).

_____. *Ploughshares into Swords: Josiah Gorgas and Confederate Ordnance*. Austin: University of Texas Press, 1952.

_____, ed. *see* Gorgas, Josiah.

Verner, Clara L. *Amelia Gayle Gorgas: A Sketch*. Montgomery, AL: Paragon Press, 1937.

Walker, Fannie. See Miller, Fannie Walker.

Walmsley, James E. "Break-up of the Confederate Cabinet." *The Mississippi Valley Historical Review* 6:3 (1920), p. 337.

Walsh, Louis J. *John Mitchel*. Dublin: Talbot Press, 1934.

"War News." *Danville Register* (April 1965).

The War of the Rebellion: A Compilation of the Official Records of the Union and Confederate Armies. 128 volumes, with index. Washington, D.C.: U.S. War Department, 1881–1901. Known popularly (and referred to in this book) as the *Official Records* or *OR*. The references relevant to the Jefferson Davis flight are to be found in Series 1, Volume 46, Part 3 (Appomattox Campaign), Chapter LVIII.

Watehall, E.T. "Fall of Richmond, April 3, 1865." *Confederate Veteran* 17 (May 1909), p. 215.

E.T. WATEHALL

The article "Fall of Richmond" opens with: *On April 3 about nine in the morning, while on my way to the Baptist church.* April 3 was a Monday. What Watehall had in mind was Sunday, April 2. His article would, perhaps, have been better titled "Fall of Richmond, April 2, 1865." *The President and Dr. Hoge were the only two who had received the news of the fall of the city during church time.* One does not quite understand this. Watehall continues: *On the street everyone was calling out: "Richmond has fallen! What shall we all do?"* And this: *There was a wild rush and hurry on all the streets, but it was magnified in the crowd that seemed going to the Danville Depot. Here trains were leaving every few minutes, and I saw Confederate soldiers, men, women, and children among the citizens going away, and a quantity of gold and money and all sorts of household articles being carried off.* Watehall says that he was 14 at the time of the evacuation. He was with General Ewell when the fire started, witnessed other celebrities doing amazing things, and saw the first Yankees come into town. He does not mention Jefferson Davis's flight. Quite rightly, only a few historians have cited "E.T. Watehall" or unquestioningly used him as a trustworthy character in their narratives. Dallas D. Irvine, for example, in his article, "The Fall of Richmond" (1939), cites Watehall for various passages in his article, and then writes: *Watehall gives a graphic account...,* which is exactly what T. Harry Williams says in his *Military Analysis of the Civil War* (1977): *E.T. Watehall gives a graphic account...* Burke Davis, who features Watehall as one of the main voices in the book, *To Appomattox* (1959), introduces the man thus: *E.T. Watehall was fourteen years old. Tonight he prowled through the crowd of strangers, searching for food. He was on hand when destruction of the city began.* James C. Clark writes in his *Last Train South* (1984): *E.T. Watehall, a fourteen-year-old lad, recalled that he went looking for food during the night.* Ernest B. Furgurson cites Watehall for a passage in the text of his book *Ashes of Glory* (1996), as does William C. Davis in *An Honorable Defeat* (2001). Those who merely list E.T. Watehall in their bibliographies include Donald C. Pfanz in *Richard S. Ewell: A Soldier's Life* (1998); Nelson Lankford in *Richmond Burning* (2002); Paul D. Casdorph, in *General R.S. Ewell* (2004); Brian Burns in *Lewis Ginter: Richmond's Gilded Age Icon* (2011); and Pfanz again, in *The Letters of General Richard S. Ewell* (2012). The Hoehlings, unable to trace E.T. Watehall in historical records, hazarded the guess that "E" stood for "Edward." It was a fair bet, but a wrong one. In *The Day Richmond Died* (1981), they wrote: *Eddie Watehall, also on the prowl...* And this, referring to Watehall's adventure with General Ewell and the burning of the city: *Young Eddie Watehall, watching this episode, thought it "entirely accidental."* There was no such person as Eddie Watehall, or even E.T. Watehall. This was known at least as far back as 1946, when Dallas D. Irvine wrote his article, "The Archive Office of the War Department," in *Military Affairs* 10:1 (Spring 1946), p. 93, in which he cites, in a footnote: *E.T. Watehall [Walthall], "Fall of Richmond, April 3, 1865."* Irvine had not known the truth back in 1939, when he wrote his own article, "The Fall of Richmond." By 1946 he did know, and so would all later historians have known, if they had done their work properly. Ernest Taylor Walthall was the son of tobacconist James Walthall and his wife Louisa. He was born in Richmond on November 25, 1848, and so he was 16 at the time of the evacuation, not 14 as he claims. After the war, he became a printer in Richmond, and died there on December 24, 1912. In 1909 he wrote this article and submitted it by mail to *Confederate Veteran*. The editor of the magazine did his best with Walthall's handwriting, but his best was not quite good enough, as one can see throughout the article. The most salient error was the correspondent's name.

Weddell, Elizabeth Wright. *St. Paul's Church, Richmond, Virginia: Its Historic Years and Memorials.* Vol. 2. Richmond, VA: William Byrd Press, 1931.

Weekly Mississippian. January 7, 1863.

Wheelan, Joseph. *Terrible Swift Sword. The Life of General Philip H. Sheridan.* Cambridge, MA: Da Capo Press, 2012.

Whitehead, A.C. *Two Great Southerners: Jefferson Davis and Robert E. Lee.* New York: American Book Company, 1912.

Wiggins, Sarah Woolfolk, ed. *see* Gorgas, Josiah.

_____. *Love and Duty: Amelia and Josiah Gorgas and Their Family*. Birmingham: University of Alabama Press, 2005.

Wiley, Bell I. *The Road to Appomattox*. Memphis State College Press, 1956.

_____, ed. *see* Pember, Phoebe Yates.

Williams, T. Harry, ed. *Military Analysis of the Civil War: An Anthology by the Editors of Military Affairs*. Millward, NY: KTO, 1977.

Wilson, James Harrison. "The Capture of Jefferson Davis." *Times* (Philadelphia) (July 7, 1877).

_____. *The Life of Charles A. Dana*. New York: Harper, 1907.

Winik, Jay. *April 1865: The Month That Saved America*. New York: HarperCollins, 2001.

Winston, Robert W. *High Stakes and Hair Trigger: The Life of Jefferson Davis*. New York: Henry Holt, 1923.

Wise, John Sergeant. "The End of an Era." *The Atlantic Monthly* (83) (1899). This article was reproduced as a book with the same title in 1901, published by Houghton & Mifflin.

Wood, John Taylor. Diary. 1947. Held at University of North Carolina, Chapel Hill, NC.

_____. "Escape of the Confederate Secretary of War." *Century Magazine* 47 (November 1893).

Woodford, Frank Bury. *Father Abraham's Children: Michigan Episodes in the Civil War*. Detroit, MI: Wayne State University Press, 1961.

Woodworth, Steven E, ed. *The American Civil War: A Handbook of Literature and Research*. Westport, CT: Greenwood Press, 1996. Foreword by James M. McPherson. This book has a chapter on Jefferson Davis, written by Michael B. Ballard.

Worsham, John H. *One of Jackson's Foot Cavalry*. New York: Neale, 1912.

Wright, John D. *The Language of the Civil War*. Westport, CT: Oryx Press, 2001.

Wright, Mike. *City Under Siege: Richmond in the Civil War*. Lanham, MD: Madison Books, 1995.

_____. *What They Didn't Teach You About the Civil War*. New York: Presidio Press, 1996.

Yearns, W. Buck, ed. *see* Oldham, Williamson S.

_____, and John G. Barrett, ed. *North Carolina Civil War Documentary*. Chapel Hill: University of North Carolina Press. 1980.

Yeatts, Todd McGregor. *Danville*. Charleston, SC: Arcadia, 2005. One of the Images of America series.

York Herald (England). April 22, 1854.

Younger, Edward E., ed. *see* Kean, Robert Garlick Hill.

INDEX

Aaron, Larry G. 24, 191
Abbeville, S.C. 24, 267
Accomac Court House, Va. 130
A.G. Green 110, 111, 116, 118
Aiken's Landing 71, 138
Alabama 14, 16, 95, 101, 122, 250
Alfriend, Frank 73, 80, 83, 218–221, 268
Allen, Felicity 60, 101, 141
Altsheler, Joseph A. 13
Amelia, Va. 122
Amelia Court House, Va. 91, 92, 154, 155, 160, 169–174, 186, 197
Amelia Springs 144
The American Civil War 277, 278, 284, 288
The American Conflict (Greeley) 45, 46
The American Iliad (Eisenschiml and Newman) 75
American Locomotive Company 118
The Americans at Home (MacRae) 45
"Amicus" 230
Anderson, Joseph Reid 86, 87
Andersonville 130
Anglo-Brazilian Times 234, 235
Annals of the War (McClure) 40
Antebellum Railroad Compendium (Taber) 110
"Antebellum Tragedy" (Melton) 108
Antoni, Andrew 199–201
Apostles of Equality (Rogers) 66, 67, 70, 76, 83, 105, 203
Appomattox Court House 14, 28, 78, 154, 170, 191, 248
Appomattox River 28, 41, 91, 169, 174
Appomattox Station 176
April '65 (Tidwell) 8
April 1865 (Winik) 7, 20, 59–61, 66–68, 80, 82, 86, 98, 101, 141
Aris Sonis Focisque (Harrison) 132
Armee, C.S. 233, 234
Ashes of Glory (Furgurson) 5, 20, 81, 86, 125, 151
Ashmore, Otis 13, 128, 129, 192, 193, 195, 197, 198

Athelings (Mrs. Oliphant) 238
Atlanta 267
Atlantic Monthly 64
Atwell, Albert Lee 108
Augusta, Ga. 231, 237, 248, 289
Augusta Constitutionalist 157
Austria 96
Avary, James Corbin 270
Averill, John H. 208

Bagby, George 227, 236
Bailey, Frankie Y. 23
Baker, Jean H. 13
Baldwin, John B. 14, 16
Ballard, Michael B. 10, 22–23, 27, 43, 59, 60, 82, 84, 120, 129, 133, 158, 183, 184, 188, 191, 221, 277, 278, 280, 284, 288, 289
Ballard House, Richmond 23
Bancroft, A.C. 190
Banister, Va. 186
Barksdale, Va. 157, 189, 190
Barnes, Ellen 10
Barnett Station 267
Barrett, John 159
Barrett Island, Va. 162
Basil Wilson Duke (Matthews) 132
Bates (express agent) 265
Battles and Leaders of the Civil War 203
Beauregard, P.G.T. 7, 19, 124, 127, 260, 261
Beauvoir 232
Beaver's 28
Beckwith, Robert T.L. 13
Before the Dawn (Altsheler) 13
The Beleaguered City (Bill) 142, 150, 191
Bell, John W. 94, 140
Belle Isle Spur, Va. 162
Belleview Hospital 192
Belmont, August 234
Bemiss, FitzGerald 273
Benjamin, Judah P. 13, 22, 29, 39, 55, 57, 58, 96, 122, 125, 141, 142, 151, 166, 174, 187, 213, 225, 242, 243, 248, 249, 251, 253, 258, 259, 261, 263, 265, 268

Bennett, James Gordon 234
Beringer, Richard E. 19, 20, 54, 55, 63, 64, 77, 185, 276, 289
Berkeley, Calif. 143
Berry Hill, Va. 186
Bettersworth, John K. 289
Bevil's 91
Bill, Alfred H. 142, 150, 191
Billingsley, Andrew 78, 104
Bivin, Ken 151
Blackheath Mines 165
Blockade Runners of the Confederacy (Cochran) 150
Bloody Crimes (Swanson) 11, 60, 81, 86, 90–93, 120, 135, 151, 159, 160, 180–185, 196, 213
Bobbitt, B.B. 23, 213
Bonair, Va. 163, 164
Boney, F.N. 278
Book of Common Prayer 66, 68
Bostick, Douglas W. 133, 195
Boston, Va. 155, 186, 187
Boston Journal 11, 31, 59, 79, 81, 83, 95, 97, 101, 103, 138, 146, 275
Boston Liberator 31
Boyd & Edmonds Stage Company 165
Bradley, Mark L. 289
Bragg, Braxton 125, 126, 184
Brazil 234, 235, 238, 240
Breaking the Backbone of the Rebellion (Greene) 28–29, 43, 50, 51, 78, 81, 89
"Break-Up of the Confederate Cabinet" (Walmsley) 158
Breckinridge (Davis) 20
Breckinridge, John C. 6, 7, 12, 13, 23, 28–34, 37, 39, 41, 42, 48, 50, 51, 53–56, 71, 76–78, 82, 89, 90, 92, 93, 97, 98, 123, 127, 128, 134, 140, 142–144, 166, 167, 173, 181, 190, 195–197, 210, 218, 227, 230, 240, 243, 246, 247, 250, 251, 255, 256, 258, 261–265, 268, 277
Breckinridge, Owen 143
Bremen 96
Bridgeport, Conn. 215, 216
Bright, Dave 116
Brighton 240

295

Bringhurst, W.R. 122, 126
Brittain, S. 122, 126, 127
Broad Street Methodist Church, Richmond 30, 53–56, 134
Brock, Sallie 25–27, 59, 64, 66, 67, 73, 82, 85, 203
Brooklyn 227
Broun, William L. 25, 64, 68, 69, 82, 87, 97, 142, 147
Brown, Beth 104
Brown, Joshua 133
Brown, Lt. 123
Brown, Norman D. 278, 288
Brown's Summit, Va. 164
Brubaker, J.H. 23, 61, 65, 107–109, 122, 130, 138, 139, 155, 188, 207, 211
Bruce, H.W. 22, 58, 65, 73, 74, 82, 85, 89, 97, 102, 103, 121, 134, 139, 177, 252, 257
Bruce family 186
Buena Vista, Mexico 125
Burger, Nash K. 289
Burkeville, Va. 10, 11, 13, 89, 155, 157, 166, 171, 174–178, 183, 186, 197, 249, 250, 259
Burns, Brian 118
Burrows, John Lansing 248

Camberwell, London 240
Cambridge 229
Cambridge Modern History 46, 47
Campaigns of the Army of the Potomac (Swinton) 171, 172
Campbell, Given 211
Campbell, John A. 35, 39, 44, 48, 49, 55, 68, 69
Canada 16, 122, 165, 230, 234, 237
Canfield, Cass 158, 159
Cantley, A.G. 122, 127
Caperton, Allen T. 14, 16, 18
Capt. Coe's Company, President's Guard 123
Capt. Huckstep's Guard 123
"The Capture of Jefferson Davis" (Harrison) 8
"The Capture of Jefferson Davis" (Wilson) 39, 95, 237
"The Capture of Richmond" (Prescott) 26
Carrington, Isaac H. 85, 87, 102, 223, 245
Carroll, J. Frank 65, 107, 122, 125, 129, 132, 133, 135, 188, 193, 196, 197, 210–212
Cary, Constance 26, 59, 61, 64, 80, 83, 86, 280
Cashin, Joan 11, 51, 139, 231–233
Casimir (Stuart) 238
Casstevens, Frances H. 85, 193, 195
Castle Thunder 85
Castletown, Ireland 273, 274
Catawba River 267
Catogni, Benny 199
Catterall, Louise 112, 114
Catton, Bruce 276, 278

Cease Firing (Johnston) 27, 59, 64, 66, 68, 75, 82, 84, 86
Celbridge, Ireland 274
Central Southern Railroad 110
Centralia, Va. 154
Century magazine 134
Chamlee, Roy Z. 21, 77, 94, 102, 142
Champlin, John 25
Charles I 230
Charles Seddon 54, 107–109, 112, 113, 115–117, 139, 207
Charleston, S.C. 111
Charlotte, N.C. 8, 11–14, 22, 24, 70, 119, 120, 122–124, 132, 137, 142, 252, 253, 258, 264–267, 271, 280
Charlottesville, Va. 192
Cheesman, Capt. 262
Chesapeake & Ohio Railroad 115
Chester, Va. 154
Chesterfield Co., Va. 160, 162, 164, 165, 167, 168, 185, 208
Chesterfield Railroad Company 165
Chicago Times Herald 280
Chimborazo Hospital 286
China 239, 253
Chula, Va. 154, 155, 169, 186
Church, Maj. N. 130
Church, William C. 25, 67
City Point, Va. 71
City Under Siege (Wright) 26, 27, 60, 61, 63, 65, 67, 80
The Civil War (Foote) 61, 77, 80, 86, 89–91, 141, 151, 154, 155, 182, 183, 185, 196
Civil War Charlotte (Hardy) 24
The Civil War Months (Coffey) 139
The Civil War Naval Encyclopedia (Tucker) 144
Civil War Petersburg (Greene) 43
Civil War Times Illustrated 217
A Civil War Treasury (Nofi) 135
Civil War Weather in Virginia (Krick) 139, 175
Clare, Israel Smith 46–48, 51, 63, 65, 76, 78, 83, 87, 90
Clark, James C. 100, 102, 107, 120, 125, 126, 129, 151, 155, 158, 159, 180, 181, 183, 184, 191, 200, 201, 221, 277, 281, 289
Clark, John E. 154
Clark, Micajah H. 122–124, 127–130, 211
Clark's, Va. 178
Clarksville, Tenn. 123, 124, 126, 128
Clay, Clement 122
Clayville, Va. 168
Clover, Va. 55, 121, 122, 126, 141, 154, 155, 175, 177, 180–186, 196, 252
Clover Hill, Va. 55, 185
Clubbs, Occie 214
Coal Mines, Va. 154

Coalfield, Va. 11, 155, 165–167, 174, 186
Cochran, Hamilton 150
Coe, Capt. 123
Coffey, Walter 139
Coffin, Carleton 11, 12, 31–34, 38, 45, 59, 71, 79, 81, 83, 95, 101, 103–105, 138, 146, 200, 201, 275
Cole, R.G. 170, 171
Coleman, William D. 23, 210, 212, 213
Coleridge, Samuel Taylor 247, 250
Columbia, S.C. 204
Columbia Phoenix 210
Columbus, Ga. 23
Colyar, Arthur S. 14
Concord, N.C. 119, 265
The Confederacy (Roland) 76
The Confederacy's Secret Weapon (Bostick) 133, 195
Confederate Commissary General (Moore) 233
The Confederate Dirty War (Singer) 141
"Confederate Naval Cadets" (Harris) 192
Confederate Operations in Canada and New York (Headley) 165, 166
Confederate Railroad Bureau 111
Confederate Railroads (web site) 116
The Confederate State of Richmond (Thomas) 76, 77, 83, 86
Confederate States of America Lost Treasury Gold (Atwell) 108
The Confederate States of America, 1861–1865 (Coulter) 203
Confederate Treasure in Danville (Carroll) 107, 122, 129, 132, 188, 193, 196, 197, 210–212
Confederate Veteran 23, 68, 82, 124, 142, 188, 200, 203
Connecticut 215
Connelly, Thomas L. 278
Conolly, Thomas 46, 59, 273–275
Conrad, Charles M. 14
Conrad, James Lee 196, 197
Cook, George S. 111, 112
Cook, Huestis P. 111–115, 117
Cook, Mary Latimer 112
Cooper, Samuel 28, 64, 68, 69, 122, 126, 224, 246, 253, 256, 263, 290
Cooper, William J. 27, 49–51, 63, 64, 77, 82, 101, 141, 158, 182–184, 276
Corey, Charles H. 103
Cornwallis, Lord 265
The Corps Forward (Couper) 132
Coulter, E. Merton 203
Couper, William 132
"A Courier's Experience" (Handy) 143, 144
Cridland, F.J. 96

Index

Crounse, Lorenzo L. 71, 72, 79
Crump, Emmie 69
Crump, W.W. 69, 193
Cuba 37
Culpeper Minute-Men 271
Cunningham, S.A. 273
Cutting, Elisabeth 120

Daily Arkansas Gazette 17
Daily News (London) 238
Daily Saratogian 140
Dan River 111, 189, 190, 197, 206–208, 211
Dana, C.A. 71, 138, 139
Daniel, John M. 7
Daniel, John Warrick 101
Dansville 190
Danville (Yeatts) 24
Danville, Va. 5, 8, 10, 11, 13, 14, 16, 20–24, 33, 38, 41, 55, 63, 70, 72, 74, 85, 94, 97, 107, 108, 114, 117–119, 121, 123, 127, 128, 130, 132–137, 139–142, 144, 146–149, 151, 152, 154, 155, 157–160, 165, 166, 170, 171, 174, 175, 180, 182, 183, 188–194, 206, 208, 210–213, 221, 226, 227, 251–258, 260, 265, 271, 272, 274, 280, 190, 259
Danville & Midland Railroad 211
Danville & New River Railroad 212
Danville Blues 23
Danville in the Civil War (McFall) 26, 63, 65, 76, 102, 103, 107, 108, 121, 126, 144, 148, 159, 184, 188, 191, 193, 207, 208, 212, 213, 281
Danville Register 108, 129, 157, 188, 207, 208
Danville Register & Bee 141
Danville Revisited (Fountain and Grant) 24
Danville, Virginia (Fountain) 24
Davies, John Woodburn 101
Davies, William W. 101
Davis, Billy 10
Davis, Burke 38, 47, 48, 50–52, 58–63, 65, 66, 69, 70, 76–79, 83, 87, 99–101, 108, 126, 129, 143, 145, 151, 152, 153, 158, 180–184, 191, 192, 200, 201, 222, 281
Davis, George 22, 69, 95, 122, 149, 243, 248, 252, 253, 256, 261, 265, 267
Davis, Jeff, Jr. 10
Davis, Jefferson 5, 7–15, 17, 18, 21–24, 26, 30–58, 60–63, 65–68, 70–97, 99–101, 103, 105, 107, 108, 112–119, 122, 124, 126, 127, 130, 131, 133–144, 147, 159, 162, 166, 167, 170–174, 176, 179, 181, 183, 184, 186, 187, 189, 190, 192, 194–196, 208–216, 218, 220–222, 227, 229, 231–233, 235–237, 242, 244, 246–253, 255–269, 271–274, 276, 277, 280

Davis, Joseph R. 12
Davis, Maggie 10
Davis, Varina 8–14, 16, 39, 50, 51, 54, 60, 61, 65, 70, 74, 75, 79, 98, 99, 100, 101, 123, 129, 131, 230, 231, 237, 268, 269, 277, 280
Davis, W.W. 280
Davis, William C. 20, 26, 49, 50, 52–55, 59, 64, 65, 77, 83, 86, 98, 101, 103, 108, 119–121, 129, 134, 139, 150, 152, 158, 159, 188, 207, 211, 213, 220, 222, 227, 229, 233, 234, 276, 290
Davis, Winnie 10
The Day Richmond Died (Hoehling) 27, 49, 100, 125, 150, 152, 270
Dearstyne, Howard 111, 112
Debow's New Orleans Monthly Review 16
Deems, Charles Force 143
The Deepest South (Horne) 234
De Leon, T.C. 74, 75, 82, 88
De Voss, Edward W. 96
Diary of a Southern Refugee (McGuire) 25, 69
Dickens, Charles 222–224
Dickinson, Lt. 123
Dillon, William 74
Dinwiddie Court House 36, 246
Dixie Betrayed (Eicher) 27, 55, 64, 67, 77, 83
Dodamead, Thomas 12, 167
Dodamead, Va. 167
Dodd, William 142, 157–159
Donald, David Herbert 277
Donegal 274, 275
Dorchester (U.K.) 239
Dorset (U.K.) 239
Dorset, Va. 168
Dorset Chronicle 239
Dowdey, Clifford 32, 48
Drake's Branch, Va. 155, 179, 186
Drewry's Bluff 145, 154
Drouyn de Lhuys, Édouard 96
Dry Bridge, Va. 167
Dublin 229, 238–240
Dublin Evening Herald 238
Dublin Warder 238
Dugard, Martin 204, 205
Duke, Basil 95, 265
Dunaway, Philip 282
Duncan, James A. 30, 134, 243, 248
Dundee, Va. 190, 207
Dupuy House 90
Durham Station, N.C. 133
Durkin, Joseph 214, 220, 221, 273

Early, Jubal 271
Eastman, Margaret R. 150
Eaton, Clement 13, 277, 278, 288
Eckenrode, Hamilton 75, 80, 82, 158, 271
Edge Hill, Va. 90
Edgefield & Kentucky Railroad 110, 111

Edinburgh 45, 229, 236
Edward A. Wild (Casstevens) 193, 195
Eicher, David 27, 55, 64, 67, 77, 83
Eisenschiml, Otto 75
Ellett, Loftin N. 248
Encyclopedia of the American Civil War (Heidler) 40, 169, 170
"The End of an Era" (Wise) 125, 126, 142, 180, 181, 184
An End to Valor (Stern) 126, 150, 180–182
England 130, 232
"Escape of the Confederate Secretary of War" (Wood) 38, 138
"The Evacuation of Richmond" (Crump/Lightfoot) 69
Evans, Eli 77, 82, 125, 196
Evans, Melvin 282
Evening Star 72, 81, 84
Ewell, Richard S. 7, 34, 86, 127, 143

"The Fall of Richmond" (Bivin) 151
"The Fall of Richmond" (Brock) 25, 66, 67
"The Fall of Richmond" (Irvine) 195
"The Fall of Richmond" (Tucker) 5, 26, 68
"Fall of Richmond, April 3, 1865" (Watehall) 142, 200, 201
"The Fall of Richmond. Part 1. The Evacuation" (Sulivane) 203
Falling Creek, Va. 165
Farmville, Va. 176
Father Abraham's Children (Woodford) 8, 80
Ferdinand, King of Naples 229, 230
First Lady of the Confederacy (Cashin) 11, 139, 231
First Lady of the South (Ross) 13, 75, 80, 99
Fitz-Gerald, Desmond 273
Five Forks 50, 75
Flagg & Co. 174
Fleming, Robert 192, 195–197, 213, 281
"Flight and Capture of Jefferson Davis" (Reagan) 40
Flight Into Oblivion (Hanna) 24, 58, 61, 120, 144, 149, 150, 270
Flood, Charles B. 78
Florida 124, 214
Florida Historical Quarterly 129, 272, 273, 278, 280
Foote, Shelby 61, 77, 80, 86, 89–91, 120, 141, 151, 154, 155, 157, 158, 182–185, 196, 221
Foreigners in the Confederacy (Lonn) 275
Fort Lafayette 209, 216, 221
Fort Mill, S.C. 24
Fort Monroe 129, 230, 256

Fountain, Clara G. 24
Four Days in 1865 (Ryan) 26, 51
Four Years in Rebel Capitals (De Leon) 74, 75, 82, 88
Four Years of Fighting (Coffin) 45, 103, 200, 201
Fourth Mile Post, Va. 162, 163
Fowden, Va. 174
France 96
Francis, R.D. 23
Frank Leslie's Illustrated Newspaper 5, 6
Frankfort Yeoman 143
Fredericksburg 133, 188
Freeman, Douglas S. 28, 36, 43, 89, 91, 92, 170
Freeman's Journal 238, 239
Fremantle, Arthur L. 135
Frirwin (Oliphant) 238
Frock Coats and Epaulets (Mapp) 61
From Richmond to Texas (Yearns) 16
Furgurson, Ernest B. 5, 20, 81, 86, 125, 151, 221

Galveston 95
Galveston Daily News 17
Galway 238
Garnett, Dr. 122, 184
Gary, Ralph 66
General Lee's City (Lee) 26–27, 30
George W. Alexander and Castle Thunder (Casstevens) 85
Georgia 14, 18, 23, 37, 39, 60, 123, 188, 231, 237, 248, 267, 280
Gianal, Va. 189
Gibraltar 5, 6
Gilmer, Jeremy F. 127, 134, 143, 144, 154
Glin Castle 273
"Gold and Silver" (Parker) 148, 195, 197
"The Gold of the Confederate Treasury" (Harris) 192
Gone with the Wind 10
Goode's 28, 91
Goodwin, Doris Kearns 81
Gordon, Armistead 142
Gordon, Va. 32
Gorgas, Amelia 25, 26, 44, 45, 68, 69, 80, 82, 97, 203
Gorgas, Josiah 8, 21, 22, 25, 32, 33, 35, 37, 38, 44, 66, 69, 72, 87, 97, 122, 127, 142, 256
Gorgas, William C. 25
Gourley, Catherine 26
A Government of Our Own (Davis) 227, 229
Graham, Senator 15
Granite, Va. 162, 163
Granite Quarry, Va. 162
Granite Station, Va. 162, 164
Grant, Gary 24
Grant, James 98–101
Grant, Ulysses S. 5, 6, 8, 17, 21, 36, 37, 49, 71, 73, 75, 79, 110, 137, 158, 170, 176, 177, 222, 241, 249, 251, 252, 254, 255, 257
Grant and Sherman (Flood) 78
Graves, Capt. 23
The Great War of Destruction (LeVan) 126
Greeley, Horace 45–47, 234, 235, 237, 244
Green, A.G. 110
Green, Alice P. 23
Green Bay, Va. 177
Greene, A. Wilson 28–30, 43, 50, 51, 78, 81, 89
Greene, Nathaniel 261
Greensboro, N.C. 14, 16, 24, 111, 119, 120, 123, 124, 126, 127, 132–135, 154, 194, 206, 258–265, 271
Grigg, Don A. 141
Guilford Court House, N.C. 261

Haewirickel, F.W. 96
Hagan, Jane 213
Halifax Co., Va. 179, 180, 185, 186, 189, 190
Hallsboro, Va. 167, 168
Halpine, Charles 233, 234
Halyburton, James D. 248, 257
Hampton, Wade 266
Handy, Moses P. 143, 144, 199–203, 275, 279, 280
Hanna, A.J. 24, 58, 61, 10, 121, 143, 144, 149–151, 221, 270
Hardy, Michael C. 24, 120
Harper's Cyclopedia 45
Harper's Encyclopedia 55, 129
Harper's Pictorial History 21
Harper's Weekly 154
Harrell, Carolyn L. 119
Harris, John W. 192, 196
Harrison, Burton 8, 10, 11, 14, 26, 64, 123, 125, 131, 132, 134, 149, 213, 233, 234, 237, 246, 248, 253, 268, 280
Harrison, Mrs. *see* Cary, Constance
Harvard 142
Harvest Queen 239
Harvie, L.E. 122, 123, 158, 170
Hatcher's Run, Va. 28, 46, 274
Hattaway, Herman 54, 55, 63, 64, 77, 185, 276, 289
Havana 37, 141, 143, 222
Haw, George Pitman 281
Haw, John Hugh 281
Haw, Joseph Richardson 281
Hay, Thomas Robson 18, 19
Haytokah, Va. 175, 186
Headley, John W. 61, 165, 166
Heidler, David, and Jeanne 40, 169, 170
Hendren, John 54, 122, 127–130
Henrickson, Robert 67
Henrico Co., Va. 160
Here I Stand (Spong) 78
Herndon, G. Melvin 192
Hertfordshsire 240
Heth, Henry 32
Hickory Island, Va. 162
Hill, A.P. 190, 274
Hill, Benjamin H. 14–20
Hill, Gen. 256
Hillsboro, N.C. 266
History of the Civil War (Rhodes) 141
Hoehling, Adolph, and Mary 27, 49, 50–52, 100, 125, 150, 152, 221, 270
Hoge, Moses 72, 74, 87, 88, 122
An Honorable Defeat (Davis) 50, 53–55, 103, 108, 119–121, 129, 150, 152, 159, 188, 207, 220, 229, 290
Hood, Gen. 12
Hood's Tennessee Campaign (Hay) 18
Horne, Gerald 234
Horrors of Andersonville (Gourley) 26
Hotchkiss, Jedediah 154, 162–165, 167, 168
Howell, Jefferson Davis 235, 236, 277
Howell, Jennie 230
Howell, Maggie 10, 231, 232, 237, 268, 277
Hughes, Meg 112, 115
Hunter, Phillip Steven 173
Hunter, Senator 15
Hutcheon and Donald Siding, Va. 162, 163
Hutter, Maj. 127

Illustrated London News 133
Illustrated Sketch Book of Danville, Virginia (Pollock) 212
Inside the Confederate Government (Kean) 33
Ireland 227, 238, 273
An Irishman in Dixie (Conolly) 273, 274
The Iron Will of Jefferson Davis (Canfield) 159
Irvine, Dallas D. 195, 289
Irving, William 68–70, 75–79, 84, 86, 87
Irwinsville, Ga. 271
Isaacs, William B. 193
Ives, Joseph C. 134, 246, 259, 277

J. Patton Anderson (Raab) 135, 136
Jackson's Foot Cavalry 27
James A. Seddon 110, 111, 116, 118
James River 25, 27, 28, 36, 41, 89, 91, 94, 142, 154, 160–162, 196
James River Squadron 121, 144, 147, 148, 224
Jamestown, N.C. 262
Jefferson, Alphine W. 105
Jefferson Davis (Dodd) 142, 158
Jefferson Davis (Eaton) 13
Jefferson Davis (Gordon) 142

Jefferson Davis, American (Cooper) 27, 49–51, 63, 77, 82, 101, 141, 182–184
Jefferson Davis and His Cabinet (Patrick) 120
Jefferson Davis: Confederate President (Hattaway and Beringer) 54, 55, 77, 185
Jefferson Davis, Constitutionalist (Davis) 129, 142
Jefferson Davis: His Life and Personality (Schaff) 107
Jefferson Davis: His Rise and Fall, A Biographical Narrative (Tate) 59, 75, 81
Jefferson Davis, Political Soldier (Cutting) 120
Jefferson Davis: President of the South (Eckenrode) 75, 82
Jefferson Davis: Private Letters (Davis) 10, 13, 98
Jefferson Davis, the Unreal and the Real (McElroy) 62, 63
Jefferson Davis: Tragic Hero (Strode) 62, 64, 80, 133, 150, 155, 180, 182, 183, 196
Jefferson Davis: Unconquerable Heart (Allen) 60, 101, 141
"Jefferson Davis' Week at Danville" (Coleman) 210, 212, 213
Jennings Ordinary, Va. 155, 174, 176, 186
Jetersville, Va. 155, 171, 174, 176, 177
Jewett, Clayton E. 20
J.H. Timberlake 115, 116
"John Cabell Breckinridge" (Hanna) 143
John Taylor Wood (Shingleton) 102, 132
Johnson, Clint 12, 50, 51, 53, 60, 64, 79, 80, 84, 88, 90, 92, 108, 121, 133, 134, 147, 152, 155, 158, 159, 177, 180–184, 212, 221, 222
Johnson, Ludwell H. 278
Johnston, Albert Sidney 123, 225
Johnston, Joseph E. 7, 17–19, 133, 166, 217, 218, 260–264, 266, 271
Johnston, Mary 27, 59, 64, 66, 68, 75, 82, 84, 86, 87
Johnston, William Preston 95, 122, 123, 134, 213, 225, 231, 233, 234, 237, 246, 263
"Johnston, Lee and Davis. The Three Great Confederate Officials" 17
Jones, Evan R. 45
Jones, J.W. 79, 170
Jones, James 10
Jones, John B. 12, 25–27, 29, 39, 64, 69, 140, 191, 202, 204, 282
Jones, Katharine M. 141
Journal of the Confederate Congress 14, 16
Joyner, J.B. 288
Judah Benjamin (Neiman) 141, 142

Judah P. Benjamin (Evans) 77, 82, 125, 196
Judah P. Benjamin (Meade) 120, 158, 159

Kanawha River 94
Katie Stewart (Mrs. Oliphant) 238
Kean, R. Garlick H. 32–38, 44, 47–49, 52–55, 72, 97, 122, 130, 131, 140, 141, 209
Kean, Wicher 257
Kennedy, Ruby Mallory 215, 216, 218–221, 277
Kennedy, Thomas S. 215
Kenner, Duncan F. 122, 130
Kentucky 14, 16, 22, 82, 102, 110, 252
Kentucky State Historical Society 143
Kentucky Yeoman 143
Kepler, Rev. 85, 87
Key West, Fla. 215
Keysville, Va. 154, 155, 157, 178, 186
Kildare (Ireland) 273
Killing Lincoln (O'Reilly and Dugard) 204, 205
Kingston, N.Y. 240
Knight, Landon 59, 74, 75, 82
Knockaney, Ireland 238
Kocher, Lawrence 111, 112
Krick, Robert K. 139, 175
Kuenzi, Hans 142

Lachman, Charles 13, 79
The Ladies of Richmond (Jones) 141
Lagrange 267
Lane, Joe 227, 230, 240
The Language of the Civil War (Wright) 120, 151
Lankford, Nelson 52, 53, 60, 74, 84, 85, 147, 151–153, 201, 203, 204, 273, 274, 289
La Prade, J.E. 154, 163
The Last Capital (Brubaker) 23, 61, 107–109, 122, 130, 138, 139, 155, 188, 207
"Last Days of the Confederacy" 16
"Last Days of the Confederate Government" (Mallory) 215, 220, 272
"Last Days of the Confederate Treasury and What Became of Its Specie" (Clark) 123, 130, 211
Last Hours of Sheridan's Cavalry (Tremain) 92
The Last Lincolns (Lachman) 13, 79
Last Train South (Clark) 46–48, 51, 62, 63, 65, 76, 78, 83, 87, 90, 100, 102, 107, 120, 125, 126, 129, 151, 155, 159, 180, 181, 183, 184, 191, 200, 201, 277, 281
Last Year of the War (Pollard) 45
Lawley, Frank 171

Lawton, Alexander R. 142, 144, 247, 250
Leaders of the Lost Cause 229, 289
Lee, Capt. 258
Lee, Fitzhugh 172, 274
Lee, Richard McGowan 26–27, 30
Lee, Robert E. 5–8, 13–18, 20, 24, 28, 29, 31–54, 56, 57, 65, 66, 70–79, 81–83, 85–98, 122–124, 127, 132, 133, 137, 138, 144, 145, 154, 166, 170–173, 181, 194, 222, 224, 242–244, 246, 248, 249, 251–259, 262, 264, 271–274, 276, 277
Lee Park, Va. 164
Lee's Dispatches (Lee) 36
Lester, James H. 157
LeVan, Russell G. 126
Lewis Ginter (Burns) 118
Lexington, N.C. 119, 264
Lexington, Va. 95
Libby Prison 143
Liberty Church, Va. 177, 186
Lies Across America (Loewen) 104, 105
Lt. Dickinson's Company, President's Guard 123
Lt. Lawson's Guard 123
Life and Campaigns of General Robert E. Lee (McCabe) 73, 79, 82, 85, 139, 202, 203
The Life and Death of Jefferson Davis, Ex-President of the Southern Confederacy (Bancroft) 190
The Life and Reminiscences of Jefferson Davis 59, 101
The Life of Jefferson Davis (Alfriend) 73, 80, 83, 218
The Life of Jefferson Davis: With a Secret History of the Southern Confederacy (Pollard) 13, 26, 35, 38, 73
Life of John Mitchel (Dillon) 74
The Life of Lincoln (Coffin) 275
Lightfoot, Emmie 69
Limber, Jim 10
Limerick 238, 273
Lincoln, Abraham 13, 71, 106, 240, 264, 265, 268, 271
Lincoln Herald 67
Lincoln's Assassins (Chamlee) 21, 77, 94, 102, 142
Liverpool 101, 232
Lloyd, William Alvin 154
Lockhart, William 240
Loewen, James W. 104, 105
Logdale, Va. 185
London 238–240
London Times 137, 140, 171, 274
Long, A.L. 79
Long Branch Record 23
A Long Shadow (Ballard) 10, 22–23, 27, 43, 59, 60, 82, 84, 120, 129, 133, 183, 191, 277, 280
The Long Surrender (Davis) 38,

48, 50, 51, 61–63, 79, 100, 101, 108, 129, 152, 182
Lonn, Ella 275
Look Away! (Davis) 98, 139
Loomis, John S. 193
Lossing, Ben 45
The Lost Cause (Pollard) 139, 204
Louisiana 14, 105
Louisville Courier-Journal 123, 128
Lowry, Don 51, 52, 62, 63, 180, 183
Lubbock, Frank 33, 35, 39, 41–44, 47, 49–53, 55, 65, 66, 69, 84, 95, 122–125, 134, 225, 242, 246, 247, 251, 261, 268
Lumpkin, Mary 103, 105
Lumpkin, Robert 103–106
Lumpkin, Thurston 103
Lynchburg, Va. 89, 94, 97, 116, 165, 170, 171, 176
Lyons, W.H. 248

MacCaleb, Walter F. 39, 41, 141
Macfarland 134, 248, 257
Machen, Willis B. 14, 16
MacMurdo, J.B. 122, 130
MacRae, David 45
MacWalter, Henrietta 239, 240
MacWalter, James 238
MacWalter, John G.P. 239
MacWalter, John George 238, 239, 287
MacWalter, Lily 240
Madison, Virginia 25
Mallory, Buddy 216
Mallory, Charles 214, 215
Mallory, Ellen 215
Mallory, John 214
Mallory, Stephen R. 20, 22, 26, 27, 37, 39, 44, 52, 57, 61–64, 66, 67, 70, 73, 83, 88, 95–98, 119–122, 124, 125, 127, 140, 141, 144, 145, 147, 149–152, 158–160, 187, 209, 210, 212–226, 227, 241–269, 272, 273
The Man and His Hour (Davis) 26, 49, 52, 53, 59, 64, 65, 77, 83, 86, 101, 121, 134, 159, 213, 276
Manarin, Louis H. 48
Manassas 7
Manchester, Va. 107, 117, 127, 143–145, 147, 154, 155, 160, 162, 174, 197, 206
Manual of the Railroads of the United States see *Poor's Manual of the Railroads of the United States*
Maplewood, Va. 173
Mapp, A.J. 61
The Marble Man (Connelly) 278
Mark's Turnout, Va. 167
Marlow, Clayton C. 39, 77, 78, 90, 95
Marotta, Gary 277
Marseilles, Va. 189
Marshall Theatre, Richmond 69

Martin (Headley's companion) 166
Mary Todd Lincoln (Baker) 13
Maryland 38
Matt W. Ransom (Marlow) 39, 77, 78, 90, 95
Matthews, Gary Robert 132
Mattoax, Va. 154, 155, 179, 186
Maynard, Maj. 262
Mayo, John 160
Mayo, Mayor 70, 248
Mayo, Peter Helms 190, 191
Mayo Bridge 143
McCabe, James D. 34, 38, 39, 73, 75, 79, 82, 85, 139, 202, 203
McClure, Alexander Kelly 39, 40
McClure's Magazine 45, 62, 63, 70, 125, 140, 141, 150, 151, 158, 214, 215, 217–224, 272, 276
McClurken, J.W. 24
McDonnell, Ronnie 273
McElroy, Robert 62, 63
McFall, Fred Lawrence 26, 63, 65, 76, 102, 103, 107, 108, 121, 122, 126, 127, 135, 144, 148, 159, 184, 188, 191, 193–195, 207–209, 212, 213, 281
McGill, John 234, 235
McGuire, Judith 25, 64, 69
McMurry, Richard N. 278
Meade, George G. 176
Meade, Robert D. 120, 141, 158, 159, 222
Meherrin, Va. 155, 178, 186
Melton, Herman E. 108, 109
Melvin, Philip 214, 273
Memminger, Christopher C. 213
"Memoirs of a Confederate Senator" 16
Memoirs of Governor William Smith (Smith) 94, 140
Memoirs of Robert E. Lee (Lee) 79
Memoirs of Service Afloat (Semmes) 144
Meredith, John A. 248
Metropolitan Iron Works 117
Mexican War 122, 125, 143
Mexico 16, 96
Miami 23
Midlothian Coal Mines 165, 167
Mighty Like a River (Billingsley) 78, 104
Miller, James M. 122, 130, 193
Millers Tavern, Va. 175
Millett, Wesley 62, 65, 66, 221
Milwaukee Daily Sentinel 137
Mining and Nitre Bureau 143
Minnigerode, Charles 45, 58–60, 64, 66–69, 72, 74, 77–79, 83–87
Minor, Hubbard T. 196
Mississippi 232
Mitchel, John 7, 74, 256, 257
Mobile, Ala. 95, 127
Money Over Mastery (Schermerhorn) 104, 105
Monroe, James 230
Monroe Park, Richmond 124

Montgomery, Ala. 101, 233
Montreal 231, 232, 234, 235, 237
Monumental Church, Richmond 103
Moore, George 96
Moore, Jerrold Northrop 233
Moore, Samuel T. 55
Moore's Complete Civil War Guide 55
Moore's Ordinary, Va. 178
Morehead, Gov. 260
Moreno, Fernando J. 215
Moreton (Dorset) 239
Morgan, James M. 8, 10, 11, 14
Morning Post (London) 238
Morris, Dr. 97
Mosby, John 192, 277
Moseley, Va. 168
Moshein, Peter 110, 116
Mossingford, Va. 155, 179, 186
Muller, Julius W. 32, 34, 35

Naples 229, 230, 236, 238
Nashville, Tenn. 273
Nassau 273
Neiman, Simon 141
Nevins, Allan 18, 19, 62, 63
New Jersey 23, 114
New Orleans 125, 137
New Orleans Democrat 18, 19
New Richmond, Ohio 105
New York 27, 137, 140, 165, 227, 230, 231, 233, 234, 236, 237, 256, 273
New York Citizen 233, 234
New York Daily News 230, 240, 256
New York Daily Tribune 17, 18, 20, 68, 71, 72, 81, 84, 94, 139, 143, 146, 201, 234, 235, 244
New York Herald 21, 26, 38, 41, 57, 59, 62, 70–72, 81, 84, 95, 96, 97, 98, 102, 124, 125, 139, 140, 144, 149, 158, 160, 166, 167, 186, 187, 212, 218, 221, 227, 234, 236, 241, 275
New York Illustrated News 238, 240
New York Mail and Express 181
New York Times 23, 71, 79, 234, 278
New York World 170, 230
Newcastle (England) 45
Newcastle Chronicle 45
Newman, Ralph G. 75
Newmarket, Va. 181
News Ferry, Va. 119, 155, 189
Newton, Emily 239, 240
Niagara 236
Nichols, Roy 150
Noble, John 208
Noding, Va. 189
Nofi, Albert A. 135
Nordendorf Map 154, 207
Norfolk & Western Railroad 116
North Carolina 7, 12–14, 19, 22, 61, 70, 95, 111, 119, 120, 123, 124, 137, 145, 166, 259, 267, 271, 273, 274

Index

North Carolina Civil War Documentary (Yearns and Barrett) 159
North Carolina in the Civil War (Hardy) 120
Northrop, Lucius 143
Northside 54, 157, 206, 207, 208, 211
Nottoway Co., Va. 174
Nottoway Company 188
Nottoway Court House 138

Ockward, Va. 185
O'Dwyer, Julia 238
Ohio 105
Old Charleston Originals (Eastman) 150, 151
Old Dominion Quarries 162
Oldham, Williamson S. 14, 16, 18–20
Oliphant, Mrs. 238
Oliphant, Octavia 238
Oliphant, Sir Oscar 239
Oliver Twist (Dickens) 223
O'Reilly, Bill 204, 205
Orr, Senator 16
Ott, John 130
Otterburn, Va. 173
"Our Last Capital" (Bobbitt) 213
Overby's, Va. 179
Owl (ship) 273

Pace, Va. 189
Palestine, Tex. 39, 127
Panama 25
The Papers of Jefferson Davis 11, 12, 91, 127, 129, 131, 132, 134, 194, 195, 227, 230, 231
Parker, William Harwar 127, 128, 138, 144, 148, 159, 160, 173, 192, 193, 195, 197
Paterson, N.J. 114, 116
Patrick, Rembert 120
Patrick Henry (ship) 128, 146, 147
Paul, Alfred 96
Payne, Va. 169
Pedro II 236
Pember, Phoebe Yates 12, 72, 73, 82, 88, 96, 102, 146, 199
Pengoyd Iron Works 208
Pensacola, Fla. 214, 216, 218
Perkerson, Medora F. 195
Persia (ship) 130
Personal Memoirs (Sheridan) 45–46
Petersburg, Va. 6, 28, 34, 36, 37, 39, 43, 45, 46, 50, 56, 74, 75, 78–80, 86, 89–92, 95, 144, 154, 166, 171, 176, 191, 193, 247–249, 271, 275
Petersburg Road, Va. 168
Petre, Dr. 55, 243
Petrie, Dr. 55
Philadelphia 23, 39, 40, 95, 237
Philadelphia Press (newspaper) 280
Philbrook, Walter 193, 194
Phillips, Lance 107, 108, 117, 138

Phillips, Wilhelmina 239, 240
Phillips, William 239
Phillips Crossing 154
Pickett, Gen. 10
Picks, Tracks, and Bateaux (Melton) 108
Pickwick Papers (Dickens) 222
Pictorial History of the United States (Lossing) 45
Pictorial Reporting (Brown) 133
Piedmont Railroad 14, 111, 135, 154, 206, 253
Pilkington, Va. 169
Pittsylvania 108
Pittsylvania Co., Va. 190
Pittsylvania County (Aaron) 24, 191
Pleasants, J. Adair 138, 194
Plymouth 240
Poe, E.A. 122
Poland 229
Pollard, Edward A. 7, 13, 26, 34, 35, 38, 44, 45, 63, 64, 75, 78, 83, 139, 202–204
Pollock, Edward 212, 213, 286
Poor, Henry Varnum 154
Poor's Manual of the Railroads of the United States 154
Port Walthall 154
Porter, Isaiah J. 289
Porter, James Davis 39
Powhatan, Va. 154, 155, 159, 165, 168, 174, 186, 248
Powhatan Co., Va. 167–169
Powhite, Va. 155, 163, 164, 174
Powhite Creek 162, 163
Powhite Granite Works 164
Powhite Quarries 164
Prescott, Royal B. 26
Presidential Messages (Muller) 32, 33
President's Guard 123
The Presidents Were Here (Gary) 66
Press (Philadelphia) 17, 18
Preston, George H. 236, 237
Price's, Va. 155, 178
Prince, Richard E. 191
Prince Edward Co., Va. 178
Prussia 96
Pugh, James L. 14, 16
Pursuit (Johnson) 12, 50, 53, 60, 64, 79, 80, 84, 88, 90, 92, 108, 121, 133, 134, 147, 152, 155, 159, 180–184, 212, 221
Putnam, Richard F. 25
Putnam, Sallie 25

Raab, James W. 135, 136
Raen, Va. 173
Railroad History #167 110
Railroads in the Civil War (Clark) 154
Raines, C.W. 124
Raines, Gabriel 132
Raleigh, N.C. 126, 274
Raleigh Confederate 210
Raleigh Morning Post 23
Randolph, J.W. 238

Randolph, John 179
Rawdon, Lord 261
Raymond, Henry J. 234, 235
R.E. Lee (Freeman) 28, 89, 91, 92, 170
Rea, John 280
Reading, Conn. 215
Reagan, John H. 13, 29, 35, 39–44, 47–53, 55, 65, 90, 122, 123, 127, 141, 142, 157, 192, 213, 218, 224, 243, 248, 250, 256, 259, 261, 263, 267, 268
The Real Jefferson Davis (Knight) 59, 74, 75, 82
The Rebel and the Rose (Millett and White) 62, 65, 66, 69, 79, 81, 82, 108, 110, 121, 129, 130, 148, 150, 153, 158, 162, 190, 191, 221
"A Rebel Courier's Experience" (Handy) 201
Rebel Reefers (Conrad) 196, 197
A Rebel War Clerk's Diary at the Confederate States Capital (Jones) 12, 25, 29, 140, 191
Recollections Grave and Gay (Harrison) 26, 59, 61, 64, 80, 83, 86
Recollections of a Rebel Reefer (Morgan) 8
Reedy Creek, Va. 162
Reformation of the Irish Church (MacWalter) 239
"Retreat of the Cabinet [from Richmond]" 123, 124
"Retreat of the Confederate Government" (Swallow) 140
Rhodes, James Ford 141
Richardson, Maj. 102, 245
Richmond (Stanard) 203
Richmond, Va. 5–13, 16–21, 23–25, 27–29, 33, 35–40, 45–52, 54–56, 57, 61, 67, 68, 71, 72, 74, 75, 77, 78, 81, 85, 88, 89, 91, 92, 95, 96, 99, 101, 103–105, 107, 108, 110–112, 114, 116–121, 123–125, 127, 128, 130, 132–134, 137–139, 142–145, 147–149, 152–155, 157, 158, 160-175, 178, 180, 182, 183, 185, 186, 188, 190–193, 195–197, 199, 203, 204, 206, 208, 210, 211, 214, 219, 221, 223, 227, 230, 233, 234, 236, 237, 241, 242, 244, 245, 248, 249, 253- 260, 265, 266, 270–275
Richmond & Danville Railroad 8, 12, 24, 28, 36, 92, 106–109, 111–115, 118, 119, 123, 125, 127, 138, 139, 141, 154, 155, 157, 164, 165, 174, 175, 177–180, 189, 190, 194, 206–208, 210
Richmond & Petersburg Railroad 127, 154, 162
Richmond Burning (Lankford) 52, 60, 70, 84, 85, 147, 151, 152, 201–204, 289
Richmond Daily Dispatch 5, 8

Richmond Dispatch 119, 280
Richmond Enquirer 207, 208
Richmond Examiner 7, 157, 238, 256
Richmond Locomotive Works 118
Richmond Newspapers, Inc. 115
Richmond Sentinel 157, 230
The Richmond Slave Trade (Trammell) 105
Richmond Theological Seminary (Corey) 103
Richmond Times 124
Richmond Times Dispatch 65
"Richmond, Virginia" (Averill) 208
Richmond Whig 31–38, 44, 72, 137, 139, 143, 246, 155, 157, 199, 201–203, 227, 234, 236
Ricketts, Robert D. 206
Ringgold, Va. 157, 190
Rio de Janeiro 234–236, 240
Rise and Fall of the Confederacy (Jewett) 20
The Rise and Fall of the Confederate Government (Davis) 17, 37, 43, 74, 82, 88, 90, 91, 138, 171, 172, 208, 209, 212
The Road to Appomattox (Henrickson) 67
Roanoke, Va. 155, 175, 177, 179, 183, 186
Roanoke River 154
Robertson, James I. 276
Robiou's, Va. 165, 174, 186
Rocketts, Va. 147, 160, 161
Rockfield, Va. 162, 174
Rogers, D. Laurence 66, 67, 70, 76, 83, 105, 203
Rogers, William Warren 129, 272
Rogers, Ketchum, and Grosvenor 115
Rogers Locomotive 107, 110, 112–116
Rogers Locomotives (Moshein and Rothfus) 110
Roland, Charles 76
Roman, Alfred 19
Rosminian Order 240
Ross, Ishbel 10, 12, 13, 75, 80, 99
Rothfus, Robert R. 110, 116
Rowland, Dunbar 129, 142
Rowland, Mrs. Dunbar 10, 12
Ruggles, Daniel 122, 130, 131
"Rummaging Through Rebeldom" (Armee) 54, 227, 233, 234
Russia 96
Ryan, David D. 26, 51, 158

St. James's Episcopal Church, Richmond 68, 69
St. Jarlath's College 238
St. John, Isaac Munroe 143, 144, 158, 172, 247, 250
St. John's Church, Richmond 74, 75
St. Louis Democrat 113
St. Martin, Jules 122, 123, 125
St. Martin, Natalie 125
St. Mary's County, Md. 38
St. Paul's Church (Weddell) 65, 69
St. Paul's Church, Richmond 14, 30, 31, 35, 37, 39, 42, 46, 47, 50–53, 56, 58, 59, 61–70, 72, 74–78, 81, 85, 86, 88, 94, 97, 182, 242, 243, 248
St. Peter's Cathedral, Richmond 61, 243
Salisbury, N.C. 61, 133, 166, 264
Savannah, Ga. 237, 253
Saxe, Va. 179
The Scarlet Mystery (MacWalter) 239
Schaff, Moris 60, 68, 75, 81, 83, 87, 107
Schermerhorn, Calvin 104, 105
Scott, Mary Wingfield 112
Scott's Monthly Magazine 271
Scott's Shop, Va. 169, 174
Scottsburg, Va. 155, 185, 186
Scully, William 235
"The Search for the Lost Confederate Gold" (Kuenzi) 142
Seattle 232
Seattle Daily Times 232
Secret History of Confederate Diplomacy (Davis) 234
Seddon, Charles 109
Seddon, Charles W. 110
Seddon, James A. 77, 108–110, 285
Seltzer, Joyce 233
Seminole Wars 122
Semmes, Raphael 95, 144–148, 185, 224, 256, 259, 277
Senator Benjamin H. Hill of Georgia (Hill) 16–17
Sewanee, Tenn. 142
Shadows in Silver (Kocher and Dearstyne) 112
Shakespeare 229
Shannon 143
Sheldon 115, 116
Shepley, Gen. 137
Sheridan, Philip 10, 45, 46, 158, 159, 168, 170, 174, 176, 177, 197
Sherman, W.T. 133, 264, 271
Shingleton, R.G. 102, 132
A Short History of the Confederate States (Davis) 74, 82, 212
Shoshone, Idaho 232
Shreveport, La. 24
Silk Flags and Cold Steel (Trotter) 50, 120, 121, 125
Sims, F.W. 111
Singer, Jane 141
Six Decades in Texas (Raines) 124
Slaughter, Charles D. 211
Smith, Gustavus 230
Smith, Jean Edward 79
Smith, Lt. Col. 94
Smith, William "Extra Billy" 24, 94, 262
Smithsyde, Va. 162
South America 234
South Boston, Va. 186–189, 251
South Carolina 8, 210, 267
South Side Railroad 176
Southampton 143
Southern Amaranth 25, 66, 67
"Southern Exposures" 112
Southern Historical Society 23, 79, 95, 123, 272
The Southern History of the War (Pollard) 202
Southern Literary Messenger 218, 227, 236
Southern Methodist University 115, 116
Southern Railroad 114
Southern Times 239
A Southern Woman's Story (Pember) 12, 72, 82, 88, 96, 146, 147, 199
"A Southside Virginia Town Became Home for Thousands During One Week in April" (anon.) 129
Spain 96
Spence, Edward Lee 152
Spencer (slave) 101, 122, 131, 132
Spirit of the American Press 228, 229
Spong, John Shelby 78
Spotswood House, Richmond 71, 81, 275
Stacker, Clay 122, 132
The Stakes of Power, 1845–1877 (Nichols) 150
Stanard, Mary Newton 203
Stanton, Edwin M. 71, 75, 133, 138, 139
Staten Island 240
Staunton River 154, 175, 179, 258
Staunton River Bridge 188
Steam Locomotives and Boats (Prince) 191
Stephen R. Mallory: Confederate Navy Chief (Durkin) 214
Stephen Russell Mallory: A Biography of the Confederate Navy Secretary and United States Senator (Underwood) 27, 207, 214
"Stephen Russell Mallory: Naval Statesman" (Melvin) 214
"Stephen Russell Mallory, The Elder" (Clubbs) 214
"Stephen Russell Mallory: United States Senator from Florida and Confederate Secretary of the Navy" (Clubbs) 214
Stephens, Alexander 15, 23, 267, 277
Stern, Philip Van Doren 126, 150, 180–182
Stevens, Walter H. 92, 279, 280
Stewart, A.T. 234
Still, William N. 214, 277
Stillson, Jerome B. 170
Stoess, C.W. 232, 277
Stoess, Charles 232

Stoess, Christy 232
Stoess, Philip 231, 232
Stoneman, Gen. 12, 256, 258, 264, 267
The Story of Danville (Hagan) 213
"The Story of the Confederate Treasure" (Ashmore) 13, 129, 192, 193, 195, 197, 198
Stout, Harry S. 65, 81
Stowe, Harriet Beecher 27
Stresa, Italy 240
Strode, Hudson 10, 13, 62, 64, 98–100, 133, 150, 155, 180, 182–184, 196, 288
Strong, Charles F. 284
Strother, John 130, 193
Stuart, C.E.L. 21, 22, 25, 26, 30, 31, 35–38, 41, 54, 55, 57–59, 62, 72, 73, 81, 84, 85, 95–98, 101, 102, 121, 124, 125, 134, 140, 144, 149, 150, 153, 158, 160, 162, 166, 167, 174, 176, 177, 183, 186, 187, 189, 210, 212, 218, 219, 221, 227, 228, 230, 231–269, 275
Sulivane, Clement 203
Sunset of the Confederacy (Schaff) 60, 68, 75, 81, 83, 87
Sutherlin, William T. 14, 23, 24, 38, 212, 213, 226, 253
Sutherlin's Mill, Va. 190
Swallow, W.H. 54, 140, 289
Swan, Mr. 21
Swanson, James 11, 60, 81, 86, 90–93, 120, 135, 151, 158–160, 180–185, 196, 213, 222
Swift Creek, Va. 168
Swinton, William 171
Switzerland 96
Sydnor, R. Walton 188

Taber, Thomas T. 110
Table-Tapping (MacWalter) 239
Take Care of the Living (McClurken) 24
A Tale of Two Cities (Dickens) 224
Tales of Ireland and the Irish (MacWalter) 238, 239
Tanner and Delaney 117
Tate, Allen 59, 75, 81
Taylor, Walter H. 28, 89
Taylor, Zachary 37, 125
Team of Rivals (Goodwin) 81
Tehuantepec 116
Tell, William 225, 257
Temple Station, Va. 154
Tennessee 14, 18, 39, 110, 111, 123, 124, 126, 128, 142
Tenney, W.T. 276
Terrible Swift Sword (Wheelan) 81
Terry, Gen. 246, 253, 254
Texas 12, 14, 16, 33, 39, 47, 50, 51, 95, 122, 124, 127, 135, 137, 225, 246, 267
Thomas, Emory 76, 77, 83, 86, 173, 283

Thomas, Lee Breckinridge 143
Thomasville, Ga. 143
Three Months in the Southern States, April–June 1863 (Fremantle) 135
Tidwell, William A. 8
Times (Philadelphia) 23, 39, 40, 95, 237
Tippit's Crossing, Va. 207
To Appomattox (Davis) 47, 51, 58–60, 65, 66, 69, 70, 76, 79, 83, 99, 100, 126, 129, 145, 151, 180–184, 191, 192, 200, 201, 281
"To Danville" (McFall) 102, 135, 193, 194, 209
Tomahawk, Va. 154, 155, 167, 168, 174, 186
Tomahawk Church, Va. 167
Tomahawk Creek 167
Tompkins Mill, Va. 164
Torpedo Bureau 132
Towards an Indefinite Shore (Lowry) 51, 52, 62, 180, 183
Trammell, Jack 104, 105
Treasures of the Confederate Coast (Spence) 152
A Treasury of the World's Great Diaries (Dunaway and Evans) 282
Tredegar Iron Works 25, 87
Tremain, H.E. 92
Trenholm, Anna 10, 55, 97, 121–123, 141, 149–153, 208–210, 212, 217, 290, 291
Trenholm George A. 10, 20, 54, 121–123, 125, 150–153, 194, 195, 213, 221, 243, 248, 256, 267
Trinidad 214, 215
Trotter, William 50, 120, 121, 125
Trudeau, Noah Andre 289
"The True Story of the Capture of Jefferson Davis" (Walthall) 95
Tuam, Ireland 238
Tucker, Beverly 277
Tucker, Dallas 5, 26, 27, 58–60, 68, 70
Tucker, Spencer C. 144
"Tunstall's Folly" (anon.) 207
Turner, Dick 143
Turpin, Va. 168
Turpin, William T. 168

Ulster Democrat 240
Ulysses S. Grant (Church) 25, 67
Underwood, Rodman L. 27, 152, 207, 214, 220–222
United Kingdom 96, 137, 239
Upon the Altar of the Nation (Stout) 65, 81

Valentine Museum 107, 108, 112, 115, 117
Vandiver, Frank E. 8, 276
Venable, Charles S. 89
Vermont Watchman 139

Vey, Va. 179
Virginia 5, 13, 14, 16, 17, 20, 22, 24, 58, 94, 95, 98, 105, 111, 117, 122, 123, 133, 139, 143, 162, 186, 188, 192, 212, 213, 252, 272
Virginia & Midland Railroad 208
Virginia & Tennessee Railroad 115, 116
Virginia at War 209
Virginia Central Railroad 115
Virginia Clay Scrapbook 49, 55
Virginia Historical Society 273
Virginia Military Institute 23, 94, 132
Virginia Reserves 188
Virginia II 144, 145
Virginia Union University 105
Virso, Va. 178
Vizetelly, Frank 122, 132, 133, 195
Volunteer 227, 230, 238, 240

Walker, Gen. 180
Walker, Mayor 212, 253, 254
Walker, Senator 15
Waller, Jennie 230, 231
Waller, William G. 230, 231
Walmsley, James E. 158
Walthall, W.T. 95, 276
War for the Union (Nevins) 18, 19, 62, 63
"War News" (anon.) 108, 129, 187
Warsaw, Mo. 279
The Wartime Papers of R.E. Lee (Dowdey) 32, 48
Washington (Benjamin's asistant) 253
Washington, D.C. 71, 72, 81, 84, 137, 138, 194, 210, 218
Washington, Ga. 24, 123, 127, 130, 132, 134, 225, 266–268, 281
Watchman 143, 199, 201, 202, 275, 279, 280
Watehall, E.T. 54, 142, 200, 201, 292
Watkins, Va. 167
Watts, Governor 36
Weddell, Elizabeth Wright 65, 69
Weitzel, Godfrey 71, 137
Wellford, Beverly R. 188
Wesley, Charles 67
West, Va. 167, 168
West Point 143
Weymouth 239
What They Didn't Teach You About the Civil War (Wright) 27, 277
Wheelan, Joseph 81
Wheeler, Maj. 251, 262
Wheeling Register 17
When the Bells Tolled for Lincoln (Harrell) 119
White, Gerald 62, 65, 66, 221
White Columns in Georgia (Perkerson) 195

Why the South Lost the Civil War (Beringer) 19, 20
Why Was Lincoln Murdered? (Eisenschiml) 75
Wicked Danville (Bailey and Green) 23
Wicked Richmond (Brown) 104
Wigfall, Louis 267
Wikipedia 118
Wiley, Bell 271, 278
Wilmington, N.C. 95, 252, 274
Wilson, James Harrison 39, 40, 71, 95, 171, 172, 177, 178, 179, 237, 267
Wilson, Nathaniel 208
Wilson's Station, Va. 176
Winchester (horse) 168
Winder, John H. 130
Winder, Richard Bayley 130, 131
Winik, Jay 7, 20, 59–61, 66–68, 80, 82, 86, 98, 101, 141, 158
Winnsboro, S.C. 8
Winterham, Va. 169
Wisconsin Volunteer Infantry 45
Wise, Gen. Henry 180
Wise, John S. 122, 125, 126, 142, 180–182, 184, 185, 277
Withers, Robert 206
Wolf Trap, Va. 155, 186
Wood, John Taylor 37–39, 44, 72, 97, 119, 122, 123, 132–134, 138, 141, 166, 209, 210, 225, 243, 246, 249, 261, 268
Wood, Lola M. 38
Woodford, Frank Bury 8, 80
Woodward's Kentucky Cavalry 126
Worsham, John 27
Wright, John D. 120, 151
Wright, Mike 26, 27, 60, 61, 63, 65, 67, 78, 80, 277
Wright & Co. 235, 236
Wyanoke, Va. 173, 186

Yale 143
Yearns, Buck 159
Yeatts, Todd M. 24
Yonder Comes the Train (Phillips) 107, 108, 117, 138
Yorkville, S.C. 267
Young Folk's History of the War for the Union (Champlin) 25
Younger, Edward 33, 35
Yugoslavia 273

Zimmerman, Dwight Jon 285

www.ingramcontent.com/pod-product-compliance
Ingram Content Group UK Ltd.
Pitfield, Milton Keynes, MK11 3LW, UK
UKHW050541150426
5217IPUK00026B/2032